Paweł Włodkowic

WRITINGS (1416–1432)

The Struggle for the Self-Determination of Central Europe

Translated by Prof. Charles S. Kraszewski

Introduction and edited by Prof. Paul W. Knoll

Foreword by Prof. Ewa Thompson

Angelicum University Press
Fundacja Świętego Mikołaja
Rome—Warsaw 2023

Angelicum University Press
Fundacja Świętego Mikołaja
Rome—Warsaw 2023

Published by the St. John Paul II Institute of Culture at the Pontifical
University of St. Thomas Aquinas in Rome—Angelicum.
Founded at the Angelicum, the St. John Paul II Institute of Culture
is run in cooperation with the Saint Nicholas Foundation.
www.angelicum.it/institutes/st-john-paul-ii-institute-of-culture

Angelicum University Press
Largo Angelicum, 1—00184 Rome, Italy
editoria@pust.it—www.angelicumpress.com
Fundacja Świętego Mikołaja
Koszykowa 24/7—00553 Warsaw, Poland
redakcja@teologiapolityczna.pl—www.teologiapolityczna.pl
www.mikolaj.org.pl

ISBN: 978-83-67065-44-3 (print)
ISBN: 978-83-67065-45-0 (ebook)

Selection of Paweł Włodkowic's texts for the publication
by Marek A. Cichocki

Managing editors: Mikołaj Marczak, Adam Talarowski
Copy edited by Aeddan Shaw
Designed and typeset by Katarzyna Solecka
Cover design by Design Cooperative TAKŁADNIE, Dariusz Karłowicz
On the cover: detail from Ulrich von Richental's Chronik der Konstanzer Konzil,
Augsburg 1483, Universitätsbibliothek Heidelberg, M38152

This book has been published with the support of the
©POLAND Translation Program

Paweł Włodkowic

WRITINGS (1416–1432)

Table of contents

Ewa M. Thompson, FOREWORD 7

Abbreviations 28

Paul W. Knoll, INTRODUCTION 29

1. WITH PRUSSIAN INFIDELS RAGING *Saevientibus* (1416) 114
2. OPINION OF OSTIENSIS *Opinio Hostiensis* (1416) 171
3. ARTICLES AGAINST THE PRUSSIAN KNIGHTS OF THE CROSS *Articuli contra Cruciferos de Prussia* (1416) 193
4. THIS TRACT *Iste Tractatus* (1417) 303
5. BECAUSE AN ERROR *Quoniam Error* (1417) 327
6. THE EYES *Oculi* (1420) 479
7. TO SEE CLEARLY *Ad videndum* (1421) 533
8. LETTER TO THE BISHOP OF KRAKÓW *Ad episcopum Cracoviensem* (1432) 619

Bibliography — Primary and Secondary Sources 641

Ewa M. Thompson

FOREWORD

This book takes the reader to a remote past: the Council of Constance (1414-1418), or the most significant religious and intellectual gathering in fifteenth-century Europe. The Council's voting members were cardinals, bishops, and other members of the Catholic clergy representing four nations: English, French, Italian, and German (the Spanish were added later, during the Council's deliberations). The Poles and Czechs were counted as part of the German delegation: a medieval instance of **"cancel culture"** that also had a bearing on the issues which the Polish delegation raised at the Council: the rights of nations, international law as perceived by fifteenth-century scholars, and attitudes toward the pagan states wishing to live in peace with Christians.

The Council's goal was to solve several problems within the Catholic Church: to end the schism that had existed since 1378 by electing a pope whom the whole of Western Christendom would recognize; to resolve the matter of Jan Hus's alleged heresy; and to undertake Church reforms. The first problem was solved by electing Pope Martin V on 11 November 1417. The second did not achieve a peaceful solution. Hus was belligerent about his interpretations and refused to soften his stance, and the Church dignitaries gathered at Constance reacted to this belligerence in a predictable fashion: they confirmed the decision to declare him a heretic. Reforms were discussed but few decisive steps were taken. On and off, the Council also debated the treatment of pagan states, ownership of pagan lands, and wars waged by Christians against pagans. The discussion of these matters was initiated by the Polish delegates whose country bordered on territories that were pagan or had only recently been converted to Christianity. Under consideration were such matters as the employment in Europe of the militant orders once formed in the Holy Land. Do Christians have the right to attack peaceful pagans and bring Christianity to them by force? Do nations have certain rights that stem from natural law and trump the power of popes and synods? Are the religious Orders originally created to run hospitals in Palestine entitled to kill pagans in Europe and claim ownership of their lands? Does the Order of Brethren of the German House of Saint Mary in Jerusalem[1] (that had long ceased to assist Christians in Jerusalem) have the right to attack Prussians, Livonians, Samogitians, Lithuanians, and Poles, and take away their territory and wealth?

These questions were asked by Paweł Włodkowic (1370–1433), a canon lawyer, rector of University in Kraków, and a Polish delegate to the Council.[2] They were asked in several treatises he delivered to the assembled clerics. His treatises were carefully annotated: almost every sentence is backed up by references to theologians, canon lawyers, historians, or the Bible. Włodkowic clearly prepared himself for a major encounter and was anxious to demonstrate his scholarly competence. His appeal to the Council was related to the dispute that started in the thirteenth century between the Kingdom of Poland and the aforementioned Order of Brethren of the German House of Saint Mary. The Poles claimed that the Order had been engaged for generations in enlarging its territory in ways that cannot be called Christian. The means used in these conquests remained one of the Order's secrets, because Baltic tribes were in no position to present their side of the story to emperor or pope. Włodkowic recommended the institution of laws that would guide international relations. His ideas regarding international law precede the School of Salamanca by several generations, and his defense of the native peoples resembles that of Bartolomé de las Casas, the "protector of the Indians."[3]

Włodkowic was one of the remarkable scholars of the fifteenth century. His writings indicate that he carefully studied the history of the Teutonic Order, paying much attention to the documents from pope and emperor allegedly granting the Teutons all power over pagan lands in the Baltic area.[4] He began his crusade for justice by presenting to the Council a treatise titled ***Tractatus de potestate papae et imperatoris respect infidelium*** (July 5-6, 1416). *De potestate* is a defense of the rights of all human beings, regardless of their religion or ethnicity. The second treatise, ***Opinio Ostiensis,*** delivered to the Council in 1416, is a polemic with the notion that all pagan lands belong to the pope, and all means to establish papal rule over them are licit. This treatise consists of 52 articles summarizing and codifying the proposals contained in *De potestate.* These initial texts are dedicated to theological and political arguments, while the later ones contain evidence of the Brethren's unchristian behavior. Włodkowic argued in favor of the Baltic tribes and of his own country, which the Teutonic Brethren continued to harass even though they had recently lost a major battle with Poland (Grunwald–Tannenberg, 1410). In several treatises he mentioned Jews by name as those who should be allowed to live in peace and follow their own laws.[5] The later treatises (***Iste tractatus*** and ***Quoniam Error,*** both written in 1417) take on Poland's adversaries, Johannes Falkenberg and Johannes Urbach de Bamberg. After the official closure of the Council, Włodkowic argued his case at the papal court (Martin V left Constance for Rome in 1418).

Włodkowic's argument concerning the rights of nations and the Teutonic Brethren's violation of these rights can be summarized as follows: all individuals and nations have certain rights that stem from natural law imprinted on their minds by God. They have the right to the land where they have lived for generations. They have the right to be left alone if they do not attack their neighbors. Both Christians and pagans are children of God and should be treated accordingly. Neither the pope nor the emperor can dispose of the lands of peaceful pagans, because these lands belong to the people who inhabit them, and not to the pope or the emperor.[6] In blatant disregard of these rights stemming from natural law, the Teutonic Brethren repeatedly raided pagan territories near the Baltic Sea, thereby committing a grave sin. But they are more than sinners. They also are guilty of heresy, because they pretend to be a Christian Order while engaging in killing and stealing from their victims. A religious order cannot be dedicated solely to killing pagans and appropriating their land and wealth. The Baltic peoples did not begin wars with the Order; it was the other way round. The Baltic people's territory never belonged to Christians (unlike the Holy Land that was overrun by Muslims in years past). The Order should be declared not just sinful but heretical, and it should be dissolved. ***Haeresia Prussiana,*** or "the Prussian heresy," inflicted more harm on the Catholic Church in the fourteenth and fifteenth centuries than any other heresy.[7]

The Polish lawyer offered a passionate defense of those who were in no position to defend themselves, among them the Old Prussians, eventually exterminated by the Teutonic Order, who then assumed their name and began to call themselves "Prussians." He condemned the military conquerors whose goal has been the acquisition of land. He proposed that the Council act as an international court of arbitration that adjudicates territorial disputes. The articulation and universal acceptance of laws governing peace among nations promised a world in which wars would be rare. Włodkowic proposed that the Council formulate such laws as pertaining to the Christian world and its dealings with non-Christians and one another. His rhetoric was compelling:

"By repetition, error becomes custom, whereby Christ's faithful, believing that they are doing service pleasing unto God by fighting on His behalf... under the pretext of spreading the Catholic faith, wage cruel war upon a peaceful pagan nation. (1) In the case of pagans who wish to live peacefully among Christians, no molestation of their persons or things is to be visited upon them... The Jews especially are to be tolerated, as it is on the basis of their codices that we prove our truth, our Faith... (3) No one ha[s] the right to possess people as slaves before the law of the nations, for by nature all men were free (p. 115 below, Kraszewski)... It is not permitted to deprive the infidels of their dominion, their possessions, or their jurisdiction, for they possess the same sinlessly from the hands of God, their Creator... No man is a proper witness in his own case... (9) The Emperor is not capable of giving anyone any license for the occupation of the lands of infidels who do not recognize his imperial authority... (10) the imperial scripts conceded to the Knights of the Cross for the occupation of the lands of the infidels confer no rights upon them whatsoever permitting them to attempt their acquisition, for no one can give anyone something that he does not have... (11) It is not licit to compel infidels to the Christian faith by arms or oppressions... In cases of imminent necessity it is allowable to call to one's aid peaceful infidels, such as are not at war with us, actively or passively.[8]

De potestate contains a brief history of territories bordering on the Baltic Sea. Włodkowic admits that the people who lived there were not always peaceful, at times they attacked their Christian neighbors and wrought destruction upon Christian towns and villages. For that reason, he says, [in 1226] the Polish duke, Konrad Mazowiecki (Konrad of Mazovia) leased the areas of Chełmno and Michałów bordering pagan Old Prussia to the Teutonic Brethren, in order to secure assistance in defending his dukedom from pagan tribes.[9] Konrad had in mind a feudal arrangement, whereby the Brethren would recognize the Duke's prerogatives and assume the position of vassals. However, the Teutonic Brethren had a different idea. Unbeknownst to Konrad, in 1235 they obtained the so-called Golden Bull from Emperor Frederick II which illegitimately bestowed on them the ownership of lands leased from Duke Konrad. They secretly forged Konrad's acquiescence to their independent status[10] and began to treat the leased areas as their core dominium. They formed an independent state, just as they wanted to do in Hungary from which they were expelled for that reason.

A historical aside is in order. Poland and Lithuania became one state due to dynastic arrangements. Poland had been Christian since 966, while Lithuania accepted Christianity in 1386, when Duke Jagiełło was baptized and married the Polish Queen Jadwiga. As could be expected in so massive a change of beliefs, not all parts of Lithuania became instantly covered with Christian bishoprics and churches. Under the pretext of converting pagans to Christianity, the Teutonic Brethren continued their raids into Lithuanian and Baltic territory, terrorizing and killing the inhabitants, robbing churches of their valuables, and forcing survivors into slave labor. Rather than accepting their status of leasers of the land, they claimed ownership of not only Chełmno and Michałów districts, (Ziemia Chełmińska and Ziemia Dobrzyńska), but also other parts of Pomerania and Samogitia.

On several occasions, the Teutonic Brethren not only attacked Lithuania but also Poland, under the pretext that both countries were sliding back into paganism and that their conversion to Christianity was being faked. By the beginning of the fifteenth century, the dispute between them and the Kingdom of Poland-Lithuania became an open enmity. On July 15, 1410 at Grunwald (Tannenberg), the joint forces of Poland and Lithuania confronted the Teutons in battle. The Polish-Lithuanian armies won a decisive victory, the Grand Master of the Order was killed, and the road was opened for Poles to storm the seat of the Order in Malbork (Marienburg), and end Germanic inroads into Eastern Baltic area once and for all. But the armies of Jagiełło were weakened by the Grunwald effort and Jagiełło lacked the brutality and determination to win at any price. The siege of Malbork was unsuccessful and the Brethren remained in possession of that castle and the military victory at Grunwald did not bring significant political results. The hastily concluded Peace of Toruń (1411) returned the Dobrzyń area to Poland, set up the size of ransom for the Teutons taken prisoner by the Polish-Lithuanian forces, and declared that Samogitia would return to Lithuania, but only for the lifetimes of Vytautas and Jagiełło. Given the fact that the two brothers were about 60 years of age (old by medieval standards), it was not much of a victory.[11] Furthermore, after the Peace of Toruń was signed, the Teutonic Order continued its raids into areas inhabited by Balts and Slavs, including parts of Poland that had been Christianized centuries ago. Their excuse for the raids continued to be the alleged relapse into paganism of both Lithuania and Poland. Poles were obliged to seek other means (other than the military) to curtail the appetite for land of the Teutonic Brethren. King Jagiełło decided to appeal to the pope and bring the issue to the attention of the whole of Christendom. The forthcoming Council of Constance provided a venue for these objectives.

It was not to the advantage of the Teutonic Brethren to adopt Włodkowic's proposal concerning international law or accept the rule that pagans have the right to their land. Such laws would eliminate the possibility of enlarging the German State at the expense of other peoples. Włodkowic's treatise was first presented "to the German nation," or to the largest delegation to the Council, on July 5. On July 6 Włodkowic addressed the entire Council, rejecting the view of a the 13th century scholar Henry of Segusio that it was licit to initiate wars with pagans just because they are pagans and have not yet accepted Christ. Ostiensis belonged to the group of canon lawyers who believed that pagan land should be considered the property of the pope and all means of securing its ownership by the Church were legitimate. His ideas were used to justify the Teutonic Order's method of "christianizing" pagans by attacking them with fire and sword. In his rejoinder to Ostiensis, Włodkowic stated that acquisition of new lands for Christianity should not be done by force, and relations between nations should be maintained according to the rules that everyone accepted beforehand. He urged the Council and the Teutonic Order to consent to a set of rules that would allow nations to live in peace. The Teutonic Brethren responded with another attack. They were not able to write a rejoinder by themselves: theirs was an order that fought battles rather than engaged in scholarship. They hired a scholar to answer Włodkowic's proposals.[12]

The person the Teutonic Brethren hired to attack Włodkowic was Johannes Urbach de Bamberg, a member of the German Nation at the Council but not a member of the Order.[13] In 1416 he produced a treatise challenging Włodkowic's postion. Urbach opposed assigning any rights to the infidels. He argued that since they do not belong to Christ, they have no rights. Furthermore, if they have been called to assist an allegedly Christian king in winning a battle against the Order (as has been the case at Grunwald), they not only proved themselves to be worthy of annihilation but also bestowed the status of pagans on the allegedly Christian king that asked them for assistance. To oppose the Order is to oppose the Church, proclaimed Urbach.[14] His argument was similar to the one presented in two other treatises written by Johannes Falkenberg, a sworn enemy of the Poles, entitled ***Liber de doctrina*** and ***Satira contra hereses et cetera nephanda Polonorum et eorum regis Iagyel.***[15] Both disregarded the factual evidence provided by Włodkowic. Urbach did not even attempt to disprove that the Teutonic Brethren killed, robbed, and enslaved their neighbors, and that it was impossible to persuade the people who had been so grievously harmed to accept a new religion based, as the aggressors said, on love and forgiveness. Stanislaus Bełch remarked that Johannes Urbach strove to prove that "infidels have no right to political independence."[16]

In response, Włodkowic came forth with yet another treatise, this time concentrating on the specific crimes committed by the Teutonic

Brethren against Polish, Lithuanian, and Baltic pagan population. This treatise is the most detailed of all of Włodkowic's critiques of the Teutonic Order. In ***Articuli contra Cruciferos de Prussia*** read to the Council in July 1416, he presented a comprehensive inventory of the Order's dealings with the conquered peoples: mass murders including women and children; robbery and looting; destruction of entire towns and villages; destruction of buildings and sanctuaries; enslavement of natives and treating survivors as if they were subhuman. Of all the treatises this is the longest: the number of towns and villages mentioned in it is overwhelming. This collection of reports begins with an invocation of "**the Prussian heresy**" which, Włodkowic claims, has been worse even than that of the "Wycliffites and Hussites."[17] In 155 "articles" Włodkowic details the crimes committed by the Brethren, ending each article with "And this was and is the public and notorious truth; it was and is common knowledge and public report."[18]

The transgressions listed by Włodkowic included destroying over a hundred churches, public execution (by beheading or drowning) of those who resisted the Brethren, robbing local residents of their possessions and churches of their valuables, and then killing the former owners; and, last but not least, extortions of donations. Particularly heinous were in Włodkowic's view executions without trial and at night, performed on the Order's own subjects in territories the Order had conquered. Article 92 of the treatise says that the Teutonic Brothers did not abstain from robbing coffins at cemeteries. While they boasted of land donations and other gifts received, the documents they showed as proof of their ownership were forged or extorted. Significantly, Włodkowic remarks that the pope who gave the Brethren his blessing for their warfare could not have given them permission to christianize by the sword, because that would be contrary to Christian teaching. Ergo, the Order provided the pope with false evidence to gain his sympathy. Summing up, the Teutonic Brethren treated the Baltic area as their own and convinced the Christian world that this indeed should be so. Yet the struggle of the Baltic peoples against German militarism was ongoing even when the Council of Constance was taking place.

Włodkowic dedicated much attention to violations of treaties and extortion of documents donating land to the Order. This kind of accusation is hard to prove or disprove, because the alleged actions happened centuries ago. Circumstantial evidence indicates that he was correct in many instances. Włodkowic describes forgeries, extortions, and other forms of deceit practiced by the Brethren with a certitude that would be hard to feign. In several cases, historical confirmation is available. Thus in 1339, Pope Benedict XII made invalid all land acquisitions of the Order and ordered the return of occupied lands to their previous owners. This papal order was ignored by the Brethren who remained in possession of not only pagan lands but also those belonging to the Christian kingdom of Poland and Lithuania: Chełmno (Culm), Michałów, the Dobrzyń area, and parts of Samogitia. During the Council of Constance the Teutonic Brethren refused to return the lands they illegally occupied to Poland, and even to discuss the issue. Włodkowic concluded that the Order was guilty of "the Prussian heresy" of militarism, to the detriment of nations bordering on the Order's illegally acquired lands. In a bitter echo of Włodkowic's theses several centuries later, German historian Heinrich von Treitschke extolled Prussia and its ways of gaining power, and pointed to the Teutonic Order as a model and prototype of the Prussian state.

Włodkowic questioned the idea of a religious order whose sole goal was to wage a war of conquest. He stated that such an order defies natural, divine, and human laws. Nowhere in Christian doctrine can one find an encouragement to aggression against peaceful neighbors. No religious order can have military activity as its declared goal. The Teutonic Order has been built on false premises and it encouraged others to follow these premises: because of disinformation it has perpetuated, members of other orders joined the Teutons in their onslaught against Baltic and Slavic peoples. Włodkowic concluded *Articuli contra Cruciferos de Prussia* by saying that the Teutonic Brethren not only committed grave sins but also fell into heresy, in that their stated goal was to invade, kill, and take over. They murdered and robbed civilians instead of converting, they used slave labor to build their castles and towns, they practiced usury and falsified documents. They became heretics by proclaiming untruths about the Catholic Church.

In addition to Johannes Urbach, the Teutonic Brethren had another defender: Johannes Falkenberg, the author of the ***Satira contra hereses.***[19] This text, said to have been written in 1412, advocates the genocide of the entire Polish nation and its king. Falkenberg justifies this as follows. The pope is the legitimate owner of all pagan lands. Therefore, the Order that violently tries to wrench the pope's dominions out of the hands of the unfaithful has the right to use any means necessary to defeat and exterminate pagan peoples. A Christian king or ruler who uses pagan armies in a war with Christians condemns himself to eternal damnation and is to be regarded as worse than pagan, because he abandoned his Christian faith in using pagan allies in battle. Such was the case with the Polish king, Jagiełło. Thus the Polish king is a heretic worse than the pagans themselves, because he abandoned the Faith in order to win battles. Furthermore, the Poles defended pagan tribes by ascribing to them the rights they do not possess. Therefore, Jagiełło and his nation should be annihilated. Those who refuse to participate in the crusade against Poles are likewise heretical. Poles pretend to be Christians, but in fact they are heretics. They deserve a crueler death than ordinary pagans and should be wiped out from the surface of the earth together with their king.[20] The controversy over Falkenberg's *Satira* was taken up by the Council on February 8, 1417.

According to Falkenberg, Poles and their king are "odious heretics and shameless dogs returned to the vomiting of their unbelief. . . it is more meritorious to kill the Poles and their King than the pagans."[21] This intemperate tone differs sharply from Włodkowic's style of writing, and it certainly did not help Falkenberg when he presented his case before the Council. He was supported by King Sigismund of Luxemburg (usually called Emperor but he was not yet emperor when the Council of Constance was taking place), with whom he shared German ethnicity. However, he was compelled to tone down his opinion when Włodkowic managed to persuade the pope that the Teutonic Brethren far exceeded their rights in dealing with territories that did not belong to them.

Falkenberg did not share with the Brethren an allegiance to the same Order—he was a Dominican—but he did share their ethnicity. His unbridled attacks against Włodkowic, Poland, and the Poles can be treated as a rhetorical device characteristic of the epoch; however, given the history of German incursions into Poland, they should not be easily dismissed. Falkenberg was the first but not the last German to propose a genocide of Poles. The desire to annihilate the Polish nation was shared by the Grand Master of the Order, Henry von Plauen (as expressed in his letter to archbishop of Riga),[22] and by Johannes Urbach. The idea reappears in the nationalistic historians of the nineteenth century such as Heinrich von Treitschke, in Bismarcks's politics, and in the Nazi efforts to wipe out the Polish nation.

While it was not difficult for Włodkowic to shake off the accusation of heresy, Falkenberg was in a more precarious position. His allegation that King Jagiełło was a heretic did not convince the Council. Just the opposite, he had to defend himself from Włodkowic's allegation that he, Falkenberg, was a heretic because he accused a Catholic monarch and his country of pagan perversities. To propose the genocide of a Christian nation turned out to be too much even for the Council's participants sympathetic to German interests. The pope condemned the *Satira* in May 1418 and repeated his condemnation at the public consistory in January 1424. Falkenberg succeeded in defending himself from the accusation of heresy, but he was imprisoned for his advocacy of genocide. When the Council ended in 1418, Falkenberg was taken to Rome as a prisoner of the pope. He was the first European author to formulate the justification of genocide.

After Falkenberg delivered his accusations, Włodkowic presented another defense. In ***Iste Tractatus*** (1417), he created a model of deductive analysis. He stated that the treatise defending the Brethren wrongly assigns certain powers to the emperor and passes them on to the Teutonic Brethren. The emperor does not derive his powers from the pope and his powers are limited to the land he legitimately possesses. God did not endow him with power over the lands of those pagans who have not attacked his territories. Therefore, the emperor may not licitly bestow upon the Teutonic Brethren "lands torn from the hands of infidels conducting themselves peacefully."[23] What a fine example of the medieval understanding of separation of Church and State.

Włodkowic pointed out that the offensive words used by Falkenberg ("Poles are heretics. . .the King is a persecutor of the Church") lack substance. They are offensive generalities without specific content. Using them without proof is a trespass against morality. Furthermore, "he who is not a judge cannot administer the judicial order,"[24] and Falkenberg has done so. In contrast, in his treatises Włodkowic mentions specific territories, churches, individuals who suffered injustice because of the Teutonic *Reisen*. Włodkowic hoped that making the Council aware of what "Mary's soldiers" had done and are intent on doing would result in universal condemnation and dissolution of the Order. He pointed out that the Brethren were a predatory band masquerading as Christians, and asked for a special commission to investigate the Order's crimes. He stated that the Council was called to eliminate heresy; and here was heresy pure and simple, the heresy of Prussianism, created and practiced by a group of people declaring themselves to be "Mary's soldiers."

His victory was only partial. His arguments seem to have persuaded the pope, but not the Teutonic Brethren and their supporters at the Council. The Brethren asked Emperor Sigismund to reject Włodkowic's accusations. The decision was favorable to the Brethren: they might have committed heinous deeds, but these were sins rather than heresies. Włodkowic failed to persuade the emperor and the pope that the entire Order was unchristian and should be disbanded. Poland regained the contested territories of Dobrzyń, Michałów and Chełmno, but the Order of the Teutonic Brethren was not dissolved.

Włodkowic did not abandon his attempts to persuade the Christian world that the Teutonic Brethren were enemies of the Christian Faith. In a consecutive tract titled ***Oculi*** (1420), he rhetorically asked which hospital do the "Brethren of the Hospital of Jerusalem" own and support. They call themselves the Brethren of the Hospital of Jerusalem, but they have long broken any ties to Jerusalem, if they ever had any. Thus all donations given to them are wasted (especially if they were extorted), because presumably they were meant for a hospital, i.e., for support of the poor, whereas the Teutonic Brethren do not support the poor, do not run hospitals or engage in other forms of charitable activity. Włodkowic concluded that the Brethren "are worthy of condemnation by virtue of the very vow they professed".[25]

Then, a show of rhetoric:

"We state that this doctrine is not only false and erroneous, but, in as much as it is repugnant to divine law, it is heretical, impious, and insane; in as much as it encourages unjust homicide to be executed unjustly, it is dangerous, scandalous, reckless, and cruel; in so far as it deprives the Poles of a legitimate defense it goes against natural law, is seditious, injurious, and openly dangerous to the public order. For all these reasons it is offensive to pious ears and as such deserving of condemnation."[26]

The Teutonic Brethren did not answer Wlodkowic's accusations; instead, they continued their raids into the Polish territories of Chełmno and Dobrzyń (which by the pope's decision were returned to Poland). Whence this insolence? The main source of information about dealings of the Teutonic Brethren in the Baltic area were the invaders themselves. They surpassed their Slavic and Baltic neighbors in numbers, diplomatic experience, and access to the two power centers of medieval Europe: the pope and the Holy Roman emperor. An illustration of this situation is the post-conciliar appeal of King Jagiełło to Emperor Sigismund. The king asked for a confirmation that Pomerania, Chełmno and Michałów belong to Poland. But in 1420 the emperor ruled in favor of the Teutonic Order. In response, King Jagiełło appealed to Pope Martin V, with Włodkowic again his spokesman. The pope ruled in favor of the Polish Kingdom but the Brethren ignored the ruling.

In 1432, when Włodkowic was in Padua, he wrote a *Letter* to his ecclesiastical superior, Bishop Zbigniew of Kraków. The *Letter* contains his final assessment of the role the Teutonic Brethren played in fomenting violence and turbulence in the Baltic area. It is the work of an old man who has seen much wrong in the world and is sad that he cannot remedy it. The *Letter* also shows his deep faith and fidelity to the Church.

Włodkowic begins by underlining his limited ability to influence events: "What can I do, insignificant as I am? Who will believe me, should I assert that I see more perspicaciously than those who are seated way higher than I?"[27] But remaining silent is not an option. He points out that in contempt of the pope's verdict, the Teutonic Brethren continue their *Reisen*. There is no doubt in Włodkowic's mind that the Brethren are "the false prophets" Christ warned us against. "The Order of the Knights of the Cross of Prussia appear in sheep's clothing, while they display their true nature as rapacious wolves. . . They ought to be sentenced by the Church of God to destruction."

Włodkowic then details what happened in 1431: the Brethren invaded the Polish Kingdom again and got as far as Gniezno and Płock. "Many notable churches in this Kingdom, such as the metropolitan see of Gniezno, as well as those of Włocławek and Płock, abounding in large possessions... suffered great damage and loss... ecclesiastical benefices destroyed [as well as] the diocesan churches themselves, along with Sacraments, the relics of the saints, books, chalices... Dobrzyń and Kujawy, along with their churches and ecclesiastical goods, were almost entirely... destroyed." All this in defiance of the decision of the Apostolic See "granting Pomerania, Chełmno and Michałów to Poland, together with the great sums of money owed [Poland] in reparations." Włodkowic points out that the emperor could not have granted the Teutonic Brethren "Samogitia, Livonia, Latvia, and Ruthenia, because these lands did not belong to him." He says that he can present 23 witnesses "to the immense and inhuman cruelties committed by these Brethren against the Poles... in Chełmno and Michałów." In addition, he stands ready to present witnesses who remember the year 1408, when another incursion into Poland by the Teutonic Brethren took place, and the testimonies of those who saw "other damages and criminal detestable deeds that this Order [has] perpetrated." Finally, Włodkowic states that the Order had the habit of selling the goods they robbed in Polish lands in "Germany, Italy and other places."

His conclusion: the Order was a heretical growth on the body of the Church and should be dissolved. It should pay reparations to those whom it harmed and from whom it stole. One hears a tragic note in this judgment: Włodkowic was well aware of his inability to enforce a just outcome of international disputes.

Why are Włodkowic's treatises worth reading in the twenty-first century? First, they demonstrate the remarkable freedom of speech that at least some Catholic clerics took for granted in the late Middle Ages. Contrary to the narrative developed in the Age of Enlightenment, in those allegedly "dark times" Church gatherings and debates were places where participants could exchange opinions that might get their authors into trouble in later times. Włodkowic's bold assertion of the rights of men deserves a second look as proof of the freedom of speech that existed during the Christian Middle Ages. Włodkowic challenged the pope and the emperor, but he did not endanger himself personally by doing so. While many bishops and Church dignitaries subscribed to the view that pagan lands belonged to the pope, an opposite view was also tolerated. Why was he not burned at the stake like Jan Hus? He supported the notion of natural law which has been fundamental to Christian theology for centuries. In contrast, Hus attacked the core institutions of the Church and charged them with transgressions against Christ's teachings.

Second, Włodkowic articulated a Christian theory of international relations. Had his proposals been accepted and had the Council spent time and treasure on developing a set of rules for international behavior, many a war could have been avoided and the growth of imperialism and colonialism in subsequent centuries might have been stymied. In the fifteenth century, there appeared in Europe a scholar and cleric who spelled out the rights of each and every human being. The Council of Constance had an opportunity to oppose imperialism. It chose not to do so. It tacitly agreed that nations can pursue their imperial ambitions without consequences.

It was not for a lack of effort on the part of Włodkowic that his proposals were passed over. He argued his point persuasively, yet his attempts to persuade the Christian world that the Teutonic Brethren were a criminal sect have failed. His failure cannot be attributed to his inability to present the case or to a lack of proof that his cause was just. He argued the way Thomas Aquinas argued in *Summa Teologica*: submitting the statement he intended to refute, quoting arguments in favor of that statement, and then refuting these arguments. In some ways, Włodkowic was similar to Ralph Nader: he was a man on a mission. He so wished for righteousness to prevail that he dedicated most of his life to exposing the doings of the Teutonic Order in the Baltic area.

Why was Włodkowic's intervention consigned to oblivion? The dispute between Poland-Lithuania and the Teutonic Order ended with Teutonic victory. In 1525, or several generations after the Council of Constance, the Grand Master of the Order dissolved it and assumed the title of a secular duke, still a vassal to the Polish king but headed for full independence as the Kingdom of Prussia. In the eighteenth century, Prussia enriched itself through the partitions of Poland, an act of political violence in direct contradiction to Włodkowic's postulates. Under such circumstances, dropping Włodkowic's writings into the abyss of memory was both expedient and convenient.

The standard histories of the Middle Ages barely mention Włodkowic's writings.[28] European historians have generally ignored Latin texts written in non-Germanic Central Europe, and until now translations of these texts into Western European languages have not been available. Furthermore, in comparison to Germany and France, Poland was a new and demographically smaller member of Christian Europe, a circumstance that Poland's western neighbor deftly made use of. Włodkowic's Latin treatises have now been translated into English and his theorizing about international relations has a chance to be recognized, thereby modifying the interpretation of non-Germanic Central European history.

I submit that **ethnicity and national allegiance** played a role in the rejection of Włodkowic's assessment the Teutonic Order. As Anthony Smith demonstrated in *The Ethnic Origins of Nations* (1986), the Enlightenment idea that nationalism began with the French Revolution is at best incomplete: national identity emerged as a result of ancient and medieval wars and loyalties that the wars generated. The German delegation to the Council of Constance was the largest: it consisted of 2,000 persons, including the Polish delegation of 200. Emperor Sigismund of Luxemburg was German, the Council was taking place in Germanic lands, and the main enemies of Włodkowic's proposals were Germans. The Teutons exerted a large influence on the subsequent Church discussions on theology and history. Włodkowic came from a country that did not have a privileged place at the table. He and his fellow clerics did not have much experience in dealing with the emperor's or the pope's court. As time went on, the choice of what to remember and what to forget increasingly resided in the hands of Western Europeans, and "**cancel culture**" attitude toward non-Germanic Central Europe became prevalent.

Historians of the Middle Ages have not paid much attention to ethnicity, which means that a good deal of what happened in the late Middle Ages has eluded them. In 2006, Jack Goody published *The Theft of History.*[29] The book argues that Western Europeans have unjustly appropriated a number of achievements of humanity for themselves, while in reality these achievements and discoveries should be attributed to the peoples whom Western Europeans conquered in their voracity for other people's land. Goody meticulously enumerates a number of such "thefts." The case of Paweł Włodkowic and the Teutonic Brethren belongs here as well.

Endnotes

1 Referred to in various sources as the Teutonic Knights, Teutonic Friars, Teutonic Brethren, Knights of the Cross, or Cruciferos.

2 Some scholars use a Latin translation of his name: Paulus Vladimiri.

3 *The School of Salamanca: Digital Collection of Sources,* https://www.salamanca.school/en/index.html; Bartholomé de las Casas, *A Short Account of the Destruction of the Indies,* tr. by Nigel Griffin (London: Penguin, 1999).

4 Tomasz Tulejski, "Paulus Vladimiri and His Forgotten Concept of the Just War," *Journal of the Polish Section of* IVR (2019/2), p. 42. DOI: https://doi.org/10.36280/AFPiFS.2019.2.39

5 "The Jews especially are to be tolerated, as it is on the basis of their codices that we prove our truth, our Faith." *De potestate...*, p. 120 below (Kraszewski's translation); *Ostiensis,* p. 176 below (Kraszewski's translation).

6 In *Quoniam error,* Włodkowic put it boldly: "Not even [the Pope] is able to grant, absolutely and in general, the lands of the infidels to said Brethren or others, without just cause." P. 335 below.

7 *Articuli contra Cruciferos de Prussia* (1416), p. 194 below.

8 *De potestate,* pp. 115–150 (fragments).

9 Tomasz Tulejski, op. cit.

10 Sources that are not party to this dispute admit it. *Encyclopedia Britannica,* https://www.britannica.com/topic/Teutonic-Order.

11 Given the Polish-Lithuanian victory at Grunwald, the 1411 Peace of Toruń was very generous toward the Brethren. Norman Housley's assessment of it as "humiliating" for the Order shows a common prejudice of Western European scholars toward the Catholic nations of non-Germanic Central Europe. Norman Housley, "A Crusade Against the Poles? Johannes Falkenberg's 'Satira' (1412)," *The Templars, The Hospitallers and the Crusades: Essays in Homage to Alan J. Forey,* edited by Helen J. Nicholson and Jochen Burgtorf (London: Routledge, 2020), p. 187.

12 Their delegate to the Council, one Peter Wormdith, wrote to the Grand Master asking for money to pay a learned scholar to answer Wlodkowic's accusations. Stanislaus F. Belch, *Paulus Vladimiri and His Doctrine Concerning International Law and Politics* (The Hague: Mouton, 1965), vol. II, p. 1108.

13 Ioannis Vrebach de Bamberga decretorum doctoris, *Tractatus De statu Fratrum Ordinis B. Mariae Virginis Teutonicorum et pugna corum adversus infideles...,* Belch II:1116–1180. There is some confusion regarding this scholar's identity. Possibly, he came from Erfurt and was a canonist. Belch, II:1111.

14 Quoted from Belch II:1112.

15 *Liber de doctrina* repeated the theses of the *Satira,* but abstained from intemperate language present in *Satira.*

16 Belch II:1113.

17 Włodkowic, *Articuli contra Cruciferos de Prussia,* p. 194.

18 Ibid., p. 209 *et alii.*

19 Hartmut Boockmann states that Falkenberg's tract was written in 1412, but does not supply evidence. H. Boockmann, *Johannes Falkenberg, der Deutsche Orden und die Polnische Politik* (Göttingen: Veröffentlichungen des Max-Planck Institute für Geschichte, Bd.45, 1975). Urbach's tract was written in 1416. Belch mentions that some scholars considered *Liber a doctrina* to be identical with Urbach's work (Belch, II:1112).

20 Falkenberg's treatise was considered lost for centuries, but it was found in the 1970s among the Leipzig University manuscripts by Polish scholar Zofia Włodek. Dr. Włodek was in Leipzig on a German scholarship. Her discovery was confirmed by her German supervisor Dr. Hartmut Boockmann, She published the ms. with the Ossolineum in Wrocław (*Mediaevalia Philosophica Polonorum,* n. 18 (1973), pp. 51–95). Boockmann published it with a commentary two years later. In his interpretive commentary, Boockmann argued that Falkenberg's genocidal project amounted to a misunderstanding. See also Norman Housley, op.cit.

21 Quoted from Belch, II:1005.

22 Belch II:1006.

23 Włodkowic, *Iste tractatus,* p. 310 below.

24 Ibid., p. 319.

25 *Oculi,* p. 517.

26 *Iste tractatus,* p. 323 below.

27 Włodkowic, *Letter to the Bishop of Kraków* (1432), p. 620 below. Subsequent quotations are from the same *Letter.*

28 Typical of this approach is Dan Jones, *Powers and Thrones: A New History of the Middle Ages* (New York: Viking, 2021). Sidney Z. Ehler and John B, Morrall, eds. and translators, *Church and State Through the Centuries* (Westminster, MD: The Newman Press, 1954) mentions the Polish-German dispute *passim.* For the views of Paul W. Knoll see *'A Pearl of Powerful Learning': The University of Cracow in the Fifteenth Century* (Leiden: Brill, 2016), especially pp. 227-245, 271-273, and 429-463. A book of essays in Polish *Paweł Włodkowic i polska szkoła prawa międzynarodowego* (edited by M.A. Cichocki and A. Talarowski, Warsaw: Teologia Polityczna, 2018) introduces the Polish reader to Włodkowic.

29 Jack Goody, *The Theft of History,* Cambridge Univ. Press, 2006.

ABBREVIATIONS

(full citations in Bibliography)

Belch, *Paulus Vladimiri*	– Stanislaus F. Belch, *Paulus Vladimiri and His Doctrine Concerning International Law and Politics*
Brundage, *Canon Law*	– James A. Brundage, *Medieval Canon Law*
Długosz, *Annales*	– *Ioannis Dlugosii Annales seu Cronicae incliti Regni Poloniae*
Ehrlich, *Pisma wybrane*	– Ludwik Ehrlich, *Pisma wybrane Pawła Włodkowica*
Lites	– *Lites ac Res Gestae inter Polonos Ordinemque Cruciferorum*

Paul W. Knoll

INTRODUCTION*

Late in his life, Paweł Włodkowic (Paulus Vladimiri), learned canon lawyer, former rector of the University of Kraków, and devoted diplomat to the king of Poland, wrote a personal letter of advice and counsel, tinged with emotion, to his friend and colleague, Bishop Zbigniew Oleśnicki of Kraków. After a formal, but deeply felt, salutation, Paweł expressed the pain he felt about matters that were profoundly personal to him: "Alas, my heart sighs in deep sorrow, wounded at the desolation of my fatherland..." Paweł was referring here to the destruction wrought upon the territories of Dobrzyń and Kujavia in which he had grown up. But he was not limiting the damage to these alone. Other regions of the kingdom had been affected and, in Paweł's mind, the kingdom within which he lived had indeed suffered as a whole. He was distressed "that the peaceful Kingdom of Poland... should be submitted... to so horrible a plague."[1]

Paweł's comments were related to a complex set of conditions that are reflected in the documents translated in this volume. He was referring to the political and military conflict between the Kingdom of Poland and the Knights of the Teutonic Order that had its roots in developments dating back to the thirteenth century and in events that had continued into his own time. These had shaped Polish policy during Paweł's lifetime, and he had been an important player in supporting and arguing that policy. Some of this had been done at the Council of Constance, an assembly of European-wide significance that dealt primarily with religious and ecclesiastical matters (to be further discussed below) but a gathering that also had implications for the secular sphere. It had met from 1414 to 1418. Paweł's efforts were not limited to this venue, and his important activities had continued into the 1420s and beyond.

His engagement in policy in support of the Polish monarchy was not, however, narrowly defined and limited. It had rather been pursued within the context of a series of treatises that raised his contribution into the realm of theory. His views in these works touched upon such issues, among other, as what powers rulers — both ecclesiastical and secular — possessed, the problem of war and peace between nations and peoples, the theory of what constituted a just war, the concept of natural law and the law of nations (*ius gentium*), and problems of national identity and sovereignty.

Paweł presented these views in powerful ways that were not abstract; they had practical implications. To be specific, he believed that the Teutonic Order was an entity that not only threatened Poland and the larger region of Lithuania and the Baltic, but that it was a threat — a plague and a heresy — to Christendom as a whole and should be suppressed. In making his arguments, Paweł was essentially arguing a legal case. He was, after all, trained as a lawyer and he thought and wrote like a lawyer. Reading the treatises contained in this volume will reveal this clearly. He often reverts to cryptic legal shorthand references that lawyers from other times and places will find familiar.[2] At the same time, he quotes often from the Bible. As any individual of learning in the medieval period would do, he also drew upon elements of classical philosophy, Christian thought, philosophy, and theology. All of these are introduced by Paweł, frequently from memory, reflecting the enormous rote mastery of legal, theological, and biblical authority that was expected of one who completed the university curriculum in the Middle Ages. But, as the German scholar Eberhard Schulz emphatically concluded, he was neither a theologian nor a philosopher, he was first and foremost a jurist.[3]

Juristic law did not, however, represent the limits of Paweł's concerns. Ecclesiastical statutes and Roman jurisprudence were important for him, but they were, in the final analysis, only positive (i.e., enacted) law, made by humans. They were inferior to natural and divine law. The former consisted of those inherent rights and laws common to, and derived rationally from the human condition. All individuals possess this law in common.[4] It is, therefore, not surprising that one of the major thrusts of Paweł's writings is founded upon his understanding of natural law, and it is in this area—as we shall see—that he makes a major contribution.

This volume arose from an editorial and scholarly project, based in Poland, to present works that reflect the Polish tradition of thought about international law in the fifteenth century. In 2018 it published a very useful collection of studies by Polish scholars on Paweł Włodkowic and the Polish School of International Law.[5] Because Paweł's contributions are not well known and appreciated outside Poland (some of the reasons for this are addressed below), a subsequent decision was taken to make Paweł's treatises available in English, with introductions and annotations, ultimately leading to this publication. The excellent English versions are the work of Professor Charles Kraszewski of King's College, a worthy translator in the tradition of Harold B. Segel.[6]

Just as with his writings, Paweł's biography and the context in which he lived and wrote have received relatively little attention in western Europe and North America.[7] Thus the eight works included in this collection need to be set into a framework that addresses all three of these elements.

What follows treats first the historical environment that provided the background shaping Paweł's life and activity, second traces his biography and the events of his lifetime that provoked his treatises (and others), and third provides an overview of the themes and contents of his writings, especially those included in this volume. This will provide readers of the treatises that follow with a basis for understanding his arguments and appreciating their power and significance. More than that, it should suggest why, as Professor Thompson put it in her Foreword, they are worth reading in the twenty-first century. Equally, they should enhance an understanding of the history and significance of this region in East Central Europe.

The Past Becomes Paweł Włodkowic's Present

The region that has become known as East Central Europe (or to some simply Central Europe) had lain outside the Roman world and also, for the most part, Carolingian Europe. In the eyes of some, these entities, particularly the last, were the "older" Europe. To its east, in the territories of a "younger Europe," several polities developed by the end of the tenth century that have traditional been identified as "east central Europe" or "central Europe."[8] Among these was the entity dominated by a family, eventually identified as Piast, in a territory that eventually became known as Poland. It was originally a pagan society, but in 966 the ruler, Duke Mieszko, converted to Catholic Christianity. In subsequent generations, with advances and setbacks, Poland became a Christian society and—after 1025, when its duke was crowned king—a kingdom that was integrated into the politics, culture, religion, and economy of the western, Latin tradition.

Although other polities in the region also became Christian and were part of this same tradition, the Polish state was bordered by a number of territories populated by pagans. This included tribes along the Baltic littoral to its north, including Pomeranians in the area west of the Vistula River to the Oder, and the Prussians in the area roughly east of the Vistula and extending toward the Niemen

River. Eventually the former region was converted and in the early twelfth century it was subjugated by ambitious Piast rulers, one of whom, Bolesław III, nicknamed the Wrymouth (d. 1138), effectively completed the process. The first chronicler of the Poles, a foreigner known traditionally as Gallus Anonymous who wrote at the time of Bolesław, called the Pomeranians and the Prussians, the "most savage nations of pagan barbarians."[9]

By the reign of Bolesław, Poland had advanced from the relatively simple status of its first rulers into a *regnum* that, even if there were no king who ruled, had an identity (abstract to be sure, but also aspirational as something to be potentially revived), a clear sense of its geographic unity, a family tradition that sustained the welfare of its subjects, and a sense of its regional role.[10] These were important, for in the generations after Bolesław's death, struggles between his sons and their successors effectively divided the Polish kingdom into regional duchies. These were ruled by individuals from branches of the Piast family. There were distinct lines in Silesia, Great Poland, Lesser Poland, Mazovia, eventually Kujavia, and—for a time Pomerania, where, however, Piast rule ended for an extended period in the late twelfth century. In this period royal authority effectively ceased to exist, as each of the Piast princelings sought to emulate in their own territories the political structures of governance from previous generations. Some of them sought to achieve superior status by holding what had become the traditional seat of authority, the city of Kraków in Lesser Poland, while perhaps combining that with other territorial possessions. The traditional picture of this division[11] has been one of "internal disorder, political collapse, and weakness in foreign politics."[12]

But not everything in this period should be considered as negative. This was also a time when social and economic transformations of important parts of Poland (and other countries in the region also) took place in a process that has come to be known as *melioratio terrae* ("improvement of the lands").[13] Local dukes and other officials invited newcomers from the west to settle in their territories—peasants, knights, and even clerics—often granting them substantial rights and allowing the establishment of new rural, urban, and ecclesiastical settlements. Innovative agricultural techniques, expanded market opportunities, and privileged religious foundations followed in due course.[14] At the same time, for urban locations especially, existing legal systems required modification and innovation. What was adopted was generally known as German law (*ius Theutonicum*) with its many variations, in particular the version known as Magdeburg Law.[15] Over time this in-migration brought about a dynamic economy and flourishing society.[16] In many ways it reflected the same developments taking place in western Europe, where previously underdeveloped regions were also becoming thriving economic and social centers.[17]

While internally within Poland there were struggles between local dukes and at the same time remarkable economic and social advance, on the borders of the state there were on-going threats to territorial integrity and stability. On the west, the aggressive Ascanian family ruling in Brandenburg sought to expand territorially at Poland's expense. In the north, the Pomeranians, now Christian, sought increasingly to secure independence from the various Polish dukes who, from time to time, claimed suzerainty over them.[18] By the early thirteenth century a local ruler, Mściwój (d. 1219 or 1220) established himself independently as Duke of Pomerania and his son Świętopełk (d. 1266) extended that independence. It was, however, not a status that went unchallenged. All of this was being played out against a backdrop of efforts to Christianize the still-pagan Prussians, that "most savage nation," who often invaded Polish territories.

The approach of the papacy, following earlier efforts to Christianize the Prussians,[19] was to establish a Prussian mission that was given over into the hands of the Cistercian Order, eventually led by Christian, a monk from the monastery in Oliwa that had been founded in

1186. Christian's proselytizing efforts in Prussia were, however, unsuccessful for the most part, and, following the example of the bishop of Riga who in 1202 had founded a military-religious order, the *Fratres Militiae Christi de Livonia*, known commonly as the Sword Brothers,[20] he established a military arm of the Prussian mission. This was confirmed by the papacy in 1228 as a religious-military order entitled The Knights of Christ (also known as the Knights of Dobrzyń, a territory within the Duchy of Mazovia).[21] This duchy was ruled by Duke Conrad, the grandson of Bolesław III the Wrymouth through the line of Bolesław's youngest son Casimir II the Just, and his duchy, along with neighboring Kujavia, suffered significantly from raids by the Prussians. Independent of and impatient with the progress of the Prussian mission and seeking to respond more aggressively to the Prussians, while at the same time hoping to strengthen his own military initiatives again the Prussians, Conrad of Mazovia had begun negotiations on another approach.

Duke Conrad approached another military order, one that already had fought in the Levant and in Hungary; this was the *Ordo Hospitalis S. Mariae Domus Theutonicorum Ierosolimitani*, the Teutonic Order, or simply the Order (which is capitalized for usage in this text), whose common German name is *Der Deutsche Orden* and is known in Poland as *Zakon Krzyżacki* (the Order of the Knights of the Cross for the black cross on the white tunic the knights wore). It is this group that eventually engaged Paweł Włodkowic so profoundly. Founded in the late twelfth century to defend a pilgrim hospital in Jerusalem, St. Mary's of the Germans, it had been forced out of the Holy Land by the resurgence of Muslim power and returned to Europe, briefly helping to defend Hungary's eastern border against the Cumans before being expelled by King Andrew II in 1225. Sometime in 1226, Duke Conrad of Mazovia approached the Teutonic Order and offered them, in terms that were vague and eventually controversial, the territory of Chełmno (*Kulmerland* in German) as a base for their defense of Christian territory and for campaigns against the Prussians. Whether these were intended for conversion or conquest seemed an open question. Subsequently Conrad and others made additional grants to the Order, and in 1226 Emperor Frederick II included apparent confirmation of this in his famous Golden Bull (so-called because of its seal). These circumstances and the actual content and meaning of the grants have long been controversial.[22] The Order's understanding seemed to be that they had been given territorial control of Chełmno and of the Prussian territories they eventually conquered. Eventually the papacy also confirmed these grants and recognized the Order's ownership of all lands gained from the pagans. These developments were among the claims that Paweł challenged aggressively and argued against. Added to this were additional territories that had been part of the Polish kingdom which eventually came under the Order's control (shall see below). The rise of the Order was complemented by increasing numbers of knights and warriors who traveled to the region to participate in campaigns and battles, the pattern that eventually became famous as the *Reisen* celebrated in chivalric literature and tradition.

In the decades that followed the arrival of the Order on Poland's northern border, they eventually conquered the Prussians and established a territorial base in the region as a kind of ecclesiastical state, an *Ordensstaat*.[23] In the process they subsumed the remnants of the Order of the Sword Brothers into their own organization. This consequently involved them in Livonia, defending it against, among others, the Lithuanians, another pagan people in the lowlands of Žemaitija (Samogitia, Polish Żmudź) and the uplands of Aukštaitija. Their campaigns in these regions reflected a high intensity that combined crusading warfare with piety to such a degree that, in the eyes of one modern scholar, it was matched only by developments on the Iberian frontier during the *Reconquista*.[24] While these years of conquest and conversion (usually, but not always, by force) had considerable impact upon Prussia and Lithuania, relations with the Kingdom of Poland, while by no means completely peaceful, were relatively free of conflict.

Whatever its problems with internal strife between various Piast princelings, an external threat from the east made a major impact upon the kingdom. In 1241, the Mongols invaded Poland, successfully attacking Mazovia and Kujavia before proceeding to conquer the region of Lesser Poland (including its two major cities of Sandomierz and Kraków). They then moved on into Silesia where its duke was killed in battle near Legnica. While the Polish lands apparently suffered less than the Kingdom of Hungary, the impact was nevertheless considerable. Among the larger implications of the Mongol invasion was the reality that their attacks had resulted in the destabilization of the northern lands of Kievan Rus'. In the aftermath of the Mongol withdrawal, the Lithuanians began to expand their territories to the southwest into this growing political vacuum, and this resulted in increasing pressure upon the Polish lands and interests. Henceforth, Polish lands, especially parts of Lesser Poland, were subject to raids and military campaigns from the east. These developments were to play out in the next century with a fundamental reorientation of Polish-Lithuanian relations.

Before that happened, however, a reunited kingdom of Poland rather than a collection of local dukes was required. One suggestion that this might be possible had come early in the thirteenth century. Duke Henry I the Bearded of Silesia (ruled 1201-1238) was particularly forward looking in terms of social and economic matters, supporting some of the most important elements of the processes involved with *melioratio terrae*. He was also engaged with other Piast lands, especially the region of Lesser Poland and southern parts of Greater Poland. A later chronicle from Silesia regarded him as a precursor of the process of political unification that eventually was achieved.[25] If one Piast princeling could aspire to higher things, there were eventually others who had similar ambitions and, moreover, had a base of support to do so.

One element that reinforced this trend was associated with the canonization in 1253 of Bishop Stanisław of Kraków, who had been martyred in 1079. His mutilated and quartered body had been found to be miraculously made whole when his coffin was later examined, and this phenomenon was extended to the image of a dismembered and disunited kingdom and its potential restoration. In addition, the church in Poland, all of whose dioceses had remained subject to the metropolitan in Gniezno, represented a lobby that favored reunion. Late in the century another Silesian duke, Henry IV Probus of Wrocław, gained control of Lesser Poland, adding it to his Silesian holdings. He had the support of the archbishop of Gniezno for his coronation but died prematurely in 1290 at the age of 37. Another aspirant, Duke Przemysł of Greater Poland, who had regained control of Pomerania for the Piast line, was actually crowned king in 1295, but was assassinated the next year. Piast interests were interrupted, however, when the king of Bohemia, Václav II, gained sufficient support in Poland to be crowned in 1300, but his reign lasted only five years and his son and successor who claimed the title himself died by assassination in 1306.

The fitful beginnings of the thirteenth and early fourteenth century eventually found a successful claimant. Władysław Łokietek, Duke of Kujavia and grandson of Conrad of Mazovia, emerged as the dominant Piast political leader, regaining the ducal titles of Greater and Lesser Poland that he had previously held and lost. (One other territory he had held and lost — see below — was Pomerania with its major city of Gdańsk/Danzig). With the support of the papacy, the king of Hungary, and a broad range of Polish society he was crowned king in Wawel Cathedral in 1320.[26]

With some exceptions, Łokietek's reign (1320-1333) was not a happy one. On the positive side he was successful in developing international alliances, particularly with Hungary (he arranged to have his daughter Elizabeth marry the king there) and with Lithuania (sealing a treaty with the marriage of his son and eventual successor to the daughter of the Grand Duke). Conversely he needed to overcome challenges from Bohemia, whose king claimed the title of Polish king because he was the successor the former Bohemian ruler, Václav II and who had consolidated Bohemian political and cultural influence over a number of Silesian territories that had previously been solidly part of the Polish kingdom. But it was with the Order to his north that he had the most difficulties, and this was true even before he became king.

As the result of complex developments, and while he was still only Duke of Kujavia and was seeking to achieve control of other Polish territories in the aftermath of the deaths of Václav II and III of Bohemia, Łokietek was able to secure control of Pomerania by 1307. That same year, the Ascanian margraves of Brandenburg occupied this same territory, claiming it had previously been given to them. To help him defend against the Ascanians, Łokietek requested assistance from the Teutonic Order, with whom he had previously had good relations. In this instance, however, after the Order had expelled the margraves' forces, they attacked Łokietek's troops and on the night of 13 November 1308 seized the city of Gdańsk under complicated and controversial circumstances.[27] It was later charged that after the Ascanian siege of the city had been lifted, the knights of the Order went into the city, killed all the soldiers and nobles in the service of Łokietek, and many others, one report putting the number at 10,000. This rumor eventually triggered an papal investigation. The Poles subsequently brought witnesses to bear on these details in the trial of 1320-1321, and the Order denied the worst charges and defended itself vigorously. These events figure in important ways in the writings of Paweł Włodkowic included in this volume. Scholars today have achieved a more balanced view of these details — and some of the subsequent near term developments to be treated below — but at the time these events served to initiate a period of military and political hostility between Poland and the Order that endured for thirty-five years before a semi-permanent resolution was reached in 1343.[28]

In the aftermath of the loss of Gdańsk, Łokietek met with representatives of the Order. Nothing was resolved, and the Order moved quickly to acquire through military campaigns the rest of the territory of Gdańsk Pomerania (Gdańsk Pomorze, i.e. Eastern Pomerania). They also moved the residence of the Order's Grand Master to Marienburg (Polish Malbork) in Prussia.[29] In the following period Łokietek followed two approaches in Poland's relationship with the Order. First he initiated with papal support a legal suit against them. The tribunal assembled in Inowrocław in the spring of 1320. The Order denied the legitimacy of this procedure and refused to participate by sending representatives. Before this papal court, Polish prosecutors leveled charges against the Order, demanding that it be expelled from Pomorze and be fined a substantial amount in damages and legal costs. Twenty-five witnesses from a number of social statuses, both ecclesiastical and secular, were called to testify to the validity of the charges, and upon this basis the court found for Łokietek in February 1321.[30] (Paweł Włodkowic makes numerous references to this judgment and its legitimacy in his writings.) The Order ignored this legal outcome, and not long thereafter Łokietek abandoned diplomacy and legalities and turned to military action.

Between 1326 and 1333 Łokietek mounted almost annual campaigns against the Order to recover what he regarded as the lost territories of the *regnum Poloniae*. Practically every year the Order prevailed and, as a result the Polish kingdom lost additional lands. These included Kujavia and Dobrzyń, the latter of which was to be Paweł's homeland and was to be later invaded a number of other times as Paweł makes clear in his treatises. Only once, at the Battles of Płowce in 1331, were the Poles victorious, but their gains were lost the following years. Thus when he died, Łokietek left behind him, in the words of a later chronicler known as Traska, a "great chaos of error and license."[31] He had, however, by unifying rule in Greater Poland and Lesser Poland, successfully revived the monarchy, ending to some degree several generations of a politically and territorially fragmented Poland. His success was continued by his son and successor Kazimierz III, known eventually as The Great.

Kazimierz's relations with the Order appeared, at first, to mirror his father's policy. After arranging and extending a number of truces to stabilize Polish-Order relations, he indicated a willingness to submit outstanding issues between them to mediation by the kings of Bohemia and Hungary (the latter his brother-in-law). A preliminary effort in this direction came at a glittering congress of kings and princes in 1335 at Visegrád, the second Hungarian capital. It resulted in progress on a number of issues (including resolving some of the tensions between Poland and Bohemia over John of Luxembourg's continuing claims to the Polish royal title).[32] Yet problems still remained with the Order, so Kazimierz resolved to try to achieve success with another judicial proceeding. He and his advisors persuaded the papacy to convene a tribunal in Warsaw in 1339 to adjudicate Polish claims against the Order. On this occasion 176 witnesses were called and 126 of them testified. Presenting thirty articles of dispute, the Polish procurators asked them about many of the same issues that had been presented in the 1320-1321 proceeding, but they went further. Questions about the Order's unlawful possession of the Chełmno region were posed, complaints about the conquests of Pomorze in 1308-1309 were made, similar charges about losses to the Order in the 1320s and 1330s were detailed, and assertions as to the damages the Order had inflicted upon the *regnum Poloniae* and the *ecclesia Poloniae* itemized and fiscal losses listed. The Order refused to participate in the tribunal, stating only that it did not recognize the authority of the court. When the judges pronounced their verdict, they ruled uniformly for the Poles.[33] This decision, along with that from 1321, was a settled judgment in Paweł's mind nearly a century later, for, as one will see in his treatises, he accepted these as final and binding upon the Order. At the time, however, the Order ignored this decision and immediately appealed directly to Pope Benedict XII, who proposed an arbitrated settlement. He died before further steps could be taken, and his successor was disinclined to alter Benedict's policy. At this point, Kazimierz decided to resolve the matter peacefully instead of reverting to war or any longer to legal tribunals as his father had. He entered into negotiations with the Order, and in 1343 a treaty was signed between them at Kalisz in Poland allowing the Order to retain Chełmno, Pomorze, and a few minor possessions, but would return Kujavia and Dobrzyń to Poland.[34]

Somewhat surprisingly, given the military and political conflict between Poland and the Order that has been outlined in previous paragraphs, the Peace of Kalisz held. Despite a few instances of tension and dispute during the rest of Kazimierz's reign, this was a generally peaceful stage in the history of Polish-Order relations.[35] In that time Kazimierz increasingly turned his attention eastward, to the territories of Halych and Volhynia (Red Ruthenia), whose ruler had died without heir in 1340. It was a region that became contested between Poland, Lithuania, and Hungary (Casimir's Lithuanian wife had died in 1339, and Polish-Lithuanian relations worsened in the aftermath). Generally good Polish-Order relations continued into the twelve-year reign (1370-1382) of Louis of Anjou and beyond, following the accession of his younger daughter, Jadwiga, as his successor in 1384.[36] By the end of the 1380s, however, the situation had begun to change dramatically.

In these years the Order was able to concentrate upon the mission it claimed it had been given in the region in the first place, the crusade against the pagans. Its focus was upon Lithuania, especially upon Žemaitija (Samogitia), and its almost annual campaigns often included knightly participants from the west who came to join in what came to be called *Reisen*.[37] These decades were the era when the

Order reached the apex of its medieval power, and was remembered as a golden era (*goldene Blütezeit*), a time during which — as a contemporary remarked — "under Grand Master Winrich [von Kniprode, ruled 1352-1382] Prussia stood among great honor and praise."[38] In addition to its military activities the Order also emerged as a distinctive regional representative of medieval chivalry. Without the female component of the chivalry of courtly love which was present elsewhere, the Order celebrated the military virtues of war against the foes of Christ and the Virgin Mary. Their chivalric code included generosity, service, honor, good manners, and gracious living. It is this outlook that is echoed in Chaucer's depiction in *The Canterbury Tales* of the "parfit gentil knight," who found that he could follow "chivalrie, trouthe and honor, freedom and curtesie" and had been given a seat of honor "above alle nacions in Pruce," for "in Lettow hadde he reysed and in ruce, no christen man so ofte of his degree."[39] On the battlefield, although there was a short period when a relative degree of peaceful stability existed between the Order and Lithuania,[40] the ruthless violence — on both sides — was considerable. Details of this are reflected in some of Paweł Włodkowic's charges against the Order. Despite individual victories, by the latter years of the fourteenth century the Order had made little progress. It continued, however, to be a threat to Lithuanian leaders. By this time, however, there had been some important changes in Lithuania.

In 1341/1342 Grand Duke Gediminas of pagan Lithuania died, succeeded by two of his sons. The older, Algirdas, primarily focused his activity on eastward expansion, reaching Kiev and Moscow in 1368. The younger, Kestutis, concentrated his attention upon the border with Poland and upon the Ruthenian lands that had become contested between Poland and Lithuania. When Algiridis died, his son Jogaila challenged Kestutis for control of the whole Grand Duchy. Still a pagan, Jogaila played Kestutis's son, Vytautas, off against his father, then outmaneuvered his cousin by negotiations with the Order, implying he would convert to Christianity (he successfully misled them). By the early 1380's Jogaila had consolidated his position over the duchy as a whole, but needed to work out relations with two of his neighbors. One was the Order, still a threat to pagan Lithuania and generally unwilling to support Jogaila (whom it no longer trusted); the other was with another traditional opponent of both Lithuania and of the Order, the Kingdom of Poland.[41]

It is difficult to determine whether it was Jogaila who took the initiative to approach the Poles or whether it was they, for their own reasons (including the necessity to find a spouse for their ruler, Jadwiga of Anjou, who had been crowned *in regem* in 1384) who made a proposal first.[42] Jogaila's representatives met with the Poles in January 1385 and presented his own proposal. Accepted in principal by the Poles, details were worked out in Krėva (Krewo in Polish) in August 1385. The final version included stipulations that Jogaila would recover the lands lost by Poland to the Order, would baptize all pagan inhabitants of his duchy into Latin Christianity, and would join Lithuania and its Ruthenian lands to the Polish crown in perpetuity (*perpetuo applicare*). This agreement was to be sealed by his own conversion to Catholicism and his marriage to Jadwiga. Then in February 1386, he converted, taking the Christian name Władysław, thereby linking himself to the royal tradition of Władysław Łokietek, and married Jadwiga. (The Polonized version of his Lithuanian name, by which he is usually known, is Jagiełło.)[43]

Within a year, the conversion of pagan Lithuania was well under way, not by force, as the Order had been attempting, but by education and example. Polish officials and clergy — both regular and secular — went into Lithuania and provided church organization, liturgy, and leadership. Jagiełło himself is said to have translated the Lord's Prayer and the Apostles' Creed into Lithuanian; Jadwiga contributed financial and material resources, including such ecclesiastical artifacts as chalices, crucifixes, prayer books; and substantial endowments were provided for the newly established Catholic bishopric in Vilnius, the Lithuanian capital.[44] This process was not lost upon the leaders of the Order, who quickly realized that if Lithuania were to become Christian, the rationale behind its activity regarding Lithuania (i.e., forcible conversion) would be rendered null and void. One alternative was to ignore what appeared to have happened; and indeed, in the very year of Jagiełło's conversion and marriage, the Order's Grand Master Konrad Zöllner, mounted an invasion of Lithuania. Another option, which was quickly seized upon, was to deny that any true conversion (of Jagiełło or the Lithuanians) had taken place, that what had happened was all a sham, that they were still pagans, and that, therefore, nothing had changed about the validity of the Order's mission.[45] The one thing that was different, however, was the union of the two polities; and as a result, relations between the Order and Poland entered a stage of increasing tension and hostility. The Order tried to play the ambitions of the two cousins, Jagiełło and Vytautas, off against one another, ultimately unsuccessfully. By the late 1390s the two were increasingly working together, if not, as Robert Frost has put it, in "a harmonious collaboration based on trust and the pursuit of common goals," at least they had "established a *modus* vivendi which characterized their whole relationship thereafter."[46] Vytautas, who had suffered a shattering military defeat in 1399 at the Vorskla River on the eastern periphery of Lithuania, thus ending his expansionist policy in that direction,[47] accepted his status as Grand Duke and as Jagiełło's plenipotentiary in Lithuania, even if his cousin styled himself *Supremus dux Lithuaniae*. Increasingly after that the concerns of the two focused upon military threats from the Order, which were, at first at a relatively low level, but soon became a constant and growing problem. These built until the crisis of 1409.

On 6 September of that year the Order effectively declared war against Poland and Lithuania.[48] To strengthen his resources, Jagiełło sought to enhance the number of troops under his command by accepting support from the Tatars, who were pagans, and others who were not Catholic Christians. This was later to be an issue that Paweł addressed in his writings. After a period of miliary skirmishing between the Order and troops under Polish or Lithuanian command, in the spring of 1410 Jagiełło, along with troops led by Vytautas, marched north toward Prussian territory of the Order, crossing the Vistula on a pontoon bridge that Długosz marveled at. They were encouraged by the bishop of Płock, who pronounced their cause to be a just war.[49] After more maneuvering, in an area whose location was determined by the Poles to be near the village of Grunwald (the Lithuanians translated this as Žalgiris) and where the Order determined their location by reference to the village of Tannenberg, the two armies confronted one another on 15 July 1410.

The battle of Grunwald was one of the largest in medieval history. Although estimates vary, there may, at the high-end, have been 39,000 Polish-Lithuanian troops and 27,000 from the Order. At the low end, reasonable estimates are about 16,500 for the Poles and Lithuanians and 11,000 for their opponents. One scholar, who has had a substantial impact upon the study of this battle, puts the totals at 20,000 to 25,000 for the Poles and 12,000 to 15,000 for the Germans.[50] The Poles were slow to engage in battle, perhaps because they continued to organize and position their forces. One anecdote from the conflict comes from the moment when representatives of the Grand Master presented Jagiełło and Vytautas with two swords to assist them in battle. This has traditionally been taken as an insult, implying cowardice, and a provocation. Polish national memory has certainly taken it that way. When the fighting began, however, it was brutal and deadly, it lasted multiple hours and was filled with a broad range of military tactics and maneuvers, some of which were considered controversial. Losses may have been as high as 8,000 for each side. These included a great many of the leading commanders of the Order — including the Grand Master, the Grand Marshall, the Grand Komtur, the Grand Treasurer, the Marshall of Supply Services, and others. More than fifty heraldic banners of troop leaders were captured and taken back to Kraków, where eventually Jan Długosz commissioned a painter to depict them in a volume that he then annotated.[51]

From a military standpoint the Polish-Lithuanian victory at Grunwald was a crushing defeat for the Order. Jagiełło, however, failed to pursue the advantage the battle had given him. He delayed at the battlefield, and was slow to march further into Prussia in order to lay siege to and capture the seat of the Order at Marienburg (Malbork). The eventual new Grand Master had gathered fresh troops that successfully resisted, and the siege was raised in September 1410. The subsequent months saw little but skirmishes, and slowly the war ground down and devolved into negotiations held in Toruń. From these came the [First] Peace of Toruń, agreed to on 11 February 1411. Jagiełło received some territory — Samogitia was returned to Lithuanian rule for the lifetimes of Jagiełło and Vytautas and the Polish territory of Dobrzyń, into which Paweł had been born in 1370, went back to Poland. The Order, however, retained most of the Polish territories it had taken in the early fourteenth century, though it did have to pay a substantial ransom for the release of its troops captured in battle.

In retrospect the battle of Grunwald, whose actual location has now been determined,[52] resolved very little. There were subsequent disagreements over the actual borders of Samogitia, which were submitted to Sigismund of Luxembourg, King of Hungary and Holy Roman Emperor elect in 1412. He upheld the terms of the Toruń treaty but did agree to send his representative Benedict Makrai to the region to obtain testimony regarding border issues. This mission also did not solve matters to Jagiełło's satisfaction, although Makrai did award Lithuania possession of territory on the north bank of the Niemen River with its port city of Memel. Other contested issues led again to a short, indecisive war in 1414 (the so-called Hunger War, as it ended when Polish troops were withdrawn due to lack of food supplies). With little resolved as a result of these negotiations and military conflicts, Jagiełło, with the support of the secular and ecclesiastical leaders of Poland and Lithuania resolved to take the matter before the greatest international assembly of the fifteenth century, the Council of Constance.[53]

The last paragraphs above have revealed the world into which Paweł Włodkowic had been born about 1370. The larger treatment of this section has not attempted to provide a fully rounded history, but have rather sought to identify the details and context that are most important for understanding the traditions and problems he dealt with. The section that follows traces Paweł's biography and features the historical developments leading up to the Council of Constance that are most important for understanding and appreciating the treatises he wrote and the philosophy he presented.

Paweł's Life and What His Times Provided and Presented for Him: to 1414

Paweł was born about 1370, apparently in the district of Dobrzyń in Mazovia.[54] The noble family into which he was born was the Dołęga clan, one of the more important of such groupings in Mazovia.[55] He apparently received his earliest education in the episcopal city of Płock, where his progress was such that he was enabled to travel to Bohemia and enroll in Arts at the University of Prague, which had been recently founded by King and Holy Roman Emperor elect Charles IV in 1347/1348. He was promoted as *baccalarius in artibus* in 1389, which suggests his first enrollment may have been two or three years earlier, since this was the typical length of time to complete an Arts degree in medieval *studia*. Four years later, in February 1393, he is noted as *magister artium*, a slightly longer period required for this degree than normal. He remained in Prague, enrolling in the Faculty of

Law that same year and three years later earned the bachelor's degree in canon law. For a while he apparently remained in Prague lecturing in Arts, which was a characteristic responsibility of those who had gone on to study in the higher Faculties after their studies in Arts.[56]

It is difficult to know the degree to which Paweł was influenced by the dynamic environment at Prague in this period. He does mention that one well-known theologian, Maurice Rvačka of Prague, was one of his teachers, but this would probably have been while he was studying in arts.[57] Beyond that, one can only infer in general terms that the growing tensions — national between Czechs and Germans, theological and philosophical between those like Jan Hus and others influenced by Wycliffe and opponents of this — had any impact upon him. There was also a spirit of ecclesiastical reform evident in Prague at this time that was eventually to feature the person of Jan Hus and his followers.[58]

Following his Bohemian studies, Paweł returned to Poland and, having taken clerical orders, was appointed as a scholastic in Poznań in 1398, then canon in Płock in 1400. This ecclesiastical career was one in which neither the positions nor the income they produced required in person pastoral duty, i.e., the *cura animarum*; this, combined with Paweł's own intellectual abilities and, perhaps, his ambitions, led him to pursue his study of law further. He may have been encouraged in this by the bishop of Kraków, Piotr Wysz, who had studied in Padua, earned the doctoral degree in both canon and civil law, and served as rector of the ultramontane university there in 1385. In 1403 or 1404 Paweł went to Padua, where he earned the license in canon law in 1408. This involved becoming familiar with a very substantial body of church law that had been developing since the early Middle Ages. Paweł would have had to read — and in many instances commit to memory — the core elements of that law (the *Decretum* of Gratian, the numerous compilations that had become official since that, a vast body of commentary, and glosses and even appropriate elements from Roman civil law that related to church matters. His command of these materials will be evident in the treatises that follow this Introduction.)[59]

With one degree attained, Paweł agreed at that point to continue his studies at Padua should he seek the doctoral degree in law. One of his teachers was Francisco Zabarella (1360-1417), one of the leading canonists of the day and, after 1411, a cardinal in the conciliar line held by Pope John XXIII. It is clear that Zabarella's scholarship and politics were important to Paweł, for he cited him often in his treatises and relied upon him at the Council of Constance to support the Polish position Paweł pursued there. Whether Paul actively pursued further academic study in Italy after 1408, he was certainly active in diplomatic affairs on behalf of the Polish monarchy. On one occasion, if not on others, he served as a representative of King Władysław Jagiełło on matters related to activities of the Order in Samogitian matters. Paweł as a result became familiar with royal policy and with proceedings in the papal chancery; this knowledge was to stand him in good stead in later years. Paweł was also probably present at the Council of Pisa in 1409, since he refers in *Saevientibus* to lectures at that council delivered by Peter de Ancharano, implying that he had heard them.[60] (This council had been convened to resolve the schism within the Latin church where one individual in Avignon claimed to be the rightful pope and another in Rome made the same claim. The meeting at Pisa only succeeded in exacerbating the problem by electing a third pontifical line, thus continuing the schism.) Shortly after this, however, Paweł returned to Poland.

Whatever had drawn him back — and we know no details that bear directly on this — Paweł began to teach canon law at the newly reestablished University of Kraków. He also renewed his academic studies in law, obtaining on 24 March 1411 a papal dispensation from John XXIII that lifted the requirement he study only at Padua. This then allowed him to complete his doctoral degree in canon law under the direction of Stanisław of Skarbimierz, the dean of the law faculty and first rector of the renewed *studium*. Stanisław's sermon recommending him for that degree in 1411 made the revealing points that this degree came not only because of mastery of the laws but also because of his knowledge of secular matters and his service, as he put it, *pro profectu Rei publice*. Knowledge of God's laws and of canonical matters was important, but so too was knowledge of secular learning and participation in secular matters. Clearly Paweł's status as a skilled negotiator and articulate defender of royal and national interests were recognized.[61] That same year Paweł was appointed *custos et canonicus Ecclesiae Cracoviensis* (i.e., Wawel Cathedral in Kraków), having at some previous point been ordained a priest (he was identified as such at the Council of Constance).

For the next few years, Paweł balanced his academic teaching with his service to his king. He was an advisor to the Polish delegation that participated in the court of arbitration in Buda in 1412 and played the same role in the investigative mission led by Benedict of Macrai that Sigismund of Luxembourg had instituted in the aftermath of the unsatisfactory decision — from a Polish Jagiellonian standpoint — about what the appropriate borders between Poland, Lithuania and the Order should be.[62] Paweł was present at a number of the hearings that Benedict of Macrai held in 1413 as part of his mission northward. The next year, he was also involved in matters before Sigismund in Buda that were related to these continuing difficulties. The Polish delegation was led by Andrew Łaskarz, a distinguished Polish diplomat who had earned his arts degrees at Prague and a doctoral degree in canon law at Padua (his promoter there was Peter Wysz). He had come under the influence of Renaissance humanism while in Italy (Pier Paolo Vergerio was a close friend), and was on an a fast-track ecclesiastical career (he was named bishop-elect of Poznań in 1414), and who was to be particularly active at the Council of Constance in both ecclesiastical issues and political matters on behalf of the Polish ruler.[63] Paweł's role in the delegation to Buda was as representative for the Duke of Mazovia, but when Andrew was not available, Paweł took his place as agent for the king.

Finally, in this crucial year of 1414, Paweł was elected rector of the University of Kraków, an annual position (at that time) that insured he was the leader and speaker for the institution. Paweł was thus part of the university and part of the policy program of the Polish king.

With this we come to a point in Paweł's life and career where it is appropriate to examine briefly the university of which he was a part (*Universitas Cracoviense*) and the larger university tradition that it represented, for in many ways it defined the approach taken by Paweł; moreover, this institution was one of the most significant achievements of the Middle Ages. Having done so, we return then to the details of developments at Constance and after.

Paweł's Life and What His Times Provided and Presented for Him: the University

Medieval Europe was not a uniform, static, isolated, savage, and primitive single block of time. Throughout more than ten centuries, it was instead a dynamic, complex, and creative era. It was not the proverbial "Dark Ages;" rather it more appropriately has been recently referred to as "the Bright Ages."[64] In the broad variety of ways that medieval institutional structures developed in response to changed circumstances, multiple sources of leadership emerged. Political authority was found in kingship and lordship and subsumed collectively in the Latin terminology of the era as *regnum*. Religious authority of many kinds was recognized collectively as *sacerdotium*. These two were, by the high medieval centuries after 1100, complemented by a new phenomenon, the university — *studium* — that was original to Europe and distinct from the range of learning available from antiquity and the early medieval period.[65] Paris and Bologna take pride of place in terms of chronological evolution without formal beginnings, but they were soon complemented by others that were founded more or less *de novo* by secular or ecclesiastical rulers. By the thirteenth century the form and function of such organizations had taken clearer shape and one can speak with confidence about curriculum, organization and governance, personnel, scholarly privileges, and contributions.[66] In this century and the first half of the one that followed a number of universities were founded in Europe, but none of them lay east of the Rhine River. Then with striking rapidity the rulers of "younger Europe" moved to follow western developments. Prague was founded in 1347/1348, Kraków in 1364, Vienna in 1365, Pécs in 1367 and Heidelberg in 1385 (the first university in the German lands proper). In tracing Paweł Włodkowic's career in the course of the previous pages, there has been mention of several universities, particularly Padua, Prague, and Kraków. In what follows, the Cracovian university environment of which he was a member is the focus.

It was the Polish king Kazimierz III who first sought to found a university in Kraków. The institutional and intellectual resources of the Polish kingdom had improved to the point where it was no longer necessary to undertake the long, expensive, and often dangerous journeys to *studia* in France or on the Italian peninsula, and he saw the need for university trained individuals, especially in law, to serve in both royal and ecclesiastical administration. He sent a delegation to the pope, then residing in Avignon, in the early 1360s with a petition for a "*studium generale* in all faculties, and especially in canon as well as civil law." The response was that the pope requested that the archbishop of Gniezno gather information about what Kazimierz intended by way of licenses and privileges. What he learned from this led him to support the royal petition, for on 12 May 1364 Kazimierz issued his document of foundation. The pope subsequently modified some of the terms contained in Kazimierz's document, but the university seemed to be on the path to success.[67] Such was not the case, and in the years that followed Kazimierz's death in 1370 the institution sank into decrepitude. Only in the early 1390s were efforts made to revive it.[68] These also did not result in the reopening of the university, though in 1399 King Władysław Jagiełło, along with his wife and co-ruler Jadwiga, obtained permission from Pope Boniface IX to establish a theological faculty in Kraków.[69]

It remained for Jagiełło, urged on by Jadwiga, to complete the *instauracio studii* that both of them, along with major ecclesiastical figures, desired. This came on 26 July 1400 when Jagiełło issued his document of foundation (ironically a year after Jadwiga had died, although she provided money, garments, and jewels to help endow the new — or renewed — institution). He hoped the *studium* would help complete the Christianization of Lithuania, he desired that the university would bring the same glories to Poland as other universities bring to their countries, and he expected the *studium* would serve the good of the kingdom. He was supported in this by the clergy and citizenry of Kraków.[70] Together they secured the creation of a university that, after some early difficulties, flourished in the remaining decades of the fifteenth century and on into the early years of the next. Governed by a rector, elected annually until 1419 and semi-annually thereafter, it consisted of four faculties: Arts, Theology, Law, and Medicine, each led by an elected dean. It attracted students from throughout Poland, and by the end of the fifteenth century there were annual new matriculations often above 300 (small in comparison with Paris and Bologna, but normative for most northern European universities). Many of the students at the university came from outside Poland and Lithuania, often reaching in the last decades of the fifteenth century an average above 50% of the matriculations, thus making Kraków in general an international center of higher learning. Many of the masters and professors were also from international locations, especially from Silesia, which in the fourteenth century had been almost fully incorporated into Bohemia.

For the most part — as was true of the pattern at the other medieval universities — students studied in the Arts faculty, whose curriculum was built around the *trivium* — the three-fold way to knowledge and wisdom (grammar, rhetoric, and dialectic, i.e., logic), the *quadrivium* — the fourfold way (music, geometry, mathematics, and astronomy), and the three philosophies: moral, metaphysics, and natural. It usually required two or three years to reach the baccalaureate and another two or three before becoming Masters of Arts. In some of these fields, achievements were of very high quality and greatly enhanced Kraków's international reputation. Part of the reason for this was that there were a number of endowed chairs in specific subjects established at Kraków unlike the situation at many other institutions. The Stobner Chair, established in 1405, was for mathematics and astronomy, including the preparation annually of an Almanac. The Mężykowa Chair, established in 1420, was for grammar and rhetoric, including instruction in the art of writing letters and official documents. And the Nowko Chair, established in 1406 but implemented only in 1419 upon the death of the donor, was for rhetoric or grammar. These chairs carried special responsibilities and the incumbent often held the position for a number of years, being able to pursue a program of instruction that might well include use by the professor of a text he had developed for the subject at hand. For example, one holder of this chair was John of Dąbrówka, eventually nine times university rector and reformer of the curriculum. He used the chair as a base to teach rhetoric with reference to the *Chronica Polonorum* of the Polish historian Vincent Kadłubek (*ca.* 1150-1223), eventually bishop of Kraków. John prepared a commentary on this work that was both historical and philosophical/moral. John's own work eventually became a text that was to be used as the basis for lectures to instruct students in matters historical, moral, and didactic.[71] (One subject taken up in it was derived from the Arts — issues related to the question of moral philosophy and political theory, including the just war — and will be treated below in the context of Paweł's writings and those of other Cracovian faculty.)

The exact sciences, particularly mathematics and astronomy, were another specific area of Kraków's accomplishments. For example, one of Kraków's most famous students in this area — though his finished work came later — was Nicholas Copernicus. Kraków was recognized as being, in the oft-repeated conclusion of Aleksander Birkenmajer, "an international center of astronomical education at the end of the Middle Ages."[72] Achievements in other areas, such as logic and natural philosophy, were equally important, reflecting especially the influence of John Buridan (ca. 1295-1361), the Parisian master whose work on logic and impetus were strongly felt in Kraków.[73] Philosophically, the traditions of moderate Nominalism and the *via moderna* were strong at the university in the first half of the fifteenth century, but in the following decades the *via antiqua* of Thomas Aquinas, Albert the Great, and John Scottus Eriugena came into prominence (Kraków was the second most important center of Albertist thought after Cologne).[74]

Should students continue into higher studies — and not many at Kraków and other medieval universities did[75] — Canon Law and Theology were the chief alternatives, since the medical Faculty was weak and students interested in that profession went abroad, usually to Italy. The curriculum in Canon Law was, as was the curriculum at other universities, defined by the *Corpus iuris canonici*, though this title was not used until the late sixteenth century. It consisted of the *Decretum* of Gratian, the *Decretales* of Pope Gregory IX (which effectively superseded previous *compilationes* or *extravagantes*, though they were often still cited as *Liber extra*), the *Liber sextus* of Pope Boniface VIII, the Clemintine Constitutions of Pope John XXII along with his own *Extravagantes*, plus a very broad range of glosses upon various parts of canon law that needed to be included in what one seeking a degree must master. As noted elsewhere, this mastery also included much memorization and the ability to respond quickly in debate and discussion with appropriate references. A deep familiarity with the Bible thus was complemented by a fluid command of a very large body of law, and the impressive range of citations Paweł made in the writings included in this volume is evidence of that command. After Paweł had become a member of the law faculty at Kraków he would have taught the subject in which he was best grounded or, more probably, the subject he was assigned by the faculty dean, even though the benefice he held did not require any teaching. Since what was taught was essentially the transmission of a received tradition, reflective creativity came in special polemical treatises or in material created to support the application of law to contemporary problems of political concern, such as those written by Paweł. In this respect, he was like other learned scholars who both taught and served — either some ecclesiastical leader or, more likely, the secular official who was most in a position to utilize his expertise, the Polish ruler.[76] From 1400, when the *studium* was re-established until the time of his death in 1431, that dean was Stanisław of Skarbimierz, who had also been the first rector of the revived university. He had studied Arts and Canon Law at Prague and was known as an exceptional preacher and speaker. The body of his writings is extensive.[77] One of them, his sermon *De bellis iustis*, was prepared on the eve of the Battle of Grunwald and will figure below in the discussion of Paweł's writings.[78]

The other higher faculty at Kraków was theology. Its curriculum, too, was well defined. The Bible and the various commentaries on it, either that by Nicholas of Gorran or that by Nicholas of Lyra, were used, together with other glosses by previous European theologians. The other fundamental text was the four books of *Sentences* by Peter Lombard, on the basis of which lectures were provided at various stages of study. An individual who studied theology moved through mastery of these texts and, in some instances, wrote their own commentaries, especially on various books of the *Sentences*.[79] There were a number of important theologians at Kraków in the course of the fifteenth century, and some of them — along with some of the canonists — weighed in on some of the more important ecclesiastical issues of the century. No where is this more evident than the conciliar treatises written by Cracovian scholars in the context of the Council of Basel (1434-1449). Their contribution to larger issues in conciliar theory has only recently begun to be appreciate outside Poland.[80]

This brief overview of some aspects of the academic environment within which Paweł functioned after he completed his doctoral program at Kraków, had become a member of the Law Faculty, and then been elected the university's rector prepares us to see him further engaged with the affairs of the Polish kingdom and, in the year of his election, being sent to the Council of Constance as part of the Polish delegation pursuing, among other issues, the long-time conflict between Poland and the Teutonic Order.

Paweł Between Royal Policy and Political Theory: Constance

The Council of Constance was not convened to consider issues between Poland and the Order. Rather its primary purpose was to address the decades-long trauma within Latin Christendom known as the Great Western Schism.[81] It had endured since 1378 when the papacy, newly returned from years of residency in Avignon, had split between a pope in Rome claiming to be the rightful pontiff and one in Avignon making the same claim. After a number of unsuccessful efforts to close the schism, a council, convened by the cardinals of both popes, met in Pisa in 1409 to resolve the problem. It only succeeded in making matters worse by electing a third pope. Within a few years, however, Sigismund of Luxembourg, king of Hungary and, after 1410 Holy Roman Emperor elect, resolved to have another council called, one with more power than Pisa. In this he was successful, gaining support from both ecclesiastical and secular leaders, and it began in 1414 in Constance. One of the most important councils in the history of the Latin church, it included a very large number of clerics of all stations, along with several thousand visitors — retinues, hangers-on, and delegates representing kings, princes, and cities.[82] It was also, as a result, the greatest of all medieval representative assemblies. After organizational and procedural matters were decided upon,[83] it was generally agreed that the main purpose of the council was three-fold: ending the schism; addressing problems of heresy in England and Bohemia (followers of John Wycliffe [d. 1384] in the former and the person of Jan Hus and his advocates in the latter); and reforming the church in terms of both its head and members (*in capite et in membris*). Yet there were other issues, with their accompanying advocates, that also required attention. This eventually caused Sigismund to define the following tasks: in addition to the three central topics noted above, there were others that could be addressed when possible. These included union between the eastern and western churches, peace between France and England in their Hundred Years' War, the matter of regicide that had been part of that war, a crusade against the Ottoman Turks, and — finally — the conflict between the Order and Poland.[84] This last item that had convulsed northeastern Europe for generations was now brought officially before the representatives of Christendom.

On 9 November 1414 Jagiełło appointed his delegation to the council. At its formal head was the archbishop of Gniezno, Nicholas Trąba, and it included the bishop of Płock, the canonist Jacob Kurdwanowski, the aforementioned Andreas Łaskarz, bishop-elect of Poznań, Peter Wolfram, licentiate *in decretis* and a master at the university of Kraków, some members of the laity, and Paweł Włodkowic. He was the *de facto* head of the delegation: a royal representative and expert and not a representative of the *studium*, though he maintained very close contacts with it.[85] Although active against the Order at

Constance, the bishop of Włocławek, Johannes Kropidło, was not an official member of the Polish delegation.[86] The range of activities of the other members of the Polish delegation are of lesser concern here than what it was Paweł did. He was most active in the conciliar commission dealing with matters of the faith and of church reform, but as will be apparent below he was fully engaged in discussions within the German nation.

Even before the Polish delegation arrived in Constance, representatives of the Order had already undertaken to defend its role in the Baltic and to accuse the Poles of having opposed and hampered efforts to accomplish the mission they regarded as having been legitimated by numerous papal and imperial grants. On Christmas Day 1414, Archbishop Johannes von Wallenrode of Riga, the head of the delegation which the Order had sent to Constance, addressed those already assembled there in a sermon that accused the Poles of monstrous actions, sacrilegious tyranny, and abdominal blasphemies. Later, in a sermon before emperor-elect Sigismund of Luxembourg, he praised the martial virtues of the Order, urging Sigismund to protect the Order. Then, early in 1415, Peter von Wormditt, the General Procurator of the Order, presented a defense of the Order in a work of twenty-six points, arguing that it had been instituted out of public necessity to defend against pagan attacks upon Christians in the Baltic and to defend Christendom. In many ways his arguments would have been well received, for, as Frederick H. Russell has observed, the "Order had the weight of theory, privileges, official toleration and two centuries of success on its side."[87]

One event that occurred early in the council had a bearing on issues related to Poland, Lithuania, and the Order. Even before Paweł made the argument in his first conciliar treatise that Samogitia was part of Lithuania and that its Christianization was proceeding peacefully in accomplishing what the Order had failed to achieve by force, a visual manifestation of that reality arrived in Constance. In December 1415 a Samogitian delegation of sixty individuals arrived, coming to plead for their rights as a sovereign people to retain their liberty and to have Christian missionaries come to them rather than soldiers from the Order. This created a sensation. Paweł quickly prepared a *Propositio Samagitarum* (or *Samaytarum*) containing forty points contrasting the Order's military violence with the peaceful efforts adopted by Jagiełło and Vytautas. Supported by this, the delegation won over a majority of the delegates at the council, casting Poland in a very positive light. Later, the visit to the council of an Orthodox metropolitan, Gregory Camblak, who was increasing inclined to Catholic Christianity by missionaries from Poland, reinforced this sentiment.[88]

In what follows, there will be no attempt to provide a fully rounded picture of the council. Instead, the focus will be upon the activities and concerns of Paweł and his writings.[89]

After engagement in some of the formal activities of the Council, Paweł spent much of the winter 1415-1416 preparing materials that he later presented in the treatises to be discussed below. In doing so, he drew partly upon discussions that had taken place at the university in Kraków before his departure for Constance; these included the sermon on the just war by Stanisław of Skarbimierz[90] and suggestions from masters and professors there on issues that were to be presented to the council.[91] In doing so he demonstrated that he was speaking as both an academic and as a royal representative, a dual status at Constance that he performed brilliantly.

— *Saevientibus*

On 5 July 1416, Paweł distributed to members of the German nation the first of two works, entitled, from the initial word or words of its Latin text, *Saevientibus*.[92] It came after the Order had refused to recognize any claim the council had to discuss whether the disputed territories it held were held rightfully. The treatise did not touch closely upon questions of boundaries or claims of military and territorial aggression against Poland by the Order. Paweł's approach was rather more general, first inquiring into the validity and effectiveness of the papal and imperial privileges upon which the Order justified themselves and their actions. After an introduction, Paweł presented an analysis of eleven points regarding what powers the pope had with respect to infidels. This is followed by a second section of eleven points devoted to what powers the emperor had in the same respect. Underlying the assumptions of these section is that letters from various popes and emperors appear to have given the Order the right to conquer and convert by pagans by force and the right to wage war against the Poles and to legitimately hold the territories they had conquered. This was an assumption that Paweł rejected on the basis of both canon law and the Bible. He concluded with a series of arguments against the views of the thirteenth century canonist, Hostiensis (Henry of Segusio, eventually Cardinal of Ostia), whose position was that any action against pagans was justifiable, since they had, as of the incarnation of Christ, lost all of their natural rights.

Paweł's introduction immediately puts forward the general principal of toleration, asserting that when pagans wish to live peacefully among themselves or with Christians, their persons and property should not be molested (*nulla molestia in personis et rebus*). With respect to papal power, Paweł accepts that the pope has jurisdiction over all humanity, but that with regard to pagans, that power is paternal, only allowing the pope to punish them when they fail to obey laws they are obliged to observe, and these are natural laws. (Indeed, the principle of natural law was to be an important part of all Paweł's argument.). If, however, pagans or infidels obtain territories in contravention of natural law, then the pope, who has full power (*plenitudo potestatis*), must only act to limit them in a legal manner (*de iure*). Following the canonical laws of Pope Innocent IV (d. 1254) and the views of Cardinal Zabarella, Paweł's master at Padua and an important figure at Constance,[93] the pope should only act in the cases of a very great cause. In such an instance there should be no action that puts Christians in danger or gives rise to a great scandal.

With respect to imperial power, Paweł begins by asserting that in both temporal and spiritual matters, the pope has jurisdiction, repeating a point he had made in his introduction. He had used the familiar medieval trope of the power of "the two swords," the ecclesiastical one and the secular one, both of which are in the pope's possession, but that the emperor is minister in temporalities, having been given this power by the pope (*Imperator vero est minister in temporalibus, habens postestatem a papa iure posito*). The emperor has no right or power to give anyone authority to conquer the lands of pagans who do not recognize him because this power belongs only to the pope. All imperial grants to the Order are invalid and any war they had waged could never have been just. Nor was it justified for the Order to convert people by force, and the military expeditions (here Paweł talks about these using the term adopted by the Order, *Reisen*) are therefore sinful and those who participate in them are sinners. Elsewhere in this section Paweł raises the question of whether Christians may, without sinning, use the aid of pagans and infidels, concluding that they may. He is here echoing some of the argument made previously by Stanisław of Skarbimierz in his sermon on the just war. He even extends the right to pagans to sue Christians for the return of property or territory taken unjustly from them, basing this conclusion upon the rights that pagans have in natural law.

This brings Paweł to the crux of whether pagans and infidels have any such right, and he devotes the third part of *Saevientibus* to the ideas of Henry of Segusio, Cardinal of Ostia, known in

Latin as Hostiensis. According to him, whatever natural rights non-Christians had before the birth of Christ — jurisdictions, principates, dominions — were lost at the moment he was born. Thus, without natural rights, they have no status in law, for their rights were given to the faithful that they should be subject to Christians. By definition, Hostiensis concludes, any war against pagans for any reason was a just war. Paweł profoundly disagreed with this position, and in the rest of the treatise he presents an argument to counter Hostiensis. In doing so, he was joining a long-standing alternative tradition in Christian thought and in canon law, best presented by the thirteenth century pope, Innocent IV, and affirmed in Christian theology by Thomas Aquinas who concluded that the dominion of pagans and infidels was not taken away at Christ's birth. It was only done later by ecclesiastical and secular law, which to Paweł are inferior to natural and divine law. On this basis Paweł concludes that Hostiensis's teaching was and remained wrong and its implications for whatever the Order claims to be legitimate were invalid. The whole of this treatise, while containing a number of historical details relevant to acts by the Order against Christian Poland and pagan dominions, focused upon demonstrating principles. He was to return to these later, and from them propose conclusions that followed from them and that should be implemented.

— *Opinio Hostiensis*

The distribution of the *Saevientibus* had been limited to the German nation, but Paweł's second treatise of 1416 was provided to all four of the nations at the council. Entitled from its first words *Opinio Hostiensis*, it began with a short summary of the position taken in the thirteenth century by Henry of Segusio, Cardinal of Ostia, with respect to the rights of non-Christians. Following this, Paweł provides a rebuttal and presents an overview of the material that had been included at the beginning of *Saevientibus*, especially that focusing upon attacks upon Poland by the Order. He then lists fifty-two articles (*conclusiones*) that are drawn from his previous work. In doing so he emphasizes that he is seeking to deny the validity of Hostiensis's view regarding pagan rights. He makes explicit whom he regards as holding this position in order to justify their actions, i.e., the Order, and where the actions they have pursued have taken place. He is doing this, he argues, so that the council may remove the error that follows from Hostiensis's position (*ut removeatur talis error*). This is not, he further implies, merely a territorial and political issue; it is also a doctrinal and legal matter that allows an incorrect theory to be accepted and utilized for purposes of violence and conquest. In doing so, he makes a point that, although he is present as the representative of the Polish ruler, he is speaking as an academic and a scholar. This is an important point. Some later scholars have judged Paweł's works as merely political,[94] and at one level they were. He was indeed the head of a delegation pursuing royal policy, but he was not merely that. He was also a legal expert, an intellectual, and a scholar whose considerable accomplishments are reflected in his writings.[95]

The first nine of the fifty-two conclusions Paweł offers summarize the inviolable natural and divine rights pagans and infidels possess and the implications these have for how popes, emperors, and Christians in general should treat them. The next ten review the power of popes with respect to these pagan nations and peoples, material that Paweł treated in more depth in his previous work. Article 20 sums up papal authority, its limitations and responsibilities, what the pope can and cannot do, and how it must be done (i.e., always *de jure*). Ten articles follow dealing with imperial power and authority, especially its limitations, since it is the pope alone who possesses universal authority. In several of these articles the legal nullity of grants given the Order is emphasized and thus their wars against peaceful pagans have never been just wars. Two more articles repeat the principle that the conversion of pagans by force and conquest is wrong, although certain crusades (in Spain and the Holy Land, for example) to recover previously Christian territories are legitimate. The final collection of *conclusiones* treat problems associated with the just war (here Paweł follows traditional medieval views of this issue),[96] restitution of goods taken in an unjust war (these, by extension, included territories regarded as Polish lost earlier to the Order), and how Christians and non-Christians may cooperated in a just war of self-defense (as, for example, Poland and Lithuania had done in their war with the Order between 1409 and 1411). Finally, Paweł re-emphasizes that pagans and infidels have inalienable rights by virtue of being human, and that therefore the views of Hostiensis are wrong. The position in canon law taken by Innocent IV and in theology by Aquinas is reaffirmed. The implication of all these articles is thus that not only the error of Hostiensis should be rejected, but that developments following from accepting it should be suppressed.[97] One other point should be made in this context. In *conclusio* 43, Paweł notes that the Order's habit of launching attacks on Marian feast days, "are to be considered superstitious acts, which exclude any devotion to piety." Here he opens the possibility that acts of the Order may fall into the category of heresy, which is a theme he develops more powerfully in subsequent writings. This subtle association of the Order with this deviation from orthodox Christian piety would have resonated powerfully in a council that, as one of its chief three goals, was to deal with the heresy of Wycliffe and (potentially) Hus.[98]

— *Ad aperiendam*

This treatise is not included in the current volume, but it should nevertheless be mentioned in light of some of Paweł's later writings. A long work,[99] it had obviously been in preparation for some time and was made available to the council as a whole after mid-summer 1416 or possibly in early 1417 (in the text it is mentioned that the Battle of Grunwald had taken place less than seven years before). The work is divided into two parts, the first of which is described by Paweł as "theoretical," and deals with three main points. The initial one is whether papal and imperial grants given to the Order are legally valid; the second is whether the theory contained in the grants are valid and whether the application of that theory by the Order is such as to allow its continuance and deserves the approval of those who assess its actions; and the third raises the issue of whether these grants allowed the Order to conquer territory, acquire wealth, and establish a state (*dominium*). The second part is an analysis, with frequent glosses, of the meanings of certain key words and of the privileges given to the Order by the emperors Frederick II Hohenstaufen, Lewis IV the Bavarian, Charles IV Luxembourg and his son Václav. The treatise concludes with a critical summary of articles that had been submitted on behalf of the Order to emperor-elect Sigismund of Luxembourg during arbitration proceedings against the king of Poland.

The treatise is marked by its learned depth and by its detailed exposition of principles that Paweł had been developing for some time and expressed here with impressive force.[100] It reflects his idea that the Order is a *secta Prussiana*, that its character is heretical, and that like other heresies it should be suppressed. Since the documents first given the Order were for a hospital order in Jerusalem, and it was no longer that, the cause for which it was established no longer obtained and the rationale for its creation was therefore moot. Therefore, the Order should cease to exist. What the Order now claims to be — a military-religious order — Paweł argues, is not actually what in practice it is. Waging war is not a religious act, but a secular pursuit; the Order prizes military and chivalric virtues above love, and this is not religious; and its original aim in Prussia was illegal in that it consisted of an unjust war against pagans with rights in natural law. He concludes "it is most evidently known that not only by canon law and civil law but also by natural and divine law their colleges of this kind are prohibited and damned. And therefore, they should necessarily by the authority of this sacred Council be altogether destroyed. And let this suffice for the present."[101] The Order is a heresy, a pestiferous sect, and its status is not one of religion but of error. In subsequent sections of the treatise, these points are further developed. The tone and thrust of this work is one that Paweł would adopt in some of his other writings that are included in this volume.

— *Articuli*

Sometime between November 1416 and January 1417 Paweł distributed his treatise ***Articuli***, a work that was little known before it was edited and published by Stanislaus Bełch in 1965. In many ways it contains approaches and outlooks that had been foreshadowed in Paweł's previous works, especially in *Ad aperiendam*, but this one is structured in a different way. It reads very much like a legal indictment. Indeed, this is the way Paweł refers to himself in the opening of Prologue B: he identifies himself as neither an academic scholar dealing with theory nor as a royal ambassador pursuing a political program. Instead he emphasizes his status as "instigator, promotor, and procurator of the cause of the Faith, deputized by this Sacred Council, [who] gives, makes, and exhibits the below-inscribed articles, seething as they are with public infamy. . ."[102] His 155 articles provide concrete historical evidence, including the monetary value of destruction done, intended to prove that the Order has practiced actions that damage justice, order, and peace. The Order is guilty of heresy (*haeresis Prussiana*) and should suffer the fate of heretics. Practically every indictment contains or ends with the formula "And such was and is the public and notorious truth" (*itaque fuit et est verum, publicum et notorium*) or something very similar.[103]

When one reads *Articuli*, it is striking to see the full range of Paweł's approach. He lists what he terms crimes against pagans, identifies the problems of a state that seems to exist only for purposes of war and conquest, and the ways it has broken natural, divine, and human law, both ecclesiastical and secular. He shows how the heresy of the Order has infected European knighthood by including them in their *Reisen*. He outlines in detail the ways the Order, by its cruelty and oppression, breaks church law. He delineates the way the Order has annexed Christian territories and committed crimes therein by citing in detail campaigns and crimes against ecclesiastical property and even sought the conquest of Poland, an effort that failed in their defeat at Tannenberg in 1410. Paweł lists the numerous times the Order had disobeyed and ignored papal judgements (he mentions particularly the tribunals of 1320-1321 and 1339). Not only had the Order acted unjustly against its neighbors, it had even persecuted its own subjects. And then there are numerous instances cited by Paweł of occasions when the Order had pursued economic policies that had harmed the trading of others and that had debased the currency. Moreover it had illegally manipulated loans and practiced usuary. Overall, by way of conclusion, Paweł condemns the Order as "being masters of iniquity and enemies of the Christian religion" (*Articulus* 153).

This work was written against the backdrop of developments at the council. Paweł's early treatises had clearly struck a blow at the Order, and it is not surprising that it should undertake to respond. Whereas before, its diplomacy had been characterized by efforts related to minimal goals in negotiations, pursuing narrow political aims, Paweł's learned formulations had theoretical legal challenges. Thus the Order moved to respond in kind. Late in June 1416 their General Procurator wrote the Grand Master that he had given moneys to some doctors to prepare answers in kind.[104] One of them was Johannes Urbach of Bamberg (see below), but before anything he could prepare was able to be considered, there were polemical contributions nearer to hand. These were two works by Johannes Falkenberg (*ca.* 1364-1435), who may have received some of the money the Order expended. His first work was devoted to the powers of popes and emperors attacking the positions taken by Paweł in *Saevientibus*. A second work, apparently now lost, was also circulated at the council, and Paweł had read it. He concluded that in form and substance the two were heretical and worthy of condemnation by the council, which Paweł recommended it should do.

— *Iste Tractatus*

Issued probably late in 1416 or early in 1417, this treatise by Paweł responds aggressively to the two works by Falkenberg noted in the previous paragraph. The individual who had written them was a Dominican who had already been involved with issues in Poland. Born in Germany, he had studied arts and law at Prague and theology at Vienna. By 1405 he was a member of the Dominican *studium* in Kraków, where he was particularly critical of intellectual and theological developments among leaders of the Polish church and of trends within the university of Kraków. The works he wrote in this period reflect this and also reveal his outlook as a full-blown defender of papal theocracy. Eventually he had left and became part of the circle associated with the Order.[105] What he had written for them was a passionate criticism of Poland and filled with personal attacks upon Paweł.

His response was to adopt a different approach. He called Falkenberg's method an abstract doctrinal argument unrelated to actual data and experience. His presentation is, instead, what he terms a judicial investigation (and thus very much in accord with his status as a lawyer). It intends to be a purely objective statement of facts. In so doing, he effectively recapitulates by quotations or summaries the content of Falkenberg's work. By way of organization, he itemizes the first eleven conclusions of "this tract" (*Iste tractatus*) that have sought to demonstrate the power of the emperor, then turns to the next eight conclusions that support the actions of the Order. The final sections of this first part of the text translated here focus upon

Falkenberg's condemnation of "the Poles and their king, including those who assist them against the Order." It is evident from Paweł's treatment of these last conclusions that Falkenberg's way of reasoning had, as Bełch has put it, "led to a conclusion that the Poles even more than the pagans deserve to be exterminated."[106] This call for what, in later times, would be called a genocide, and is a theme that is reflected in the second part of the translations.[107]

The text Paweł deals with next is a work by Falkenberg formally entitled *Satira contra hereses et cetera nephanda Polonorum et eorum regis Jaghel.* Falkenberg had written this probably in 1412, and at some time thereafter — perhaps in 1417 — it had been given to the Grand Master for approval. At that point it had been deemed not to fit the style of the Order's propaganda, but it had remained available and circulated at the council. The *Satira* accused the king of Poland of being a pagan idol and the Poles of worshipping him; they and he were despised by God as heretics and shameless pagan dogs; the best service to be rendered Christendom would be to kill Poles and their king (here he was advocating tyrannicide), for they were heathen, and heaven's purposes were served by any who kill Poles; etc., etc., etc.[108] Paweł's response to this was measured, but powerful. He shows through historical example and legal argument that there is, as he put it, "in the absence of evidence confirming the crimes alleged, *de iure* it is understood that no such crimes exist, according to the cited laws... all of his claims are *de iure* false." He then turns to the issues relating to what Jürgen Miethke has called a "demand... for a Christian based [*begründetem*] genocide."[109] Paweł further notes that, in fact, with reference to the Order's principle intent, one can see that the entire doctrine can be said to be heretical.

One other aspect of Falkenberg's treatise should be emphasized here. He calls explicitly for the killing of the Polish king, a regicide. This issue resonated deeply with one other issue that had been part of the council's discussions, that of regicide or tyrannicide, put forward by the French theologian Jean Petit in support of the killing of the Duke of Orleans in the midst of the Hundred Years War between France and England. It had been condemned by the leaders of the council, especially Jean Gerson and Pierre d'Ailly, but to have it raised again created renewed discussion.[110] In the course of this, the Polish representative at council, especially the bishops, pushed hard to have the *Satira* condemned and Falkenberg accused of heresy.[111] They were at least successful in the short run in persuading the council to appoint a commission to investigate the matters. This included Cardinals Zaberella (Paweł's mentor), Orsini, and D'Ailly. By the end of the council in 1418, the group was prepared to condemn the author and his work, but nothing was decided, and the newly elected pope, Martin V, ruled that only matters that had been formally on the agenda (i.e., the main three: ending the schism, eradicate heresy, and reform the church in head and members) could be acted upon. Since Polish issues, including those connected with Falkenberg, had not been formally presented, nothing could be done. He promised, however, to investigate the matter further. This infuriated Paweł, who, along with others in the Polish delegation, in the closing session of the council on 22 April 1418, demanded condemnation, protested the failure to do so, and threatened to appeal to a future council. Paweł even tried to read out a text of protest, but was interrupted and silence was imposed upon him. The formal appeal was made on 1 May, with Paweł reading it before witnesses and notaries, but it was annulled by the pope. (The papacy having been challenged in its authority by the conciliar movement was understandably reticent about an appear to another council.) Thus the matter ended without the Falkenberg matter having been fully resolved from the Polish standpoint. This was to come only in the mid-1420s,[112] but before this and while the council was still in session Paweł presented one more important treatise.

— *Quoniam error*

Johannes Falkenberg was not the only individual who accepted the invitation of the Order to prepare responses to Paweł. A second was a German canonist who had studied at Erfurt and Heidelberg, Johannes von Urbach of Bamberg. Little was known about him until the early 1970s beyond the information that he prepared a defense of the Order and a systematic critique of Paweł's views.[113] They are contained in a work known by its short title as simply *Tractatus*.[114] Once it was circulated, Paweł responded almost immediately with his own treatise, *Quoniam error*. It is divided into two parts. In the first, Paweł analyzes — and judges negatively — the legal basis upon which the Order justifies its existence and activities. Many of the points he makes had appeared in his previous works, but they are deployed effectively and systematically here. In this Part One there are three main points, each subdivided into three or more questions or considerations. These, in turn, are further subdivided into rubrics or explanatory comments that Paweł analyzes.

Part Two directly addresses the treatises of Urbach and Falkenberg, with Paweł often seeking to equate the work of the former with the heretical nature he had attributed to the latter in *Iste Tractatus*. Urbach had organized his work first into fourteen conclusions in which he dealt with the legal status of the Order and with their wars against pagans. He then ended with four final conclusions that focus upon the use of pagans by Christians (i.e., Poles) and what he termed the unjust aims of Poland in the war from 1409 to 1411. In doing so, he does not explicitly refer personally to Paweł, dealing rather with positions and interpretations in the abstract. He clearly disagrees with Paweł regarding the status of pagans and infidels, for he regards Hostiensis as correct on these matters rather than the position of Innocent IV. Indeed, his strategy was to focus his attack on what he regarded as key points in Paweł's arguments, seeking to undermine his impact by showing, as Timothy Brennan has argued, Paweł's "arguments to be radical attacks on the traditional understanding of the faith, and not in keeping with centuries-old interpretations of canon and civil law."[115] In his response Paweł systematically addresses each of the conclusions and draws upon his impressive mastery of canon law and of the writings of other scholars, including Cardinal Zabarella, Maurice (Mařik) Rvačka, and others. Whenever possible he sought to link Urbach's positions to those — such as Wycliffe — that had already been condemned as heretical by the council.[116] Elsewhere he contradicted Urbach's implications (vis-à-vis Poland) that Christians could seek aid from pagans for simple defense but not for attack and offensive warfare. Paweł showed that the Poles had not waged an offensive war that culminated in the battle at Grunwald, that no tribunal had convicted Poland on this count, and that canon law allowed the Christians to communicate with pagans.[117] He also drew upon his earlier works, especially his critique of Hostiensis. Where appropriate he also provided, as he had done in *Articuli*, factual material. In other instances he seemed casually dismissive of whatever it was that Urbach was arguing, simply saying — as he did in his response to Urbach's sixth conclusion — "this conclusion, similarly to the other, is as easily spurned [*contempnitur*] as proven."[118] Some modern scholars have recognized the relative sophistication of Urbach's treatise and the impressive textual argumentation of Paweł and concluded, as Frederick Russell has put it, that both "argued their cases impeccably" and that "the debate was at an impasse."[119] Others in their conclusions have leaned in Paweł's direction, noting in a chapter title "Wlodkowic Almost Overturned: Urbach's *Tractatus* and the Final Victor for the Rights of Unbelievers."[120]

* * * * * * * * * * * *

At Constance, the Poles achieved limited success. By their demonstration through the presence of the Samogitians and the approval of the Orthodox bishop Gregory Camblak that Poland could achieve the peaceful conversion of Lithuania that the Order had not been able to accomplish by military force, western Europe's perception of Poland was significantly altered for the better. The Poles also were able, in significant measure through the distribution and discussion of Paweł's treatises, to weaken western Europe's trust in the Order. At a more individual level, Paweł performed multiple roles in Constance. He was active as a royal diplomat pursuing Polish policy and seeking to have the council condemn the Order. He was a learned jurist articulating in his treatises an argument grounded in canon law, the Bible, the teachings of the medieval church and presenting it in a logical and factual manner. Finally he was a theorist of ideas touching the just war, the rights of non-Christians, principles of natural law, of international law and the law of nations, and ultimately the limitations of both ecclesiastical and secular authority. We shall return to these matters below after tracing the remainder of his career and examining the other three writings contained in this volume.

Paweł After Constance to the End

Following the council Paweł returned to Poland and resumed his academic life at the university. For the academic year that began in the fall of 1418 he was chosen by the rector, Jan of Fałkow, to assist him as vice-rector. (This office was an irregular one that only existed from time-to-time, depending on the needs of the rector.) Paweł's role did not last long, however, as he was called back into royal service the next year. In 1419 conflict broke out again between the Order and Poland, and to avoid an extended conflict the parties were persuaded by envoys from Sigismund of Luxembourg, King of Hungary and still only emperor-elect, to put their concerns before him for arbitration. In September, Paweł was appointed by Jagiełło as procurator for the kingdom, and he prepared to go to Wrocław (Breslau) where Sigismund was scheduled to attend the *Reichstag* in the coming January.

The document he intended to present there opened by calling upon Sigismund to, in effect, open his eyes so that he would see matters in an equitable manner.

— *Oculi*

Paweł organized his intended presentation into three parts. In the first, he set forth the historical facts regarding Polish-Order relations during the reigns of Władysław Łokietek (d. 1333), Kazimierz III the Great (ruled 1333-1370), and Jagiełło (king after 1386), emphasizing the misfortunes Poland (and Lithuania) had suffered at the hands of the Order in these three generations. Second, he recapitulated his previous arguments — developed in *Saevientibus, Ad aperiendam, Articuli*, and elsewhere — about the legal validity (or, more precisely, the illegitimate status in his eyes) of the Order's claims. And third, he proposed a set of remedies that Sigismund should adopt to resolve these contentious matters. One of his main points was that the papacy had already reached conclusions in the legal judgments brought against the Order by its own courts in 1320-1321 and again in 1339, that these were still valid, and they should be approved by all. While Paweł is often direct in the thrust of his arguments, in a few places his approach is far subtler. For example he seeks to tie Sigismund to the Order by suggesting that should he not oppose the errors of which they are guilty (errors that are contrary to divine law, null, void, and iniquitous), he would appear to be favoring them and thus — by extension — be guilty of these same errors.[121]

* * * * * * * * * * * *

When Sigismund finally arrived at the *Reichstag*, it was only one day before the expected oral arguments were to be presented to him. Paweł may, therefore, have prepared a shorter version of *Oculi* that could have been a summary to be quickly presented to Sigismund.[122] But apparently not even this was to be. Without an oral hearing,

Sigismund rendered a decision that favored the Order.[123] Outraged, Jagiełło and his council considered renewing the war against the Order. Not all, however, favored this, and they proposed trying to negotiate a treaty with the Order directly. Paweł favored neither of these approaches, arguing in an eloquent letter to the king that an appeal be made to the pope.[124] His position carried the day. The papacy agreed to hear the appeal, and arranged a process in which materials relevant to the matter would be gathered and submitted to Cardinal Guillaume Fillastre, who would then process them for papal consideration.

From Paweł's standpoint this was a fortunate choice. The Cardinal of Aix and Archpriest of the Lateran basilica, Fillastre (1348-1428) had been a very active individual at the Council of Constance, where Paweł had the opportunity to get to know him personally. He had been instrumental in the election of Martin V as the pope who ended the schism and was, therefore, a favorite in the papal chancery and might have been thought to be knowledgeable about Polish-Order affairs and perhaps somewhat favorable to their concerns. (He also had kept a very full diary at Constance that has proved to be of great importance to historians of that council.) Some of the materials prepared at this stage were intended to prove that an appeal from an imperial judgment to a papal review was legally valid. At the same time Paweł began the preparation of what was to become his treatise *Ad videndum*.[125]

— *Ad videndum*

This treatise reflects, as expected, Paweł's command of canonical literature and the historical materials that have underlain his other works (indeed, he freely drew upon them when necessary). It was apparently originally intended to be composed of an introduction and three parts: the articles and privileges claimed by the Order; a section on what the law touching these items was; and, finally, a discussion of theological issues. If originally all of these parts were written, only the introduction and the second part, supplemented where necessary by implied references to some of the Order's claims, have been transmitted and form the basis for the work translated in this volume.[126]

From a stylistic standpoint, this treatise is divided into twenty-three *capitula* (chapters), each starting with a letter of the alphabet in consecutive order, A to Z (but without J, U, and W). Paweł argues that the arguments used by the Order to justify itself were false and void: these had been issued to a hospitaller order and the Order had no such hospital. Further, the grants and privileges had only provided lands to compensate them for their efforts against the Prussians and when that was complete, their possession of these lands was forfeit; the Order had acted in an entirely different way. Moreover, any grant given by an emperor was invalid (Paweł especially singles out Emperor Frederick II of Hohenstaufen), for — as he had shown elsewhere — emperors do not have this power. In developing his argument Paweł uses the logical analysis based upon Aristotle's four causes, though in no systematic order. The final cause (the intent of the emperor) was the propagation of the faith, but this fails as it lies outside the competency of any emperor, being rather the responsibility of the pope. With respect to the efficient cause (Frederick's claim to have inherited the power of Roman emperors) this is also not valid; imperial power in the Middle Ages, Paweł argued (in agreement with many others in this period), was derived from the pope as vicar of Christ. Thus, Frederick's supposed donations have no authority since they lack an efficient cause. To the extent that a material cause would relate to the lands of pagans and other non-Christians, these territories are not subject to imperial jurisdiction, but only — as Paweł had argued in *Opinio Hostiensis* and *Saevientibus* — to natural law; thus, again, the emperor's acts were invalid, being contrary not only to natural law but also to divine law. Finally, with respect to the formal cause, natural law also plays a role. Here Paweł develops an important theme, which will be further discussed below, that of an international system of justice that would deal with international disputes. Here again, the emperor fails to have legitimate authority. In developing this argument, Paweł has clearly concluded that the authority of the emperor — any emperor — lacks the degree of competence to deal with issues the arise between states — both Christian and pagan.

* * * * * * * * * * * * *

Once again, the Poles were disappointed.[127] Pope Martin V delayed rendering a judgement on the appeal that had been brought before him, determining that more information was needed. On 24 November 1421 he commissioned Antonio Zeno of Milan as a legate to go in person to the territories disputed between Poland, Lithuania, and the Order to gather first-hand testimony. The Order was not pleased at this turn of events, but Zeno eventually undertook his mission gathering much valuable information.[128] In the course of this, a truce between Poland and the Order that had been arranged earlier expired, and a brief military campaign was waged by both sides. It was ended by the Treaty of Melno on 27 September 1422 and achieved some important things, while complicating others. The border between the Order and Lithuania was clearly established and remained virtually unchanged for centuries. But another clause in the treaty dealing with territorial issues between Poland and the Order opened what, in the eyes of many, had been a closed matter. Jagiełło agreed in effect to annul the papal adjudication of 1339 that had resolved, in Poland's favor, the possession of Gdańsk Pomorze, Chełmno, Michałowo, and other smaller territories.[129] Thus in the next years, there was continuing diplomatic and eventual military conflict between Poland and the Order, although there was nothing on the scale of the war between 1409 and 1411.

During much of this time Paweł had remained in Rome, supporting Poland's interests in whatever way he could. At some point he returned to Poland, and for about four years he was involved in diocesan matters in Poznań, where Andrew Łaskarz, his friend and fellow diplomat from Constance, was now the bishop. During that period, on 30 September 1426, he was appointed by Wojciech Jastrzębiec, archbishop of Gniezno, to serve on a Commission, chaired by Stanisław of Skarbimierz, to investigate the miracles of Queen Jadwiga, with an eye to her canonization.[130] Shortly thereafter he returned to Kraków, where he is mentioned in 1427 in a document from the cathedral chapter. Whatever else he might have done is not known. Jan Długosz, whose archival knowledge was unmatched in the fifteenth century, remarks in his notice of Paweł 's death, that he was active in "Constance, Rome, Buda," and "aliis plurimis locis — many other places".[131] Unfortunately, he does not spell out where and when these were. Before his death, however, Paweł left us one last important work, called by Jan Fijałek, at the beginning of the last century, his "last word."[132]

* * * * * * * * * * * *

This "word" was a letter sent by Paweł to Bishop Zbigniew Oleśnicki of Kraków from Padua in March 1432. What he was doing there is unknown, though it may have been somehow associated with his academic ties to the location where he had studied. How he had learned of the subject he took up in the letter is also unknown, though it had taken place in 1431, and that would have allowed considerable time for information to have been transmitted to Paweł in Italy. The individual to whom he is writing was one of the most remarkable figures of late medieval Poland. Oleśnicki was one of the leading figures among the nobility from the region of Lesser Poland (*Polonia minor, Małopolska*). Born in 1389, he matriculated at the University of Kraków in 1406 and only studied in the Arts Faculty. Following his time there, he entered the royal chancery of Jagiełło and accompanied him on the field of battle at Grunwald in 1410, and it is said he saved his life there. Subsequently he rose in royal favor and, already a cleric, in 1420 he become the king's secretary. Three years later he was named as bishop of Kraków, a position that included his status as the Chancellor of the University of Kraków.[133] He was eventually (thrice) appointed a cardinal by the pope,[134] and served as bishop until his death in 1455. He was rightly regarded as one of the most influential politicians within the realm, and in 1454 Aeneas Sylvius Piccolomini, eventually Pope Pius II, praised him as "the leading person in Poland after the king."[135] With respect to his policy vis-à-vis the Order, he was ambivalent.[136] He supported them as a religious order but also found them a frequent enemy of the Polish kingdom. Thus, it is not surprising that Paweł would have chosen to write him.

The letter was occasioned by yet another moment when Poland was invaded by the Order. While engaged in Lithuania with matters relating to the succession to Vytautas following his death in 1430, Jagiełło found himself in conflict with his own younger brother, Švitrigaila, whom he aimed to name as the new Grand Duke, though with diminished territorial control. Švitrigaila, however, had different ambitions and allied with the Teutonic Order. Their invasion of northern Poland in 1431 aimed to support Švitrigaila but broke the 1422 Treaty of Melno.[137] Before Poland resolved upon a response, Paweł contacted Oleśnicki to advise him on the options he saw.

— *Epistola ad Sbigneum episcopum Cracoviensem*

First, it should be said that this letter, despite some similarities to his other writings, was a profoundly personal one. Echoes of the destruction that Paweł's homelands and the kingdom within which he has lived and served resonate as he expresses his sorrow and the events that have led to this.[138] After his brief salutation he moves to counsel Oleśnicki about how to proceed. He notes the ways (*viae*) that exist: the first is the only true way, Christ. After that, three exist. One is the way of agreement or concord. Here Paweł can barely conceal his contempt for this approach with the Order. They are rapacious wolves dressed in sheep's clothing; they are the cruel sect hostile to

Christianity that he has depicted in previous writings; they must be destroyed. In support of this he presents analyses of the Order's previous deeds, documents, and declarations (rehearsed again by Paweł in detail), all of which led him to conclude that no just and lasting concord can be achieved with them.

A second way to respond is through war. This leads him to discuss what kind of war could be considered a just war, and here he draws upon a long-standing medieval tradition about the criteria for such a conflict. It is obvious that the synthesis reached on this by Ramon de Penyafort is his point of departure, together with the refinements made in the thirteenth century by Thomas Aquinas.[139] Although he does not develop the arguments he had presented at Constance regarding the just war in this letter, it is clear that he had made some modifications to them that are significant.[140] In this letter, having raised issues related to the just war, he concludes — decisively — that the Order has "never waged a just war," and its "warring has always been unjust." He follows this up with five specific reasons why the foregoing is true, recapitulating in effect his more fully developed arguments in his previous writings.

The *via* Paweł accepts — the middle way — is adjudication, which he terms "short and secure." One approach of this way is evangelical denunciation, but he is less inclined to rely upon it. There are too many examples of bishops and other making such denunciations without any effect being achieved. In too many instances they are themselves guilty of the same sins by virtue of neglecting their responsibilities. Wolves among the sheepfold of Christ have been tolerated (the Order being chief among the wolves), and therefore the Order has been allowed to persevere. As a result, sinners simply don't restore goods gained illegally, so the denunciation does not achieve its goal. What Paweł prefers is judicial or official denunciation. He does not explicitly in this section develop the principle that the pope is the one who, by virtue of being the vicar of Christ, is the one to achieve this, but it is implicit from what he has said earlier and elsewhere that this is the case. His telling allusion to the reference to Jeremiah is particularly revealing: "I have set thee this day over the nations, and over the kingdoms. . . "[141]

With this, Paweł humbly closes his letter, making sure it is clear that he, himself, had written it.

****

Little is known of Paweł's final years. Whatever it was that had taken him to Padua, he did not stay there. He may have contemplated taking monastic vows either before or after he returned to Kraków, though this is unclear.[142] In Kraków he lived out his last years in the handsome house he had built on the street where canons of the cathedral had their homes (*platea Canonicorum*, ul. Kanonicza 16). Jan Długosz indicated he died in 1435, but in fact he lived for some time after that, probably until 2 March 1436.[143]

Themes Reflected in Paweł Writings

Reading Paweł's writing can often be difficult. There are numerous citations to canonical and other legal material and to the writings of earlier theologians and philosophers (in the Middle Ages the two are often difficult to separate) that are not as familiar to modern audiences as they would have been to his contemporaries. Moreover, his points are often developed in the framework of immediate political issues he was pursuing as a diplomat in service to Polish royal policy, and it is not always easy to separate the abstract from the political. Yet there are several important themes that exist in his treatises, even if they are not always systematically developed. What follows is an overview of the most important themes to be found in his works.[144]

As noted above, Paweł was a lawyer and a jurist.[145] But he was not narrowly this, for his sense of the law included much beyond what is often called "positive" law, i.e., law enacted in human institutions, in the medieval case ecclesiastical and civil statutes enacted by religious or secular bodies, including the traditions of Roman jurisprudence. Above any positive, enacted law, were divine and natural law. Divine law was, of course, the revealed law contained in Holy Scripture, and Paweł was a believer. This is why there are so many biblical citations and references, for this is where medieval Christians believed revealed law was to be found.[146] When he made these references he was not merely reflecting what one might consider God's wisdom, he also saw these as reflecting God's real power in the temporal world. For Paweł, as indeed for most medieval Christians, natural law was something that arose from the nature of humanity.[147] All individuals — whether pagan or Christian (or of any other religion) — possess this law in common. Thus, Stanisław of Skarbimierz in his sermon *De bello iustis* could assert "Likewise natural law is present among all."[148] Paweł built upon this by making natural law something guaranteeing certain rights to everyone. Rather than being something ontologically part of the warp and weft of the universe as antiquity had understood it, Paweł saw natural law as being of divine origin, since God created humanity and defined what human nature was. Natural law was thus something that could be determined rationally and was applicable to all. From this, he would draw the conclusion — as had others before him, including Hostiensis in one of his works! — that human law and judicial decisions that violated rational natural law were untenable and lacking any binding force.[149] More than this, natural law implicitly carries with it the moral principle that one should not do to another that which one would not wish to have done to oneself, i.e., a principle that is traditionally called the "golden rule."[150]

From his understanding of natural law, Paweł derives the law of nations.[151] Originally God gave dominion over the whole earth to be held in common. When eventually this proved unworkable, by the law of nations, dominions were identified and divided, and from this

Paweł concludes that pagans, Christians, and others all legally possess their dominions, that this is a right that includes the right of defense, and that it is immutable. This is a status that prevents the emperor (always) and the pope (except in grave cases) from seizing their lands. This right confirms the moral principal established in natural law that one should observe the aforementioned "golden rule." The law of nations defines inviolable rights for all and establishes norms of justice that, as Paweł put it, even a simple and undeveloped mind can grasp.[152] These rights include humanity's right to life (he repeatedly quotes the commandment "Thou shalt not kill") and protection against force, plunder, and cruelty; the right to freedom (slavery and subjugation are artificial, caused by other humans) and it belongs to everyone, including pagans; the right to property (again, the commandments include one that says "Thou shalt not steal"); and — perhaps most creatively — the right to a just process in which judgment comes by the law and be administered by an impartial judge.[153]

When Paweł had fleshed out the principles of divine and natural law and the law of nations, he was in a position to move on to the question of how power over individuals had developed, and this led him into issues of the authority of spiritual and temporal rulers. As he understood it, this was derived in several ways. The first is from the will of God, who allowed the establishment of government on earth (Paweł often cited Old Testament passages in which God gave power to kings and leaders and this was later transferred by Christ to Peter and his successors by the command "feed my sheep"). A second way comes from violence, an unjust alternative derived *de facto* and not *de jure*. And neither of these can justify claims made by the empire over pagans, since God did not sanction it and violence respects neither natural rights nor the law of nations. A third way of establishing temporal rule exists for Paweł; it can come from the consent of the governed, which arises from natural law whereby inhabitants of an area agree to preserve peace and order by accepting governance from above. This is not a "social contract" arrangement; it assumes that the best government is one supreme ruler, a monarch, who serves the common good and takes no action that harms the ruled. (This can't be the emperor, for he is without spiritual jurisdiction, so this ruler must be the pope).[154] Here we also see Paweł concluding from both divine and natural law that spiritualities are greater than temporalities, and ascribing full power to the pope as representative of both.

As noted above, another theme that Paweł developed is related to the theory of the just war. He modified the long medieval tradition by adding the requirement that in order "that a war might be shown to be just *de iure*, it is necessary for the just cause to be inquired into and declared legitimate..."[155] What is presented here, albeit in an embryonic form, is the idea that an international tribunal able to summon experts and specialists and hear witnesses should be created. It would be presided over by an individual of great moral and spiritual authority who would be given appropriate legal jurisdiction to which all other authority would be subordinated. In Paweł's eyes, the supreme such authority would be the pope, who would establish the principles of international relations assuring the security of all countries — Christian and non-Christian. This is, in the final analysis as Paweł argues, derived from the aforementioned principle in natural law, the "golden rule."[156]

What then, is the outlook Paweł Włodkowic presents in these themes? One answer to this has been argued recently by Thomas Wünsch, who argues that Paweł introduced "realistic thinking" in the teaching and theory of international relations.[157] Set against the backdrop of modern political theory, Wünsch describes realistic thinking (or realism) as looking at political things as they are, not as they should be. It is an outlook rooted in antiquity (Thucydides), expressed in the Renaissance (Machiavelli) and early modern era (Hobbes), and propounded in the twentieth century (Weber and Hans Morgenethau). Wünsch sees the Renaissance era as a period in which the idea of a transcendent deity was beginning to weaken or disappear from political thinking, with empirical evidence being brought to bear on such issues rather than idealistic or ethical concerns rooted in a traditional religious outlook. He finds that this outlook can be found (though it should be taken, as he puts it, *cum grano salis*) in Paweł's thinking and writing, especially in his "last word," the letter to Zbigniew Oleśnicki. (In his argument at this point Wünsch provides the background of extended conflict between Poland and the Order.) In his letter, as described above and in the translation printed below in this volume, Paweł rejects political agreements and wars as a way of achieving peace, and instead argues for the "middle way" of adjudication. There is a good deal of insight here by Wünsch into the practicality of Paweł's approach, and, of course, Paweł's argument against the other two *viae* is a strong one, as reflected in his other treatises. Paweł is beginning to develop an approach to international politics that reflects his ideas about international law. The one weakness in Wünsch's argument is that there is less secularism in Paweł's thought than might otherwise be thought. Instead he puts his hopes into the possibility that in a reformed church and curia it would be the pope who could provide dispassionate adjudication, rising above the narrower concerns of princes, kings, and states.[158] In so doing, Paweł in many ways attributed to him the *plena potestas* of absolute papal monarchy.[159] Nevertheless, Wünsch's approach is one that reflects the possibilities of future analyses of what Paweł's contribution is. Paweł sought to rise above the limitations he saw present in war and unreliable treaties and hoped to find in something traditional the basis for a new approach.

This outlook reflects a process that is in many ways characteristically medieval. By drawing upon traditional sources — ancient and medieval — and applying them to novel situations such as the wars waged by the Order against pagans and the wars waged by the Order against Poland in ways he tried to demonstrate as unjust, Paweł achieved something creative, something that pointed to the future rather than the past. As Marcia Colish has indicated in her insightful and stimulating intellectual history of the Middle Ages, although medieval Europeans strove faithfully to adhere to tradition and did not seek originality and innovation, they nevertheless created new forms of thought that "achieved Europe's intellectual modernization" by the end of the medieval period.[160] This was achieved by methods to deal with changed circumstances that resulted in new forms of thought and institutions. The university as an institution of higher learning — as described above while tracing Paweł's biography — is only one example of this.[161] And Paweł's feeling his ways toward a new version of the potential in a reformed and transformed papal monarchy, one rising above the needs that war or treaties fail to meet, pointed toward the modernization that Colish attributed to medieval Europeans. The explicitly transcendental character of the higher court Paweł imagined, when sufficiently modified by secularized elements of natural law and the law of nations had, in the long run, the potential to achieve what he only hoped for. He sought a just judge in a tribunal that rose above local, national, and even religious constraints. His argument against Hostiensis about the permanency of natural rights for all humanity (and revisited in a variety of ways in the works translated in this volume) is one that resonates to this day. It is one of the most important reasons to echo Professor Ewa Thompson's observation in her Foreword as to why reading Paweł is not only worth doing, but also more important now than ever.

Final Observations

— *A Kraków School of International Relations*

Paweł Włodkowic and the writings he produced were by no means the only examples of what has frequently been called a Kraków school of international relations. Mention has already been made of the contribution of Stanisław of Skarbimierz and his sermon on the just war.[162] It introduced some new elements that had a particular focus upon issues of public war, whereas many previous works had dealt with these matters more generally. It also emphasized the rights of pagans and non-Christians and their status according to natural law, and it was written in a context quite different from earlier medieval treatments of feudal warfare, focusing instead upon states and princes who were in the process of consolidating their political and even national sovereignty.[163] Another example of a focus on international matters is the anonymous and undated work *Revocatur*, which deals with whether the Christian Polish king may accept help from and ally himself with heretics.[164] Probably written in the early 1430s at the time of heightened tensions with Hussites in Bohemia and bearing some similarity to the views of Stanisław of Skarbimierz (and incorrectly attributed to him by Ehrlich, who first edited the work),[165] it is a typical scholastic treatise: five arguments against the proposition followed by the author's own view, then five arguments rebutting the *contra* position, finishing with a restatement of the author's position. While concluding the Polish king may accept help from and ally with heretics, the author bases his argument in natural law, which allows self-defense, permits Christians coming to the aid of pagans in a just war, and legitimates entry into relations with pagan, and that — because of these considerations — concludes that these also apply to matters dealing with heretics. In addition to these three sources, there clearly were other individuals — most of them at the university — who were engaged in one version of political discussions or another. The specific political issues of the day lent themselves to a discussion on the rights of pagans, the proper relations between states, and questions of peace and order.[166]

Clearly, fifteenth century Kraków was the *locus* of much political discussion involving issues of natural law and the rights of those within the Christian community and those outside Christendom.

Many of these had been evoked by specific political developments — war, conversion, conquest — but they transcended the particular and mundane to become general and theoretical. How systematic and cohesive these contributions were has been the subject of considerable modern scholarship, with some (often — but not only — from the Polish side)[167] making a maximalist argument. On balance, this conclusion is warranted, and the views and contributions of Paweł in particular repay careful attention.[168]

The assertion, however, that this Polish school, and in particular Paweł, were influential upon the later development of modern international law is more difficult to support. Generalized assertions to this effect have often been made, in particular by Stanislaus Bełch, who concludes that Paweł "influenced his colleagues, the Italian canonists and civil lawyers of renown" and was "not without influence upon the tradition common to European Christianity."[169] But the line of development from Paweł to developments that flourished in the sixteenth century in the Iberian peninsula with Francisco Vitoria, Francisco Suárez, and Luis de Molino on into the seventeenth century culminating with Hugo Grotius is one that is not clear or convincing, though some have made efforts to make the connections.[170] Indeed, the prevailing judgment has been that his views were not widely known outside the context of Polish-Order relations and that, even in the international gathering of Christendom at Constance from 1414 to 1418, the focus of the council was really upon the question of closing the schism, dealing with heresy, and reforming the church in head and members. This is unfortunate, for within two generations Europe was to confront precisely the issues that Paweł raised in a very different way and on a different front.

In a dissertation unfortunately too little known, Timothy Brennan made the shrewd observation that "there is no concrete evidence, for instance, that Wlodkowic's *concilia* were ever used in the debate over shaping policy for the conquest of the New World beginning later within the same century as the Council of Constance."[171] Europe's views of the peoples with whom it came in contact was implicitly that of Hostiensis; they were without natural rights and could therefore be ruthlessly conquered. Only isolated voices such as Bartholomé de las Casas (1484-1566), a Dominican priest charged with the protection of the natives saw them in a different light and, as he put it in his *Short Account of the Destruction of the Indies*, strove to prevent them from being abused, enslaved, and their civilization being destroyed.[172] The early stages of European colonialism thus were without the moral standards Paweł had articulated. What he could have provided is suggested by Frederick Russell, who sagely concluded "The problems Paulus addressed would soon resurface with the European conquest of American. Though no direct influence of his thought has been shown, Paulus adumbrated the doctrines of early modern international law and historical jurisprudence."[173] Indeed, significant developments of the modern European tradition would have been impacted had Paweł's views been disseminated and followed. It was a great missed opportunity, a potential turning point in the direction of development that over the generations could have shaped a European tradition less wedded to war and conquest, and less committed to what became, during the time of Social Darwinism, the survival of the fittest. Paweł's views haven't changed. Yet another reason why it is a good idea to read him, for if he were read more, we might be influenced to change.

— *Concluding Remarks*

Why was Paweł's influence at Constance and after of little influence and why has his tradition been largely overlooked in the larger understanding of European history? What follows addresses these two questions briefly. First, Paweł's treatises and the policy it represented at Constance were peripheral to the central purposes of the council. Afterward, the complexities of East Central European politics were compounded by the outbreak of the Hussite revolution, and Polish-Order matters played a background role. This was also the time when advances by the Ottoman Turks focused the attention of the papacy and other European leaders upon its southeastern flank. Eventually Poland successfully waged war against the Order for thirteen years after 1454, and in the aftermath of the [Second] Peace of Toruń, the Order was an institution in decline, so the issues raised by Paweł appeared irrelevant. Polish matters and Europe's knowledge of its development were of lesser concern than the opening of the Atlantic and the great geopolitical struggles between France, Germany, and England — or, to put it differently, the dynastic conflicts between Habsburg, Valois, and Tudor Europe. The Reformation movement, centered in Germany, France, and England was also a distraction. Even though the Polish-Lithuanian state — after 1569/1572 a Commonwealth of Two Nations — was the largest polity in Europe, its focus in the seventeenth and eighteenth centuries was increasingly upon eastern matters with the rise of Tsarist Russia. Ultimately that focus was resolved — at Poland-Lithuania's great cost — with the partitions of the late eighteenth century wrought by Prussia, Russia, and Austria. Poland-Lithuania was removed from the map and in some important ways ceased to exist for a century and a half. Culturally, it is not without significance that intellectual life ceased to be dominated by the Latin language. Vernacular languages became localizing instruments of discourse while, on the international scene, first Italian, then French served to facilitate international discourse. Against this, the Polish language, a difficult Slavonic tongue for the Romance and Germanic worlds, had little hold upon Europe's attention as whole. But perhaps the greatest reason why Paweł's influence in the centuries after his death was not sustained, was that the history of Europe was being written by the winner states of the modern period. Poland was a non-entity on the European map after the 1790s. It was little regarded by French, English, and especially German historians after the historiographical revolution wrought by Leopold von Ranke and his contemporaries in the nineteenth century. From the perspective of that historiography, the history of Europe was the history of the Romance and the Teutonic peoples. If you were not in either of those categories, and moreover were not a country, you did not have a history of significance. This was an unconscious but very real conclusion of that historiography. Whatever it was that Poland and the tradition of Paweł could offer was of little interest to others. In the twentieth century a *Polonia restituta* had an all too brief existence after 1919, and the Second World War and the Cold War meant that much of the twentieth century was lost to the creativity that Poland was able to provide. All of this is unfortunate from the perspective of assessing Paweł's significance and contribution.[174] At least the works translated in this volume will provide a partial remedy to this situation.

Endnotes

* The documentation in what follows privileges material in English and Western European languages somewhat, while at the same time giving due credit to the very rich tradition in Polish historiography.

1 „Heu! cor meum ingemiscit dolore intimo sauciatum super desolatione patriae meae. . . " "Quodque Regnum Poloniae facificum. . . tam horribilem plagam. . . excepit." Belch, *Paulus Vladimiri*, II, 1091.

2 For only one of many examples, see in *Ad Aperiendam*: "Sunt tamen mali nichilominus excitandi quandoque exhortacionibus (dicto canone Qui sincera), quandoque premijs (XXIII questione IIII canone ultimo) et qualiter hoc intelligatur habetur Extra De baptismo: Maiores et dicto canone Qui sincera et canone De Iudeis." Ehrlich, *Pisma wybrane,* II, 40.

3 Eberhard Schulz, "Paulus Vladimiri und das jagiellonischen Polen. Eine Untersuchung zu den Wirkungen der italienischen Rechtswissenschaft auf den jagiellonischen Staat" (Unpublished Ph.D. dissertation, Göttingen, 1951), p. 106.

4 One example where Paweł argues this is in his treatise *Ad Aperiendum* in Ehrlich, *Pisma wybrane*, II, 71: "si peccant contra legem nature que omnibus gentibus est communis. . ."

5 Marek A. Cichocki and Adam Talarowski, eds., *Paweł Włodkowic i polska szkoła prawa międzynarodowego* (Warsaw: Narodowe Centrum Kultury/Teologia Polityczna, 2018). This volume included, in addition to an original Introduction by Wojciech Kozłowski, previously published studies by Stanisław Krzyżanowski (from1908), Andrzej Niesiołowski (from 1935), Stanisław Bełch (from 1959), Juliusz Domański (from 2011, originally published

in 1982), two from Tadeusz Jusudowicz (from 1992 and 1993), Stanisław Wielgus (from 1996), two by Krzysztof Ożóg (from 2006 and 2008), and Tomasz Graff (from 2014).

6 Professor Kraszewski used the following editions for his translations: *Savientibus*, in Belch, *Paulus Vladimiri*, II, 792-844; *Opinio Hostiensis*, in Belch, *Paulus Vladimiri*, II, 864-884; *Articuli*, in Belch, *Paulus Vladimiri*, II, 916-988; *Iste Tractatus*, in Belch, *Paulus Vladimiri*, II, 994-1001; *Quoniam Error*, in Ehrlich, *Pisma wybrane*, II, 216-315; *Oculi*, in Ehrlich, *Pisma wybrane*, III, 2-78; *Ad videndum*, in Ehrlich, *Pisma wybrane*, III, 91-194; *Epistola ad Sbigneum*, in Belch, *Paulus Vladimiri*, II, 1091-1103.

7 One exception to this was the massive (and relatively expensive) two-volume work of Belch, *Paulus Vladimiri*. While it was reviewed in some scholarly journals and was acquired by a limited number of libraries outside Europe and North America, it received less attention outside the circle of Polonia than it deserved. Despite its weaknesses (see, for some of which, the review by Howard Kaminski in *Speculum* 42 [1967]: 918-920), it remains a major study of Paweł's life and work. A second important contribution, though limited in its impact outside Poland, is the three volume edition of Paweł's works, with text and commentary in Latin, Polish, and English by Ludwik Ehrlich, *Pisma wybrane*; it is not widely available in the Anglophone world, despite having been published in a relatively large edition of 3350 copies.

8 For the distinction between "older" and "younger," the clearest argument in this regard is Jerzy Kłoczowski, *Młodsza Europa* (Warsaw: Państwowy Instytut Wydawniczy, 1998). For the questions bound up with the issue of "east central" or "central" Europe see now Nora Berend, Przemysław Urbańczyk, and Przemysław Wiszewski, *Central Europe in the High Middle Ages. Bohemia, Hungary and Poland, c.. 900—c. 1300* (Cambridge: Cambridge University Press, 2013), pp. 1-39; Antoni Podraza, "Central Europe as a Historical Region," in Kłoczowski, ed., *Europe Centrale entre l'Est et l'Ouest / Central Europe Between East and West* (Lublin: Instytut Europy Środkowo-Wschodniej. 2005), pp. 30-45 (Polish version in Krzysztof Baczkowski and Janusz Smołucha, eds., *Europa Środkowowschodnia od X do XVIII wieku—jedność czy różnorodność?* [Kraków: Societas Vistulana, 2005], pp. 25-39); and Nada Zečević, "Introduction: 'Central Europe': Perceptions, Definitions, and Comparisons in a Historiographical Context," in Zečević and Daniel Ziemann, eds., *Oxford Handbook of Medieval Central Europe* (Oxford: Oxford University Press, 2022), pp. 1-20.

9 *Gesta principum Polonorum / The Deeds of the Princes of the Poles*, trans. Paul W. Knoll and Frank Schaer (Budapest: Central European University Press, 2003), p. 12/13. This work has traditionally been described as a chronicle, but Thomas N. Bisson has suggested its character, glorifying Bolesław as a heroic warrior and recording his varied achievements, bears more relationship to the type of "narrative or versified commemorations of deeds in western lands during the century after the Norman Conquest," likening "Gallus" to Henry of Huntingdon and Geoffrey of Monmouth; see his "Preface" to the *Gesta principum Polonorum*, p. x. Bisson's influence was important in the choice of the title for the English translation. The identity of the author of this work has been widely debated. He has been thought by some to have come from France, or from Flanders, or from Provence; others have linked him to Italy, one of the Dalmatian cities, or some part of Germany. For an overview of the relevant historiography, see Wojciech Drelicharz, *Unifying the Kingdom of Poland in Mediaeval Historiographic Thought* (Kraków: Societas Vistulana, 2019, Polish original 2012), pp. 53-55.

10 These elements are themes that run through the presentation of Wiszewski, *Domus Bolezlai: Values and Social Identity in Dynastic Traditions of Medieval Poland (c. 966-1138)* (Leiden and Boston: Brill, 2010, Polish original 2008); see specially pp. xiii-xxxiv.

11 Often referred to in the Communist era as "feudal division," a term with multiple implications. A good example is Henryk Łowmiański, ed., *Polska w okresie rozdrobnienia feudalnego* (Wrocław: Ossolineum, 1973). On the question of whether there was "feudalism" in Poland, see generally Florin Curta, *Eastern Europe in the Middle Ages (500-1300)*, 2 vols. (Leiden and Boston: Brill, 2019), I, 463-469 (in a chapter entitled "The Construct of a Tyrant: Feudalism in Eastern Europe"); and more specifically Sławomir Gawlas, "Dlaczego nie było w Polsce feudalizmu lennego?" *Roczniki Dziejów Społecznych i Gospodarczych* 58 (1998): 101-123; and Marian Dygo, "Czy istniał feudalizm w Europie środkowo-wschodniej w średniowieczu?" *Kwartalnik historyczny* 120, 4 (2013): 667-717.

12 This is the observation of Marcin R. Pauk, "Language of Power and Communication in the Piast Dynasty: Toward a Reappraisal of Polish Political Culture of the 12th-13th Century," in Grischa Vercamer and Dušan Zupka, eds., *Rulership in Medieval East Central Europe. Power, Ritual and Legitimacy in Bohemia, Hungary and Poland* (Leiden and Boston: Brill, 2022), pp. 178-197, here p. 3, citing the assessment of Marek Barański, "Książęta i społeczeństwo wobec zjednoczenia Polski na przełomie XIII i XIV wieku," in Wojciech Fałkowski, ed., *Polska około roku 1300. Państwo, społeczeństwo, kultura* (Warsaw: DiG, 2003), pp. 9-56. Pauk disagrees with this interpretation and provides an alternative view in his article, some elements of which are included above in the text that follows.

13 For this process in a comparative regional treatment, see Adrienne Körmendy, *Melioratio terrae*: *Vergleichende Untersuchungen über die Siedlungsbewegung im östlichen Mitteleuropa im 13.-14. Jahrhundert* (Poznań: Wydawnictwo Poznańskiego Towarzystwa Przyjaciół Nauk, 1995). More specifically for Poland, see the classic overview by Benedykt Zientara, "*Melioratio terrae*: The thirteenth Century Breakthrough in Polish History," in J.K. Federowicz, ed., *A Republic of Nobles. Studies in Polish History to 1864* (Cambridge: Cambridge University Press, 1982), pp. 31-48; and Halina Manikowska, "*Melioratio terrae* and System Transformations on Lands to the East of the Odra during the Thirteenth Century and the Late Middle Ages," in Simonnetta Cavaciocchi, ed., *Poteri economici e poteri politici, secc. XIII-XVIII* (Florence: Le Monnier, 1999), pp. 303-323.

14 The traditional term for this development was the German *Drang nach Osten*, that carried with it, certainly by the nineteenth century at least, if not before, a heavy load of imperial and colonial ambition. The break-through to a new understanding is reflected in the important publication, Walter Schlesinger, ed., *Die deutsche Ostsiedlung des Mittelalters als Problem der europäischen Geschichte* (Sigmaringen: Jan Thorbecke Verlag, 1975), based in famous conferences in Reichenau between 1970 and 1972. See the materials collected in Jan M. Piskorski, ed., *Historiographical Approaches to Medieval Colonization of East Central Europe* (Boulder, CO: East European Monographs, 2002).

15 Most recently on this process, see Maciej Mikuła, *Municipal Magdeburg Law (Ius municipal Magdeburgense) in Late Medieval Poland. A Study on the Evolution and Adaptation of Law* (Leiden and Boston: Brill, 2021; Polish original 2017).

16 For a case study of this process in one part of the Polish lands, though one that eventually slipped into the political and cultural orbit of its neighbor Bohemia, see Wiszewski, "Politics and Change: The Silesian Dukes and the Transformation of the Land in the Thirteenth and Fourteenth Centuries," in Sunhild Kleingärtner, Timothy P. Newfield, Sébastien Rossignol, and Donat Wehner, eds., *Landscapes and Societies in Medieval Europe East of the Elbe* (Toronto: Pontifical Institute of Mediaeval Studies, 2013), pp. 183-203.

17 On this point, the observations by Piotr Górecki, *A Local Society in Transition. The Henryków Book and Related Documents* (Toronto: Pontifical Institute of Mediaeval Studies, 2007), pp. 36-39, and in his *The Text and the World. The Henryków Book, Its Authors, and Their Region, 1160-1310* (Oxford: Oxford University Press, 2015), p.256 and 258, are well taken: medieval Europe, whether west, central, or east central, had a variety of [internal] frontiers and that there was not just Poland on an "eastern frontier." These "frontier" lands each underwent their own process of *melioratio*.

18 Pomeranian affairs in these decades may be followed in detail in Gerard Labuda, "Stanowisko prawno-polityczne książąt Pomorza Nadwiślańskiego na przełomie XII i XIII wieku," *Zapiski Historyczne* 66 (2001):195-226; and Paul Milliman, *"The Slippery Memory of Men." The Place of Pomerania in the Medieval Kingdom of Poland* (Leiden and Boston: Brill, 2013), pp. 30-40.

19 In the tenth century the bishop of Prague, Vojtěch/Adalbert, inspired by a passion to convert the pagan, had travelled to Prussia and been martyred there in 997. He was friend of Emperor Otto III and of the then duke of Poland, Bolesław I, nicknamed the Brave, who was crowned king of Poland in 1025. His body had been revered by Bolesław and buried in Gniezno. Otto came there to worship at his tomb in 1000 and was hosted by Bolesław in a meeting that has become known as "the Congress of Gniezno." At that time, Otto confirmed the independence of the Polish church, established Gniezno as an archbishopric and authorized three bishoprics (Kraków, Wrocław, and Kołobrzeg) in addition to the already existing missionary bishop with its seat at Poznań. See Roman Michałowski, *The Gniezno Summit: The Religious Premises of the Founding of the Archbishopric of Gniezno* (Leiden and Boston: Brill, 2016; Polish original 2005). Other efforts to Christianize the Prussians had been made. Bruno of Querfurt traveled into Prussia and on to the border between Kievan Rus' and the lands of Lithuania; he was martyred in 1009 and his body was recovered by Bolesław. In the 11th century Bishop Otto of Bamberg (1060/1061-1139) was sponsored by Polish Duke Bolesław III the Wrymouth to work at converting the Pomeranians (where his success complemented Bolesław's military triumphs) and later sought unsuccessfully to convert the Prussians.

20 The tradition of monastic knighthood in the Baltic was foreshadowed by the crusading orders established to support the Latin cause in the Holy Land (the Knights Templars and the Knights Hospitallers) and the Iberian Peninsula and elsewhere (the Knights of Calatrava). From the outset, these armed monks were crusading orders seeking to recover formerly Christian territory. The Baltic phenomenon was rooted rather in efforts at conversion. On this point, see Eric Christiansen, *The Northern Crusades. The Baltic and the Catholic Frontier, 1100-1525* (Minneapolis, MN: University of Minnesota Press, 1980), pp. 70-79.

21 The Prussian mission has had a long-standing controversial status in Polish scholarship; on this point, see Mikołaj Gładysz, *The Forgotten Crusaders. Poland and the Crusader Movement in the Twelfth and Thirteenth Centuries* (Leiden and Boston: Brill, 2012; Polish original 2002), pp. 178-181, with extensive reference to Polish historiography p. 178, n. 12. For a fuller treatment of Bishop Christian's activities, see Darius von Güttner-Sporzyński, *Poland, Holy War, and the Piast Monarchy, 1100-1230* (Turnhout: Brepols, 2014), pp. 204-211.

22 There is a very substantial body of scholarly literature on these issues. The following citations are only representative and illustrative of this. See Gerard Labuda, "Die Urkunden über die Anfänge des Deutschen Ordens im Kulmerland und in Preußen in den Jahren 1226-1235," in Joseph Fleckenstein and Manfred Hellmann, eds., *Die Geistliche Ritterorden Europas* (Sigmaringen: Jan Thorbecke Verlag, 1980), pp. 299-316; Tomasz Jasiński, "Złota Bulla Fryderyka II dla zakonu krzyżackiego z roku rzekomo 1226," *Roczniki Historyczne* 60 (1994): 107-154, and in a condensed English version with reduced documentation, "The Golden Bull Allegedly Issued in 1226 by Frederick II for the Teutonic Order," *Quaestiones Medii Aevi Novae* 3 (1998): 221-224; and Jasiński, *Kruschwitz, Rimini und die Grundlagen des preussischen Ordenlandes: Urkundenstudien zur Frühzeit des Deutschen Ordens im Ostseeraum* (Marburg: N.G. Elwert, 2008). A German perspective is provided by Hartmut Boockmann, *Der Deutsche Orden. Zwölf Kapitel aus seiner Geschichte* (Munich: C.H. Beck, 1982), pp. 66-92; see also his notes pp. 264-269, esp. p. 266, n.51.

23 Boockmann, *Der Deutsche Orden*, pp. 93-114, provides a brief overview. Fuller treatment of this process is available in Marian Biskup and Gerard Labuda, *Dzieje Zakonu Krzyżackiego w Prusach. Gospodarka—Społeczeństwo—Państwo—Ideologia* (Gdańsk: Wydawnictwo Morskie, 1986), pp. 139-161, and 178-188; this book is available in a German translation: *Die Geschichte des Deutschen Ordens in Preußen. Wirtschaft— Gesellschaft—Staat—Ideologie.* Klio in Polen 6 (Osnabrück: Fibre, 2000). In English, the best treatment is William Urban, *The Teutonic Knights. A Military History* (London: Greenhill Books and Mechanicsburg, PA: Stackpole Books, 2003), pp. 41-108.

24 Steven C. Rowell, "Baltic Europe," in Michael Jones, ed., *The New Cambridge Medieval History*, vol. 6: *ca. 1300-1415* (Cambridge: Cambridge University Press, 2000), p. 729.

25 See Drelicharz, *Unifying the Kingdom of Poland*, p. 196.

26 The steps toward reunification are well analyzed by Tomasz Jurek, "Polska droga do korony królewskiej 1295—1300—1320," in Martin Wihoda and Lukaš Reitinger, eds. *Proměna středovýchodní Evropy raného a vrcholnéo středověku. Mocenské souvislosti a paralely* (Brno: Matica moravská 2010), pp. 139-191. See also Milliman, "*The Slippery of Men*," pp. 101-119.

27 The details of these developments up to the night of 13 November 1308 are analyzed by Błażej Śliwiński, *Pomorze Wschodnie w okresie rządów księcia polskiego Władysława Łokietka w latach 1306-1309* (Gdańsk: Muzeum Archeologiczne w Gdańsku, 2003). See also Biskup and Labuda, *Dzieje Zakonu Krzyżackiego w Prusach*, pp. 241-258; and Milliman, "*Slippery Memory of Men*," pp. 112-114.

28 Publications from the nineteenth and the many of the decades of the twentieth century reflect the powerful influence of modern nationalism. For an overview of more balanced current scholarship, the following are particularly helpful: the items in Śliwiński,

ed., *"Rzeź gdańska" z 1308 roku w świetle najnowszych badań. Materiały z sesji naukowej 12-13 listopada 2008 roku* (Gdańsk: Muzeum Historyczne Miasta Gdańska, 2009), especially his own article therein, "Wydarzenia w Gdańsku i w okolicach w okresie od września do 12/13 listopada 1308 roku," pp. 79-114. In English, the best treatment is now that of Milliman, *"Slippery Memory of Men,"* pp. 142-151, who also provides the text of and an English translation of the statement submitted by the Procurator-General of the Teutonic Knights to the papal curia concerning the putative Gdańsk massacre; see also Paul W. Knoll, *The Rise of the Polish Monarchy. Piast Poland in East Central Europe, 1320-1370* (Chicago: University of Chicago Press, 1972), pp. 29-30.

29 See Sławomir Jóźwiak and Janusz Trupinda, *Organizacja życia na Zamku Krzyżackim w Malborku w czasach Wielkich Mistrzów 1309-1457* (Malbork: Muzeum Zamkowe w Malborku, 2019), p. 21.

30 Biskup and Labuda, *Dzieje Zakonu Krzyżackiego w Prusach*, pp. 342-345. The documents associated with this papal tribunal were originally published in the nineteenth century in *Lites*, 2nd ed., I, 1-51, in an inadequate edition. In the last century, they were successfully re-edited in a much improved version by Helena Chłopocka: *Lites ac Res Gestae inter Polonos Ordinemque Cruciferorum*, vol. I: *Sprawa Wytoczona w Inowrocławiu i Brześciu Kujawskim w latach 1320-1321*, 2nd ed. (Wrocław: Ossolineum, 1970). Older Polish and German studies of this proceeding are treated in Knoll, *The Rise of the Polish Monarchy*, pp. 43-44; see also Milliman, *"Slippery Memory of Men,"* pp. 119-124, who also provides an English translation of the claims submitted by the Polish procurators.

31 *Rocznik Traski*, in *Monumenta Poloniae Historica* II (Lwów: Nakładem Własnym [August Bielowski], 1872), 858. Some modern scholars have provided a more nuanced and positive assessment; see Janusz Kurtyka, *Odrodzone Królestwo. Monarchia Władysława Łokietka i Kazimierza Wielkiego w świetle nowszych badań* (Kraków: Societas Vistulana, 2001), pp. 37-40.

32 See now Stanisław Szczur, "Zjazd wyszheradzki z 1335 roku," *Studia Historyczne* 35 (1992): 3-17; and György Rácz, "The Congress of Visegrád in 1335: Diplomacy and Representation," *Hungarian Historical Review* 2 (2013): 261-287.

33 The record of these proceedings is printed in *Lites*, I, 2nd ed, 55-408. On the course of this trial, see Janusz Bieniak, "Przebieg procesu polsko-krzyżackiego z 1339 roku," *Pamiętnik Biblioteki Kórnickiej* 23 (1993): 5-22; Milliman, *"Slippery Memory of Men,"* pp. 135-137 and 171-179, who also prints the Latin text and English translation of the claims submitted by the royal procurator in 1339 pp. 269-277; and Knoll, *The Rise of the Polish Monarchy*, pp. 100-107.

34 Szczur, "Traktat pokojowy Kazimierza Wielkiego z Zakonem Krzyżackim z 1343," *Zapiski Historyczne* 56 (1991): 439-464; and, more briefly, Biskup and Labuda, *Dzieje Zakonu Krzyżackiego w Prusach*, pp. 349-351.

35 See the observations by Boockmann, *Der Deutsche Orden*, p. 150: "Im Jahre 1343 wurde der Friede von Kalisch geschlossen... Damit war für sechsundsechzig Jahre wiederum Frieden zwischen Polen und dem Deutschen Orden;" and Sebastian Kubon, *Die Außenpolitik des Deutschen Ordens unter Hochmeister Konrad von Jungingen (1393-1407)* (Göttingen: V & R Unipress, 2016), p. 55: "Obwohl mit dem Frieden von Kalisch 1343 zwar zeitweilige

militärische Auseinandersetzungen beendet und ein immerhin 66 Jahre haltender Friede geschlossen werden konnte, blieb das Verhältnis von nun an latent angespannt."

36 This is particularly evident by the absence of any treatment of Polish-Order relations in Andrzej Marzec, "New King and New Elites. The Reign of Louis the Great in Poland 1370-1382," in Dániel Bagi, Gábor Barabás, and Zsolt Máté, eds., *Hungaro-Polonica. Young Scholars on Medieval Polish-Hungarians Relations* (Pécs: Történészcéh Egyesület, 2016), pp. 189-224.

37 The classic work on this topic remains Werner Paravicini, *Die Preussenreisen des europäischen Adels*, 2 vols. (Sigmaringen: Jan Thorbecke Verlag, 1989-1995).

38 Cited by Marian Tumler, *Der Deutsche Orden im Werden, Wachsen und Wirken bis 1400* (Vienna: Panorama, 1955), p. 350.

39 Quotations from Geoffrey Chaucer, *The Canterbury Tales*, "General Prologue," in F.N. Robinson, ed. *The Works of Geoffrey Chaucer*, 2nd ed. (Boston: Houghton Mifflin, 1957), pp. 17-18. An expanded depiction of that chivalry is depicted by Urban, *The Teutonic Knights*, pp. 137-150. In some of his writings, Paweł depicts this chivalry — the *Reisen* and the Table of Honor among other things — as a negative element of the Order's life and activity.

40 See, for example, Alvydas Nikžentaitis, "Die friedliche Periode in den Beziehungen zwischen dem Deutschen Order und dem Großfürstentum Litauen (1345-1360) und das Problem der Christianisierung Litauens," *Jahrbücher für Geschichte Osteuropas* 41, 1 (1993): 1-22.

41 A good overview of these developments is provided by Robert Frost, *The Oxford History of Poland-Lithuania*, vol. I: *The Making of the Polish-Lithuanian Union, 1385-1569* (Oxford: Oxford University Press, 2015), pp. 28-33.

42 For the alternatives, compare Michał Giedroyć, "Lithuanian Options Prior to Kreva (1385)," in *La Cristianizzazione della Lituania* (Vatican City: 1989), pp. 87-105; Urban "The Teutonic Order and the Christianization of Lithuania," in *La Cristianizzazione della Lituania*, pp. 105-135, esp. pp. 128-130; and Frost, *The Making of the Polish-Lithuanian Union*, pp. 33-35.

43 The Union of Krėva/Krewo formed the basis of the Polish-Lithuanian union, but what the nature of that union was continued to be debated by its rulers, officials, and nobles until 1569. Even after that scholarly opinion has been divided and interpretations have often reflected the assumptions and outlooks of modern nationalism: Polish, Lithuanian, Ukrainian, and Russian. Not least of the problems has been what the word *applicare* meant. The recent treatment of the origins of this union by Frost, *The Making of the Polish-Lithuanian Union*, is remarkable for its evenhandedness; see especially his Chapter 5: The Krewo Act, pp. 47-57.

44 A good overview is provided by Marek T. Zahajkiewicz, "Théorie et pratique de l'Évangelisation dans le processus de Christianisation de la Lituanie," in *La Christianizzazione della Lituania*, pp. 179-192. For Jagiełło's activities, see the comments of Jan Długosz: "This done, the king... remains in Lithuania for the rest of the year, travelling the country and encouraging those not yet baptized to be christened, building and endowing churches and chapels, so that he can rightly be considered the apostle who converted the Lithuanians." This English-language quote is from the translation by Maurice Michael (from the Polish translation made by Julia Mrukówna), *The Annals of Jan Długosz. A History of Eastern Europe*

from A.D. 965 to A.D. 1480 (Charlton, Chichester, West Sussex: IMPublications, 1997), p. 349 (from the year 1387). For the full Latin text, see Długosz, *Annales*, VI, 170 (*Liber decimus, sub anno 1387).*

45 This approach was to play a significant role in Paweł's responses in *Iste tractatus* and *Quoniam Error* (see these texts below) to treatises by Johannes Falkenberg and Johannes Urbach of Bamberg.

46 Frost, *The Making of the Polish-Lithuanian Union*, p. 86. This whole complicated period is, in Polish historiography, best treated by Grzegorz Błaszczyk, *Dzieje stosunków polsko--litewskich*, vol. II, part 1: *Od Krewa do Lublina* (Poznań: Wydawnictwo Poznańskie, 2007)

47 Prior to that, to avoid a military challenge from the west, he had signed a treaty with the Order at Salinwerder in 1398 in which he had given up Lithuanian claim to the territory of Samogitia — although without reaching an agreement on this with Jagiełło. For these details, see Sebastian Kubon, *Die Außenpolitik des Deutschen Ordens under Hochmeister Konrad von Jungingen (1393-1407)* (Göttingen: V & R Unipress, 2016), 66-123.

48 The war from 1409 to 1411 has elicited a very substantial body of scholarship. In Poland there is the multi-edition history by Stefan M. Kuczyński, *Wielka Wojna z Zakonem Krzyżackim w latach 1409-1411*, 5th ed. (Warsaw: Wydawnictwo Ministerstwa Obrony Narodowej, 1987); and the briefer Biskup and Labuda, *Dzieje Zakonu Krzyżackiego w Prusach*, pp. 363-367. See now, however, Andrzej Nadolski, *Grunwald 1410*, 3rd ed. (Warsaw: Bellona, 2010). In English there is the sound treatment by Urban, *The Teutonic Knights*, pp. 195-220, and the excellent brief summary by Patrice M. Dabrowski, *Poland. The First Thousand Years*, 2nd ed. (Dekalb, IL: Northern Illinois Press, 2021), pp. 61-67.

49 Długosz, *Annales*, VI, 44 (*Liber decimus, sub anno 1409*): "Disponunt insuper fieri pontem sublicium **nunquam alias visum** ex navibus. . ." The issue of a just war is one that Paweł addressed later, since the Poles had been accused of doing something against Christian teaching and canon law by waging an "unjust war."

50 These figures are summarized by Frost, *The Making of the Polish-Lithuanian Union*, p. 106.

51 There are two modern editions of this. Karol Górski, ed., *Jana Długosza Banderia Prutenorum* (Warsaw: Państwowe Wydawnictwo Naukowe, 1958); and Sven Ekdahl, *Die "Banderia Prutenorum" des Jan Długosz. Eine Quelle zur Schlacht bei Tannenberg 1410* (Göttingen: Vandenhoeck & Ruprecht, 1976). For the importance of this book, see Paul W. Knoll, "Jan Długosz and His *Banderia Prutenorum*" *The Polish Review* 25, 1 (1980): 93-97.

52 Ekdahl, "Battlefield Archaeology at Grunwald (Tannenberg, Žalgiris). A Polish--Scandinavian Research Project during the period 2014-2017," *Przegląd Historyczny* 109, 2 (2018): 239-266.

53 There is a good overview of the Order's relationship with Poland and Lithuania by Adam Szwede, "Zakon Krzyżacki wobec Polski i Litwy w latach 1411-1414," *Prace Historyczne* 141, 2 (2014): 531-553.

54 The other part of the name by which he is known — Włodkowic — means "son of Włodko," short for Włodzimierz (Vladimir in Latin). For his biography see first the entry by Karol Górski, "Paweł Włodkowic z Brudzenia," *Polski Słownik Biograficzny* 25 (1980) 377-381. The biographical information provided by Tadeusz Brzostowski, *Paweł Włodkowic*

(Warsaw: PAX, 1954), p. 46; Belch, *Paulus Vladimiri*, I, 115-117; and Ehrlich, *Pisma Wybrane*, I, 11-12, is very useful and will be cited in what follows when there is a specific point to be made. The general biographical material that follows relies largely upon the four authors cited above in this note.

Dobrzyń has been characterized as land "soaked in blood and tears amid constant attacks and violence by the Knights of the Teutonic Order," by Jan Fiłajek, "Ostatnie słowo Pawła Włodkowica o zakonie krzyżackim," *Przegląd Kościelny* I (1902): 92-93, a theme that Paweł himself implicitly expressed in his attacks upon the Order.

55 Polish clans and their origins — as indeed the origins of the nobility in medieval Poland — is something not yet fully understood by scholars, although some recent contributions have been important. See particularly Eduard Mühle, "Genese und frühe Entwicklung des Adels in polnischer Sicht," and Tomasz Jurek, "Die Entstehung des polnischen Adels," in Mühle, ed., *Studien zum Adel im mittelalterlichen Polen* (Wiesbaden: Harrassowitz Verlag, 2012), pp. 1-12 and 13-117 respectively.

56 Details concerning the University of Prague's development at this point are best treated in the chapters of František Kavka and Josef Petráň, eds., *A History of Charles University*, vol. I (Prague: Karolinum, 2001, Czech original 1995); these are Michal Svatoš, "The Studium Generale 1347/8-1419," pp. 22-93; František Šmahel, "The Faculty of Liberal Arts," pp. 93-122; Jaroslav Kadlec, "The Theological Faculty," pp. 123-148; and Jiří Kejř, "The Prague Law Faculty and the Law University," pp. 149-170.

57 See below in Paweł's treatise *Quoniam error*, n. 71, for this reference and for Maurice's career at Prague and eventually at the University of Kraków.

58 The most recent work on this is reflected in Šmahel, ed., in cooperation with Ota Pavlíček, *A Companion to Jan Hus* (Leiden and Boston: Brill, 2015); and in Michael van Dussen and Pavel Soukup, eds., *A Companion to the Hussites* (Leiden and Boston: Brill, 2020). Belch, *Paulus Vladimiri*, I, 119-120, has strongly suggested that Paweł knew Hus and spoke up in his defense at the Council of Constance, but this is a position that not many others have accepted.

59 A good overview of canon law and how it developed is provided by Brundage, *Canon Law*; see especially his appendix on the Romano-Canonical citation system, pp. 190-205, and his appendix on the major canonists of the classical period, pp. 206-230.

60 See his comment in *Saevientibus*, n. 70.

61 Stanisław's sermon was based upon the text from Proverbs 3:13, *Beatus vir, qui inveniat sapienciam*. For the sermon, Bożena Chmielowska, ed., *Stanisław ze Skarbimierza. Sermones Sapientiales*, 3 vols. (Warsaw: Akademia Teologii Katolickiej, 1979), III, 232-244. Further on this general point, see Krzysztof Ożóg, "Stanisław ze Skarbimierza," in Piotr Dymmel, Krzysztof Skupieński, and Barbara Trelińska, eds., *Droga historii. Studia ofiarowane Profesorowi Józefowi Szymańskiemu w siedemdziesiątą rocznicę urodzin* (Lublin: Wydawnictwo Uniwersytetu Marii Curie-Skłodowskiej, 2001), pp. 47-61.

62 For these last two developments see below *Articuli*, n. 10; and Wiesław Sieradzan, "Benedek (Benedict) Makrai as a Subarbiter in the Conflict Between the Teutonic Order and Neighbor Countries in 1412-1413," in Sierdzan, ed., *Arguments and Counter-Arguments. The Political Thought of the 14th-and 15th Centuries during the Polish-Teutonic Order Trials*

and Disputes (Toruń: Wydawnictwo Naukowe Uniwersytetu Mikołaja Kopernika, 2012), pp. 157-168.

63 On Andrew, see Ożóg, "Udział Andrzeja Łaskarzyca w sprawach i sporach polsko--krzyżackich do soboru w Konstancji," in Ożóg and Szczur, ed., *Polska i jej sąsiedzi w późnym średniowieczu* (Kraków: Societas Vistulana, 2000), pp. 159-186.

64 Matthew Gabriele and David Perry, *The Bright Ages. A New History of Medieval Europe* (New York: Harper Collins, 2021).

65 These early institutions were not known as "universities" at first. The Latin term *universitas* that eventually came to be used to describe them and that, by extension is the source of the term in many modern vernaculars by which they are known, had as its original general meaning simply "whole" or "entirety," often used to indicate a legal corporation of people, associations, or collectives. Eventually, in the context of higher education, the term was applied to the whole body of masters and students (*universitas magistrorum et scolarium* or *universitas doctorum* etc.). See Mariken Teeuwen, *The Vocabulary of Intellectual Life in the Middle Ages* (Turnhout: Brepols, 2003), pp. 147-149.

66 For these developments the standard treatment remains the several individual chapters in Hilde de Ridder-Symoens, ed., *Universities in the Middle Ages* (Cambridge: Cambridge University Press, 1992 [vol. 1 of Walter Rüegg, General Editor, *A History of the University in Europe*]), especially Rüegg, "Themes," pp. 3-34; and Jacques Verger, "Patterns," pp. 35-74..

67 The foregoing is best treated in current Polish historiography by Szczur, *Papież Urban V i powstanie uniwersytetu w Krakowie w 1364 roku* (Kraków: Societas Vistulana, 1999), who analyzes the extensive older scholarly literature. In English, see now Knoll, *"A Pearl of Powerful Learning." The University of Cracow in the Fifteenth Century* (Leiden and Boston: Brill, 2016), pp. 11-22. Much of what follows in the text above is reflected in this volume and in general it will not, for the most part, be cited further.

68 We know this from the series of speeches and sermons delivered by Bartholomew of Jasło; see Maria Kowalczyk, "Odnowienie Uniwersytetu Krakowskiego w świetle mów Bartłomieja z Jasła," *Małopolskie Studia Historyczne* 6, no. 3/4 (1964): 23-42 and reprinted in a volume of her collected writings *Colligite fragmenta ne pereant... Studia z dziejów Uniwersytetu Krakowskiego w średniowieczu* (Kraków: Societas Vistulana, 2010), pp. 111-131.

69 See Mieczysław Markowski, *Dzieje Wydziału Teologii Uniwersytetu Krakowskiego w latach 1397-1525* (Kraków: Wydawnictwo Naukowe Papieskiej Akademii Teologicznej w Krakowie, 1996), pp. 42-51.

70 There are a number of individual works that address specific aspects of the university's history at this point and during the years to come, but the multi-authored study prepared in connection with the first 600th anniversary of Kazimierz's foundation remains a reliable and useful work: Kazimierz Lepszy, ed., *Dzieje Uniwersytetu Jagiellońskiego w latach 1364-1764* (Kraków: Uniwersytet Jagielloński Wydawnictwo Jubileuszowe, 1964), with important chapters by Zofia Kozłowska-Budkowa, "Odnowienie Jagiellońskie Uniwersytetu Krakowskiego (1390-1414)," pp. 37-89; Krystyna Pieradzka, "Uniwersytet Krakowski w Służbie Państwa i wobec Soborów w Konstancji i Bazylei," pp. 91-137; Ignacy Zarębski, "Okres Wczsnego Humanizmu," pp. 151-187; and Józef Garbacik, "Ognisko Nauki i Kultury Renesansowej (1470-1520)," pp. 189-220. See also, in a work prepared for the second 600th

anniversary of the university's founding, Krzysztof Stopka, "From Foundation to the Late 18th Century," in Stopka, Andrzej Kazimierz Banach, and Julian Dybiec, *The History of the Jagiellonian University* (Kraków: Jagiellonian University Press, 2000), pp. 9-76.

71 For John, see the study by Marian Zwiercan, *Komentarz Jana z Dąbrówki do Kroniki Mistrza Wincentego zwanego Kadłubkiem* (Wrocław: Ossolineum, 1969); and his subsequent edition of this work, Zwiercan, ed., *Ioannes de Dąbrówka Commentum in Chronicam Polonorum Magistri Vincentii dicti Kadłubek* (Kraków: Polska Akademia Umiejętności, 2008). See also Knoll, "*A Pearl of Powerful Learning,* pp. 282-285 and pp. 301-308. John has a treatment of the humble ruler (*humilis*), who is successful, and the arrogant or proud ruler (*superbus*), who is doomed to failure, by discussing the *humilitas* of Jagiełło and Vytautas versus the *superbia* of the Order's Grand Master that determined the outcome of the Battle of Grunwald; see *Ioannes de Dąbrówka Commentum*, p. 76

72 Aleksander Birkenmajer, "L'Université de Cracovie. Centre international d'enseignement astronomique à la fin du moyen age," in his *Études d'histoire des sciences en Pologne* (Wrocław: Ossolineum, 1972), 483-495.

73 The most important study of this influence was the work of Mieczysław Markowski, *Burydanizm w Polsce w okresie przedkopernikańskim. Studium z historii filozofii i nauk ścisłych na Uniwersytecie Krakowskim w XV wieku* (Wrocław: Ossolineum, 1971).

74 There is a very good brief overview of achievements in the Arts at Kraków in this period by Ożóg, *The Role of Poland in the Intellectual Development of Europe in the Middle Ages* (Kraków: Societas Vistulana, 2009), pp. 94-104.

75 In Kraków, only about 20% of students who matriculated in Arts earned a first degree (bachelor) and of those who did, only about 20% of them achieved a second (master). Thus, those able to embark upon a higher, professional, degree was very small indeed, and those who began did not always complete. See Knoll, "A Pearl of Powerful Learning," pp. 196-201.

76 There are a number of useful studies point out this kind of service. See Ożóg, "University masters at the royal court of Hedwig of Anjou and Władysław Jagiełło," in Piotr Górecki and Nancy van Deusen, eds., *Central and Eastern Europe in the Middle Ages, A Cultural History. Essays in Honor of Paul W. Knoll* (London and New York: I. B. Tauris, 2009), pp. 147-160, and, more fully, his volume *Uczeni w Monarchii Jagwigi Andegaweńskiej i Władysława Jagiełły (1384-1434)* (Kraków: Polska Akademia Umiejętności, 2004); and Knoll, "Working for the King (and the Queen): Krakovian Scholars in the Royal Service in Late Medieval Poland," *The Polish Review* 59, 2 (2014): 3-18.

77 For his biography, see *Filozofia w Polsce. Słownik Pisarzy* (Wroclaw: Ossolineum, 1971), pp. 364-365.

78 This sermon was first edited and analyzed by Ludwik Ehrlich, *Polski wykład prawa wojny XV wieku. Kazanie Stanisława ze Skarbimierza De bellis iustis* (Warsaw: Wydawnictwo Prawnicze, 1955); for an insightful treatment of it, see Wojciech Świeboda, *Innowiercy w opiniach prawnych uczonych polskich w XV wieku. Poganie, żydzi, muzułmanie* (Kraków: Societas Vistulana, 2013), pp. 143-156.

79 The anonymous commentary known as *Utrum Deus Gloriosus*, derived from Prague and upon which a number of Cracovian masters wrote questions and glosses of their own, has received the most careful analysis; see Zofia Włodek, "Krakowski Komentarz z XV wieku do

Sentencji Piotra Lombarda. Część pierwsza: Wstęp historyczny i edycja tekstu Księgi I i II," *Studia Mediewistyczne* 7 (1966): 125-355; and her follow-up study "Krakowski Komentarz z XV wieku do Sentencji Piotra Lombarda. W poszukiwaniu tendencji doktrynalnych na wydziale teologicznym Uniwersytetu Krakowskiego w XV wieku. Cz. 2: Tendencje doktrynalne komentarza," *Studia Mediewistyczne* 9 (1968): 245-291. See also Zenon Kałuża, "Podręcznik teologii używany na Uniwersytecie Krakowskim: Komentarz do *Sentencji*, zwany *Utrum Deus Gloriosus*," *Przegląd Tomistyczny* 17 (2011): 235-254. There remain many other Cracovian commentary on the *Sentences*, and Ożóg, *The Role of Poland in the Intellectual Development of Europe*, p. 105, has noted that no in depth contrastive analysis of these commentaries has yet been made.

80 The first Polish scholar to address their importance was Jan Fijałek, *Mistrz Jakób z Paradyża i Uniwersytet Krakowski w okresie soboru Bazylejskiego*, 2 vols. (Kraków: Nakładem Akademii Umiejętności, 1900). They have now been edited by Wacław Bucichowski, ed., *Polskie Traktaty Koncyliarystyczne z połowy XV wieku* (Warsaw: Akademia Teologii Katolickiej, 1987); and one of them, that by Thomas Strzempiński, has been reedited by Zofia Włodek, *Scripta Manent. Textus ad Theologiam Spectantes in Universitate Cracoviensi saeculo XV conscripti* (Kraków: Wydawnictwo Naukowe Papieskiej Akademii Teologicznej w Krakowie, 2000), pp. 227-292. See now, with reference to Strzempiński's treatise, the comment by Antony Black, *Council and Commune. The Conciliar Movement and the Council of Basle* (London: Burns and Oates, 1979), p. 112: it represented "the most complete... defense of Basle conciliarism ever produced outside Basle itself." All of the treatises have now been brilliantly studied and analyzed by Thomas Wünsch, *Konziliarismus und Polen. Personen, Politik und Programme aus Polen zur Verfassungsfrage der Kirche in der Zeit der mittelalterlichen Reformkonzilien* (Paderborn, Munich, Vienna, and Zürich: Schöningh, 1998), especially pp. 72-122 and 128-386.

81 The schism is now well treated by the several chapters in Joëlle Rollo-Koster and Thomas M. Izbicki, eds., *A Companion to the Great Western Schism (1378-1417)* (Leiden and Boston: Brill, 2009), though the classic work of Noël Valois, *La France et le grand schism d'Occident*, 4 vols. (Paris: A. Picard et fils, 1896-1902) is still valuable.

82 Citing the contemporary writer Ulrich von Richental's *Chronicle of the Council of Constance*, Francis Oakley, *The Western Church in the Later Middle Ages* (Ithaca, NY and London: Cornell University Press, 1979), p. 64, n.42, lists the numbers in attendance: two popes, a host of other officials temporal as well as spiritual, five patriarchs, thirty-three cardinal, forty-seven archbishops, 145 bishops, ninety-three suffragan bishops, 132 abbots, 155 priors, 217 doctors of theology, 361 doctors of both laws, 5,300 simple priests and scholar, more than 3,000 merchants, shopkeepers, craftsmen, musicians, and players, and more than 700 harlots in brothels distinguished from those who lay in stables and wherever they could, beside the private ones who I could not count.

83 One of the most important decisions was to establish voting at the council on the basis of *nationes*. These, four in number originally, were geographically defined and bore little relationship to modern "nations" (though there certainly was nation feeling expressed within them). These nations were the English (north), the French (west), the Italian (south) and the German (east) , in which the Polish, Czech, Hungarian, and Scandinavian delegations

were included. Each nation had one vote, no matter how many individual members it had. Eventually the College of Cardinals (collectively), as a corporate body equal to the nations, was given a vote, and after 1416, a fifth nation was added, the Spanish. The work of the council was done in commissions or committees organized around themes or issues, and voting was done in general sessions, of which there were forty-five. The commissions and general sessions often took up some of the peripheral issues beyond the main three identified below.

84 Heinrich Finke, et al., eds., *Acta concilii Constanciensis*, 4 vols. (Münster: Regensburgsche Buchhandlung, 1896-1928), II, 413. For an overview of Polish activity at the council, see Biskup and Labuda, *Dzieje Zakonu Krzyżackiego w Prusach*, pp. 369-372.

85 Early in the activities of the council, during a meeting of a general session, Paweł was also appointed canon and prebend of Poznań, recently made vacant with the confirmation of Andreas Łaskarz as bishop of Poznań, thus adding to the offices he already held in the cathedral of Kraków; see Belch, *Paulus Vladimiri,* I, 133.

86 For these individuals, see the brief descriptions of Wünsch, *Konziliarismus und Polen*, pp. 53-58.

87 Frederick H. Russell, "Paulus Vladimir's Attack on the Just War: A Case Study in Legal Polemics," in Brian Tierney and Peter Linehan, eds., *Authority and Power. Studies on Medieval Law and Government Presented to Walter Ullmann on his Seventieth Birthday* (Cambridge: Cambridge University Press, 1980), pp. 237-254, here 241. For the activities of representatives of the Order described in the previous sentences, see the nice overview by Timothy M. Brennan, "Just War, Sovereignty, and Canon Law: Legal Arguments Over the Lithuanian Crusade and the Rights of Unbelievers at the Council of Constance (1414-1418)," (Unpublished Ph.D. dissertation, University of Kansas, 2006), pp. 119-126.

88 On this point see Frost, *The Making of the Polish-Lithuanian Union*, p. 125.

89 It is generally agreed that the fullest history of the council as a whole remains that by Walter Brandmüller, *Das Konzil von Konstanz*, 2 vols. (Paderborn: Schöningh, 1991-1997, with a revised edition of vol 1 published in 2000). Also important is the study by Ansgar Frenken, *Die Erforschung des Konstanzer Konzils (1414-1418) in den letzten 100 Jahren* (Paderborn: Schöningh, 1995). In English, see the recent chapter by Phillip H. Stump, "The Council of Constance (1414-18) and the End of the Schism," in Rollo-Koster and Izbicki, *A Companion to the Great Western Schism*, pp. 396-442; and Stump, *The Reforms of the Council of Constance (1414-1418)* (Leiden, New York, and Cologne: Brill, 1994). For the specific question of Poland and the Council, an issue that includes other matters than those treated here, see Tomasz Graff, *Episkopat monarchii jagiellońskiej w dobie soborów powszechnych XV wieku* (Kraków: Societas Vistulana, 2008), pp. 199-219, which is broader than its title suggests.

90 See above, n. 78.

91 In a letter Paweł wrote to Jagiełło on 22 January 1416, he described these matters: "Eadem universitas sum ministerium ad hoc realiter prestitit, licet per me cuius rector eram anno preterito et nunc prestat ministrando dictis negociis bonum principium atque causam, que divina gratis operante videtur posita in fundamento solido, cui non poteuerit resistere omnis adversarii vestri hostesque dicti Regni." See Jacek Wiesiołowski, "Prace i projekty Pawła Włodkowica—Konstancja, zima 1415 i 1416 roku," *Roczniki Historyczne* 35 (1969):

93-123, here pp. 118-120. Paweł here is speaking as an academic and as a royal representative, a duplex status at Constance that he performed brilliantly.

92 Belch, *Paulus Vladimiri*, I, 165, entitles this work *De potestate papae et imperatoris respectu infidelium*. The work is undated, through the second work Paweł distributed bears a specific date of 6 July 1415. In that treatise he states that *Saevientibus* had been given to the German nation the day before. Thus the traditional dating for that work is in the year 1415. For reasons that are complex, and argued compellingly by Boockmann, *Johannes Falkenberg, der Deutsche Orden und die polnische Politik. Untersuchungen zur politischen Theorie des späteren Mittelalters* (Göttingen: Vandenhoeck & Ruprecht, 1975), pp. 225-228, especially n. 21, the date should be in 1416. See also Knoll, *"A Pearl of Powerful Learning,"* p. 239, n. 57. Most recently the date of 1416 has also been adopted by Wojciech Kozłowski, "Wstęp," in Cichocki and Talarowski, eds., *Paweł Włodkowic i Polska Szkoła prawa międzynarodowego*, p. 15, following Karol Górski's entry in *Polski Słownik Biograficzny*, p. 378, who in turn was perhaps convinced by the argument made by Boockmann.

93 See Izbicki, "The Authority of Peter and Paul: The Use of Biblical Authority During the Great Schism," in Rollo-Koster and Izbicki, *A Companion to the Great Western Schism*, pp. 375-393, here pp. 390-391: "The third leading intellectual present at the Council of Constance, together with d'Ailly and Gerson, was the Italian canonist Francesco Zabarella." See also Thomas E. Morrissey, "Cardinal Franciscus Zabarella (1360-1417) as a Canonist and the Crisis of his Age: Schism and the Council of Constance," *Zeitschrift für Kirchengeschichte* 96 (1985) 196-208, reprinted in Morrissey, *Conciliarism and Church Law in the Fifteenth Century. Studies on Franciscus Zabarella and the Council of Constance* (Farnham, Surry, England and Burlington, VT: Ashgate, 2014), as item VIII, with original pagination.

94 This is the position taken by Schulz, "Paulus Vladimiri und das jagiellonische Polen," p. 107.

95 On this point, see below in *Opinio Hostiensis*, n. 31

96 See the standard history of this topic by Frederick H. Russell, *The Just War in the Middle Ages* (Cambridge: Cambridge University Press, 1975).

97 Several convenient brief summaries of the contents of *Opinio Hostiensis* are available; see, for example, Belch, *Paulus Vladimiri*, I, 856-859; Brennan, "Just War, Sovereignty, and Canon Law," pp. 204-213; and Knoll, *"A Pearl of Powerful Learning,"* pp. 434-436.

98 This point is nicely made by Brennan, "Just War, sovereignty, and Canon Law," p. 216, n. 779.

99 Not included in Belch, *Paulus Vladimiri*, who gives it the title *Causa*, I, 169, it runs 272 pages in the edition of Ehrlich, *Pisma Wybrane*, I, 144-259 and II, 2-167. It opens with the words *Ad aperiendam pregnantem materiam grandi periculo involutam ac incautos suis gravissimis reticulis pestiferis involventem huic sacro Constanciensi generali consilio*. . . ("To open a pregnant matter, entangled in great danger and implicating the incautious most gravely in its pestiferous nets, before this sacred General Council at Constance. . .")

100 See the observations by Belch, *Paulus Vladimiri*, I, 173, and by Knoll, *"A Pearl of Powerful Learning,"* pp. 436-440.

101 ". . .evidentissime non solum iure canonico et civili sed eciam iure naturali et divino ipsorum collegia huiusmodi esse prohibita et dampnata. Et ideo auctoritate huius sacri

concilij necessario penitus destruenda. Et hec sufficient pro presenti." Ehrlich, *Pisma wybrane*, I, 189.

102 See below in the treatise *Articuli*, n. 6.

103 This is precisely the point made by Norman Housley, "A Crusade Against the Poles? Johannes Falkenberg's 'Satira' (1412)," in Helen J. Nicholson and Jochen Burgtorf, eds., *The Templars, the Hospitallers and the Crusades* (London and New York: Routledge, 2020), pp. 183-198, here pp. 190-191.

104 "Ich habe etlichen doctoribus gelt gegeben, Redlich entwert doruff zu schriben." See Boockmann, *Johannes Falkenberg*, pp. 234-247, here p. 235.

105 For more details, see *Iste tractatus* below, n. 5.

106 Belch, *Paulus Vladimiri*, II, 993.

107 The text translated to this point is identified by Belch as *Scriptum I*; what follows is a separate work in Belch's taxonomy, one that he designates as *Scriptum II*. That work is Falkenberg's notorious *Satira*. See *Iste tractatus* below, nn. 13 and 14.

108 There is a good, brief summary of Falkenberg's points provided by Boockmann, *Johannes Falkenberg*, pp. 9-10, a volume that remains the authoritative treatment of Falkenberg's context. Boockmann, *Der Deutsche Orden*, has remarkably little treatment of the Order and Poland at the Council of Constance.

109 Jürgen Miethke, "Heiliger Heidenkrieg? Theoretische Kontroversen zwischen Deutschem Orden und dem Königreich Polen vor und auf dem Konstanzer Konzil," in Klaus Schreiner, ed., *Heilige Kriege. Religiöse Begründungen militärischer Gewaltanwendung: Judentum, Christentum und Islam im Vergleich* (Munich: Oldenbourg, 2008), pp. 109-125, here p. 117.

110 This issue has been neatly treated comparatively by Anna Lisa Merklin Lewis, "Tyrannicide: Heresy or Duty? The Debates at the Council of Constance," (Unpublished Ph.D. Dissertation, Cornell University, Ithaca, NY, 1990), pp. 101-159. It is worth noting that Falkenberg had already distributed three of his treatises on tyrannicide at Constance; see Władysław Seńko, "Trzy traktaty Jana Falkenberg na temat tyranobójstwa przedstawione na Soborze w Konstancji w 1416 r.," *Przegląd Tomistyczny* 10 (2002): 87-127.

111 The focus in this section has been upon Paweł for obvious reasons, but at the council members of the ecclesiastical hierarchy were of major importance, and the same is true of those from the Polish church. See Graff, *Episkopat monarchii jagiellońskiej*, pp. 199-219; with particular reference to their role in the effort to condemn Falkenberg, see pp. 209-212. Graff has also treated this subject briefly in his *Kościół w Polsce wobec konfliktu z Zakonem Krzyżackim w XV wieku. Studium z dziejów kultury politycznej polskiego episkopatu* (Kraków: Księgarnia Akademicka, 2010), pp. 44-45.

112 For an analysis of why Poles failed to achieve complete success in the Falkenberg case, see Graff, "Servants of the Devil or Protectors of Christianity and Apostles among Pagans? Shaping the image of Poland and Poles in the Context of Steps taken by Wladyslaw II Jagiello's Diplomacy against 'Satira' by John Falkenberg," *Folia Historica Cracoviensia* 23, 1 (2017): 143-176. For developments at the end of the council and beyond, see the treatments by Belch, *Paulus Vladimiri*, I, 133-136; Boockmann, *Johannes Falkenberg*, pp. 263-288; Wünsch, *Konziliarismus und Polen*, pp. 63-67; and Ożóg, *Uczeni*, pp. 217-222. The dénouement of the

affair of Falkenberg came after further negotiations. On 17 January 1424, a Polish delegation led by Andrew Łaskarz and Paweł met in Rome with Martin V and Falkenberg. The Dominican formally abjured his satire on the Polish king and his subjects and the Poles retracted their appeal to a future council.

113 His identity was first established, together with an analysis of his treatise, by Boockmann, "Aus den Handakten des Kanonisten Johannes Urbach. Die Satire des Johannes Falkenberg und andere Funde zur Geschichte des Konstanzer Konzils," *Deutsches Archiv* 28 (1972): 497-532.

114 Its full title is *Tractatus: De statu Fratrum Ordinis B. Mariae Virginis Teutonicorum et pugna eorum adversus infideles necnon de imploratione adiutorii infidelium per christianos ad defensionem suam*, edited by Belch, *Paulus Vladimiri*, II, 1116-1180; he terms it (II, 1108) "one of the longest, the most thorough and learned treatise[s] written on that occasion." It has been translated into English by Brennan, "Just War, Sovereignty, and Canon Law," pp. 422-532. For more about Johannes Urbach, see below, *Quoniam error*, n. 5.

115 Brennan, "Just War, Sovereignty, and Canon Law," p. 233.

116 See *Quoniam error*, the material following n. 99.

117 See *Quoniam error*, the material following n. 172.

118 See *Quoniam error*, the material immediately following his quotation from Urbach, n. 151. The Polish and English translation of *contempitur* at this point in Ehrlich, *Pisma wybrane*, II, 365 is *odrzuca* and *rejected* respectively.

119 Russell, "Paulus Vladimiri's Attack on the Just War," p. 246.

120 Brennan, "Just War, Sovereignty, and Canon Law," p. 233. Belch, *Paulus Vladimiri*, I, 425, whose views about Paweł were always favorable, is more explicit: He concludes that his works at Constance "dealt a blow against the very idea of conversion by force." For an analysis of Belch's outlook, see the review of his two-volumes on Paweł by Howard Kaminsky in *Speculum* 42 (1967): 718-720.

121 See the text of *Oculi*, n. 57.

122 This version, not included in the translation of *Oculi* below, is printed in Ehrlich, *Pisma wybrane*, III, 62-78.

123 Sigismund was trying to balance his own interests against his general support of the Order and his need for support from Poland on other matters. See below, *Ad videndum*, n. 1 and the literature cited there. For a fascinating treatment of how arbitration was expected to work in these contexts, see the study by Rafał Wojciechowski, *Arbitraż w doktrynie prawnej średniowiecza* (Wrocław: Wydawnictwo Uniwersytetu Wrocławskiego, 2010); the practical aspects of this, though without reference to the Wrocław judgment, are analyzed by Jean--Marie Moeglin, "Krieg und Vermittlungsverfahren in Europa in den letzten Jahrhunderten des Mittelalters," in Werner Paravicini, Rimvydas Petrauskas, and Grischa Vercamer, eds., *Tannenberg—Grunwald—Žalgiris 1410: Krieg und Frieden im späten Mittelalter* (Wiesbaden: Harrassowitz, 2012), pp. 211-222

124 Printed by Belch, *Paulus Vladimiri*, II, 1027-1032.

125 The standard overview of this process is Stanisław Zajączkowski, "Studia nad procesami Polski i Litwy z Zakonem Krzyżackim w l. 1420-1423," *Ateneum Wileńskie* 12 (1937): 282-403. See now, however, Ożóg, *Uczeni w Monarchii Jadwigi Andegaweńskiej i Władysława*

Jagiełły, pp. 234-241; and the insights in Adam Szweda, et al., eds., *Lites ac Res Gestae inter Polonos Ordinemque Cruciferorum/ Akta postępowania przed wysłannikiem papieskim Antonym Zeno z Mediolanu w latach 1422-1423* (Toruń: Wydawnictwo Naukowe Uniwersytetu Mikołaja Kopernika, 2015), pp. 15-19. The transmission of the various documents prepared in connection with this papal review is best traced by Szweda and Anna Adamska, "Notariusz przy pracy. Akcja transumowania dokumentów krzyżackich jesienią 1421 roku," in Grażyna Rutkowska and Antoni Gąsiorowski, eds., *Memoria viva. Studia historyczne poświęcone pamięci Izabeli Skierskiej (1967-2014)* (Poznań: Instytut Historii PAN, 2015), pp. 487-501.

126 Compare the treatments of the structure of *Ad videndum* by Belch, *Paulus Vladimiri*, I, 194-195; and Ehrlich, *Pisma wybrane*, I, xxxvii-xxxviii.

127 Political and diplomatic developments after this are summarized effectively by Belch, *Paulus Vladimiri*, II, 1065-1089.

128 The relevant documents from this mission, including the testimony of twenty-nine witnesses, have now been printed, in a model edition, in Szweda, et al., eds., *Lites ac Res Gestae inter Polonos Ordinemque Cruciferorum*. For the mission itself, see Krzysztof Baczkowski, "La missione del nunzio Antonio Zeno in Polonia negli anni 1422-1423," *Prace Historyczne* 86 (1987): 15-27; and Ożóg, *Uczeni*, pp. 241-249.

129 See Ekdahl, "Der Krieg zwischen dem Deutschen Orden und Polen-Litauen im Jahre 1422," *Zeitschrift für Ostforschung* 13 (1964): 614-651; and Biskup and Labuda, *Dzieje Zakonu Krzyżackiego w Prusach*, pp. 372-374.

130 Roman Maria Zawadzki, "Początki kultu Królowej Jadwigi," in *Jubileusz Sześćsetlecie Wydziału Teologicznego w Krakowie 20 X 1996 – 20 X 1997* (Kraków: Wydawnictwo Naukowe Papieskiej Akademii Teologicznej, 1998), pp. 283-298, here p. 290. Jadwiga was eventually canonized in 1997 during the pontificate of John Paul II.

131 Długosz, *Annales*, IX (*Liber duodecimus, sub anno 1435*), p. 162.

132 Fijałek, "Ostatnie słowo Pawła Włodkowica," Przegląd Kościelny I (1902)1-13, 92-104, 180-189, 258-273, 342-352.

133 For the position of university chancellor, see Knoll, *"A Pearl of Powerful Learning,"* pp. 81-86.

134 The figure who was most important in both these appointments (the first by Pope Eugene IV in 1439, the second by the Council of Basel in 1441, the third by Pope Nicholas V in 1449) was the Polish historian Jan Długosz, who was in these years a ranking member of the chancery of Oleśnicki; see Knoll, "Jan Długosz, 1480-1980," *The Polish Review* 27, 1/2 (1982): 3-28, here pp. 12-14, reprinted in Charles Kraszewski, ed., *Fifty Years of Polish Scholarship: The Polish Review 1956-2006* (New York: PIASA Books, 2006), pp. 259-295, here 271-274.

135 For an overview of his biography, see the entry (by Maria Koczerska) in *PSB*, XXIII, 776-784; for his role as bishop, see Koczerska, *Zbigniew Oleśnicki i kościół krakowski w czasach jego pontyfikatu (1423-1455)* (Warsaw: DiG, 2004); and for an appreciation of the range of his accomplishments and influence, see the contributions in Feliks Kiryk and Zdzisław Noga, eds., *Zbigniew Oleśnicki Książę Kościoła i Mąż Stanu* (Kraków: Secesja, 2006).

136 Dariusz Wróbel, "Zbigniew Oleśnicki a kwestia pruska i krzyżacka," in Kiryk and Noga, eds., *Zbigniew Oleśnicki*, pp. 85-101.

137 See Marian Biskup, "Najazd krzyżacki na Polskę i bitwa pod Dąbkami 1431 r.," *Zeszyty Naukowe WAP* 48 (1967): 15-28. Melno was one of five "eternal peaces" that were signed between Poland and the Order between 1398 and 1435. None lasted very long. Klaus Neitmann, "Vom 'ewigen Frieden'. Die Kunst des Friedensschlusses zwischen dem Deutschen Orden und Polen-Litauen 1398-1435," in Paravicini, Petrauskas, and Vercamer, eds., *Tannenberg—Grunwald—Žalgiris 1410,* pp. 201-209, sets these kinds of developments into context. The complexity of this set of developments is well presented by Frost, *The Making of the Polish-Lithuanian Union*, pp. 131-176, especially pp. 151-157. The impressive contribution to this from the Polish side is best represented by Grzegorz Błaszczyk, *Burza koronacyjna: Polska-Litwa 1429-1430: Dramatycznych fragment stosunków polsko-litewskich w XV wieku* (Poznań: Instytut Historii Uniwersytetu im. Adama Mickiewicza, 1998).

138 See below, *Epistola*, n. 3.

139 For these, see Russell, *The Just War in the Middle Ages.*

140 See Russell, "Paulus Vladimiri's Attack on the Just War," pp. 237-254, especially pp. 240-241. Paweł's modification here is most clearly seen in his treatise *Quoniam error*; see below in *Quoniam error,* after n. 65 (the third conclusion in Version I): "so that a war might be shown to be just *de iure*, it is necessary for the just cause to be inquired into and declared legitimate. . ."

141 See below, *Epistola*, n. 40.

142 See Belch, *Paulus Vladimiri*, I, 150.

143 Długosz, *Annales*, IX (*Liber duodecimus, sub anno 1435*), 161, and n. 50 (384), which provides the editorial information for this date. See also Knoll, "*A Pearl of Powerful Learning*, p. 445, n.147. The standard mid-twentieth century Polish biography of Paweł provides only an approximate period in which his death falls; see Brzostowski, *Paweł Włodkowic*, pp. 52-54.

144 For the most part, what follows makes no systematic effort to illustrate the details regarding these themes in Paweł's writings by reference to his specific works included in this volume. Those who read them will readily recognize where and how Paweł developed these themes. For more extensive analyses of these themes (including detailed references to Paweł's texts) see Belch, *Paulus Vladimiri*, I, 237-688; and Ehrlich, *Pisma wybrane*, I, xlii-lxv. There is a briefer set of analyses, with references, in Knoll, "*A Pearl of Powerful Learning*," pp. 445-458.

145 See above, n. 3.

146 The classic work on the Bible in the Middle Ages remains Beryl Smalley, *The Study of the Bible in the Middle Ages* (Oxford: Oxford University Press, 1952 and later editions). For biblical studies in Poland, especially at the University of Kraków, see Stanisław Wielgus, *Średniowieczna łacińskojęzyczna biblistyka polska* (Lublin: Redakcja Wydawnictw Katolickiego Lubelskiego, 1992).

147 The medieval canonical tradition which was so much a part of Paweł's intellectual make-up drew heavily upon natural law and its rights as shown by Brian Tierney, *The Idea of Natural Rights. Studies on Natural Rights, Natural Law, and Church Law, 1150-1625* (Atlanta, GA: Scholars Press, 1977), pp. 43-77 in particular. The relationship between canon law and natural law is discussed also by Brundage, *Canon Law*, pp. 156-158.

148 "Ius naturale idem est apud omnes," quoted by Ehrlich, *Polski wykład prawa wojny XV wieku*, p. 130.

149 Here I paraphrase Brundage, *Canon Law*, p. 157, who is describing the views of Hostiensis, who had expressed this position in his *Summa* on the *Liber extra* of Pope Gregory IX. There is a profound irony in this, as in other contexts at the Council of Constance Paweł rejected Hostiensis' position about what the effect of Christ's birth had been with reference to the rights on non-Christians.

150 This principle is reiterated in a number of instances; see *Saevientibus*, sentence after n. 17: "And by natural law it was prohibited for one to do unto another that which he would not wish done unto himself."

151 What follows is greatly indebted to Wielgus, *Polska średniowieczna doktryna* Ius Gentium (Lublin: Wydawnictwo Katolickiego Uniwersytetu Lubelskiego, 1996), and the English translation of this, with significant additions for an Anglophone audience, *The Medieval Polish Doctrine of the Law of Nations* (Lublin: Wydawnictwo Katolickiego Uniwersytetu Lubelskiego, 1996). See also Władysław Seńko, "Z badań nad historią myśli społeczno-politycznej w Polsce w XV wieku," in Ryszard Palacz, ed., *Filozofia polska XV wieku* (Warsaw: Państwowe Wydawnictwo Naukowe, 1972), pp. 20-57; and Tadeusz Jasudowicz, *Śladami Ludwika Ehrlicha. Do Pawła Włodkowica po naukę o prawach człowieka* (Toruń: Wydawnictwo Comer Jacek Waloch, 1995), which includes material from his two articles included in Cichocki and Talarowski, ed., *Paweł Włodkowic i polska szkoła prawa międzynarodowego*. (see above, n. 5).

152 In the *Propositio Samagitarum*, which Paweł either wrote or participated in the preparation of, this phrase is used to justify the status of the Samogitian delegation that had come to the Council of Constance to plead their condition against the Order. See Knoll, "*A Pearl of Powerful Learning*," p. 448, n. 160.

153 See the way this is developed by Jasudowicz, *Śladami Ludwika Ehrlicha*, pp. 37-149; and Wielgus, *The Medieval Polish Doctrine of the Law of Nations*, pp. 95-101.

154 See, for example, the argument in *Opinio Hostiensis*, conclusion 21: "It is clear from natural law that the best rule is there, where all are subject to the general rule of one ruler. It is therefore necessary to have one monarch in the world. . . therefore said ruler must be the Pope." A similar argument is found in Paweł's treatise *Oculi*, *Ad aperiendam*, and *Ad videndum*; see the analysis by Ożóg, *Uczeni*, pp. 92-100.

155 See above, n. 140.

156 This argument is most clearly developed by Wielgus, *Polska średniowieczna doktryna* Ius Gentium, pp. 66-71 and in his *The Medieval Polish Doctrine of the Law of Nations*, pp. 89-95, building upon the arguments especially of Jasudowicz, *Śladami Ludwika Ehrlicha*.

157 Wünsch, "Paulus Wladimiri und die Genese des 'realistischen Denkens' in der Lehre von den internationalen Beziehungen: Der Krieg zwischen Polen und dem Deutschen Orden als Stimulus für ein neues politiktheoretisches Paradigma," in Paravicini, Petrauskas, and Vercamer, eds., *Tannenberg—Grunwald—Žalgiris 1410*, pp. 27-42.

158 Although Paweł was active at the Council of Constance (where in other contexts some important principles of conciliarism were articulated) and he appealed to a future council for a decision on the Falkenberg issue, he was not a conciliarist, as Wünsch, *Konziliarismus und Polen*, pp. 60-72, shows by tracing his activity there. He was, however, a reformer, especially with respect to questions relating to papal annates (see Wünsch's further comments

p. 344.) Belch, *Paulus Vladimiri*, I, 161-162 identified two works by Paweł on simony and on annates. For the question of reform efforts at Constance, and the involvement of Paweł therein, see Phillip H. Stump, *The Reforms of the Council of Constance (1414-1418)* (Leiden, New York, and Cologne: Brill, 1994), pp. 173-205, esp. pp. 173-175. It should be noted, however, that subsequent to the work of Stump, the work *Speculum aureum* he attributed to Paweł, has been shown to be written by Piotr Wysz; see Władysław Seńko, *Piotr Wysz z Radolina i jego dzieło* Speculum aureum," (Warsaw: Instytut Tomistyczny, 1995).

159 For an example of this, see below in the treatise *Saevientibus*, n. 40.

160 Marcia Colish, *Medieval Foundations of the Western Intellectual Tradition 400-1400* (New Haven, CT and London: Yale University Press, 1997), p. xi.

161 See above, n. 65. And see Colish's comment, *Medieval Foundations of the Western Intellectual Tradition*, p. 265: scholastics "had to show their mastery of past authorities and to demonstrate their ability to winnow out those that were irrelevant, inconsistent, or addressed to outdated conditions, to harvest those that illuminated their subject, and to offer principled reasons for agreeing or disagreeing with their sources."

162 See above, n. 78.

163 See Ehrlich, *Paweł Włodkowic i Stanisław ze Skarbimierza* (Warsaw: Państwowe Wydawnictwo Naukowe, 1954), especially his comment (p. 6) "Both scholars created at that time the Polish school of the law of nations;" and Wielgus, *Polska średniowieczna doktryna* Ius Gentium, pp. 21-24 and his *Medieval Polish Doctrine of the Law of Nations*, pp. 25-28.

164 Edited by Bożena Chmielowska, "Notatka *Revocatur* w rękopisie Biblioteki Uniwersyteckiej w Gandawie," *Studia Medievistyczne*, 30 (1993): 33-39; see also the treatment by Świeboda, *Innowiercy*, pp. 156-160; and Knoll, "*A Pearl of Powerful Learning*," pp. 425-428.

165 Ehrlich, *Polski wykład prawa wojny*, pp. 198-203.

166 These individuals are identified by Wielgus, *Polska średniowieczna doktryna* Ius Gentium, pp. 15-18 and his *Medieval Polish Doctrine of the Law of Nations*, pp. 17-20. One of them was Benedict Hesse of Kraków, who took up many of these issues in his extensive commentary on the Book of Matthew; see Świeboda, *Innowiercy*, pp. 243-268.

167 A sampling of Polish opinion can be found in Knoll, "*A Pearl of Powerful Learning*," p. 458, n. 192. The best example of someone outside the Polish scene is the overview provided by Jean Moreau-Reibel, "Le droit de société interhumaine et le "Jus Gentium." Essai sur les origins et le developpement des notions jusqu'a Grotius," *Recueil des Cours de l'Academie de Droit International* 77 (1950): 481-598, esp. pp. 523-536.

168 See the comment of Norman Davies, *God's Playground. A History of Poland*, 2 vols. (New York: Columbia University Press, 1982), I, 166: "[Pawel's (*sic.*)] detailed charges against the excesses of the Teutonic Order were supported by arguments from theology and philosophy which provide one of the earliest expositions of a specifically Polish concept of international law." An especially negative assessment of whether one can talk about a "school" of international law is given by Boockmann, *Johannes Falkenberg*, pp. 229-231.

169 Belch, *Paulus Vladimiri*, I, 744.

170 See, for example, Jan W. Woś, "Un débat ouvert: Paulus Wladimiri et Francisco de Vitoria," *Mediaevalia Philosophica Polonorum* 20 (1975): 85-88, and his "Paulus Wladimiri aus Brudzen—Vorläufer oder Fortzetzer," *Zeitschrift für Ostforschung* 25 (1976): 438-461;

and Zenon Kałuża, "Paweł Włodkowic i problem jego doktryny," *Zeszyty Naukowe KUL* 21 (1978): 85-92, esp. pp. 91-92. One recent effort to connect Paweł's contribution to the School of Salamanca (i.e., Vitoria et al.) has been to argue that, with respect to the idea of the just war, similar ideas to those of that school appeared "a hundred years earlier in the Kraków Academia" and that, therefore, Salamanca's claims to originality are invalid and — by extension — Kraków should be recognized as the source of modern international law; see Tomasz Tulejski, "Paulus Vladimiri and His Forgotten Concept of the Just War," *Archiwum Filozofii Prawa i Filozofii Społecznej* 2019, 2: 39-52, here p. 41. This approach side-steps the question of actual ties and influence and argues instead that the approaches of both "schools" were similar. This is an assertion that needs to be more fully analyzed, for the outlook of the sixteenth century was much changed from that of the early fifteenth.

171 Brennan, "Just War, Sovereignty, and Canon Law," p. 296.

172 See Lewis Hanke, *Bartolomé de las Casas. An Interpretation of his Life and Writings* (The Hague: Martinus Nijhof, 1951) and Hanke, *Bartolomé de las Casas: Bookman, Scholar, and Propogandist* (Philadelphia: University of Pennsylvania Press, 1952).

173 Russell, "Paulus Vladimiri's Attack on the Just War," p. 253.

174 The most recent foregoing paragraphs have been very "textbookish" in character. There are two excellent textbooks, with good suggestions for further reading, for an Anglophone audience that provide a reliable fuller treatment. They are Jerzy Lukowski and Hubert Zawadzki, *A Concise History of Poland*, 3rd ed. (Cambridge: Cambridge University Press, 2019); and Patrice M. Dabrowski, *Poland: The First Thousand Years.*

WITH PRUSSIAN INFIDELS RAGING

(*Saevientibus*, 1416)[1]

With Prussian infidels, and others, raging against the Christian Poles, the Knights of the Cross were once summoned into Poland as an aid in the struggle against them by some princes of Poland. These knights are known as the Brethren of the Holy Virgin Mary of the Hospital of Jerusalem of the Teutonic House. To these, certain possessions near the borders with the above-mentioned pagans were delimited and granted by said princes of Poland.[2] From these possessions, and with the aid of the Poles and other Christians, the Knights sought, at successive times, to subject the — at the time — cruel and pagan Prussian nation, occupying their lands. It is for this reason that they are also referred to as the 'lords of Prussia.'

And here they built firm and well-defended cities and fortresses of the greatest strength; so firmly establishing all and securing the lands they occupy that it would take a force ten times greater than their own to overcome them, if indeed they not be impregnable even so.[3] Now, although the Prussians have been subjected to their dictate and have ceased, for many years now, to wage war against the Christians and to inflict pagan cruelties upon them, still these Knights of the Cross have not ceased from battling them down — even the gentle and peacekeeping, quiet pagans — invading their lands under their old pretexts, as if rabid pagan savagery were still being directed at the followers of Christ. Gathering other Christians to their aid, they have become accustomed to invading these pagan lands twice a year with a powerful armed force, namely, on the feasts of the Assumption and the Purification of the most glorious Virgin Mary. In their vulgar speech they call these periodic raids *Reisen*.[4]

Thus, by repetition, error becomes custom, whereby Christ's faithful, believing that they are doing service pleasing unto God by fighting on His behalf, gather there in great numbers, and, under the pretext of spreading the Catholic faith, wage cruel war upon a peaceful pagan nation. The result is homicide, whereby both the faithful and the infidels run the risk of eternal damnation, committing rapine and other shameful acts.

And thus grows the fame of the Order, as well as their wealth and their power, as they stuff their treasuries with the riches obtained from both sides — from Christians as well as pagans. They procure letters patent from Roman Pontiff and Roman Emperor, so that whatever regions, lands, or dominions they should wrest from the hands of pagans or otherwise occupy, might belong to them.

At last, through the ministry of the Poles, the Spirit of God, Who bloweth where He listeth, did lead the most powerful pagan princes out of their gentile error and into the acknowledgement of the Faith, whereby they were washed clean by the sacred waters of baptism.[5] One of them became King of Poland,[6] while another remained governor and ruler of Lithuania and other neighboring regions inhabited by schismatics as well as pagans.[7] And these were also followed to the profession of the Holy Faith by an immense number of gentiles, whose formidable power once smote the Christian regions of Prussia,

Livonia and Poland with dread, but who now rushed in droves to the sacred baptismal font. So that practically all the subjects native to the lands of Lithuania, etc., have accepted the sacred rite of baptism one after the other. Those still remaining in their infidelity have voluntarily made themselves subject to their Christian governors.

But the Knights of the Cross, looking upon these wondrous doings and, as if becoming worried at them, sensing that their further possession and occupation of the lands and goods of the aforesaid peoples should be threatened thereby, continue, often, successively, and according to their old custom, to invade these regions, with ever greater ferocity slaughtering the aforementioned neophytes, priests included, and many others both baptized and unbaptized. They slay them cruelly, burning their new churches to the ground, and committing other shameful acts of which modesty implores us to pass over in silence.

What is more, they even gravely insult Christians of old standing, the benefactors of their own Order, taking captive their donors, Christian dukes, and threatening in the most shameful manner those who have endowed their own Order. Convoking copious multitudes of Christ's faithful to their aid, and, coloring their intents cleverly, as if their aim was to move against pagans, they set their power against the Catholic King of Poland, invading the Kingdom of Poland with hostility, demolishing fortress and town, reducing all to ash, despoiling, raping, and committing many other such shameless deeds there as the pen can hardly express.

Poland began to wail, no longer at cruelties suffered at the hands of the pagan Prussians, but at those of the Knights of the Cross. In just such a way, those whom she summoned to herself as a shield had become a ferocious scourge, lashing her. Yet Poland did not merely moan on account of the pestiferous atrocity she had nursed in her own bosom; indeed, she was at last led to armed resistance in response. The armed forces of both sides have been drawn up against one another in battle, the result of which has been that the Order was toppled from the summits of its power. Battlefields are now, alas! covered in human remains, and Polish swords have drunk deep of the blood of the Knights of the Cross in the year of Our Lord 1410, on the fifteenth day of July, and afterwards, several times now, in succession.[8]

But although the martial mission of those Hospitallers in these parts came to an end with the cessation of hostilities from the side of the pagans, now regenerated in the waters of holy baptism, as well as those others now fully subject to Christian rule, that is, to the power of the aforementioned orthodox princes, it seems that the aforesaid letters patent that the Knights assert to have in their possession, from Emperor and Roman Pontiff, have provided them with the occasion and pretext to do all the things mentioned above. Now, having laid out this most true and most manifest report on the state of things as they now stand, and with the aim of helping Christian knights to become more cautious in their chivalric metier, I, master Paweł Włodkowic, Custodian and Canon of the Church in Kraków, the very least of the doctors of the decretals,[9] present three treatises for consideration, humbly submitting the same to the correction of those to whom such a thing pertains:

The first, of the power of the Pope in regard to infidels,

The second, of the power of the Emperor in regard to infidels,

each of which treatises contain XI questions for the fuller clarification of the matter;

while in the third I shall concern myself with a certain erroneous opinion regarding this issue, which shall be refuted by responding to each of its rationales.

As to the first treatise

First, the question arises as to whether princes may, without sinning thereby, expel Saracens and Jews from their realms and expropriate their goods, and whether the Pope may persuade such princes to such action, or dissuade them therefrom.

Second, we shall discuss whether infidels possess realms and provinces independent of ours, exercising legal jurisdiction over the same and holding all rightfully, and whether it is permissible for Christians to declare war, without sinning, upon such as are living in peace and occupying what belongs to them.[10]

Third, in relation to the above, whether it is licit for Christians to defend the Holy Land and the faithful who reside there.

Fourth, if, on account of the Roman Empire, the Pope is allowed to deprive the infidels of their jurisdiction, such as they have despoiled and arrogated to themselves.

Fifth, whether the Church of Rome, and all other churches, possess their holdings licitly, since all of this was acquired by violence, through the force of arms employed by the Roman Emperors.

Sixth, if it is licit to occupy the goods of heretics and schismatics.

Seventh, if the Pope is allowed to punish infidels in any sort of case.

Eighth, if the Pope is capable of exercising jurisdiction over such infidels as do not hold lands that were once in the jurisdiction of Christian princes.

Ninth, the question is whether the Pope is empowered to command infidels to admit preachers of the Gospel into their lands.

Tenth, the question is what will occur if the Pope is unable *de facto* to punish them.

Eleventh, the question is what sort of law applies in such a case, when the people of a certain pagan prince are converted to the faith, but the prince himself is not?

As to the second treatise

We shall firstly enquire as to the power of the Emperor; that is to say, what sort of power does the Emperor have over infidels and their goods? Here we preface the question with several arguments containing efficient proof that the Pope alone is foremost in the world, to whom both swords belong. As to the Emperor, he is merely a minister in temporal things, whose power derives from that of the Pope by virtue of positive law.[11]

Second, the question is whether the Emperor may grant anyone a licence for the occupation of lands belonging to the infidels, especially in the case of those infidels who do not recognize his Empire over them.

Third, it shall be asked whether letters patent conceded to the Knights of the Cross by Roman Pontiffs and Emperors accord them any rights concerning the occupied lands of the infidels as to their acquisition by force or suit.

The fourth question is whether the battles waged by the Knights of the Cross against peaceful infidels may be considered a just war.

The fifth question: whether in general it is licit to compel infidels to the Faith by force of arms or oppression.

The sixth: whether it be tolerable or licit for Christians to gather in aid of the Knights of the Cross so as to do battle with pagans on the mere grounds of their being pagans, or if it be said that the aim of the expedition is the spreading of the Christian faith — or for exercising the army in the arts of war.

Seventh, whether it be permissible to fight, or to prepare for war against the infidels, on holy days, absent pressing necessity.

Eighth, whether those subject to the Knights of the Cross may be absolved of sin for warring against the infidels or invading their lands or undertaking *Reisen* against them twice a year, as mentioned above, or knowingly waging unjust war against Christians on account of their being commanded to do so by their lords.

The ninth question concerns goods, lands, or dominions occupied in this sort of war: Whether they effectively become the property of the occupiers, and whether they can be retained without incurring sin thereby? And if no, is the war leader, or the principal person or persons obliged to restore what has been taken away or damaged by them or others, as a condition of their sin being forgiven?

Ten. Can a Christian make use of the aid of infidels for his defense or that of his land?

Eleven. Should an infidel who seeks restitution of what has been seized or taken from him be accorded justice when he makes appeal to a Christian judge?

AS TO THE FIRST QUESTION, it is to be stated that in the case of pagans who wish to live peacefully among Christians, no molestation of their persons or things is to be visited upon them (Codex *De Iudeis*, the law *Nullus* and the chapter *Multorum* of this same title). Here is what is prescribed them in regard to Christians (XVI question III: *Porro* and the note there, XXIII question VIII: *Si de rebus*, by the Archdeacon).[12] And therefore that prince sins who despoils them without just cause. Even the Pope should not deprive them of their goods, but rather tolerate them as long as possible (XLV distinction *Qui sincera, De Iudeis*: *Etsi Iudeos*). The reason for the foregoing is that by commerce with them we might make of them a profit to the Lord (XXIII question III *Infideles* and argument XI question III: *Ad mensam*: *De divorcijs*: *Gaudemus* and the chapter *Quanto*).

The Jews especially are to be tolerated, as it is on the basis of their codices that we prove our truth, our Faith. As St Augustine says, if they do not wish to believe our scriptures, let them believe these (On Psalm XL). St Jerome adduces another reason: Since it is stated in the law that the remnant of Israel shall be enlightened at the end of this age, and shall be saved, this cannot come about if it be lawful to expel them from the world entire. Thus Jerome in the homily 'Innocentium.' And these things are true where Christians are not threatened by danger or scandal (as is noted in the chapter *Quod super hijs*: *De voto et voti redempcione*). Only on account of these latter causes may they be expelled and deprived of their goods. For if out of piety and grace they are tolerated by the Church (as the text says in the aforementioned chapter *Etsi Iudeos*) if they abuse this goodwill, they shall be deemed ungrateful and deserving of the loss of their privilege, according to the example of the servant woman and her son. For when she proved ungrateful and irksome to her lady — who here is a metaphor of the Church — it was said against her: 'Cast out this bondwoman, and her son' (XXIII question III: *Si ecclesia*). For through the death of Christ they have become bondmen (as the above-cited *Etsi Iudeos* puts it). And accordingly, the Archdeacon says that the prince who is their lord may sell them (XLV distinction: *Qui sincera*), and also take away their goods (LIV distinction: *Fraternitatem,* by the Archdeacon), and all the more expel them (the argument in the Codex *Si servus exportetur,* law I and II). Now these things are true, as I say, only where they do not keep the peace or where they cause scandal. Otherwise, the Pope ought not to command or persuade princes to act in such a way (as we find in the note to the aforesaid chapter *Quod super hijs*). And it does not belong to him 'to judge them that are without' (*De divorcijs*: *Gaudemus*). And on this Oldradus stands (question XCI).[13]

BEFORE I COME to the solution of the second question, it should be known that however the illustrious Fathers Innocent and Ostiensis seem to be on opposite sides in this matter, all the most capable doctors of both laws in general follow that father of the laws, Innocent, in their writings, saving what is to be said below. And so, all things considered, in accord with the common school of thought, the opinion of Ostiensis will be stated, and sufficient response will be made to all of his reasoning.[14]

And so, taking the matter sufficiently in hand, Innocent and the doctors following him in general (in the chapter *Quod super hijs*: *De voto et voti redempcione*) conclusively state that goods, jurisdictions and possessions can justly and without sin belong to infidels.

That the infidels justly possess goods is proven:

The first proof is given in regard to possessions. In truth, 'the earth is the Lord's and the fulness thereof' (*De decimis*, the chapter *Tua nobis*), but God Himself subjected all this to man, his reasonable creature, on behalf of whom He created it all (*Genesis*, chapter one,[15] and the law *In pecudum ff De usuris*). From the beginning all of this was held in common by all, until it was so instituted by the use of our first parents that some should possess some things, and others, others, appropriating them to themselves and their use, and this because it is a natural thing for men to neglect the proper care of things held in common, and common possession gives rise to discord (*ff De legatis* II: *Cum pater* § *Dulcissimis*).

§ *Dominions.*

And thus by the law of the nations dominions and realms are distinct and divided one from another (I distinction *Ius gencium* and *ff De justicia et iure*, the law *Ex hoc* and the note *De summa Trinitate et fide Catholica*, chapter 1 concerning the word *Disposuit*).

§ From which it clearly follows that from the beginning nothing belonged to man save what was God's, and what he occupied by God's concession to him; hence we read (Deuteronomy XI):[16] 'Every place, that your foot shall tread upon, shall be yours.' And it reads here 'shall be yours' as if to mean that which is first occupied by one, no other may licitly occupy thereafter. Hence we read (Proverbs XXIII)[17]

'Touch not the bounds of thy neighbor,' etc. And by natural law it was prohibited for one to do unto another that, which he would not wish done unto himself (as at the start of the *Decretals*).

§ From these foregoing it is clear that for the rational creature, man, these things have been ordained of God 'Who maketh His sun to rise upon the good, and the bad,' and 'Who feedeth all the birds of the air' (Matthew V, VI),[18] and 'Who giveth food to all flesh' (PS 149).[19]

Furthermore, our first parents also had special dominion by division, as is clear from the cases of Abraham and Lot, one of whom took on the left hand, the other on the right (Genesis XIII).[20]

§ And further, Innocent says the following of dominion, that no one had the right to possess people as slaves before the law of the nations, for by nature all men were free (*Institutiones, De libertinis* §1).

§ *Jurisdictions.*

Now, concerning rule and jurisdiction, Innocent states that by natural law the paterfamilias had such authority over his families from the very first as was a general and universal authority. Today, however, his authority holds only in a few things (See the entire chapter *De patria potestate*), etc. and in singular fashion. From this it is argued that all jurisdiction derives from the authority of the paterfamilias, although this is not to be expressly inferred from Innocent's words. Innocent also states that God Himself has exercised jurisdiction from the beginning, which thought he expounds upon broadly (*De foro competenti*, *Licet* 1).

§ These things having been said, Innocent states that dominions, possessions, and jurisdictions may be licitly and without sin held by infidels, because they were created not so much for the faithful, as for all rational beings, as stated above. From this statement by Innocent we are to deduce that it is not permitted to deprive the infidels of their dominion, their possessions, or their jurisdiction, for they possess the same sinlessly from the hands of God, their Creator. To this he appends the text of Exodus XX, *scilicet* 'Thou shalt not kill, thou shalt not steal,'[21] whereby all rapine and all violence is prohibited (as in Canon XIV, question V and following, up until § *Contra in Exodo*).

THIRDLY THE QUESTION IS POSED whether it is allowable to defend the Holy Land and the faithful who reside therein.

Innocent says that there is no doubt but yes (XXIII question VIII: *Omni*, and the canon that follows); much further on Innocent states that even though the Holy Land is in the possession of the Saracens, the Pope is within his rights to declare war upon them, because his motivation is just if he intends the recovery the Holy Land, which has been sanctified by the birth, the residence, and the death of Jesus Christ, but where it is not Christ Who is worshipped but Mahomet — so that it should be inhabited by Christians. Further, the Holy Land had been conquered in a just war after the death of Christ by the Roman Emperor, and hence on the basis of the claims of the Roman Empire it is licit for the Pope to obtain it, revoking to his jurisdiction what he had been unjustly despoiled of by those who had no right to do such a thing. According to Innocent, this reason can be sufficiently applicable to all other lands over which the Roman Emperors once had jurisdiction.

This position is opposed by that which states that it seems that even the Holy Land cannot be recovered by the Pope, since the Church has no empire save in the Occident (XCVI distinction: *Constantinus*). Innocent explains in response to this that if the Pope cannot act as the Emperor, or for other reasons, just stated, at least the Emperor can act on his own behalf, or the King of Jerusalem can, to whose realm the Holy Land pertains, as we are bound to believe, since there appears to be nothing to contradict this. Now, as to the canon *Constantinus*, he says that there the matter spoken of is ownership, while here we are speaking of protection, and one sword ought to aid the other. And the spiritual sword has pride of place, hence, the Pope may punish the Emperor for neglect or offence (XCVI distinction: *Quis dubitet*, and the canon *Duo*, and the canon *Si Imperator*). The Pope may also aid the King of Jerusalem, to whom this matter belongs.

THE FOURTH QUESTION asks whether on behalf of the Roman Empire the Pope might take away jurisdiction from the infidels who first usurped it from the Empire.

My Lord Francis, Cardinal of Florence, states that even against Empire and Pope prescription can be made, as he notes (*De postulacione*: *Bone* II), responding to the question, following Innocent: Can an inferior prescribe papal rights?[22] He says: If the matter concerns the plenitude of papal rights, no inferior may so prescribe, for that power is granted the Pope alone (see infra *De usu palii*: *Ad honorem*). No inferior is capable of such a thing; what is more, such a prescription goes against obedience and is null and void (*De prescripcionibus*: *Cum non liceat*). But if he wishes to prescribe some particular rights, which the Pope possesses in a particular place, he may, whether these rights be spiritual or temporal (*De prescripcionibus*: *Ad audienciam*, and the chapter *Cum vobis*). And whereas no rights of empire can be prescribed against him so that some regions become autocephalous (*De prescripcionibus*: *Cum non liceat*), still there are many Christians as will prescribe such in that *de facto* they do not recognize the authority of the Empire over them, as is said of the King of France (*Qui filij sint legitimi*: *Per venerabilem*).

Likewise, the Romans had some confederates who were not subject to them. And whatever the case may be with ancient law, empires have been overthrown in various ages, and so many times, that it is impossible to sustain this rationale: that because some provinces were once under Roman law, war can now be waged to recover them. So there is a better reason to say that while it is licit for Christians or at least the King to recover the Holy Land according to what is said in question three, as far as other lords are concerned, this is not true unless there be some special causes according to which such a war might be waged. We shall discuss such reasonable causes below in question ten.

THE FIFTH QUESTION arises from what has been stated above in the third question, because the Church has its empire in the Occident. Does the Roman Church, and all other Churches, and even other Christians, licitly hold what they do possess there, and otherwhere?

It would seem not, because the Church came into the possession of all that from the Roman Emperors, who occupied all those lands by violence and force of arms. Therefore, they possess them in bad faith.

Now, according to Innocent, all, in general, both clerics and laypersons, may securely hold onto what they have, and in good faith, because we do not know whether those who occupied the above-mentioned had been taking advantage of their rights, recovering, perhaps, what had been previously lost to them through violence, or perhaps by matrimony or donation these things came to them legitimately, although they contained many rebels whom they overcame. Of churches, however, we can state, following Innocent, that they well might hold onto what they have, for if it be unknown who their lord was before their occupation, they must be restored to the Pope as the vicar of Christ and to the other churches who possess them from the hands of the Pope and by his authority. For the Pope and the churches possess all things in the name of all, as they come with aid to all who are in need (XII question 1 *Videntes*), which is a peculiar service (for this: XVI question I: *Quoniam quidquid*), from which it arrives that clerics possess their goods as in common, and not as though they were their own property (*De prebendis*: *Racio*).

THE SIXTH QUESTION posed concerns the goods of schismatics and heretics, whether these might be occupied or seized.

It seems illicit to occupy or seize the goods of infidels, as above in question 1.

But Innocent says that yes, indeed, as long as these things are deeded one through the concession of a prince (VIII distinction: *Quo iure*; XXIII question VII, the entirety thereof, as in *De hereticis*: and according to book VI), for it is especially provided that in certain cases their goods can be seized by the faithful, with proper authorisation, whereas in others, no (On this, see the chapter *Presidentes*: *De hereticis* book VI in *Novella* and as Ostiensis notes in *Summa*: *De hereticis*, the verse *Numquid catholici*), in other cases it does not seem licit to seize the goods of such persons (as in *De hereticis*: *Excommunicamus*).

THE SEVENTH QUESTION asks whether the Pope may in any case punish infidels for their offences.

For the explication of this question Innocent says that the Pope, who is the vicar of Christ, has authority not only over Christians, but also over all infidels, since Christ had authority over all (as in the Psalm 'Give to the king thy judgment, O God,' etc.,[23] and the final Chapter of Matthew: 'All power is given to me in heaven and in earth').[24] And the Redeemer Himself would not be seen to be the Father of his family if he had not left unto His vicar on earth complete authority over all (for this, see what is noted in *De homicido*: *Pro humani*, book VI).

Furthermore, having given to Peter and his successors the keys to the kingdom of Heaven, He set him up as the shepherd of his flock, saying 'Feed my sheep.'[25] Consequently, all persons, whether faithful or infidels, are sheep of Christ, by virtue of their creation, even if they are not of the sheepfold of the Church. And by virtue of this, according to Innocent, it is apparent that the Pope has jurisdiction and authority over all — *de iure* if not *de facto* (*De eleccione*: *Significasti*, *De maioritate et obediencia*: *Solite*, *De iudicijs*: *Novit*).

§ From this, Innocent infers decisions concerning certain things, which my Lord Francis, Cardinal of Florence, collects in five conclusions.

The first is that if a gentile who possesses no law save natural law offends against natural law, he may be licitly punished by the Pope, according to the pattern of Genesis XIX,[26] where the Sodomites, who sinned against the law of nature, the law of nature, were punished by God. Now, since the judgements of God are examples to us, it does not appear that the Pope, who is the vicar of God, should not be able to do this; indeed, he even ought to do so, as long as the faculty for so doing be present.

The second conclusion: The Pope may punish infidels who worship idols. For it is natural to worship the one and only God, the Creator, and not creatures.

The third conclusion: The Pope may punish the Jews if they offend against the law in moral matters, and likewise, if against their own law they invent heresies. Motivated by this reasoning, Popes Gregory[27] and Innocent have ordered the combustion of such books in which many heresies are contained, as well as ordering that those who follow or teach said heresies be punished. These books are spoken of in *Speculum historali*, book XXVI, chapter XXVIII and the following.

The fourth conclusion: There is no doubt but that the Pope may judge those who offend against the Gospel, also if they gravely sin in other matters (*De iudicijs*: *Novit*).

The fifth conclusion is that, while in the foregoing matters it is possible for the Pope to set aside from time to time just and merited punishments to be meted out to all the aforementioned, whether because he does not possess the actual faculty for executing them, or whether he restrains from so doing in order to avoid imminent harm or scandal, still and all the authority for so doing is his.

THE EIGHTH QUESTION posed is whether the Pope is able to exercise jurisdiction over such infidels who possess no land that was not formerly under the jurisdiction of Christian princes.

Innocent states that the Pope is able to justly make rules and precepts prohibiting the unjust molestation of Christians who are subject to pagan jurisdiction. Indeed, what is more, he may absolve those Christian subjects entirely of such jurisdiction and their obedience to such rulers (the argument *De Iudeis*: chapter 1 and the final chapter; LIV distinction: *Mancipia* and the canon that follows). What is more, if they treat Christians evilly, Innocent says, the Pope has the power of depriving them of their dominion and jurisdiction such as they have over Christians. He may so absolve by virtue of his privilege, and he may so deprive *de iure*. Now, Innocent also says that there must be a grave cause for the Pope to arrive at such a determination. For the Pope ought to tolerate infidels as long as possible, as long as the Christians are not faced with danger, or grave scandal may be caused by his hesitation, which is similarly noted by my Lord Francis, Cardinal of Florence, etc., following Innocent.

THE NINTH QUESTION poses whether the Pope may command infidels to admit preachers of the Gospel into their lands.

Innocent replies in the affirmative, even though according to him infidels should not be coerced into accepting the Faith, as all men should be left to their free will in this question, and only the grace of God can effect such a vocation (XLV distinction: *De Iudeis*; XXIII question V: *Ad fidem*). As far as the first statement is concerned, that they may be forced to admit preachers, Innocent refers to the fact that all rational creatures have been created to give glory to God (as in Book 2 of the *Sentences*, LIV, 1). Should they prohibit preachers from announcing the Gospel, they would be sinning and consequently should be punished.

THE TENTH QUESTION asks what will happen if the Pope is *de facto* incapable of punishing them? Innocent states that, in all of the foregoing cases, in which the Pope may licitly command them to do something, if they do not obey him, they should be compelled by the secular arm. War is to be declared by the Pope, and by no other, unless someone be acting in defense of his own rights. Now if it be objected that it does not belong to you to judge them that are without (II question 1: *Multi*): Innocent replies that this is understood in reference to the fact that we should not introduce them to the Faith by excommunication or compulsion, as men are called to conversion by the grace of God alone (XLV distinction: *De Iudeis*). It is a different matter if they are disturbing Christians or otherwise offending (note, to the same effect, what is noted in *De divorcijs*: *Gaudemus*).

St Thomas says the same thing (*Secunda secunde* question XII article 2): That it is not for the Church to punish for unfaithfulness those who have never accepted the Faith in the first place — according to the words of the Apostle (1 Corinthians):[28] 'For what have I to do to judge them that are without?' But according to the same St Thomas, if anyone commits sin through infidelity, he may be deprived of his human rights judicially, just as he may in the case of any other sin.

THE ELEVENTH QUESTION: What if some people ruled by a great pagan prince should convert to the Faith, while the prince himself remains in his infidelity?

Innocent states that he should be tolerated by the Pope in his jurisdiction and dominion as long as no danger be imminent to the Faith, or to those faithful, in which case he could be forced to accept a ransom or an exchange (*De Iudeis*, final chapter).

Concerning the second treatise

THERE REMAINS FOR US TO CONSIDER the question of the Emperor's authority, and thus question XII asks what sort of power, in general, does the Emperor have over infidels?[29]

For it would seem that all nations are subject to him (XI question I § *Hec si quis*, the verse *Nolumus*), for he is the prince and lord of the world (*ff* the law *Rodiam*: *Deprecacio*) and even the Jews are subject to him (the codex *De Iudeis*: *Iudei*), as well as all provinces (LXIII distinction: *Adrianus*). And all is in the power of the Emperor (VIII distinction: *In iure* and XXIII question VIII: *Convenior*; the codex *De quadrienij prescripcione*: hence to Zeno; as the gloss *Sic ergo* in the chapter *Venerabilem*: *De eleccione* notes) for the Empire depends on God (in *Autentica*: *De consulibus*, the final § of collection IV where it is stated that God sends us the Emperor as if His law animate on the earth) or is he merely the lord of those who are subject to his rule (codex *De summa Trinitate*: *Cunctos populos*, and there by Cynus; LXIII distinction: *Adrianus* II; see the chapter *De eleccione* of *Venerable*, the gloss *Et in Germanos*).

Concerning this matter it is to be considered whether the Emperor is subject to the authority of the Pope in temporal matters, or not.

In law, there seem to be contrary opinions here, and so (XCVI distinction: *Cum ad verum*, to wit *Cum ad verum, id est Christum, ventum est*): 'Let neither the Emperor arrogate unto himself the rights of the Pope, nor let the Pope usurp the title Emperor.' On the contrary, consider XXII distinction, canon 1, where it is stated that both the rights of the heavenly and earthly Empires have been entrusted unto Peter, etc.

And so for the clarification of this matter let it be known that, according to the notes of my Lord Francis, Cardinal of Florence (in the chapter *Venerabilem*: *De eleccione*) many great intellects have been vexed to arrive at an understanding of the beginnings of terrestrial monarchy. Many volumes and tracts on monarchy have been produced, and according to the Cardinal, there can be no more worthless enquiry than this. For the truth is that it has been ascertained that the kingdom known as the Babylonian was an empire. The same is true of the kingdom of Macedonia, which flourished under Alexander, and the Carthaginian, which flourished at the time that Hannibal, the Carthaginian leader, was devastating Italy through many a year, as is apparent from Titus Livius' work on the Second Punic War.

For this reason Johannes notes (XCVI distinction *Si Imperator*):[30] That before any constitution was enacted, no layperson had any power over men unless by usurpation.

There is also a new book on Monarchy that strives to prove that in both Old and New Testaments the authority of both swords was always in the possession of the supreme pontiff.[31] There is another book entitled *De Monarchia*, compiled by the Florentine poet Dante.[32] Because he was a Ghibelline, he strove to prove that the Empire does not depend upon the Pope in the least, and on account of that tractate he but narrowly escaped being burnt at the stake for heresy. Likewise, another book on Monarchy was published by Menardino of Padua, an illustrious doctor of sacred scripture, who took the part of the Bavarian when the Church came out against him. In the same way, Marsilius too strove to display that the coercive power, that is to say, the power to force a person to a particular sort of action by arms cannot be found with the Pope, but belongs to the Emperor — in spiritual matters as well.[33] In this, many other rationales might be set forward.

And yet the truth of the matter is that both jurisdictions, that is, in temporal and spiritual matters, belongs to the Pope; this is proven by many arguments.

The first of these[34] is that the terrestrial order ought to be uniform with the order of the heavens, for the lower world is regulated according to the image of the higher (see the first book *Meteorologicorum*), for on the higher order all of nature depends (*De Summa Trinitate*, final chapter; the first book of *Meteorologicorum*, and the first book *De Caelo*). As the regulation of the higher urges that what exists in the corporal genus arrive at the most noble celestial sphere, toward which all inferior spheres tend, so in the spiritual genus there should be a motion towards the most noble principle upon which all that is, depends (as in chapter 1, just now referred to). But what is most noble corporeally is the instrument of the most noble spiritually, since both what is spiritual and what is corporal issues therefrom; therefore, in the terrestrial order, things tend to the temporal principle, which is the Emperor, and thence to the spiritual principle, which is the Pope, and therefore the Emperor is to be the instrument of the Pope as heaven is of God, as above.

Likewise, that there ought to be but one principle in the universe, because among all things in the world possessed of an essential order, while they differ in species, it is impossible for there to be two that are equally perfect; therefore, these are not equals. And as the Emperor is not the greater of these two, consequently, the Pope is the greater.

Thus, as the Philosopher[35] puts it, there should be one lord of an entire monarchy. Beings do not wish to be badly disposed of; a plurality of rulers is bad, ergo, there must be but one ruler. This is the deduction made by the Philosopher (XII *Metaphysics*) where he demonstrates that there is but one God. Plurality is evil for this reason, that destruction is the outcome where there are two powers in opposition. If they are of disparate strengths, one would be supreme; if their strengths are equal, one would be superfluous. Thus, there can be but one ruler.

These matters having been settled, it is argued that because the Pope is the ecclesiastical judge of all, he is quite capable of secular jurisdiction, but the opposite does not hold true (the reason for this is set out in the chapter *Decernimus* and in the chapter *Qualiter*: *De iudicijs*). No secular judge, who is a prince, can be acknowledged as possessed of both swords, and thus as a spiritual judge — for the only such is the Pope. And so, as no one negates the fact that the Pope enjoys the plenitude of spiritual authority, it necessarily follows that he possesses the temporal authority as well. For as the superior perfection contains the inferior, the opposite cannot be true. Hence the intellective spirit in man contains both sensitive and vegetative perfection, and there can be but one spirit in any man.

From which it is inferred that just as the spiritual power is more perfect than the temporal — because temporalia, as accessories, are ordered in subjection to spiritualia, as toward their proper end (I question III: *Si quis obiecerit*), but they are not perfect in and of themselves, nor were they created directly by God and principally, but rather in consequence and accessorily for the use of men in pursuit of things spiritual (*ff De usuris*: the law *In pecudum*). Thus, the spiritual authority, as the more perfect, possesses the temporal authority subject to it (*De maioritate et obediencia*, chapter *Solite*); ergo, the Pope has power both in spiritual and temporal matters. This conclusion holds, as it implies both an end and what is ordained to that end (*ff De procuratoribus*: the law *Ad legatum* and the law *Ad rem*). And so it is confirmed: the Pope has power over souls, the Emperor over bodies, but the soul rules the body as the master rules his servant (as is said in II *Politics*). Now, the master of the master is also master of the latter's servant, as the rule holds in consequence: Having conquered him who hath conquered thee, I conquer thee as well (*De concessione prebende*: *Auctoritate*, book VI). From this I confirm: the Pope is the master of the soul and its operations; the Emperor is master of the flesh; but the flesh is the instrument of the soul's operations, ergo, etc. This conclusion holds because the principal agent is more perfect than that which operates instrumentally, as the one who wields the axe is more perfect than the axe (II question VIII § *Item Balaam*).

Likewise, the principate of the Pope was bestowed by God (XXII distinction: *In novo*); the principate of the Emperor was instituted by man (XCIII distinction: *Legimus*); the immediate effect of God exceeds the effect of man — arguing thus from the nobility of cause over the nobility of effect (*De celebracione missarum*: *Cum Marthe*).

Likewise, Christ had power over all things; the conclusion holds then that the vicar should have the same consistory as the ordinary (*De consuetudine*, chapter II book VI).

Likewise, to argue from the heavenly bodies, the sun illuminates the day and the night; the day by itself, and the night through its minister, *scil.* the moon, hence, according to the variety of the lunar aspect in respect to the sun, the light of the moon varies. In the same way, the Pope, like the sun, illuminates by himself the day, i.e. the soul, and the night, i.e. the dark temporalities and material things, through the agency of his minister, *scil.* the Emperor.

Inferring from these things it can be demonstrated as it were naturally that the power of the Pope is one and unique, while that of the Emperor is so to speak servile thereto. To this matter many laws and canons may well be adduced pro and contra, but I give them little heed, for though the Pope issue decrees and the Emperor legislation, no man is a proper witness in his own case. Giovanni da Legnano.

Furthermore, it is demonstrated that there ought to be but one sole prince and that principate is best where one principally rules (this is demonstrated in the second book of *Politics*, where the figure employed is that of the Steward, as is written in the first book of *Economics*). Ergo, it is necessary that there be but one prince in the world. This cannot be the Emperor, to whom no spiritual authority belongs.

Likewise, from the creation of the world God exercised jurisdiction Himself in punishing Adam and Eve (Genesis III and V),[36] which was transferred by Him to Noah, following the flood, to whom God committed government (Genesis V and VI)[37] — in whom the Church is prefigured, for Noah himself exercised the sacerdotal office (Genesis VIII).[38]

There then succeeded kings and others, of whom the Old Testament speaks.

But the law of the Old Testament has been done away with in this era of grace. And Christ had the plenitude of jurisdiction and was our natural King, of Whom it is said (in the psalm)[39]: 'Give to the King Thy judgement, O God,' etc. and this he transmitted to Peter and his successors, of which you may read more in Innocent (*De foro competenti*, the chapter *Licet* I). There are other reasons as well spoken of in the bull *Unam sanctam*, where it is concluded, at the end, that it is necessary to salvation to believe that all human creatures are subject to the Roman Pontiff;[40] in support of this John (XVIII) is adduced: 'Put up thy sword into the scabbard,'[41] and the authority of Bernardus (*Ad Eugenium* in the book *De consideratione*).

By these it is concluded that the Pope, in so far as he is considered to be the vicar of Christ, is in possession of both jurisdictions. However, the Emperor possesses an executive power in temporal matters, because it would not be proper for the Church to use the temporal sword which puts to death the wicked, and is used for separating the soul from the body, for it belongs to the prelate, above all, to foster the union of the soul, properly regulated, with the flesh.

It is possible that there are other reasonings, but those who negate principles cannot be convinced; you have nothing more to do than deny that Christ assumed all jurisdiction, and indeed declared that His Kingdom was not of this world.

Whatever might be the case in this matter, which according to the above mentioned Cardinal, is ever conditional, it should be taken into consideration that, accepting the opinion that temporal jurisdiction is subject to the Church, it cannot be that one may make an appeal to the Pope following a decision made by the Emperor, since the subordination of the latter is not of such a type that would make the Pope superior in regard to the actual exercise of Imperial power, but only by way of precedence, unless it be in cases expressly noted in law, such as the vacancy of the imperial throne (*De foro competenti*: *Licet* I). And according to this mode of expression, the imperial jurisdiction can even be said to proceed from God, for it was the will of God that it be exercised by the Emperor, and in this manner proceed the laws which state: he is not impeded in his temporal jurisdiction, unless in certain specific cases such as the above-mentioned (*De eleccione*: *Venerabilem*, and others similar thereto).

But whatever may have been noted before the age of grace, following the acquisition of the Empire by the Romans, so that arguments may be put forward inferring the Emperor's independence from the Pope, today, the decision lies in many chapters (above all *De maioritate et obediencia*: *Solite*; *De iudicijs*: *Novit*; *Qui filij sint legitimi*: *Per venerabilem*; *De eleccione*: *Fundamenta*; *De re iudicata*: *Apostolice* book VI): that both powers belong to the Pope, and this is of the most ancient custom, the contrary to which is in the memory of no person, according to which the Pope, as the superior of the Emperor, transferred the Empire from the Greeks to the Germans (as it is noted in the gloss of the word 'Transtulit' in the chapter *Venerabilem*: *De eleccione*), which translation took place (as testified in *Speculum historiali* book 24, chapters 54 and 56), at the hands of Pope Stephen, who was later martyred.

It is therefore proper to admit that the Empire depends upon the power of the Pope, for to him belongs the examination, approbation or rejection of him elected to the throne. And what is more, the election of the Emperor is in the hands of the prince electors, *scilicet* those of Cologne, Trier, Mainz, etc. (who are enumerated in *De re iudicate*: *Apostolice,* in the penultimate gloss to book VI), and this law holds by papal concession (as in the aforesaid chapter *Venerabilem*), even though Ostensis expounds 'de iure' as meaning common sense, which as the aforementioned Cardinal said is far from that, for to say such a thing is to say nothing at all. Now, this right accorded to the prince electors has been confirmed by ancient custom.

Furthermore, whenever any difficulty is encountered in these opinions, it is that declared by the Church which is to be followed (for this, see the text of *De consuetudine*, final chapter, *De iuramento calumnie* chapter 1; *Qui filij sint legitimi*: *Per venerabilem*, where the case is clear; see also the text *Ut lite non contestata*: *Quoniam*. It is also noted in *De foro competenti*: *Licet*) and he who speaks to the contrary is deserving of an evil death (as in the above-mentioned chapter *Per venerabilem*) by the hand of God. In this chapter, Johannes Andreae states, following Ostiensis,[42] 'Where an ambiguity of opinion arises it is better to trust canon law than the statements of the saints or learned men, because it is to the Pope and to no other that such interpretation of dubious matters has been entrusted — hence even the Emperor has recourse to him (codex *De Summa Trinitate*, in the final law; Ostiensis says the same). So Abbas[43] argues against those lawyers who in their cases do not rely upon the precedents expressly determined in the decretals.

And so to make response to those who are of a different opinion, saying 'Everything is subject to the Emperor,' that is true in so far as guardianship and jurisdiction are concerned, but not as to particular dominion (as noted in *De constitucionibus*: *Que in ecclesiarum*: XXIII question VIII: *Convenior*). He is the lord of the world in aptitude, but not in fact (argument *ff De natalibus restituendis*, the penultimate law). Ebra[44] says that he is lord in guardianship and solicitude (argument *ff De negociis gestis*: the law *Si pupilli*). What was said to Peter is here adduced: 'Put up thy sword into the scabbard' (John XVIII),[45] the significance of which words is that the power of the sword is not therefore established, but rather the right of exercising the same; the gloss even wishes to say that Emperor and kings possess the exercise of the sword as granted them by the Church, for at one time the Church also had jurisdiction over civil matters, which was exercised by priests (as XI question III: *Relatum*). But the exercise of this power, especially in criminal matters, was committed to others because it was not proper for the Church to wield it in such cases herself. Now, we may frequently do things through others which we cannot do ourselves, and commit to others what we cannot ourselves retain (*De institucionibus*: final chapter; LXXXVIII, distinction: *Episcopus gubernacionem*; *Ne clerici vel monachi*, last chapter, book VI).

And from the foregoing it might be inferred that according to the opinion that holds that the Pope has a superior, it is to be stated that the Donation of Constantine to the Church[46] was null and void. For he gave nothing to the Church, but rather released to her what was hers already. The gloss in *Authentica* (*Quomodo oportet episcopos*) at the beginning of collation V) can be seen to signify that he promised it as property, but not as jurisdiction (on this question see what is noted in *Qui filij sint legitimi*: *Per venerabilem*). Ergo it says that powers of execution are distinct, but as to whom they belong, both were given to Peter, although the Pope entrusts the power of the temporal sword to the Emperor (on this matter see X distinction: *Quoniam idem*; *De privilegijs* chapter II, first gloss).

THESE THINGS HAVING BEEN STATED, when we ask, firstly, what sort of power or jurisdiction does the Emperor have over infidels, especially those who do not recognize his imperial authority: in order to clear up this matter it must first be seen that kingly authority on this earth arises in three ways: first, by the will of God as revealed to men in some fashion; second, by the consent of the governed; third, by force. The first and second manners establish just authority, the third does not. The authority of the Pope is justified according to the first of these, beginning with the authority granted to the patriarchs in the Old Testament, and later taken up by Christ and transferred by Him to Peter and his successors. Furthermore, the Pope's authority is likewise justified in the second fashion, as the entire Catholic Church and the whole congregation of the faithful consent to his rule, which has the approbation of the most ancient custom, and no position contrary to this exists in the memory of any man. There is no need to continue with the third proof, which is something *de facto* rather than *de iure*.

Now, since it cannot be said in general that the imperial authority over the aforesaid infidels is justified in either the first or second manner, the Emperor cannot be said to hold any power over the aforesaid infidels except in the third way, that is, by violence and tyranny, as stated above.

The answer to the second question.

From this, in answer to the second question, it is inferred that the Emperor is not capable of giving anyone any licence for the occupation of the lands of infidels who do not recognize his imperial authority — this is on account of his lack of said authority, which is not to be found with the Emperor, but rather with the Pope. The only thing in the possession of the Emperor is the executive or ministerial power, as has been sufficiently deduced above. For only the Pope, and no other person, may declare war against them, according to Innocent — as is found above in the first treatise, question X.

The answer to the third question.

WITH THIS SAID, in response to the third question it is inferred: that the imperial scripts conceded to the Knights of the Cross for the occupation of the lands of the infidels confer no rights upon them whatsoever permitting them to attempt their acquisition, for no one can give anyone something that he does not have (I question VII: *Daibertum*). And that which is done contrary to law should be considered as never having been done (according to the rule *Que contra ius*: *De regulis iuris* book VI).

The answer to the fourth question.

From these things arises a clear response to another question: that the Knights of the Cross, etc., doing battle with peaceful infidels, as such, were never engaging in any just war.

It is clear that all law is against those who do battle against those who wish to live in peace. Civil law: the codex *De paganis et eorum sacrificijs*, the law *Christianis*, and all others in agreement with these that affirm that the law commands that those who are living peacefully should not be molested. Canon law: *Extra. De Iudeis* chapter II and the chapter *Sicut* and XXIII question VIII *Dispar* by argument 'a contrario,' with concordances. Natural law is also opposed, *scilicet*: 'Do unto others as you wish others to do unto you,' etc., at the beginning of the *Decretals*. Divine law opposes: 'Thou shalt not kill,' 'Thou shalt not steal' (Exodus 20),[47] by which words 'Thou shalt not steal,' all rapine, and by which words 'Thou shalt not kill,' all violence is prohibited, as is made clear in XIV question V: *Dixit Dominus* and following, up to § *Contra in Exodo*. For in his *Book Concerning Exodus*, III chapter (which has been taken over in the canon *Penale* XIV question V), St Augustine states: 'By the term theft, all illicit usurpation of another's goods is well understood, for He who disallowed theft did not permit rapine, and certainly in the law of the Old Testament He wished that rapine too be understood by the name theft, for it clearly signifies all cases in which the goods of another are illicitly taken away.' For rapine is a species of theft, according to the gloss to the above-mentioned canon *Penale*. Because all robbers are thieves (as we read in the Institute *De verbo raptorum*, at the commencement of the passage).

Furthermore, such warring against infidels, especially without just cause, is not compatible with love of one's neighbor, for the entrance of one contrary thesis causes the exit of the antithesis, and, according to the Truth, both faithful and infidels are our neighbors, without distinction (*De penitencione*, distinction II: *Non illi tantum proximi*, in the text and in the gloss to the canon *Proximos*). And because the scripts of Roman Pontiff or Emperor do not grant them any privilege, especially such as would be contrary to natural and divine law, therefore, etc.

The answer to the fifth question.

FROM WHAT HAS BEEN SAID ABOVE it is also easier to respond to another question, i.e., that it is not licit to compel infidels to the Christian faith by arms or oppressions. For this method does injury to one's neighbors and evil cannot be done so that good may result (XXII question IV: *Sic non sunt*; XIV question V: *Forte* and the canon *Neque*). And hence (in the canon *Quid autem*: XLV distinction) we read: 'It is a new and hitherto unheard of preaching that elicits faith by blows.' And (in the chapter *Sicut*, *Extra*: *De Iudeis*) it says 'Indeed they are not to be believed to have faith in Christ who did not approach Christian baptism of their own free will, but by coercion,' where this is proven according to the gloss stating that no one is to be compelled to the Faith (XXIII question V: *Ad fidem*). For faith should not come about through necessity (XLV distinction *De Iudeis*, and the canon *Qui autem*, and the canon *Qui sincera*), because God is not pleased by compelled service (the above-mentioned canon *De Iudeis*). And for this reason it was established at the Council of Toledo (in the aforesaid canon *De Iudeis*) that those who are to convert others ought to employ blandishments and not bitterness. For this reason: 'That those who might be called by an appeal to reason ought not to be repulsed by adversity.' And it is added thereto: 'For whoever acts otherwise proves to have his own agenda more in mind than the cause of God.'

And what is said here of the Jews applies wholly to any infidel, as the same law (arguing from the chapter *Nam concupiscenciam* and the chapter *Translato*: *De constitucionibus*; *De rescriptis*: *Inter ceteras*, at the end; *De translacione*: *Inter corporalia*): for where power operates rather than charity, those men are seeking that which should belong to them and not to Jesus Christ, and thus they easily depart from the rules of divine law, and whenever one wishes to dominate others rather than to care for them, one's sense of personal honor inflates one's pride and that which was intended to foster accord leads, rather, to harm (the text here is XLV distinction in canon *Licet non numquam*).

The answer to the sixth question.

FROM THE FOREGOING IT IS CONCLUDED that it is an error, completely intolerable, any way one looks at it, that Christians should gather there to do war against the infidels solely because they are infidels, or because it is said that their goal is the spreading of the Christian Faith, for under the color of piety impieties are not to be committed (XXX question 1: *Nosce*; XIV question V: *Forte*, I question 1: *Non est putanda*) or even if it be said that the aim is chivalric exercise, etc. No one who voluntarily offers aid to the Knights of the Cross in warring against peaceful infidels may be absolved of mortal sin, whether they be subjects of the Knights or no. For he aids no one who aids in the commission of sin (XIV question VI *Si res*) and in consequence, those who die impenitent while supporting an illicit war of this sort are the sons of ire, and it is proper to assume that their fated portion is among the damned.

The war being waged by the Spaniards against the Saracens is a just war, according to Oldradus (in his *Questions*, question LXXII), because it is being fought in order to recover Christian lands previously inhabited by Christians.

Now, for the Christian soldier who is not a subject of a prince engaged in a given war, he ought to be entirely certain of the justice of the war in which he would fight. Otherwise, if he is doubtful or uncertain in this regard, he is exposing himself to grave peril. For as St Ambrose says: If it is impossible to help someone without doing wrong to another, it is better to help neither than to wrong one of them (XIV question V: *Denique*). For only a subject of one of the warring princes is excused, in a matter where the justice of the conflict is in doubt, for aiding his lord. For in that case we are talking about a bond of obedience; it is the case of someone who is obliged to obedience. No such obligation exists, however, when a person is certain that the war is unjust, or believes it probably so (to this point, see the text of the canon *Quid culpatur*: XXIII question 1). But the reason given earlier, concerning obligation, ceases to hold in the case of non-subjects who are not bound by the law of obedience, but are acting of their own free will. According to Ostiensis and Raymundus,[48] this is also true of the subject who has enquired into the matter as closely as he could, consulting those more experienced in such things, yet who still remains in doubt. Otherwise, pretended ignorance will be punished in the same way as definite knowledge (as in c. *Cum inhibicio*: *De clandestina desponsacione* § *Si quis vero*). Nor will such a one be excused on the grounds of his fearing the loss of temporal goods, for although fear extenuates guilt, it does not completely exclude it (*De hijs que vi metusve causa fiunt*, in the chapter *Sacris*). On this in full, see Ostiensis in his *Summa*: *De penitencijs et remissionibus* § *Quibus et qualiter*, the versicle *Quid de rapina*).

For in this, the authority of the law or of a judge is required. From hence, for an even clearer grasp of this and what follows, it should be known that five things are required for any war to be considered just. According to Ostiensis, following Raymundus (in the text just mentioned), these are: the person, the thing, the cause, the spirit, and the authority. The person, that is, he who is capable of waging war, that is, a secular person who is not forbidden the shedding of blood — for this is not permitted any clergyman unless it be a case of dire necessity. The thing, that is, that the war should be about recovering what has been wrongly taken from one, or for the defense of one's country. The cause: whether one be fighting to as to establish peace thereby (XXIII question 1: *Noli*). The spirit — that one not be moved by hatred or revenge or cupidity, but rather to redress wrongs, and with charity, justice, and obedience. For it is no sin to engage in war *per se*, but it is so when military action is undertaken in order to loot. That is sinful. Authority — that is, whether one be fighting with the authorisation of the Church, in matters where faith is the issue, or with the authority of the prince (XXIII question 1: *Quid culpatur*).

One might also add a sixth element here: *scil.* the proper time. For certainly there are times when even a just war is prohibited (*De treuga et pace*, chapter 1). In particular: days of solemn festival are subject to the prohibition of refraining from all servile work in favor of prayer and spiritual works. And only in cases of necessity, which knows no law, can anyone be absolved of sin for fighting on such days: in defense of one's self or one's own, but not attacking others first (*Extra*: *De regulis iuris*: *Quod non est licitum*; XXIII, last question: *Si nulla*). Thus did the Maccabees fight on the Sabbath without incurring sin (II Maccabees, last chapter[49]) but even these, when no longer compelled by necessity, refrained on the Sabbath from pursuing the enemies of the faith, who had invaded with the intention of oppressing the Jews (II Maccabees VIII chapter).[50]

And hereby appears the response to another question.

FROM THESE IS CONCLUDED another error of the Prussian Knights of the Cross, who call themselves the Brethren of the Blessed Virgin Mary. For however many times they make their customary *Reisen* against the infidels with the intent of waging war upon them, this they do regularly, twice a year, particularly on holy days devoted to the Blessed Virgin, i.e. on Assumption Day and the feast of the Purification of Mary, invading their territories or leaving their own to do so, etc.

And because it is this error, wholly contrary to the Christian religion, that gives them licence to violate the law of the Lord and transgress the precepts concerning the observation of the Sabbath:

therefore, so as to make this all the clearer, it is good to draw attention to the fact that the commandment on the observation of the Sabbath contains two things: one, as to the purpose, so that man should keep himself free for divine things, as signified by the words: 'Remember that thou keep holy the Sabbath day' (Exodus XX).[51] 'Keeping holy' here means attending to divine liturgy. The second enjoins one to refrain from work, as the text adds: 'thou shalt do no work,' which is explained (Leviticus XXIII):[52] 'You shall do no servile work,' it says there.

Now, all works are known according to the object of their service: one is service to God — this is known as *latreia* — which is not prohibited. The second is service to sin (John VIII):[53] 'Whosoever committeth sin, is the servant of sin.' The third is when man serves man. Here, one man is the servant of another, not according to the soul, but according to the flesh. It is for this reason that servile works are called corporal works, in which one man serves another. And they are called servile works in so far as they properly belong to servants. On the other hand, in so far as such works are common to both servants and free men, they are not known as servile, according to St Thomas Aquinas. For example: Everyone, whether free or servant, is bound to provide things necessary not only to himself, especially in the things pertaining to the health of the body, which recognizes no distinction of time, and in cases of emergency according to this (Proverbs IX):[54] 'Deliver them that are led to death.' Subsequently, in the avoidance of damage being done to things, according to this (Deuteronomy XXII):[55] 'Thou shalt not pass by if thou seest thy brother's ox, or his sheep go astray, but thou shalt bring them back to thy brother.' And therefore any corporal work that pertains to the corporal welfare of oneself or one's neighbor, whether it be to rescue him or any thing belonging to him, does not go against observance of the Sabbath. Hence (John VII):[56] 'Are you angry at me because I have healed the whole man on the sabbath day?' And (Matthew XII):[57] 'Which man shall there be among you, that hath one sheep, and if the same fall into a pit on the Sabbath day, will he not take hold on it and lift it up?' etc. (The argument: *Extra De ferijs*; *Licet*; XXIII question VIII: *Si nulla*; *De consecracione*, distinction I: *Sicut*). Any work done after the second or third fashion is therefore prohibited, because it is contrary to the observance of the Sabbath in so far as it impedes a man from applying himself to things divine. And because a man is impeded even more by a work of sin, therefore, all the more does a person act against this precept, who sins on a holy day.

Or it can also be stated, following Richardus,[58] that the work of a servant or a free person ought to be judged in reference to its proximate aim. Thus, it is not so much the work in itself which is in question, but rather the intent with which it is carried out by its agent, whether he be a servile person or a free man. For, as the Philosopher states (V *Ethics* chapter III): 'If one indulges in luxury so as to amass wealth, he is a miser. If someone indulges in luxury for the sake of delight, he is debauched.' And hence, although a spiritual work properly concerns the good of the soul, which is free, and thus is called a liberal work, and a corporal work properly concerns the body, according to its proper aim, and for this reason is known as servile, because the body is in servile subjection to the soul, still a liberal work can be servile in so far as how the intention of the agent is principally ordained — if it is so to the benefit of the body, which is proper to a servile work — for example, in the case of a lawyer who applies himself today to study what he is to present tomorrow for material gain, or in that of a farmer planning today how he shall plough tomorrow. Such a work, therefore, however in itself it be liberal, materially speaking, is nonetheless formally a servile work in respect to the agent. And vice versa: a corporal work that is servile in itself can formally be a liberal work, as when one writes something so as to educate others.

Thus, a work which is servile both materially and simply, as well as formally and in respect to its aim, that is, in respect to its agent, is prohibited on the Sabbath. Those, on the other hand, which are solely materially or formally servile, are not strictly prohibited, nor is a person strictly bound to abstain from them on the aforementioned days, because it is easier to abstain from those than from these. And therefore, he who engages in them is not sinning mortally unless thereby he excludes the free time necessary to divine worship.

And because there is no doubt that to invade, to war, or to ride to war or to provide oneself with arms — save in cases of necessity — is materially in and of itself a servile work, and also formally so, in so far as the intention of the agent is directed toward temporal advantage, as in truth such things cannot be otherwise, therefore, they are all the more worthy of vituperation in relation to the degree in which the end aimed at by those engaged in such warring is condemnable. For if they engage in such fighting so as to subject said infidels to them: this is desire for domination! Or, if their aim is to obtain their goods and occupy their lands — this is greed, which is the root of all evil! And such a war is considered unjust by the spirit — as has been said above. For such a war is one that destroys the peace of God, and is forbidden (Jeremiah, chapter IX):[59] 'they have labored to commit iniquity,' etc.

The answer to the eighth question.

AND FROM WHAT HAS ALREADY BEEN SAID there arises the response to another question: whether those men subject to the Knights of the Cross, who participate with them in their biannual *Reisen*, as described above, against infidels who they know are living in peace, or who they believe with great probability to be peacefully inclined, can be absolved of mortal sin; and by the same token, whether they can be forgiven if they wage war against Christians without the authority of the law or a judge who determines that the cause for which they are fighting is just, or if they obstinately resist a just attack undertaken by such. For in this case the law of obedience is taken away, because one is to obey God in preference to man (XI, question III: *Qui resistit*, and the canon *Julianus*). Nor are they excused on the grounds of ignorance of the law — especially natural or divine law; nor are they excused on the grounds of fearing material loss, as has been said above, for Ostiensis also holds (in his *Summa*: *De treuga et pace* § *Quid sit iustum bellum*; the versicle *Ergo qui auctoritate*, and what follows): whoever on the authority of a legitimate judge, who is not mistaken in his judgement, or on the authority of a law that permits it, wages war against another, does so justly. He, on the other hand, who opposes a person battling in a cause that is just, defends himself unjustly and thoughtlessly, because it is all the more apparent that his resistance is presumptuous and contumacious (the argument *De penitentia*, distinction VI § toward the end; *Extra. De maioritate et obediencia*: *Si quis*: *ff De rei vindicacione*: *Qui restituere*). It would be better for him, then, if he mended his ways, etc.

The answer to the ninth question.

TO ANOTHER QUESTION an easier answer may be made: whether a thing acquired in war becomes in that way the property of him who seizes it. Now, considering that a war is unjust, especially when it occurs contrary to any one of the five aforesaid conditions, or the law is against it, as described in the response to the above question, there is no doubt but that the occupier is not permitted to retain such a thing without incurring sin thereby; nor may he ascribe to himself that which he has occupied by force. For such things as have been stolen or acquired by force are known as defective, and cannot be acquired through usucapation or prescription, neither by the thief nor the looter, nor anyone else, even if he were to purchase or otherwise receive it in good faith (*De usucapacionibus* § *Furtive* and § *Quod autem*). This holds true in the case of a war unjust by cause, spirit, person and authority, but if the object of the war be the recovery of things unlawfully taken, the one who initiates the war is obliged to restore to his adversary that which he has taken, or the value thereof, beyond that which the adversary had unjustly taken from him — which must be returned to him, or the value thereof. And this I state according to the judgment of the court of conscience, where even compensation of non-liquid to liquid takes place — something that, according to Vilhelmus, does not occur in the legal arena.

From this it is inferred that all things so occupied or seized are subject to restitution, and it is necessary to salvation that such restitution take place as far as this is possible. For sin is not absolved unless what has been unjustly taken away is restored, as in the rule *Peccatum* (*De regulus iuris* book VI). As to the instigator of the war, or the war leader, there is no doubt but that he is responsible not only for the looting and depredations that he himself has carried out, but also for those of all others whom he led to war, and for all crimes committed in such a war — and not only those committed by his own men, but also those committed against his men (as in the law *Quantum*: *Ad legem Juliam de vi publica*, and in Ostiensis' *Summa*: *De penitencijs et remissionibus* § *Quibus et qualiter*, the versicle *Quid de rapina*).

The answer to the tenth question.

AS TO THE QUESTION POSED whether a Christian may, without sin, make use of the aid of infidels for his own defense and that of his land,[60] I reply that this question has been dealt with adequately by Johannes Andreae (in *Addiciones Speculi*: *De Iudeis et Saracenis*, near the beginning of the second half). He says: 'In cases of imminent necessity it is allowable to call to one's aid peaceful infidels, such as are not at war with us, actively or passively, otherwise, no — that is, if the war is almost won, or if our war be an unjust one, or if it were just, but absent urgent necessity.' (And so has the decretal

Quod olim of that same title, which also distinguishes the times and circumstances accordingly).

For the Maccabees, who were saintly men and warriors on behalf of the faith, entered into a pact of mutual aid with the Romans (1 Maccabees VIII chapter),[61] even though the Romans were pagans at the time. So also did Abraham enter into a confederacy with Eschol, leading them into battle though they were not of his law (Genesis XIII,[62] 1 Maccabees V is in accord with this). Nor is any obstacle presented by (II Paralipomenon, chapter XIX):[63] 'Thou helpest the ungodly, and thou art joined in friendship with them that hate the Lord, and therefore thou dost deserve indeed the wrath of the Lord,' or that which we find in Isaiah (XXIII question III § 1st verse *Item sicut legitur*), for these are understood to be references to unjust wars.

To this, especially as he could not otherwise protect himself, there is adduced *ff Ad legem Aquiliam*: *Scienciam* § *Qui cum aliter*; which agrees well with the Clementine *De homicidio* chapter one, rubric II. And what is said of Paul (Acts XXIII[64] and given in XXIII question III § *Item ab aliquo* near the end).

Likewise, when sorely pressed, a man may employ deceit (XXII question II *Utilem*; XXIII question II: *Dominus*). Even dogs we tolerate out of concern for the peace of the Church (XXIII question III: *Quidam*). And God has used evil men to vindicate wrongs (XXIII question V, the beginning of the final §), Whose deeds are examples to us.

Just the same, vice versa, infidels are aided by the faithful in a just war (XXIII question I: *Quid culpatur*; XI question III: *Julianus*).

Likewise, when pressed by necessity, we have converse with the excommunicate (*De penitentia excommunicacionis*: *Si vere*).

Likewise, for the health of crops we make use of the magicians' art, which is condemned in both testaments (Codex *De mathematicis*, the law *Eorum*). Oldradus concurs (in *Questiones*, question LXXI).

The answer to the eleventh question.

TO ANOTHER QUESTION, namely, whether an infidel may demand justice of a Christian judge in the case of a stolen item, or one carried off, the reply is that there can be no question of their being disallowed this, according to Innocent, because they have no less just rights to property than we do (as noted in the chapter *Quod super hijs*: *De voto et voti redempcione*, which we touch upon in question 1). Ostiensis differs in this matter; his opinion is as if there has never been any such possession or dominion amongst infidels.

Therefore, it seems that Ostiensis sees it like this: that Innocent's opinion holds only for those infidels who acknowledge the dominion of the Church.[65] For according to him, the Church may well tolerate such men because they are not to be compelled to the Faith as it has been said, and many are the passages that can be adduced in support of this (1 Peter II):[66] 'Servants, be subject to your masters with all fear, not only to the good and gentle, but also to the froward,' and (1 Timothy VI, at the start):[67] 'Whosoever are servants under the yoke, let them count their master worthy of all honor.' But other infidels, who neither acknowledge the authority or dominion of the Roman Church, are unworthy of all realms, principalities, and dominion; this is true of those, for example, who have occupied the Holy Land or regions which Christians had acquired; those ought to be warred against on the authority of the Church.

For according to Ostiensis, with the advent of Christ, all jurisdiction, principality and dominion were taken away from the infidels and transferred to the faithful, and this for just cause, as proven (Ecclesiasticus XI):[68] 'A kingdom is translated from one people to another, because of injustices, and wrongs, and injuries, and divers deceits' (to this see the chapter *Translato*: *De constitucionibus*). Hence Christ Himself, the Son of God, predicted to the Jews (Matthew XXI):[69] 'The kingdom of God shall be taken from you, and shall be given to a nation yielding the fruits thereof.' This He entrusted to Peter and his successors as is clear from what is written and noted (in the chapter *Pro humani*: *De homicidio*, book VI, and the chapter *Qui filij sint legitimi*: *Per venerabilem* § *Racionibus*). And for this reason, according to Ostiensis, the infidels *de iure* ought to be subject to the faithful, and not vice versa (this is clear from what is written and noted in chapter 1 and the chapter *Multorum* and the chapter *Etsi Iudeos*: *De Iudeis*).

This opinion is to be seen as also followed by Oldradus (in the question he poses: *Whether the war of the Spaniards against the Saracens be legitimate?*); the reason being that the entire province there once belonged to the Christians, and there were churches, monasteries and other pious places there where Christ was worshipped, subject to the Roman Church, which the Saracens occupied, despoiling us of them on account of our sins — with God's permission. Hence, where the question is one of recovering lands from which we had been violently expelled, war is just and should be judged a defensive war, not an invasion. And although Oldradus adduces this as an opinion of Ostiensis', still it is not contrary to Innocent, for he says that this rationale is sufficient for all lands in which the Roman Emperors ever, etc., as above in question III. From this Oldradus concludes, in accord with Ostiensis, that infidels today possess no jurisdiction, nor dominion, nor honor, nor power, since they are utterly incapable of the same — as he notes in question LXVII.

Now, many absurdities have followed upon this opinion, such as that Christians may, without incurring sin thereby, steal, carry off, rob, invade, and occupy the goods and the lands of infidels who do not recognize the Church or her authority, even if they wish to live with us in peace. It would then follow that this rule has no place here, namely: 'A sin is not absolved unless,' etc., for according to the aforesaid no sin has been committed at all.

It would seem, nevertheless, that Ostiensis and Innocent intimate that for all this there need be authorisation of the Pope and the

Church, but then there also can be no doubt in such a case, for such a determination must be strictly observed, and therefore, he who occupies on the authority of the Church sins not. But, even taking into account the circumscription of Papal authority, it must be said that according to the opinion of Ostiensis, dominion, jurisdiction, and possession by such infidels is null and void, and their goods are as things left vacant and derelict, for which reason they may be conceded to the occupiers just as the birds of the air, the fish of the seas, the stones upon the seashore, and other such things (*Instituciones*, *De rerum divisione* § *Si vero*). It would even follow that the prohibition 'Thou shalt not steal,' 'Thou shalt not kill,' etc., as well as that commandment 'Do not unto others what you would not have others do unto you,' and many other divine laws, are not binding upon Christians who pilfer the goods of infidels.

This opinion is therefore seen to be full of danger. For it gives licence to injure one's neighbors and presents the occasion for limitless homicide — for which reason it is generally not recognized.

Hence in his revisiting of the chapter *Peccatum non dimittitur* (*De regulis iuris*, Book VI), which he delivered at Pisa during the general council, Master Pietro de Ancorano repudiated this opinion[70] (Question III article 2), stating: 'I am struck, first of all, by the statement that the goods of our enemies thus become our property and those captured become our slaves, since war has been declared upon them (as in the law *Hostes*: *De captivis*) and that, from the time when they are seized in war; hence up until this time the property was theirs, according to the dictum that what is permitted at one time is prohibited at another (the law *Statu liberum ff De legatis* II, as according to the chapter *Nonne*: *De presumpcionibus*). Furthermore, even Christians taken captive in such a war are made the captors' slaves, as is clear from the entire title *De captivis*.' Moreover, as he himself puts it in the same repetition, it is not permitted them to escape without incurring sin thereby, or to steal from their masters, and that Ostiensis himself thinks so (in the *Summa*: *De penitencijs et remissionibus* § *Quibus et qualiter*, sub § *Quibus accusatoribus*, the versicle *Quid si Christianus*). But now if they were wholly incapable of dominion and the possession of goods, as he himself says, that would mean that our men taken captive by them would not become their slaves, of which he himself affirms the contrary to be true.

Second, it is proven that infidels are not to be forced unto the reception of the Faith, but induced to it through holy exhortations (XLV distinction: *De Iudeis*; XXIII question V: *Ad fidem*): But if they were to learn that, according to our divine law, they were not the masters of their possessions, and that without sin these may be taken from them, certainly they would become even more firmly grounded in their faithlessness, and out of a just fear of losing their goods, would be drawn away from our Faith (the argument of the chapter *Abbas*: *Que metus causa*, where fear of losing one's goods is most just).

Likewise, if the Church tolerates persons remaining in their faithlessness in matrimony and similar things (as in the chapter *Gaudemus*: *De divorcijs*), why should she not tolerate them in their jurisdiction, dominion, and in the goods that they possess? There is no reason not to; indeed, on the contrary, for things and accessories always follow the condition of the person (chapter 1 *De iure patronatus*, Book VI).

§ Likewise, what sort of toleration on the part of the Church would that be, what sort of exhortation to the Faith, if she were to take away from them their goods, dominion, and honors? For sure, this would not be exhortation or encouragement, but dire coercion, since absent such temporal goods human life cannot long endure (argument c. *Si quis obiecerit*: I question III). And since such coercion is forbidden, as we find in the question above, thus, it cannot be admitted by some other road (*De procuratoribus*: *Tuae*, and the chapter *Cum quid una via*: *De regulis iuris* Book VI).

Moreover, for confirmation of the aforesaid, however (in *Addiciones speculi*, the title *De Iudeis et Saracenis*) Johannes Andreae treats of the question: Are Christians permitted to invade the lands of pagans or infidels, and without just cause take away the dominion of their lands and possessions? he refers us to his major gloss (in the chapter *Quod super hijs*: *De voto et voti redempcione*), where though seeking to limit the dicta of Innocent according to the opinion of Ostiensis, he still states (in the chapter *Si a subdelegato*: *De officio delegati*, Book VI in *Novella*, on the gloss *Quid dices*) that even infidels beyond the Church have jurisdiction, adding to this (in the *Addiciones speculi*, the title aforesaid), quotations from the sayings of others in this matter:

'I have seen some clear writings that conclude on the basis of seven rationales that peaceful infidel princes must not be expelled from their lands without legitimate cause.'

§ The first of these seven is founded upon the precept 'What you would not have others do unto you,' etc., of which enough is said at the beginning of the Decretals. The same is true, as, along with us, they share in natural law (here is adduced the canon *Caritas,* in III before the conclusion I believe, in the verse 'Item non illi tantum' up to the verse 'Illi vero plus'). And thus by that law of nature and by charity we are bound to come to their aid in their need (XLII distinction: *Quiescamus*; LXXXVI distinction: *Non satis*).

§ 2° the text is introduced: *Causa* XXIII question I: *Noli* at the end, and question V: *Prodest* from the verse *Proinde* all the way to *Nichil inhumaniter*. And because we are to act not out of fury, but out of charity (XII question II: *Fraternitas*).

§ 3° adduces the gloss *Per hoc* (in the canon *Si de rebus*: XXIII question VII). Likewise, their right of possession is based on the law of nations, and therefore they possess things justly (XXIII question IV: *Quid dicam*). Moreover (the canon *Quando*: XXIII question IV and question V: *Unum solum*) where cruelty is disapproved of.

§ 4° they are sheep of Christ's fold (John X):[71] 'other sheep I have, that are not of this fold,' that is, the Church; and Peter was commanded 'Feed my lambs' (John, final chapter[72]) without any distinction being made among them. So, the successor of Peter also has to feed and defend them; thus, not to battle against or to allow them to be harmed (*De natis ex libero ventre*, the final chapter).

§ 5° introduces texts that seem appropriate: *Qui sincera*, and the canon *De Iudeis*, and XXIII question IV in the final canon, and what is noted of XXVIII question I: *Iudeorum*, in the first gloss, where it is stated that indeed it is impossible to win them for God unless we consort with them (XXII question IV: *Infideles*; XI question III: *Ad mensam*).

§ 6° the words of the Apostle (to the Ephesians, last chapter),[73] teaching the manner in which masters ought to treat their obedient servants. And (Colossians, the last chapter at the beginning),[74] where he speaks of how we punish the unfaithful for their crimes (*De raptoribus*: *In archiepiscopatu*), therefore, without good cause they are not to be punished (LVI distinction: *Satis perversum*), nor to be driven from their homes nor deprived of their possessions, as the Church supports co-existence with them (the same title: *Etsi Iudeos*; in agreement with XI question III: *Nolite*, the verse *Audi ergo*).

§ The final text adduced (in the law *Christianis*: the codex *De paganis et eorum sacrificijs*) where we are commanded not to molest those who are living in peace. Likewise, on the Jews: *Extra*, the same title chapter II and the chapter *Sicut*). Likewise, 'a contrario,' the canons XXIII question VIII: *Dispar*, where it is noted and XVI question III: *Porro*, where it is also noted. Likewise, 'the heavens to the Lord of Heaven, the earth to the sons of man,' therefore, it is not allowed to refuse them what is conceded them by the law of human society (XXIII question II: *Notandum*; and in argument V distinction *Ad eius vero*); at last, he adduces XXIII question V, the last §.

Thus Johannes Andreae in the place spoken of above.

Response is thus made to the reasoning of Ostiensis, to wit: what he suggests is not to be assented to; indeed, it is to be negated as erroneous, the opinion that all honor, dominion, and jurisdiction has been taken away from the infidels by the advent of Christ.

For St Thomas states that although the infidels should not set themselves up over new territories as lords or prelates having power over the faithful, out of concern of the danger to the Faith that this would constitute, and the scandal it would cause, still they are not to be deprived of their pre-existing dominion over the faithful, for dominion and prelature were introduced by human law, while the distinction between faithful and infidel is a matter of divine law. Now divine law, which comes of grace, does not do away with human law, which arises of natural reason. If therefore the dominion of infidels over the faithful has not been taken away at the advent of Christ, so much less can that be said of the dominion of infidels over other infidels, and still so much the less in the case of their dominion over possessions. Therefore, that same St Thomas says (2a 2e q. XII a. 2) that infidelity is not in disaccord with such dominion, introduced *de iure* by the law of nations, which is human law having its source in natural reason. And such law is also called natural law, as St Thomas states (2a 2e q. LVII a. 3), declaring that natural law or natural justice is that which by its nature is adequate or commensurate with equality, and this can be seen in two ways. One of these is by considering it an absolute, as the male is commensurate to the female in that he may reproduce through her agency, she bearing him a son to nourish. Another way in which something is naturally commensurate to something else, is not according to any absolute characteristic, but according to what results from it — for example, ownership of property. For if we were to consider a field from an absolute point of view, there is no reason why one should have more right to it than another. But if it is considered according to its appropriateness for tilling, and its peaceful agricultural use, according to this it is somehow naturally commensurate to one rather than another (as is made clear by the Philosopher in 2nd *Politics*). For the absolute nature of a thing is not apprehended solely by the categories of its convenience to man, but also in regard to other creatures as well. And it is for this reason that that which is called natural law is common to us, and to other creatures. Therefore, he who is learned in the law states that the law of the nations branches from this. So, to consider something from the perspective of that which results from it is proper to reason and therefore indeed is something natural to men, according to natural reason, which dictates this. Thus, the learned jurist: 'That which natural reason has established amongst all men, that which is kept in all nations, is known as the law of the nations.'

§ And so according to that same St Thomas, holy men may be found who faithfully served infidel lords. In the Old Testament Joseph served the Pharaoh, Daniel Nebuchadnezzar, and Mordecai Ahasuerus. In the New Testament, we have St Sebastian. Hence (Philippians IV)[75] 'All the saints salute you, especially they that are of Caesar's household,' i.e. Nero's, and he was an infidel. And it was useful for the faithful to be members of the Emperor's household for the defense of others of the faithful, as St Sebastian was to those Christian souls whom he saw could not hold up under torments.

§ Still St Thomas admits (2a 2e q. IX a. X) that by verdict or ordinance of the Church such dominion of infidels over the faithful may be done away with in the case of said infidels meriting such, on account of the infidels over whom they rule converting to the Faith, becoming sons of God. And therefore, concerning such as are subject to the temporal authority of the Church and its members, the Church has established that any slave of the Jews who becomes a Christian is immediately freed from his servitude, with no restitution being due in exchange, if he be native to that state, that is, born into slavery. Similarly, if he be an infidel sold into service. If, however, he was purchased in order to be sold again, his owner is obliged to offer him for sale within three months (fuller information on this may be found in the gloss *Distingue* LIV, distinction § *Hoc tunc observandum* and the canon *Fraternitatem*; *Extra, De Iudeis* final chapter).

§ Nor does the Church do them any injury in this because as the Jews themselves are in servitude to the Church, she may dispose of their matters just as secular princes enact many laws binding upon their subjects on behalf of liberty. However, St Thomas says, as to those infidels who are not temporally subject to the Church or her members, the above mentioned law has not been enacted in their regard by the Church although *de iure* she might; she acts in this way so as to avoid scandal as even the Lord (Matthew XVII)[76] shows, stating that they may be excused from paying tribute because children of God are free. And yet He commands that tribute be paid, so that scandal might be avoided. Paul as well says the same, when he says that servants must honor the masters to whom they are subject, adding: 'lest the name of the Lord and His doctrine be blasphemed." It is thus to be concluded from the aforesaid that the infidels did not lose their dominion at the advent of Christ, but afterwards, through legislation of the Church and secular princes, and only in regard to those who became Christians (LIV distinction: *Mancipia*; *Extra, De Iudeis* c. 2). And what has been said of the slaves of the Jews we say too in regard to all those of the Saracens, with Laurentius and Johannes and many others following Raymundus. He, however, disagrees as to the native slaves of the pagans, who, even though they become Christians, still ought, he says, to serve their masters according to what the Apostle says (I Timothy):[77] 'Whosoever are servants under the yoke of infidels, let them count their masters worthy of all honor' and (in the Epistle to the Ephesians VI):[78] 'Servants, be obedient to them that are your lords according to the flesh, with fear and trembling,' even if they be infidels, as stated in the gloss. And so a pagan may be the master of a Christian, but he may not become one, which Raymundus develops (in *Summa* §). With this concurs the final gloss toward the end of § *Hoc tunc observandum*, LIV distinction. The reason for this disparity in the question is because the Jews, through their abuse of the scriptures and the contempt in which they hold our food fight against our Faith to a greater degree. Therefore, we should not accept them unto our banquets nor eat with them or live with them (XXVIII question I: *Nullus*), whereas we may eat in the company of Saracens (XI question III: *Ad mensam*). Others, *scilicet* Laurentius, Johannes, and many others following them, make no such distinctions, holding — better than Raymundus — that, just as a Christian ought not to have such dealings with a Jew as described above, by the same token neither should he with Saracens. For today's Saracens are Judaisers, practicing circumcision and discerning among clean and unclean meats, as according to Wilhelmus, Raymondus' glossator — and thus the same danger holds in both cases, as consequently does the same prohibition. As to the permission enunciated by the Apostle and mentioned above, this should be understood, according to Raymundus, as referring to the Primitive Church when such Judaisation was not yet taking place; or in speaking of a time when they were approaching them in order to preach.

But it is not true that this solution can be applied to those who live with the Jews promiscuously, nor can it be applied in the case of other infidels.

FINALLY, answer is made to the authorities adduced by Ostiensis, *scilicet* (Matthew XXI):[79] 'The kingdom of God shall be taken away from you,' etc., where He is speaking of the Jews who received the law of the Old Testament; nothing can be taken away from infidels who received nothing in the first place, because they never received the law of the Old Testament, just as they do not receive the law of the New Testament. And so, what is said here of the Kingdom of God, according to the gloss, is multiplex: First, the Kingdom of God is the grace of God by which He reigns in us; Second, according to

Gregory, the Kingdom of God is that familiarity with the scriptures, according to this (Luke XVII):[80] 'the Kingdom of God is within you.' Third, the Kingdom of God is the government of the Church, and it shall be given to them who bring forth fruit therefrom; thus — the Apostles and their successors.

Furthermore, it does not hold (see the chapter *Translato*: *De constitucionibus*) that all possessions, jurisdictions, and dominion have been translated from the infidels to the faithful. For by this the Apostle[81] wished to prove that as the Levitical priesthood, which began with Aaron, has been transferred from the Jews, by Christ, to Peter as to the head and to others as though to the members, it was necessary also that the transfer of the laws concerning the observance of circumcision and the keeping of the Sabbath, etc., was also effected. Thus St Augustine assumes the reason for the necessity of the transferal as written in the above-cited chapter: Because both at the same time and with the same will were given, so what is said of the establishment of one is to be understood of the other as similarly established. This operates by reason of connectivity, as the glosses mention. And understand that 'with the same will' otherwise under the same promise, id est, to the same effect, is brought together both in respect to Him who wills or promises, *scil.* God, who promised the bestowal of a land flowing with milk and honey (Deuteronomy VI)[82] and also in respect to the Hebrews willing or promising to observe both, *scil.* the Law as well as the priesthood (Exodus XXIV).[83] They are also connected from another aspect, because the interpretation of the law belongs to the priests (Deuteronomy XVII;[84] *Qui filij sint legitimi*: *Per venerabilem*, the verse *Racionibus*). Therefore, the translation of the priesthood signifies the translation of the law as well, i.e. the authority to interpret the law. This is a connexion of accessory and principal, because the law depends upon the priest.

Now since other infidels neither received said law nor was the priesthood found among them, it does not seem possible that the said allegation can prove anything else, save that the authority of pronouncing or interpreting the law has been transferred from the Jews to Peter, etc. This is however not true of the dominion, jurisdiction, and possessions of the infidels, which are not held by virtue of this sort of divine law, but rather by the law of the nations, as stated above. And because certainly the law of the nations has no connexion with the priesthood, therefore, etc.

Finally, the dictum (Ecclesiasticus X)[85] is alleged: 'A kingdom is translated from one people to another, etc.' In response to this we note that, as justice — of which there is no greater than the righteousness of God — dictates that on account of a person's unrighteousness, he ought to be deposed so that he should not be the judge of other men, his power and authority are taken away from him so that he might not be able to harm his neighbor, thus it is in regard to others. Therefore Solomon says this in his aforesaid authority: 'A kingdom is translated from one people to another, because of injustices, and wrongs, and injuries, and divers deceits.' Of which saying Nicholas de Lira states: That dominion is transferred on account of pride is exemplified by the monarchy of the Assyrians, which was translated to the Babylonians, thence to the Persians and the Medes (Daniel V)[86] and from others unto the Greeks (1 Maccabees)[87] and from the Greeks to the Romans (Luke 2).[88] For shortly before this Solomon states: 'Do thou nothing by deeds of injury,' that is, 'thou shalt do no injury through thy power,' and because such things come of pride, he adds there: 'Pride is hateful before God and men.'[89]

This too must be said of the Pope who acts as the vicar of God: he may justly punish, for these reasons, whichever infidels, and however many times they exceed the limits of the law of nature, should the faculty present itself, as has been said above in the first tractate concerning the solution to question VII. So much for that. Thanks be to God.

Thus concludes the tractate of Master Paweł Włodkowic, doctor of the decretals, custodian and canon of Kraków, on the war of the Prussians against the infidels, and of the authority of the Pope and the Emperor in respect to the infidels.

Endnotes

1. This Latin title, derived from the first word of the treatise, is the traditional one. It is used by Ehrlich, *Pisma wybrane*, I, 2-98, who, however, does not include the closing phrase and *explicit* in the edition by Belch, *Paulus Vladimiri*, II, 844, used by Charles Kraszewski as the basis of his translation. Belch, I, 165, however, assigns this work a different title: *De potestate papae et imperatoris respectu infidelium*; see his discussion of its publication history II, 789-791. The traditional dating of this treatise is 5 July 1415 because in the text of Paweł's *Opinio Ostiensis* he refers to *Savientibus* as having been given to the German nation the day before (see the last sentence of *Opinio Ostiensis*). There are, however, a number of scholars—not, including Belch and Ehrlich—who have concluded this is in error and that *Savientibus*—and by extension *Opinio Ostiensis*—should be dated to 1416. On this issue, see the discussion in Paul W. Knoll, "*A Pearl of Powerful Learning*." *The University of Cracow in the Fifteenth Century* (Leiden and Boston: Brill, 2016), p. 239, n. 57, who follows the argument of Hartmut Boockmann, *Johannes Falkenberg, der Deutsche Orden und die polnische Politik. Untersuchungen zur politischen Theorie des späteren Mittelalters* (Göttingen: Vandenhoeck und Ruprecht, 1975), pp. 225-228, particularly p. 226, n. 179.

2. Paweł is here referring to Duke Conrad of Mazovia (1187/88-1247) who sought assistance from the Knights of the Teutonic Order (or often, in this context, simply The Order), a military-religious corporation, to defend his and neighboring territories. What he granted them in the way of rights and privileges and what eventually was granted by the papacy, has long been a contentious subject in Polish and German scholarship, with the question of possible forgery present from almost the beginning. See the treatment by Paul Milliman, "*The Slippery Memory of Men.*" *The Place of Pomerania in the Medieval Kingdom of Poland* (Leiden and Boston: Brill, 2013), pp. 40-42, especially p. 40, n. 60. The standard Polish history of the Order is Marian Biskup and Gerard Labuda, *Dzieje Zakonu Krzyżackiego w Prusach. Gospodarka—Społeczeństwo—Państwo—Ideologia* (Gdańsk: Wydawnictwo Morskie Gdańsk, 1988), pp. 96-161, 178-188, 241-258 for the early development to *ca.* 1310. See also Boockmann, *Der Deutsche Orden*: *Zwölf Kapital aus seiner Geschichte* (Munich: Beck, 1981), pp. 66-92; and, more briefly, Knoll, "The Most Unique Crusader State. The Teutonic Order in the Development of the Political Culture of Northeastern Europe during the Middle Ages," in Charles W. Ingrao and Franz A.J. Szabo, eds., *The Germans in the East* (West Lafayette, IN: Purdue University Press, 2008), pp. 37-48, especially pp. 37-39.

3. An overview of these fortifications can be found in Aleksander Pluskowski, *The Archaeology of the Prussian Crusade. Holy War and Colonisation* (London and New York: Routledge, 2013), pp. 140-195 especially (in a chapter entitled "A Land of Red Castles").

The most important of these fortifications was that at Marienburg (today Malbork in Poland). For an up-to-date treatment of its construction, see Sławomir Jóźwiak and Janusz Trupinda, *Organizacja życia na zamku Krzyżackim w Malborku w czasach wielkich mistrzów 1309-1457*, 3rd ed. (Malbork: Muzeum Zamkowe w Malborku, 2019), pp. 45-113.

4. The authoritative work on the *Reisen* of the Teutonic Knights and participants from elsewhere in Europe is Werner Paravicini, *Die Preußenreisen des europäischen Adels*, 2 vols. (Sigmaringen: Thorbecke, 1989-1995). It should be noted that not only knights of the Order and western European adventurers were involved in these *Reisen*; Polish military participants were also part of the forces that embarked upon these campaigns; see Anna Supruniuk, "O wyprawach do Prus rycerzy polskich i wojnie domowej w Koronie w latach 1382-1385," *Zapiski Historyczne* 65, 2 (2000): 31-56.

5. The Christianization of Lithuania and its peoples was a long and complex process that here Paweł compresses considerably and that has evoked conflicting historiographical interpretations. For example, compare the differing viewpoints of William Urban, "The Teutonic Order and the Christianization of Lithuania," in *La Cristianizzazione della Lituania. Atti del Colloquio Internazionale di Storia Ecclesiastica in Occasione del VI Centenario della Lituania Cristiana (1387-1987)* (Vatican City: Liberia Editrice Vaticana, 1987), pp. 107-138; and Jerzy Kłoczowski, "La Pologne et la Christianisation de la Lituanie," in *Ibid.*, pp. 139-159. In the same volume see the article by Michał Giedroyć, "Lithuanian Options Prior to Krėva (1385)," pp. 87-105. The political as well as the religious context of these developments is well treated, with reference to both older and new scholarship, by Robert Frost, *The Oxford History of Poland-Lithuania*, vol. I: *The Making of the Polish-Lithuanian Union, 1385-1569* (Oxford: Oxford University Press, 2015), pp. 5-35, 71-73.

6. i.e., Grand Prince Jogaila, who converted to Latin Christianity in 1385 and married Jadwiga, the ruler of Poland, taking the Christian name Władysław and known by the Polonized version of his pagan name as Jagiełło.

7. i.e., Vytautas (often referred to by the Polish form of his name, Witold).

8. Paweł refers here to incursions that eventually led up to the Polish-Teutonic Order war between 1409 and 1411, ended by the (first) Peace of Toruń. Its crucial battle came at Grunwald/Tannenberg/Žalgiris in 1410 and was a major defeat of the Order. See, for example (among a large body of scholarship), Andrzej Nadolski, *Grunwald 1410*, 3rd ed. (Warsaw: Bellona, 2010); and, in English, Urban, *The Teutonic Knights. A Military History* (London: Green Books, 2003), pp. 195-220. Military and diplomatic conflict continued after the war. For a brief overview of these developments after 1411—the position of emperor-elect Sigismund of Luxembourg, the misguided campaign mounted in 1413 by Grand Master of the Order Heinrich von Plauen, and the equally unsuccessful Polish campaign of early 1414 known for its disastrous food and supply shortages as "the Hunger War"—see the comments in the still valuable work by Eric Christiansen, *The Northern Crusades. The Baltic and the Catholic Frontier, 1100-1525* (Minneapolis, MN: University of Minnesota Press, 1980), pp. 222-223; and the brief treatment in the excellent text-book by Tomasz Jurek and Edmund Kizik, *Historia Polski do 1572 roku* (Warsaw: Wydawnictwo Naukowe PWN, 2013), pp. 386-388. These elements were important in the formulation of Polish policy as presented at the Council of Constance and in the treatises of Paweł.

9. Paweł is here presenting himself as a scholar in law and a responsible ecclesiastical leader. He thus seeks to de-politicize his remarks and de-emphasize his role at the council as a representative of the Polish ruler. In reality he was both.

10. In these two questions Paweł relies here directly upon the canonist Peter of Ancharano (*ca.* 1330-1416), who may have been one of his teachers at Padua, and whom he most probably knew. See Belch, *Paulus Vladimiri*, I, ii, 795, n. 1. Peter, who had studied under Baldus de Ubaldis (*ca.* 1327-1400, among the best known canonists of his time) was particularly influential in the last decades of the fourteenth century and the beginning of the fifteenth century; see the comments of Brundage, *Canon Law*, p. 180 and p. 207.

11. i.e., legislated law, not Divine or Natural law.

12. Guido de Baysio (*ca.* 1250-1313), Archdeacon of Bologna and Archchancellor of the University of Bologna, author of *Rosarium*, a rich commentary on Gratian's *Decretum*. He was a master teacher, and one of his students was Johannes Andreae (about whom, see below, n. 42). See Brundage, *Canon Law*, pp. 212-213.

13. Oldradus da Ponte (d. post 1337), a canonist eventually teaching at Bologna and part of the Colonna household. This family, based in Avignon, was a bitter enemy of Pope Boniface VIII. After his death they were once again in favor when the papacy settled in Avignon. There Oldradus made good friends with Petrarch, who regarded him as the most illustrious jurist of the day. See Brundage, *Canon Law*, pp. 221-222.

14. Reference is here made to Pope Innocent IV (reg. 1243-1254) and Henry of Segusio, Cardinal of Ostia (1190/1200-1271), about whom more, with respect to the treatise *Opinio Ostiensis*. Innocent (Sinibaldo dei Fieschi) was an important and influential canonist before becoming pope. During his pontificate, he promulgated three important decretal collections; see Brundage, *Canon Law*, pp. 225-226.

15. Gen. 1:26-29.

16. Deut. 11:24.

17. Prov. 23:10; see also Prov. 22:28.

18. Matt. 5:45; and Matt. 6:26.

19. Ps. 146:9; see also Ps. 103:27 and Ps. 144:15-16.

20. Gen. 13:9-12.

21. Ex. 20:13 and 20:15.

22. On this question Paweł largely followed the writings of his mentor at Padua, Franciscus Zabarella (1360-1417, bishop-elect of Florence in 1409, cardinal 1409-1417, and one of the three most important intellectuals at the Constance of Constance 1414-1418); he was arguably the leading canonist at Padua in the late fourteenth century. See Thomas E. Morrissey, "Cardinal Franciscus Zabarella (1360-1417) as a Canonist and the Crisis of His Age: Schism and the Council of Constance," *Zeitschrift für Kirchengeschichte* 96 (1985): 196-208, and reprinted as item VIII, with original pagination, in Morrissey, *Conciliarism and Church Law in the Fifteenth Century. Studies on Franciscus Zabarella and the Council of Constance* (Farnham, Surrey England and Burlington, VT: Ashgate: 2014).

23. Ps. 71:1.

24. Matt. 28:18.

25. John. 21:17.

26. Gen. 19:12-25.

27. Pope Gregory IX (Hugolinus *ca.* 1171-1241); see below n. 48.

28. 1 Cor. 5:12.

29. Although Paweł had previously defined an organizational structure for considering in his first part of his treatise the power of the pope vis-à-vis infidels in eleven questions and then, in the second part, the power of the emperor vis-à-vis infidels in eleven questions, he here provides an extended general disquisition as—in a sense—a twelfth question to introduce his treatment of imperial powers. Following this he then proceeds to examine specific powers. He then concludes *Saevientibus* with an analysis of what he had termed "a certain erroneous opinion."

30. Johannes Teutonicus (Johannes Zemeke, *ca.* 1170-1245), who was based in Bologna. He prepared his own *glossa ordinaria* on Gratian's *Decretum*, and later collected the decretals of Pope Innocent III. His work also included glosses on the Fourth Lateran Council of 1215 and later complications that were eventually incorporated into the body of canon law. See Brundage, *Canon Law*, pp. 219-220 with additional bibliography n. 22.

31. Not clear to what work Paweł is referring.

32. Dante's political philosophy is effectively summarized by Antony Black, *Political Thought in Europe 1250-1450* (Cambridge: Cambridge University Press, 1992), pp. 96-100.

33. Paweł here is, according to Ehrlich, *Pisma wybrane*, I, 105, n. 82, apparently closely following his notes of Zabarella's comments mentioning Marsilio of Padua as "de Menardino." In what follows he refers clearly to Marsilio, implying a second individual. (This is repeated later in his work *Ad aperiendam*; see Ehrlich, *Ibid.*, II, 145.) A further problem with the text at this point is his description of Marsilio as a "great doctor of divine scripture," when in fact his listeners or readers at the Council of Constance knew that Marsilio was a writer rejected by the church for presenting, among other things, a position on imperial versus papal power that Paweł himself rejected. The Bavarian referred to in Paweł's text was Duke Lewis of Bavaria (1282-1347), who had claimed the imperial title and vigorously opposed papal power. His claim was in varying degrees recognized in the imperial lands, but was eventually withdrawn, and the electors in 1346 selected Charles of Luxembourg as eventual Holy Roman Emperor (crowned in 1355).

34. Without identification, Paweł begins here—according to Belch, *Paulus Vladimiri*, II, 811, n. 26—an argument based, among other sources, upon the writings of Johannes de Legnano (Giovanni da Legnano, *ca.* 1320-1383). Johannes was active politically as well as productive as a legal scholar. His *corpus* included a treatise *De bello* and another entitled *De pace*; his work, according to some, represents a precursor to modern international public law. See Brundage, *Canon Law*, p. 218.

35. The works discussed by Paweł in previous sentences are by Aristotle, who was simply known in the Middle Ages as "the Philosopher."

36. Gen. 3:24; Gen. 5 has nothing related to this.

37. This assertion is only tenuously reflected in Gen. 6:8-9 and 6:18.

38. Gen. 8:20

39. Ps. 71:2 (Vulg. numeration)

40. Pope Boniface VIII (Benedict Gaetani, *ca*. 1235-1303) was an important canon law scholar in additional to being a successful ecclesiastical politician. His decretal collection (*Liber sextus*) was promulgated in 1298. Equally important, his decree *Unam sanctam* (1302) summed up more than two centuries of the growth of concept of papal monarchy, in which papal power is regarded as supreme over both the lay and the ecclesiastical sphere. A clear explication of this politico-ecclesiastical theory is provided by David Zachariah Flanagin, "Extra Ecclesiam salus non est—sed quae ecclesia? Ecclesiology and Authority in the Later Middle Ages," in Joëlle Rollo-Koster and Thomas M. Izbicki, eds., *A Companion to the Great Western Schism (1378-1417)* (Leiden and Boston: Brill, 2009), pp. 333-374, here 339-348. The theory of absolute papal monarchy included papal claims to jurisdiction over non-Christians, including the power to make laws that apply to them. See Brundage, *Canon Law*, p. 164 and, for Boniface VIII, pp. 208-209.

41. John 18:11; see also Matt. 26:52.

42. Johannes Andreas (*ca*. 1270-1348) studied at Bologna, then taught at both Bologna and Padua, serving also from time to time as an ambassador from Bologna. A married layman (only the second to become a professor of canon law), he produced a number of important and influential works. He died in the plague in 1348. See Brundage, *Canon Law*, pp. 216-217.

43. Abbas Antiquus (d. 1296) is the name applied to Bernard of Montemirat, who was abbot of Monte Cassino. His cognomen distinguishes him from Nicholas de Tudeschis (1386-1445, called Abbas Modernus), a distinguished fifteenth century canonist also known as Panormitanus. See Brundage, *Canon Law*, pp. 209-210.

44. Both Belch, *Paulus Vladimiri*, II, 818, n. 94, and Ehrlich, *Pisma wybrane*, I, 105, n. 103 note this individual as an unidentified scholar.

45. Again John 18:11.

46. This fictional donation of the 8th century purported to be a decree by the early 4th century Roman emperor gifting "the western provinces" to the Latin church in the person of Pope Sylvester I. It became the foundation for medieval papal claims to temporal sovereignty to Rome, its environs, and the generalized lands of the west. See Thomas F.X. Noble, *The Republic of St. Peter: The Birth of the Papal State, 680—825* (Philadelphia: University of Pennsylvania Press, 1984), pp. 134-137 especially. The text of the *Donation* is printed in Paul E. Dutton, ed., *Carolingian Civilization: A Reader* (Peterborough, Ontario: Broadview, 2004), pp. 13-22. Often regarded as a forgery in the Middle Ages, the most convincing demonstration of this was provided by Lorenzo Valla in 1433.

47. Ex. 20:13 and 15.

48. Ramón de Penyafort (1180/1185-1275), a Catalan who studied and taught at Bologna, whom Pope Gregory IX (Hugolinus)—himself an expert canonist—commissioned to prepare the compilation of canons that eventually was published as the *Liber extra*). For Ramón, see Brundage, *Canon Law*, pp. 222-223; for Gregory IX, see Brundage, *Canon Law*, p. 215.

49. 2 Macc. 15:1-11

50. 2 Macc. 8:26-27.

51. Ex. 20:8.

52. Lev. 23:7.

53. John 8:34.

54. Prov. 24:11.

55. Deut. 22:1.

56. John 7:23.

57. Matt. 12:11

58. Ricardus Anglicus (Richard de Mores d. 1242), the first Englishman to study and teach at Bologna. He produced an impressive body of writings and eventually served King John in his negotiations with Pope Innocent III. See Brundage, *Canon Law*, pp. 223-224.

59. Jer. 9:5.

60. The point being treated here by Paweł was a particularly controversial one that he addressed more fully elsewhere. The Polish-Lithuanian army that had fought the Teutonic Order and defeated it at Grunwald in 1410 included troops from the Lithuanian lands—Tatars and perhaps others—that were still pagans. Their utilization was vigorously condemned by the Order. Paweł's justification of the Polish position and his treatment of this issue here, reliant—as he notes—in many ways on the works of Johannes Andreas, is further developed in his treatise *Opinio Hostiensis*. An earlier, equally important treatment of this issue, had been provided by Stanisław of Skarbmierz, professor of canon law at the University of Kraków and the first rector of that refounded institution in 1400; see the analysis of his *Sermo de bellis iustis* by Wojciech Świeboda, *Innowiercy w opiniach prawnych uczonych polskich w XV wieku* (Kraków: Societas Vistulana, 2013), pp. 143-156.

61. 1 Macc. 8:17-30

62. The text incorrectly cites Gen. 13; the correct citation is Gen. 14:13

63. 2 Chron. 19:2

64. Acts 23:17-22.

65. At this point, Paweł begins the third part of his treatise. It is explicitly devoted to an attack upon Ostiensis' position. Significant parts of this, in one form or another, are included in Paweł's treatise *Opinio Hostiensis*.

66. 1 Pet. 2:18.

67. 1 Tim. 6:1.

68. Ecclus. 10:8.

69. Matt. 21:43.

70. This information is an important part of the evidence that led Jan Fijałek to conclude that Paweł had attended the Council of Pisa where he heard Petrus deliver these comments, had copied them, and could incorporate them into his treatise; see his analysis in *Polonia apud Italos scholastica saeculum XV* (Kraków: Typis Universitatis Jagellonicae, 1900), p. 9, and his "Ostatnie słowo Pawła Włodkowica o zakonie krzyżackim," *Przegląd Kościelny* 1 (1902): 101. Belch, *Paulus Vladimiri*, I, 128, n.2. See also Ehrlich, *Pisma wybrane*, I, 111, n. 162.

71. John 10:16.

72. John 21:17.

73. Eph. 6:9.

74. Col. 4:1.

75. Phil. 4:22.

76. Matt. 17:25.

77. 1 Tim. 6:1.
78. Eph. 6:5.
79. Matt. 21:43.
80. Luke 17:21.
81. Heb. 7:12.
82. Deut. 6:3.
83. Ex. 24:7-8.
84. Deut. 17:8-12.
85. Ecclus. 10:8.
86. Dan. 5:28.
87. 1 Macc. 1:1.
88. Luke 2:1.
89. Ecclu. 10:6-7.

THE OPINION OF OSTIENSIS

(*Opinio Hostiensis*, 1416)[1]

The opinion of Hostiensis[2] is as follows: With the advent of Christ all jurisdiction, principality, honor, and dominion were transferred from the infidels to the faithful; nor does any jurisdiction or any power or dominion or property remain among the infidels today, as, according to the said opinion, they are incapable of this. Further, those infidels who refuse to recognize the Roman Empire are to be pacified in battle, etc.; he also states that wars waged against infidels who do not recognize the Roman Empire are always just and licit for Christians. Although this opinion has found favor amongst some later thinkers, in general, the learned who express themselves in writing on this subject are of the contrary opinion. In this they follow Innocent,[3] as he treats of these things in the chapter *Quod super hiis*: *De voto et voti redempcione.*

Now, this opinion is seen to be seditious and opens the way to much slaughtering of people, and looting as well, since if they are not lords of their property, it will be allowable to any person to occupy and pillage them. And so it is clear that the explanation of such material, so full of dangers, by this holy Council, is urgently necessary.

Whence, in his lecture on this rule of law given at the Council of Pisa, *Peccatum non dimittur* that most famous jurist of both laws in Italy, Pietro de Anchorano,[4] disapproved of this opinion on the grounds of the many absurdities to be deduced therefrom, such as: Christians may steal, take away, and pillage the goods, and occupy and invade the lands of infidels such as do not recognize the Roman Church or Roman Empire without sinning thereby — even if said pagans wish to live in peace with us, and so it follows that this rule 'sin is not remitted,' etc., has no place here. And further, it follows that the prohibitions of divine law: 'Thou shalt not steal,' 'Thou shalt not kill,' by which, according to St Augustine, all plunder and violence are prohibited, have no application. And further, even the law of Nature, such as 'Do not do unto others what you would not have done to yourself,' etc. and many other such prohibitions are not binding upon Christians, etc.[5]

Now, for the easier extirpation of this error, I shall draw up fifty-two conclusions, in which I shall also touch upon their doings [that is, those of the German Knights of the Cross], indicating as well in which circumstances this error is committed; and so that these gentlemen, with whom this business is concerned, should not think that these writings have arisen merely to bring upon them the vituperation of men — let them know that I am not getting myself entangled in their hidden practices, but that I concern myself only with such of their doings as are notorious, for which there is such an abundance of evidence in various lands that there is no way for them to turn their backs on them. Nor am I acting from any motive of vituperating any person or persons, but only to this effect, that such error be done away with by this sacred Council — in so far as any error may be found, and all doubtful matters clarified. And so that all evil suspicions concerning my person be fully allayed, although I am counted amongst my lords as an Ambassador of His Most Serene Majesty, my Lord the King of Poland,[6] etc., I speak here not so much as an Ambassador as a doctor, who does not intend to stubbornly insist upon any erroneous statement, but who rather submits himself to the correction of this Council in all humility.[7] Of course, if there be anything in what I have said or written, or in what I had done in the past, or if there be anything that shall proceed from me in the future, that is noted to be erroneous in law or offensively injurious to anyone, this I do now revoke and declare my will that such be considered as never having been said or written or done. This I solemnly declare, and would have this declaration applied to all of my acts.

Paulus Wladimiri, doctor of the decretals and master of arts, Custodian and Canon of the Church in Kraków.

On Saturday, 6 July, Master Paulus Wladimiri, the doctor stated above, has presented this schedule along with the conclusions of which mention is made in one of its sexterns.

TOPIC.[8] Since the Prussians, infidels at the time, along with others, were raging against the Christian Poles, the Knights of the Cross, also known as the Brothers of the Order of the Blessed Virgin Mary of the Jerusalem Hospitallers of the Teutonic Nation, were admitted into Poland by the princes of that nation. Certain possessions near the territories of the above-mentioned infidels were assigned and given them, and from these possessions, with the aid of the Poles and other Christians, over the course of time they subjugated the cruel Prussians (erstwhile pagans) occupying their dominions in Prussia — for which reason they became known as the 'lords of Prussia.'

In those regions, they have already built cities to be reckoned with, and the strongest and best fortified defensive works wherewith their dominion is so firmly protected that they have been shown to be impregnable to forces up to ten times greater than those who hold them. And although since their subjection the aforementioned Prussians have desisted from inflicting their pagan cruelties upon the Christians, except for such times as, provoked by the Christians themselves, they were wont to pay the Christians back in kind, the Knights of the Cross did not cease in their attacks upon the now gentle and peaceful infidels, but attacked their lands and invaded their dominions, provoking them by irritations of this sort to clash with them, and others, as far as they were able. And so, under the color of the pagans' continual threat to the faithful of Christ, as if they were still raging against us, they summoned other Christians to aid them. As a rule, they invaded the infidel regions twice a year, with a powerful armed force, on the following days and seasons: that of the Assumption and Purification of the glorious Virgin Mary. In their own tongue they call these armed excursions *Reisen*.

And thus the great deception occurs, by which the Christian faithful, wishing to engage in a pious military work, believing thus to be doing service to God, gather there in multitudes, and, motivated by the desire of spreading the Catholic faith, instead are made to attack a peaceful pagan nation with cruelty. What then follows is great homicide, in which the faithful on par with the infidels run the risk of eternal damnation, committing pillaging and other unworthy deeds without end.

In this way the reputation of the Order grows, as does its wealth and its power; the Knights of the Cross make their treasuries swell at the cost of Christians as well as pagans. For they have succeeded in obtaining scripts of both Roman Pontiffs and Emperors that grant them the lands and goods of all infidels they conquer or occupy.

At last, the Spirit of God, Who blows where He lists,[9] inspired the mightiest of the pagan princes, leading them out of their error to the recognition of the true faith, conducting them to the waters of Holy Baptism where they were washed clean of their sins through the ministry of the Poles. One of these assumed the government of the Kingdom of Poland; another remained governor and ruler of Lithuania and other parts thereabout, both pagan and schismatic.

And thus a great multitude of pagans, who had in former times filled the Christian regions of Prussia, Livonia and Poland with such terror and such loss, now, in multitudes, raced to the font of Holy Baptism, to the profession of our sacred faith. Nearly all of those native to Lithuania and subject to the aforesaid princes received the laving of the sacred waters. Others continually request baptism on their own, while still others subject themselves to the government of the newly Christian leaders.

Considering these wonders, the Knights of the Cross, as if concerned at the loss of a pretext for the occupation of lands and the amassing of wealth to the detriment of the aforementioned peoples,[10] with still greater ferocity did they make multiple invasions of these lands, successively, and with wonted cruelty, slaying the above-mentioned neophytes and even the newly baptized, with no regard paid even to priests or religious, burning their new churches to the ground and committing other innumerable outrages, such as modesty enjoins us to pass over in silence.

For they dared insult even their own benefactors, Christians of old, gravely turning upon them, imprisoning Christian princes who had earlier funded them, treating in most foul fashion those who had outfitted their own Order in material goods. At last, calling to their aid a great number of Christians, as if summoning them to wage war against pagan peoples, by this deception did they, unexpectedly, raise a great power against the Catholic King of Poland, hostilely invading the Polish Kingdom. They destroyed its fortified castles, burning others to the ground, looting, raping, and committing many other shameful acts such as the pen is hardly able to express.

Now, while Poland was bewailing the manner in which the Knights of the Cross continued to inflict upon her the very same cruelties that she had suffered at the hands of the Prussians, bemoaning the fact that those, whom she had summoned to her as a defensive shield, should, in their ferocity, have become a scourge to her, Poland did not merely sigh at having fostered such a pestiferous atrocity in her own bosom, for she felt compelled to arise at last in opposition.

The two sides drew up in pitched battle, at the conclusion of which, the battlefield, alas, was strewn with corpses, but the might of the order had been cast down from the heights. The blades of the Poles were slaked with the blood of the Knights of the Cross. This took place on the fifteenth day of July in the year 1410, and then several times afterwards, at intervals.[11]

Now, because the writings aforesaid, worse yet than any sorrow, are seen to have been the occasion for the fomenting of such great calamities, on this topic — quite rightly and evidently — certain questions have arisen, which I have addressed in my tractate on the power of the Pope and the Emperor in respect to infidels.[12] Responses have been made to these questions in the form of fifty-two conclusions. These follow below, extracted from the above-mentioned tractate.

The first conclusion: Even though the infidels are not of the Church's sheepfold, all of them are no less of the flocks of Christ, without a doubt, on account of their very creation. As the Lord says in John 10: 'Other sheep I have, that are not of this fold,'[13] *scil.* the Church. Pope Innocent.

2. And the words spoken to Peter by the Lord Himself, *viz.* 'Feed my sheep,'[14] are to be understood as referring to both the faithful and infidels without distinction. And therefore the successor of Peter ought not only to feed them, but to defend them as well. Those, of whom he is to keep in his care with paternal solicitude, he ought not to attack nor allow to be injured unless a rational cause urges the same. The justification for this is that injury should never proceed from the very font of the law (*De natis ex libero ventre capitulo unico*, Innocent).

3. No Christian prince ought to expel Jews or other infidels from his territories, or despoil them, without just cause. The justification: For the law prohibits those who are keeping the peace from being molested (*Codex De Iudeis* law *Nullus* and the chapter *Multorum*, etc.).

4. Although from the beginning of creation all things were given in common to all, by the law both natural and human distinctions in possession and governance were established (I distincition: *Ius gencium*), therefore, natural law prohibits the occupation of things already occupied by others, according to the rule 'Do not unto others what you would not have others do unto you, etc.' and divine law 'Do not transgress the boundaries set, etc.' (Proverbs XII).[15] Innocent, and others, in general.

5. It is not lawful to take away the dominions or possessions or jurisdictions even of those infidels who do not recognize the Roman Empire, for they possess these things sinlessly, from God who created them for man, without distinction, whom He created in His image and likeness, placing all at his feet, all flocks and herds, etc.[16] St Thomas, Innocent, and others in general.

6. The Holy Land, of which the Saracens are in possession, having been conquered by the Roman Emperor in a just war, is therefore liable to be recalled into his jurisdiction by the Pope, or by others acting in the interest of the Roman Empire. And that also for this reason, that there, where Christ had been worshipped, now the worship of Mahomet has been instituted. Innocent, and Francis.

7. No sufficient cause exists for depriving pagans of dominions and jurisdictions simply because they keep the same out of Roman control. Justification: because these things may never have been subject to the Romans in the first place, due to their lawful occupation by the infidels, for the Romans also had allies who were not at all subject to them. Innocent and Francis de Zabarellis.

8. The Roman Church, which has her authority in the West, and furthermore all other churches, are in lawful possession of their

holdings, there and wherever else, whatever may be asserted concerning their having received the same from the Roman Emperor, who came into the possession thereof by force of arms. Innocent and Francis.

9. Whatever the case may be with heretics and schismatics, that is, that they might well and lawfully be dispossessed of their holdings, still, the faithful are not permitted to occupy these without the sanction of law or a legitimate judgment so passed to that effect. Innocent.

10. In so far as he is the Vicar of Christ, the Pope enjoys power and jurisdiction not only over Christians, but also, in general, over all infidels, though this be only *de iure* and not *de facto*. The justification: Because Christ first possessed the same: (see the final chapter of Matthew):[17] 'All power is given to me in heaven and in earth,' etc. Nor would He be seen to be a diligent father of His family if He did not transfer that power over all to His deputy. Innocent and Francis.

11. Should a pagan who has no law save the law of nature transgress against the natural law, it is right for the Pope to punish him, accordingly as the Sodomites were punished by God for their having sinned against the law of nature (Genesis XIX).[18] Innocent and Francis.

12. Similarly, the Pope has the power to punish those pagans who worship idols. For it is natural to worship the one and only God, and not creatures. Innocent and Francis.

13. The Pope has the power to pass judgement on the Jews if they transgress the law in so far as morality is concerned, or if it is found that they invent heresies against their own law. Innocent and Francis.

14. Although the Pope may, at times, forego the execution of penalties due to all of the above-mentioned, either because he does not possess the faculty to execute such things, or because he restrains himself from doing so on account of the danger or scandal feared to arise upon such actions being carried out, still and all, the jurisdictional power for this does belong to him. Innocent and Francis.

15. The Pope is empowered to declare precepts and constitutions declaring that infidels may not unjustly molest the Christians subject to their temporal authority. Innocent and Francis.

16. Even though the Pope is empowered to entirely remove Christians from the jurisdiction and dominion of infidels, and may even deprive such infidels, by his just sentence, of the dominion and jurisdiction they have over Christians, still he should not do so absent grave cause. On the contrary: he ought rather to sustain the same, as long as this does not result in danger for said Christians nor give rise to grave scandal. Innocent and Francis.

17. Although pagans should not be forced to accept the faith, and their free will should be respected, as only the grace of God may call them to that vocation, as canon law states, still the Pope is empowered to require of the infidels that they admit the preachers of the Gospel into their lands. The justification for this is that all rational creatures have been created to praise God (as in *II libro Sentenciarum* distinction I). Therefore, should they forbid such preaching to take place, they would be sinning and this would merit punishment. Innocent and Francis.

18. In all of what has been said above, in those things in which the Pope is permitted to command the infidels, if they do not obey him by their own free will, they may be compelled to do so by the secular arm. Innocent and Francis.

19. Only the Pope, and no one else but he, is empowered to declare war upon the infidels, unless it be one who is contending for his own rights.

Innocent and Francis take note of nearly all the above points in the document *Quod super hijs*: *De voto et voti redempcione.*

20. From all that is said above, we deduce that when the writings of the Roman pontifex concede to any man or any order the occupation of the lands of the infidels, these concessions are to receive such an interpretation that no violation of anyone's rights should ensue. And if the nature of what is written is not capable of such an interpretation, it is plain that, since an infringement upon someone's just rights is occurring, these letters should be considered suspect, falsifications. And if they are made use of to deprive others of their rights without legitimate reason, they are by law null and void, especially in such cases where the certain knowledge of the Pope is not apparent. The justification: because the act or disposition, which is invalid by its very nature, as it comes not of a legitimate source, if it expresses no sufficient cause, is null and void unless it is apparent that it arises with the full knowledge of the proper authority, who is not able to do any such thing without just cause. And such especially, among all other writings that the Knights of the Cross of Prussia assert themselves as having in their possession, is the letter of Pope Clement. This document not only lacks the full knowledge of the Pope, but nor does it contain any sufficient cause whereby the infidels ought to be despoiled by them, as is clearly proven from the tenor of the copies examined.

The above-cited conclusions concern the first tract: On the power of the Pope respective of the infidels. The conclusions that follow concern the second tract: On the power of the Emperor respective of the infidels.

21. However many minds have been occupied with investigating the foundations of earthly monarchy, the point of view more consonant with the truth and more universally held among the learned is that both jurisdictions, that is, the spiritual and the temporal, belong to the Pope. This opinion is clearly based not only on canon law, but also on natural law and divine law. As far as canon law is concerned, it can be found in many places, for example, in the *extravagans* of Pope Boniface VIII which begins with the incipit *Unam sanctam*, and ends with the conclusion that it is necessary to salvation to believe all human creatures subject to the Roman Pontiff.[19] It is clear from natural law that the best rule is there, where all are subject to the general rule of one ruler (2 *Politicorum*). It is therefore necessary to have one monarch in the world. However, this cannot be the Emperor, because he has no spiritual jurisdiction. Therefore, said ruler must be the Pope. On divine law, Innocent speaks further (in the chapter *Licet*: *de foro competenti*) as does Francis.

22. The Romans amassed their Empire *de facto* through their oppression of other peoples. The same thing must be said of other realms that possessed monarchies, such as Babylon and Macedonia, etc. Cardinal Francis.

23. Although the Emperor may be termed the ruler of the world according to civil law, *de iure*, no lay person has ever had power over other lay persons precedent to a constitution, unless by usurpation of the same, according to John (XCVI distinction: *Si imperator*).[20]

24. Now, however the empire is dependent upon the power of the Pope, who wields both swords, it shall not be allowed anyone to appeal from a decision of the Emperor to the Pope in temporal matters on account of this subordination. Justification: because this

subordination is not of such a nature as to permit the Pope to be understood as the Emperor's superior in so far as actual exercise of power in matters temporal is concerned, but only in a formal sense, except in cases where this is expressed explicitly in law. Caspar and Francis.

25. However true it is that the Church has executed civil jurisdiction through its clergy from time to time, it is more reasonable for the Emperor and kings to wield temporal power, especially in cases of criminals, where soul is separated from body. Justification: For it shall not be fitting for a minister of the New Testament to undertake such things, as the minister of the Gospel is a minister of the sacrament of unity. The first is clear from XI question III: *Relatum*. Caspar, etc.

26. Governance in this world arises in three ways. 1) by the will of God, as revealed unto men in some fashion; 2) by the consent of the governed, and hence justly; 3) by violence and tyranny, and hence unjustly. Now, since it is not clear that the rule of the Emperor over all infidels can be generally justified by the first or second of those measures, as can by said of the Pope according to the most probable proofs aforesaid, it is wrong to assert that the Emperor has any power at all, generally speaking, over the infidels.

27. The Emperor has no right to license the usurpation of pagan lands such as do not recognize his authority. Justification: because his power is not primary, but secondary and subordinate, that is, he possesses the exercise of only such power as is delegated to him.

28. Any writings of the Emperor that grant the Knights of the Cross of Prussia, or anyone else, the right to occupy the lands of the infidels, confer no such power at all. They effect nothing save to deceive faithful Christians, since the Emperor cannot give to others what he does not possess himself. Nor can any letter of the Roman

Pontiff grant them such a privilege, any more than can the rescripts of the Emperor, seeing that such would go against both natural and divine law.

29. Thus, by doing battle, or, rather, by invading the lands of the peaceful pagans in Prussia, on such false authority, the Knights of the Cross have never been waging a just war against them. Justification: All law, natural, divine, canonical and civil, is opposed to those who would invade such peoples as desire to remain at peace. Thus, Natural law: 'Do not unto others as you would not have done unto you;' Divine law: 'Thou shalt not kill,' 'Thou shalt not steal' (Exod. XX),[21] by which words all rapine and all violence are prohibited (XIV question V: *Dixit Dominus*); Canon law: (XXIII, question VIII: *Dispar,* etc.) and Civil law: (*Codice De paganis et eorum sacrificijs,* the law *Christianis*, etc.)

30. Such invasions of pagan lands by the faithful not only exclude love of one's neighbor, but also constitute the illicit usurpation of the goods of others, including the sins of theft and rapine. Justification: Both faithful and infidel, without distinction, are our neighbors (*De penitencia* distinction II: *Non illi tantum proximi*, and the canon *Proximos*).

31. It is not permissible to compel pagans to the Christian faith by force of arms or oppression. Justification: because in so doing, injury is caused to one's neighbors, and evils are not to be done so that good may result therefrom; as the canon says: A novel and unheard-of thing is this preaching that enforces the faith by blows (XLV distinction: *Quid autem*).

32. Although the decretal of the general council of Toledo commanding that blandishments, and not roughness, ought to be used to

persuade men to convert was formulated with the Jews in mind, by the fact of the law applying to all men, this ought to be extended to all infidels in general. For whoever proceeds otherwise proves himself to have his own affairs, rather than those of God, in mind. (This text is literally excerpted from XLV distinction: *De Iudeis* etc.)

33. It is an error completely intolerable that Christians should gather to the aid of the aforesaid Prussian Knights of the Cross for the invasion of the lands of peaceful pagans simply because the latter are pagans, or because such a cause is offered for the exercise of their knightly profession or the spreading of the Christian faith. Justification: piety cannot be the pretext for the commission of impious acts, etc. (XXX question 1: *Nosse*, etc.) The exception to this is the war waged by the Spaniards against the Saracens, which was undertaken for the recuperation of lands long occupied, which had earlier been inhabited by Christians (according to Oldradus in question LXXII).

34. Those who fall impenitent in such an unjust war are to be esteemed as having merited the fate of the impious and the damned. For one does not bring help to anyone by aiding him to sin (See canon XIII question VI: *Si res*).

35. However it be that a soldier, particularly a Catholic soldier, who is not a subject of the lord waging a war, ought to be certain as to the justice of said war in which he is to fight, otherwise he would be exposing himself to grave danger should the justice of the conflict be dubious, still, if he is subject to the lord in question he is excused of blame for engaging in the dubious struggle on account of his serving his liege lord in so doing. This is true if he studied the matter as closely as he could and consulted those more experienced than he, but still remains unsure (according to Raymundus and Ostiensis).[22]

36. Now, fear of being deprived of temporal goods is no excuse for a subject to engage in a war he knows or is inclined to believe to be unjust. Justification: Because even though fear extenuates guilt, it does not exclude it entirely (see the chapter: *Sacris*: *De hijs que vi metusve causa*). Ostiensis.

37. Although, according to the doctors, five conditions are necessary for a war to be declared just, that is: the person, the object, the cause, the spirit and the authority, still a sixth ought never to be omitted, that is: the proper time. Justification: because there are times in which even just wars are prohibited (*De treuga et pace*, chapter 1, etc.).

38. Only in cases of necessity, which has no law, can one be held sinless for doing battle on holy days and days of festival. But this exemption does not apply to those who invade the lands of others of their own free will. This is proven by the example of the Maccabees (II Maccabees, final chapter, etc.).[23]

39. Any work that is servile in a material sense, that is, in and of itself, as well as in a formal sense, respective to the agent thereof, is prohibited on the Sabbath. Richardus.[24]

40. Those works that are servile solely in a material sense or solely in a formal sense are not to be considered strictly prohibited. Justification: Because it is more difficult to abstain from them than from the first. And therefore he does not sin mortally who engages in them, unless in so doing he excludes the free time that is necessary for the respect due to divine worship. Richardus.[25]

41. There is no doubt but that to invade pagan lands and also fight, or to draw to the attack especially with armies or arms and other

materiel convenable to war making, is in and of itself both materially and formally a servile work, save in cases of necessity in so far as the aims of those so acting are for temporal gain. This is all the more worthy of vituperation, the more damnable is the aim in respect to the invaders, to wit: the lust of domination or appropriation of the goods and realms of others, the occupation of their lands; this is that cupidity, which is the root of all evil.[26]

42. It is an error that violates the Lord's Commandment of keeping holy the Lord's Day when the Knights of the Cross, from the mere desire of waging war, are used to set out on their customary *Reisen* twice a year, and chiefly on the solemnities especially dedicated to the Blessed Virgin Mary, that is to say, the Feasts of the Assumption and the Purification. For this act of theirs, spurred by cupidity or the lust of domination, is prohibited, as it extinguishes the spiritual peace of God (Jeremiah IX: 'they have labored to commit impiety,' etc.).[27] Ostiensis.

43. The observances of the Knights of the Cross, invading the lands of the pagans and prosecuting other belligerent activities of this sort, in so far as they are especially carried out on the aforementioned holy days, are to be considered superstitious acts, which exclude any devotion to piety. And in so far as they consider waging war on these particular days to be a guarantee of their successful outcome, this rite of theirs is entirely contrary to the Christian religion. The justification for this may be found in the canon *Illud quod est*: XXVI question II, and is proved on the authority of St Augustine (Book I *De doctrina Christiana* and the same case, question V: *Non licet*, etc.). And thus the Apostle (Galatians 4):[28] 'You observe days, and months, and times, and years,' etc. For it does not seem that in respect to the Blessed Virgin, such a day should provide such justification, as if the Blessed Virgin were more amenable to such activity on account

of her holy day, as if her power to aid were restricted to such days, or as if such 'homage' done her then would render such things any more honorable or acceptable to her, etc. But as far as the agents are concerned, it is not that the day should be considered as supposedly more propitious to the success of their intentions, as rather that such action on such a day excludes the very piety that ought to be the first principle of all action.

44. Those subjects of the Knights of the Cross who participate in their twice-yearly *Reisen* against peaceful pagans are not absolved of sin, and this for the same reason as if without the authority of law or judge they were to make war against Christians. The justification: Because God must be obeyed before man, nor is ignorance of the law, especially natural law and divine law, any excuse. Ostiensis.

45. The party attacking justly cannot be resisted by the attacked without sinning thereby. Rather, he is obliged to seek a wiser solution. Ostiensis.

46. Goods taken in an unjust war cannot lawfully belong to the takers, nor can any such thing be retained by them without sin. Justification: For such a thing stolen or possessed by force is said to be wrongly held, and neither thief nor bandit nor anyone else who purchases it or otherwise comes into its possession from the hands of such even in good faith can hold it by adverse possession or any common-law title. (*Institucionibus*: *De usucapionibus* § *Furtive et* § *Quod autem*). Ostiensis.

47. At the risk of salvation itself, all things held in such a manner must, as far as possible, be restored to their rightful owner, nor may any portion thereof be retained, save as compensation of a liquidated nature for items of a liquidated nature; but such compensation can

only be effected in court penitential. Justification: Because sin cannot be absolved without the restitution of what had been wrongfully taken, etc.

48. The leader of an army in such a war, or any other authority, shall be held accountable not only for the rapine, murder, and other crimes that he himself commits, but also for those perpetrated by others. And these include not only his own men, but also those fighting against his troops. Ostiensis.

49. Justice must not be denied to infidels who appeal to a Christian judge for the restitution of what has been stolen from them or taken from them by force. Justification: According to Innocent, they too have a right to just dominion over what belongs to them.

50. A Christian ruler may, in cases of imminent need, in his own defense and that of his lands, sinlessly take advantage of the aid of pagans — and not only those who are subject to him, but others as well. It is to be understood that we are speaking here of peaceful pagans such as are not at war with us, actively or passively. This is proven by the example of the Maccabees who, although they were holy men and champions of the faith, compacted with the Romans, pagan at the time, to aid one another reciprocally (I Maccabees chapter VIII),[29] nor were they impeded in doing so by the Law (II Paralipomenon XIX):[30] 'Thou helpest the ungodly, and thou art joined in friendship with them that hate the Lord, and therefore thou didst deserve indeed the wrath of the Lord,' because these words to the contrary are to be understood as concerning the case of an unjust war. Such is the conclusion of Johannes Andreae *in Addicionibus Speculi de Iudeis et Saracenis*, in which tract multiple proofs are given, with which Oldradus is in agreement (question LXXI).

51. It is impious and absurd to assert that today pagans are entirely incapable of possessing any jurisdiction, honor, power, or dominion, because this seditious assertion opens wide the path to homicide and rapine. For if they were incapable of such things, it would be allowable for anyone to loot or occupy that, which is theirs. From which the conclusion derived would be that Christians might, sinlessly, steal, loot, or invade the lands and goods of infidels, even such as wish to live in peace with us, giving no regard to the prohibitions of the Law, that is: 'Thou shalt not steal,' 'Thou shalt not kill,' by which all rapine and violence are prohibited, as stated above. Thus, what is generally conceded to the pagans by the law of human society must not be denied them (XXIII question II: *Notandum,* etc.).

52. So great an error as to suggest that all honor, dominion, and jurisdiction has been taken away from the pagans at the advent of Christ is not to be asserted; rather, it is to be denied. For as St Thomas states: 'Although the infidels should not now be newly set up as lords or authorities over the faithful, on account of the danger that such would present to the faith, still and all, such preexisting dominion as they enjoy of old is not to be taken from them. For infidelity *eo ipso* is not contrary to dominion, on account of the fact that dominion and authority are things instituted by human law, that is, by the law of nations, while the distinction between faithful and infidel is a matter of divine law, and divine law, which proceeds from grace, does not do away with human law, which proceeds from natural reason' (*Secunda Secunde*, Question IX, art. X).

Given at the General Council in Constance before all four nations of which it is constituted, that is to say, the Italians, the Gauls, the English, and the Germans by myself, Master Paweł Włodkowic, doctor of the decretals, Custodian and Canon of the Church in Kraków, being also concurrently rector of the University of Kraków,[31] with the intent that all doubtful matters in this issue should be solved and all erroneous things reformed to the salvation of all by this same sacred General Council. And should anyone wish to see the above-given conclusions, he shall be able to do so along with the allegations more amply laid out in the above-mentioned tractate[32] presented to the German Nation on 5 July in the year of Our Lord 1415.

Endnotes

1. It is clear that this treatise was presented after the distribution of *Saevientibus*. If the dating issues connected with *Saevientibus*, noted above in its translation, n. 1, lead to the conclusion that it is a product of 1416, then *Opinio Ostiensis* also should be dated 1416. This problem, which was raised earlier by the Polish scholar Paul Nieborowski, *Der Deutsche Orden und Polen in der Zeit des grössten Konflikts*, 2nd ed. (Wrocław [Breslau]: Wahlstaat-Verlag, 1924), pp. 159 and 190, is discussed by Belch, *Paulus Vladimiri*, II, 852-854, who concludes that both treatises should be dated to 1415. Apart from possibly altering some chronological matters in the history of the Council of Constance, the dating issues affect neither the substance nor significance of Paweł's work.

2. Hostiensis (Henricus de Segusio, 1190/1200-1271) studied canon law at Bologna at the same time as Sinibaldo dei Fieschi (the future Pope Innocent IV). He subsequently taught at Paris and was named cardinal-bishop of Ostia in 1261. His important body of canonical writings and his influence ensured he was highly regarded. Dante includes him in *Paradiso* in his *Commedia*: 12:82-97. See Brundage, *Canon Law*, p. 214.

3. Pope Innocent IV (reigned 1243-1253), who studied canon law and eventually taught it at Bologna. His very successful career led him eventually into the papal curia, where he was assistant and counsellor to Cardinal Hugolino of Ostia, later Pope Gregory IX (d. 1241). See Brundage, *Canon Law*, pp. 225-226.

4. Peter of Ancharano (*ca.* 1330-1416), perhaps one of Paweł's teachers at Padua and whom he most probably knew. He was especially influential in the late fourteenth and early fifteenth century and was, as Paweł notes, a participant in the Council of Pisa (1409) and of Constance, where he was an adherent of Pope John XXIII. See Brundage, *Canon Law*, p. 180 and p. 207.

5. This general principle in natural law (in another version known as "the Golden Rule") is mentioned multiple times by Paweł, but without reference to any specific source. Along with the law of nations, natural law is central to much of Paweł 's thought. See the comments of Belch, *Paulus Vladimiri*, II, 860.

6. i.e., Władysław Jagiełło (*ca.* 1348?-1434), former pagan Grand Duke of Lithuania, who converted to Latin Christianity in 1385.

7. Unlike his self-identification in *Saevientibus* that made no mention of his status as a royal representative, Paweł here includes this information, even while emphasizing his status as scholar. For further information on his academic status, see Paweł's statement below, n. 31.

8. What follows, until reaching the section of the numbered fifty-two conclusions, is a summary that covers much of the same material Paweł presented in the first part of his treatise *Saevientibus*. For the most part, annotation there is not here repeated.

9. John 3:8.

10. The crucial word here is "pretext." Paweł's point lays the foundation for his argument in other contexts in these several treatises that the cause for which the Teutonic Order was established no longer exists and that therefore the effect of their creation (i.e., their very existence) should also cease and that the Order should be abolished. This is particularly evident in the arguments in his treatise *Ad Aperiendam*, part I of 1416 (entitled *Causa inter reges Poloniae et Cruciferos coram Concilio Constantiense dicta A.D. 1416* by Belch, *Paulus Vladimiri*, I, 169). See the edition and translation in Ehrlich, *Pisma wybrane*, I, 144-259, here pp. 162-163, and the discussion in Paul W. Knoll, *"A Pearl of Powerful Wisdom." The University of Cracow in the Fifteenth Century* (Leiden and Boston: 2016), p. 437.

11. This is the battle of Grunwald. See the similar statement in the treatise *Saevientibus*, n. 8.

12. i.e., *Saevientibus*. Many of the points that follow are treated by Paweł at greater length in it.

13. John 10:16.

14. John 21:17.

15. Prov. 22:28.

16. Ps. 8:8

17. Matt. 28:18.

18. Gen. 19:12-29.

19. See *Saevientibus*, n. 40.

20. The canonist Johannes Teutonicus is meant here (see *Saevientibus*, n. 30), not the Gospel of John.

21. Ex. 20:13 and 15.

22. Hostiensis, whom Paweł is apparently quoting negatively, may, according to Belch, *Paulus Vladimiri*, II, 879, n. 178, be quoting Ramón de Penyafort (1180/1185-1275), a Catalan who studied and taught at Bologna, whom Pope Gregory IX (Hugolinus)—himself an expert canonist—commissioned to prepare the compilation of canons that eventually was published as the *Liber extra*). For Ramón, see Brundage, *Canon Law*, pp. 222-223..

23. 2 Macc. 15:1ff.

24. Belch, *Paulus Vladimiri*, II, 879, n. 137, suggests this is a reference to a writing of Richard of S. Victor (*ca.* 1123-1173), a mystical theologian and eventual prior of the abbey of St. Victor in Paris.

25. See previous note.

26. Paweł here implicitly quotes 1 Tim. 6:10, where the Latin reads "Radix enim omnium malorum est cupiditas." In the twelfth century, the cleric and satirist Walter Map changed *cupiditas* (cupidity) to *avaritia* (avarice or greed) to make the first letters of the words in the phrase spell **R**[adix] **O**[mnium] **M**[alorum] **A**[varitia] = **ROMA**, a not so-subtle critique of the papacy. This outlook would have resonated well with parts of the academic and political leadership Paweł would have been familiar with in Kraków. These included Matthew

of Kraków, whose treatise *De praxis* [*squaloribus*] *Romanae Curiae* of 1405 was a scathing indictment of the papacy's leadership. (It also was to figure in the role Johannes Falkenberg played in the Cracovian and conciliar scene.) Another treatise from this period was the *Speculum aureum de titulis beneficiorum ecclesiasticorum* of Peter Wysz, bishop of Kraków, which attacks papal simony. (This work was at one time attributed—but incorrectly—to Paweł Włodkowic.) On these two works, see the treatment, with reference to Polish and other European scholarship, in Knoll, "*A Pearl of Powerful Learning*," pp. 509-511.

27. Jer. 9:5.

28. Gal. 4:10.

29. 1 Macc. 8:17-30.

30. 2 Chron. 19:2

31. This is an important statement of Paweł's status: he was both a royal ambassador and a distinguished academic. These qualifications marked him out as someone of particular importance and are reflected in a summary of his career path. He had undertaken university studies in Bohemia and later legal studies in canon law in Italy, where he gained the license in decretals at Padua in 1408. After returning to Poland, he pursued, with papal permission, the doctoral degree in canon law at the newly reestablished University of Kraków. He was promoted to Doctor of Decretals, probably in 1411 upon the recommendation of Stanisław of Skarbimierz, professor of canon law, who argued—in part—that in addition to his studies, Paweł's knowledge of secular matter and service *pro profectu Rei publice* qualified him for promotion. Within three years he was elected rector of the *studium*. Though there is no formal record of his re-election, he is listed as rector for 1415 also. See Antoni Gąsiorowski, Tomasz Jurek, and Izabela Skierska, eds., with the assistance of Ryszard Grzesik, *Metryka Uniwersytetu Krakowskiego z lat 1400-1508*, 2 vols. (Kraków: Societas Vistulana, 2004), here I, liii and 81-82. What this means is that the treatise *Opinio Hostiensis*—and by extension also *Saevientibus*—had been prepared and presented to the *nationes* of the Council of Constance by a figure of substance and status and deserved to taken seriously.

32. i.e., *Saevientibus* (or, as Belch entitles it, *De potestate papae et imperatoris respectu infidelium*).

ARTICLES AGAINST THE PRUSSIAN KNIGHTS OF THE CROSS

(*Articuli contra Cruciferos de Prussia*, 1416)[1]

Prologue A[2]

And because Our Savior promised in the Gospel that you are to 'beware of false prophets, who come to you in the clothing of sheep, but inwardly they are ravening wolves,' adding immediately thereafter 'by their fruits you shall know them,' because 'an evil tree cannot bring forth good fruit,' etc. (Matthew VII):[3] Now, the fruits of this pestiferous sect are seen to consist not only in said erroneous letters and the aforementioned articles, but also in their criminal deeds and works which are wholly contrary to the Christian religion. And therefore, having considered the abovementioned, which are seen to concern more the theory of this matter, we must now approach its practical aspect, and initiate an investigation by virtue of the office of this sacred Council, before which these articles have been denounced, as we believe them to be notorious and seething with public infamy; these are inscribed below.

Prologue B

In the Name of Our Lord Jesus Christ. Amen. Because the present General Council of Constance has chiefly been convoked, and congregated in the Holy Spirit, for three things: First, that pestiferous schism be cleansed from the Church; second, that heresies be extirpated; and third, for the reformation of the Church to be made in its head as well as its members, not omitting the other two:[4]

As far as the second of these is concerned, Our Savior teaches us how we are to proceed (in the Gospel of Matthew, chapter VII): 'Beware of false prophets, who come to you in the clothing of sheep, but inwardly they are ravening wolves,' adding 'by their fruits you shall know them,' and a little afterward 'an evil tree cannot bring forth good fruit,' etc. Therefore, the fruits of the Prussian heresy — which are to be seen as not less, but indeed much greater, more horrible, much worse and much more damnable than those of the Wycliffites and Hussites, *viz.*, those of the Brethren known as the Brethren of the Hospital of the Blessed Virgin Mary of the Teutonic House in Jerusalem, otherwise, of Prussia, are set forth in the articles inscribed below.

The instigator, promotor, and procurator of the cause of the Faith, deputized by this Sacred Council, gives, makes, and exhibits the below-inscribed articles, seething as they are with public infamy, to the effect, as far as [...][5] against them, etc.[6]

1. First of all,[7] it is lain down, stated and asserted, that the aforesaid Brethren of the Teutonic House, alias of Prussia, known as the Brethren of the Hospital of the Blessed Virgin Mary in Jerusalem, falling away from the path of the Catholic Faith to wander the treacherous

wastes, rather than to proceed along the right path, erring among the steepest cliffs of guilt, firmly continue to maintain and assert, as ever they have maintained and asserted, however falsely, erroneously, brashly, impiously and insanely, against evangelical law as well against as the Catholic and apostolic Faith and against the truth of the divine Scriptures, that each and every infidel 'on account of their perfidy should without a doubt be propelled beyond the bounds of this world by the faithful.'[8]

Likewise, they say, firmly maintain, and assert, however tacitly and implicitly, that a religious order may be instituted for the purpose of exterminating whatever sort of infidels, and wresting their dominions from their hands; they maintain furthermore and even expressly assert that this order of theirs, which pretends to be — to use their own words — 'chiefly and specially instituted' or confirmed *de facto* 'by the Roman pontiffs' to these very tasks: 'in order to invade the lands of any enemies of the Cross of Christ whatsoever, exterminating them with might, and wresting their lands or dominions from their hands, converting the same to their own use for the augmentation of the Catholic Faith, which not only can be, but indeed is, and should be, the case.'[9]

Likewise, that it was licit for this Order of theirs, albeit extended, to invade all neighboring lands held by infidels, and to wrest the goods, possessions, lands and dominions from their hands, converting the same to their own use. And indeed they state, maintain, and assert things of this sort, and quite a few others similar thereto — these and other statements are clearly and more broadly contained in their articles, and offered and produced by them at judicial appointment, with the Most Serene King of Poland as the adverse party. And these they did offer and produce, *viz.*, before the Most Serene Prince, Lord Sigismund, King of the Romans and of Hungary, acting as principal arbiter in the case, and also before that noble man, Lord Benedict of Macra, of Hungary, sub-arbiter and deputy of the same

King of the Romans,[10] both of whom had been chosen and accepted by the consent of both parties. It is to these articles and acts and legal entries produced in this case that said promoter and procurator refers. Thus it has been, and remains, true, public knowledge, and notorious, thus held publicly and notoriously, just as they have maintained, *viz.*, offering and producing, as said above, and as they continue to maintain such things — that they are and have been public and notorious heretics,[11] and for such they are to be held, judged, and taken.

2. Likewise, as the said Brethren, being as they are public and notorious heretics, intending by falsehoods and false means to obtain in this way the dominions of others, and to color their heresy in some way, they made use of, and they continue to make use of, some sort of letters, privileges, or pretended bulls, producing them in the abovesaid legal process, as indeed they did produce these letters, privileges, and so-called bulls however utterly false, unjust and iniquitous, heretical and weakening of charity towards one's fellow man, thereby providing a path to homicide, rapine and many other evils; letters and writings that contain many scandalous errors offensive to pious ears, and that not only in law, but in Faith as well, as is clearly proven and can be proven by their very tenor, to which, or at least to the words of their privileges thus delivered in the legal process and contained in the Register of the same case, the aforesaid promoter and procurator makes reference. And such was and is the public and notorious truth.

Now, these letters, privileges and bulls differ amongst themselves evidently in two ways: there are two ascribed to Emperor Frederick II, and one ascribed to Emperor Lewis IV. Similarly, two are ascribed to the Roman Pontiffs, viz., Alexander IV and Clement IV.[12] Upon these aforesaid pretended letters, privileges, or bulls, more than any other letters, privileges or bulls produced by these Brethren in the aforesaid legal case, these most set forth their intention, however erroneous, unjust, iniquitous and heretical, as if they were a foundation, however null and invalid, upon which their claims are seen to be based — and thus they have founded and continue to found said claims, however, invalidly, still de facto, upon them. By both groups of these letters, privileges, or bulls, by any one or by all them together, they pretend to the ownership of some lands, viz., Lithuania, Rus, and Samogitia (Żmudź), as if due to them *de iure*; but this they do pertinaciously, brashly, iniquitously and unjustly, because possession of any thing may be acquired only from one cause at any particular time. Furthermore, they even claim to have received of the aforesaid Emperor Frederick a donation of these lands, expressly and specifically, viz., Prussia, Lithuania, Courland, Lettonia, and Żmudź, possessed and inhabited by infidels, and moreover the land of Russia, inhabited by schismatics, as if they were pagans, too. They make the same claim in regard to all other lands of any pagans whatsoever, such as said Brethren might succeed in penetrating and conquering, banners and standards aloft. This claim they make falsely, erroneously, unjustly and iniquitously. For the Emperor is unable to make any such pretended donation of anything that is not his own, or is not in any way in his power, for no man can give away anything which does not belong to him. And notwithstanding the fact that they award themselves this 'donation' of said lands from said Roman Pontiffs, who in these letters, privileges, or bulls seem to give these Brethren all lands of any infidels, whatsoever, that they, aided by Christian armies, should succeed in wresting from the hands of infidels — this donation is likewise false, erroneous, unjust and iniquitous. For saving legal cases where justice is served thereby, neither Pope nor Emperor can transfer a single thing belonging to someone else, something which is not his own, to another, except in cases of evident exigency, in which public utility is concerned, and due recompense is given to the party so deprived. Otherwise, such an act would go against natural law and divine law, although recompense might be withheld in cases of the insolence or the malice of an offender — which might be more the case amongst unbelievers not subject to their authority. And unbelievers are not to be considered as subject to any civil or canon law, but rather natural law, although in that case, consequently, divine law, too.[13] Now, because such does not, legitimately, appear to be the case with these letters, in consequence, it cannot appear that these pretended donations are valid, and said letters, privileges, or bulls are false and erroneous. As indeed they are: for it would not seem probable, indeed it would savour of impiety and brashness, to think that such princes of the world, leaders of the law, would be so gravely and deliriously deficient in the law — seeing that 'And the Roman Pontiff' has 'all laws within the coffer of his breast' (Chapter 1 *De constitucionibus* I, 2), or that they should be so depraved and insane as by such pretended letters or privileges to give to another licence to loot the dominions of others, or to wish to clear the way for homicides and so many other evils, or that in planting the seeds for so impious an error they should wish to plant this heresy which is not only contrary to natural law, but also contrary to the commandments of divine law, evangelical truth and the Catholic and apostolic Faith. The consequence of this is that said Brethren, in so thrusting this heresy upon the aforesaid Pontiffs and Emperors, are overbold, impious, and insane, injurious and obnoxious, guilty of the crime of lèse-majesté. And as they themselves are the authors of the aforesaid heretical letters, pretended privileges or bulls, they are iniquitous counterfeiters and masters of falsity. And thus, by common law they are and have been excommunicated twice over, and that by a double excommunication: for they are not just as it were falsifiers, but also as it were heresiarchs and the inventors of a new heresy. Similarly, by producing said letters and making use of the same, notoriously and publicly, as they have used and continue to use them, said Brethren have been and are public and notorious counterfeiters, heresiarchs and excommunicate, and as such they are to be understood, judged, and held.

3. Likewise, said Brethren, heresiarchs and counterfeiters and, moreover, public and notorious excommunicates, somehow under the cloak of religion wish to palliate this heresy of theirs, having pretended as they continue to pretend, that their society or sect is a religious order instituted and confirmed by the Roman Pontiffs by virtue of the aforesaid letters, privileges, or bulls, for the spreading of the Faith, *viz.*, by force of arms and by warmaking, just as they assert in said articles of theirs, to which the aforesaid procurator makes reference. However, falsely they assert this, temerariously and iniquitously: for they are not a religious order, but an erroneous sect, entirely immersed in the greatest of errors as shall appear from the following — a sect invented by the temerity of these Brethren, flouting canonical sanction — not for the amplification of the Faith, but seeking — 'the things that are their own, not those [...] of Jesus Christ' (Phil. II),[14] as their manner of converting people to the Faith by arms of war is not what Christ taught, but rather the promptings of the fallen angel, Satan. For Christ taught His disciples differently, saying: 'Go ye into the whole world, and preach the gospel to every creature,' etc., 'He that believeth and is baptized shall be saved' (Mark XVI).[15] He never said 'those who believe not shall face the sword,' or 'have their earthly goods taken from them.' But said Brethren, also, wishing to simulate religion of some sort for this sect of theirs, call themselves Brethren of the Hospital of Jerusalem of the Blessed Virgin Mary of the Germans.' So do they call themselves, so have they called themselves and thus have become used to calling themselves, however fictionally and falsely: for such was and might have been the case — but minus the existence of such a hospital in the real world, as no such thing is considered to be, nor ever was, at least for such a long time absent from the memory of man as to be unremembered, thus their nomenclature is fictive. And even though it is said that such a thing as said hospital did once exist in Acre, a city in the province of Jerusalem, from which said Brethren are said to have emerged, and where their pretended

order is said to have had its origins, this supposed fact still exceeds the memory of every person living at the present time. Now, moreover, these same Brethren, pretending, under the name of the aforesaid hospital, however fake that name be, and even cloaking themselves in the habit of some order of regular religious, although it be a simulated order, having no rule at all, unless so simulated and pretended a one, their 'iniquity hath lied to itself' (Psalm XXVI).[16] For as is, was, and has been the case, that they are far away from leading, of having led, a religious life in any religious hospital or hospitals, *viz.*, where they have made the vows of a religious regular, there or in any other establishment subject to such a hospital intended for the use of a religious order and said religious rule — and, as they do not lead such a religious life in it or in them (as none such exist), they make a profession which is not a profession at all, nor have they professed such a vow or led such a life nor are in they in the habit of so doing, even for such a long time as exceeds the memory of man. Since such does not exist as far as memory stretches backward, it cannot be said that they are what they pretend to be — men living in a regular, professed religious order, *scilicet* Brethren of the aforesaid hospital. And this is a notorious public fact. And therefore, doing so, they do it, as has been said, publicly and notoriously, seduced by their cupidity, thus they are, were, and have been, simulators, public and notorious hypocrites, and as such they should be understood, held, and even judged.

4. Likewise, said Brethren, simulators and notorious public hypocrites as they truly are, just like false prophets clad in the aforesaid habit of religiosity, wish to appear as it were in sheep's clothing, so that they might disguise their inner, wolfish rapacity and all the more rage against men as they have raged, savaging wildly as they have been accustomed to savage — among men who, even granting that they are infidels, were still creatures created by God and sharing our nature, participating therein as our fellow men — attacking them with the

most ferocious wars, perturbing, molesting, and oppressing them, seizing their possessions and dominions and usurping them in such a way as to gain control of them for themselves, however overboldly, unjustly, and iniquitously, infringing thereby natural law and the laws of human society, however much against the charity owed one's neighbor and against the commandments of the Decalogue, subverting the Gospel and the orthodox Faith, even against the laws, both human and divine, and vilely doing evil. And this was and is the truth, public and notorious. And as they do so publicly and notoriously, as they do and have done, they are, were, and have been false prophets and heretics, as well as public and notorious persecutors of the Christian faith, and for such they are to be considered, held, judged, and even repudiated, according to the Lord's words in the Gospel: 'Beware of false prophets, who come to you in the clothing of sheep, but inwardly they are ravening wolves' (Matthew VII).[17]

5. Likewise, the aforesaid Brethren, being publicly and notoriously false prophets, heretics, and persecutors of the Christian Faith, from time immemorial, and from the time of the given letters, privileges and bulls aforesaid and pretended, and before this and continually, every year or just about every year, as expressed below, were, and now are in so far as it is in them, or in their sect or society, their use, practice, and custom to invade with strong forces of armed men the aforesaid lands of the infidels, attacking, perturbing, molesting, and even oppressing them, looting their possessions and usurping their dominions. And this is public, notorious truth. In so doing, publicly and notoriously, as they had and have done, they are and have been not only heretics, but public and notorious nurturers of ancient heresies, and should be held and understood as such.

6. Likewise, not only are they public and notorious heretics and nurturers of ancient heresy, as they are, but also by said letters, privi-

leges, or pretended bulls offered in their defense, as they do and have done, even though these letters, privileges and bulls are wholly erroneous in morals and in faith, as has been said above — and this is also true concerning the goods and dominions so erroneously acquired by these Brethren or which may be acquired by them henceforth in their contentions, litigations with, and stubborn resistance to the Most Serene King of Poland, or others; which letters, privileges, or articles abovesaid have been produced in legal process as has been mentioned, or fabricated in their defense, as they do and have done publicly and notoriously, however pertinaciously, temerariously, iniquitously, and unjustly, just as is clear from all these acts and entries in the said legal process — they are and have been public and notorious, pertinacious heretics, and as such should be considered, held, and even reputed, and what is more, according to the Evangelical doctrine, they are as it were a sterile fig, a desiccated tree, which bringeth forth evil fruit, and which is to be cut down and destroyed (Matthew VII).[18]

7. Likewise, said Brethren, notorious heretics notoriously pertinacious in their heresy, of entirely hardened heart, indeed, obstinately devoted as they are to the pursuit of their heresy with all their strength, as it were by law or rule, twice every year, gather together in strong forces of armed men, at times which they consider most apt and accommodating, *viz.*, in the month of February in the winter, and in the month of July[19] in the summer, to invade lands once pagan, but now indeed by the grace of God operating there converted to the Faith. They invade various regions, now these, now others, excepting such times as when because of flooding or other such natural impediments, they are unable to move their armed forces there — forthwith to fall upon said infidels there residing, even those peaceful and gentle ones who in no way molest the Christian people, unless so provoked by said Brethren, irritated and vexed and disturbed by the Christians first. And here they indeed attack, invade, disturb,

and molest the lands, possessions, and dominions belonging to these infidels, and also rape and seize the families there resident as well as seizing other goods for themselves and committing and perpetrating arson, homicide, and many other evil acts, however injuriously, temerariously, unjustly, cruelly, and iniquitously. And these things are not merely done twice yearly, but indeed however many times and whenever it seems to please said Brethren to do so. And indeed in their vulgar speech they call these invasions, or turns of invasions, *Reisen*. And this has been and is so in use by them, in practice and in custom, conducted and commonly practiced, that it is believed by many of Christ's faithful to be not merely permissible, but pious, religious, and meritorious, however it was and is impious, erroneous, temerarious, illicit, heretical, and unjust. This has been and is the public and notorious truth.

8. Likewise, the aforesaid brethren, being pertinacious heretics and even hardened in their error, going from bad to worse, contemptuously disregarding Almighty God and His Holy Mother, the glorious ever-Virgin Mary, conduct and have conducted their invasions, turns, or *Reisen* aforesaid on major holy days specifically dedicated to the Blessed Virgin Mary, *viz.*, on Assumption Day and the Day of the Virgin Mary's Purification, at the times and months aforesaid, as commonly and regularly it has become customary of them to do, although in vile contempt of ecclesiastical constitution and the custom of the Church universal, that is, as on such days and other days of festival there is to be no fighting, even if the war were otherwise a just one, unless urgent necessity dictated it at such an untimely period. This is the public and notorious truth.

9. Likewise, said Brethren, depraved with their heretical perversity, wishing to fulfil, as it were, the object of their desire more easily by begging the assent of others, attracted many Christian soldiers

and Christian men of arms to their aid, convincing them, as they continue to attract and convince such unto them, according to their custom, although underhandedly, with lies and iniquitously: and these, *viz.*, under the above-mentioned cloak of piety, were and are seduced as if fighting on behalf of the spread of the Catholic Faith, deceived by the error of these Brethren's heresy as if they were infected by some damnable and pestiferous toxin. Thus, men of divers status from various parts of the Christian world, seduced by such an error, deceived, and equally infected, have gathered and continue to gather every year in great numbers unto the aid of these Brethren for purposes of warmaking, as has been their custom to congregate and gather, especially at the above-mentioned times and seasons, to undertake such *Reisen* along with these Brethren against the infidels, in such manner to invade, attack, disturb, and molest said infidels, as well as to perpetrate upon them all the aforesaid crimes, however erroneously, impiously, temerariously, and unjustly, except for the last six years or so, during which the *Reisen* against the infidels have been suspended.[20] This was and is the truth, public and notorious, and such it has been proclaimed, held, believed, and reputed, as it is proclaimed, held, believed, and reputed openly, publicly, and notoriously; it has also been and remains public knowledge and report.

10. Likewise, by so attacking and invading the aforementioned infidels and setting foot upon their lands and dominions, however cruelly, injuriously, temerariously and unjustly waging wars of this sort aided by said armies of fighting men and the powers of Christ's faithful, as mentioned above, many notable lands and great dominions of whole regions have been eviscerated year by year of such infidels, depriving them of their power, however unduly, injuriously, violently, and unjustly — *scilicet*: Prussia, Courland, Lettonia and a great and notable portion of the land of the Samogitians, as well as other lands and dominions so subjected to expulsion and extraction,

such as they either hold now in their power, or occupy, however less than justly, unduly, and iniquitously, to the great danger of their own souls, while they inflict great prejudice and grievous injury upon those suffering harm at their hands, and upon their successors. And such has been and is the truth, public and notorious.

11. Likewise, although *de iure* it truly is that whatever regular religious one choose to mention, who profess to be of some hospital, monastery, or any other such religious establishment of this or any sort, observing their rule or way of life by virtue of their profession and solemn vow, whether in a community or on their own, the same being incapable of possessing any dominion of any sort, whether over possessions or things, outside of the goods belonging to their hospitals, monasteries, or pious establishments provided by the pious devotion of the faithful, accordingly, by those who found communities of religious persons, in which they should fulfil their profession or have fulfilled the same, living as they should, or otherwise from the alms of the faithful; nor may they usurp any other dominion, whether held in common or by individuals, at all. Although they may possess said goods or dominions, nevertheless they are not to be held in their own name or that of their community, but rather in the name of some hospital, monastery, or establishment, and they are to be as procurators, the legitimate dispensers or administrators of said goods, not the lords or owners thereof. And whatever is acquired by such regulars or professed religious, these things are not acquired for themselves or for their order, but rather for hospital, monastery, or other establishment. These things being true as they are, these Brethren aforementioned are seen to reverse the order and are oriented towards the aforesaid in a completely contrary manner.

And even though for the palliating of the iniquity of their heresy they seem to make profession to a regular order, both by name and exterior habit and vesture, and even simulate religiosity, in their hypocrisy they pour out upon others the venom of their heresy, which they furnish all the more easily as they have poured and furnished it in multiple ways, as was said above and as shall appear more clearly below, however these Brethren do not, nor have they ever, professed their vows in any hospital or other establishment of religion dedicated or even deputized for religious use or founded for religious persons, nor have they ever been in the habit of doing so, so that, *viz.*, by such regular truly religious profession they might to any degree be said or even reputed to be in some way true religious. Instead, they have professed and continue to profess it in their camps and assemblies or other places in which they tarry, or in which it has been their custom to tarry, although also in camp oratories, assemblies, and other places of that sort, which assemblies of theirs, camps, or other establishments of this sort, said Brethren, holding them as such and even possessing them by force, and formally, and to the end and effect as expressed in their articles, letters, or pretended privileges stated above, *viz.*, as having done battle with the infidels, they obtain the goods of the infidels and convert the same to their own use, and they do so hold and possess these as they did hold and possess them, and have become used to holding and possessing them, not in the cause of religion, nor for any religious order at all, nor for any public utility, but for their own gratification, and in their own name, for their own profane use — it is thus that they hold and possess and have become used to holding and possessing them. These said convents of theirs, camps, or other such establishments are not religious in nature, but profane; not public, but private, and thus they should be spoken of and also reputed to be; and since they ought not to possess any dominion of goods, nor should they be capable of acquiring anything, neither do they acquire, and as they must not possess anything in their own name, so do they possess nothing. For thus, said Brethren, bound by their aforesaid professed vow, and with it, however simulated a vow as it is, by holding possessions and having dominion over things in their name or in that of their aforesaid pretended order, as they do hold, as has been said, are damnably in prejudice to their aforesaid profession and, as proprietors, are to be censored not only in common and in general, but also as it were in species; as according to the ratio of the whole and its constituent parts. And thus as has been said was, and is, the truth, public and notorious, as has been stated, held, and reputed, and is stated, held, and reputed openly, as public and notorious truth.

12. Likewise, although it is doubtlessly seen to go against faithfulness not to fulfil the promises one has made to God, which faithfulness man owes to God both out of obedience and because of the benefits received of Him, nevertheless said Brethren proceed against the vows they made previously unto God, in that: the possessions and dominions of the aforesaid lands, whether given or said to be given them by others — even if mistakenly: for none of these donations can be upheld, nor are they valid, both on account of their incapacity and on account of the error of those who have 'given' them — whether because of the aforesaid wars, however iniquitous and unjust, and because of the aforesaid looting, or however they were acquired by these same Brethren in such a way for themselves and in their own name, and for their own gratification or that of their abovesaid pretended order, damnably usurping the same, as they hold and possess, have held and possessed, as they have become used to do, even though they should not have done, nor should they do; nor should they be able to do *de iure* on account of their profession as Brethren of the aforesaid rule, with which they have bound themselves and made public, as they do bind and make public, and have become used to do, however many times and whenever anyone is received by them into this pretended order or sect of theirs. For they solemnly vow and promise three things, *viz.*, poverty, chastity, and obedience, pronouncing thereby their will to live by them, and to keep to them

firmly, in the same way that any other professed regulars you should care to mention are used to do. And thus said Brethren, paying no regard to what is written (in Ecclesiastes, V):[21] 'If thou hast vowed any thing to God, defer not to pay it: for an unfaithful and foolish promise displeaseth Him;' not only are they unfaithful to Almighty God with an infidelity contrary to the Christian faith, which is given the special name of heresy, of which mention has already been made, but even with an infidelity that opposes and is repugnant to moral fidelity. For in doing as has been said, having made a solemn promise of worshipping God, which cult is due Him by all, especially those so professed, still these men, conquered by the iniquity of mammon and riches, exhibit to the world the idolatry unto which they cleave, as they take idolatry for religion, simulation and hypocrisy for truth, and horrible heresy in the place of Christian faith; the crime and contempt of infidelity in the place of faithfulness to God; these things, as well as many other evils and enormities that follow upon them, said Brethren, as sectaries and adherents of multiple crimes which they firmly embrace and honor, however tacitly, and still are so used to embrace and honor. And this, as has been said, was and is the public and notorious truth.

13. Likewise, however said Brethren solemnly vow to be profitable unto God as they vow their will to cleave unto poverty — to which the possession of things is repugnant — no less than to be subject and obedient, entrusting themselves into the hands of others — to which the desire of ruling and dominating over others is repugnant, still and all said Brethren, like unto 'a perverse generation' and 'unfaithful children' (Deuteronomy XXXII),[22] not only hold and have held possessions and dominions of land, being degenerate and even withdrawing from the poverty that they had solemnly professed to God; but even rule and dominate their subjects of the lands and dominions aforesaid — which lands or dominions they occupy

according to the method described above — in this way they usurp the principate and dominion in respect to their subject peoples and continue to usurp them unto themselves, in their own name, however tyrannously, wrongly, and unjustly, as well as contrarily to their very own vow. And despite the fact that they should not mint their own coinage — for *de iure* they should not on account of their incapacity, notwithstanding any privileges or concessions or indults of whatever sort abovesaid, however false and null, they produce, nevertheless these Brethren, making themselves princes and lords of their commonwealth as they do and have done, mint said coinage, and have minted it, cause and have caused it to be minted. And thus having vowed with their tongues subjection and obedience, they give the lie to the same with their deeds, as they dominate and rule others contrarily to their promise, and that not without grand blasphemy on their part, as well as grave insult to their Creator, and with tyrannical oppression of those subject unto them. And this was and is the public and notorious truth.

14. Likewise, after these same men had evicted the infidels from Prussia and wrested the power there from their hands, having exterminated the more noble, powerful, and capable men of said land — as they had exterminated them, *viz.*, cutting some down, decapitating others, drowning still others, and doing others to death in other ways, while expelling others from their possessions and dominions, sending them off from said land into perpetual exile — wishing to seize for themselves and occupy the camps, towns, cities, and other possessions of the infidels, of whatever sort, and however many they had, which having occupied and seized, they held on to and continue to hold on to, however violently, unjustly, temerariously, and iniquitously, to the grave danger of their own souls, and to the injury of those harmed by them, and to the injury of their heirs, with grand prejudice and physical detriment; which they have done as well in other lands and

dominions, wherever they have wrested the same from the hands of the infidels, or otherwise hold them as they do and have done, and have become used to doing; and this was and is the public and notorious truth.

15. Likewise, having occupied said possessions, goods, and dominions, usurping the same for themselves, and fortifying said land with cities, camps, and other fortresses and munitions — as they have fortified and continue to fortify — with varied and extremely heavy burdens and torments they oppress the infidels as they have oppressed them. Not only this, but they have become used to compelling these same Prussians to divers servile works, even many gravely onerous ones, imposed upon them by these Brethren, *viz.*, now the edification of munitions, the greatest defensive walls and the stoutest fortresses; now the excavating of the deepest fosses; now the felling of measureless forests; now this, now that, and not just such things, but they even force them to participate in said *Reisen*, making them accompany them as often as they set out upon them, even having them abandon their homes, their women, and their own children, even at their own expense, and even forcing them to the commission of savageries and cruelties, which is worst of all. And thus said Prussian nation, which was free at the time of their gentile state, now, even after their reception of the sacrament of Holy Baptism, subjected and compelled to a yoke of such servitude, which is hard to find among any other people in the entire world similarly bound and oppressed, has doubtlessly been made to submit to a grave injury, which is a reproach and great prejudice to the Faith as well as to the Christian religion, even though these knights have done the same things to men of other lands, which in this way they have had of the infidels. And this was and is the public and notorious truth.

16. Likewise, wishing to appear zealous defenders of the Christian Faith, these Brethren, being prevaricators of the divine law and notorious heretics, so that these aforementioned *Reisen* of theirs, and all wars waged against the infidels, be believed by other men to be according to Catholic reason, not only Prussians of both sexes, but also other men inhabiting the aforesaid lands, whom they subjected to the aforementioned miserable servitude, they baptized and made to be baptized, however deceitfully, by force and tyrannical oppression, unduly, cruelly, and unjustly, though it be against the prohibition of the General Council of Toledo, which orders that 'no man [...] is to be brought to belief by force [...] so that the form of justice should be correctly served. For just as man perished by obeying the serpent of his own free will, so by the vocation of the grace of God,' not by force but 'by his own free will, the conversion of his own mind, every man [...] is saved'.[23] They did not instruct these so baptized into the Christian Faith at all, just as they do not instruct or cause to be instructed, as they themselves, *viz.*, these Brethren rulers, are inexpert idiots as far as letters are concerned, hardly knowing the Creed themselves, indeed, wholly ignorant. And so, baptized in such a way, commonly uninstructed in faith and morals, they live as pagans or near to that state, just as they were used to live when not possessed of the Christian Faith. And this is the public and notorious truth.

17. Likewise, said Brethren, blinded by their heretical cupidity, seeing that much wealth and other advantages would increase to them from the frequent gathering of Christ's faithful unto them, as described above and desiring in some way, even the way of deception, however vainly and iniquitously, to attract allies all the more strongly to them for warmaking, proclaimed at certain times and caused to be proclaimed among them at such times as seemed to be most proper for the making of *Reisen*, a so-called *mensa honoris*, or, as they say in their vulgar Teutonic speech, an *Ehre Tisch*, or 'table of honor,' to

be provided for such as gather unto them, sending out letters to this effect to kings, and princes, and other lords and persons of great status among the Christians.[24] Now the nature of these so-called 'tables of honor,' although invented by the vanity of said Brethren, was and is such that a meal for a certain number of persons, guests to the number of ten or twelve, or some other small amount, is solemnly prepared by the Brethren, as long as such persons selected by heralds from among the knights there present could be seated at the aforesaid table. And these persons, on the testimony of those heralds of theirs, had travelled through many parts of the world in order to wage war, as is testified to by the heralds who have seen them in many kingdoms and other regions. And according to the merits by which some of these knights and persons are recognized to surpass others, thus are they seated at the table and served in turn. And such seating there they take to be a great honor, just as they are accustomed to be honored. And in special pursuit of this honor, knights from the divers regions of the Christian world, in great multitudes — some among whom, as more than one person reports, places himself in great debt, selling his home, possessions, and sometimes property as pledges — so as to flow towards these Brethren in Prussia in order to make war. Here they spend months and months waiting upon said *Reisen*, during which time they spend great amounts of money among the Brethren, leaving behind great treasures of money there. And thus, with customary slyness and clever cunning, said Brethren extract gold and silver from them. Much of this occurs under the veil of honesty, i.e., by middlemen who provide them with victuals in exchange for their money.[25] And this was and is publicly and notoriously true.

18. Likewise, after already having taken possession, sequentially, of Prussia, Courland, and Lettonia, in order to obtain other dominions belonging to others, breathing an insatiable voraciousness, they turned their blades and their army of warriors against other regions,

with wolfish rapacity, although injustice is done to wolves by the comparison. They invaded and also attacked, molested, and perturbed on the one hand the Samogitians, and on the other the Lithuanians, and still again the schismatic Ruthenians under the specious color of their being pagans, and making in this way their *Reisen* against their lands and dominions, now against one of them, now against many, now against this land, now against that, where they practiced devastation, arson, and rapine, even destroying said lands year after year or nearly so.[26] And from such times, the beginning of which exceeds the memory of man, up until the times of the conflict mentioned below,[27] more or less, they perpetrated many and divers acts of homicide, burning cities, towns, castles, and habitations to the ground, committing adultery, debauchery, rapes of persons of both sexes, as well as the seizure of goods of others, and almost innumerable murders and the slaughter of many citizens. Such cruelties they frequently perpetrated during their wars with those who at the time were infidels, however temerariously, impiously, unjustly and iniquitously; and many other shameful acts of this sort did they wrongly commit and oversee in the aforementioned lands. Such have they done, such do they, and such are they used to do. And this was and is true, publicly and notoriously so. And such has been stated, held, and reported, and is stated, held, and reported openly, publicly, and notoriously.

19. Likewise, in so attacking the aforesaid Samogitians, a notable part of their land bordering upon Prussia where the river vulgarly known as the Memel flows, having wrested from the power of the Samogitians, just as it is expressly confessed in their aforementioned articles — although, in effect, the material evidence provides the best testimony — to which articles the instigator and promotor, by his office, makes reference: said Brethren assert (there in their first article) in such words or others similar thereto: this was and is

publicly manifest, and notorious, that said pretended Order of theirs is, as they put it, making use of two fortresses successively constructed by the infidels on a certain district of the land of the Samogitians in which may be found the fortress called Velina, with other lands surrounding it below and above, from which they expelled the infidels 'which they conquered and totally destroyed [...] at great cost and labor and with the shedding of no little Christian blood.'[28] Thus, there. Also, in the same land and in the same part thereof they have extracted and abstracted, holding for themselves and even occupying, the remarkable castle of Memel (as it is vulgarly known), as well as other divers goods and possessions, which they continue to hold and occupy, however violently, temerariously, iniquitously and unjustly, to the danger of their very own souls and with grave prejudice and harm being done to the community of the Samogitians in general as well as in particular, to those who have suffered directly from them and to their heirs. And such was and is true, publicly and notoriously.

20. And lastly, said Brethren, who with much application and effort, and for a long while, as has been said, had their hands full with extracting the land of Lithuania from the power of the Lithuanians, seeing that that most Serene Prince, Lord Władysław, the current King of Poland, along with his brother Alexander, alias Witold, the Grand Duke of Lithuania, had already become Christians through the reception of the holy Sacrament of Baptism, and that consequently also a great multitude of people in Lithuania followed the lead of their princes and had received, or were about to receive, the Sacrament of Baptism, at which the pretended cause of said Brethren for the aforesaid acquisition of said Lithuania would disappear, still and all, regardless of the foregoing, *scilicet*, that said Lithuanians had already received Baptism in due succession — claiming that they still had a right to oppress said Lithuania on the might of their papal donations and even those imperial ones, as well as the aforesaid pretended

letters, just as they had claimed, as can be gathered from these abovesaid pretended articles, desiring to wear down the aforesaid princes and their peoples in said Lithuania by constant, disruptive wars, so that they might be driven to despair, molested, and also exhausted, and thus that they should drive Lithuania into subjection to them, with more armies gathered together than usual, or just about, they entered and devastated said Lithuania. And with more ferocity and greater atrocities than usual,[29] they killed and miserably murdered old people and youths, and with even greater avidity the neophytes, and others as well, paying no respect to the female sex, sparing none. They burnt to the ground their new churches, as well as villages, cities, camps, and other of their habitations, as well as their things and movable goods, of whatever sort they were able to find, according to their pleasure. What is more, they also removed people of both sexes, and indeed entire families, from thence to Prussia and Livonia and to other of their locations. Many other enormities and abominations did they commit and have they committed, just as they have become used to doing, as said above, of which there is no doubt but that they bring the Faith into detriment and the name of Christian into vituperation. And such was and is the public and notorious truth, as it was and is publicly known and commonly reputed.

21. Likewise, said Brethren, wishing to exterminate the aforesaid princes and their peoples, already Christians, so as to occupy their lands, and extinguish the young faith newly planted there with their heretical cruelty, as much as was in their power to do, for the space of two and twenty years, or thereabouts, did, every year, at least twice each year, according to their custom, traverse the length and breadth of said Lithuania, with strong armed forces of great power, crosswise, as it pleased them, doing maximum harm to the neophytes there, burning, killing, inflicting upon them the greatest wars, and many other things, much more than even when they were infidels, expelling

priests from their land and burning down to the ground the new churches there, as much as they had been rebuilt in preceding years, which doubtlessly verges upon persecution of the Christian faith. And this has been and is the public and notorious truth, common knowledge and public report.

22. Likewise, after these had so devastated said land and cruelly persecuted the aforesaid neophytes, occupying the same with as large a force of armed warriors as they were able to gather — while the aforesaid King with his brothers, and many others, at least the most powerful men of said land, were already Christian — attacked the city there known as Vilna.[30] This city contains three fortresses, *viz.*, the lower, the middle, and the higher. It was to the lower castle that lord Kazimierz of blessed memory, the brother of the aforesaid King, a Catholic man and a good Christian, fled the rabid rage and insults of said Brethren, along with many nobles and the most notable men of said land, enclosing themselves there to regroup.[31] Here, when said fortress was more or less taken and received by said Brethren, although with great numbers of men killed on both sides, they led said prince, captive, out of the fortress and into their territory, that is the camps where their armies stood, and here said Brethren savagely raging in their heretical cruelty, without any human mercy had the said prince's head struck off miserably, in public. And not being content with this, but glorying in their malice, they dealt with the head atrociously, ignominiously, their soldiers carrying it about publicly on the head of a lance — not without great vilification of the Faith of the Christian religion. And this has been and is the public and notorious truth, common knowledge, and public report.

23. Likewise, unable to advance in their acquisition of said land through such effort, with such a great force, *viz.*, however great a one they could have gathered, and by laboring for such a space, as an evil tree is unable to bear good fruit, but only wild grapes (Isaiah

V),[32] pretending all the same, however deceitfully, unjustly, slyly and iniquitously, on the strength of their apostolic and imperial donations, as well as the aforesaid pretended letters, to have a right to said Lithuania, to fetch it back from said princes as has been stated, and also desiring at least, under the same color, to obtain from them said land of the Samogitians, which land borders upon that of these Brethren, *scil.* as it is located between Livonia, Prussia, and Lithuania, which, once in their possession, would make the taking of Lithuania all the more easy too — by some subtlety, however underhanded and iniquitous, they induced the King and the Duke aforesaid to grant them said land, *viz.*, by way of compensation for the aforementioned right so pretended, just as they assert in their abovementioned pretended articles, to which also the instigator and promotor of the afore-introduced office also refers.[33] Now these princes, incapable of obtaining peace with these Brethren on any other terms, although themselves being incapable of making such a donation, both because of the incapacity of the Brethren, as well as because of the deceptive reason set forth by the latter, who pretend to be religious, whereas they are heretics; it is not probable, indeed it is overbold to presume that said princes should wish to nourish this heresy. The donation is also impossible on account of the residents and inhabitants of said land, who are most concerned in the business, and who admitted the Brethren into their lands only reluctantly and under compulsion, although by law and simple justice this should not have happened. And this was and is the public and notorious truth.

24. Likewise, as said Brethren so invaded this land in certain numbers, against the will of the reluctant people native to the place, and tarried there for a certain while, just as they tarried, desiring things 'which are theirs, not [...] those of Jesus Christ',[34] *scilicet* erecting camps and fortifications for themselves and burdening the peoples of the land with unusual and extremely grave labors, depriving

them of liberties, goods, and afflicting them with divers burdens, also committing enormities, *viz*., debauchery, unchastity, and other such, just as they have gravely oppressed, deprived, and committed — the Samogitians, unable to bear such damages, burdens, and scandals, expelled them and drove them from their land.

25. Likewise, said Brethren, 'delivered up to a reprobate sense' (Romans I)[35] and avid in their malice, neither capable of, nor willing to keep peace with men, whether they be infidel or even faithful Christians, after being expelled from the land of the Samogitians on account of their great malice (as described above) pretending, however falsely, that such things had not happened to them because of their wickedness, but rather on account of the conniving or approbation of the aforesaid King of Poland, they made hostile entrance into the Kingdom of Poland with a very strong armed force of warriors, at such a time as the King of said Kingdom was busy in a remote part of Poland. This was entirely unexpected; they proceeded to devastate said Kingdom even though such was contrary to their pacts of perpetual peace, not only the aforesaid, but even such as before had been solemnly made and affirmed between King Kazimierz and the entire Kingdom of Poland as party of the first part, and said Brethren as party of the second part.[36] Falling upon the dukedom of Dobrzyń, which belongs to the aforesaid King and Kingdom, *viz*., in 1409, in the month of August,[37] and, what is worse, on the very feast day of the Assumption of the glorious Blessed Virgin Mary, they committed much rapine, sacrilege, arson, homicide and many other evils, burning to the ground churches, villages, and cities, devastating and despoiling them. Such things they brought about and executed, however villainously, brashly, and unjustly, giving no little offence to God, to the grave oppression of Christ's faithful and scandalising many. And this was and is the public and notorious truth.

26. Likewise, at this time they devastated Dobrzyń, the capital city of said dukedom, by which name it is known in the vulgar tongue. During the course of this they perpetrated great atrocities, raping the virgins they came across during their reduction of the fortress. Also, they led out a certain valiant soldier, whom they had captured there, and ferociously struck off his head.[38] They would have done the same to many other of their captives, as much as they were able to, had their own retainers, as it is said, not resisted their command. Afterward, they completely destroyed said fortress with a raging fire, reducing it to ash. This was and is, the public and notorious truth.[39]

27. Likewise, at the same time, having taken another fortress in that same dukedom known as Slotoria, the walls of which they destroyed, throwing them prostrate to the ground, they entirely ravaged it, carrying off and having carried off the stones and bricks thereof to their own dominion. Then, to a third fortress, known commonly in Polish as Bobrowniki and in vulgar Teutonic as Bebrar, which they similarly took, they returned by themselves to remain there and to maintain their position in the dukedom they occupied. And in this castle some of their Brethren remained, continually keeping that dukedom in their hands and under their power for the space of two years or so, until the time of the conflict which will be described below, however injuriously, violently, and unjustly, not only to the grievous injury of said King, but also to the great prejudice of the entire Kingdom of Poland, which received of them similar offence. This was and is the public and notorious truth, common knowledge and public report.

28. Likewise, these Brethren, raving in their malice and thus devastating the aforesaid dukedom, did not only plunge their sacrilegious hands into ecclesiastical goods to carry them off, burn them to ash and wholly destroy them, but, even breaking into churches and places

where churchmen bided, *viz.*, churches in the villages and cities listed below, which they shattered, they cast to the ground the books, chalices, ornaments and other precious things deposited therein for sacramental use, despoiling them nefariously. And in despoiling them they not only profaned, but even combusted them. This they did not without great vilification and contempt being offered to the Christian religion, *scilicet* in old Rypin, in Szale, in Brosze, in Sadlowo, in Górzno, in Seczyn, in Rokicze, in Jastrzębie, in Ossek, in Nowogród, villages and cities so-called in the vulgar tongue, as well as others, both of the Płock diocese and that of Włocławek. This was and is the public and notorious truth and is common knowledge and public report.

29. Likewise, casting aside all reverence and fear of God, contemptuously, in the aforesaid city of Górzno, which is in the Płock diocese, they laid their hands on the rector of the parochial church, a priest and religious man, whom they beat to death in his own church. Having dealt mortal blows unto him, they left him lying there, half-dead, and indeed he did expire on the next day from his wounds and afflictions. And not only him, but many other priests and clerics as well did they atrociously beat, wound, kill, and cruelly treat, not without great contempt being shown to the ecclesiastical state and clerical order. And this was and is the public and notorious truth.

30. Likewise, said Brethren, the perpetrators of so much evil, wishing to cruelly wreak their savagery against the Church in Płock and its bishop, went so far as to completely destroy and wholly burn to the ground the aforesaid city of Górzno, along with its millworks, which served the bishop's table, along with the bishop's residence and many other structures belonging to the episcopal curia there. What is more, they carried and drove off to their own lands many things

and animals: draught animals, herds, and flocks. And this was and is the public and notorious truth.

31. Likewise, raging even more against this local Church, they had their way with freehold land in the village known as Łaszewo, which belongs to the bishop, carrying off divers grains and produce, as well as other things pertaining to the nourishment of men, existing there in copious and even opulent amounts. And indeed they dealt similarly with other freeholds comparable to this, in Miesiączkowo, where, after having first driven off moveable goods and livestock, they burnt it to the ground. And this was and is the public and notorious truth.

32. Likewise, scheming further to wreak even greater destruction upon the aforesaid Diocese of Płock, similarly they totally destroyed and then burnt to ash twenty notable and great villages or thereabouts, as well as cities constituted in that dukedom and pertaining to the episcopal holdings. These they similarly despoiled of divers things and utensils, moveable goods and livestock. And thus, the bishop who headed the diocese at the time, who from these possessions did have and was used to having, by annual yield, according to true accounts, conferred to him some six hundred Prussian marks, more or less, which has a value much greater than a thousand gold ducats in coin of the realm, of so much was he despoiled. This figure does not include the value of services, businesses and interests, of considerable estimated value — so that the Church in Płock will hardly ever be able to recoup or restore the same to its original condition. The names of the villages and cities referred to above are as follows: Brzosza Pauli, Brzosza Janowa, the double settlement of Gęboczek, the double settlement of Górzno. Likewise Szalesze, Nowogród, Gółkowo, duplex, with mills, Trębowo, Czernikowo, Miesiączkowo, duplex along with the aforesaid episcopal freehold, Jastrząbek, Gręszczewo, Zaworów, Sułkowo, Łaszczewo,

along with the aforesaid episcopal freeholds. These are the cities and villages burnt to the ground along with other possessions of the said Church. And this was and is the public and notorious truth.

33. Likewise, the aforesaid Brethren, sacrilegious plunderers, and arsonists, at the time of those visitations raged similarly against the Church in Włocławek. There they fired and entirely destroyed and made to be destroyed a notable village in that dukedom known as Ciechocino, one with its freehold, that is, the church and the bishop's residence there, having first looted it of divers objects and victuals there abounding that pertained to the bishop. And breaking into the parochial church there, it too they despoiled of divers items devoted to divine worship and other uses. This was and is the public and notorious truth.

34. Likewise, panting with lust of even worse outrages, not just this village, but fifteen others, or thereabouts, belonging to the diocesan bishop, along with five notable mills and the entire surrounding district, they treated in the same manner. Having first despoiled the Church in Włocławek, as well as the inhabitants of these villages, of their moveable goods and livestock, as well as divers furnishings and utensils and other things of theirs, they reduced the towns to ash with flame voracious, completely burning them to the ground. This was and is the public and notorious truth.

35. Likewise, not content with such, they drained eleven notable fishponds in the aforesaid villages, releasing their waters and the fish pertaining to the episcopal table of that diocese, into the nearby river known as the Drwęca. They destroyed and caused to be entirely destroyed the dams and habitations of the persons living there. This was and is the public and notorious truth.

36. Likewise, after the passage of some time, when the inhabitants of the aforesaid villages of said Diocese of Włocławek had somehow re-collected their strengths and recuperated the things necessary for life, leading back their flocks and herds and other divers animals they possessed, rebuilding their houses and re-establishing the aforesaid villages so that they once more appeared in their original pristine condition, and when that most reverend father, the current bishop of the aforesaid Diocese had re-erected his residence and episcopal curia in said village of Ciechocino, at great expense, and had reorganized his freehold there so that flocks and herds and other necessary things were again in abundance, the aforesaid malefactors, greatly avid for the destruction of that Church, once more fell upon said district of the aforesaid Diocese with a force of armed men. And just as before, they despoiled said residence and freehold of that bishop — all the above-mentioned villages that had been rebuilt, destroying them entirely and burning them to the ground. And thus, they not only damaged the Church, but even gravely pauperized the men of the villages belonging to the Church, oppressing them. And this was and is the public and notorious truth.

37. Likewise, at this same time, or thereabout, these sacrilegious men, incendiaries and heretics, so obstinate in their malice, wishing to afflict the Church with even greater damages and still more gravely to oppress it, despoiled all cures or freeholds of that Church, property of and pertaining to the episcopal table, in the villages listed below, *viz.*, Komersko, Gaszewo, Sechotowo, Małebądź, Brodna, Sobców, Klasztorek, and in several others found in the land of Pomerania, which said malefactors retain in their power, despoiling them of agricultural tools, divers beasts and animals, grains, corn, and other things of nourishment, as well as household furnishings and other apparatus in which said cures abounded, actually despoiling and abducting them from their homes, converting the same to their own

use and retaining them, just as they still retain them now, however violently, unjustly, wickedly, and iniquitously. And this was and is the public and notorious truth.

38. Likewise, not content with the aforesaid spoils, but continually aspiring to greater crimes, having plundered all the abovesaid cures and freeholds, as well as notable villages to the number of forty or thereabout, pertaining to the property of the diocese of that same Church in Włocławek, and found in the aforesaid land of Pomerania, for upwards of ten years or thereabout, they despoiled and occupied these villages, cures, or freeholds for many years, holding them in subjugation. The fruits, returns, and produce resulting from these they converted to their own use, while oppressing the men of these aforesaid villages belonging to the Church, encumbering them with divers and grave services, labors, exactions, corvées and burdens. And this was and is the public and notorious truth.

39. Likewise, not being content with the aforesaid, collecting all the moneys which were paid by the common people found in all the villages in said land of Pomerania and the diocese of Włocławek, and which are customarily paid to said Diocese and its bishop each year in place of tithes, collecting them in the same way for themselves during the many years abovementioned, they poured them into their own purse and converted them to their own use, however unjustly, boldly, and iniquitously, with no small oppression and annoyance to the abovementioned Diocese. And such was and is the public and notorious truth.

40. Likewise, not content with the foregoing, but striving to overthrow and fundamentally destroy said Church at Włocławek, finally, all the abovementioned cures and freeholds of the Church, along with all their edifices, including homes and habitations, noble and notable

ones raised at great expense and in splendid fashion for the residences of the bishops of said Church, these they destroyed and totally burnt to the ground. For example, the episcopal residence belonging to this Church, a grandly ornate building constructed at great cost, which was acknowledged to be fit for a king and which stood at the city of Gdańsk before it was burnt to ash by these sacrilegious incendiaries, by common estimation could not be rebuilt to its former condition without the outlay of more than ten thousand gold florins in coin of the realm. The same is true of the village of Małebądź, where the cost would be more than two thousand florins. As for the village of Sobców with its adjacent neighborhoods — more than six thousand. In the village known as Brodna — more than six hundred. In Klasztorek, near Toruń, a city in the Diocese of Chełmno, the common estimation of the costs of rebuilding stand at more than one thousand five hundred florins, not including the houses of the villagers and the buildings of the village itself there burnt to the ground, of which more will be said below. This was and is the public and notorious truth.

41. Likewise, not content with the foregoing, having occupied the villages belonging to the Church in Włocławek, and despoiling the inhabitants there of their moveable goods and livestock, they burnt to ash all of said villages or just about, along with the churches located therein and all their sacramental utensils and relics of the saints, just as they irreparably destroyed even the millworks, fishponds, and other possessions of the Church in the aforesaid land of Pomerania. All these things have been irrecoverably destroyed, or nearly so. Although the army of the Poles, in pursuit of said malefactors who occupied said villages, may also have burnt some of them, still it was the Brethren and the aforementioned evildoers who provided the cause or at least the nearest opportunity for this to happen. This was and is the public and notorious truth.

42. Likewise, not satisfied with the aforesaid, *viz.*, with having inflicted such grave harms upon the Church in Włocławek as well as upon the men of the Church in the two lands or dukedoms aforementioned, that is, Dobrzyń and Pomerania, falling upon them so nefariously, as has been said, continually still and even more strongly aspiring to the destruction of said Church, cruelly raging, they hostilely invaded the land of Kujawy belonging to the Kingdom and King of Poland with a great number and power of armed men. First, they attacked the city known as Raciąż, a notable locality of said Church; they despoiled it of many divers and indeed precious objects, carrying off the same as loot, along with moveable goods and livestock, after which they reduced to ash said city along with its church known as All Saints', which stood at the gate of the city; all of this they cremated or made to be destroyed by fire. And this was and is the public and notorious truth; it was and is common knowledge and public report.

43. Likewise, not content with the foregoing, they also delivered up to the flames and completely burned down one significant freehold adjacent to the abovesaid city, along with all its buildings, after first having taken as plunder all its flocks and herds, and a copious multitude of other animals, along with divers grains, fruit, produce, and other things and victuals existing there in abundance. And it would require more than a thousand gold florins in coin of the realm in order to return said freehold to its original state, rebuilding all the structures as they were. And this is the public and notorious truth; it was and is common knowledge and public report.

44. Likewise, not content with the aforesaid, they reduced to ash and ember by fire voracious some other notable villages, fifteen in number or thereabout, a little more or a little less, adjacent to the aforesaid city, pertaining and belonging to the table of the bishop of

that Church at the time, just as above, after first having carried off as plunder the moveable goods and livestock they found there. And these objects, after having been rebuilt, were despoiled once more by these malefactors, cremated and actually burnt to the ground along with the churches that existed in some of these villages, including their sacramental furnishings and the relics of the Saints. Thus, on this side of ten years in the immediate past, the aforesaid Church in Włocławek has suffered such harm at the hands of these malefactors that, individually calculated, according to common estimation, some three hundred thousand gold florins in coin of the realm could hardly have sufficed to balance it out. And this is the public and notorious truth.

45. Likewise, not only from the times immediately aforesaid, but even before, *viz.*, during the reign of Kazimierz, the immediate predecessor of the current King of Poland,[40] this same Diocese of Włocławek was grievously oppressed. The same abovesaid renowned city and castle existing there, as well as all the villages, cures, freeholds and other of its possessions that pertained both to Dobrzyń and Pomerania and even Kujawy, the aforementioned lands and dukedoms, to which they continue to pertain, were despoiled by these Brethren of all goods mentioned previously. They were for many long years occupied and held in their occupation, while they usurped to themselves the fruit, revenues, and produce thereof and converted the same to their own use. This was and is the public and notorious truth, common knowledge and public report.

46. Likewise, these Brethren, the said oppressors of the Church and occupiers even still of its goods, are unwilling to restore to the Church and its current bishop said goods, and especially the aforesaid city and fortress, unless the Church and bishop are first compelled to remit unto them maniple tithes, such as they are supposed to be

obliged to do under the terms of an agreement of some sort extorted from them by said Brethren. These tithes are to be in divers grains and produce as said Church had or possessed or is used to having and possessing from all and singular fields and tillages, supposedly throughout the land of Pomerania and in the Diocese of Włocławek, to which agreement they harried the negotiators, however deceitfully, fraudulently, and iniquitously. Having oppressed the bishop in the name of said Church so despoiled and oppressed, they made them to stipulate or promise, in such a manner, however unfreely, unwillingly, and under duress, that from this time forward in lieu of the aforesaid maniple tithes they should pay to them a fourfold scot[i] in Prussian coin for every manor there, every year, to the value of two gross[i]in coin of the realm (which today is equivalent in value to less than one gross) — and this is to be observed and had in perpetuity. And vice versa, said Brethren promised, although deceitfully, fraudulently and iniquitously, as evidence was later to prove — under the terms of the pretended agreement — to protect all the goods of the Church found in the dominions of these Brethren against all and sundry, and never to molest the Church again in its goods. And in this way, by virtue of this pretended agreement, the Church was and is being oppressed since that time under such yearly maniple tithes to the amount of four thousand gold florins in coin of the realm, by common estimation. And in this way, said oppressors still, that is, for every year this side of sixty years or thereabout, have so been defrauding the Church of four thousand florins, more or less, and they continue to do so. And there is no doubt but that in so doing they risk the salvation of their souls, acting in such prejudice unto and burdening so the Church, as well as its bishops then and now. And this was and is true, publicly and notoriously, and it was and is common knowledge and public report.

47. Likewise, not only in this way did they deceive and do they continue to deceive the Church in this tithing, but even having pur-

chased certain possessions and villages, from the produce of which the Church was supported in tithes, they made of these farms and tillages, and, tending them, they refuse to pay the tithe due from these to the Church. Thus, they neither resolve nor are they used to resolve the tithes, claiming to have a privilege granted them by the Apostolic See that absolves them and their possessions from the obligation of paying tithes. This is, however, false, iniquitous, and fraudulent, for it is not the Apostolic See's custom, nor should it be, to grant a privilege to one party that wrongs another, or to allow one to gorge himself on another's right in such a manner.

48. Likewise, not content with all the foregoing, but all the more persecuting said Church and scheming to weaken its jurisdiction in spiritual as well as material things, they impeded and continue to impede the most reverend father Jan, the current bishop of the diocese,[41] and his officials in the aforesaid dukedom of Pomerania, and the Diocese of Włocławek, in the free exercise of their jurisdiction in spiritual matters, *viz.*, not permitting them to excommunicate or to publicly denounce the excommunicate among their subjects, and at times not even those who are not subject to them, even though the sentence of excommunication be a just one. They also impede them in the exercise of their temporal jurisdiction, *viz.*, interfering with judgments and legal matters among men even in villages and goods belonging to the Church, acting as judges even though overboldly, unjustly, and iniquitously. This they have done and continue to do, so that neither the bishop himself nor his officials aforesaid dare, out of their horror of the cruelty of said Brethren, with which they have been terrorized so many times, to administer justice against the will of said Brethren. This they have not dared to do, and still do they dare not. And so evil men and rebellious souls have recourse to the Brethren, whether in matrimonial matters or other spiritual things, and in temporal matters, and, as such, they are protected in their evil

doing by them. And this they did and continue to do, to other bishops of said Diocese and their officials as well, as they did and do, and are used to doing. And this is the public and notorious truth.

49. Likewise, when the most reverend father, Lord Jan, the aforesaid bishop of said Church in Włocławek, saw that his officials in the aforesaid land of Pomerania were unable to freely exercise their jurisdiction, he sought to remedy the situation by recalling the officials in said land of Pomerania and constituting them about his cathedral church, *viz.*, in the city of Włocławek, which is beyond the reach of said Brethren, *viz.*, in the Kingdom and dominion of my lord the King of Poland. In this way, he wished to work it that whoever had a matter to be considered in his presence, or before his officials, would be obliged to be take himself to the city of Włocławek. Said Brethren, sons of iniquity, wishing, contrariwise, to foment rebellion amongst the clergy as a whole and the people of said Diocese of Włocławek against their mother Church and its bishop, wishing thus to sever the body of the Church and its members from its head, procuring schism as they strove to procure, caused them in the name of the entire clergy to file an official appeal to the Apostolic See and the Pope, containing more than a few notorious pamphlets against the bishop, such as they were inserting and causing to be inserted. And thus, under the aforesaid pretended appeal, even though it had no issue, the aforementioned clergy and people remained for a long while in rebellion against their mother Church and its bishop, so that even today they are not entirely obedient to them, but only accordingly as it pleases the Brethren. And this was and is the public and notorious truth.

50. Likewise, not content with the aforesaid, but wishing also to usurp the dominion of the Church in its men and goods, not only did they, and do they, oppress the villagers and peasants of the villages belonging to the Church in said dukedom of Pomerania with many

and varied levies of tribute, penalties, exactions, and distresses, at their pleasure requiring them, and even compelling them as they did compel them, to work the lands of the Brethren, hewing and carting lumber, bricks, and stones for the construction of battlements, digging trenches and performing other most difficult labors; not only did they all the more frequently compel them, as they do compel them, to accompany them on their usual *Reisen* made against the aforesaid infidels, but also to many diets, at the expense of these villagers themselves. And thus they have been burdened and oppressed by them, so much so as to make them unable of resolving effectively the pension and census constituted to them, on behalf of said Church. And this they do, have done, and are used to do, however much there is no little detriment done to the Church thereby. And this was and is the public and notorious truth.

51. Provocatively, all the more this depraved and perverse generation of Brethren, not content with what has been said above, but desiring still to subject the clergy to their servitude, to place the priesthood under tribute, that they might be found hateful, just as they placed and subjected them; just as if they were faithless sons, said Brethren, dominating the clergy, compelled the rectors of the parochial churches of said land, as well as other lands that they hold in their power, it is believed, according to the means of each of these churches or benefices, to purchase horses, keep them, and even pledge them for the making of war against the King of Poland, even though this goes against the prohibitions of the General Lateran Council, which forbids such collections to be made among, or burdens to be set upon, the clergy, or for the latter to consent to the same, under the penalty of excommunication *latae sententiae* (as in the chapter *Adversus*: *De immunitate ecclesiarum* X, III, 49, 7). And such is the public and notorious truth.

52. Likewise, being the cruellest persecutors, not only of the aforesaid churches but also of religious orders, spiritual institutions, and convents or monasteries, recently, *viz.*, shortly after the year 1400, a certain significant monastery of monks of the order of the Cistercian Brethren, located in the city known as Koronowo, in the Diocese of Włocławek, was not only despoiled by them, who arrived there with a large force of armed men, as they did despoil said monastery, the aforesaid city, and also many villages and notable possessions of said monastery, to the number of twenty-four large villages and holdings pertaining to the monastery and adjacent thereto, but they burnt these to the ground and reduced them to ash, or caused them to be so combusted, along with many churches, sacramental furniture, and the relics of the Saints. And when said city belonging to the monastery was rebuilt, they burnt it to the ground once again.[42] And this was and is the public and notorious truth.

53. Likewise, they not only despoiled the abovementioned Churches, but also the Metropolitan Archdiocese of Gniezno in the Kingdom of Poland. This they did cruelly persecute, despoiling it of its possessions in the district known as Kamień, belonging to said Archdiocese. They ravaged this district in its entirety, or nearly so, occupying many villages and other notable possessions of said Archdiocese, holding them in such occupation for the space of many years, usurping the fruit, revenue, and produce thereof and converting the same to their own use. And this they did not only once, but many times: *viz.*, occupying the aforesaid district, just as they had become used to occupying it, however many times they make war against the aforementioned King or Kingdom of Poland. And this is the public and notorious truth.

54. Likewise, not only have they occupied the aforesaid district of the Church in Gniezno many times, but they have also many times

devastated the villages and possessions of the aforesaid in such a manner, ravaging and destroying them, along with their churches, by fire. And so have they done, especially for eight years or so this side of the aforesaid events, driving the men of the aforesaid villages and possessions in that district of the Church to such poverty, that many of these victims of theirs have been driven to beggary. And so have said Brethren, these most evil enemies of the Church, oppressed the Archdiocese of Gniezno, that the archbishop of said Church at the time, who had and was used to having a regular yearly income of fourteen hundred gross Bohemian marks from the district and its possessions, exceeding, more or less, the value of three thousand gold florins in coin of the realm — and this not taking into account the many freeholds pertaining to the table of the archbishop of this Church — all plundered and combusted by these Brethren, and other things falling to him, services, and other utilities — today he has or may have hardly one hundred marks, or two hundred gold florins. And this was and is the public and notorious truth.

55. Likewise, not content with the foregoing, but panting in their lust for ever greater destruction to this Church, having invaded the aforesaid city of Kamień along with its stronghold in the aforesaid district of the Church, they made a pact with those who held said fort, *viz.*, that these men would be allowed to withdraw safely with their possessions if they left the stronghold in the Brethren's hands. Now they trusted the words of these Brethren, however fallacious and deceptive. And as soon as they descended from said stronghold or fortress, they were quickly taken captive. The Brethren took possession of the fortress as stipulated in the pact, but as soon as they had it in their power, they destroyed it, along with the city, to its very foundations, burning it entirely to ash. The men themselves were kept in captivity for many years, and, it is believed, they are still so held, although two priests from among their number were released after

first being publicly paraded, with their hands bound behind their backs, among men, for two days and in divers places, as if they were common thieves — however this is great vituperation and contempt of the clerical order. And this was and is the public and notorious truth, common knowledge and public report.

56. Before the destruction of said stronghold and city, in the year previous to this, having no reverence for the divine or sacred, nor any respect for ecclesiastical immunity, falling upon said city, straightaway they dragged a once famous and notable man, a captain of said fort at the time, out of church while Mass was being celebrated and in the view of multitudes of people, with violence. They wished to hang him and decapitate him, even though there had been no judicial trial, and they were in an alien territory not belonging to them, and he was not a man of their own, but a stranger to them. And this they would have done had they not been turned aside by the entreaties of many and the intervention of others there who resisted them. And this is the public and notorious truth.

57. Likewise, a village called Gozdno, a great and notable one, with an abundant freehold belonging to the archiepiscopal table in Gniezno, the annual rents of which village were rising to a significant sum each year, and the cure of which village was used to be entrusted to certain ministers or vicars appointed to the divine office there, said Brethren delivered up to the flames and had totally burnt to the ground, along with the freeholds belonging to the Archdiocese, *viz.*, Sucha, Wielka Cerekwica, Kamień, etc., to the grave detriment of said Church, as well as to the aforesaid ministers and to the diminution of the divine cultus. And this was and is the public and notorious truth.

58. Likewise, not satisfied with the aforesaid, but oppressing the Church ever more, they impeded, as they continue to impede, its jurisdiction — spiritual as well as temporal — in said district, and especially in the villages of the Church located in the aforesaid land of Pomerania, subject to said Archdiocese, or others, obeying no sentences or mandates received or gathered therefrom. Not only do they deflect through their machinations these sentences and mandates, but they scheme and connive so that the officials of the archbishop of Gniezno present in the district have no free hand in the exercise of their duties at all, making them unable to excommunicate persons on account of their excesses or to punish them otherwise, or administer justice. In so doing they not only doubtlessly subvert justice and present an occasion for rebellion, but they also weaken the jurisdiction of the Church. And this is the public and notorious truth.

59. Recently, after the year of Our Lord 1400, falling upon the Kingdom of Poland aggressively, with a large force of armed men, banners erect, and devastating said Kingdom, they completely delivered up to flames, or just about, a great land, district, or significant county, *viz.*, Nakło, commonly known as Skrajna, belonging to the Kingdom of Poland. Many villages, cities, forts and divers other objects, the great number of which were notable possessions, as well as churches and other sacred edifices, were turned to ash by them or completely levelled in destruction. And this was and is the public and notorious truth.

60. Likewise, invading the Kingdom in such a way and ravaging the same, not once, but many times, repeatedly, and not only in the abovementioned land or county of Nakło, but also in the region of Bydgoszcz, as well as in the aforementioned dukedoms, that is, Dobrzyń and Kujawy, and also in the dukedom of Mazowsze, they destroyed by arson and the most grave rapine — as mentioned above — many

villages, cities, forts, and divers other possessions, spiritual as well as secular, belonging to many noble persons, and the dominion of others. The objects levelled included many churches; all these they destroyed or made to be destroyed. Thus these malefactors, Brethren not of any militia indeed, but rather and most profoundly Brethren of iniquity and malice — wreaked such and so great harms in the Kingdom of Poland as seem to be well-nigh innumerable and inestimable! So much and so great crimes did they perpetrate, as seem to be well-nigh beyond the capability of human speech to describe! And thus did they bring many nobles and divers other worthy persons to extreme want and miserable poverty. These are the fruits of their glorious order! And this is the public and notorious truth.

61. Likewise, having oppressed said Kingdom as described above, not content with these evils, but panting in lust, going from bad to worse, and wishing to overthrow the Kingdom of Poland, they gathered together a maximum number of armed men from many regions of the Christian world, wishing to cruelly rage against the Christian Poles.[43] They armed themselves most stoutly in cannon and other instruments of war,[44] providing themselves sufficiently therewith, as well as wagons laden with iron chains with which to bind and fetter captive men, as the evidence later witnessed. The abovesaid King, sensing such to be afoot, and judging from past experience what sort of future was brewing, desiring to prudently forfend the same, gathered together armies of his own, along with his brother, *viz.*, lord Witold, the Grand Duke of Lithuania. Both of the brothers, wishing to meet these Brethren with their armies, progressed with them even unto the dominions held by the Brethren, wishing all the same, through solemn and official envoys, to incline said Brethren to some sort of peace and concord, at least at the sight of such a great multitude of men and hearing such a clatter of arms opposing them. But said Brethren, so haughty in their pride and prepared most strongly

for war, hastening towards the spilling of Christian blood, having set their warriors in armed ranks, they sent two swords by two heralds to said princes, *scilicet* one to the aforesaid King and the other to his brother aforementioned, saying (as has been asserted by more than one witness): 'take these two swords to aid you, for today you will be unable to avoid warring with us.' Which having done, soon after they rushed with vehemence upon the army of the aforesaid princes with their men.[45]

This resulted in a great loss of life, such as had never been known or heard of before, up until our own time. Many thousands of armed men on the part of the Brethren fell in battle. And in this way, in their bold recklessness, the Brethren brought to their death in this conflict not only said multitude, but also many of their superiors in great numbers, as if by their own hand. Thus did they bring themselves and their own to a damnable end — God grant that it were not unto their perpetual perdition as well! And speaking according to the common report of those who had witnessed these things with their own eyes, the number of their own men that they slaughtered in this way came to one hundred thousand or so — which verges upon grave insult being offered to God, the detriment of the faithful, and serves as a pernicious, bad example and scandal to many. And this was and is the public and notorious truth.

62. Likewise, after their triumph in the aforesaid conflict, the princely brothers, the King and the Duke, although having recovered many camps and cities from these Brethren, finally, among other things, the aforesaid Duke, brother of the King, stationed a great number of armed men in the city known vulgarly as Elbląg, in the Diocese of Warmia, to guard the camp there. Later, said Brethren, having recuperated their strength, gathered anew a great force of armed men, with whom they laid siege to said camp, after the aforesaid princes had returned home with their armies. At last, with blan-

dishments and amicable persuasion, though cunning and deceitful, in such a way as to wrest said camp from the hands of the abovesaid men, they presented them with letters of safe conduct. Then, under the pretence of safe conduct and friendly concord, they led the same, with all their possessions, along the road leading to Lithuania. Arriving at a certain city belonging to the Brethren called Holand, in said Diocese of Warmia, they fell upon those two hundred eighty men, along with other capable men and principals, good Christians all, along with their servants, despite there being great numbers of them. For after they had lain aside their weapons, whether at table, in the baths, or while resting in dormitories, they were killed atrociously, murdered by the Brethren, so that no more than three or four of the original number were spared. And thus, of the trains of those same two hundred eighty men slaughtered in this way, only a very few of their retinue, indeed a very small number, evaded death by fleeing the shambles destined them by these murderers. And this is the public and notorious truth; common knowledge and public report.

63. Likewise, since a pact of peace between these two parties in the abovesaid war had been concluded and agreed upon here and there, when these Brethren, by force and effect of the pacts and concord agreed upon by both parties were to release and pardon all men whom they held captive and distant from the dominions of said princes, permitting them to return from thence freely, these Brethren, nevertheless, violators of their own given word and masters of fraud, pretending to hold to the pact so made, committed nefarious crimes against the same, releasing the captives as pardoned only to ambush them on their way, insidiously, and inhumanly to murder them or cause them to be murdered, cutting down some and drowning others. And thus of the very many taken, only a very few of these aforesaid captives returned home. And this was and is the public and notorious truth, common knowledge and public report.

64. Likewise, after the abovementioned King and Duke returned with their armies from the dominions of these Brethren, as stated above, the Brethren, incapable of doing good but avid for great rapine, immediately proceeded to ravage the Diocese of Warmia and its bishop at the time in those regions of Prussia of all possessions and other moveable goods, including precious items, occupying camps, villages, cities, and other possessions for themselves just as they have occupied them for three years or so, holding them under occupation, usurping for themselves their fruit, revenue, and produce, and converting the same to their own use, however iniquitously, brashly, and unjustly. Said bishop, having, like his Church, been despoiled of all of his goods as said above, terrorized by the cruelty of the Brethren, was forced into exile from his homeland, leaving his Church derelict, to find refuge in the dominion of the King of Poland — just as for three years or so he remained there, continually suffering poverty. And this was effected by said Brethren so that said bishop should not be capable of residing freely in his Diocese aforesaid nor enjoying the free and peaceful possession thereof, even though in so doing they gravely oppressed said Church and displayed no little contempt for the pontifical dignity. And this was and is the public and notorious truth.

65. Likewise, the abovesaid things are true, even though later, on the part of both parties aforesaid, *scilicet* on the part of the aforementioned King of Poland and his coadjutors on the one hand, and on the part of the aforesaid Brethren and their coadjutors on the other, a case concerning all controversies, damages, and injuries whatsoever was set before His Most Serene Majesty, Lord Sigismund, King of the Romans and Hungarians, etc., by whom an arbitration of compromise concerning the suits of these parties had been pronounced, judged, and approved between said parties under the threat of the gravest penalties and with the consent of both, which also declared and

compacted, among other things, that all the items of the aforementioned Dioceses of Włocławek and Warmia such as had been taken off and detained by said Brethren, were to be restored to said Dioceses and to lord Andrzej Łaskarz as well — the provost of Włocławek at the time.[46] Now, as the aforesaid King of the Romans, etc. was unable to deal with the aforesaid personally, he appointed and deputized to these regions, and with the express consent of both parties, a certain nobleman of the Hungarian Kingdom, *viz.* Benedict de Macra, laureate of both laws and master of the liberal arts, to see to it. And he gathered information, testimonies, claims and defenses such as the parties in question wished to produce both here and there concerning the borders of dominions in the regions of Poland and Prussia, and concerning several other matters which were then being contested by these parties; he was also to demand the execution of the verdicts already passed by the King of the Romans, etc.[47] Before this lord Benedict said Brethren, now by themselves, and now through their legitimate representatives, produced as legal evidence some acts prepared such as were to display and describe the rights they claimed to have in the lands of the Samogitians, in Lithuania, and in other places, as well as the borders thereof, and with the intention of showing a firm foundation for these pretended claims, the articles aforesaid, along with certain letters, described above, pretended to be of Roman Pontiffs and Emperors, however fabricated and erroneous in both faith and morals, as has been stated above.

Therefore, that the abovementioned lord Benedict, both for the execution of the arbitrated verdict and, proceeding to other matters according to the mandate entrusted him, commanded said Brethren to restore effectively all the possessions, as well as other moveable goods, to the aforementioned Dioceses of Włocławek and Warmia, and to their bishops, as well as to the aforementioned lord Andrzej, who was set over the Włocławek Diocese — this can be proven and is proven by the acts and procedural records of this case, to which the instigator and procurator abovesaid refers. Still, said Brethren, obstinate in their malice, nor having any regard for the King of the Romans, nor caring about those gravest penalties threatened by the verdict of arbitration, to which they had voluntarily submitted themselves, content with none of the foregoing and fearing neither God nor man — did not wish to admit the aforesaid Churches and their bishops to their rightful possessions, nor did they wish to restore to any persons whatsoever the aforementioned goods, carried off and detained, just as they have not restored them. Rather, they interposed and had an appeal made on their behalf to the imperial electors, however frivolously, overboldly, and iniquitously; for *de iure* such an appeal is null and void. And this is sufficiently proven and can be so proven according to the acts and legal entries and the transcripts of the abovesaid legal case, to which said promotor and prosecutor refers. And they did so with great detriment to the Churches, and prejudice shown to the abovementioned persons, as can be clearly proven and is proven, both *de iure* and *de facto*. For the imperial electors are not the judges of the King of the Romans and the aforesaid parties and persons. And this is the public and notorious truth.

66. Likewise, the abovementioned verdict of arbitration handed down by the aforesaid King of the Romans was published, which among other things stated that merchants and any other persons whatsoever should enjoy full security and freedom of passage here and there between the aforesaid parties, whether by land or by water, as they travel from Poland to Prussia and vice versa on account of their needs or their business interests — just as is contained, along with other statements, in that verdict to which the aforesaid instigator makes reference. Now, many merchants and other persons of both sexes did cross over into Prussia from the dukedom of Mazovia and from other dominions of the King and Kingdom of Poland, along

with their goods, on account of the practice of their enterprises, believing said Brethren to wish to respect said concord, affirmation, or arbitrated sentence. But these Brethren, inexperienced in human pity and all too blinded by their heretical impiety, which seems so proper and peculiar to them, wretchedly put to death as many of said merchants and other persons from the Kingdom of Poland and the dominions of the aforesaid princes as they could lay their hands upon, and that with great cruelty. Some they cut down, others they hurled into the waters to drown them, taking from them their wages and money and other goods — such as has been deduced and, one believes, sufficiently proven before our reverend father in Christ, the lord Archbishop Johann Strigenensis [Esztergom, Gran] and his colleague, lord Nicholas de Gara, grand palatine of Hungary, who served in lieu of the aforesaid King of the Romans for this case, with the express consent of both parties aforesaid; just as can be proven and is proven from the acts and transcript of the trial conducted before them, to which acts and legal entries the procurator and promotor aforesaid makes reference, in the absence of other proofs, in the event of the aforesaid or any other of the premises being denied by the adverse party.

67. Likewise, wishing to pile 'iniquity upon iniquity' (Ps. 68),[48] notwithstanding the aforesaid verdict of arbitration of the King of the Romans, indeed after its publication and contrary to said verdict, the Brethren renewed their attacks again and again, invading the Kingdom of Poland with banners erect and a great multitude of armed men in order to ravage it, no less than they ravaged said Kingdom before the sentence was pronounced, burning and despoiling, abducting, and committing many homicides, robberies, sacrileges, acts of arson, and many other enormities, sparing neither churches and sacred edifices nor women nor priests in Holy Orders, but perpetrating crimes upon them all. And thus in said Kingdom, especially

in the dukedoms of Mazovia, Dobrzyń, and Kujawy, but also in the districts of Bydgoszcz and Nakło aforesaid, they brought men, both religious and secular, nobles, plebeians, and peasants, to utter poverty through this pillaging and arson of theirs. And this was and is the public and notorious truth.

68. Likewise, notwithstanding said sentence of arbitration, which also concerned and included the illustrious prince, lord Bogusław, Duke of Słupsk as coadjutor of my aforementioned lord, the King of Poland, similarly entering his dukedom of Słupsk, not once but multiple times, devastating the same with banners erect, they burned to the ground, broke into and also despoiled many villages there along with many churches, consuming with flame the Sacrament and the relics of the Saints. They decapitated several men, nobles and others, and turpidly oppressed both honest women and virgins, facilitating too their oppression and decapitation, committing multiple homicides, rapes, robberies, sacrileges, acts of arson and other of the most villainous enormities. Said dukedom was so grievously ravaged and destroyed at their hands, and many divers men as above, were impoverished by them. And this was and is the public and notorious truth.

69. Likewise, following and contrary to said arbitrated verdict, they wreaked no less damage upon the aforesaid Churches, *viz.*, the metropolitan see of Gniezno, the Włocławek and Płock Dioceses, as well as the aforesaid lord Andrzej Łaskarz — at the time provost of the Diocese of Włocławek, and currently bishop-elect of the Poznań Diocese — despoiling them of their goods with looting and arson. Indeed, some of these suffered even more following the sentence than they had before it — for example, three notable villages pertaining to lord Andrzej, *scilicet* Węgiersko, Sitno and Maciejkowo as they are called, of the Diocese of Płock, these even following and contrary to

said verdict they burned and caused to be cremated. And this was and is the public and notorious truth.

70. Likewise, when at last the aforesaid King of Poland, seeking a remedy for so many evils, and wishing to draw said Brethren in some way to making some sort of satisfaction, or at least an efficacious truce, took himself and his armies into the dominions of these Brethren, some poor men from various villages and cities in the Kingdom of Poland set off on a journey to said army, with well over seven hundred or so wagons laden with victuals, which they hoped to sell to said army, in hopes of making a profit from such lucrative trade. But said Brethren, thirsting for human blood, those most atrocious butchers, insidiously ambushed these men near the castle known as Działdowo, in the Diocese of Chełmno. Not only did they rob them of the aforesaid wagons of victuals, but thereupon they also cruelly put to death as many as were there, drowning some and having others cut down or drowned, so that only the very smallest number of them succeeded in fleeing this mortal danger. And this was and is the public and notorious truth.

71. Likewise, when some of the soldiers had been separated from said armies on their own business, said Brethren fell upon them. And, not being content with merely taking them captive, they murdered and made to be most cruelly murdered some fifty of them, or thereabout. And not content either with their murder and slaughter, but like shameful curs unable to slake their rabid thirst for cruelty, they sliced off the private member of each of the murdered men, and, placing one in the mouth of each corpse, they left them there as a spectacle to be wondered at by all who passed that way. This, done not without great prejudice to the Christian religion, was and is the public and notorious truth.

72. Likewise, a truce of some sort was again effected, which brought the warring to a pause through the efforts of the aforesaid King of the Romans and John XXIII, who was Pope at the time. The Pope had sent a special nuncio for this purpose, *viz.*, Rev. Fr. Wilhelmus, then bishop of Lausanne.[49] And although the aforesaid King of Poland was diligently encouraged as to the truce, when he demanded insistently that said Brethren should make and confirm such a pact with him, that whenever it should fall out that they should engage in war with him, during which they should succeed in taking men captive, they must not kill them or commit outrages upon them — said Brethren, going from bad practices into ever more evil ones, desiring not to diminish their cruelties at all, as it turned out, but to augment them all the more, declined to enter into any such agreement or to consent to anything of the sort, and indeed they did not. And this is the public and notorious truth.

73. Notwithstanding the aforesaid truce having been established, as has been noted above, these Brethren, unable to abandon their old habits, hesitated not to extract by violence some villages from the hands of the captains of the King of Poland, effectively procuring divers acts of arson in the Kingdom of Poland to be committed by the most iniquitous people, just as the arsonists freely confessed when they had been arrested. Meanwhile, the Brethren had entered the dukedom of Słupsk, belonging to the above-mentioned Duke Bolesław, with a great force of armed men, and they proceeded to devastate his dominions with arson and looting. They despoiled as well the Church in Gniezno and its current archbishop of their tithes and revenues — now doing this, now that, in spite of and contrary to said truce. And again other truces, or the extension of earlier ones, such as that made recently between the aforesaid parties in Paris,[50] through the offices of the most illustrious Kings of the Romans and Franks, they recklessly broached and similarly violated, being un-

willing to restore said villages, just as they have not restored them, and committing ever more crimes. And this was and is the public and notorious truth.

74. Likewise,[51] as for some time several dukes of the Kingdom of Poland, especially of the dukedom of Mazowsze, at the time having the land of Chełmno, which borders on the land of Prussia, in their dominion, located in the Kingdom of Poland, not attentive to how said Brethren, not yet having possession of Prussia, were coming to them in sheep's clothing, *viz.*, wearing the habit of a regular order, pretending religion, whereas inwardly they were, as they are today, like unto ravening wolves, just as later became apparent from the fruits they bore, as is even today clearly apparent, made certain donations unto them, and granted them certain possessions in the land of Chełmno.[52] And this they did, as several men assert, to the effect, *viz.*, that they should fight against the Prussians, who were infidels at the time — although such donations were null *de facto*, as they were invalid *de iure*, nor could they have any validity, both on account of the incapacity of said Brethren to receive them, and because of the deception of the givers, who deceived, gave in error. For it would not be probable, indeed it is impious and overbold to hold the contrary, *viz.*, that the aforesaid princes should wish so to nourish the hypocrisy of the Brethren and favor their impiety. And thus the pious simplicity of the dukes and princes aforesaid forged a hammer to strike at their own heads, and the most severe, the stoutest whip, knotted not only against their descendants and their own posterity, but also against the whole Kingdom of Poland, albeit they did so in their ignorance. Now, these possessions having been given to said Brethren, and their land, as stated above, occupied, the Brethren, with the elimination of the Prussian might, following their lust for rapacity, in the end, really excluded said dukes from the entirety of the dominion of said land of Chełmno, however temerariously, iniquitously, and unjustly. From

that time forward, they occupied and held under their occupation said land, as they still do hold it, however to the grave peril of their own souls and with great prejudice to and burdening of the dukes and their legitimate successors. And this was and is the public and notorious truth.

75. Likewise, not only did they so exclude said dukes from the dominion of this land, but they also defied the Kings of Poland. For in all this time, they did not wish to subject themselves to them nor to recognize them as their superiors, just as they have not subjected and do not recognize, however temerariously, unjustly, and iniquitously, this land as belonging to the Kingdom of Poland. Thus, abstracting so damnably a portion of said Kingdom from its whole, they tore the Kingdom apart and divided it, as much as was in their power to do so, not without grave harm being done to said Kingdom of Poland, or grave prejudice and contempt shown to the Kings of Poland. And this was and is the public and notorious truth.

76. Likewise, not content with the dominion they obtained by having said land, abstracted from the Kingdom of Poland, in their power, they also usurped to themselves the dominion of the Church in Chełmno, which is found in that land.[53] And this Church had been granted many temporal goods and notable possessions by the aforesaid dukes of the Kingdom of Poland, as it had been similarly richly established — these Brethren, sons of iniquity, wretchedly oppressing this Church so abundantly supported by donations, drew off for themselves many of these possessions. This they did, now by violence, and now by agreement, such as they were, deceitful certainly, unjust and iniquitous, claiming, as reported by some, in said pretended agreements, to be receiving said possessions as recompense for granting freedom to said Church and those subject to it from the burden of accompanying the Brethren on their customary *Reisen* against

the abovesaid infidels. Now, this was done wrongly, deceitfully, and fraudulently, wheedling the Church out of its possessions abovesaid, for by law the Church is to be free in its goods and subjects, and to subject it to such servitude would be a great sacrilege, a violation of ecclesiastical immunity. And said possessions they continue to occupy and hold, to the peril of their own souls, and with the greatest oppression of the Church. This was and is the public and notorious truth.

77. Likewise, not only did they oppress the Church in temporal matters but also spiritual things they infected with their error, like some pestiferous venom, *viz.*, by introducing to that Church both bishops and canons of their pretended order, or heretical sect, whenever a vacancy occurred in the episcopal see or even in any other inferior benefice. And thus the aforesaid land, as well as the aforesaid Church in Chełmno, was ruled in such a way in temporal and spiritual things as it is ruled now by these Brethren, the abovesaid public and notorious heretics. And thus — O, the pity of it! — the flock of the Lord Christ's faithful, through the miserable negligence of its prelates, has been betrayed to the mercy of rapacious wolves, who batten themselves upon them, exposed as they have been for such a long time to their cruel maws, and no good shepherd appearing amongst them for so long to lift onto his own shoulders and lead back into the fold these lost sheep of Christ. Not only is this amazing, but it is doubtlessly impious, execrable, and horrendous. And this was and is the public and notorious truth.

78. Likewise, not only have they so abstracted, as has been said, the land of Chełmno from the aforesaid Kingdom of Poland, but also, tearing the Church in Chełmno from its metropolitan see, *scilicet* that of Gniezno, which is found in the Kingdom of Poland, and of which the Chełmno Diocese was, and used to be, a suffragan diocese, they attached it to the metropolitan see of Riga in the region of Livo-

nia, which is greatly distant, although in the power of said Brethren. They added and caused it to be adjunct thereto as a suffragan diocese, however unduly and unjustly, and with no little prejudice being done both to said Archdiocese of Gniezno and the Diocese of Chełmno, as said Church in Riga and its diocese is ten times more distant from the Diocese of Chełmno than Gniezno is from the same. And this was and is the public and notorious truth.

79. Likewise, not content with the aforesaid land and Church, but strongly yearning even towards other lands and dominions of the aforesaid Kingdom, extracting and even wrenching away in such a fashion the land of Pomerania, which is found within the borders of the Kingdom of Poland and belonging thereto, which land is a significant dukedom, from the Polish dukes who had leadership or governance of it at that time.[54] So extorted or extracted it was, despite the fact that such an act was null and merely *de facto*, undue, deceitful, unjust, and iniquitous, as there was no legitimate contract, so the transfer of property of this sort to said Brethren was invalid, nor could it be valid, nor can it be, as stated above: *viz*., both on account of their own incapacity, as well as by reason of the dukes aforesaid being in fact mistaken, and in substance of fact deceived, where the reason for such a contract was provided by the trickery and hypocrisy of those so deceitful Brethren, if even there was any such reason, and this is what is presumed *de iure* — for it is not a probable thing that in making such a translation of dominion, said dukes wished to nourish such heresy — and also out of consideration of the King and Kingdom of Poland, as no such contract can, nor should be, made to their prejudice. And all the same they so detained said dukedom as if they had every right to possess it, and have detained it under their occupation for quite a long time now, unwilling to recognize the King of Poland as their superior although being under his power, within his realm, at the time; still they do not submit to nor do they

recognize him. And this dukedom they also hacked away from the aforesaid Kingdom of Poland and even divided it, however injuriously, temerariously and *de facto*, with mortal danger to the souls of said Brethren and to the prejudice and burdening of the aforesaid King and Kingdom of Poland, as well as with the tyrannical oppression of the subjects inhabiting said dukedom. And this was and is the public and notorious truth. And in doing as described above, publicly and notoriously, as they do and have done, they were and are reckless occupiers and harmful detainers, as well as public and notorious tyrants and oppressors.

80. Likewise, not content with the aforesaid, they truly wrenched away another land, consistent with and found within the Kingdom of Poland, *viz.*, the land of Michałów, similarly belonging to the dukes of the Kingdom of Poland. And in wrenching it away, they did so invalidly, merely *de facto*, unjustly, and iniquitously, so that its occupation is null, as *de iure* there can be no such valid contract, for the reasons said above. Yet this land they similarly extracted from the Kingdom, and, as much as was in their power to do so, they divided it, and similarly they have held it and continue to hold it under long occupation, to the danger of their own souls, and with prejudice to and burdening of said King and Kingdom. And this was and is the public and notorious truth.

81. Likewise, not content with the aforesaid lands, but wishing to invade other lands of the Kingdom of Poland at their pleasure, whenever they wished, they built themselves a strong castle named Nesów, deep in the Kujawy dukedom of said Kingdom, occupying similarly some villages, woods, and other possessions in that dukedom, the same as said castle. These they held under occupation, as they continue to hold them, however unjustly and iniquitously, with great prejudice to and burdening of the aforesaid King and Kingdom, and

with grave injury and oppression of said dukedom and those who inhabit it. Now, as neither by title of donation nor by purchase are they able to possess these, so they do not possess them, as such would not be possible, for such a donation is by the law itself null. Nor might they even by title of prescription, for a *possessor in bad faith* similarly possessing something *by force, doubtfully, or secretly, does not prescribe at any time* (Reg. 2, R. 5, in VI). From this castle, very often, they invaded said dukedom and indeed the Kingdom itself, most grievously damaging them as they were used to do, by rapine and arson, whenever they wished or wish. And to such an extent have they injured the Kings and Kingdom of Poland, as well as the dukes and their dukedoms aforesaid in the Kingdom, inflicting upon them again and again atrocious and divers injuries, that even if such pretended donations should be somehow recognized as valid *de iure* — as they are not, nor could they ever be — they would have proven themselves to be unworthy of the same. And this is the public and notorious truth.

82. Not content with the aforementioned lands, but also, notwithstanding the fact that the river known as the Wisła is the common border dividing said land of Chełmno, occupied by them, from the other lands of the Polish Kingdom, *viz.*, Kujawy, Bydgoszcz, and Nakło, and as a common border between them, it ought to serve both of these lands, *viz.*, those just mentioned on the one hand, and said land of Chełmno on the other, so that navigation might be made from one part to the other, and vice versa, said Brethren, grave and notorious enemies of the Crown of the Kingdom of Poland, wishing to invade said Kingdom in its many parts, districts, and localities whenever they wish, made said river their own, however iniquitously and unjustly, usurping to themselves alone all navigation, not wishing to allow any others to travel upon the river, to or fro, unless carried in the Brethren's own vessels, so as to appropriate unto themselves any profit that may proceed from it. And this they have done, which

profits and takings amount to a significant sum annually, and not, however, without grave injury being done to the King and Kingdom aforesaid. And thus they have invaded and become used to invading the Kingdom, in the manner of bandits making sorties from their caverns. And such is the public and notorious truth.

83. Likewise, not content with such navigation, as from another side of said land of Chełmno a certain river named the Drwęca flows between this land of Chełmno and Dobrzyń in the Kingdom of Poland, dividing these lands and forming a common border between them, these Brethren, even more intensely stubborn in their accustomed rapine and savagery, so that they might be able to invade the land of Dobrzyń, and consequently, other lands of said Kingdom of Poland whenever they should wish, not only usurped said river as if it were their own exclusive property, as they continue to do, but, occupying both banks thereof, they constructed in three places the most powerful bridges with great castles and the strongest fortifications for themselves, facing the land of Dobrzyń. These are found in Lubicz, in Golub, and in Strasburg, also known as Brodnica, cities of the Chełmno Diocese. From these places and castles they make and have made sorties like unto brigands emerging from their caverns, invading as they have invaded and have become used to invading said land of Dobrzyń. Taking which, at times they occupy it entirely, and at times they course about it like rapacious wolves: beating and slaughtering men, raping, robbing, taking captive, committing sacrilegious acts and acts of arson, as well as many other evils. This they do as they have done and are used to doing. This is the public and notorious truth.

84. Likewise, since they had so occupied the aforesaid lands in the Kingdom of Poland, or at least some of them, not willing to rest on such laurels or be content with them, for a long time, *viz.*, for the

space of eighty years past or so, congregating a great multitude of armed men, they also invaded said Kingdom, vehemently aspiring, consequently, to occupy other territories of said Kingdom. Now, when lord Kazimierz of happy memory, King of Poland at the time, resisted and triumphed over them in war, many thousands of their armed men and their nations fell by the sword. This is known by the Poles as the Battle of Płowce, so named for the village in the Diocese of Włocławek, on the fields of which it took place.[55] And thus these Brethren, deceivers of Christ's faithful, murdered and wretchedly made to perish, by their own hand, as it were, that multitude of men they had attracted to themselves, however deceitfully and unjustly, by their falsehoods. This they did with grave prejudice to Christ's faithful, and to the Christian religion. And this was and is the public and notorious truth; it was and is common knowledge and public report.

85. Not wishing thus far to desist from what they had begun, with renewed energies, raging with even greater malice, grievously persecuting the King and Kingdom, they once again gathered together an even greater force of armed men, with which they invaded so as to devastate said Kingdom, which, cruelly ravaged, they drove to great harm: cities, towns, villages, castles, and churches as well in great numbers and in divers lands and districts of said Kingdom. They set fire to and made to be combusted said places and objects, perpetrating many sacrileges, rapes, robberies, homicides, and many other enormities. Other lands from the aforementioned, *viz.*, Brześć, Włocławek, and Dobrzyń, they occupied and even held under occupation for many years. And this was and is the public and notorious truth.

86. Likewise, an exposition of these facts was finally made before Benedict, the XII Pope of that name, reigning at the time, in public consistory, and to the effect: that said Brethren, tarrying in parts of Prussia, hostilely invaded and violently occupied several lands and

dominions pertaining to his Kingdom of Poland, *viz.*, Chełmno and Pomerania for some time, as well as Włocławek, Brześć, Dobrzyń and Michałów, all of which lands belonged *de iure* to his progenitors, and constitute portions of his Kingdom.[56] They did this not without great slaughter of Christ's faithful and the concremation of one hundred or so churches, and up till now, as was said, they were detaining these lands under occupation, with grave danger to their own souls, and with prejudice to and burdening of the King, to whom by the reasons listed above these lands, as previously stated, are known to belong. Thus supplication on the part of the King was made, that a suitable remedy be made unto him. The aforesaid Pope, having received in his curia summary information concerning the aforesaid infamies of said Brethren, not wishing to wink the eyes of his conscience at them in passing by, commissioned two delegate judges to see to the matter, commanding them, by proceeding simply and plainly, to administer justice. These judges, according to the force and form of the mandate they received, followed the case as it preceded. And it became clear to them from the legitimate proofs provided in their presence that, as they state:[56a] *Brother Theodoricus de Aldenberg*, pretended *Master* of the Order at the time, and the commanders and pretended advocates of his pretended Order, of the land of Chełmno, *viz., of Toruń, Grudziądź, Lipowo, Radznensis, Elgiburgensis otherwise known as Koprzywnica, Golub, Strasburg otherwise known as Brodnica, Popów, Włocławek, as well as from the old city of Toruń and the land of Kujawy*, which at the time they occupied: *Nesów, Orłów, Murin, Brześć, Cavolovicensis, Radzegoviensis, Masburg otherwise known as Przedzeć, and from the land of Pomerania, Swecensis, Gdańsk, Tczew, Kamień, and also of the land of Prussia*: *Malbork, Stumensis, Lessinensis, Elbląg, Lesseck, and Riga, as well as Brethren of said Order of the aforesaid and other places and parts aforementioned, where they were at the time with a powerful and hostile army, and standards erect, casting behind them the fear of God, and under the persuasion of the devil, devastated the Kingdom of Poland, churches, viz., of Nakło, Warta, Szadek, Błądzikowo, Konin, Stupcza, Pobiedziska, Gaczów, as well as that belonging to the Friars Minor and the Brethren of the Holy Cross in Pyzdry, consuming there by fire after first taking from them books, chalices, treasures, and other deposits of said churches, burning said churches to ash along with their sanctuaries, relics of Saints, and sacred images.*

And therefore, all the aforementioned, in species and as well as many others in genus, who set fire to and burned down said churches, and who provided occasion from them to be burned, were proclaimed excommunicate, on the apostolic authority granted to the judges, as well as by bishops and prelates and other rectors of ecclesiastical communities, in the dioceses of Gniezno, Poznań, Włocławek, Płock, Kraków, Lubusz, Wrocław, and Chełmno, commanding these, under the penalty of suspension from their offices, to announce this sentence in their churches on Sundays and feast days, when people would congregate for divine worship. Likewise, the Brethren were ordered by the verdict *to rebuild said churches as well as to restore and emend other non-moveable goods* damaged by them.

Likewise, it was similarly stated to be proven that the aforesaid lands, *viz., Chełmno, Pomerania, Włocławek, Brześć, Dobrzyń and Michałów, with their cities, castles, towns and villages, and their rights and all that pertain to them, are situated within the borders of the Kingdom of Poland, and that being within said Kingdom, pertaining to the Kingdom and its King, and to the Kings and princes of the Kingdom of Poland, the progenitors of said Kazimierz, King of Poland* [...] *by whom at the time* [...] *they were possessed* [...] And that said Brethren and pretended commanders *with great slaughter of the faithful, to the great offence of God, and to King Kazimierz and his father of illustrious memory, lord Władysław, also King of Poland, invaded these lands with hostility and occupied them with heavy loss and injury done* [...]

and holding them with all rights and interest [...] *they occupy them unjustly.*

Likewise, it is similarly agreed by them *that having entered and invaded with a powerful hostile army, banners erect, the land of Greater Poland belonging to this Kingdom, they wholly combusted, devastated, and desolated said land, castles, villages, cities and towns*: viz: *Gniezno, the metropolitan city of said Kingdom of Poland, Znenia, Nakło, Lancitia, Uniejowo with its castle, Sieradź with its castle, Warta, Szadek, Błądzików, Charłupia, all villages in the territory of the district of Kalisz, Pyzdry with its castle and cloister or monastery of Friars Minor, Konin, Słupca, Kłecko, Pobiedziska with its castle there too, and Kostrzyn, cities or towns fortified, with all the villages adjacent thereto, and all constituted in their districts and territories, which previously despoiling of all their moveable goods and livestock, and having killed many men, and carried off many from said land into captivity, having denuded and oppressed women, wholly combusted, devastated, and desolated the areas aforesaid, bringing upon said lord King, his Kingdom and subjects, many other harms.*

Therefore, the aforesaid judges compelled the Brethren *to the restitution of said lands of Pomerania, Włocławek, Brześć, Dobrzyń, Chełmno, and Michałów, fully and integrally, to said* [...] *King of Poland, as well as the fruits, revenues, and produce, and all moveable goods taken therefrom, consumed by flame and destroyed, along with compensation for damages caused to non-moveable goods.* All of this was taxed them at the rate of ninety-four thousand, five hundred marks in Polish weight and currency [...] as well as costs and expenses of the lawsuit, assessed to the amount of one thousand, six hundred marks. Thus the judgment condemnatory went against said invaders, occupiers, arsonists, and sacrilegious malefactors. And this sentence, suspended by no appeal, passed into *res iudicata*. All this is contained in the verdict of the aforesaid judges, to which the instigator of the aforementioned office makes reference. And this was and is the public and notorious truth.[57]

87. Likewise, taking no notice whatsoever of all the aforesaid, nor being at all concerned with the abovesaid sentences of excommunication, they were unwilling in the least to rebuild the aforesaid churches, restore the goods they stole, or render back the aforesaid lands invaded and even occupied by them, to any extent, unless first some agreement was reached, however iniquitous and in such a way extorted, by the Brethren, however null and *de facto* undue and unjust — but such, *viz.*, as several have reported, that a perpetual peace would be effected between the present King and Kingdom of Poland on the one part, and said Brethren on the other, should three of the abovementioned lands, *scilicet* Chełmno, Pomerania, and Michałów, now under their occupation, remain under the control of said Brethren. Three others, which they also occupied at the time, *scil.* Brześć, Włocławek, and Dobrzyń, near to the aforesaid King and Kingdom, they directly restored to the latter, simulating thus to enter into a perpetual peace with the King and Kingdom, although fraudulently and deceitfully, so as to deceive said King and Kingdom, so that they should desist from further pursuit of regaining their lands and others owed them by right. But as the law does not assume that one who has been despoiled of something renounces his right thereto — according to canonical sanctions, indeed, it is the contrary that is presumed (see ch. II *De restitucione spolaitorum*). For any renunciation must be freely-willed, and uncertain actions, though they may be temporal as far as the penalty is concerned, are all the same perpetual as to prosecution.

Nor did they hold to said peace, but later, nevertheless, they devastated said Kingdom from these lands, not without grave injury, wreaking much harm upon the Kingdom, and more frequently than they had done to any infidels. And thus said Brethren, having extorted an agreement of such sort, however null by very law, both on account of the incapacity of the aforesaid Brethren, and on account of the King and Kingdom aforesaid, who *de iure* are not considered to have withdrawn in such a way from these lands, as has been stated — they held, as they continue to hold said lands under their occupation as if they belonged to them by hereditary right — to the perdition of their souls and with great prejudice to the King and Kingdom of Poland, and with the tyrannical oppression of the subjects of said lands as well. And this was and is the public and notorious truth.

88. Likewise, a certain time having passed, a certain castle, vulgarly known in Polish as Bobrowniki, and in Teutonic called Bebrar, in the abovementioned dukedom of Dobrzyń, was surrounded by the armed forces of His Most Serene Majesty Władysław, the present King of Poland, at his order — some twenty-six years ago. This he did because a certain László Naderspan, Duke of Opole, who had obtained said castle and the dukedom of Dobrzyń as a fief from the King of Poland, arranged to deliver the entire dukedom with the castle into the hands of said Brethren, with prejudice to and also against the will of the King and the Kingdom to which they belonged.[58] So did he betray them. Said Brethren, mindless of their own given word, the enemies of peace, without regard to the aforesaid pact, fell with a great force of armed men upon the dukedom and, by consequence, upon the Kingdom itself. Repulsing the captain and aforesaid forces, and lifting the siege of the castle, said castle and dukedom they received as their own and indeed occupied. They have held it under occupation for many years, however, not without doing great injury thereby to the aforesaid King and Kingdom. What is more, following this, they inflicted many other evils upon said Kingdom. And nevertheless, so obstinate are they in their malice, relying on the aforesaid pretended pact, they contend, as several men assert, that they are to retain

said lands, as if the King and Kingdom of Poland were obliged by the terms of said pact to acquiesce to this. And yet this contention is malicious, temerarious, obstinate and insipid, seeing that according to the rule of law, even if said pact were valid, *vainly he demands that a word given to him be observed, who* wishes not *to observe* or *refuses to observe his own word given to another* (Reg. 75, R.J. in VI). For he who breaks his faith cannot expect that the faith of another given to him, even if confirmed by oath, should be kept. And this was and is the public and notorious truth.

89. Likewise, after the aforesaid prince, lord Władysław, the present King of Poland, following so many grave harms done unto him in his Kingdom by said Brethren, being so many times baited, as has been said, finally resisting with the sword such rabies and malice of said Brethren, with divine justice favoring him, as it is believed, he laid prostrate their power, mutilating it indeed in the most fierce battle, which is spoken of above, decimating them significantly by taking captive in this conflict great numbers of their dukes, counts, soldiers, and others of their helpers, and taking many of their camps and castles. And after this King, as the friend of peace, nonetheless solemnly entered into a covenant of perpetual peace and concord[59] with them near the city of Toruń in the diocese of Chełmno, paroling said captives and releasing them from their captivity, with the restoration of all castles and cities, although with certain monetary encumbrances upon said Brethren, which were negligible indeed, and beyond that, condescending to them the aforesaid lands which they wished to have, although this should not have been done — so that, at least through the resignation of said lands due unto him *de iure*, he might purchase from them said peace at such a price, for himself and for his Kingdom, which he might not obtain otherwise — said Brethren, jealous of peace and masters of iniquity, an order of malice and villainy and not a militia at all, having recouped their strengths

shortly after said pact so solemnly celebrated, just a short time later, burst the bonds of the aforesaid peace and, with a great armed force, invaded said Kingdom again with banners erect, devastating it just as before. And nevertheless, as asserted by some, they claim to be respecting said concord as it was confirmed by His Most Serene Majesty Sigismund King of the Romans and Hungarians, however frivolously, obstinately, and iniquitously, as according to the rule of law, *no one should derive any fruit from assault* (Reg. 38, R.J. in VI). And so they assaulted said sentence, doing violence to said concord by deeds contrary to it, *viz.*, ravaging said Kingdom of Poland as they ravaged it, as is stated above. And this was and is the public and notorious truth.

90. Likewise, some twenty years ago, or thereabouts, an illustrious prince, lord Jan, Duke of Mazovia, which is in the Kingdom of Poland, procured the edification of a certain fortress or castle in his dukedom, causing it to be built with much labor and expense. One night, said Brethren snuck into said dukedom secretly and furtively, with a power of armed men. As the duke was sleeping in his bed, these men fell upon him cruelly, and instead of the reverence due him, they captured him and many of his soldiers and other noble men, taking them completely unawares. Taking these captives torn from their beds in a state of nakedness, having nothing upon them but one tunic, and hardly allowing them time to place slippers on their feet, they set lord Jan upon a horse without a saddle and led him out of his dukedom. Making such sport of this honorable and magnanimous prince, shaming him so grievously, they treated him with turpidity. And notwithstanding this, said edifice or castle of his they caused to be demolished and totally destroyed. In such a way did they pay him back for his expenses and benefices rendered, *viz.*, for those donations in the land of Chełmno which, it is said, were made to them by his progenitors, according to the facts recalled above. And this was and is the public and notorious truth.

91. Likewise, after they had already been received by the Poles and had begun to wax in Prussia, growing stronger and increasing, the prelates of the Churches in Livonia, seduced just as the Poles had been by the crafty simulation of said Brethren — which prelates at the time in question, from their conversion onward, had been governing their fatherland, *viz.*, Livonia and Lettonia, in temporal as well as in spiritual matters — especially he, who at the time presided over the Church in Riga as the principal see of these parts, which is now the metropolitan see — believing these Brethren to be religious (as they were not nor are they, however in the habit of feigned religion they go about), piously desiring that their militia be of benefit to their Churches in these parts — assigned certain possessions and a certain portion of the land there in Livonia to the Brethren, so that, owing obedience to the aforesaid prelates and churches, they should defend said Churches against the incursions of the infidels.[60] Said Brethren feigned for a while such obedience, so that later they might strike at them with the venomous sting in their tail and inject their poison into them, as they still do. They remained so long pacifically obedient to said prelates until they became satisfactorily satiated, strengthened, and enriched by the goods of those Churches. Having then constructed for themselves castles and fortresses, this wretched and perverse generation, sons of infidelity, actually retreated from their given word of obedience, first plunging their sacrilegious hands into their own mother and lady, *viz.*, the Church in Riga, from which they had received so many goods in fief. Successively and immediately, one after another, they took captive three archbishops of the Church in Riga, *viz.*, the most reverend Father Albertus, the first archbishop of said see, then Johann de Vechten, with many persons of his household, several of whom they decapitated immediately upon taking them, and Johannes Zwerin. These they detained long in captivity, treating them cruelly, nor did they release them until they had extorted

from them what they desired. And this was and is the public and notorious truth.

92. Likewise, the aforementioned most revered Father lord Johannes Zwerin, archbishop of said Church at the time, being held captive and detained by them, said Brethren, breaking open the caskets and chests belonging to the archbishop, took a great quantity of silver in vessels and in bulk, and in other precious items, as well as his mitre, his pallium, and other of his pontifical apparatus including divers vestments, altogether valued at six thousand silver marks, more or less, converting the same to their own use. And not content with this, they then occupied all the goods pertaining to the archiepiscopal table and detained the same under their occupation, as they detained all fruits, revenues, and produce that they found there, entirely filling their coffers with the same for many years, from the time of the archbishop being taken captive, up until the times of his successor, with the grave oppression of the aforesaid archbishop and his Church. And this was and is the public and notorious truth.

93. Likewise, as they continually lusted after supreme dominion in these parts, they first usurped the castles, villages, fishponds and other divers possessions of the aforesaid Churches neighboring their borders, abstracting these successively over time from the Churches, especially that of Riga. Afterwards, not only despoiling said Churches, especially that of Riga, of their lands and districts for their own gain, as they continue to usurp them at present, so did they set themselves up in opposition to their aforesaid lords and prelates, neither submitting to them, obeying them, nor in any way at all wishing to obey them, as they continue in their obstinance today. They constructed for themselves castles and fortresses in these lands and districts belonging to the Churches, which buildings they continue to hold, as they have held them, with grave prejudice to the Church in

Riga particularly, and also to the detriment of the Christian religion in these regions. And this was and is the public and notorious truth; it was and is common knowledge and public report.

94. Likewise, wishing to oppress said Churches all the more, and desirous of blocking access thereto, lest anyone from other Christian lands might come to the aid of these Churches, they so obstructed the seaport belonging to said Church in Riga, known colloquially as Dünemünde, through which merchants and other people had been used to enter and depart from the city of Riga by boat, sinking therein large ships, which they first burdened and filled with great loads of stone before scuttling them. This they did with great prejudice to these regions of the Christian world. And this was and is the public and notorious truth.

95. Likewise, they occupied the monastery and castle belonging to the Order of Cistercian Brethren located near the port, also known in the vulgar tongue as Dünemünde, with all goods and possessions adjacent and belonging to said monastery, which they continue to occupy to this very day. Expelling the friars and monks, some they killed outright, others they cast into the waters, where they drowned, after which they made over said monastery into a castle for themselves. And thus they completely destroyed and exterminated the aforesaid Order of Cistercian Brethren, who had been in that place for no little time for the support and advancement of the Christian faith, which they did with great prejudice to the Christian faith. And this was and is the public and notorious truth; it was and is common knowledge and publicly reported among such men as are intimate with the matter.

96. Likewise, they persecuted with their machinations the most reverend Father Fredericus Bohemus, archbishop of said Church in

Riga at the time.[61] Wishing to force him to exile from his abovesaid Church and diocese, they straitened and compelled him to tarry in foreign parts, as he did; meanwhile, during his absence, the Brethren not only stealthily entered the castle belonging to him and the aforementioned Church in Riga, occupying it as they did many other goods belonging to that Church, but finally, they seized the dominion of those regions, subjecting the entire land or province to their authority and holding it subject, as they continue to do today. With banners erect, they proceeded to surround the vassals of said Church in Riga, along with the city of Riga, urging and compelling them to abandon the fortifications of the Church. Some of these they slaughtered cruelly, and others they forced to be exiled from their fatherland, seizing the goods of those who went unwillingly. And this was and is the public and notorious truth.

97. Likewise, when said city belonging to the diocese of Riga felt the oppression of these Brethren so keenly, seeing that the aforesaid seaport, through which succour might have come to them from Christian lands, had been obstructed and destroyed by these Brethren, the inhabitants of the city were obliged to beseech the aid of neighboring infidels, calling upon the Lithuanians, who were pagan at the time, for aid. This notwithstanding, said Brethren having acquired and made subject to themselves the city, had a most strong fortress built in it from the bricks and lumber of said Church, and forced the men of the Church, at their own expense, to labor most onerously at said fortress on their behalf. And having impressed them to such service, they had them erect mill-houses in the manner of fortifications at the entrance to the city, and on land belonging to the Church, and other things, building and causing to be built whatever they pleased.

98. Likewise, the Brethren having set themselves up in the aforesaid city of Riga, which they now held, they began to oppress the cit-

izens of said Church, and others, too, with the most severe exactions and taxes, as they continued to do and have become used to doing. What is more, whenever they invaded lands belonging to infidels, making their customary *Reisen*, a certain number of citizens, as well as other men of said Church, were compelled to go along with them, again at their own expense. This they were compelled to do many times, as the Brethren became used so to compel them. And this was and is the public and notorious truth; it was and is common knowledge and public report.

99. Likewise, the archbishops of the Church in Riga at the time were engaged in a long-running suit against said Brethren before the Roman Curia, concerning these occupations of the city of Riga and other goods of the Church there. They won their case by definitive sentence, although the power of execution of the same was in the form of an admonishment, that the Brethren desist from said occupation. Sentences of excommunication and other ecclesiastical censures were passed and legitimately executed, as at last, by apostolic authority, they were officially published in the aggravated regions, as well as in many other lands and places. And thus the case remains, although the Brethren, and others, were also at the time strictly prohibited by the Emperor Charles the Fourth from invading the land, or infringing up the goods, immunities, castles, courts, borders, or persons belonging to the Church, or to do them any harm, or to dare to erect any castle or fortress against the wishes of the archbishop of the Church in Riga.[62] Yet still these Brethren — so obstinate in their malice as to be contemptuous of both ecclesiastical and secular authority, not only desired not to restore said city and other goods to the Church and to desist from said occupation, just as they desire not to do today, but even invaded other lands belonging to this same Church, which the archbishops of the diocese possessed up until then — *viz.*, the dioceses of Ruthenia and Selburg in Latvia, at one time destroyed by

the pagans in these parts, wherein they erected for themselves two strong castles of stone, vulgarly known as Selboch and Antea. And they acted contrariwise towards the Church in other, similar ways, wallowing in the filth of said excommunication for thirty-four years or thereabouts, holding the keys of the Church in contempt, up until the times of Boniface IX, the absolution of whom, such as it was — as it was purchased, as several assert — they obtained. And such was and is the public and notorious truth; it was and is common knowledge and public report.

100. Likewise, although for a long time successive archbishops of said Church were involved in many litigations with these Brethren, and many varied and divers sentences of excommunication and ecclesiastical censure have been pronounced by the legates and subdelegates of the Holy See, as have been handed down, and are, against said Brethren,[63] nevertheless, they, piling *iniquity upon iniquity* (PS 68),[64] never appeared to care a jot about them, or the obligations imposed upon them thereby. They had no desire of restoring said city or any other goods belonging to said Church, just as even today they do not wish to do — but rather always and frequently, wallowing in the filth of the sentence of excommunication, in contempt of the keys of the Church, for forty years or so, they drew out the processes at the Roman Curia by their various calumnies and corruptions, resisting said archbishops, however calumniously and unjustly, while squandering the goods of the Church of Riga all the while. And thus, the most reverend Fathers, *viz.*, the aforementioned Fredericus, Vromoldus, Engelbertus, Siffridus, and Johannes, who were archbishops of said Church, unable to live in their own regions due to their fear of the cruelty of said Brethren, all died impoverished in foreign lands, particularly at the Roman Curia during their litigations against them. And thus said Brethren, persecutors of the Christian faith, do, as

they have become used to doing, with grave prejudice to the faith and contempt for the offices and status of the Church. And this was and is the public and notorious truth; it was and is common knowledge and public report.

101. Likewise, after these legal sentences, sentences of excommunication and renewed declarations of excommunication imposed upon them for non-compliance with the first sentences, were published in many places, they seemed somewhat confused among men; for not reforming themselves in any way, but joining evil to evil all the more, not seeking to cure their malice but rather to avoid their own destruction, receiving these sentences of excommunication and tumbling from one such excommunication into another, with sacrilegious hand they took hold of the archbishop's general vicar in spiritual and temporal matters, *viz.*, their own superior, and all canons and prebendaries and other dignitaries of said Church in Riga, and tossed them into dire prisons, holding them there for many long years in actual captivity or something just short thereof. Several of these, particularly Scholasticus, who was seen to be more fierce in his defense of the rights of said Church, were tortured and put to death in those prisons. And this was and is the public and notorious truth, it was and is common knowledge and public report.

102. Likewise, at that time, several secular clerics of said city of Riga, overly terrorized by the cruelty of said Brethren, assumed a regular habit in divers monasteries so as to avoid the mortal danger they feared looming. Consequently, compelled by such necessity, *viz.*, the fear of death, they became religious regulars. And this was and is the public and notorious truth.

103. Likewise, said superior and other ecclesiastical persons, among them several other presbyters who had been taken captive, had their

homes and habitations violated. Chambers, trunks, and chests were burst open and shattered. The Brethren took as plunder all books, money, letters, rules, instruments and documents, vestments, and divers precious items, indeed all things they were able to find, both in archiepiscopal holdings as well as those belonging to the aforementioned prebends and chapter-houses, from the least to the greatest, carrying off what they seized and converting the same to their own use as they saw fit. The letters, rules, and documents, however, they stifled. And this was and is the public and notorious truth.

104. Likewise, not content with the foregoing, but indeed with hearts hardened by a diabolical obstinance, breaking through the locks and bolts of said Church in Riga, they foully despoiled it of privileges, books, chalices, ornaments, and other things and precious items. They also despoiled the archiepiscopal library of its resources of books, tearing in pieces and scattering at their pleasure all the aforesaid, while converting to their own use those items among them that pleased them, although they did this with grave prejudice to the Christian faith in those parts. And this was and is the public and notorious truth; it was and is common knowledge and public report.

105. Likewise, said Brethren, the aforementioned heretics and sacrilegious men, wishing that so much foul crime of theirs should be in some way hidden, that the rulers of the would should be ignorant of so many shameful acts of theirs — so shameful! — the crimes and sins they committed, and that news thereof should not come to the public notice of people in other parts of the Christian world, so that, having at last exterminated the entire clergy of these regions of Livonia, they might be enabled to occupy the entirety thereof themselves, alone — as subsequent evidence clearly proved — they shut off all roads and passes into said region, by sea as well as by land, so that no person would be able to enter or to leave these parts of Livonia without their

knowledge and permission. And in as much as any man happened to be allowed passage out, the Brethren first compelled him to swear a solemn oath not to reveal to anyone in any other region anything of the acts of violence, injuries, sacrileges, and other crimes aforesaid, perpetrated by them. And this was and is the public and notorious truth; it was and is common knowledge and public report.

106. Likewise, the aforesaid truths being what they are, at last, said Brethren, those sons of iniquity, wretchedly trampling beneath their feet their own proper lady, *viz.*, the aforesaid Church in Riga, and treasonously transforming the defense of the faith due her on their part into the maximum offence presented her, after the manner of infidels — and this not without perpetrating the crime of lèse-majesté and showing great ingratitude — they occupied all cities, castles, fortresses, freeholds, and all other possessions of said Church in Riga, those belonging to the household of the archbishop as well as to the chapter-houses and all other persons of said Church, along with all their rights and appurtenances. These they continually held under their occupation for more than thirty years as they continue to hold them, wickedly spilling into their own purse all fruits, revenues, and produce of the same. And so it was not only the aforesaid archbishop, but also canons, prebendaries, and other clerics who were finally driven into exile from their fatherland: some fleeing the threat of prison there, and others narrowly escaping imprisonment at the hands of the King of the Romans and Bohemians at the time, and other instances too. And this was and is the public and notorious truth; it was and is common knowledge and public report.

107. Likewise, said Brethren, to whom previously the Church in Riga had been mistress and lady, now wished to transform her perpetually into their own handmaid. And in order that said church should never be enabled to escape their clutches by any power or

authority whatsoever, they practiced upon the Pope at the time, Boniface IX. Having taken money from these Brethren, despite their being heretics, and having neither the counsel nor the consent of the Cardinals of the Church of Rome, and without taking any knowledge of the true state of things, but acting with undue speed in such a difficult matter, entirely misusing and abusing his apostolic authority, he incorporated unto them and their pretended order the said Church. He so established and even ordained that henceforth and in perpetuity, no title of prebendary, nor superior, nor dean, nor any other dignity, whether assumed or official, being a cure in said Church or not, whatever the title should be, could be received by or due to any person unless he had first made the pretended regular profession, which said Brethren are used to make. And thus, following the profession of all these, or at least the great majority thereof, from this time forward and in perpetuity they were deemed to be and known as — not being of the Augustinian order, but rather of the Order of the Blessed Virgin of the Teutons. This is laid out at more length in the letters concerning these matters, in which they are contained, however to the grave detriment of the faith and the Christian religion, to which letters said corporation refers in the absence of other evidence. And this was and is the public and notorious truth.

108. Likewise, standing upon this aforesaid and accomplished fact, soon they once again approached the aforesaid Pope Boniface, and — through the means of money, as before — they worked it so that the most reverend Father Johannes, being at the time archbishop of the Church in Riga, just as he was litigating against said Brethren before the Roman Curia, be translated — although unwillingly — to the titular patriarchate of Alexandria, so that he should enjoy only the title of that Church. They then proceeded to procure the Archdiocese of Riga for some other person from among their own pretended Order, or sect. They paid a high price for this act of simony, becoming as

it were participants in Simon Magus' own malediction, as the Apostle Peter declared: *Keep thy money to thyself to perish with thee, because thou hast thought that the gift of God may be purchased with money* (Acts VIII),[65] for without a doubt the gift of God is belongs to the authority of the Church, along with all its appurtenances. And this was and is the public and notorious truth.

109. Likewise, the aforesaid provision notwithstanding — such as it is, procured and effected through simony — nevertheless, those simoniacal Brethren, who had already, even before the provision, occupied all the temporal goods of the Church in Riga, which they continually occupy even now, still they did not wish to permit even this brother of theirs so provided for to enter into the possession of the city of Riga, its castle and other possessions, and so they do not admit him still, doing as they have done lest said brother, the so-called archbishop of Riga, might and may reside in said Church, having full and free use of its possessions, rights, and appurtenances. And this was and is the public and notorious truth.

110. Likewise, so that their Church would be seen by men as having an archbishop, said Brethren, the aforesaid simoniacs and heretics, so set about discussing, or, better, bargaining with, that brother of theirs, that disciple of Simon Magus, who was provided for by way of simony, until they contented him with a certain quantity of money as an annuity so that, residing in whatever part of the world he chose, he should not seek to be invested in any manner with the possessions, rights, or appurtenances of said Church, at least in so far as temporalities are concerned. And indeed this brother of theirs, so abandoning and betraying his Church, having received thirty silver pieces, went off in the footsteps of Judas Iscariot. For, catching sight of the wolves, he had no concern for his sheep, being as he is a mere hireling (John X).[66] And in this way said solemn Church, at one time

planted and watered by pious Christians and zealots for the faith, and possessed and governed happily for the longest time, now — O the sorrow of it! — has been made over into such a heretical sect by said Brethren, those terrible enemies of the faith and most cruel persecutors thereof, and is so occupied these days and destroyed, to the gravest reproach of, and indeed detriment to the Christian faith! And this was and is the public and notorious truth.

111. Likewise, the Brethren, fearing lest afterwards this brother of theirs, the so-called Archbishop of Riga, or his successor, should reclaim from them the Church's possessions, and fearing lest he might offer resistance to them from said holdings, they proceeded to make them less useful than they had been before. Some of them they destroyed utterly, *viz.*, burning to ash several castles, and annihilating or destroying other edifices in other manners. They devastated villages, turning them into desolate wastelands, just as they had destroyed, annihilated, and desolated villages before. They moved the men who had inhabited these villages to their own, and, collecting materials from the objects they destroyed, used them to better their own proper possessions. And this was and is the public and notorious truth.

112. Likewise, shortly thereafter, about four years having passed since the foregoing, they seized this aforesaid brother of theirs, the so-called Archbishop of Riga — a pretended title, that — paying no deference to his pontifical orders, nor caring at all for ecclesiastical censures nor taking note of them, indeed, damnably contemning them. Him they held captive in the castle of Malbork in the Diocese of Chełmno for such time until they succeeded, constantly working on him, to extort from him whatever it was they wished. And this was and is the public and notorious truth.

113. Likewise, the Brethren not only received and damnably subjected the Church of Riga to themselves, but not long ago they treat-

ed in the same way other Churches being suffragan dioceses to the Riga Archbishopric, *viz.,* those of Courland and Reval in parts of Livonia, Sambia and Pomezania in parts of Prussia, and Chełmno in the Kingdom of Poland. In these abovesaid Churches there are both bishops and prebendaries, and also those who preside during a period of vacancy, of whom it has become a matter of course that both those installed and those merely presiding should belong to the Brethren's sect, as heretical and damnable as it is. And therefore the authority over bishops, canons, and other clerics remains with the Brethren and laypersons, and not the other way around, as the latter ought to be necessarily obedient to the former — by which situation canon law is held in grave detestation. You might well say that the aforesaid bishops dare not, for the most part, exercise their ecclesiastical jurisdiction, whether in spiritual or temporal matters, against the will of their pretended lay preceptors — to the grave oppression of both the Churches in question, and of justice itself. And this was and is the public and notorious truth.

114. Likewise, wishing yet to subject to themselves other Churches in the regions of Livonia as were subject to the Church in Riga as suffragan sees, *viz.*, the Diocese of Saare-Lääne and Dorpat, just as they did with those others mentioned above, so as actually to usurp unto themselves said Churches and their cities, castles, villages, towns, and whatever other goods they possessed, gathering the same and uniting them unto the holdings of their pretended Order, they attempted many and varied machinations with this goal in mind, as even today they desist not in employing, however much it lies in their power to do so. Such was their treatment of the most reverend father, Lord Henricus, bishop at the time of the aforesaid Diocese of Saare-Lääne, the immediate predecessor of the present bishop of said Church. Conspiring with fraud and deceit, they captured him and proceeded to throttle and suffocate him. Then, strangled to death,

they foully tossed him into a dungheap, that is, a sewer, as they have done before and are used to doing. And this was and is the public and notorious truth; it was and is common knowledge and public report among such men as are aware of the matter.

115. Likewise, they grievously oppressed and wounded the aforementioned Church in Dorpat many times over, by their acts of arson, rapine, and other evil doings, such as they are used to perpetrate. This they did for some fourteen years before and after the years about which we are now speaking, more or less, *viz.*: stealthily entering said Diocese with a force of armed men, after first driving away all flocks and herds, domestic, farm, and draught animals, they burnt to the ground the villages and towns belonging both to the Church and to other men inhabiting this diocese, after first despoiling them of their yearly produce by igniting the grain in the fields and ravaging it with flame. They massacred some men, slaughtering some themselves and causing others to be killed at the hands of others; some they took captive, committing many other evil crimes against said Church while damnably transporting others, both subjects of said Church and not, into said Diocese so as to work their will upon them. As has become their custom, they brought much molestation upon the bishops of the Church both in Saare-Lääne and Dorpat, frequently afflicting them with disorders and injuries. And this was and is the public and notorious truth.

116. Likewise, some four years ago or so, a most notable and renowned soldier of Livonia, a vassal of the Riga and Dorpat churches, named Johannes von Dalen, was making his way home from Prussia towards Livonia. He was taken prisoner near the city of [ ][67] in the diocese of Warmia and there, without having been given any reason for his arrest, he was held by the Brethren until nightfall, at which time, by the light of a candle, having been led into a horse stable and

still being completely ignorant of what was to happen to him, he was most cruelly and wretchedly decapitated by them, who caused his head to be struck off. And this was and is the public and notorious truth; it was and is common knowledge and public report.

117. Likewise, a certain man named Johannes Schmidt, alias Faber, from the city of Lübeck, being a captain in command of a company of armed men, came, at the call the aforesaid Brethren, leading a multitude of soldiers to the aid of the Brethren in the war they were waging at the time against the King of Poland. This was around the year 1400. He did serve these Brethren with his men for some time. At length, when he reminded the Brethren of the salary they had promised him, demanding the same for the service he rendered them, said Brethren stuffed this Captain Johannes into a sack, which they securely fastened, and there, in the city of Gdańsk, which belongs to the Włocławek Diocese, they tossed him into the river known as the Wisła, where he sank and drowned. Such was the reward and salary he received for his service. And this was and is the public and notorious truth, for which they were and are publicly infamous.

118. Likewise, in that same year or thereabouts, in the aforesaid city of Gdańsk, said Brethren summoned to the castle of which they had taken possession in said city, the most prominent men of the city, *viz.*, Konrad Leczków, a city alderman, Arnold Hecht, and Bartholomew Gross, both consuls. And these men, unprovided and suspecting nothing, without any knowledge of any reason why, were decapitated and cruelly murdered as the Brethren caused them to be. Many days later the Brethren buried them and caused them to be buried, their bodies bound in rope, within the walls of the castle. And this was and is the public and notorious truth; it was and is common knowledge and public report.

119. Likewise, in the same year or thereabouts, certain of said Brethren entered into a castle belonging to the church in Chełmno called Lubovia. There, following a meal, they seized a certain canon of the church in Chełmno, a resident of said castle named Nicholaus Swaveswel. Him they led out to a cart and drove to the river known as the Drwęca, where, having bound him and enclosed him in a sack, they tossed him into the river waters where they submerged him and caused him to be submerged. Later, the other canons of the Church found his body sunk in the river and recovered it. They reported what had happened to their cathedral church, and buried him with ecclesiastical honors. When the bishop of that Church, also one of their pretended Order, as is attested by several men, deposed on this matter before their superior, who among them is known as the Master General, demanding satisfaction for the aforesaid Church on account of the murder of its canon, their pretended Master wholly refused to do anything, nor did he. And this was and is the public and notorious truth.

120. Likewise, in our own most recent times, *viz.,* in the present year of Our Lord 1416, in the month of July or thereabout,[68] the Brethren cruelly decapitated and caused to be decapitated fourteen consuls and other important men of the same city of Gdańsk, who were neither convicted of nor confessed to any crime, with the great neglect of the rule of law. And this was and is the public and notorious truth.

121. Likewise, some time afterwards in this same year, the Brethren seized, sometimes by twos, sometimes by threes or more, some inhabitants of this city, successively, even pulling some of them from their beds, until they had arrived at a large number of them, *viz.*, some fifty or so, whom they then wretchedly killed and similarly caused

to be killed, without any rule of law being observed. Many others of these they drowned and caused to be drowned, and even to this day do they successively kill and drown whomever they suspect of being opposed to them. And this was and is the public and notorious truth.

122. Likewise, having witnessed cruelty of such sort being perpetrated by these Brethren upon their fellow citizens, and acknowledging that this would never come to an end or ever be limited at all, as it continually seemed to grow and grow, some hundred and eighty citizens of Gdańsk, unable to bear such a doubtful state of mortal danger as loomed over them, fled the city here and there for other dominions, abandoning their own wives, children, houses, and other goods. And this was and is the public and notorious truth.

123. Likewise, said Brethren, those adherents of cruelty and malice, neither able nor willing to restrain their own cruelty and malice, nor indeed to temper it, they totally seized, as is their custom to do, all the houses and all the goods of all the aforesaid decapitated, murdered, and drowned men. In repulsive fashion they ejected, expelled, and had ejected and expelled all the women and children of the aforesaid from their homes. And thus these aforesaid women, honest women all, so excluded and expelled from all their possessions along with their children, under the fardel of poverty were driven by wretched penury to hard labor. And this was and is the public and notorious truth.

124. Likewise, these Brethren cruelly cut down, murdered, decapitated, and drowned, and caused to be drowned, decapitated, cut down, and murdered many other persons at divers times. Some of these were secular priests; nor did they even spare those in regular religious orders, nor did they show any respect unto the female gender, doing such things without any cause therefor being known, and

quite beyond the pale of the rule of law, merely at the pleasure of their own free will, however iniquitous and perverse. And this they do, have done, and have become used to doing. And this is the public and notorious truth. Thus it has been stated, held, and reckoned; thus it is spoken abroad, held, and reckoned openly, publicly, and notoriously.[69]

125. Likewise, whenever they receive any new person into their pretended Order, wishing to disburden themselves of the faculty of proof, immediately and without any probation whatsoever, or at least any legitimate sort of probation, they demand of him and receive his solemn religious profession, however iniquitous, devious and unjust it be, thus binding him unto themselves, in so far as in them this lies, lest, discovering later the wickedness of the Brethren, he should be able to break away from them. Now, the canonical institutes do not allow for such a precipitous profession, but, with good reason, provide rather for an entire year of probation. Thus said Brethren act, have acted, and have become used to acting in such a way. And so it often happens that such men, having made a blasphemous profession in the Name of the Lord, later curse those who so deceived them. And this was and is the public and notorious truth.

126. Likewise, with indifference they receive unto their pretended Order wicked, cruel, and infamous men, sometimes even such as have been banished from foreign parts on account of their crimes and demerits, or indeed such as have fled from justice. This they do, have done, and have become used to doing. And this is the public and notorious truth.

127. Likewise, two, three, four, or more of these Brethren are regularly sent from Prussia into Germany each year in order to recommend their pretended Order and extol its customs, uses, habits, and observances, such as they were and are, with the aim of enticing

men unto them. And these, running to and fro and traversing divers parts of Germany, recommending their pretended Order with many and various praiseful narratives and even making promises, as some men assert — like false prophets, they seduce men in this manner and lead them unto the precipice of their heresy, as indeed they have become used to doing. And thus sometimes these Brethren collect bastards and other men born illegitimately from damnable couplings, who abandon their homeland on account of their father's crime. At other times they easily entice poor men, even such as are without blemish, and noble-born, who, however, do not find themselves capable of sustaining their father's material position as befits the nobility. These also they gather and receive unto their pretended Order. This they do, have done, and have become used to doing. And this is the public and notorious truth.

128. Likewise, by this kind of aforesaid religious profession clerics and priests, as well as laymen, whenever such profession takes place, entrust themselves into the hands of laymen — as they have done and have become used to doing — *viz.*, into the hands of the *commendatores* or other superiors of their pretended Order, however erroneous this is. The Brethren claim that such a profession to warmaking has been in their rule since their pretended Order was first instituted, as has been said above. Yet this vow is in no way binding, at least as far as clerics are concerned; indeed it is and has always been erroneous, contrary to good morals, and also contrary to canonical institutions, repugnant to the clerical state and rules, and indeed impossible *de iure* — even if such warmaking should be in itself licit and honest. And thus it happens, *de facto*, and frequently, that said Brethren and the laypersons who claim such superiority, treat their priests with irreverence. And not only simple priests, but even their own bishops, *viz.*, those belonging to their abovesaid society or sect, these they address with little reverence, *viz.*, in vulgar Teutonic per *du Pfaffe*,[70]

which has a disrespectful ring to it. Sometimes they even drown their brother priests. And this is the public and notorious truth.

129. Likewise, not only are they cruel murderers and bandits, and are also entangled in the many crimes abovesaid, but they are also in fact men of business and merchants.[71] For each year they bank a certain amount of money, *viz.*, eight hundred thousand Prussian marks, of which each of these is valued at two gold florins in coin of the realm, and is used to be so valued, with a certain brother of theirs. The purpose of this official, known in their vulgar Teutonic speech as the *grosz schaphar*, which in Latin would be *magnus dispensator* (or Grand Steward), is the conducting of various businesses for profit and the multiplication of lucre. And their rule for such banking was such, that with the passage of each year, beyond the stated principal of eight hundred thousand marks, which he was bound to account for, preserving it in full, an additional six thousand marks, or whatever sum they determined upon as interest, should be deposited into their common treasury, augmenting their wealth each year. Beyond this, he was obliged to provide the superior of these Brethren, who amongst them is known as the Master General, and his court and household, with copious amounts of woolen cloth and an abundance of items for the kitchen, as well as other necessary items, from the profits he had earned. And said Grand Steward, engaging in commerce of various sorts with the use of said money, according to the rule established for him, did restore said capital and deposit the aforesaid profits in their treasuries. He sufficiently provided the cloth and the other items to said Master General and his court, and whatever remained from said profits beyond the abovesaid he reserved for his own use. And thus said Brethren do, have done, and have been accustomed to do, engaging thus in trade. And this is the public and notorious truth; such is said, held, and reckoned openly, publicly and notoriously; such was and is common knowledge and public report.

130. Likewise, whenever any vessel laden with ware from beyond the seas should apply to put in at the aforesaid city of Gdańsk, where there is a notable port under the power of the Brethren, none of the other merchants is permitted to buy anything until said brother, the Grand Steward, should select and purchase whatever amounts of said wares please him. Thus they are obstructed by the prohibition of the Brethren. And then, whenever the other merchants wish to purchase said wares from the Brethren, they are made to pay a steeper price for them. And this was and is the public and notorious truth.

131. Likewise, whenever said ships are unloaded, they are immediately laden anew with the wares of the Brethren, to be carried by them beyond the sea. And no ship is permitted to, or dare, set out from that port, forbidden to do so by the aforesaid Brethren, until such time as a ship laden with the wares of the Brethren might first be unloaded at the port of destination, at their pleasure, and before any of the above-mentioned ships might arrive. And this process might take, for example, a month, or some other long term, to complete, according to the pleasure of the Grand Steward. And this was and is the public and notorious truth.

132. Likewise, when said Brethren, being as they are merchants, disciples of trade and mercantile pursuits, realized that grains such as wheat and rye are valued more in certain lands beyond the sea than other items, and because it was customary that great abundances of grain from the Kingdom of Poland would transit through their port, wishing to convert such grain to their pecuniary advantage alone, they prohibited all and sundry from exporting, or even daring to export, such grain from their possessions, although this was fraudulent and deceitful, deceiving other merchants by such iniquity so as to exclude them from such profits. And thus they did exclude them,

scilicet, by having said grain laden only onto their own vessels and thus monopolising its transport beyond the sea. Only they gathered in and thus obtained such lucre, however, not without great prejudice being done to other merchants. And this was and is the public and notorious truth.

133. Likewise, not only, as has been said, did these Brethren engage in common trade, but also, specifically, their *commendatores*, or pretended superiors, commonly, and as a rule, do not permit their subjects to own flour mills. Rather, they themselves possess nearly all the flour mills that exist in the lands subject unto them, so that thus constrained — though with tyrannical subtlety — their subjects must mill their grain in the flour mills of the brethren, rendering directly unto said Brethren a certain quota or portion of said flour or grain. And thus they wax in wealth from said milling, every year, to their great profit.[72] The flour thus acquired and extorted they ship beyond the sea, selling it and having it sold for some thousands of florins, or other large amounts of money.

134. Likewise, said Brethren, wishing to be the only ones in Livonia permitted to engage in trade — as they are, although they also operate through other agents of theirs — and so that they might sell their goods more freely and profit therefrom, as much as lies in their power, they do not permit other merchants to enter said regions with their wares. Nor do they permit entry to anyone, unless as a special mark of favor, or unless said merchants have learned how best to please said Brethren. And thus they set divers obstacles before other merchants, both by sea and by land, by various machination of theirs often blocking access to their seaport, though maliciously and unjustly, and with prejudice burdening not only the merchants in question, but indeed the country as a whole. Thus merchants existing under the rule of these Brethren are not able to well sustain themselves. And

this they have done, do, and are used to doing. And this was and is the public and notorious truth.

135. Likewise, not content with this sort of profiteering from trade, but aspiring to even greater dominions of lands through the perversity of usury, not yet thirty years have past since they obtained the dukedom of Dobrzyń in the kingdom of Poland from a certain Duke of Opole named Naderspan, a vassal of the King of Poland, who offered it to them as collateral for a certain sum of money lent to said duke upon such guarantee. Now, having so received it, for many years, *viz.*, fourteen, more or less, they held it in their possession, retaining for themselves the fruit, revenues, and produce arising therefrom without in any way reckoning these profits into the debt as partial or gradual repayment thereof, as still they do not. Nor did they wish to restore said dukedom to the aforesaid duke, nor to the King of Poland, nor would they restore it, unless first having received, as they really did receive, monetary satisfaction in the total amount that they had originally loaned. And this was and is the public and notorious truth.

136. Likewise, long before said duke, as stated above, had entered into debt in regards to a loan received, for which he staked his dukedom as collateral, the Brethren set a notable castle in that same dukedom, colloquially known as Sloteria, under obligations, along with many villages and divers other possessions belonging thereto, for a certain amount of money. Here too the brethren held said castle and its aforesaid appurtenances in their possession, and as far as the fruit, revenue, and produce that they obtained from it during the time under our consideration, they wholly refused to deduct or subtract anything from the amount of money owed them. Rather, they demanded the entire sum on top of the aforesaid, nor would they restore said castle with its aforesaid villages

and possessions until they did. And this was and is the public and notorious truth.

137. Likewise, a notable district in Mazovia known in the vulgar tongue as Zawadzkie containing within it many divers and notable villages, towns, and other possessions, lying in said dukedom of Mazovia and thus in the Kingdom of Poland, was offered as collateral by the Duke of Mazovia, *viz.*, lord Ziemowit, and received as such, in exchange for a certain amount of money lent to said duke on such terms. For a long time, for many years, they so held and indeed possessed said district, retaining for themselves all fruit, revenue, and produce resulting therefrom, nor for all that did they compute the same as any extenuation or payment in kind for the money lent — nor do they — as is the practice of usurers. And so would they have held it in perpetuity, as much as would be in their power to do so, retaining it still until the debt had been fully repaid, even though the full value of the debt had been sufficiently repaid in species of said fruits, revenues, and produce, had not the hand of the Lord, as it is believed, smote them in their overweening pride through His Most Serene Majesty, the King of Poland, who with an iron rod wrested said district from their hands. And this was and is the public and notorious truth.

138. Likewise, yet another notable district in said Dukedom of Mazovia known as Wizna was tendered by the same duke to the Brethren under obligation for a certain amount of money. This they held as collateral for some fourteen years or so, similarly retaining its fruit and produce to themselves, without in any manner reckoning them in reduction of the capital sum — just as usurers are wont to do. Nor did they restore said district until the aforesaid sum had been repaid totally and integrally. And this was and is the public and notorious truth.

139. Likewise, in the Nakło district of the Kingdom of Poland, a certain military leader of the King of Poland at the time offered a large and truly notable tract of woodland, known as Babsko, as collateral for a certain amount of money. And this, along with the exploitation thereof, they have held for a long time now, as they continue to hold it. What is more, they are attempting to usurp it to themselves in perpetuity. A great portion of said woodland they have already reduced and converted to agricultural purposes, locating several villages therein. And this was and is the public and notorious truth.

140. Likewise, a dukedom or margravate in Saxon lands, known as Nova Marchia, was similarly offered them by his Most Serene Highness lord Sigismund, King of the Romans and Hungarians, as collateral for the loan of a certain amount of money. They have held this land for many years, retaining all of its produce and enjoying quite all of its rights. Indeed, they hold it still after the manner of usurers, thus enjoying the fruits of usurious profit, however unjust and iniquitous they be — damned and declared iniquitous by divine as well as human law — for, in the end, according to the common estimation of many, they have already been repaid sufficiently for the loan offered on the basis of said margravate. And this was and is the public and notorious truth.

141. Likewise, said usurers, wishing to have subjects worthy of such masters as they, have asserted — however falsely, erroneously, and just like false prophets denying the truth of sacred Scripture and even canon law (see *De usuriis* X, V, 19; X. II. 24, 7) — that it is permissible to charge interest of one mark, every year, for each and every ten marks of money loaned, as clear profit, and that such a small profit is not to be understood as usury. And this they caused to be approved among their subjects as a sort of law. These subjects

of theirs did approve of the same, and not a few of them, seduced by this action, began to practice usury as they continue to practice it: *viz.*, loaning ten or twelve Prussian marks at an interest rate of one mark per year. And this was and is the public and notorious truth.

142. Likewise, the aforesaid Brethren, ever eager to engage in usury, as well as to exchange their money for lands, castles, cities, and whatever other sort of possessions, in whatever amount might be offered them on account of the aforesaid lucre — however being thus usurious, damned, and unjust — they have received and continue to receive such usurious obligations, whenever offered to them, and they are used to receive the same, *viz.*, through the exercise of such usury, damnably usurping as collateral more than a few such possessions and dominions, as they have done in the past. And this was and is the public and notorious truth; on account of the aforesaid they were and are publicly infamous.

143. Likewise, the aforesaid Brethren began minting their own coinage, causing the same to be minted, however iniquitously and unjustly, some seven or so years past, and continuously thereafter. And yet they have so continually diminished it in weight that, whereas one mark of their coinage had been worth two gold florins of coin of the realm, as it continued long to be valued, presently it is hardly worth half a florin, or even three-quarters. Accordingly, what previously cost one of their marks, presently can hardly be purchased for three or so. And thus said Brethren, so devoted to their lucre — however to the maximum detriment of their subjects — have already pauperized no small number of them, oppressing them and grievously harming them in their possessions, however tyrannically, iniquitously, and unjustly. And this was and is the public and notorious truth; it was and is common knowledge and public report.

144. Likewise, when said subjects, unable to bear such a burden, made humble supplication unto said Brethren, requesting them to ameliorate the situation of the coinage described above, the Brethren, conceiving a great rancour in their spirit against these petitioners, cruelly cut down, made to be cut down, and decapitated many of them, both natives of that region and other citizens and inhabitants of regions and lands subject to said Brethren. This happened just recently in the present year of Our Lord 1416.[73] Some they had thrown into dire prisons, shackling them and causing them to be shackled. Several of these they snatched from their homes, indeed from their very bedrooms in the middle of the night, after which they hurled them into the waters and drowned them, causing them to be so hurled into the water and drowned, with no regard to any rule of law. And this was and is the public and notorious truth; it has been stated, held, and reckoned, and it is stated, held, and reckoned openly, publicly, and notoriously today. And thus on account of the foregoing they are publicly infamous.

145. Likewise, when any secular cleric, especially a parish priest or rector, dies in any of the lands and dominions subject to these Brethren, they first despoil, as they have despoiled and have become used to despoiling, their parishes of all their objects and goods. Thereupon, declaring the same derelict upon the death of said rector, however wretchedly and indeed sacrilegiously, they usurp and seize the derelict objects to themselves. Thereupon, they present said seized and usurped, vacant churches to clerics of their choice, pretending to be authorized to do so by privilege received of the Apostolic See, although this be a false claim, and they proceed to emburden and grievously oppress said parochial churches, as they continue to do, and have become used to doing. And this was and is the public and notorious truth; it was and is common knowledge and public report.

146. Likewise, claiming simultaneously to be absolved by privilege from the paying of tithes, this they do falsely and in order to deceive the Churches in their lands, depriving them of the tithes owed them, refusing to resolve the tithes from their lands under cultivation and their other possessions — thus defrauding as they have defrauded many Churches of the tithes owed them. Thus they do, and have done, and have become used to doing, however unjustly and iniquitously, for tithes are due by divine law, and are *de iure* to be rendered unto parish churches, especially estate and agricultural tithes. This was and is the public and notorious truth; it was and is common knowledge and public report.

147. Likewise, the laymen among these Brethren, wretchedly usurping to themselves the authority of superiors in the abovesaid lands subject to them, not only in temporal matters, but even, sometimes, in matters spiritual, impede the ecclesiastical jurisdiction as they have impeded it, not permitting the bishops to freely administer justice to those subject to them. Nor do they permit their subjects, even if these be clerics, to pursue justice before the bench of their bishops, whether in suit against the Brethren, or at times even against others, to say nothing of appealing to the Apostolic See on account of any grievance, if it be against the will of the Brethren. As they have not permitted this in the past, nor do they permit it now. Said subjects, even if they be clerics, fearing the cruelty and tyranny of these Brethren, are unable to pursue, let alone achieve, justice, nor dare they make such a motion, as they are unable to, they dare not to, whenever such a case should present itself. And thus said Brethren, being the oppressors of justice, do not only dominate laypersons with such tyranny, but even the clergy — not without grievous vituperation of the ecclesiastical state and Holy Orders. And this was and is the

public and notorious truth; it was and is common knowledge and public report.

148. Likewise, at the time of the pontificate of Pope Gregory XI of blessed memory, several erroneous articles of the Saxon Mirror, which in vulgar Teutonic is known as the *Magdeburghische Recht* — in Latin *Ius Magdeburgense*,[74] were for a long period of time condemned and prohibited under a sentence of excommunication *latae sententiae*, at least to all judges in Germany, of which several are still in effect, *scilicet*: 'Whenever a legal matter is moved against a person, be it a criminal or civil question, it is not up to the accuser to prove the accusation, but rather up to the defendant to prove his innocence' — which is entirely erroneous, for *denial of a deed, by nature, is no direct proof of anything* (ch. XXIII, X, *De eleccione* I. 6; ch. 2, C. 6, *ff* and ch. V, X, *De renunciacione* I, 9). Or: 'The testament or gift of one bedridden on account of illness, even though he be of sound mind, is null and void if the testator, clad in his armour, be unable to bestride a horse aided by no more than one stone or wooden block raised no higher than one cubit above the earth.' These, and others similar thereto, were rightly condemned. Nevertheless, caring not a fig for ecclesiastical censure, pronouncing thus judicial sentences among those subject to them, however erroneous, iniquitous, and unjust, and prohibited on account of the condemnation of the abovesaid articles and errors, still do the Brethren judge as they have judged. And this was and is the public and notorious truth.

149. Likewise, being as they are in rebellion against the Roman Church and her Sacred Councils, really opposing themselves to and resisting the apostolic authority after the manner of heretics, *viz.*, in refusing to obey said Councils, and, in general, neither obeying the decretals of the Holy Fathers, or the apostolic constitutions, mandates and letters, which they continue to spurn, transgressing

and violating them, whenever such apostolic letters, sentences, and verdicts of any sort are issued by the Roman Curia, they forbid the presentation, publication and execution thereof, contemning and impeding them. With such and many other evils do they counter all such decretals, constitutions, mandates, and apostolic letters, doing as they have done, and have become used to doing and perpetrating, however temerariously, contumaciously, iniquitously and unjustly. And this was and is the public and notorious truth.

150. Likewise, poorly and ever worse oriented to the keys of the Church, continuously caring nothing at all for sentences of excommunication or interdict or other ecclesiastical censures, bearing them as they have borne and have become used to bearing them [...] being as they are [depraved] legalists, under this color they despise [... and] flee discipline. A[nd this was and is the public and notorious truth; it was] and is common knowledge and public r[eport.][75]

151. Likewise, wishing to present this to [...] being unable, they wrote and [caused to be written] [...] in large letters in vulgar T[eutonic] [...] they were rather seen among them to be in [...] in effect, that whatever sort of sentence of ex[communication] [...] is entirely null and void, however being not without a g[reat] [...] and deceptively, and with the aim of deceiving the people [...] of authority. And this was and is the public and [notorious] truth.

152. Likewise, although, as has been said, they became sufficiently wealthy *in their own lands*, authority over which they obtained through rapine and other illicit practices, — *still unwilling* to put an end to their cupidity and malice, but rather *elated still in their pride*, yearning to obtain still more from the neighboring Christian kingdoms, *a certain while ago* having received unto them a certain Goliardus, they dissembled *his marriage* to Her Most Illustrious Maj-

esty, the Queen of Denmark, although they did so mendaciously and deceitfully, *quickly arranging the betrothal* with suitable conduct, they arranged the match and had it arranged. And they *led him* to the Kingdom of Denmark as the heir to said Queen, so that, under such color and *fraudulently* they might stealthily *enter* the castles, cities, and towns of said Kingdom and obtain the same *through deception*. This Goliardus, although having been reverently received and well treated by some bishops who had been deceived themselves, the *depravation* of said Brethren being discovered at last, he was arrested, set on trial, and sentenced to death, executed, *as well as* burnt at the stake. And this was and is the public and notorious truth; it was and is common knowledge and public report.

153. Likewise, said Brethren, masters of iniquity and enemies of the Christian religion, entering by stealth a certain sacred monastery in Gotland, near to the city, or town, of Visby, of the Linköping Diocese of the Order of St Bernard and known as the *Mons solis*, it [...] the relics of the saints completely

[...] [tr]eating them there from said [monastery expelling them?] [...] they occupied as they continue to occupy [dest]roying and having it destroyed. And this was [and is the public and notorious truth; it was and is co]mmon knowledge and public report.

[154. Likewise] [...] in neighboring regions and round about
[...] [publi]c and manifest was and is, that,
[...] [I]n ecclesial and ecclesiastical persons, than
[...] that the most grievous oppressors of their neighbors
[...] innumerable [injur]ies and evi[l]s in general
[...] and of the worst condition, *viz*, men
[...] destroying, despoiling temporal goods
[...] to the Christian kings and princes and others
[...]ing, oppressing their own subjects, the ecclesiastical state

[...] to [ma]ny other priests, cursing God and the Saints

[...] blaspheming the Body of Christ, abusing the word

[...] condemning [...]deemer's Gospel. Nor do they fear God

[...] prideful, deceitful, perverse, grasping, greedy, invidious, drunkards

[...] incontinent, lazy, seditious, makers of scandal and all vices [the following categor]ies, sorely hated of men and noxious, having not the least true vestige [of religion/piety] in them, however [they bear upon their white mantles] a black cross outwardly, not without significance, that: since with good reason the color black is not understood as a sign [of light, but?] the darknesses, not the Cross of Christ, but truly the gibbet of some bandit condemned to hang, in whose foot[steps] they follow and whose work[s] they imitate. And such are the fruits of the abovesaid iniquity of their heretical, most cruel and horrendous [sect]. And this was and is the public and notorious truth, even so that all the aforesaid has made and makes all and sundry of them to be publicly and notoriously defamed and uncovered for what they are, as in all the regions wherever notice is taken of them, they have been so taken, proven, and been reckoned, openly, publicly, and notoriously.

155. Likewise, all the foregoing was and is common knowledge and public report concerning all them, collectively and individually.

Endnotes

1. The complicated process by which this treatise was identified as an independent work of Paweł is described by Belch, *Paulus Vladimiri*, I, 176 and II, 906-911, and his conclusion has generally been accepted. His dating—between November 1416 and January 1417—is based on internal evidence from articles 73, 120, and 144; see his comments II, 912 and below in the translation of these articles.

2. This prologue, originally intended for another work and appearing in only one of the two manuscripts upon which this edition is based, was abandoned and replaced by the Prologue B below; see Belch, *Paulus Vladimiri*, II, 910.

3. Matt. 7:15-16 and 18.

4. The primary reasons the Council of Constance was held and the main foci of participants were indeed ending the schism, extirpating heresy, and reforming the church "in capite et in membris" as Paweł notes here. But there were other European issues that some participants argued should be given attention. Emperor Sigismund outlined them in an address before a general convocation on 13 July 1415. They included union between the eastern and western churches, peace between France and England, Jean Petit's ideas on tyrannicide that had been used to justify the assassination of the brother of the French king by agents of the duke of Burgundy, a crusade against the Turks, and—central to Paweł's treatises and the Polish delegation—the conflict between the Teutonic Order and Poland. See Heinrich Finke et al., eds. *Acta concilii Constanciensis*, 4 vols (Münster: Regensbergsche Buchhandlung 1896-1928), 2:413.

5. Word[s] in manuscripts unreadable.

6. Paweł here identifies himself in an official capacity; he has been given the status of "instigator, promotor, and procurator" by the Council. Thus he is neither a royal ambassador nor an academic scholar, and this is not a theoretical disquisition or a political program in pursuit of Polish policy. What he argues he is providing is an indictment, with concrete historical evidence intended to prove the Teutonic Order has practiced actions that damage justice, order, and peace. They are guilty of heresy and should suffer the same fate as Wycliffites and Hussites.

7. In this first article, and in the several that follow immediately, Paweł's argument is that the Teutonic Order is heretical because it has broken natural, divine, and human laws, a theme he takes up in a theoretical way in his treatise *Saevientibus* and elsewhere.

8. Paweł is here quoting directly from the deposition given on 20 January 1413 by the Order's procurator. It was part of an investigation led by Benedict de Macrai (see below, n. 10), who had been charged by newly elected emperor Sigismund of Luxembourg to arbitrate issues that had arisen between Poland and the Order following the [First] Peace of Toruń in 1411. See *Lites*, II, 93, and compare with Belch, *Paulus Vladimiri*, II, 917, n. 5.

9. Deposition by the Order's procurator on 23 January 1413; see *Lites*, II, 97.

10. Benedictus de Macra (Benedek Makrai) was a Hungarian nobleman educated at Prague, Vienna, Paris, and Padua who eventually became a legal advisor to Sigismund of Luxembourg. He was sent by the emperor-elect to Poland and Lithuania in 1413 to arbitrate between Jagiełło and the Order. The testimony he received eventually became part of the body of evidence Paweł and other Poles drew upon in their arguments against the Order. See Wiesław Sieradzan, *Misja Benedykta Makraia w latach 1412-1413. Z dziejów pokojowych metod rozwiązywania konfliktów międzypaństwowych w Europie Środkowo-Wschodniej w późnym średniowieczu* (Malbork: Muzeum Zamkowe, 2009), and—more briefly, Sieradzan, "Benedek (Benedict) Makrai as a Subarbiter in the Conflict between the Teutonic Order and its Neighbor Countries in 1412-1413," in Sieradzan, ed., *Arguments and Counter-Arguments. The Political Thought of the 14th-and 15th Centuries during the Polish-Teutonic Order Trials and Disputes* (Toruń: Wydawnictwo Naukowe Uniwersytetu Mikołaja Kopernika, 2012), pp. 157-168.

11. The phrase "public and notorious" (sometimes "true, public, and notorious" with other variations) is a characteristic expression of condemnation aggressively repeated by Paweł throughout this treatise.

12. For the documents attributed to Frederick II, see Tomasz Jasiński, "The Golden Bull Allegedly Issued in 1226 by Frederick II for the Teutonic Order," *Quaestiones Medii Aevi Novae* 3 (1998): 221-244; for documents by Lewis of Bavaria and the two popes, notes the references by Belch, *Paulus Vladimiri*, II, 919, n. 10, 11, and 12.

13. Paweł is here reprising many of the theoretical arguments made in *Saevientibus* and *Opinio Hostiensis*.

14. Phil. 2:21.

15. Mark 16:15.

16. Psalm 26:12.

17. Matt. 7:15.

18. Matt. 7:16.

19. The month should be August, not July; the Assumption of Mary is celebrated on 15 August.

20. Paweł is referring to the apparent weakness of the Order in the years following its defeat at the Battle of Grunwald in 1410.

21. Eccl. 5:3.

22. Deut. 32:5; see also Luke 9:41.

23. Paweł is referring to the Fourth Council of Toledo in 633, and its decree on whether Jews might be forced to convert. It is the same issue he discussed in his answer to the fifth question about imperial authority in *Saevientibus*.

24. Among the most famous participants from abroad were John of Luxembourg, King of Bohemia, the great knight and chivalric poet Oswald von Wolkenstein, Henry Bolingbroke (later King Henry IV of England), and Geoffrey Chaucer's "parfit gentil knight" who found he could follow "chivalrie, trouthe and honor, freedom and curtesie," who was given a place of honor (the *Ehre Tisch*?] "above alle nacions in Pruce" for "in Lettow hadde he reysed and in ruce, no cristen man so ofte of his degree."

25. The table of honor, rooted in larger European chivalric traditions—some associated with King Arthur and his knights—was indeed a feature of the Order's life, especially at Marienburg and during the time of Winrich von Kniprode (Grand Master from 1351-1382) and after. See the treatment by Werner Paravicini, *Die Preußenreisen des europäischen Adels*, 2 vols. (Sigmaringen: Thorbecke, 1989-1995), here II, 316-325; and, more briefly, Sławomir Jóźwiak and Janusz Trupinda, *Organizacja życia na Zamku Krzyżackim w Malborku w czasach Wielkich Mistrzów*, 3rd ed. (Malbork: Muzeum Zamkowe, 2019), pp. 300-301. Whether the Order profited as greatly from this as Paweł asserts is another question. It is quite clear, however, that by the early decades of the fifteenth century, the Order was generally in financial difficulties, especially as a result of the terms of the [First] Treat of Toruń; see, in general, Michael Burleigh, *Prussian Society and the German Order. An Aristocratic Corporation in Crisis* c. *1410-1466* (Cambridge: Cambridge University Press, 1984), especially pp. 70-73 and Appendix 2, Table 1.

26. Not counting border skirmishes, between 1345 and 1382, the Order mounted 96 raids on Lithuanian territory (and the Lithuanians responded with 42 campaigns of their own against the Teutonic Knights); see the comments of Robert Frost, *The Oxford History of Poland-Lithuania*, vol. I: *The Making of the Polish-Lithuanian Union, 1385-1569* (Oxford: Oxford University Press, 2015), p. 33, drawing upon Lithuanian scholarship.

27. i.e., The Battle of Grunwald.

28. Paweł is here quoting from a document written by the Order; see Belch, *Paulus Vladimiri*, II, 930, n. 29.

29. The Order recognized its rational of Christianization by force and conflict had been undermined by Jagiełło's (and Vytautas's) conversion, along with some inhabitants under Lithuanian rule (see treatment of their response below with respect to Paweł's treatise *Iste Tractatus*). They therefore focused their military efforts upon the remaining pagans in the Grand Duchy, especially in Samogitia. Militarily the decade of the 1390s saw warfare whose intensity and brutality outstripped the conquests and campaigns earlier in the century. Paweł's comments here are thus much to the point. Conversely, the approach of Sebastian Kubon, *Die Außenpolitik des Deutschen Ordens unter Hochmeister Konrad von Jungingen (1393-1407)* (Göttingen: V & R, 2016), especially pp. 53-192, emphasizes diplomatic developments and gives little direct attention to ongoing military conflict.

30. An example of the specificity of many of Paweł's charges, this *articulus* describes—perhaps somewhat sensationalized—the Order's campaign of 1390, in which Henry Bolingbroke, Duke of Lancaster, participated. See Chris Given-Wilson, *Henry IV* (New Haven, CT: Yale University Press, 2016), pp. 66-69.

31. Paweł is here using the Christian name of the previously pagan brother of the foresaid king (i.e., Władysław Jagiełło). This younger brother of Jagiełło, born Korigaila (or Karigaila), was Prince of Mstislavl. See Grzegorz Błaszczyk, *Dzieje stosunków polsko-litewskich*, ii/i: *Od Krewa do Lublina* (Poznań: Instytut Historii Uniwersytetu im. Adama Mickiewicza, 2007), pp. 148-149; and William Urban, *The Samogitian Crusade* (Chicago: Lithuanian Research and Studies Center, 1989), pp. 204-205, who calls him Karijotas. According to Urban, using sources from the Order's records, the crusaders denied having anything to do with this death, having found his body only five days after the battle.

32. Is. 5:2-4.

33. Paweł is referring here to the 1404 Treaty of Raciąż between Poland-Lithuania and the Order bringing to an end a brief conflict, one relatively unsuccessful for Poland, over border definitions as well as matters in Samogitia. This is one of the "eternal peaces" discussed by Klaus Neitmann, "Vom 'ewigen Frieden'. Die Kunst des Friedensschlusses zwischen dem Deutschen Order und Polen-Litauen 1398-1435," in Werner Paravicini, Rimvydas Petrauskas, and Grischa Vercamer, eds., *Tannenberg—Grunwald—Žalgiris 1410: Krieg und Frieden im späten Mittelalter* (Wiesbaden: Harrassowitz, 2012), pp. 201-209, here pp. 201-202. The terms for Poland were not particularly favorable and included Jagiełło's renewal of the Peace of Kalisz signed by Poland's king Kazimierz III (the Great) and the Order in 1343. This agreement had ushered in a general era of peace and stability between the two polities that lasted until the late 1380s/early 1390s.

34. Phil. 2:21.

35. Rom. 1:28.

36. The Peace of Kalisz, 1343.

37. i.e., the beginning of the war 1409-1411. In part because Paweł's home territory was the region of Dobrzyń, he pays special attention to its misfortunes. Jan Fijałek, "Ostatnie słowo Pawła Włodkowica o zakonie krzyżackim," *Przegląd Kościelny* 1 (1902): 92-93, gave voice to Paweł's sensitivities by describing Dobrzyń as a land "soaked in blood and tears as a result of constant attacks and violence by the Knights."

38. This was apparently Iohannes de Plonini, the *advocatus* (*Wójt* or *Vogt*) of Dobrzyń. See the description on this by Długosz, *Annales*, VII, 331 (*Liber decimus, sub anno 1409*), who identifies him as Iacobus de Plonini; this is corrected by the editors, p. 229, n. 223. Paweł's specificity of detail in this, as in many other instances, lends weight to the reliability of his charges against the Order.

39. The next several *Articuli* in Paweł's argument focus *seriatim* on details from the 1409-1411 war, with the Battle of Grunwald as crucial turning point.

40. Paweł's reference to Kazimierz (d. 1370, the last Piast ruler in medieval Poland) as Jagiełło's immediate predecessor ignores the reign from 1370 to 1382 of Louis the Great of Hungary, Casimir's nephew. In a narrow, legalistic aspect, he also skips over the fact that Jagiełło's first wife, Jadwiga (Louis's daughter) had been crowned *in regem Poloniae* on 16 October 1384. This status meant technically she exercised royal power and that she was, as some of the contemporary sources state, that she was *rex Poloniae*—king of Poland. This issue has recently been carefully analyzed by Stephen C. Rowell, "1386: The Marriage of Jogaila and Jadwiga Embodies the Union of Poland and Lithuania," *Lithuanian Historical Studies* 11 (2006): 137-144, here pp. 139-140.

41. This is Ioannes (Jan) Kropidło (*ca.* 1360-1421) who was bishop of Włoclawek 1384-1389 and again 1402-1421. The grievances he brought against the Order were specific and detailed; see, for some examples, *Lites*, III, 29, 36-37, 42, 68. Ioannes was present at the Council of Constance, though not in an official capacity, and may have provided Paweł with some of the information he utilized in *Articuli*. There is a good overview of his life and career by Antoni Liedtke, *Polski Słownik Biograficzny*, X (1963), 436-438.

42. On the substance of these accusations by Paweł, see *articulus* 86. Note the relatively specific chronological details Paweł provides here and elsewhere.

43. Paweł turns now to specific events in the war from 1409-1411, in particular to the battle of Grunwald.

44. The long standard Polish history of the "Great War" of 1409-1411, Stefan M. Kuczyński, *Wielka Wojna z Zakonem Krzyżackim w latach 1409-1411*, 5th ed. (Warsaw: Wydawnictwo Ministerstwa Obrony Narodowej, 1987), p. 280, suggests that the Polish army had an artillery of 60 guns, the Lithuanian army 15, and the Teutonic Order 100, which is more reasonable than earlier estimates.

45. Paweł here retells one of the more dramatic—and controversial—elements in the battle, that is, the moment when (from the Polish standpoint) the haughty leadership of the Order tried to shame Jagiełło and Vytautas into battle by sending two swords to tempt the Poles out of the underbrush where—the Order taunted—they had been hiding to avoid fighting. From the Polish side, Długosz, *Annales*, VII, 101-103 (*Liber decimus, sub anno*

1410), described Jagiełło's magnanimous response that he had plenty of his own swords, but he would accept the Order's gift, taking whatever God gives him to help him destroy his enemies (for the fate of the swords, see p. 262, n. 364). There are two English translations of Długosz's treatment (both done from Polish translations rather than directly from the Latin): *Medieval Literature of Poland. An Anthology*, transl. Michael J. Mikos (New York and London: Garland, 1992), pp. 33-61, here pp. 48-49; and *The Annals of Jan Długosz. A History of Eastern Europe from A.D. 965 to A.D. 1480*, transl. Maurice Michael (Charlton, Chichester, West Sussex: IM Publications, 1997), p. 388. Nationalistic traditions of the nineteenth and part of the twentieth century have made this event one of the singular nexuses of mutual hostility between Germans and Poles. See, however, the dispassionate and scholarly analysis provided by Sven Ekdahl, *Die Schlacht bei Tannenberg 1410*, vol. I: *Einführung und Quellenlage* (Berlin: Duncker & Humblot, 1982), pp. 156-168. With respect to the "two swords" incident, this has traditionally been seen in Polish historiography as an insulting, shaming maneuver. But see also the different interpretations, including a presentation of Jagiełło's action as based in his own *humilitas*, described by Klaus Militzer, "Kommunikations- und Verständigungsprobleme vor und nach der Schlacht bei Tannenberg," in Werner Paravicini, Rimvydas Petrauskas, and Grischa Verkamer, eds., *Tannenberg—Grunwald—Žalgiris 1410: Krieg und Frieden im späten Mittelalter* (Wiesbaden: Harrassowitz, 2021), pp. 301-305, here pp. 301-302, especially nn. 3-5.

46. The reference to the arbitration by emperor elect Sigismund took place in Buda in 1412 when a considerable body of testimony was gathered, now printed in *Lites*, 2nd ed., II, 1-72. The Order did not accept the terms of Sigismund's decision. Andrzej Łaskarz, a member of a noble family from the region of Greater Poland, who had studied law at Prague, become provost in Włoclawek and was elected bishop there (but did not hold that office). He later studied in Padua under Francisco Zarabella and was an important participant at the Council of Constance, but not as a member of the Polish delegation. A brief overview of his biography is given by Thomas Wünsch, *Konziliarismus und Polen. Personen, Politik und Programme aus Polen zur Verfassungsfrage der Kirche in der Zeit der mittelalterlichen Reformkonzilien* (Paderborn, Munich, Vienna, and Zürich: Schöningh, 1998), p. 55.

47. See above, n. 10.

48. Ps. 68:28 (Vulgate numeration).

49. This is Guillaume de Challant (d. 1431), a noble from Savoy, whose ecclesiastical career had included being appointed bishop of Lausanne by a pope from the Avignonese line during the western schism; surprisingly his role in the church was confirmed by Pope John XXIII, a pope from the conciliar line established at Pisa. Pope John was supported by emperor elect Sigismund, which is how Guillaume became involved in issues between the Teutonic Order and Poland after Sigismund's Buda decision in 1412. Guillaume's efforts at arbitration were unsuccessful, though he did play some minor roles at the Council of Constance and was mentioned favorably by Cardinal Fillastre in his diary, an important source for our knowledge of the personnel at the council. For Guillaume's career, see Sophie Vallery-Radot, *Les Français au concile de Constance (1414-1418). Entre resolution du schism et construction d'une identité nationale*, 2 vols. (Turnhout: Brepols, 2016), II, 96-97.

50. This is a reference to an agreement recently made between Poland and the Teutonic Order made at the abbey of St. Denis, then outside of Paris, on 8 April 1416, thus helping one to date the *Articuli*.

51. Having summarized some of the recent history of what Paweł saw as crimes by the Order against Poland (and Lithuania), he here returns to the story of how the Order established itself in Prussia. The standard Polish history treating this process is Marian Biskup and Gerard Labuda, *Dzieje Zakonu Krzyżackiego w Prusach. Gospodarka—Społeczeństwo—Państwo—Ideologia* (Gdańsk: Wydawnictwo Morskie Gdańsk, 1986), pp. 118-161, 178-188, and (including their conquest of Gdańsk Pomorze) 241-258. For an overview of the political and ecclesiastical structures of the Order in Prussia, see Roman Czaja and Andrzej Radzimiński, eds., *The Teutonic Order in Prussia and Livonia. The Political and Ecclesiastical Structures 13th-16th Century* (Toruń: Towarzystwo Naukowe w Toruniu, and Cologne, Weimar, and Vienna: Böhlau Verlag, 2015), pp. 9-166.

52. In addition to Paweł's critique of papal and imperial privileges, along with what he regarded as questionable and invalid grants by Polish dukes that he presented in *Saevientibus*, he reiterated these in many of his other treatises; see particularly his *Ad Aperiendam*, not included in this present collection but available in English translation by Ehrlich, *Pisma wybrane*, I, 144-259, especially pp. 162-166 and 208 and II, 2-167; see the discussion of it, together with bibliography in Paul W. Knoll, *"A Pearl of Powerful Learning." The University of Cracow in the Fifteenth Century* (Leiden and Boston: Brill, 2016), pp. 436-440.

53. The circumstances and controversies connected with the Order's acquisition and control of the territory of Chełmno (Kulmerland) are well analyzed by Tomasz Jasiński, "Okoliczności nadania ziemi chełmińskiej Krzyżakom w 1228 roku w świetle dokumentu łowickiego," in Zenon Hubert Nowak, ed., *Balticum: Studia z dziejów polityki, gospodarki i kultury XII-XVII wieku ofiarowane Marianowi Biskupowi w siedemdziesiątą rocznicę urodzin* (Toruń: Wydawnictwo Towarzystwa Naukowego w Toruniu, 1992), pp. 151-163. The ecclesiastical endowments in the early thirteenth century were made by Duke Conrad of Mazovia and confirmed by Popes Honorius III and Gregory IX.

54. Implicit in this assertion is the Order's acquisition of Gdańsk (Danzig) in 1308, which, according to some, was the result of a massacre of 10,000, a claim that was eventually investigated by the papacy and was the subject of testimony taken in legal proceedings in 1320 and 1339 in Inowrocław and Warsaw respectively. The most reliable recent analysis of this remains the materials in Błażej Śliwiński, ed., *"Rzeź Gdańska" z 1308 roku w świetle najnowszych badań* (Gdańsk: Muzeum Historyczne Miasta Gdańska, 2009), but see also Biskup and Labuda, *Dzieje Zakonu Krzyżackiego w Prusach*, pp. 256-258. Subsequent to the events of 1308, the Order took control of additional lands traditionally part of the Polish kingdom. For a sampling of the Order's defense and of accusations against the Order, see *Lites*, I (3rd ed.), 103-105 (statements by the Order); pp. 22-23 (statement by Polish procurators in 1320).

55. The Battle of Płowce in 1331 was one of the few Polish military victories against the Order in the first third of the century. Paweł has some of the details wrong: Kazimierz was present at the side of the Polish king, Władysław Łokietek, his father, but—according to the information provided by the Order, he left the field of battle ("der junge Kunic gegen Crakau vlôh/Das er wênic den zogil zôch," quoted by Knoll, *The Rise of the Polish Monarchy. Piast*

Poland in East Central Europe [Chicago: University of Chicago Press, 1972], p. 57, n. 50). It was really Łokietek who led the Polish forces to victory. The battle was indeed a bloody one; the bishop of Włocławek reported counting 4,187 bodies after it.

56. Paweł is referring here to the tribunal Pope Benedict had convened in Warsaw in 1339, in which testimony was taken from 126 Polish witness on 30 articles of dispute. See *Lites*, I, 2nd ed. 57-408 (pp. 94-98 for the articles; pp. 99-408 for the testimony). The most recent treatment in English of the 1320 and 1339 tribunals is Paul Milliman, "*The Slippery Memory of Men.*" *The Place of Pomerania in the Medieval Kingdom Poland* (Leiden and Boston: Brill, 2013), pp. 139-254. See also two studies by Janusz Bieniak, "Przebieg procesu polsko-krzyżackiego z 1339 roku," Pamiętnik Biblioteki Kórnickiej 23 (1993): 5-22, and "Geneza procesu polsko-krzyżackiego z lat 1320-1321 (inowrocławsko-brzeskiego)," in Nowak, ed., *Balticum*: *Studia z dziejów politiki, gospodarki i kultury XII-XVII wieku*, pp. 49-59.

56a. The following text in italics is being quoted by Paweł from the conclusions of the papal judges at the Warsaw tribunal of 1339. He had access to the manuscript material later printed in *Lites*, ed. 2, I, 68-69 and 137-141.

57. This detailed *articulus* is impressive in its specificity, lending weight and credence to Paweł's accusations. It suggests he had direct access to the manuscript material eventually printed in the nineteenth and first third of the twentieth century in *Lites*.

58. Duke Władysław of Opole, a controversial political figure in late Piast Poland, in the era of Louis of Hungary as king of Poland that followed, and well into the reign of Jagiełło, especially with respect to relations with the Order. See the solid treatment of his career by Jerzy Sperka, *Władysław książę opolski, wieluński, kujawski, dobrzyński, Pan Rusi, Palatyn Węgier i namiestnik Polski* (Kraków: Avalon, 2012).

59. This came seven years after the "eternal peace" of Raciąż that was intended to be different from a general peace treaty that were little more than cessation of hostilities. See, for this distinction, Neitmann, "Vom 'ewigen Frieden,'" p. 201, who notes that the eternity of peace often seemed to last only about a decade.

60. Paweł begins here a series of *articuli* regarding the Order's activities in Livonia leading eventually to their control over this region, with its chief city Riga. For the political and ecclesiastical structures of the Order in this region, see the overview in Czaja and Radzimiński, eds., *The Teutonic Order in Prussia and Livonia*, pp. 169-288.

61. The context of the Order's relationship with Archbishop Friedrich of Riga (and the details contained in some of the *articuli* that follow) are briefly treated by Hartmut Boockmann, *Der Detutsche Order. Zwölf Kapitel aus seiner Geschichte*, 2nd ed. (Munich: C.H. Beck, 1982), p. 147

62. Charles of Luxembourg (1316-1378), King of Bohemia from 1346 and Holy Roman Emperor (crowned in 1355) as Charles IV. He was generally sympathetic to the Order, but as this example reveals, this was not always the case. For an overview of his policy in one particularly crucial period, see the older study Karl Conrad, "Der Deutsche Order und Karl IV. 1352-1360," *Zeitschrift für Ostforschung* 21 (1972): 20-41.

63. In addition to the condemnations listed by Belch, *Paulus Vladimiri*, II, 970, n. 104, there are the two judgments issued by papally appointed procurators after the tribunal of 1320 (*Lites*, I, 3rd ed., 68-70) and after the 1339 Warsaw tribunal. *Lites* I, 2nd ed. 137-142.

64. Again Ps. 68:28 (Vulgate numeration).

65. Acts 8:20.

66. John 10:12-13.

67. This segment of the manuscript is blank.

68. Paweł's comment helps establish a date prior to which the *Articuli* could not have been written.

69. As the leading historian of late medieval crusading, Norman Housley, puts it in "A Crusade against the Poles? Johannes Falkenberg's 'Satira' (1412)," in Helen J. Nicholson and Jochen Burgtorf, eds., *The Templars, the Hospitallers and the Crusades* (London and New York: Routledge, 2020), pp.183-198, here p. 191, the numerous misdeeds that Paweł singles out in the foregoing *articuli* have "an impressive specificity." They are consistent with other tales of atrocities—from both sides—that characterize the polemics of this era (he notes other sources, p. 191, n. 39), but Paweł's are distinctive by virtue of having reasonably precise dates and financial damage amounts included in them.

70. i.e., "Du ("You"), Priest" in the informal second person rather than the polite, formal form "Sie."

71. For the financial details Paweł presents here, see the most recent analysis by Jóźwiak and Trupinda, *Organizacja życia na Zamku Krzyżackim w Malborku*, pp. 26-28 (central finance organ of the Order) and pp. 273-292 (the offices of the Treasurer and the Dispensor [Scheffer]), together with references to the older literature.

72. The Order's milling policy is well covered by Wiesław Długokęcki, Jan Kuczyński, and Barbara Pospieszna, *Młyny w Malborku i okolicy od XIII do XIX wieku* (Malbork: Muzeum Zamkowe w Malborku, 2004). A telling example of the hostility to the Order's control of mills is cited by Belch, *Paulus Vladimiri*, II, 982, n. 126.

73. This event led Belch, *Paulus Vladimiri*, II, 912, to conclude that early 1417 was the latest this part of the *Articuli* would have been written.

74. i.e., Magdeburg Law. This law was widely adopted in east central Europe during the process known as *melioratio terrrae* (the improvement of the lands), a period from the late twelfth century onward. It served a broad range of emerging rural and urban communities. German law (*ius Theutonicum*), one version of which was the form utilized in Magdeburg, served these settlements and towns by providing forms of self-government, including guarantees of personal freedom for burghers, a written catalogue of reciprocal duties for both the grantor and the grantee of the law, and a collegiate court system. How this worked in general is treated by Adrienne Körmendy, *Melioratio Terrae. Vergleichende Untersuchungen über die Siedlungsbewegung im östlichen Mitteleuropa im 13.-14. Jahrhundert* (Poznań: Wydawnictwo Poznańskiego Towarzystwa Przyjaciół Nauk,, 1995). How it developed and functioned on the Polish scene, including Pomerania and to a very great extent the territories of the Oder, is treated by Maciej Mikuła, *Municipal Magdeburg Law* (Ius municipale Magdeburgense) *in Late Medieval Poland. A Study on the Evolution and Adaptation of Law* (Leiden and Boston: Brill, 2021; original Polish ed. 2017). Current scholarship views the extension of German settlement and law into the region of east central Europe very differently from the nationalistic scholarship of the nineteenth and part of the twentieth centuries: "Landesausbau" has replaced "Drang nach Osten." See the classic revisionist presentation in the articles contained

in Walter Schlesinger, ed., *Die Deutsche Ostsiedlung des Mittelalters als Problem der Europäischen Geschichte* (Sigmaringen: Thorbecke, 1975). More recently, see Jan M. Piskorski, ed., *Historiographical Approaches to Medieval Colonization of East Central Europe: A Comparative Analysis* (Boulder, CO: East European Monographs, 2002); and Stefan Donecker, "Locals and Immigrants in Medieval Central Europe," in Nada Zečević and Daniel Ziemann, eds. *Oxford Handbook of Medieval Central Europe* (Oxford: Oxford University Press, 2022), pp. 191-212, here pp. 191-197

75. From this *articulus* to the end of the treatise, the manuscript conditions are fragmented. Some possible readings are more certain than others. In any case, however, the multiple points that Paweł has been making are clear enough.

THIS TRACT

(*Iste Tractatus*, 1417)[1]

This tract, which begins with the words 'Rereading the old accounts,' and ends with 'Thus concludes the book on the doctrine of papal power and that of the Emperor, drawn up against Paweł Włodkowic the Pole, his heresy and his errors,' is the same in matter and form as that, which begins with 'Receive the sword,' and is of the same author; these differ not except wherein this tract contains additions, which that other lacks.[2]

And so it contains the doctrinal investigation and argumentation wherewith an attempt is made to demonstrate that the war waged by the Poles against the Knights of the Cross of Prussia was unjust, and that the King of Poland and the Poles committed sacrilege in devastating the Church, which word it applies to the Knights themselves, etc., offering XXIII conclusions.

Now, because war is such a thing that cannot be justified except on the basis of facts and the particular circumstances peculiar to it, which determination is not arrived at through contemplation, but by the experience of the senses, and therefore, because it is not possible to come to such a determination via doctrinal investigation, which deals not with particular data, but proceeds rather from universals and things more widely known, again, not through experience but rather through the natural light of the intellect; thus, if a determination as to the justice or injustice of a war, to all and sundry, is to be arrived at, another sort of investigation must be resorted to, that is to say — a judicial investigation, in which proofs will be established by the testimony of legitimate witnesses to whose senses the singular facts that would justify said war are familiar.[3]

From this it is evident that their entire earlier 'investigation' is false and erroneous, and sinful in matter and in form. In matter, because in it much persuasion is based on things false and contrary to divine law. In form because such an investigation is an improper method wherewith to pronounce on the matter. And thus it is established that both materially and formally it is itself heretical and, by consequence, worthy of condemnation as such by this Holy General Council.[4]

The author[5] seeks to prove his argument in two principal ways. In the first eleven of his conclusions, he strives to shore up the power of the Emperor, and in the following eight, that of the above-said Order of the Knights of the Cross, beginning with conclusion number twelve and continuing to the twentieth (exclusive). From here on until the end, he infers the above-mentioned deduction and many other erroneous things. And in all of this he employs such mordant, exquisitely malicious words, stating many falsities in vituperation of the Poles and the King of Poland, to whom he does manifest and atrocious injury, especially unto Paweł,[6] even making use of Sacred Scripture to wound, through the perversion of the same. Accordingly, the entire tract is of three parts, after the manner of a syllogism.[7]

I now proceed to list the individual errors found in this tract.[8]

God, and not the Church, endows the Emperor with the right of exercising legal authority in criminal cases. This first conclusion is found near the end of the tract *Accipe gladium*, and the opposite is called an error, with which he charges Paweł.

Empire derives from God and not from the authority of the Pope. Conclusion II at the end.

The authority of the Emperor is not necessarily subordinate to the papal authority. This is clear because they are mutually repugnant. Conclusion III is found to be so formulated.

It is an error to state that the Imperial authority is, in practice, subordinate to that of the Pope. In the tract *Accipe gladium*, conclusion II, proof II.

The authority of the Emperor and that of the Pope, formally constituted, suffer not co-existence in the same matter. In this form, conclusion IV, and conclusion III of the tract *Accipe gladium*.

And there, in the same third conclusion, in proof VI or VII near the end, it reads: That the decretal *Per venerabilem*, the portion entitled *Qui filij sint legitimi*, expounds Holy Scripture in a manner inconsistent with that solicited by the Holy Spirit, *viz.*, in the way the author himself reads Deuteronomy XVII[9] in his own favor: 'If thou perceive that there be among you a hard and doubtful matter in judgment between blood and blood, cause and cause, leprosy and leprosy: and thou see that the words of the judges within thy gates do vary: arise, and go up to the place, which the Lord thy God shall choose. And thou shalt come to the priests of the Levitical race, and to the judge, that shall be at that time: and thou shalt ask of them, and they shall shew thee the truth of the judgment. And thou shalt do whatsoever they shall say, that preside in the place, etc.' And he adds: 'But he that will be proud, and refuse to obey the commandment of the priest,' etc. 'that man shall die,' etc.

Likewise noteworthy are proof II of the said fourth conclusion, and proof IV as well, beginning: 'Thus to serve as a soldier of God and to mix oneself up in secular matters is irreconcilable' (2, with reference to Timothy 2).[10] And for this reason, he claims that what the conclusion states is all the more certain.

Now, note that the arguments that lead to his conclusion are the same as the error of those who claim that spiritual jurisdiction and temporal jurisdiction are incompatible in one and the same man of the cloth. And therefore that no churchman is permitted to wield temporal jurisdiction. Likewise, toward the middle of the sixth proof, he makes a statement formed thusly: 'It is most certain that the Pope neither possesses both jurisdictions, nor both swords.'

His fifth conclusion is: The whole world was subject to Imperial Edict in matters temporal — the proofs of which are worth noting. And please note that in proof IV, towards the middle, he says that whereas the Pope's authority springs from the authority of God, so does the authority of the Emperor arise therefrom — and that much earlier than the Pope's — as is manifestly evident to any thinking person. And so, likewise, that in all things that pertain to the civil good, the papal authority is subject to the imperial.

Conclusion VI: The Emperor is the general vicar of God in temporal matters. And in the tract *Accipe* we find added to this 'over the world entire.' He bases this claim on the foregoing, and adds other reasons too. In the same way, near the beginning of proof IV, he thus concludes: 'Therefore, it is true beyond a doubt that the Emperor possesses power of precedence in temporal matters.' Likewise, following the middle portion, he claims that the infidels who do not acknowledge the authority of the Roman Empire do not legally possess what they have, for those possessions they have not according to Imperial law, and therefore, it couldn't be clearer that, since they possess these things lawlessly, they unjustly possess what they have. In the same manner, he states in conclusion: 'And therefore, indubitably, he who professes the Christian religion will affirm, as soon as he hears the issue broached — however Paweł denies it — that the Emperor possesses the right to grant a licence for the occupation of lands of those infidels who do not acknowledge his Empire. And by granting to the Knights of the Cross of Prussia, or others, his letters patent for the occupation of pagan lands, he bestows such rights upon them.'

Conclusion VII. The Emperor may legitimately call back under his jurisdiction all lands of pagans not recognising his Imperial authority. And here he introduces arguments leading to the conclusion that the same holds for all Christian kings and their faithful realms, who do not recognize the authority of the Roman Empire over them. Let the kings of France, England, Castile, etc., respond to that!

Conclusion VIII. The Emperor is permitted *de iure* to wage war against infidels living and conducting themselves peacefully. This he proves from the foregoing, introducing other rationales of the most seditious nature, which are contrary to the rites of the Church and inimical to kings who are not subject to the Empire. The same is to be noted here in reference to Jews living peacefully among Christians. Let those who are not in the habit of killing them respond.

Conclusion IX. The Emperor is permitted *de iure* to declare war on infidels living and conducting themselves peacefully. This he proves from the foregoing, adding other rationales as well.

Conclusion X. It is permissible and licit for the Emperor to deprive infidels living and conducting themselves peacefully of the lands they cultivate and inhabit. This he proves from V and VI and by other rationales belligerent to Christian kings. Likewise, in proof IV, near the middle, he concludes that the lands cultivated and things owned by infidels are possessed unjustly and sinfully; he adds that to deny this is blasphemy.

Just the same, in proof V near the middle of conclusion XI he states that in reference to infidels there remain but two options open to the Pope in the case of such pagans who refuse the invitation to accept the true God when encouraged by word: they must either be taught by the sword to recognize the truth of the faith, or, confounded in humiliation, they perish out of the fold of the Church indeed, as not being of the flocks of Christ even *in potentia*, as they have not been since their very creation, though Paweł so stupidly asserts the contrary.

So that this matter of the papal power and that of the Emperor be better displayed, and so that the above-mentioned errors be even more clearly seen, I list below, in the end, the sayings of the doctors which I have assembled.

Here begins the second principal part of this tract.

Near the end of conclusion twelve, in the proof, we read: 'As for the Ruthenian clergy, because they are manifest heretics, it is no less meritorious to kill them as it is to kill pagans.' And he justifies the Brethren of the Teutonic House who so butchered and killed such priests in Lithuania and Ruthenia.

Conclusion XIII. It is legitimate for the Brethren of the Teutonic House to wage war against the Poles and their kings and dukes. He argues that the latter have no grounds save greed and the desire to dominate for their frequent falling upon the Brethren in armed attack, and laying them prostrate. And in conclusion he states that it is doubtlessly true that, by any sort of law or legal licence, it must be granted that the Brethren have the right to do as they have done in response. Likewise, in proof 4, near the middle, he states that anyone who believes the King of Poland to be a good Christian is a fool.[11] Evident proof of this is that the gentiles who followed him into the profession of the holy Faith are false Christians; in general, he makes many other atrocious, insulting claims. And thus he justifies those Brethren who, on such account, cruelly butcher the neophytes and burn their new churches to the ground, stating that these gentiles merit not the name of Christian. He says in conclusion: 'Thus, the fact that the King of Poland and Witold were laved in the sacred waters of baptism through the ministry of the Poles was certainly not inspired of the Holy Spirit, as

Paweł asserts, but of their father the devil, to whose desire they were obedient,' etc.

Towards the end of the fourteenth conclusion, in the first proof, he states that to wage war against infidels because they are infidels, in order to spread the Christian faith, is legitimate and may be seen as a work of charity. And for this reason, he says, Paweł's conclusion is multifariously erroneous as it asserts the contrary, that is, that it is not licit to do battle against peaceful infidels, neither on account of their being infidels, nor in order to spread the faith. And he argues that none of these are really at peace with us, for none of them have concluded any orderly pact of peace with us according to all the movements of their will, and then he concludes thus: 'And so the infidels are neither peaceful in themselves nor amongst themselves.' The same thing might be alleged against certain Christians, as well.

He brings proof II to a conclusion by claiming that, despite the stated laws, i.e. the codex *De paganis, sacrificijs et templis eorum,* the law *Christianis* — the Emperor and other princes are within their rights when they wage war, and grant the right to or command Christians to gather in military support of the Brethren of the Teutonic House in waging war against infidels for the sake of spreading the Christian Faith. And just a little further on he concludes in the same way: 'And this is most true — while the contrary is heretical — that those Christians who from charity gather in support of the Brethren of the Teutonic House for the purpose of waging war against infidels — even pagans conducting themselves peacefully — on behalf of the Faith, merit the Kingdom of Heaven.' And he says that Paweł evidently errs when he writes in his prologue that 'error becomes custom whereby Christ's faithful, in the belief that they are rendering service to God as soldiers, gather in multitudes there, that is, with the Knights of the Cross, in support of them, and under the pretext of spreading the Catholic Faith, and wage war against the pagan people living peacefully,' 'noting not, in his envy, that what they do, they do with an aim of repairing, not damaging,' and so thus he calls their battling by no means cruel, but rather an act of mercy. Toward the end of his proof IV he concludes: 'And therefore, without any new allegation, it is evident, and we are bound, consequently, to concede, that all things being equal, those Christians who, of their charity, congregate in support of the Brethren of the Teutonic House for the purpose of waging war, be it against the pagans or the Poles and their kings and dukes, are deserving of an equal reward from God in the Kingdom of Heaven.'

Conclusion XV. The Emperor may licitly bestow upon the Brethren of the Teutonic House, in perpetuity, lands torn from the hands of infidels conducting themselves peacefully. And at the end of proof II he claims that Paweł errs in asserting that the Emperor is not to grant a licence for the occupation of the lands of infidels that acknowledge not his imperial authority. And in proof III he claims that Paweł errs when he affirms that the writs conceded to the Knights of the Cross of Prussia by the Emperor concerning the occupation of pagan lands bestow no rights upon them.

Conclusion XVI. The Pope may licitly concede to the Brethren of the Teutonic House, in perpetuity, the lands they wrest from the hands of pagans. This he proves on the basis of Paweł's statement that the Pope possesses both powers. And he states that Paweł's argument is unreasonable when he asserts that, in the writs conceded by the Roman Pontiff, the reason why the infidels ought to be despoiled by the Brethren of the Teutonic House is not expressed, i.e. so that the cult of the Catholic Faith might be spread.

Conclusion XVII. In a just war, the Brethren of the Teutonic House may deprive infidels conducting themselves peacefully of the lands they occupy. And in the second proof he states that the Brethren of the Teutonic House are waging war under the banner of the Empire, and therefore, the Emperor's command obliges them to the same, and the war they wage is just. And he adds that because it is declared by their privileges, and known in fact that more than one emperor has commanded and advised them to occupy the lands wrested by arms from infidels conducting themselves peacefully, possessing them and ruling them in perpetuity under the authority of the Empire,' in proof IV he infers as in conclusion: 'so no further declaration is needed to prove that the Brethren of the Teutonic House have deprived, or may deprive, infidels of the lands they occupy or had occupied, in a just war. And that Paweł errs in affirming the contrary. Likewise, later he infers the same: 'And thus the Brethren of the Teutonic House, in fighting against infidels, although they often kill men thereby, still are not committing murder in so doing.

Conclusion XVIII. All lands wrested from the hands of infidels by the Brethren of the Teutonic House are justly held by them. He proves this from the foregoing. Likewise, toward the end of the fourth proof, he concludes that in stating that such an attack amounts to theft of another's goods and rapine, etc., on account of illicit usurpation, Paweł errs.

Conclusion XIX. It is allowed to the Brethren of the Teutonic House to fight or to initiate war against infidels on the feasts of the Purification and Assumption of the Blessed Virgin Mary.

Conclusion XX. It is a damnable heresy to state that the Poles and their King and dukes licitly devastated the Church with the aid of the infidels. By 'Church' he means the above-mentioned Brethren and those who supported them. And in the other tract *Accipe gladium,* he so says: 'It is a damnable heresy to state that the King of the Poles legitimately won a victory over the Brethren of the Teutonic House with the aid of infidels.' Here he is speaking of the rout of the Brethren which began on the ninth day of July, in 1410.[12] He strives to prove this conclusion by varied rationales which are found in the tract against the Poles. Likewise, in the 5th proof he says: 'It is most certain that in defeating the Church with the aid of infidels, the

Poles and their King and dukes were in league with the devil,' and that, therefore, it is true what is stated in the conclusion. Likewise, in proof 7 he states: That Paweł's conclusion is manifest heresy, that is, his statement that a Christian prince may, in case of pressing necessity, for his defense and that of his land, make use not only of those pagans subject to him, but others as well, without sinning thereby. By these 'others' we are to understand peaceful pagans who are not in a state of active or passive war with us. And in the end he says: 'And as for those assertors of Paweł's, as he calls them, whom he found to uphold this heresy, and other errors in favor of the pagans and to the humiliation of Christians, for this reason they should be condemned the same as he, and never cited in support of any argument.' And note that by similar rationales, which he introduces here and at the end of this book, he deduces that no prince may licitly fight against any Christians with the aid of any men whom he would know to be sinners and adversaries of God, lacking the charity which makes one a friend of God. It is also to be noted that he equivocates when he uses the very name of the Church in statements claiming that the Poles, etc., have made war against the Church.

Conclusion XXI. On account of all harms, general and singular, that the Poles and their King and dukes have inflicted on the Teutonic House and on those subject to them, with the help of infidels, they are obliged to render them satisfaction as a condition of their eternal salvation.

Conclusion XXII. All Christians who die while battling against the Brethren of the Teutonic House on behalf of the Poles, their King and dukes, with the aid of pagans, descend into the bitterness of eternal damnation. For it is said that all of them died in a state of mortal sin, and no prayers should be offered for them.

Conclusion XXIII. The Poles and their King and dukes deserve to be deprived of the crown of the Kingdom. And in proof three he says that the Poles, their King and dukes are the most vehement enemies of the Church and have wounded her more than the pagans themselves. And it is to be noted that he bases these conclusions on his prior statements, adding the most atrocious insults and adducing means that lead to manifest error if the argumentation they present should be followed to the end. Likewise, of special note is the clause that begins: 'But because he is not clad in the vestments of revenge,' etc., which is set in the fourth proof.[13]

A SCRIPT IN DENUNCIATION OF THE ERRORS OF THE SATIRE OF JOHANNES FALKENBERG, OP PRESENTED TO THE COUNCIL OF CONSTANCE BY MASTER PAWEŁ WŁODKOWIC, DOCTOR OF THE DECRETALS[14]

And because this pestiferous doctrine appears repugnant to both human and divine law: by virtue of the first it appears morally erroneous; by virtue of the second it appears heretical. The first is an object of moral consideration, legal consideration above all; the second is a matter for theological discussion. Having now disposed of the former, we come to the latter, which is easier to recognize after the former has been taken care of.

Entering upon this matter, I determine to divide it into four types of causes, according to Aristotle, as he says in his first book of *Physics*: 'we may then reckon that we know something when we have come to know its causes, even to the very elements thereof.' The end cause, which is the chief cause of all, is that all Poles, along with their King, are to be slain. The efficient cause is the author of the little book himself. The true matter or subject is the King of Poland and the Poles in so far as they merit extermination, because all this he strives to demonstrate concerning the King himself and the Poles: that they are hypocrites;[15] that they are sacrilegious, persecutors of the

Church, heretics, etc., as is supposedly made evident throughout all the chapters, and at last, in the final ones, he advises and concludes that these persons ought to be exterminated. The formal cause is the manner of proceeding, which is doctrinal and argumentative, and indeed imprecatory, because he does not merely strive to prove this by arguments, but indeed promises eternal life to all who have girded their loins to the task of exterminating the Poles and their King.

These thing having been said, it should further be noted that, in evidence of all that follows, it is fundamentally presupposed that the war waged by the Poles against the Prussian Brethren was unjust on the part of the Poles, as he says in his first chapter: 'That just as the factual evidence demonstrates, against which no appeal may be heard, the King of Poland has done all this, that is, the evils and enormities here enumerated.' And this he also announces to the universal Church through his tract. Later on, in chapter III, he seeks to prove the same by argument, using many means: i.e. that the King and the Poles have committed these evils. And thus he would prove the thing by itself, completing a vicious circle and committing the fallacy of *petitio principii*.

Now, because words are to be received according to their subject matter, and the entire matter of this little book is moral and juridical, it is therefore to be understood according to the law, and all of the injuries it lays out are to find their resolution, according to him, in the injustice of the Polish war. And so it is to be noted that just as the definition of a war as just or unjust does not fall within the purview of the arts and sciences, or the recognition of any other virtue or attitude save justice itself, which is a moral virtue, the object of which is law, or what is just, as is clear from the fifth book of *Ethics*, where Aristotle says the following, in defining justice: That it is the attitude whereby we act justly and seek what is just, thus similarly it should be said that if it is to be stated that someone is a hypocrite, or sacrilegious, or a heretic, etc., which are all aspects of injustice, this cannot be determined unless by way of jurisprudence. *Ex facto*, thus, it occurs that if anyone is spoken of in this way, it is because a legal situation has arisen from the fact, as the laws state, and as proven in the chapter *De muliere, De sponsibus,* and the chapter *Symoniace*: *De symonia*. For just as justice is to determine what is just, as such is its proper subject, so it is to determine the unjust, for the discipline of contrarieties applies here. And so all such propositions which are to be resolved as to their factual basis, and are to be verified *ex facto*, such as the propositions 'The King is sacrilegious,' 'The Poles are hypocrites and heretics,' etc., 'The Poles have done such and such,' are not knowable by way of doctrine or science, as if arising from allegedly self-evident statements, as this fantast has dreamed up in this matter, but may only be arrived at by way of the law, by juridical process, with the presentation of legitimate evidence, observing what ought to be observed and holding true to all solemnities of the law. Such judicial examination and knowledge proceeds from the consideration of the particular circumstances of a given deed, which justify the deed or not, which aggravate it or not (as in the canon *Homo Christianus*, XL distinction: *De iure iurando*: *Cum quidam*). For just as if a blind man were to judge of colors by his sense of hearing, or a deaf man sounds by his sense of sight, so it is impossible in this case to decide the juridical matter doctrinally or theoretically. It is, as I say, to ask a blind man to determine color by sound.

From the above it necessarily follows that all these conclusions set forth are false, all the proofs erroneous, and in consequence, all his doctrine erroneous, pestiferous and unjust.

I say 'false,' which in the matter before us means 'unjust.' In matters theological, 'false' means 'heretical,' etc. I say 'false' because in the law there appears to be no truth in his claims. In the present legal matter 'to appear not' and 'to be not' are equivalent things (which is proven in the chapter *Ordinari*: *De officio ordinari*, book VI, and as noted in the gloss 'Quod non' by the law *In lege* and the law *Rutilia*

Polla ff De contrahenda empcione, and in the canon *Solempnitates: De consecracione*, distinction I).

And so all such propositions: 'The King is a persecutor of the Church,' 'The Poles are heretics,' etc., are evil-sounding, criminal, scandals in themselves, as scandal and crime are not presumed *de iure* of anyone unless they are legitimately proven, as the good is always presumed of everyone unless the contrary be made apparent (*De presumpcionibus*, final chapter). And therefore, in the absence of evidence confirming the crimes alleged, *de iure* it is understood that no such crimes exist, according to the cited laws. And by consequence, all of his claims are *de iure* false.[16]

Having taken care of this preamble, I now come to the second matter, the chief one in this business, that is, the encouragement of the unjust slaughter of the Poles and, by way of this encouragement, the spreading of this heretical dogma, which he intends, as the following conclusions demonstrate.

First, that the allegedly 'pestiferous community of all Poles ought to be smote in retributive punishment until full revenge has been meted for crimes committed.' And he sets forth the cause in the very same chapter: 'because the pestiferous community of all Poles is guilty as a whole of having been contaminated by heresy and thus separated from the Church.'

2nd conclusion. The secular princes are obliged to raise the sword of vengeance against all Poles along with their King, without any dissimulation, exterminating them all or the greater portion of them, or hanging all their noblemen and the King from high gallows.'[17]

3rd. That without any sort of sly shirking the secular princes are indispensably obliged to revenge the injury done to God by the Poles and their King Jagiełło by putting the same to death. And this he places in chapter XII.

4th. All secular princes who have consented to the crimes of the Poles, although they were able to check them, are deserving of eternal death. From chapter XII.

The fifth conclusion. All things considered, the Poles and their King Jagiełło are more deserving of being killed in battle than the pagans. From chapters XI and XIII.

The sixth conclusion. All secular princes who kill the Poles and their King Jagiełło for the sake of God are doing pious works.

Seventh conclusion. That those who do so are deserving of eternal life thereby.

The eighth. Not only the princes, but also, most certainly, all their inferiors who gird themselves, for charity's sake, against the Poles merit eternal life. This is set in chapter XIII.

These conclusions, and others similar to them, are false and erroneous not only in morals, but also in faith. That they are indeed false has been stated above, and for that reason are to be completely denied. And because they unjustly encourage the commission of unjust homicides, they are contrary to good morals. Certainly, because such murders are prohibited by law divine in both Testaments (Exodus XX: 'Thou shalt not kill,'[18] and in the New Testament in many places: I Peter 3 and 4, Matthew 5,[19] etc.) — so they are strictly heretical and repugnant to Catholic truth. For according to St Jerome, a dogma that is contrary to the Catholic faith is termed a heresy.

Now, the fact that such homicides as encouraged in these conclusions are unjust is clearly evident in multiple respects.

The first is that homicide itself is a sort of evil that is evil by nature and thus contrary to all law: divine, natural, and human, and thus prohibited. For in law such a rule is stated: When a thing is promulgated in an expressly negative manner, or is prohibited, it is understood as always prohibited, unless it is to be found permissible by law. Such is stated in the gloss that is part of the argument in the chapter *Inter corporalia*: *De translatione prelati.* And there, Ostiensis expounds upon the negative precepts: 'Thou shalt not kill,' 'Thou shalt not steal,' as being understood as prohibited in all cases, unless a concession be found (as is clear from question V of chapter XXIII *Non licet,* where it is stated that killing is not allowed, neither of oneself nor of another, unless the law permits it, for example, in self defense — as in *De homicido*: *Si quis*).[20] Likewise, theologians hold that negative precepts are in force always and forever, whereas affirmative precepts, even those that are always in force, are not so in every single case.

They are also unjust by reason of their manner, as they present false claims such as that Poles are idolators and persecutors of the Church, heretics, etc,. for all that is false. And so it is clear that there is no possible application here of the dictum 'Workers of evil thou shalt not suffer to live,' whereby the execution of persons is conceded for good cause.

The third reason why these are unjust is that not only do they encourage the killing of the King of Poland and the Poles as well, without just cause, but their author also slanders them with many unjust and false calumnies, impugning them by charging them with an unrighteous cause, as stated above. And he does this by appealing to doctrine and science, such as does not admit proofs offered in contrary, thus effectively depriving the Poles and their King of legitimate defense, which is their right on the basis of natural law. Consequently, he shunts them outside the bounds of natural law. For the nature of doctrine or science is such that it excludes all doubt and therefore admits no proofs to the contrary, for its propositions are self-evident, as Aristotle teaches in book one of the *Posteriora*. This is not the case of opinion, which fears the opposite and therefore admits contrary proofs.

He worked expressly to deprive the Poles of this defense, as he says in the third chapter: 'So as not to relinquish to our adversary any place from which to mount a defense, we wish to demonstrate — as it is useful to do — by scripture and reason, that Jagiełło and the Poles are responsible for all this.' Such a demonstrative process is not compatible with judicial process in respect to this issue, since theory and justice being diverse causes, diverse must be their effects, too.

They are unjust, fourthly, in respect to the princes whom he would persuade to such homicides, and also in respect to others, their subalterns. In this respect he does away with judicial order and juridical investigation. For he who is not a judge cannot administer the judicial order. Because a sentence passed by someone who is not a judge is not valid (*De iudicijs*: *At si clerici*, with other similar statements). For as Raymundus puts it,[21] the judge who condemns a person to death and the minister of the sentence who executes said person commit mortal sin if they act not according to judicial order (which is proven by *Ad Romanos* XIII;[22] XXIII question V § the penultimate); and in the same cause the question *Miles*, the canon *Cum minister*, the canon *Officia*, the canon *Lex eterna*, and the canon *Qui percutit*, with which Gamfredus concurs; so much more grave a mortal sin does he commit who, not being a judge, kills someone without cause and beyond the judicial order — which is exactly what the conclusions stated above urge, dogmatically!

And although in some of the above-cited conclusions such phrases as 'of charity' and 'on behalf of God' are employed, nevertheless, nothing is in operation here but venom; those phrases are employed merely so as to cloak the heresies set forth — such as where it is stated that the subjects of the princes who 'out of charity' gird themselves against the Poles are deserving of life eternal. For there can be no place for charity where evils are committed — no one can do evil 'out of charity' without sinning. If something is evil, it cannot be said of him who does it that he is acting 'out of charity.'

Even he who kills an evil person without the sanction of public office will be charged with homicide. All the more so is this true of those who dare to usurp such power not granted them by God (as St Augustine states in his first book *De Civitate*, and as is stated in canon XXIII question VIII, at the end). How much greater an evil it is when an inferior person slays a man who is not malevolent, or whose evildoing has not been proven — as in the present case — surely, no one of sane mind can doubt that. And yet that is exactly what this conclusion urges, cloaking the error in that phrase 'out of charity.' Now, as St Thomas says (*Secunda Secunde* question LXII, articles II and III): 'For just as the amputation of a putrid member belongs to the physician to whom care of the entire body has been entrusted, so it belongs only to the prince, or to him to whom public authority has been entrusted for the care of the entire community, to put evildoers to death.' Petrus de Tarantasia concurs with this in his writings in Third *Sententiae*, distinction XXXVII;[23] so does Alexander de Hales in the third part of his *Summa*;[24] so do other learned men, commonly. The same must be said of this conclusion, as follows: 'Whoever kills the Poles and their King on behalf of God is performing pious works.' That is absolutely heretical, just as it would be to say 'whoever kills the consuls of this city on behalf of God is performing pious works,' or any similar things that do outrage to the precepts of divine law, God's commandments, as has been stated. *Eo ipso* such things cannot be done on behalf of God.

From the foregoing it is clear that such words are adduced so as to further fraud, in support of the aforementioned heresies. Now, the law pays heed to intentions rather than words (XXXVIII question *Sedulo*; I question VI *Marchion*, and many other similar to those), for it is not that intention is to serve words, but rather words intention (*De verborum significacione*: *Propterea*, and the chapter *In hijs*). Therefore, where the intention of the writer is known, it is not the sense of the words themselves that is to be our primary concern (as the above-cited laws, and others similar to them, state); rather, they are to be accepted according to the intention of him who promulgates them. For the meaning of words is to be derived from the causes that give rise to their utterance (this is proven in the text *De verborum significacione*: *Intelligencia*). And because the express intention of him who utters them here is clearly evident, that he seeks the extermination of the Poles and their King on false and calumnious bases, here instructing, there begging the favor of God upon those who should follow his instructions, asserting the Poles to be shameless dogs, calling the King, in insulting fashion, by a name other than that which was given him at his baptism, and inflicting other most atrocious injuries, it is therefore manifestly evident that he uses the aforesaid words to color and cloak his heresy.

Now, as I have stated that the above-listed conclusions are absolutely and certainly heretical. although statements may be understood as heretical on several accounts (as stated in XXIV question III § *Qui vero*, in the chapter *Firmissime*: *De hereticis*), still according to St Thomas (*Secunda Secunde* question XI article 1), heresy properly consists in reference to something that has been handed down to us by Christ, when a person chooses not that to which Christ would give His assent, but that which his own mind suggests to him. From this derives the general definition: heresy is a false dogma that is contrary to Catholic truth. So does Jerome understand it (XXIII question III: *Heresia*). Now, according to our Catholic truth, which is the Faith, there are three things to consider: things that by way of primary principles are articles of the Faith; things that by way of conclusion are singular truths demonstrated to us by divine law and comprehended in the canon of the Bible, and third: whatever sort of writings there be, for the declaration of the Faith, such as the writings of the holy doctors, which expound the sacred scripture, or are promulgated for the instruction and stability of the faithful — such as divine decrees and Apostolic decretals. And according to these three heresy is usually understood in a threefold manner, that is: most strictly, as something that is a false dogma contrary to the articles of the Faith (XXIII question I: *Hec est fides*). Secondly, not as strictly: as a false dogma that is contrary to divine law, as in the above-cited canon *Heresis*. Because there can be nothing contained in divine law but truths credible in the light of the Faith, whatever is repugnant to divine law is repugnant to our Faith.

For, according to Aristotle (first *Posteriora*), just as science is a firm and true attitude acquired by demonstration, so is the faith a firm and true attitude acquired by giving heed to the word of God. This is according to the Apostle (Romans 10): 'Faith cometh by hearing, and hearing by the word of God.' And the word of God is what we call the sacred scripture preached or read, acquired by instruction or study.

Thirdly, broadly speaking, heresy is acceptably defined as a dogma that is false in the light of the sayings, statutes, or decrees of the Holy Fathers, or contrary to the determination of the Church (as proven in XIX distinction *Nulli fas*, and XXV question II: *Si quis dogmata*).

From what has been said it clearly follows that the doctrine presented by the above-listed conclusions is not merely simple heresy, but doubly heretical; heretical twice over. For it is plain that it is not only contrary to divine law, but also to canon law and ecclesiastical institutes, as can be seen clearly from *De homicidio*: *Pro humani*, book VI and in many other passages).

Therefore, as the means they propose savour of an extreme nature (which is proven by XLV distinction: *Disciplina*; *De donationibus*: *Cum Apostolica* and other such), and as many other of these conclusions serve as means tending to infer, with finality, the above-mentioned heretical conclusions, it follows that all such are said to savour of heresy. For example: 'The King and people of Poland are persecutors of the Church,' 'hypocrites,' 'heretics' etc. For all of these statements, although not heretical in and of themselves, nonetheless savour of heresy in relation to the end to which they intend.[25] And when we note all in reference to their principal intent, we see that the entire doctrine can be said to be heretical.

To conclude from the foregoing: We state that this doctrine is not only false and erroneous, but, in as much as it is repugnant to divine law, it is heretical, impious, and insane; in as much as it encourages unjust homicide to be executed unjustly, it is dangerous, scandalous, reckless, and cruel; in so far as it deprives the Poles of a legitimate defense it goes against natural law, is seditious, injurious, and openly dangerous to the public order. For all these reasons it is offensive to pious ears and as such deserving of condemnation.[26]

Endnotes

1. The dating of this work has been generally established by Belch *Paulus Vladimiri*, II, 991, as late 1416 or early 1417 (he did not explicitly assign a date to it in his earlier listing of Paweł's writings, I, 174). Ehrlich, *Pisma wybrane*, I, xxx, is in general agreement. Instead of using the incipit of *Iste tractatus*, Belch entitles it *Scriptum denunciatorium errorum in duobus tractatibus Ioannis Falkenberg, O.P. contentorum* and abbreviates it as *Scriptum I* (see below, n. 13).

2. Paweł is here referring to two works by Johannes Falkenberg, a Dominican author (see n. 5 below) whom the Order had apparently commissioned to write a response to *Saevientibus* and *Opinio Hostiensis*. The first was entitled *Liber de doctrina potestatis papae et imperatoris editus contra Paulum Vladimiri Polonum*, though it is more generally known by its incipit *Veteres relegentes historias*. The second work, whose incipit is *Accipe gladium* and which was circulated at the council, is now apparently lost. As Paweł notes in his text, however, it is essentially identical in substance and form (*in materia et forma*) to the first and he explicitly refers to it several times.

3. Paweł's argument is that the doctrinal and theoretical approach (*processus doctrinalis*) taken by Falkenberg is fundamentally flawed and that only a judicial process in which evidence is presented can establish the truth of the matter under consideration.

4. This is Paweł's larger goal, to have the Council of Constance condemn Falkenberg's treatise[s].

5. i.e., Falkenberg (*ca.* 1364-1435). He was born in north-western Germany, studied arts and law at Prague and theology at Vienna. At some point he entered the Dominican Order, becoming eventually a prior and an inquisitor. He was a member of the Dominican *studium* in Kraków in 1405 and 1406, where he was particularly critical of intellectual and theological

developments there. He engaged in an on-going polemic with Matthew of Kraków, by then bishop of Worms, over the latter's *De praxis* [or *squaloribus*] *Romanae Curiae* that criticized clerical corruption; with the bishop of Kraków, Piotr Wysz (who had written a work, *Speculum aurem de titulis beneficiorum ecclesiasticorum*, that was equally critical of many current church practices), and Stanisław of Skarbimierz, the first rector of the refounded University of Kraków and dean and professor of Canon Law, who in 1410 was the author of an important sermon, *De bellis iustis*, that among other issues took up the question of Christian alliances with pagans; see Stanisław Wielgus, *The Medieval Polish Doctrine of the Law of Nations*: Ius Gentium (Lublin: University Press of the Catholic University of Lublin, 1998 [original Polish version *Polska średniowieczna doktryna* Ius Gentium, 1996], pp. 25-28): and Wojciech Świeboda, *Innowiercy w opiniach prawnych uczonych polskich w XV wieku. Poganie, żydzi, muzułmanie* (Kraków: Societas Vistulana, 2013), pp. 143-156. Falkenberg's massive *De monarchia mundi* was a full-blown defense of papal theocracy and has been twice edited by Władysław Seńko: in *Materiały do Historii Filozofii średniowiecznej w Polsce* 9 (20) (1975): vii-lvi, 1-289, and as *Krakowska redakcja Jana Falkenberga* De monarchia mundi (Warsaw: Akademia Teologii Katolickej, 1986 [Textus et Studia Historiam Theologiae in Polonia excultae spectantia 20]). Falkenberg's *Satira* and Paweł's reaction to it are treated elsewhere in this current volume. His life and work is addressed by Norman Housley, "A Crusade Against the Poles? Johannes Falkenberg's 'Satira' (1412)," in Helen J. Nicholson and Jochen Burgtorf, eds., *The Templars, the Hospitallers and the Crusades* (London and New York: Routledge, 2020), pp. 183-198, especially pp. 184-186. The authoritative treatment of him, his biography, and his infamous *Satira* in the context of relations between the Order and Poland remains Hartmut Boockmann, *Johannes Falkenberg, der Deutsche Order und die polnische Politik. Untersuchungen zur politischen Theorie des späteren Mittelalters* (Göttingen: Vandenhoeck & Ruprecht, 1975).

6. This is Paweł's stylistic approach in this treatise. He refers to himself in the third person when dealing with attacks upon him by others, but uses the first person when he assumes the status of author. Ehrlich, *Pisma wybrane*, II, 212, n. 5, observes that the fifteenth-century Polish historian, Jan Długosz, often adopts this same mode.

7. Here Paweł categorizes Falkenberg's organization as consisting of three elements: what the powers of the emperor are with respects to his grants to the Order; a characterization of the legitimacy of the Order's wars against the pagans and the Poles; and, finally, the validity of the Order's condemnations of the Poles and their king, including those who assist them against the Order.

8. What follows in this section is essentially Paweł's summary of the points Falkenberg made in his treatise (and in the third part of this translation, which is a separate treatise; see below, n. 13).

9. Deut. 17:8-10, 12.

10. 2 Tim. 2:4.

11. Implicit in this is one of the core arguments made by the Order against Jagiełło, namely that his "conversion" was invalid, a hypocritic sham meant merely to deceive others. On this, see Falkenberg's assertions treated below n. 15, among other places.

12. i.e., the Battle of Grunwald.

13. This marks the formal end of *Iste tractatus* as edited by Belch, II, 994-1001, abbreviated in his listing of Paweł's writings, I, 174, as *Scriptum I.* The text that follows immediately in this present translation is a separate work in Belch's taxonomy, *Scriptum denunciatorium errorum Satirae Ioannis Falkenberg, O.P., Constantiensi Concilio datum* that he abbreviates as *Scriptum II.* Ehrlich, *Pisma wybrane*, II, 196-209, presents this as the third part of *Iste tractatus.*

14. The work referred to by Paweł is Falkenberg's *Satira contra hereses et cetera nephanda Polonorum et eorum regis Jaghel*, or *Satira*, which was discussed in the Introduction above in the section devoted to a description of Paweł's *Iste tractaus.* Falkenberg wrote the *Satira*, probably in 1412, and by 1417 the general procurator of the Order indicated it had been offered it to the Teutonic Knights by Falkenberg, but they had rejected it, because elements of it were "scandalous" and "injurious." Nevertheless, Falkenberg had seen that it was circulated among the members of the council, where it was indeed found to be a vitriolic polemic that accused the king of Poland of being an idol and the Polish of worshiping him. According to Falkenberg, they and he were despised by God as heretics and shameless pagan dogs, and Christendom's best service would be to kill all the Poles and their heathen king, for heaven's purposes would be served by any who kill Poles. Poland, its king, and population were a plague besetting the church. Many at the council were outraged at this, not least the Poles, and Paweł strove in this response to convince the council that it should condemn Falkenberg for heresy and punish him. Though the general content of the *Satira* was known, its text appeared lost until the third quarter of the last century (neither Ehrlich nor Belch had knowledge or access to it). Hartmut Boockmann and Zofia Włodek both discovered a copy of it in Leipzig and separately published a modern critical edition (Boockmann added to his edition a second MS he discovered at Zeil). See Zofia Włodek, "Odnaleziona Satyra Falkenberga," *Studia Historyczne* 14 (1971): 477-491, and Włodek, "La Satire de Jean Falkenberg. Texte inédit avec introduction," *Mediaevalia Philosophica Polonorum* 18 (1973): 51-120; and Boockmann, *Johannes Falkenberg*, pp. 312-353.

15. Jagiełło's hypocrisy, in the eyes of Falkenberg—and, in general, of the Order's defense—lay in his conversion, which was regarded by them as a political sham intended merely to mislead Christendom into accepting the justice of their continued policies vis-a-vis the Lithuanians and other peoples of the Baltic region.

16. Paweł's summary here of the contents in the thirteen chapters of the *Satira* is complemented by the comments of Boockmann, *Johannes Falkenberg*, pp. 9-10; and Housley, "A Crusade Against the Poles? Johannes Falkenberg's 'Satira' (1412)," pp. 187-189. For a much fuller description of the *Satira*, see the treatment by Anna Lisa Merklin Lewis, "Tyrannicide: Heresy or Duty? The Debates at the Council of Constance," (Unpublished Ph.D. Dissertation, Cornell University, Ithaca, NY, 1990), pp. 101-118.

17. Falkenberg's call for the killing of the Polish king raised issues of tyrannicide that, to greater-or-lesser degree, mirrored previous discussions on this topic at the Council, particularly connected with the views of Jean Petit justifying such actions (on the issue related to him, see the translation above of *Articuli*, n. 4). The classic work on this question for Petit is Alfred Coville, *Jean Petit. La question du tyrannicide au commencement du XVe siècle* (Paris: A. Picard, 1932, reprinted Geneva: Slatkin, 1974). Treating Petit and Falkenberg in the same

context, however, has now been nicely done in her, unfortunately unpublished, dissertation by Lewis, "Tyrannicide," pp. 119-159 (the Petit Case) and pp. 160-197 (the Falkenberg case).

18. Ex. 20:13.

19. 1 Peter 3:8-9 and 4:5; Matt. 5:21.

20. Hostiensis (Henricus de Segusio 1190/1200-1271), studied at Bologna, taught at Paris, and eventually became cardinal-bishop of Ostia; see Brundage, *Canon Law*, p. 214, and above, in the translated text of Paweł's treatise *Opinio Ostiensis*, n. 2. While in Paweł's treatise on Hostiensis he fundamentally disagreed with him on one central point, here, on another matter, he accepts his views.

21. Ramón de Penyafort (1180/1185-1275), a Catalan who studied and taught at Bologna; see Brundage, *Canon Law*, pp. 222-223.

22. Rom. 13:1-4.

23. Peter of Tarantasia, a canonist, who was briefly Pope Innocent V in 1276.

24. Alexander of Hales (d. 1245), English Franciscan and theologian who taught at Paris after 1210, lecturing especially on Peter Lombard's *Sentences*. See Robert E. Bjork, ed., *The Oxford Dictionary of the Middle Ages*, 4 vols. (Oxford: Oxford University Press, 2010), I, 36.

25. That end, as Falkenberg made clear in a variety of ways, was—as the result of heresy—that the Polish king and the Poles should be killed; Paweł's conclusion was that this constituted all of the things he so eloquently defined in his next, and final, paragraph. Earlier in our own century, the doyen of German historians of late medieval political theory observed that Falkenberg's "shrieking demands resulted unexpectedly in the demand for a Christianity based genocide." ("Die schreienden Forderungen... münden unversehens in die Aufforderung zu christlich begründetem Genozid."). Jürgen Miethke, "Heiliger Heidenkrieg? Theoretische Kontroversen zwischen Deutschem Orden und dem Königreich Polen vor und auf dem Konstanzer Konzil," in Klaus Schreiner, ed., *Heilige Kriege. Religiöse Begründungen militärischer Gewaltanwendung: Judentum, Christentum und Islam im Vergleich* (Munich: Oldenbourg, 2008), pp. 109-125, here p. 117.

26. The Council eventually condemned Falkenberg's *Satira*, but not in a way that satisfied the Polish delegation. The first stage of the process came in the solemn closing session of the Council on 22 April 1418; see Belch, *Paulus Vladimiri*, I, 133-136. Later developments that culminated in 1424 and 1425 are summarized by Ehrlich, *Pisma wybrane*, II, 215, n. 52.

BECAUSE AN ERROR

(*Quoniam error*, 1417)[1]

Part I

Version 1[2]

In the Name of the Lord, Amen

Because an error unopposed is an error approved, and a truth undefended is a truth suppressed (as is said in canon LXXXIII), for this reason, so as to confute a certain screed erroneous not only in law, but in good morals, as it appears *prima facie* inimical to Catholic truth, fabricated and concocted in favor of the Knights of the Cross of Prussia and against the King of Poland and his subjects by a certain Johann von Bamberg,[3] a doctor of the decretals, and recently presented to several nations gathered at this sacred Council of Constance, in which it is seen that said Johann asserts two chief points: in the first of which he strives to establish said Order and justify the warring of its Brethren, and in the second to reprove the war waged by the Poles against said Brethren, I have thus determined to compose, likewise, two scholarly tracts, determining nothing myself, but rather laying out the matter for others who should wish better to consider them, leaving the determination of the same entirely to our most holy lord, the Pope,[4] and this Synod of the universal Church.

In the first tract, all that should be known of the aforesaid Order *de iure* will be examined. In the second, responses will be made to what is said in the aforementioned writings.[5]

As far, therefore, as the first tract is concerned, in order that the issue be set clearly upon its proper foundations, at the start we shall present the factual truth.

Version 2

IN THE NAME OF THE LORD, AMEN. Because error unopposed is error approved, and truth undefended is truth suppressed, here in the presence of the General Council of Constance, which, among other things, has been convoked chiefly for the extirpation of errors and heresies, I therefore present a matter containing certain errors of the Brethren of the Knights of the Cross of Prussia — which Brethren are known as the Brethren of the Most Holy Virgin Mary of the Teutonic House — for the consideration of this sacred Council, and our most holy lord the Pope, in the writings which follow.[6] And so that this matter should appear most clearly set upon its proper foundations, let us first set out the factual truth.

TOPIC. Discord having arisen between our Most Serene Prince, His Majesty Lord Władysław, King of Poland, etc., on the one hand, and the aforesaid Brethren of the Knights of the Cross on the other, concerning several lands and dominions, etc., these Knights, setting forth their pretensions to said lands before our Most Illustrious Lord

Sigismund, King of the Romans and King of Hungary, as well as his deputy or commissary, selected for the task of arbitration and invited thereto by common accord of both parties, produced multiple and divers writings claiming the authority of the Roman Pontiffs and the Emperors as well. One of these writings produced, emitted under the name of Emperor Frederick II, contains a donation made unto them, of three lands, in particular: Prussia, Courland, and Lettonia,[7] which they were then to acquire for themselves by military action for the spread of the Faith and that of the borders of the Roman Empire, which accordingly they did acquire and which even now they occupy *de facto*. And this donation also grants unto them all other lands of infidels whatsoever they are able to penetrate with their armies, banners erect.[8]

Now in the second of these letters, under the same title, he is seen to donate to them three other lands, *scilicet* Lithuania and Żmudź, the land of the Samogitians, who were pagan at the time, and the land of Russia, which is inhabited by schismatics. These lands they do not possess, excepting a certain part of said land of the Samogitians, which they did obtain.

To speak briefly of some letters produced under the authority of the Roman Pontiffs, *viz.* Alexander IV and Clement IV, they are to the effect that, whatever lands of the infidels in general they succeed in wresting from the hands of said pagans with the aid of Christian armies should belong to them in as much as exploitation is concerned, while their ownership is reserved to St Peter and the Roman Church. In all of these aforesaid letters, said Brethren insist that the principal cause of these donations is, first of all, the spread of the Catholic Faith. Second, although in all of the above-mentioned letters these Brethren are spoken of as Brothers of the Hospital of Jerusalem of the Blessed Virgin Mary of the Teutonic House, the fact is that they never inhabited nor were used to inhabit any sort of hospital, nor did they ever profess nor have they professed any regular vows by serving in any such hospital in living memory. Nor does there exist in the world, nor has anyone ever heard of there actually existing any such hospital to which they have had a principal association since then. So much for part two.

Third, in the same cause, they have produced several articles asserting and maintaining as confirmed, defending it likewise, that their Order has been instituted and even confirmed for the very reason of invading the lands of whatever enemies of the Cross of Christ and exterminating them with violence, and wresting their lands from them, converting the same to their own use, so that the Catholic Faith might be spread and established there.

In this article they assert and maintain, even if tacitly, that a religious order might be instituted for the extermination of infidels of whatever sort and the wresting of their dominions from their hands! Likewise, they claim in this same article that it was legitimate for this order of theirs to invade all neighboring pagan lands and wrest from their hands their goods, possessions, lands and dominions, converting the same to their use.

Likewise, they assert and maintain that, on account of their perfidy, whatever infidels there may be are to be propelled beyond the confines of the world, of which there can be no doubt, etc.

In this manner, they confess to having acquired several lands from infidels at the cost of the greatest shedding of Christian blood during the extermination of said infidels, etc. So much for point three.

From this prelude, a triplex question arises.

First: whether the aforementioned donations are valid *de iure* or might be valid to the effect that all the aforesaid letters can be somehow acquitted of the taint of falsehood.

Second: whether the aforesaid Brethren are, or were, capable of licitly acquiring dominion over material possessions or taking advantage of the same.

Third: whether this society or sect of these Brethren might be in conformity with canonical writings or acknowledged to be a religious order, or be approved in any way by the Church.

It is useful to call all these into question.

Rubric. This chapter is dedicated to a general proof of the fact that this warfare of theirs is not for the promotion of the Christian Faith, but rather an impediment thereto.

And lest under any color or pretext this matter be pretended to be anything other than what it is: thus, reducing these Brethren to their fundamental essence through these letters of theirs, it is to be known that, because said letters contain matters of the faith as an end, and as such is a theological matter, reducing all to the rule of charity, etc., and because they also contain matters of war, the occupation of dominions, the invasion and subjugation of infidels, etc., as means to said end, and as such are matters above all for moral consideration, and especially that of the judicial faculty, which reduces all to the rule of justice:

therefore, this matter of faith is to be considered here according to its subject matter, scilicet according to the matter of justice, which is a moral virtue inferior to charity.

It shall therefore be the business of jurists to debate these means, *viz.*, whether they be just or unjust, because if unjust, then they are untrue, nor is it possible for the Faith to be promoted by such means, rather, it would be impeded thereby, and a theologian would be bound to conclude that it is not faith we see here, but heresy. For to suggest that the Faith may be amplified by an unjust war, or spread by the illicit occupation of lands and dominions, seems heretical.

And because such wars, etc., are being waged on the basis of the aforesaid letter, if, therefore, the first, instrumental and efficient cause, *viz.,* said letter, cannot be reduced to the cause or rule of justice, it necessarily follows that this sort of war is erroneous, as is all the rest that follows from these letters.

Now, so that said letters might be reduced to the terms of justice, it would be necessary for them to contain just causes of the acts which they proclaim, *scil.* the donations made and privation of the infidels' dominions. Because as such acts are indifferent in themselves, they can be properly done, or wrongly done. In order for them to be acknowledged good or just it is necessary that they arise from an evidently just cause or due circumstances. And as such are apparently not present in this case, these writings cannot be deemed just. For in such cases the law would have us consider the cause more than what results therefrom, and thus concerning the law it is not sufficient to speak of the accomplished fact, one must also speak of its cause (which is proven in the chapter *Dilectus*: *De rescriptis*, with many others similar thereunto adduced in the first gloss).

Not only can they not be deemed just, indeed, they ought actually to be adjudged unjust and considered so. Because in so far as just causes for such actions are not apparent, *de iure* they are understood as non-existent, and by consequence, not contained in the letters. Because in this matter 'not apparent' is equivalent to 'not existent' (which is legally proven in *De eleccione*: *Ut circa*, the penultimate § of book VI; *De consecracione* distinction I: *Solemptnitates*, with others similar).

And so that these things should be seen in ever clearer light, pay particular attention to what follows.

There is nothing missing here.

Now, because I have somewhat more broadly dilated upon the texts of the abovesaid letters,[9] here I will be as brief as possible, not luxuriating in a multitude of allegations, but contenting myself with a few, for brevity's sake.

As far as the first, chief proposition is concerned, we must consider the causes preceding all such donations, according to the words of the poet:

'In giving gifts, consider these four things:
Who gives, who gets, what's given, and wherefore.'

Which is noted in the gloss beginning 'Aliud est' in the chapter *Etsi questione*: *De symonia*.

And thus, according to the four types of cause, a quadriplex consideration arises here.

Rubric. Here first it is proven that by reason of efficient cause the aforesaid letters are utterly invalid, as neither the Pope together with the Emperor, nor the Emperor by himself, is able to do such things *de iure*.

By the first reason, concerning the givers, it is clear that *de iure*, both of them, that is, the Pope and the Emperor, along with their authorities, are seen to be distinct and diverse, and thus they are incapable of making a donation of these lands to said Brethren. The rationale: Because although it sometimes occurs that one possesses something by different causes, still, possession is acquired only by virtue of one cause, for that which is mine because of one cause cannot be mine from another cause, unless it first ceases to be mine (as in the chapter *Inter dilectos*: *De fide instrumentorum*, in concord with the chapter *Ut quis duas*: *De eleccione* book VI. Nor is an Imperial donation valid *per se* because, according to the writings of learned men in general, and as

Johannes Andreae[10] writes (see chapter I: *De constitucionibus*) those infidels who do not acknowledge a Christian superior are subject in temporalities to the Vicar of Christ, that is, to the Pope, as Innocent sets forth (in the chapter *Quod super hijs*: *De voto et voti redempcione*). And even should we grant that they are subject to the Emperor, still the abovesaid donation of the Emperor, especially on account of the amplification of the faith (as mentioned in the Topic above), could not be valid *de iure*, nor might it be maintained as such. The rationale: because no one should be deprived of his goods without cognisance of the cause, and as the cognisance of a cause of the faith, as the principal matter, does not belong to the office of the Emperor, nor does its accessory, *scil.* such a donation. For, according to Ostiensis,[11] permission to wage war on behalf of the faith pertains to the Church (in his *Summa*: *De penitencijs et remissionibus* § *Quibus et qualiter*, the verse 'Quid de rapina'). Therefore, such permission to wage war conceded by the Emperor is invalid by law, and by consequence so is the donation invalid. For anything done by a judge that exceeds the authority of his office cannot he maintained (as in chapter *De regulis iuris*, book VI); this is true (according to the gloss there) even if what the judge does is good: for example (XCVI distinction: *Bene quidem*), even though it was a good thing for the Emperor to enact a statute to the effect that a holding of the Church cannot be alienated, still the statute was invalid, because such a determination does not belong to the Emperor's office. So, generally speaking, it is not sufficient merely to do good; that good must be well and properly done.

Rubric. Here it is proven that even the Pope cannot make such donations himself without just cause.

And even though the Pope is the Supreme Vicar of God upon the earth, not even he is able to grant, absolutely and in general, the lands of the infidels to said Brethren or others, without just cause. For to do so would be contrary to both natural and divine law. This is true both in relation to the infidels, who must be judged according to natural law, and in relation to the Pope, whose authority is subject to both natural and divine law.

By reason of the first, because the Pope may not punish them unless they sin against natural law, for example, as the Lord punished Sodom and Gomorrah, as Innocent and the learned men in general note (in the chapter *Quod super hijs*: *De voto et voti redempcione*) and here certain cases are given whereby the Pope may legitimately punish them, *scilicet* if they seize and occupy Christian lands, if they impede Christians in their worship of the true God, if they refuse to admit preachers of the Gospel into their lands, or if they do not allow the Christians who live among them to live in peace, if they worship idols, since it is natural that all men worship but the one sole God, the Creator of all, rather than worshipping creatures.[12] For to deprive someone of his temporal goods is a harsh punishment to inflict upon a person without his guilt having been proven, or at least without just cause having been shown, especially when this is being done without said person having been convicted, or allowed to defend himself — which is against natural law, seeing that self-defense is a natural right. Likewise, to grant someone the faculty of looting someone else's goods by violence is contrary to natural law and the commandments of the Decalogue, *scil.* 'Thou shalt not kill,' 'Thou shalt not steal' (Exodus XX).[13] For according to St Augustine, by 'Thou shalt not kill,' all violence is prohibited, and in the word 'steal'[14] all rapine is contained (*viz.* Canon XIV question V: *Dixit Dominus, ff*).

By reason of the second it is repugnant to the pastoral office of the Pope to expose the sheep of Christ to the rapaciousness of wolves; however much they exist in an infidel state, he should rather lead them into the fold of the Church as much as this is possible, according to the saying of the Savior (John X: 'Other sheep I have, that are not of this fold,' *scil.* the Church, and 'them also I must bring').[15]

Rubric. The second consideration in respect of the final cause, in which it is shown that, because these Brethren cannot be said to be of the Hospital of Jerusalem, any donation made unto them as such is null and void.

In respect to whom the gift is given, that is, on behalf of whom such a grant was made, it cannot be said that it was principally or finally made on behalf of these Brethren. Because whatever is given to them is understood as a gift made on behalf of the Hospital of Jerusalem (see the chapter *Cum in officijs* and the chapter *Requisisti*: *De testamentis*) which will appear clearer later. I say 'on behalf of the hospital,' *viz.* one actually existing at the time, to the exclusion of all houses and all hospitals that these Brethren may have in Prussia and in other regions later acquired, for no donation may be understood to be made to a monastery not yet in existence — such a donation would be invalid (see the text in the chapter *Abbate Sane*: *De re iudicata*, the verse 'Allegabatur,' book VI) just as things which are not yet in existence cannot be given any privilege or can any easement be constituted thereunto (*De ecclesijs edificandis* chapter *Ad audienciam* II, where this is spoken of), nor can a matrimony be dissolved, which has not yet been consummated (*De desponsacione impuberum*: *Ad dissolvendum*). I also say 'on behalf of the Hospital of Jerusalem,' to which the Brethren insist they belong in all the aforesaid letters, and others, and since no such place exists; therefore, in the absence of a final cause, the donation is null and void. From which it follows that these Brethren of the Hospital of Jerusalem are Brethren of a hospital that does not exist, and this is tantamount to an effect existing in the absence of a cause, which is repugnant to the very order of things in the universe. From which it also follows that all of the aforesaid letters are utterly of no advantage to these Brethren, as they cannot be verified or justified, since they have nothing to do, principally, with any hospitals. And by consequence, in asserting themselves to be hospitallers, while not pursuing their lives in hospitals nor being bound to any hospital by monastic vows, as can be seen — they are committing a falsehood. Because names ought to be consonant with the things they represent and things are to be received according to their effects (*De clericis non residentibus*: *Relatum*).

Rubric. The third consideration in respect to the material cause, or the thing given, in which it is proven that the infidels justly possess their dominions, which cannot be bestowed upon another nor licitly occupied.

And because by the natural law of nations the pagans justly possess their dominions, these same cannot be licitly occupied. Innocent and other learned men in general following him pursue this matter broadly (see said chapter *Quod super hijs*: *De voto et voti redempcione*) and St Thomas (*Secunda secunde* question IX article X). And this is generally maintained by theologians as well as canonists and jurists. Therefore, that which is in the power of enemies and not in the power of the putative donor cannot be given to another; this is proven verbatim by the text of chapter *Abbate Sane*: *De sentencia et re iudicata*, the verse 'Allegabatur,' where in the sixth gloss the reason is given as follows: Because man is free and the land is the enemy's, and what nature does not grant cannot be disposed of by stipulation (*ff De verborum obligacionibus*, the law *Liber homo*, etc.). This is true in the case of things which always belonged to the enemy. If, however, they were once ours, and if they were now occupied by these enemies, they may be donated unconditionally and made the matter of stipulation on our hopes in the law *postliminii* (as is found in the law *Id* for which see *ff De legibus* I) as Bartolus infers[16] and as lord Petrus de Ancarano[17] re-cites in said chapter *Abbate*, where it is stated that the concession of the Kingdom of Jerusalem made by the Pope to King Charles and his successors is valid even though he hold no part of it, simply on the basis that the Kingdom once belonged to the Christians and thus constituted a concession according to the hope of *postliminii*.

In his *Questiones*, Oldradus[18] is of the same opinion, as he states in question LXXII, which begins with the query 'Whether the war waged by the Spanish against the Saracens is a just war.' He responds in the affirmative, even presupposing that now and in the future they wish to live with us in peace, giving the rationale that the entire province of Spain had once been Christian. Churches, monasteries and other pious locales had been established there, in which Christ was worshipped and which had been subject to the Holy Church, which these Saracens later occupied by violence, despoiling us thereof. To this he adds: 'And thus, if we are acting in order recuperate the fatherland of which we have been despoiled by violence, our war is just,' and, according to him, ought to be judged a defensive action, and not an invasion. From which the manifest error of those who hold that there is no just dominion amongst the infidels, etc., is clearly shown, and held as a heresy by the most capable theologians, because this error is not only contrary to natural law, it is contrary to divine law as well. Against which error Ockham[19] (in the third part of his book of dialogues, chapter XXV) adduces many citations from Holy Scripture and the sayings of sainted doctors, which shall appear even clearer below, in the second tractate in reference to the second conclusion. Said Brethren are seen to base themselves upon this error given these aforesaid articles of theirs, above all where they offer in defense of their claims what I cite here verbatim: 'Because the Samogitians have always been pagans, and the majority of them remain so to this day, hostile to our faith, possessing no right, it is therefore nefarious to state that they and their lands are comprehended within certain bounds and limits. Because, on account of their perfidy, there is no doubt about it but that they should be propelled by the faithful beyond the bounds of the world,' etc. Said Johannes von Bomberg seeks to defend them in this error too, in the above-mentioned writings, *viz.*, in his desire to justify and salvage their war making, as he sets down for this purpose the very error aforesaid.

Version I

The fourth consideration in respect to the formal cause.

The reduction of infidels to the Catholic Faith through oppression, *viz.* by armed force or the subtraction of their temporal goods, seems repugnant to the truth of Sacred Scripture, as stated above. Likewise, it is repugnant to canon law. For these reasons, such a reduction is neither a sufficient nor just cause for the bestowal upon anyone of the lands or goods of infidels, or for the looting thereof, as piety is no pretext for the commission of impieties (XXX question I: *Nosce*), nor may evils be committed so that good may result therefrom. As we read in the canon *Quid autem*: XLV distinction: 'For it is a new and unheard of preaching, that Faith may be compelled by beatings.' And in the chapter *Sicut Iudei*: *De Iudeis* it is said: 'Because they are not believed to have faith in Christ, who come to Christian baptism not spontaneously, but are driven there by force,' where it is proven (in the second gloss) that no one is to be compelled to the Faith, as faith should not be a matter of necessity (according to the laws there alleged). For the General Council of Toledo[20] prohibited the forced conversion of any person, stating: 'For the unwilling are not to be led to salvation, but rather those who wish it, so that the form of justice be preserved. For just as man perished by his own free will in his obedience to the serpent, so being called by divine grace is he saved by the conversion of his own mind' (XLV distinction in the canon *De Iudeis*) and (in the canon *Qui sincera*, the same distinction) it is said that 'he who leads others to the faith not by blandishments, but by asperities, proves himself to be more concerned with his own advantage than that of God,' etc. Hence St Thomas (*Secunda secunde* question X article VIII) says that 'it is for this reason that Christ's faithful wage frequent wars against the infidels: indeed, not so as to compel them to the Faith — for even if they are victorious over them and hold them in captivity, still they allow them freedom of religious belief — but rather to compel them not to impede those among them who do believe in Christ.'

Version II

Rubric. The fourth consideration in respect to form, in which it is shown that this manner of spreading the Faith, by armed force, especially there, where there does not seem to be any impediment to the Faith, is reprehensible both according to divine and human law, and entirely contrary to the Christian Faith.

Now the manner of spreading the Catholic Faith contained in this letter, *viz.,* by armed force, by the subtraction of temporal goods, and by the oppression of the infidels, is not seen to be compatible with the Christian Faith, but repugnant to both the Faith and the soldier's occupation itself, as in such fashion men are violently and unjustly oppressed, contrary to the precepts of the Decalogue, since without guilt or legitimate cause; nor is the order of justice duly observed, as, in respect to this, the spread of the Faith cannot be a legitimate cause for such a method or for warmaking — for evils must not be committed so that good may result therefrom, nor can piety be a pretext for the commission of impieties (as canon XXX question I: *Nosce* reads). And so it is manifestly clear that such a method works not to the amplification of the orthodox faith, but rather as an impediment thereunto. And hence one reads in the canon 'it is a new and unheard of preaching, that Faith may be compelled by beatings' (XLV distinction: *Quid autem*), for by its very nature war cannot be a causative of faith, nor vice versa, unless by coincidence and indirectly, *viz.,* where the Faith is imperilled. And since no such impediment is alleged to be at issue in these letters, it ceases entirely to be the cause of a just war. And for that reason, because the mode is unjust, it is prohibited by divine law by the words 'thou shalt not kill,' in which all violence is prohibited, as is all illicit usurpation of goods not belonging to one by the words 'thou shalt not steal,' as said above. It is therefore prohibited by canon law (in the chapter *Sicud Iudei*: *De Iudeis*) where it is proven (in gloss II) that no man is to be compelled to the Faith, because faith ought not to come of necessity (see the laws there alleged), wherefore the text reads 'because they are not believed to have faith in Christ, who come to Christian baptism not spontaneously, but are driven there by force.' The same is prohibited by the general Council of Toledo,[21] which forbids the compulsion of anyone to accept the Faith (on which see XLV distinction in the canon *De Iudeis*) where it says 'For the unwilling are not to be led to salvation, but rather those who wish it, so that the form of justice be preserved. For just as man perished by his own free will in his obedience to the serpent, so being called by divine grace is he saved by the conversion of his own mind.' Likewise, this is repugnant to the nature of warfare, or the métier thereof, the aim of which is to put up resistance to those who would impede the Faith or any other common or civil good — to this end the vocation of arms was naturally instituted. Hence Egidius (*De Regimine principum*, in the third part of chapter I),[22] says: Because just as man has two virtues in himself, one by which he pursues good and and flies evil, the other by which he attacks and repulses those who disturb others, *viz.,* the rapacious and irascible, thus every city and every kingdom, etc., requires a duplex virtue and duplex prudence, *viz.*, positive laws so that what is advantageous may be preserved and what is noxious may be avoided, and an army with which it might attack and overcome in military operations such enemies as would prohibit it from enjoying these good things. And therefore the end of war should be peace, according to St Augustine (*De civitate Dei*),who says: 'It is obvious that peace is the acceptable aim of warring.' Also (*Ad Bonifacium*): 'War is waged so that peace might be acquired. Be, therefore, peacefully minded when waging war so as to lead those you overcome and conquer to peace.' Thus, the spreading or support of the Faith in and of itself is contrary to this end, and in consequence, the warmaking of these Brethren is contrary to peace, and because the amplification of the Faith is principally an act of faith, which is a theological virtue, it pertains to the theologian and not to the soldier. And even though it can be promoted by means of other, inferior virtues and moral acts, ministerially, still, it cannot be promoted or brought about by the waging of war unless, as we say above, by coincidence. Therefore, etc. This is what St Thomas says (in *Secunda secunde* question X article VIII): 'it is for this reason that Christ's faithful wage frequent wars against the infidels: indeed, not so as to compel them to the Faith — for even if they are victorious over them and hold them in captivity, still they allow them freedom of religious belief — but rather to compel them not to impede those among them who do believe in Christ.' Hence it is, according to Isidore, that a war is said to be just when it is declared for the recuperation of things unlawfully taken or in order to resist enemy invasions (and this can be found in XXIII question II canon II); yet neither of these two things are at the root of the matter here. And so it evidently follows that said Brethren, waging war in such fashion, are pursuing their own aims and not those of Jesus Christ (which is also proven in the canon *Qui sincera*: XLV distinction, where it says: 'he who leads others to the faith not by blandishments, but by asperities, proves himself to be more concerned with his own advantage than that of God,' etc.). This they seem to confess themselves in the above-cited articles, where they state 'Because this Order has been instituted and even confirmed for the very reason of invading the lands of whatever enemies of the Cross of Christ and exterminating them with violence, and wresting their lands from them, converting the same to our own use, so that the Catholic Faith might be spread and confirmed there.' Here is their religion, here is their devotion — to obtain the possessions of others for their own! What is more, they declare that they have acquired some lands from the infidels at the cost of a maximum effusion of Christian blood. See what cruelty! What need have we of further witnesses![23] For one thing is certain: given such efficacious testimony, with such notoriously evident truth before us, there can be no denying the same. See the cruel perversity and the perverse cruelty — as St. Bernard says to you (in the book *Ad Hugonem magistrum militie Templi*, c. 2), where he writes to the Templars, from whom these Brethren derive as from their predecessors, when they would ratify their privileges, *viz.*: that for such causes it is neither safe to kill nor to die, *scil.*, when the cause is moved by some irrational lie or the cupidity to obtain any terrestrial possessions, etc. Hear further what he says in this same place: 'Him therefore who wages war with the aim of obtaining secular goods or aims I call not a militia-man, but a malicious man,[24] since both the killed and the killer die an eternal death, the killer for having mortally sinned.' And a little after this he adds: 'Indeed, pagans are not to be killed if there exists any other manner of prohibiting them from excessively persecuting or oppressing the faithful.'

Rubric. Here it is inferred from the foregoing that the abovementioned donations are completely invalid, in support of which many other particular reasons are touched upon.

From all of the above it follows that the abovementioned, and pretended, donations, of the Roman Pontiffs as well as the Emperors, are entirely invalid. Nor are they capable of being valid, and they are invalid, as has been said, for divers reasons: on account of their being contrary to divine law, and by reason of it being contrary to natural law to despoil the infidels of their goods; and by reason of the means, which do not serve lawful order, and this again is contrary to natural law, of which more is said below; and because the Imperial donation is deficient in the root of its power, concerning which see below, where it is more broadly discussed in the second tract near the fourth conclusion;[25] and because there is no such thing as the Hospital of Jerusalem, of which they claim to be, and in respect to the Brethren of the Knights of the Cross themselves, who are incapable of receiving such donations, which also will become more fully apparent below; and in respect to the cause, which is both insufficient and unjust; and because said donations have been made that grant things that do not belong to the granting party — and such a donation is invalid as prejudicial to the actual owner (Codex: *De donacionibus*, law II), for no one may donate anything unless he is the true owner thereof (according to Ostiensis in his *Summa*: *De donacionibus* § *Quis posit donare*; by the law *ff De regulis iuris*: *Cui ius est donandi*), because according to the law no one may transfer to another any more right than he is known to possess himself. And it is known that neither the Pope nor the Emperor is lord of those lands belonging to the infidels, especially in so far as singular and proper ownership is concerned. Nor are any laws which claim that everything belongs to the Emperor of any account here. Just the same with any that claim that he is the ruler of the world and its lord, because these and similar statements are understood to suggest that all things are the Emperor's, which rather refers to jurisdiction and protection, i.e. all things in a kingdom belong to the king as far as jurisdiction and defense are concerned, but not in any sense of real property and individual ownership, according to the Archdeacon[26] (XXIII question VIII § *Quamvis*). Just so the Emperor is said to be the lord of the world, which is understood in terms of aptitude but not act, and, according to others, in terms of care and solicitude.

Therefore, as these lands were not the property of said donors, the donations can be worth nothing, because he who has not, cannot transfer to any other what he does not have himself (Codex *De donacionibus*: *Si filius*: I question VII Daibertum).

And if it be objected: That a prince can take a thing from one person and bestow it upon another, as some learned men claim publicly and in writing, the response to this would be that he may only do so when public utility is in question, and the recompense given for the appropriation does not outrage justice; otherwise no. And so is this generally understood by the doctors of both laws, especially Bartolus in I *Constitucione* of the Digest and expressly in the law *Ne lacius* and the law *Omnes*, Codex: *Si contra ius vel utilitatem publicam*. The same is upheld by the glosses and the doctors in the law *Rescripta* and in the law *Quociens*: Codex *De precious Imperatori offerendis*, and the Archdeacon (IX question III: *Per perincipalem*), etc.

I omit the other allegations for brevity's sake, concerning which see the text itself. There are multiple other particulars of the falsity of the cause of the aforesaid letters, which are obvious to the careful observer, and which I have touched upon in my discussion of the text.[27]

Version I

Rubric. Here it is shown that the aforesaid letters are not only deficient in just cause, but that they also contain a manifestly false cause. And because they tend to the usurpation of the rights of others, etc., they are iniquitous, scandalous, and cruel.

Furthermore, not only on account of a defective cause, but also because the aforesaid letters, especially those that pretend to papal authority, contain a manifestly false cause, *viz.,* in so far as they state in respect to their cause: As the evidence of the work evidently declares that said Brethren fervently insist that they spread the cult of the Faith in both the Orient as well as Prussia and Livonia, etc., this certainly cannot be true, on the evidence of their works, to the Pope himself sitting in Anagni or Perugia (as the dates of their letters shows). The idea is repugnant on account of the distance between the two places, as there is a distance of at least fifty days between Anagni and Prussia. The evidence of the work cannot declare itself otherwise than in a manner open to his exterior senses, as the meaning of the words themselves indicates. According to which, it is to be known that by 'evidence' we mean a thing perceived without any sort of hesitation on the part of the perceiver (and this is proven by the text of the chapter *Cum contingat*: *De rescriptis* and the chapter *Auditis*: *De integrum restitucione*). For certitude is of two sorts: one as presented to the exterior sense by a corporal object, the other, certitude of reason, which infers one thing from another. And for this reason, evidence is also of two types, *scilicet,* evidence of a fact or a work, and evidence of proof by legal argument, as learned men are wont to note (in the chapter *Vestra*: *De cohabitacione clericorum et mulierum*).

Nor does he say whose work or what sort of work; if it is war being spoken of, as we may determine from the evident sequence in these letters, this is not of itself the amplification of the Faith, as appears above, for sometimes what succeeds determines what precedes it, and sometimes it's the other way round (as proven by the laws XXVII question II: *Egressus*, and XXXIII question VII: *Apostolus*, where the gloss concurs). For one does not presume a war to be just unless it is evidently so; indeed, war is always presumed to be unjust unless the justice thereof is obvious (*De resitutcione spoliatorum*: *Olim*; *De pugnacione canonica*, c. I and II, with others similar thereto). Because he who fights with the sword, *viz.*, on his own authority, will perish by the sword (Mt XXVI[28] and in canon XXIII question IV: *Tres personas*, near the end). Nor was religion so instituted for the waging of war, that consecrated persons should be permitted to wage war on their own authority, as St Thomas says (in *Secunda Secunde* question CLXXXVIII, article III) and as is noted by learned men (in the chapter *Sane*: *De regularibus*).

Nor can any other work, which claims to be of itself for the spreading of the Faith, be understood here, for example: the preaching of the word of God, etc., because, as is clear from the above, this does not pertain to the office of said Brethren, and thus *de iure* may not be presumed. Now, therefore, as falsity of cause vitiates all dispositions (*De consaguinitate et affinitate*: *Quid circa*, in the final gloss): for such a sentence handed down on the basis of false evidence does not hold, so is the same true of concessions arising from a false cause (Codex: *Si ex false instrumento,* I and II): thus, it evidently follows from what has been said that all of the aforesaid letters are entirely false and iniquitous, and consequently contrary to written law, fabrications concocted without the knowledge of Pope or prince, which can be assumed from the chapter *Licet* and the chapter *Quamquam*: *De crimine falsi*, for under such species of piety, *scil.* the cause of spreading the Faith, what they really are after is the absorbing of the rights of others without just cause, and contrary to all natural, divine, and human law. And for this reason they are iniquitous and unjust, and because they are intent upon waging war upon others who are guiltless, they boldly provide a path towards rapine, and the introduction of violence — and by consequence, to homicide and other crimes arising therefrom, and thus are injurious, seditious, and cruel.

Rubric. Here we deal with the errors which are virtually included in these letters and tacitly approved, because it is impossible to justify these letters unless such things are taken for granted. From which it necessarily follows: first, that the letters are erroneous; second, that this militia or order of theirs is heretical; third, that they are entirely incapable of any dominion.

It is true that in the aforementioned letters some things are at times supposed as if foundational, and at other times things are inferred from them and continued onward. For example, it is supposed that the Catholic Faith may be spread by arms and wars even in the absence of any nearer and more specific *casus belli*. And that even peaceful and gentle infidels, who impede the Faith in no way, etc., can be warred against licitly with the spread of the Faith given as a chief cause therefor. And that in this way it is lawful to occupy the lands and possessions of infidels even though they previously never belonged to Christians, maugre the fact that said infidels possess the same justly and in accord with natural law. And that such infidels may be licitly subjugated in war by Christians, or reduced to slavery, despite the fact that they are of free condition and are naturally free men. And further, that all these aforesaid things may be licitly accomplished even in the absence of any guilt of these infidels, or any other cause or even despite the fact that the order of the law is not served in any way thereby. And that such things may not only be done licitly, but that they are even acts of piety meriting eternal life, and that such a religious order or monastic rule may be instituted upon such premises, or that such activities might be engaged in by religious.

Such are the principles to which said letters resolve. And such are the foundations of the order of the Knights of the Cross of Prussia if it is true, as they themselves assert on their part, what these letters declare concerning their institution, as above in the Topic.

Now, that such foundations contrary to the Christian Faith and unsustainable in any way without damage to Catholic truth and divine law are reproved indeed by learned theologians and jurists, this can be clearly seen from a mere consideration of the response given to the triplex question elicited above from the Topic. It therefore follows, first: that all such letters as these are erroneous. Second: it follows that the aforesaid order is heretical. Third: it follows that said Brethren are incapable of acquiring anything in such a manner, and that if they ever had any such, these necessarily fall away from them by the very rule of law (see the chapter *Cum secundum leges*: *De hereticis* book VI).

Version II

Now, because in the matter of the aforesaid letters, by virtue of which this order is said to have been instituted, it is taken for granted, as a foundation of sorts, that it is permissible for Christians, especially those who are endowed with the authority of the Emperor or Roman

Pontiff to this end, to wage war against infidel pagans so that the Faith might be spread, without any respect being given to any other cause for a just war, and that in such a war it is permissible for infidels to be subjugated to Christians, and that in this way their lands and possessions may even be occupied from the same cause: because indeed such a supposition or foundation is not only false, but does not appear sustainable without damage being done to Catholic truth, divine law, and the Christian faith, as will be made clear below — it is sufficient to consider our response to the triplex question in the Topic for this to be manifestly evident. It therefore follows, first: that all such letters as these are erroneous. Second: that the aforementioned Order is heretical. Third: that they are incapable of having acquired any sort of dominion. And if they had any rights in any lands or dominions, these must fall away from them by the nature of the law itself, the crimes they committed there rendering their claims null and void from the very moment said crimes were committed (see the chapter *Cum secundum leges*: *De hereticis* book VI).

But they base all of these letters upon this, and it is clear that these same are finally reduced to the idea that the cause for all their claims and activities is principally, and indeed solely, the spread of the Faith. Hence, such warring and rapine, and even the concession of the Pope, and other things of which mention is made in these letters refer to this: to this end being finally reduced, and consequently, according to this, it is understood that they are to be accomplished. For this reason no other cause may even be tacitly understood for the possible justification of these donations, wars, and rapine, which cause might be a sufficient means thereto, or necessary to arrive at said end (which is proven *a contrario* by the law in the chapter *Preterea*: *De officio delegati*). For the understanding of what is said is to be accepted on the base of the cause for why the thing is uttered (as in the chapter *Intelligencia*: *De verborum significacione*).

Rubric. Here it is shown that by virtue of said letters it is not proper for these Brethren to possess any right whatsoever to wage war against the infidels, and, consequently, no right to subjugate or despoil them either, nor can these letters be said or adjudged to be of any Roman Pontiff or Emperor, as they are repugnant to divine law, to which no right of opposition exists.

Since therefore the aforesaid letters contain no just causes for the things moved in them, *viz.,* the aforesaid donations, as is clear from the above, or for the war, as they do battle not for the recuperation of things unjustly taken from them nor to resist invading enemies, as is likewise clear from the above:

And because they also contain a judgment according to which it is tacitly accepted that it is licit to deprive infidels of their possessions, which should not occur unless the cause thereof has been at least summarily looked into, *viz.,* on account of the Faith being impeded by said infidels and thus, for this or other reasons, because of which they might be licitly punished, as mentioned above:

These aforesaid letters are seen to exceed the due order of justice, and even divine law, which demands said order and includes it.

Hence it follows that they are in no way reducible to the rule of justice, and consequently are erroneous, as are all that follows upon them, *viz.,* wars, the occupation of dominions and possessions, etc. It is also evident here that the infidels are being deprived of their goods without any fault of their commission, and without legitimate cause, which these very letters prove in that they are so repugnant to natural law, divine law, and human law as well, for *de iure,* guilt or reason are not presumed unless proven, as is clear from the above. Nor is cognisance understood as having taken place unless it is evidently explained (as proven by the laws in the gloss *Sed numquid* adduced before, in the chapter *Quoniam contra*, *De probacionibus*; *De renunciacione*: *In presencia*, in the gloss *Hic est*; *De apellacionibus*: *Cum speciali*, in the third from the final gloss, along with others similar thereto).

Therefore, since none of the things they claim are apparent or proven on the basis of these letters, nor is the cause of the spread of the Faith in and of itself a sufficient reason to wage war against the infidels, and deprive them of their possessions, especially in reference to this sole cause being given as rationale, it is given us to understand *de iure* that there is no other particular reason for the execution of such deeds, in so far as truly and chiefly it is given us here to understand as the only, the prime and principal cause of the wars, the lootings, and all other things which are here mentioned, and as this one cause is included in the writings, or is so expressed, by this all other causes are excluded, which is proven by law, for when one thing is conceded, it is clearly understood that others are negated (XXV distinction: *Qualis*, with others similar).

From this it necessarily follows that the pretended provision of said letters, as it is contrary to law natural, divine, and human, is not only unjust but even dishonest, and incapable of achieving the end to which it is directed, *viz.*, the spreading of the Faith. By consequence, said letters are false, and what is false proves no truth, but rather the privation of truth. Thus, by these letters it is neither proven nor confirmed that said Brethren have any right to wage war, subjugate infidels, deprive them of their goods, etc. Nor, furthermore, *de iure*, may it be presumed to the discredit of Pope or prince that they conceded such letters; indeed, *de iure*, it is the contrary that is presumed and proven, *scilicet*, that these writings emanated rather against the will or without their knowledge (see the chapter *Licet* and the chapter *Quamquam*: *De crimine falsi*). Therefore, it cannot be said now *de iure* that they proceed from any Pope or Emperor, but rather are to be deemed fabrications.[29]

Rubric. Here by way of conclusion some deductions are drawn from these letters. And first it is said that as these letters presented said Brethren with a cause to wage war against the infidels, they have never waged a just war.

From what has been stated above, therefore, the conclusions below evidently follow.

Rubric. Certain conclusions are arrived at from deductions made from these letters.

The first conclusion: That by virtue of these donations or letters the Brethren have never waged a just war against the infidels.

Firstly: fighting against the infidels on the authority of such pretended donations, said Knights of the Cross have never been engaged in a just war. For even granting, despite the falsity of the aforesaid letters, that it might be stated that a concession had been given them to engage such infidels in battle, even if the error of the authorising authority arose from a probability, this is no excuse for not making reparations and satisfaction once the error was discovered. This according to Ostiensis (in his *Summa*: *De treuga et pace* § 1, the verse *Item error*). Now this error, being not of fact, but of law, and that not solely human law but also natural and divine law, cannot in any way be seen as probable. For neither the Pope nor the Emperor may provide a licence for the looting of alien goods and offering violence unto men, as has been said. Therefore, etc.

Rubric. The second conclusion, in which it is stated that said Brethren have no right or title to the lands in Prussia, Courland, and all other places that they obtained in this way, *viz.,* by wars cruel and unjust.

It also follows in consequence that these Brethren have never been licensed, nor may they be licensed, on the basis of the aforesaid donations and letters to invade, detain, or also to occupy the land and dominions of Prussia, Courland, Lettonia, Żmudź, or to despoil these of anything, as *de facto* they do detain and occupy. These invasions, detentions and occupations having been, and being, illicit, and unjust, said Brethren of the Knights of the Cross may pretend to no rights in regard thereto, and in consequence it is evidently manifest that these Brethren have never had any title to the lands of Prussia, Courland, Lettonia, or any other which they occupy in this fashion, as on the authority of those letters and donations aforesaid they wrested the same from the hands of the pagans, and with the maximum effusion of Christian blood, by force and potency of arms and wars of this sort — just as they expressly admit in the aforesaid articles of theirs, and as in fact is notoriously known throughout practically the whole world. Therefore, etc.

Rubric. The third conclusion, in which it is stated that they are obliged, as a condition of their salvation, as far as this is possible, to restore all of these lands, etc., or really and truly to abandon the same.

It also follows that, as a necessary condition of their salvation, these Brethren must abandon and restore said lands of Prussia, Livonia, and all others that they have acquired by rapine; that is, that part of the Samogitians' lands, with the fortress named Memel which these Knights of the Cross confess to having acquired by such means. The truth of this conclusion is clear to see as said donations and letters are incapable of providing them with any just title to these lands; therefore, said lands cannot belong to the occupiers, and in consequence the sin of these Brethren cannot be absolved unless they first restore what they have taken.

Rubric. The fourth conclusion. That the Church is obliged to compel the Brethren to abandon these lands, even if the secular arm must be invoked for this purpose.

It also follows that, should they not wish to abandon these lands as they are obliged to do, and immediately, then, the Church is obliged to compel them to the same, even if the aid of the secular arm must be invoked to effect this. Now, by law, there is no doubt that they are obliged to abandon these lands without delay, because a thief is always in arrears (*ff De condiccione furtiva*, see *Si pro fure*). Hence Saint Thomas (*Secunda secunde*, question LXII, article VIII) says that he who is obliged to restore something must restore it at once. For as to receive goods belonging to someone else is a sin against justice, the same is true of their retention. And for this reason the text states that there is no great difference between unjustly retaining something and invading that which does not belong to one, as far as danger to the soul is concerned (see the chapter *Sepe*: *De restitucione spoliatorum*). For all men are obliged to desist from sinning immediately, according to this (Ecclesiasticus XXI):[30] 'Flee from sin as from the face of a serpent.' Now, as for the Church being obliged to compel them, the Archdeacon maintains the following (II question I: *In primis*, near the beginning), that a person who has gravely and publicly sinned is to be compelled to penitence, but no penitence can take place without the restitution of the thing. Therefore, etc.

Rubric. The fifth conclusion. Wherein the manifest iniquity of these Brethren is set forth, as to their aspirations to fight to obtain the land of the Samogitians.

From these is patently manifest — to speak without prejudice to the peace — the deceit and iniquity of the aforesaid Brethren in regards to His Majesty the Most Serene King of Poland, as mentioned above in the Topic, concerning their contentions with him over said dominions, *viz.*, Żmudź or the portion thereof. Their iniquity is made manifest by the rule of law, according to which 'his petition is deceitful, who demands the restoration of that, which he himself is obliged to restore' (*De regulis iuris* book VI). For anything stolen or occupied by force is considered faulty possession, as there may be no uscupation or prescription of the same from thief or seizer by anyone else, even if it were to be purchased by him or otherwise received in good faith (*Insitutcionibus*: *De usucapionibus* § *Furtive* and § *Quod autem,* and by Ostiensis in his *Summa*: *De penitencijs et remissionibus* § *Quibus et qualiter*, the verse 'Quid de rapina'). For this reason, such notorious looters are denied absolution *de iure,* and ecclesiastical burial as well, because they cannot be saved unless they first restore what they had stolen. And those clerics who grant them ecclesiastical burial, or who even absolve them of sin or participate in their rapine, are deprived of their office and benefices (which is proven in the chapter *Super eo*: *De raptoribus*, where this case is covered).

Rubric. The sixth conclusion, wherein is established the temerity with which they defied the King of Poland in the matter of the land of the Samogitians using these letters as their basis; entering upon a war with him, during the course of which they led many of their armed men to destruction.

From the aforesaid, clearly evident, in fact, is the temerity of these Brethren who, on account of the possessions and above all the dominions of the aforesaid Samogitians, which they attempted to usurp, waging fierce war against the aforementioned King of Poland after first defying him with their letters patent, led many thousands of their armed men to their death, and that not without great slaughter of the common people. They have ever been guilty of all of the homicides, sacrilegious acts, and other crimes, however many and of whatever kind have occurred during these wars, of which they themselves supplied the cause — i.e. their desire to obtain said lands. Because they are to be held accountable not only for their own rapine, and the murders, and the other crimes they committed, but also, even for those others not committed by their own men, but against them, too (as we see in *Quoniam*: *Ad legem Iuliam de vi publica*, and Ostiensis in his *Summa*: *De penitencijs et remissionibus* § *Quibus et qualiter*, the verse 'Quid de rapina').

Rubric. The seventh conclusion. Because of their use of said erroneous letters, especially in a legal process, as noted above in the Topic, they are considered excommunicate, gravely so, by virtue of the law itself, until proper satisfaction be made.

It also follows from the foregoing that in making use of these letters, especially in the course of a legal process, they not only offend God, deceive the judge and do harm to their fellow men, but are also guilty of committing in damnable fashion the crime of falsity. Obviously, thus they incur, as the law itself dictates, the sentence of major excommunication. And I say that they are excommunicated until the proper satisfaction is rendered, *scilicet*, through restitution (see the chapter *Ad falsariorum*: *De crimine falsi* § *Qui vero*). Now this is the difference between one who falsifies papal letters, or procures their falsification, and one who makes use of such falsifications: He who merely uses them is accorded twenty days to provide for himself and evade punishment by making use of the days given him to examine said letters and prove if they be false or no. Once these twenty days are passed, it is too late for penitence; laypersons are excommunicated, and clerics, besides this, are despoiled of their benefices and offices. But falsifiers and procurers of falsifications, along with their supporters and defenders, are excommunicated and deprived of their benefices by the same law (said chapter *Ad falsariorum*).

Rubric. The eighth conclusion. That those producing these letters in court of law are *de iure* just as deserving of being punished as the falsifiers thereof, even in the absence of accuser or any other proof.

From these things it follows that in producing these letters in the aforesaid court case, as mentioned above in the Topic, in order to obtain the dominions of others, or so as to retain those they already occupy, these men are *de iure* just as deserving of punishment as the falsifiers thereof. And I say more: they are deserving of being punished even in the absence of accuser or other proofs, according to Ostiensis (in his *Summa*: *De falsarijs* § *Qualis probacio*), near the beginning, where it is stated that there are certain special aspects to questions of falsification: for even though from the very beginning proof shall be required such as is clearer even than light itself, still, because there exists a certain suspicion of falsehood concerning the document produced, it shall be deemed a falsification unless he who produces it can prove its authenticity definitively lacking which one moves on to the penalty (as in the Codex: *De probacionibus*; see *Iubemus*), which does not occur in other cases. Second, a falsification may be condemned even without an accuser, which generally does not occur in other cases (II question I: *Nichil*; *ff De muneribus et honoribus*, see *Munorum* § *Defensores*). Ostiensis.

Rubric. The ninth conclusion. That those who defend said letters are seen as subject to the same excommunication, as participants in falsehood.

Finally, it is inferred from what has been said that those who defend said false and manifestly erroneous letters are not free of suspicion of being in secret collusion, and therefore, *de iure*, are understood as participants in the crime of falsity, no less than the foregoing, and are thus subject to the same sentence of excommunication (see the chapter *Nuper* and the chapter *Si concubine*: *De sentencia excommunicacionis*).

So much for the first principal proposition.

Now follows the second principal proposition.

Rubric. Here commences the second part of the tractate, or the second principal proposition, where first it is shown that said Brethren are in unjust occupation of all that they possess, nor can they possess anything justly, for a triplex reason.

As far as the second principal proposition is concerned, the general conclusion is as follows: In all that these Brethren possess, or detain rather, they have never had any right to the same, nor have they at present, rather, all that they obtain they unjustly detain, remaining unjust occupiers thereof.

And this is manifest by a triplex reason:

Rubric. The first reason.

The first reason for this is the illicit end of their actions, which is understood *de iure* to prohibit any and all means thereto (see the rule *Cum quid prohibetur*, *De regulis iuris* book VI). Now, there appears to be no doubt of the fact that the spreading of the faith by force and the use of arms and rapine is not only prohibited by the General Council of Toledo,[31] but is also contrary to natural law and divine law, as is said above. Therefore, their dominions also, understood as their aim, are prohibited by said Council, and, according to all the aforesaid laws, are illicit and unjust. Hence Ostiensis (in his *Summa*: *De hereticis*, in § *Qualiter devitetur*, the versicle 'Et licet'), where he says that all goods of heretics are to be taken from them by military force, the rationale given for this is that, according to Isidore and Augustine and other saints, said heretics have no right whatsoever to possess these things. Neither have they by natural law, as according to it all things are held in common (I distinction: *Ius naturale*), nor have they according to divine law, as the Son of God demonstrates when He says 'the kingdom of God shall be taken from you, and shall be given to a nation yielding the fruits thereof.'[32] Thus, the just are to consume the fruits of the labor of the impious (VIII distinction: *Quo iure*). Thus, neither by civil nor by canon law have the latter any such right.

Rubric. The second reason.

Secondly, by reason of their heresies, special positive law provides, not only tacitly but also expressly, that such men are declared unjust possessors from the time their heresies were committed, depriving them of their goods, even those justly possessed heretofore, and making them from that time incapable of the possession thereof.

For from that time forward the law itself considers their goods to be confiscated (see the chapter *Cum secundum*: *De hereticis* book VI), as is stated above. And even Ostiensis is in accord with this (in his *Summa*, the title just alluded to, § *Quia pena*), where he says that the places held by heretics are to fall to the Church (see the Codex of the same title, *Cuncti*), which notwithstanding it is said that they should be confiscated (as we find in the same title, see *Si qui orthodoxe*), still, according to him, today the Church is to be preferred (as in *Autentica*: *De ecclesiasticis titulis* § *Si autem ortodoxus*). Ostiensis. For a more full treatment of this matter, refer to Henricus Bock in his chapter *Vergentes*: *De hereticis.*[33]

Rubric. The third reason.

Thirdly, by reason of their vows as regular religious, they are incapable of any dominion, in that by their profession they have abdicated their rights to private possessions and all dominion (which is proven by the chapter *Cum ad monasterium*, towards the end: *De statu monachorum*, and XII question I: *Non dicatis*).

And concerning this it is to be noted that there are two manners of understanding their order: an absolute one, in which they are considered in and of themselves, and in their relations one to another in the order itself, according to which their possession of things as individuals and even in common is a thing repugnant to their profession, both as individuals and in common, as is stated in the laws adduced, whereby not even the *peculium castrense* earned by military service falls to them, either individually or all together, as the same law must apply to the whole as it does to the part (*De eleccione*: *Clementis Ne Romani I Rubrica*; XII distinction canon I and *De prebendis*, the chapter *Maioribus,* where gloss I is in concord with this).

They may also be considered in respect to the end at which they aim, which to encompass they need to possess what is necessary for life. And in this case it is not repugnant that they possess property in common (as Johannes Andreae[34] notes in the chapter *Cum Iohannes*: *De regularibus*, following the gloss in question II). Now, I speak here of property administered, not property owned. Because although said Brethren hold, by some reason of subjection, such means ordered to the end at which they immediately aim, still these means cannot be a final foundation, but only an extreme of the same genus or order. By the same token, these means cannot root and found in them any sort of dominion, but in their proper place are things to be employed for the common good and deputized according to what they are, what their use is (as to this see *Civitatibus*: *De legatis* I). For this very reason, such regular religious are spoken of as 'denuded' ministers, and in law are compared to slaves (LIV distinction: *Multos*, and the aforementioned canon *Non dicatis*). And just as the slave acquires nothing for himself, but rather for his master (*ff De acquirenda possessione* law I), thus whatever is acquired by such regulars is acquired by the hospital or monastery in which their profession was made (which is proven in *De officio ordinarij*: chapter *Quanto*, and *De regularibus*, the final chapter). For *conversi*, i.e. those who inhabit a religious institution, serving it without taking vows, like the monks themselves, belong to the Church (*ff De acquirenda possessione*: see *Cum heredes*, in the gloss 'de iure'). Hence, such as renounce their own possessions are to live on the fruits or gifts of their hospital or monastery (as is noted in the chapter *Iohannes*: *De regularibus*, by Iohannes Andreae and others) and for this reason neither hospital nor monastery ought to be founded without sufficient donation (I question II: *Placuit*; *De institucionibus* chapter I; in *Autentica*: *Ut determinatus sit numerus clericorum*, at the beginning). As for mendicant orders, alms take the place of donations. Iohannes Andreae.

Now, said Brethren, although they have the outward appearance of a religious order that pretends to serve the common good, still are not such in respect to others, but only in respect to themselves, acting in their own private interest and not in that of the common good at all — *viz.*, in order to obtain the possessions of the infidels for themselves, converting the same to their own use, as is clearly apparent from their own letters and the above-mentioned articles. And so it cannot be said that they are acquiring these things for their convents, fortresses or other places they inhabit. There are multiple reasons for this. First, because these things necessarily serve their own private comfort, and thus are seen to serve them, for what serves my cause is mine (note *De arbitris*: *Dilecti*) and what serves me is mine (*ff Si servus vendicetur, Si cito* § I), and thus it is repugnant for them to possess dominion. And what occurs or comes about on behalf of someone is his. For he that is possessed by another possesses nothing of his own (*ff De adulterijs*: *Sic eveniet*, as noted in XII question I: *Non dicatis*, in the major gloss);

Also — the aforesaid and pretended donations, by virtue of which the acquisition of such dominions ought to occur, are null and void, the letters being erroneous, as is shown clearly above.

Also, third, even if they were in some way legal, because it is seen that they presuppose the real existence of a hospital as an end, the grants by no means extend to convents later acquired, which have nothing to do with either the actual being, or even the name, of any hospital. For nothing can be given to anything which does not exist — such a donation would be invalid (as is proven by the chapter *Abbate Sane*: *De re iudicata,* the verse *Allegabatur,* book VI), to which the concordances adduced above. Thus, accordingly, there could not have been, nor can there be now, anything acquired by them (which is also fully covered by *Clementina Litteras*: *De rescriptis*).

Likewise, fourth, we have the reason of the Brethren themselves, to whom acquisition or possession of anything is repugnant, no matter what donation even, contract or cause. Now, because an action ought to be attributed to a principal agent, not an instrument, and as it seems they wish to be seen as a principal agent in respect to such convents and, consequently, all other things that follow upon these as possessions, these Brethren are said to acquire or even to possess the same (XXIII question V § *Hinc notandum*). And yet if said Brethren were to possess these things in the name of their convent, on the contrary, they would not be the principal agents thereof, but instrumental agents. Because he is said to possess something in whose name the thing is possessed (as per the chapter *Cum venisset*: *De restitucione spoliatorum* with others similar). And thus the same would be seen to be effect and cause in itself, principal and secondary, agent and instrument, possessor and possessed in respect to the same, and by consequence active and passive in the same cause, which is repugnant to the natural order of things in the world.

Nor are said Brethren capable of acquiring anything for their order, or possessing anything in its name, as their order has no absolute rationale, seeing as no dominion falls to it according to the first consideration. Therefore, such possessions must be reduced to something else as to their end, to which also said order must have a relationship subjective and respective, *viz.*, a hospital, not imaginary, but real, and of Jerusalem, truly, or interpretatively, to which said Brethren assert their adherence. For the law is not made in regard to mere words, but facts. And so, they would needs have a hospital in which to labor, or on behalf of which they could administer such things, according to the second consideration. Because as a slave is to the benefit of his master, and not vice versa, so these brothers regular ought to be to the benefit of their hospital, and not vice versa. For a hospital ought not to exist primarily on their behalf, but rather on behalf of the poor and infirm (XXIII question VIII *Sanccimus*) as whatever is given or deeded to a hospital is understood as being given to the poor (which Johannes Andreae notes in the chapter *Dudum*: *De conversione coniugatorum*, on the word 'Pauperum'). Hence it also is that whatever is given to these Brethren is understood as being done on behalf of the hospital *De testamentis*: *Cum in officijs*, and the chapter *Requisisti*).

Now, because there exists no such Hospital of Jerusalem as is spoken of here, therefore, no dominion thereof exists either. Nor is there any other such hospital, which they inhabit and live their rule, or in the name of which they administer its goods. It therefore necessarily follows that there can be no possessions or dominions at all belonging to them.

Rubric. Certain things are deduced from the aforesaid by way of conclusion. First, that no dominion may be transferred to the aforesaid Brethren by virtue of any contract or any definitive sentence.

It may be definitively stated from the foregoing that all transactions, donations, and in general all contracts by which any dominion is transferred to these Brethren is invalid. It also follows, similarly, that any sentence of definitive adjudication in their favor concerning any possession or dominion is null and void. The rationale for this: Because they are neither capable of suing nor of contracting anything unless in the name of a religious hospital of the sort upon which a dominion is founded, of which they ought to be the procurators and not the owners. For under the name of procurator all administrators are understood (I question III: *Salvator*). For the first, see Johannes Andreae (in the chapter *Quanto*: *De officio ordinarij*, on the gloss 'hic patet'), where he says that where a suit is moved concerning money or any other civil complaint is lodged against a regular religious, there can be no question of a trial, as said monk possesses nothing of his own (XII question I: *Nolo*, and the canon *Non dicatis*). Concerning the second, see Johannes Andreae (in the chapter *Cum olim* II: *De privilegijs*, on the word 'Promotus'), where he says that whether a regular religious stipulates for himself or for his monastery, whether contracting personally or in any other way, it is the monastery that acquires what is stipulated. It is a different matter if he stipulates for another, for this he cannot do at all (on this see *De procuratoribus*: *Constitutis*, in gloss I with its reference), nor even can his master, or monastery, acquire it, as such was not the intention (*ff De stipulacionibus servorum*, *Servus*). Johannes Andreae.

Rubric. Here is deduced the error of suing or contracting in the name of the order and not in the name of the hospital.

From these things becomes apparent the manifest error of these Brethren who, having neither hospital nor religious house in which they live, sue, contract, and effect all other things in the name of their order. For although secular colleges or congregations, to the membership of which possession and dominion is not repugnant, may sue and contract in the name of their college or congregation, this has no place among religious orders. Hence it is that although sometimes an abbot might sue on his own behalf and that of his convent, he does so improperly, as Johannes Andreae states (in the chapter *Abbatem*: *De re iudicata*, book VI, on gloss II at the end), following Johannes Monachus[35] and the Archdeacon.

Rubric. Wherein it is clearly shown that those who hold possessions and dominate others, even in the name of their order, are acting contrarily to the substance of the monastic profession.

From these things it is deduced by consequence that these Brethren, holding possessions and dominion over great swathes of land in the name of their order, and not in the name of any hospital, etc., are damnably in prejudice to their own monastic vows, as has been shown, and as proprietors they are liable to punishment under the law (as per the chapter *Cum ad monasterium*: *De statu monachorum*). The rationale: Because the Hospital of Jerusalem, to which these Brethren assert that they belong, does not exist in the real world, so they are incapable of possessing anything in its name, because something is said to be possessed in the name of the possessor (*De restitucione spoliatorum*: *Cum venisset*) and in consequence of their holding something in the name of their order they thus hold it in their own name, as the whole includes its parts (according to the rule *In toto*: *De regulis iuris* book VI), and the same rule applies to the whole as to its parts (XIV question, V *Penale*). Thus, what follows is the usurpation of property. For mine is what I hold in common with others, and, vice versa, he who swears that something does not belong to him, swears too that it is not his in common with others (*ff De verborum significacione, Si pupillus*, the final §, with which the chapter *Cum in illis*: *De prebendis* book VI concurs, as does what is noted there in the final gloss). Whereas, therefore, these three things are said to be of the essence of any monastic profession, *scilicet* poverty, obedience, and chastity (as in the chapter *Cum ad monasterium* adduced above): property and the possession of dominion is repugnant to the vow of poverty; the wish to rule over or dominate others is repugnant to the vow of obedience, vowed solemnly to God, by which one places oneself in the hands of others; and by virtue of these things, without infringing on the peace, I state that said Order is seen to be clearly degenerate, acting contrarily to the faithfulness owed to God by man, both on account of dominion and on account of the advantages usurped: *viz.*, holding dominion over large swathes of lands and dominating other men, as well as minting their own coinage, governing thus a community, which is contrary to the rationale of the monastic profession and, by consequence, contrary to their own vows, by which they effectively become infidels themselves in the eyes of God, according to this (Ecclesiastes V):[36] 'If thou hast vowed any thing to God, defer not to pay it: for an unfaithful and foolish promise displeaseth Him.'

Version II

Cancelled[37]

Now, as far as the second principal question is concerned: The general conclusion is that in all things that these Brethren possess, or rather retain (which seems the more proper term), they have never, ever, had any right or dominion thereto, nor had they, nor have they at present. Rather, everything whatsoever that they obtain, they detain unjustly, and of all things of theirs they are seen to remain the unjust occupiers. The rationale: Because said Brethren are seen to be regular religious, with professed vows, and thus are incapable of any sort of dominion, for in consequence of their monastic vows they have abdicated all right to property, and all dominion (as per the chapter *Cum ad monasterium*: *De statu monachorum*, near the end). For such men are 'denuded ministers,' comparable to slaves (LIV distinction: *Multos*), and just as a slave acquires nothing for himself, but rather for his master (*ff De acquirenda possessione*, I), in the same way anything at all acquired by them is acquired on behalf of the hospital in which they professed their vows (*De officio ordinarij*, chapter IV; *De regularibus*, the final chapter). For both *converses* and monk belong *de iure* to the Church (*ff De acquirenda possessione*, *Cum heredes* in the gloss), hence such as renounce their right to property ought to live off the fruits or gifts of their hospital or monastery (as is noted in the chapter *Iohannes*: *De regularibus*, by Johannes Andreae and others), and for this reason no hospital or monastery ought to be founded without sufficient funds donated (I question II: *Placuit*; *De Institucionibus* chapter I; in *Autentica*: *Ut determinatus sit numerus clericorum*, at the beginning). Now, as for the mendicant orders, alms take the place of donations.[38] Johannes Andreae.

From which it follows that dominion and the possession of goods principally and regularly belongs to hospital or monastery, or any other place deputized to a religious order, not to the Brethren themselves. The rationale: Just as we find in the relation between master and slave that the slave is for the benefit of the master and not the other way round, so these regular Brethren ought to be for the benefit of the hospital to which they are supposed to belong, and not the contrary. For the hospital should not be chiefly for them, but for the poor and infirm (XXIII question VIII: *Sanccimus*). As Johannes Andreae notes, whatever is deeded or donated to a hospital is understood as a donation made to the poor (in the chapter *Dudum*: *De conversione coniugatorum*, following the word 'Pauperum'). Hence also it is that whatever is given to these Brethren is understood as being given on behalf of their hospital (*De testamentis*: *Cum in officijs*, and the chapter *Requisisti*). And because the hospital to which these Brethren insist that they belong does not in fact exist, therefore, there can be no dominion belonging to them either, because it is repugnant to the profession of regular religious to possess dominion either individually or in common. However, administration, that is, the administration of property, is not repugnant thereto. Hence it is that whoever acts as the administrator of a hospital acts in his own name and in the name of the community as a whole, according to which all power or administration of a monastery is said to pertain to the abbot (as is noted in XVIII question II: *Nulla*). On the other hand, there can be no property of dominion amongst individuals as the individual's professed vows are opposed to this, nor may it be held in common amongst all, because the same law pertains to the whole as to its parts

(XII distinction, canon I, which is also proven by the gloss in the chapter *Maioribus*: *De prebendis*, with others similar).

Rubric. Here it is shown that all goods, however obtained by said Brethren, are understood *de iure* as being vacant, without owner, in so far as they are concerned.

The conclusions below are deduced from what is said above.

First, that all goods acquired by these Brethren in general, or obtained by them, are *de iure* vacant and ownerless, as far as said Brethren are concerned; in each case, they are illicitly occupied by them. It is noted, I say, as far as they are concerned, because as far as others are concerned, to whom *de iure* belongs the right of demanding the recuperation and restoration of that of which they had been violently despoiled, etc., this vacancy does not apply, as right and dominion belong to them.

Rubric. Wherein it is shown that those subject to these Brethren are under no obligation to obey them as their superiors. Even if they swore fealty unto them, their oaths would be invalid, and even if they were valid, they would be *de iure* released from them.

Moreover, it follows that both the homage of vassals and the subjugation of cities, lands, and any community whatsoever, including their subjects and individual citizens, are not legally bound in subjection to said order, even if this were confirmed by oaths. Neither such communities, nor the individuals themselves, are obliged *de iure* to obey these Brethren in anything as their superiors. The truth of this is manifest in that it is clear that there can be no dominion belonging to this order or its convents: no jurisdiction is founded in them and thus, conversely, there is no subjection; thus, there is no obligation of vassalage. Ergo, by the law itself, no fidelity to any oath is required of them, as no oath of mine to any master, who is not my master by law, can be anything worth. For there can be no derogation of public law by contracts made between private persons (*De foro competenti*: *Si diligenti*, with its concordances, and the rule *Nemo potest*: *De regulis iuris* book VI is best in accord with this, and what Dinus notes, above). Ostiensis too is in accord with this, in his *Summa*: *De hereticis* § *Qua pena*, although his rationale runs otherwise: 'Let them know, that they are free from fidelity, homage, and all sorts of obsequy whatever to those who are manifestly lapsed, i.e. notoriously heretical, if they bound themselves to them in any sort of pact or assurance' (as we see in the chapter *Absolutos*, of the same title). Thus, they are not bound as vassals by any special stipulation or oath (arg. XV question VI: *Iuratos*, and the chapter *Nos sanctorum*), because a vow is understood as having a tacit condition, *scilicet*: if faith is kept (arg. XXIII question I: *Quid culpatur,* etc.). According to Ostiensis following Raymundus and Goffredus.[39]

Rubric. That the obligation Nova Marchia, etc., made to the benefit of these Brethren is null and void.

Moreover, it follows that the obligation known as Nova Marchia, etc., made in their favor was, and is, by law null and void, and hence said

Dukedom may be demanded from their hands without any payment being given for it in return. This is clear as said Brethren have no right to detain the same nor any right to demand the return of the money lent.[40]

Rubric. That they unjustly occupy lands belonging, in particular, to the Kingdom of Poland.

From the foregoing it clearly follows that these Brethren have never had, nor are they capable of having, any cause to detain dominions belonging *de iure* to the King and Kingdom of Poland, such as they now occupy *de facto*. By consequence, it follows that they have no right to the lands of Pomerania, Chełmno, and Michałów, and the same applies to other lands as well.

Rubric. That the guilt and cause of all evils resulting from wars with them have ever been theirs.

It also follows that these Brethren have always been the guilty party in all wars and slaughter of people consequent to such wars, which have occurred because of the frequent fighting between the kings and Kingdom of Poland on the one hand, and them on the other. Moreover, the same is true of any other conflicts between them and other princes, etc.

Rubric. That they should be compelled to render back to the rightful owners all that they possess.

Since, therefore, it can be clearly stated from the foregoing that said Knights of the Cross have no right whatsoever to any of the aforesaid goods, lands, and dominions occupied by them,

and because they are entirely incapable of any such possession or occupation,

and because they base the rationale of said occupation upon the false and clearly erroneous nature of the abovesaid falsely fabricated letters and donations,

and because the law declares the goods of heretics liable to confiscation from the date of the commission of their crime,

and because what they detain they do so detain in the name of a hospital, the non-existence of which in the real world is a notorious fact,

and because they obtained these things by way of notorious rapine:

Therefore, it is a notorious fact that they have no right at all to these things and, by consequence, they have no right to engage in any action concerning the retention of said dominions, nor is any exception or even defense on their part possible, but, quite simply, they are to be effectively and really compelled to return them to their rightful owners by our most holy lord the Pope, and by this sacred Synod.[41]

And thus it is clear what is to be said concerning the second principal proposition.

Here follows the third principal proposition.

Rubric. Here follows the third principal part, or the third principal proposition, to which there are three considerations.

The first, which follows immediately, is in respect to the essence of the order.

Concerning the third principal proposition, *scilicet*: May this society, or sect, be reputed to be a religious order? a triplex consideration arises, *viz.,* concerning the state of a religious order, that is, its essence, its means, and its end. Now, religion, properly understood, imports an order directed toward God, to Whom we ought to adhere as to a never-deficient principal. According to St Thomas, religion, therefore, is a portion of justice that takes preeminent place amongst the moral virtues in so far as it more closely orders man to God than all other moral virtues, *scilicet* in as much as it directly and immediately orients all things that pertain to it, to the honor and glory of God, and divine worship. And therefore it has a duplex action: some of these are such as it properly and immediately elicits, by which man is immediately oriented towards the one true God, to adore Him, and to offer sacrifice unto Him. It has other acts, which it produces by means of the inferior virtues, by which it commands and ordains said acts toward divine reverence, for the virtue that operates toward an end impels its subject virtues to that same end. Hence (James I):[42] 'Religion clear and undefiled before God and the Father, is this: to visit the fatherless and widows in their tribulation, etc.' According to what has been said, the religious act in the form of a command is to visit the infirm in their tribulation, and this is an act elicited; to keep oneself entirely unspotted from this world is an imperative of religion elicited by temperance, etc. One can also say of the soldier's vocation that it is impelled by piety, in as much as it is for the defense of the honor of God, yet it is elicited by another, inferior virtue.

Rubric. Here some things are deduced by way of a conclusion. The first is that the clerics and laypersons of this society or sect cannot be considered as belonging to the same rule or order.

From this it follows the clerics and priests of this society or sect are not of the same order or rule as their lay soldiers. The rationale: Because warmaking is not compatible with a clerical order, clerics cannot be immediately and finally ordained to the soldier's trade. Now, the distinction between religious orders is not compassed by the proper and immediate acts of the rule, for all rules agree in such, but by acts impelled by the inferior virtues, as according to Johannes Andreae (in the chapter *Sane De regularibus*) where he says that religious rules can distinguished in two ways: one, according to the diversity of their aims, as one order is ordained to the reception of pilgrims in their hospitals, another for the redemption of captives, another for the visitation of the sick, etc. Another way is according to the diversity of spiritual exercises, whereby one order mortifies the flesh by abstaining from food, another does so by manual labor or the asperity of their vestments, etc. But because the end is the most important thing in all matters, the diversity of the ends to which each order is ordained is greater than that which is found among diversity of exercise and means. For comparisons according an end are absolute, as we search out the end for its own sake, but the second matter is something relative, because exercise is not carried out for its own sake, but rather in pursuit of an end.

Rubric. That even though it appears that both clerics and laypersons of this sect make the same profession, still they do not make it in respect to the same thing, and thus cannot be said to be of the same order.

From these things it follows of necessity that even though both clerics and lay soldiers in the convents of said Brethren make a profession to the rule of St Augustine, still these clergy and these soldiers cannot be said to belong to the same order, or even profession. The rationale: Because although both these and those are professed, their vows are still not made to the same end, and quite simply, diversity of means implies diversity of order, and identity of rule does not imply identity of religious order, because multiple orders distinctly profess the same rule, *viz.,* that of St Augustine, etc.

Rubric. That the profession of clerics made into the hands of laypersons in this sect is especially erroneous.

From this it further follows that clerics who in this way make their profession into the hands of the laymen and aforesaid soldiers are making professions erroneous, and inimical to the sacred canons. I say they are erroneous because it is contrary to the prohibition of the general Council (of which see the final chapter: *De religiosis domibus*), which prohibits anyone from making a profession to an order unless such has been approved by the Apostolic See; the same may be found in the same title, book VI, rubric 1. They are likewise erroneous because those whose disciplines are divers cannot adhere to one another and be joined together (XVI question VII: *In nova accione*), and this is also true of those living in cloisters according to Johannes Andreae (which he notes in the chapter *Cum deputati*: *De iudicijs*, concerning the word 'Studijs'). And therefore it is said that men of divers professions or disparate cultus should not be brought together in one office (*De eleccione*: *Cum causam*); this is true, that they ought not to socialize collegially as if they were one body or college, but this does not prohibit them from doing so singly, as, for example, to be arbiters or judges, according to my Lord Francis, Cardinal of Florence (in *Clementina* I *De eleccione*, a little bit on after the beginning).[43] Likewise they are erroneous because it is natural for each that tends toward an aim to direct everything contained under said aim, to that aim. Therefore, no clergyman who is subject by vow of obedience to a lay soldier can be directed at any other aim save that of warmaking, and by consequence, at something that is not agreeable to the clerical state at all (XXIII question VIII: *Clerici*). And the same order, or the same thing, or the same body, cannot be judged by divers laws (*De decimis*: *Cum in tua*); because it is directed at something else, there necessarily follows a diversity of order from diversity of end. And if it is directed at nothing, it will be a mockery, not a profession.

Rubric. That even a vow solemnly made does not oblige these Brethren to the observation of this supposed rule.

From this it even follows that the vow of such clergymen and laymen, however solemnly made, does not oblige them to the observation of this rule, indeed, quite simply, it does not oblige them to any rule, in so far as their intention was to make such a profession, and no other. For the first of these statements there is the rule *Nemo potest* (*De regulis iuris*, book VI), and what Dinus[44] notes there, for if he who was making the profession knew of the impossibility, it does not seem that he would consent (*ff De accionibus et obligacionibus*: *Non solum*): while if he was ignorant of it, the error itself would impede his consent (*ff De iurisdiccione omnibus iudicum*: *Si per errorem*), therefore natural obligation is lacking, and in consequence such a profession is contrary to the reason of the vow. For according to Johannes Andreae (in *Novella*: *De voto*, the sole chapter, book VI), a vow is a promise made to someone's benefit, upon deliberation. Now, according to Raymundus and Goffredus (see *Remissiones*), there is no obligation to a thing that is evil, or to a thing that is good absent deliberation.

As to the second statement of the above conclusion, we have the gloss beginning with the incipit *Quo ad recipiendum* (the sole chapter of the aforesaid), where it is determined that if he making profession intended to profess this rule and no other, he is not obligated, if otherwise, he is, and he is to be believed as it is rather improbable that such a person would act without concern for his own salvation (I question VII: *Sanccimus*, etc.). The reason for this is that in such a case the professing man would be wishing to live according to this way of life and according to this rule, otherwise he would not be making the profession. For where the principal is not, there is no accessory either (*De fide instrumentorum*: *Inter dilectos*). The matter appears to be different in the case of one who wishes an absolute change of life, for in such a case, although he would not be obliged to that rule, he would be obliged to some order in general (as in the chapter *Non solum* and what follows *De regularibus*, book VI).

Rubric. That if said Brethren were to strip themselves of the habit of their order in order to return to the world, there would be no reason thereby to consider them apostates, nor excommunicated by the law.

From this it also follows that if such a professed person were to abandon his religious habit to return to the world, he would not thereby incur the sentence of excommunication, or be deemed guilty by law of having committed the crime of apostasy as is usual in such cases (see chapter II: *Ne clerici vel monachi*, book VI). This rationale is confirmed by gloss II, where it speaks of the case of such who profess to a religious order approved by the Apostolic See.

Rubric. That if such a man, not ordained to Holy Orders, contract a marriage, said marriage is valid *de iure*.

Moreover, it follows that if a layperson who has made profession to this order, or a clerk not ordained to Holy Orders, contracted a marriage following such a profession, his matrimony would be valid no matter the previous vow. This is true even if the professed person believed that his vow had been approved. This is clearly proven by the chapter *Quod votum*: *De voto et voti redempcione*, book VI, in text and gloss.

So much for the first consideration.

The second consideration concerning the religious state.

Rubric. Here now follows the second consideration in respect to the means, or the religious state, where it is first shown that such warring as theirs is not chiefly for purposes of defense but rather to the offending of others. It is to be said that this is not religion, but superstition.

As far as the religious state is concerned, it is to be noted that: According to what St Thomas says (*Secunda secunde* question CLXXXVIII article II): That the religious state is ordained to the perfection of charity, which extends to the love of God and one's fellow man; the contemplative life directly pertains to the love of God, as the contemplative wishes to devote himself to God alone, while the active profession pertains to the love of one's fellow man, as it serves the needs of one's brothers. And just as charity toward one's fellow man arises on account of one's love of God, in the same way the service rendered to one's fellow man redounds to God, according to this (Matthew XXV):[45] 'Whatsoever you did to one of these my least Brethren, you did it to me.' Hence this manner of serving one's fellow man in as much as it is directed to God is said to be a sacrifice, according to this (Hebrews, final chapter):[46] 'And hospitality do not forget: to do good, and to impart: for by such sacrifices God's favor is obtained.' And because it properly pertains to religion to offer sacrifice unto God, in consequence some religious orders have been ordained to active labor, such as hospitality, warfare, etc. Now, as to wage war so as to wrest the goods of the infidels from their hands and convert them to the use of these Brethren is to wage war on their own behalf, and not on behalf of God, not for the utility of one's neighbor and the public good, but to their private advantage and comfort, not in defense of those oppressed, but so as to oppress others, is something entirely contrary to the nature of religion, it is therefore evident that such an organisation cannot be considered a religious order, but is a profane one. As the Doctor says (in the chapter *Sane*: *De regularibus*). And that such is the present case is made plainer than the light of day by their very own letters and the aforesaid articles, which give notorious testimony to the same. There are absolutely no grounds to deny that their status is contrary to all religion. And because an error opposed to religion is superstition, this warmaking of theirs must be called superstition, not religion. Now, according to the gloss of Colossians, chapter three, superstition occurs when the name of religion is applied to human tradition. And whatever does not in and of itself pertain to the glory of God or elevate the mind toward Him, or rein in the inordinate concupiscence of the flesh, or is contrary to God and the constitution of the Church, or opposed to common custom, which, according to Augustine, is to be respected like law, all of this is considered superfluous in respect to the divine cultus, and superstitious (the words are those of St Thomas, *Secunda secunde* question XCIII article 2). St Bernard upbraids such warmaking, writing to the Temple Militia[47] such words (second chapter): 'It is not healthy otherwise to initiate wars or quarrels amongst you by irrational wrath or on account of an appetite for inane glory or any sort of cupidity for worldly possessions; it is neither safe to kill or to die on behalf of such things, for such causes,' etc.

Rubric. Here it is said that, although other orders have been established and approved by law for military reasons, when just cause so dictated, such is not the case of this sect.

It clearly follows from the foregoing that we are not to think of this society or sect in terms of other religious orders established for military aims. For such have been instituted by the Church out of necessity and for the utility of the public good, *viz.,* for the defense of the Holy Land, for which it is confirmed that they were approved by law. Likewise, St Thomas states that on account of the deficiencies of secular princes, the Church has at times established certain orders for military purposes. Hence Ostiensis notes (in the chapter *Ad liberandum*: *De Iudeis*, in the part cut off, concerning the words 'religiosis eximendis'), that Hospitallers and Templars have been especially deputized to the task of defending the Holy Land. And for this reason they have been endowed with many privileges (as is clearly seen from *De privilegijs*: *Porro* and the chapter *Dilecti; De decenis*: *Ex parte tua*. On the Hospitallers and others, *viz.,* those of the Holy Sepulchre, their case is taken up in the chapter *Inter dilectos*: *De donacionibus*, etc.). Now it is seen that this sect, despite being reproved by both canon law and civil law, has been invented by the temerity of the Brethren themselves. As to this it should be noted that colleges and congregations are distinguished by the learned it two ways (in the chapter *Dilecta*: *De excessibus prelatorum*) because some colleges arise as it were naturally, such as those which come of the law of the nations, such as the societies of cities and villages, etc., and others come not by the law of the nations, but are merely voluntary associations, such as colleges of religious canons. These are spoken of in the second rule of my Lord Francis, Cardinal of Florence: That all colleges are prohibited unless it is found that they have been expressly approved by law (to this is addressed *ff De collegium illicitis*, see the end). On the other hand, all colleges are approved by law which in a city or municipality devote themselves to a particular licit art, as are those which are instituted for pious purposes, and for bringing aid to the oppressed or to the care of those cast-off (*ff De collegijs illicitis*, I). This is true for secular organisations, but in the case of religious congregations or colleges, these are not approved unless they are of approved religious orders (*De religiosis domibus*, final chapter, and the sole chapter of the same title, book VI).

Rubric. A response to the tacit question, should they allege any other privilege seen as instituting them for the defense of the faithful, and not in order to offend any others.

However, because of what is stated above, these Brethren, in an effort to rationalize and find excuses for their sins, so it seems, assert that their order derives its institution from the city of Acre, in the province of Jerusalem, pretending thereby to have been instituted initially for the defense of the Holy Land. Whereby, if they so understand the matter of their establishment, this contradicts the privilege granted them by Pope Honorious III, to which they pretend above, as it is seen to express things in this manner: 'We propose with the dew of apostolic grace to irrigate your new plantation, and with the favor of divine clemency to aid the crops that spring so fecundly therefrom at present, and shall so do in the future, with our ready and vigilant care. For this reasons, O sons beloved of the Lord, we give our clement nod to your postulations, and take under out protection and that of St Peter your house or hospital in which you are congregated to the glory of God, and for the defense of His faithful, and for the liberation of the Cross of Christ, along with all possessions and goods which it is known to justly possess, and which in the future, with the Lord's favor, you shall obtain; this we confirm with these present letters, etc.' And a few sentences later, it is added: 'We establish the order of the Brethren of the Hospital of Jerusalem for the care of paupers and the infirm and the order of the Brethren of the Temple Militia as clerics and warriors, to be observed in perpetuity. Dated Anagni by the hand of Master Symboldus of the Vice-chancellory of the Holy Roman Church on the V Calends of August, XV Indication of the Incarnation of the Lord, 1217.'

Rubric. Here it is stated in what manner said privilege does not agree with warring, nor is it in accord with their aforesaid letters and articles.

As can be seen, two things are confirmed in this same privilege: First, this hospital of said city of Acre in which at the time the Brethren were congregated for the defense of the faithful, with all of their possessions justly acquired by that time and yet to be (justly) acquired in the future, were taken under the Pope's protection. Second, he establishes them as an order, *viz.,* in that hospital where they are perpetually to observe their vows: *scilicet* the order of the Brethren of the Hospital of Jerusalem for the care of paupers and the infirm, and the order of the Templars as to clergy and warmaking.

Considering the first part, it is to be noted that what is said here is 'your house or hospital,' and not 'your houses or hospitals.' Likewise, it is said 'in which you are congregated,' and not 'in such as you shall be congregated, having abandoned this one.' Moreover, it speaks of their establishment 'for the defense of the faithful,' and nowhere does it speak of 'for the wresting of the goods of infidels from their hands, and converting the same to your own proper use,' but rather of 'the liberation of the Cross of Christ,' in so far as the Holy Land is spoken of.

Concerning the second part, it is to be noted that this is to be 'observed in perpetuity,' that is, 'this' order and no other, nowhere else, because a privilege given to one location is not to be extended elsewhere unless this be expressly enunciated.

Rubric. Here it is said that at the destruction of the Hospital of Jerusalem, in which said Brethren were reputed to be established, all of their privileges were destroyed as well.

From this it follows that, as this privilege, and all others similar thereto, were not given to the order, but rather to the hospital, as long as they were acting in defense of the Holy Land, consequently, at the destruction of the aforesaid hospital by the enemy all of its privileges were also destroyed. This is notably upheld by the final gloss of the chapter *Abbate*: *De verborum significacione*, with its concordances. And there, speaking of these, Johannes Andreae states: 'destroyed and not rebuilt, otherwise, that which is rebuilt would possess the same privileges (following Innocent, *De eleccione*: *Quia diligencia*)' or, according to the privilege in question, given to the order, it would endure as long as the order itself lasted, whereas given to a place or to particular possessions belonging to the order, it so belongs to those even when the order is absent (*De religiosis domibus*, chapter II; *De statu monachorum*: *Recolentes*), and in consequence, when the privilege ceases, so does the order established by it.

Rubric. Here it is stated that these Brethren hospitallers do not look after the poor and the infirm, and as this rule of theirs is no longer fulfilled, their privilege too has ceased. And that they are rather to be known as Templars than Hospitallers.

Moreover, even should we grant that this privilege was conceded to the order, and not to the hospital alone, because the chief task of this order was to care for paupers and the infirm, while only their secondary task was to make war on a religious basis, as far as this was done by laypersons, *viz.*, for the defense of the Holy Land, an occupation that is in no way convenable to these Brethren, therefore, with the cessation of the cause there also follows the cessation of the privilege in this regard (which is proven by gloss III, XVI question I, *Generaliter*). For if any privilege is granted a religious order, when the religious rule ceases, so does the privilege (as in XXV question II, the final §, and said chapter *Abbate*: *De verborum significaccione*). As for the first, it is the most evident fact, clearer than the light of day, that these Brethren are not chiefly concerned with hospitals, caring for paupers and the infirm. As too for the second, it is not seemly to them, *viz.* warfare, because the warfare of those aforesaid was necessary, and therefore had the approval of the Church as something just. But the warmaking of these Brethren is, rather, merely something of their own free will, and therefore hostile to the sacred canons, reproved thereby, and as such unjust in spirit and in cause (as is clear from XXIII question I: *Quid culpatur* and question II chapter I and there in the major gloss). Hence St Augustine: 'To have peace is a thing of the will; war on the other hand ought to be a thing of necessity. For peace is not sought so that war might be waged, but rather war is waged so that peace might be had' (XXIII question I: *Noli*), of which I treat more fully concerning the text, and below, in tractate 2 near the conclusion. As, therefore, it is clearly stated that this order of theirs is not one and the same order as that found in the privilege of the aforesaid Pope Honorious III, it follows that it is false to say that this order takes its beginning from that in Acre, unless according to other conditions that no longer apply, and that they falsely call themselves Brethren of the Hospital of Jerusalem, as they are completely different from those, and it would be much more convenient to call them Templars.

Rubric. Here it is stated that as this sect is reprehensible by law, it is therefore to be destroyed.

From this it follows clearly, that this sect, invented for the obtaining of alien dominions by those Brethren under the cloak of religion, is false and has been established contrary to legitimate and canonical sanctions. For as St Thomas says (*Secunda secunde* question XCIII article I) that the sin of falsity is committed by those who on the part of the Church practice the worship of God contrary to the divine authority constituted by the Church and as usually found in the Church, hence, he is in violation of the law who, lacking the licence of the prince, institutes a new order or college on his own behalf (*ff De collegijs illicitis*, I and III, *De religiosis domibus*, the final chapter). This is seen to have occurred in the present case, as said Brethren, having abandoned the aforesaid hospital, made themselves a new order, asserting on the basis of the aforementioned letters that this order of theirs was instituted to the extermination of infidels — which is not only something novel, but fully erroneous in the light of the Christian religion. Now, according to Johannes Andreae (in the afore-adduced chapter *Dilectam*: *De excessibus prelatorum*), although they have a good name, i.e. a religiously-sounding name, because they work evil, they are illicit and prohibited by law. Therefore, according to him, they are to be destroyed (which he supports with the law *De collegijs illicitis* and the Greek law set there).

And this suffices for the second consideration.

Version I

THE THIRD CONSIDERATION is in respect of the End to which the Order ought to be directed.

Now, in respect to the articles,[48] it is to be noticed that said Order has been instituted by said letters so that they might invade the lands of any enemies of the Cross of Christ whatsoever, exterminating them and wresting their lands from their control, converting the same to their own proper use for the augmentation of the Faith, etc. What has already been said is declared even more plainly by these articles. From these things it clearly appears that, while the state of the religious is ordered to the perfection of charity, as is said above, according to which all religious orders of whatever type ought to be directed toward charity, we have here a sect that is in conflict with all religion, as has been said; ordered, as can be seen, to the very opposite of charity, and nothing is so opposed to charity as mortal sin (*De penitencia* distinction II: *Caritas*, and the canon *Quia radix*). From this it follows that this sect is finally and fundamentally rooted in mortal sin, and consequently heretical. For whatever weakens love or induces to mortal sin is offensive to the Faith, for there can be no charity without faith (the above-mentioned canon *Caritas*), nor can the Faith be at all utile without love as the Apostle says (in chapter XIII of I Corinthians):[49] 'If I should have all faith, so that I could remove mountains, and have not charity, I am nothing,' etc. It therefore follows that this sect is erroneous in faith and thus heretical, for as they themselves confess in their articles, with which all the aforesaid letters concur, their Order has been established for the extermination of infidels and the occupation of their dominions and in consequence it must be acknowledged that their Order is not directed toward the perfection of charity, but rather is impious and cruel; not to offer beneficence unto their fellow men, but to exercise savagery; not to aid their neighbor but to bring him harm, which is repugnant to the love of God and neighbor and in consequence, is repugnant to the Evangelical truth. Hence St Bernard in his book addressed to Hugo, master of the Temple Militia, writes to the Templars (chapter two): 'Him then who seeks secular goods and pursues secular aims I call not a militiaman but a malicious man; in killing he sins mortally and in being killed perishes eternally.' A little farther on he adds: 'Indeed, pagans are not to be killed if they can be restrained in any other way from overly falling upon or oppressing the faithful,' etc. Now, no true Christian doubts but that infidels of whatever sort are our brothers, too (according to what we read in *De penitencia*, distinction II): *Si ex caritate* § *Proximus* and what follows, in text and gloss). And therefore, however their sin of infidelity, just as any other sin in any man, is not to be loved, still, according to the human nature that each man possesses, having been created in the image and likeness of God, he is to be loved according to God's commandment (Luke X, Mark VII).[50] Hence Augustine says: 'We do not accept sinners on account of their being sinners, but because they are humans, we treat them with human consideration. We persecute our own iniquity in them, and we take pity upon them on account of the nature we have in common' (see the canon *Duo ista*: XXIII question IV).

Because therefore this order is profane and heretical, it is also to be noted, according to Petrus de Tarentesia[51] (4 *Sentenciarum* distinction XXIII) that heresy is translated as division. And because the prime unity of the faithful is by faith, thus, division from the community of the Faith is specially known as heresy (with this Thomas is in accord in that same writing, and the Archdeacon notes the same in XXIV question III, in the canon *Heresis*). Hence according to the aforesaid articles, etc., this Order contains this error, contrary to the Faith, which, according to the Apostle (Galatians V)[52] 'worketh by charity,' in this, *viz.,* that it includes violence and rapine and by consequence, seditions, homicides, etc. Who, therefore, will doubt that this order is the very rudest of errors and cruel, excluding the Apostolical Faith, the form of which Faith is charity, and without which it is impossible to be pleasing in the eyes of God (Hebrews X),[53] the act of which Faith is not merely to believe in God as the devils believe, and tremble (James II),[54] for such indeed is a formless faith, and dead (as in the same chapter),[55] but to believe in God as the Apostles' Creed says, that is, believing by loving God and one's neighbor, walking in that faith according to Augustine, verified by the Apostle: 'saints by faith conquered kingdoms, wrought justice, obtained promises,' etc. (Hebrews XI)?[56]

Indeed, these heresies can also be considered to be triply rooted in mortal sin, according to the doctrine thereof, and on this triplex sin, this sect is seen to be fundamentally based.

THE FIRST ROOT is noted in respect to their neighbors, whom they offend directly, contrary to the precepts of divine law. For this order has been instituted chiefly for the extermination of infidels and the reception of their temporal goods, which, in other words, is to say that this order of theirs has been established or founded upon freely-willed homicide, theft, rapine, and banditry! Certainly such must be admitted, necessarily that this is in no small measure offensive to pious ears, because whatever is opposed to divine truth, scriptural or canonical, is also opposed to the supreme Truth, which is its wellspring (which is proven by said canon *Heresis* XXIII question III, and XXV question I: *Violatores*), and in consequence, is opposed to the Faith which is directed toward the Supreme Truth as to its object. Indeed, there is no doubt but this pestiferous error rages against the commandments of the Decalogue, *viz.,* 'thou shalt not kill,' 'thou shalt not steal,'[57] etc. Therefore.

Furthermore, as the Apostle says, 'all the law is fulfilled in one word: Thou shalt love thy neighbor as thyself' (Galatians V).[58] And elsewhere he writes: 'He that loveth his neighbor hath fulfilled the law.' From these it follows that this heresy, in that it excludes love of neighbor, is even contrary to all law and rebels against the Majesty divine. As it includes violence and rapine, it includes the lust of domination and pride, which is the mother of all vices, all sins, spawning both spiritual and carnal sin, as the Apostle (in said chapter V of his Letter to the Galatians)[59] enumerates: *scilicet* 'fornication, uncleanness, immodesty, luxury, idolatry, witchcrafts, enmities, contentions, emulations, wraths, quarrels, dissensions, sects,' etc., saying that 'they who do such things shall not obtain the kingdom of God.'

From these things it is deduced that this order is not merely not established to the perfection of charity, but is truly an abyss of the sinful and a sect of the deepest impiety and iniquity, and in consequence, it follows that it is the most cruel heresy.

The Second Part or Consideration

The second root is in respect to the Brethren themselves in that, according to the temporal goods they would obtain or have already obtained, they simulate a religion that they have not, so as to retain the same — which is the height of blindness. Now, blindness of the mind and hebetude of the senses are sins opposed to the gift of the intellect, as St Thomas holds. The former blinds, the latter debilitates the intellect. As St Gregory (*Moralium* XXXI) and St Thomas (*Secunda secunde* question XV, articles I and II) has it, the first is born of lasciviousness, the second arises from gluttony. Indeed, by its sinfulness, this blindness blurs the sharpness of intellectual vision twice over. Firstly, by wilfully turning away from it, as the Psalm says: 'He would not understand that he might do well.'[60] Secondly, by occupying the mind with that which one loves more, for example, temporal things, as the Psalmist writes: 'fire (*scil.* concupiscence) has fallen on them, and they shall not see the sun (*viz.,* justice).[61] Hence, to make a show of religion so as to obtain temporal goods which one makes one's goal, or the dissemination of false doctrine, is a mortal sin according to St Thomas (question XII article 4), because, as he states it, simulation is properly mendacity, which reveals itself in the exterior signs of the facts. For the exterior habit of the religious is a sign of sorts of his religious status, representing him as obliged to the works of perfection, just as in the case before us: although these Brethren cloak themselves in the habit of religious persons, there is no religion in them, as is clearly revealed from what is said above, and as is sufficiently gathered from their own articles and above-mentioned writings. And for this reason we see here such hypocrisy as we have persons who don't give a fig for sanctity or religion, but merely wish to appear saintly or religious, and this is a mortal sin (said question, article 4). The sainted doctor alleges the same (in the same question, article 2), citing St Gregory (XXXI *Moralium*) where he states: 'There are such as wear the habit who are unable to achieve the merit of perfection. It is not to be believed of them that they are to be numbered amongst the hypocrites, as infirmity is one thing, and the maliciousness of sin another. But those who wear the habit of sanctity, but do not strive to achieve the merit of perfection, are simulators, because the exterior habit of sanctity signifies the works of perfection.'

And because this simulation, mendacity, or hypocrisy, is not seen to be alien to this sect, and that in and of itself, setting aside any offence to one's neighbors, is a mortal sin, which will not cease to be until the sect itself ceases to be — here, consequently, one clearly sees the second root.

THE THIRD ROOT is the weakening of ecclesiastical authority, which authority that sect boldly opposes. For even though the prohibition of the General Council, which expressly prohibits anyone from assuming whatever pertains to religious institutions unless the same is approved by the Apostolic See (*De religiosis domibus*, the final chapter, and the only chapter of book VI of that same title, still this sect resists this prohibition, holding the contrary to be licit, however tacitly, still *de facto*, which is nothing less than to resist the same by word, for Christ, Who is the Truth, can be denied by act as well as by speech (XI question III: *Existimant*), not only false words, but also simulated works are lies (XXII question V: *Cavete*) and by consequence ecclesiastical authority is defied. Nor is ignorance of the prohibition any excuse (I question IV, the final §). Whence such a profession is nothing other than transgression of command, which, according to Ostiensis, leads to mortal sin (as is noted in the chapter *Illud*: *De maioritate et obediencia* and chapter II). Nor does it suffice for one to believe that the order has been approved, since, because such a prohibition exists, it is necessary for the one wishing to profess such vows, by a thorough discussion of the issue, to flee the guilt of omission and negligence, which also arises from ill will, according to which the assumption is always against him who professes in cases where doubt exists. For the law considers him guilty of transgression who dares hope for that which is not licit (*Codex*: *De peticionibus bonorum sublatis*, I, at the start).

From these it is manifestly clear that according to these foregoing, this sect is not simply, but multifariously, heretical, which I state here, ever wishing to keep the peace.

FRAGM. EXCISED H

...in this way it may be stated that this triple root is triple heresy, or triply heretical, however according to the first root we have heresy proper, the second refers more to hypocrisy, and the third, truly, to idolatry, which should be stated *de iure*. This is proven by the words of St Gregory (set in the canon *Si qui presbyteri*: LXXXCI distinction), stating that disobedience is equal to the sin of fortune-telling and that it is foul idolatry to refuse acquiescence, and that it is the sin of paganism to be contrary to Apostolical precepts (as in IX distinction: *Nulli*) although by reason of the third it is also called heresy broadly understood, according to Ostiensis (in his *Summa*: *De hereticis* § I in the verse 'Et qui transgreditur'), which is understood in the case of someone who asserts that the Roman Church is unable to establish canons, etc. (as in gloss I of the I canon *Nulli fas* XIX distinction, with its concordances).

FRAGM. EXCISED H

The sainted doctor considers such sectarians and heretics as being much worse than Jews and Saracens, as the infidelity of heretics is a graver sin than the infidelity of those others, being that the heretics confess to the Evangelical Faith yet corrupt it, sinning more gravely thereby than Jews who have never accepted it, while those Jews who have accepted the figure of the Faith in the Old Law and corrupt it by evil interpretation sin more gravely than the gentiles who have never accepted the Gospel in any form (*Secunda Secunde* question X article VI).

Now, as no one of sound mind doubts but that the aforementioned articles of these Brethren are heretical, which is notoriously obvious from them and from the aforementioned letters, and is established in documents, it consequently follows that these Brethren themselves are notorious heretics and must be proceeded against accordingly.

FRAGM. EXCISED H

Hence Innocent notes (in the chapter *Cum dilecti*: *De accusacionibus*), stating that in the case of bringing notorious facts to trial there is no need of taking note of all circumstances, otherwise no crime could be considered notorious, which might have any extenuating circumstances by which it might be excused, and this suffices in notorious cases: that the fact cannot be denied, however it may be rationalized, for proceedings to take place outside the normal judicial order. The same is noted by lord Francis, Cardinal of Florence (in the chapter *Vestra*: *De cohabitacione clericorum et mulierum*). Now, in the present case, not only the facts of the aforesaid articles, but also the fact of the cruel warring waged by said Brethren according to the same articles and letters, not only cannot be denied, but they also take away any manner of their being excused on the basis of these letters and articles.

FRAGM. EXCISED H

From which it follows that to defend such erroneous letters as theirs is to defend error. For what else can it be, to support their pretended cause, or to come to their aid in their cause, but to nourish heresy and to favor heretics against the General Council (on this see the chapter *Excommunicamus*: *De hereticis*), for those, for example, who shelter, defend, or support heretics are likewise excommunicated by the same law. And should they remain excommunicate for a year, they become infamous, ineligible to hold public office, and incapable of offering testimony, whether active or passive; nor are they capable of receiving an inheritance. No one is responsible to them in any business, yet they are responsible to all others. Their word and their script are alike null and void. If they be clerics, they are deposed from office and benefice, etc. (said chapter *Excommunicamus* § *Credentes*). And beyond what has already been said, today, by the new law, those who trust, receive, defend, and support heretics, along with their sons unto the second generation, are not admitted to any ecclesiastical benefice, and should they somehow arrive at this, their position is null and void by the law itself. And whoever presumes to offer them burial in sacred ground, knowingly, is *ipso facto* excommunicated and shall remain so until proper satisfaction is made. Nor is his sin forgiven him unless he digs up with his own hands, publicly, and then casts aside, the bodies of the condemned, as we find here and elsewhere in the chapter *Quicunque*, book VI of the same title.

It is said that one can support heretics in fact or in speech (which Johannes Andreae lays out in his *Novella*, following the Archdeacon (in the same chapter, on the word 'Fautores,' and on the word 'Defensores'). By fact, for example, when one intervenes on their behalf in a legal matter. For, as he sees it, proof arises from the very fact (II question I § *Quis autem*, with its concordances, where it is noted that nothing else can be proven concerning that person's real feelings;

XXXII distinction: *Erubescant*, at the end). Likewise, those are said to support them in speech who justify a heretic, not jokingly, or with a slip of the tongue, but with such as those of advocates who in their defense seek to justify their actions, and can thus be called their supporters (as is clear from XI question III *Timendo*; II question and canon I, the final canon). Therefore, those who defend them, speaking in their favor, can be said to support them. Johannes Andreae.

Beyond this, sometimes a person defends the error, and sometimes the person who errs. The former is more worthy of condemnation, quite simply, and is called a heresiarch (XXIII question IV: *Qui aliorum*). And he is to be more bitterly punished than the errant party himself (as we find in the same canon: see what is also said in the previously adduced chapter *Excommunicamus*, at the word 'Defensores').

From all this it is clear what is to be known concerning the Third principal proposition. I shall pass over other things for brevity's sake, and because I have set these comments more broadly where I speak of the text of the aforesaid letters.

So much for the first tractate.

FRAGM. EXCISED H

And just as Our Savior, after warning us to be on our guard against false prophets who come to us in the clothing of sheep, but inwardly are ravening wolves, immediately adding 'By their fruits you shall know them. Because an evil tree cannot bring forth good fruit,' etc. (Matthew VII):[62] that the pestiferous fruit of this sect is seen not only to consist in said erroneous letters and in the articles mentioned, but also in their deeds and criminal works, which are wholly contrary to the Christian religion: Thus, taking all the aforesaid into account, which seems more to concern itself with theory, it is now incumbent upon us to pass on to the practical and to inquire, on the authority of this sacred Council, into the articles with which we charge these Brethren, believing them to be notorious and in accord with which they lobor in public infamy — which follow, inscribed below, etc.[63]

Version II

The third consideration in respect of the end toward which this order ought to be directed.

> Rubric. Here follows the third consideration, in respect to the end toward which this order claims to be directed. And that it is not for the amplification of the Faith, but rather to the destruction of the same, this is proven via two arguments, the first concerning the means, as follows.

And even though the end at which they pretend to be directed is the amplification of the Faith, as can be gathered from the abovesaid letters and articles, that this is nevertheless impossible is proven by the means they employ, which are contrary to the faith, evil in and of themselves, and prohibited by law divine, *viz.,* violence, injury, rapine, and unjust wars. Such are the means they employ to attain their stated end. Indeed, these means have already been sufficiently touched upon, and can be ascertained from their letters and articles. Thus it necessarily follows that said order has something quite different in mind, in reality, than might be suggested by the spin they give it. As therefore it is necessary to say what they intend via means of this sort, other than the supposed aim with which they color and cloak their deeds, pretending to act on behalf of the spread of the Faith, while there can be no doubt about it but that these means are contrary to the Faith and prohibited by divine law, therefore, nor will there be any doubt as to the true end of this order, according to the law of necessary consequence and the nature of the correlatives in relation to one another, which offer ample proof. From which it must be deduced as a matter of course that this order, or militia, is heretical.

Rubric. The second argument concerning the end to which they pretend.

The same can be inferred from said end at which they pretend to aim, taking the argument for granted, that said aim is to be the amplification of the Faith. And because the end is the cause for all that tends unto said end, accordingly, it ought to be conceded that the Faith is the cause in itself of all these wars, unjust as they are, as having no just cause at all, as is clear from the above, and as is clear from the letters themselves; and that faith is the cause in itself of injury, rapine, and, by consequence, homicides and all other evils that occur in such wars. But there can be no doubt but that this is repugnant to the faith, and so it must be conceded that said order, basing itself on such a foundation, is contrary to the Faith.

Version III[64]

FRAGM. EXCISED

The third consideration in respect to the End toward which this order ought to be directed.

AND AS THE LETTERS spoken of above in this controversy (in which see the Topic above) are pretended to be Papal and Imperial, and are seen to be the ultimate and final refuge of the aforementioned Brethren, to these they have absolutely restricted themselves. Because if there were any other stronger basis...

Version I[65]

Rubric. Here after the manner of an epilogue the whole matter is reduced to three principal conclusions.

Reducing therefore the entire matter before us to three principal conclusions, by which the entire structure of this supposed order is destroyed, the following conclusions are presented as reliable:

The first conclusion

FIRST. It is not licit to oppress pagans by warring against them, invading their lands and subjugating them, or wresting from their hands the goods belonging to them without just cause, or, to speak precisely, for the absolute and immediate cause of the spread of the Faith, i.e. without respect to any other prime and principal cause of a just war.

As far as the first part is concerned, this conclusion is evident from what has been said.

As for the second part, the conclusion has been proven (John XX)[66] where Christ says to His Apostles and disciples: 'As the Father hath sent me, I also send you.' For it is well known that Christ spread the Faith by His humble teaching, benign admonition, and peaceful and virtuous conversations, just as Holy Scripture testifies. Just the same did the Apostles and disciples, and this did they hand on to their successors. Furthermore, that the law of the Gospel is the law of love, concord, and peace, and not the law of fear, discord, and war, is testified to by Sacred Scripture many times over. Here the Apostle states that the arms of our warfare are spiritual ones, therefore Christ sent His Apostles and disciples off to preach the Gospel and spread the Faith amongst the gentiles, unarmed, and in so doing He instructed that this mission of ours amongst others is to be like His — one of instruction. Hence St Augustine (speaking of John's gospel, in the person of Christ), says: 'Hear, ye circumcised; hear, ye uncircumcised; hear, all ye kingdoms of the earth: I impede not your domination in this world, but call you to Me believing; serve not in fear.' With this conclusion the most able theologians concur; some of them have written about it during this sacred Council, setting it on efficacious and theological bases. And this too is clear from what has been said above.

It therefore follows that the contradiction of this conclusion is error, to which in the end this warmaking of theirs is reduced, as to its final and ultimate foundation, as it either has no cause at all, or its cause is this aforesaid erroneous one.

Rubric. The first corollary.

And from this conclusion three corollaries may be deduced.

The first is that the aforesaid writings, of whatever sort, in basing themselves upon this error, virtually contain heresy, and by law are thus null and void and invalid, and by consequence provide no authority to anyone to invade the lands of infidels, subjugate them, despoil them, etc.

Second Corollary

Secondly, it follows that such warmaking as based on such letters as its foundation, conducted for no other immediate, just cause as has been said above, is necessarily founded upon heresy. By consequence it is clearly and convincingly proven from their own principles that this order or militia of theirs is heretical.

Third Corollary

Thirdly, it follows from these same principles that it is false what said Brethren assert in their articles, that is to say that this order was established on the basis of these letters for the invasion of the lands of any infidels whatsoever, etc., for these letters, as null and void, contain no authorisation of Roman Pontiff or Emperor, as has been said, and, by consequence, no establishment or foundation for their order, either.

Rubric. The second conclusion.

The second conclusion. A religious order established generally to fight against infidels, cannot initiate war against them for any special reason, unless the authority of their superior intervenes and permits them to do so. This conclusion is in agreement with St Thomas (in *Secunda Secunde,* question CLXXXVIII article III at the end) where he states that no religious order is established for the waging of war in such a way that the religious themselves might determine of their own authority whether it is licit to conduct such war but may engage in it only upon the authority of prince or Church. This is also seconded by all canonists, especially Johannes Andreae (in the chapter *Sane*: *De regularibus*).

The First Corollary

From this conclusion three corollaries are inferred.

The first is that the cause of the spreading of the Faith, because it is a cause, *per accidens*, general and remote to any sort of order established for warmaking, cannot be to any degree more of a special cause for this particular military order than any other, nor may any one military order be more directed to the spreading of the Faith in and of itself than any other, unless by circumstance and any other special reason, such as preaching or another, which does not appear to be the case here, and therefore, no special authority for warmaking is seen as belonging to these more than to any other orders instituted for that purpose, etc.

The Second Corollary

Secondly, it follows that where there is no apparent impediment to the Faith, in fact or in probability, as it were imminent, there is no cause for warring in order to spread the Faith. But such is asserted in the aforesaid letters, therefore, etc. It is clear that the Faith cannot be spread by warmaking otherwise than indirectly, *viz.,* by removing an impediment to the Faith. If, therefore, it does not arise as such means to the end, i.e. if there is no impediment to be removed, nor can it appear to belong to the end. Now, where both proximate and final causes cease to be, there ceases the remote cause as well. Therefore, etc. Now, the laws rather pay attention to proximate causes than to remote, because the effect is named thereby (*De concesione prebende*: *Quis diversitatem*, and what Innocent notes in *De Testibus*: *Tesimonium*, etc). Now the proper and natural end of warmaking is the removal of that which prohibits or impedes the Faith or the common or public good, and just warmaking cannot be immediately directed at anything other than the removal of such an impediment as its cause, and because it cannot be stated in the case before us that such an impediment exists, it cannot be stated that there is any sort of special cause for their order's warmaking. Consequently, nor can any such thing be stated on the basis of these letters, that they are moved to action on behalf of the spreading of the Faith, however much they pretend to the same.

The Third Corollary

Thirdly it follows that, granting (without prejudice to the truth), that the order of these Brethren had been established in Jerusalem, generally for military purposes, still, without special licence, especially of the Apostolic See, they have no right to invade lands belonging to infidels in order to occupy their dominions, etc. And therefore it follows that, for this reason too, this warmaking of theirs is and has been repugnant to divine law and, consequently, heretical.

Rubric. The third conclusion.

The third conclusion. So that a war might be shown to be just *de iure*, it is necessary for the just cause to be inquired into and declared legitimate whenever doubt as to such may exist. According to St Thomas (in *Secunda Secunde* question XL, article I), it is clear that for this three things are required, *scilicet* authority, just cause, and righteous intent. If, however, these three things are to be established by law where there is a lack of other factual evidence, it is necessary for these two things to concur: first, that the cause must at least be summarily known. Second, that a legitimate declaration should ensue. For there should be no doubt as to the authority of the attacking party, nor of the legitimacy of the cause of the attack, nor of the injustice of the attacked party's resistance. For ignorance of such things, even if probability exists in their regard, provides no excuse to the attackers unless they are acting out of the obedience of subjects who have good reason to assume that the war is just (as in canon XXIII question I: *Quid culpatur*). Thus, legal or factual evidence is required. Now, legal evidence cannot be had except by way of a legal process, via the path of justice, *viz.,* by proof established by law or by legal verdict and by consequence by legitimate declaration, and to this end many laws exist.

Not even in the case of the Pope is it seen to be licit to deprive the infidels of their dominions without legitimate cause or due legal process permitting such, and therefore, such deprivation is unjust, because it is clearly repugnant to natural law and divine law. As the cause consists in a particular fact, just as in the case of other facts particular to a distant location, by law it is assumed that the Pope is ignorant of it (see chapter I: *De constitucionibus* book VI). Because although something may be notorious in itself, because it is all the same not considered notorious to the judge, it must still be proven before him (as in the chapter *Ad nostram*: *De iure iurando*, the third, with others similar thereunto).

And thus legal necessity demands that such a cause ought to be looked into, a process of proving this same ought to be carried out, thus, some legal order is needed.

From this conclusion three corollaries are inferred.

The First Corollary

The first corollary. Unless such a legal process is established as having taken place, the authority of the Pope, the legitimate cause, and the righteous intention in depriving the aforesaid infidels cannot be otherwise justified or proven *de iure*. Thus it cannot be judged that the authority of a superior has intervened in this warmaking, granting his consent whether tacit or understood. By consequence the above-mentioned letters prove nothing, as no mention of any such legal process is to be found in them. Actually, they prove the contrary, *scil.* as for the Pope to deprive them thus, tacitly, without just cause, and absent any guilt on their part, would be contrary to natural and divine law. The reason for this is that by law guilt is not presumed until it is proven, and ignorance of cause is *de iure* presumed when knowledge thereof has not been proven (by the rule *Presumitur*: *De regulis iuris* book VI).

The Second Corollary

Secondly, it follows that the warmaking of said Brethren, in that it is taking place in the absence of just means and in consequence is unjust and does not serve legal order, is not only in opposition to the proper order of justice and unjust, but, what is more, it is thus culpable, both actively and passively, in respect to others. It is to be understood as prohibited by divine law and on such grounds must be judged heretical. I say both actively and passively on the one hand on account of the scandal to which it gives rise, and on the other, because of the harm done to both life and things, which cannot be in any way unjustly offended or attacked.

The Third Corollary

Thirdly, it follows that unless the attacked party, even if they be infidels, do not know the cause for which they are attacked, they are just in resisting their attackers however much the latter have cause to wage war, because such a cause does not do away with the natural right of self-defense.

From this it is manifestly clear whether the Church can or should tolerate this error, or compel said Brethren to restore, actually and effectively, all goods and dominions occupied by them or acquired in any way whatsoever, as has been expressed above.

This suffices for the third consideration, and by consequence also for the third principal proposition.

And may it be said in so far as the first tractate is concerned: with probability, and also as a setting forth of the matter to the effect that so presented it might receive due determination and end, as is expedient, or as it should be, by the Pope, our most holy lord, above all in this sacred general Council.

And may these things be considered as having been stated not determinatively, but as probabilities to be so submitted.

Version II[67]

Reducing this issue to three principal conclusions:

Neither Pope nor Emperor may licitly give anyone the faculty of invading infidels' lands, subjugating them, and occupying their dominions, with the absolute and immediate cause of spreading the Faith without any respect to any direct and chief cause for a just war. To hold the opposite opinion is heresy.

The rationale: Because the end is the cause in and of itself of all that exists in pursuit of that end it is repugnant to the Faith that it should be the end and principal cause of any sort of war, violence, homicide, or rapine.

Three corollaries are inferred from this conclusion.

First, because any sort of letters alleged to be papal or imperial, based upon this error, virtually contain heresy, and they are also *de iure* null and void and invalid nor can they endow anyone with any general or special authorisation to invade the lands of infidels, subjugate them, despoil them, etc.

Second, it follows that this warfare, taking letters like this for its foundation, in which there is no other principal cause for a just war moved, except the cause of spreading the Faith, it is founded in heresy. And by consequence, on the basis of their own claimed principles, it is clearly convincing and proven that this order of theirs is heretical.

Third, it follows from these same letters and principles that it is manifestly false what said Brethren assert therein, *scilicet* that their order had been established by these letters for the invasion of the lands of whatsoever infidels you please, because, as has been said, these letters contain no authority of Roman Pontiff or Emperor, and by consequence, no establishment or foundation of their order.

II Conclusion. No religious order generally established in opposition to the infidels may initiate war against them for any special reason, however just in itself, unless indeed the authority of a superior intervenes to grant them special authorisation. To hold the opposite opinion appears to be heretical.

This aforesaid conclusion is that of St Thomas (*Secunda Secunde* question CLXXXIX, article 3 at the end). This is also upheld by Johannes Andreae and other canonists in the *Decretals* (book 3 title 31 chapter 10: *Sane, De regularibus*).

From this three corollaries are inferred. The first is that any religious militia waging war otherwise, *viz.,* without special edict of Church or Prince, is acting contrary to divine law and as such is to be judged heretical.

Second, it follows that, granting (without prejudice to the truth) that the order of these Brethren has been generally instituted for warmaking, still it is not legitimate for them to invade infidel regions with the aim of occupying their dominions, without special licence from the Apostolic See.

Third, it follows that all dominions acquired in such a way by them, as stated in fact, are unjust and must necessarily be restored or remitted really and effectively, as far as this is possible, at the risk of them losing their chance at salvation.

III Conclusion. For a war to appear just, the prerequisites are: the authoritative cognition of its cause and its legitimate declaration, wherever there may be a verisimilitude or probability of doubt in the matter. To hold the contrary is seen as heresy and contrary to Sacred Scripture, which lays out the obligation that in such cases the due process of justice is to be observed. There can be no doubt about the authority of the part that brings suit, or takes up the sword on account of imminent danger of war: or as to the just cause on the part of the defendant or the attacked party, concerning injuries committed by them or their error. And in the case of both of these, in respect to those whose interest it is to know these matters so as to avoid active and passive danger.

Three corollaries are inferred from this.

First, the authorising intervention of the superior or his consent to this warmaking cannot be assumed as tacit or understood. For no man can give tacit approval to something of which he is in ignorance (VI *Decretals* book 1 title 2 *De constitucionibus* chapter 1) concerning which ignorance is presumed *de iure* where certain knowledge is not proven (*De regulis iuris*: *Decretalium liber* 6, rule 47).

Second, it follows that such warmaking waged in the absence of just means, having no approval by the order of law, is not only contrary in itself to the due order of justice and unjust, but also culpable in respect to others, actively and passively, and for that reason it ought to be understood as prohibited by divine law. Now, I say 'actively and passively' both by reason of the scandal caused, and by reason of the offence and harm done not only to persons but also to things, which it is not licit to harm or offend at all, unless there is an evidently just cause. Nor is ignorance of the justice of the cause, however probable that just cause may seem to be, any excuse, except in the case of subjects acting in obedience even though they are not completely certain of the justice of the cause — these are so excused (as in canon XXIII question 1: *Quid culpatur*, etc.).

Third, it follows that unless the infidel who is attacked is aware of the cause of the attack, he is just in his resistance to the attacker however the latter may have good cause to attack, because such cause does not do away with the natural right of self-defense, etc.

BECAUSE AN ERROR

(*Quoniam error*, 1417)

Part II

Here follows the second tractate.

AS FAR AS THE SECOND TRACTATE IS CONCERNED, it shall be constituted of responses to the XVIII conclusions set forth in a little booklet by some fellow named Johannes von Bamberg, doctor of the decretals, which pamphlet seems to be identical in material and effect to that of Brother Johann Falkenberg, OP, which in turn contains XXIII conclusions[68] (I speak here not of that pamphlet of his which has already been condemned,[69] but another one rather, which is still awaiting judgment). Because both of these have arisen from the same yeast of malice, doing detriment to the status and Regal honor of his most exalted excellency the King, and the inhabitants of the Kingdom of Poland, in vehemently prejudicial fashion supporting the Knights of the Cross of Prussia: indeed the touchwood of their odium and the manner of their progression is the same in both, although their means be divers: thus, the judgment will apply to both of them equally, at least in certain things. Nevertheless, so that such screeds of the aforementioned Johann von Bamberg not remain unanswered, as they attack certain conclusions drawn from the expressions of divers learned men that I collected and brought forward as a submission to the Nations gathered at this sacred Council for the wholesome reformation of the status of these Brethren, by gathering his aforesaid conclusions together, along with certain errors asserted therein in attempted proof of their conclusions, thoroughly tearing apart his inutile legal allegations, I give clear and very brief responses to the same — not as a final determination, but rather as a submission uncovering the matter[70] to the eyes of those who wish to occupy themselves with them to better use.

Now, as my adversary is seen to falsely assert my conclusions to be fabricated to the detriment of papal and imperial authority, etc., thus, in self-defense and in order to remove all such calumnies of my adversary, I here protest that I intend to say nothing by manner of assertion which would be contrary to the Faith, good morals, and healthy doctrine, or that would be contrary to the state, reverence, or persons of the Supreme Pontiff or Emperor. And if there should occur, amongst the things I have said or am to say, either principally or incidentally, anything even seeming to be so, I would rather that these things be considered as not having been said at all. I also desire that this protestation of mine be considered ever current and valid, as if I were specially to resume or repeat it in every case of anything I shall say, or anything I have already said.

And first, I mention at the start some things said by my master, Mauricius of Prague, that most able of theologians, in response to my first conclusions.[71] He thus begins:

In accord with the judgment of the doctors, who accept as fact that heresy is defined as dogma that is assertively contrary to Holy Scripture, thus the tractate on behalf of the Prussians that begins with the words 'In the Name of the Holy and indivisible Trinity,' etc., and concludes with the words 'under the authority of St Jerome: *Ad militem*,' part of said tractate is heretical, and part of it smacks of heresy in all of its XVIII conclusions,[72] collectively, by which the warfare of the Prussians against the infidels is deduced as having been licit and founded in law. Hence in the Proemium it is stated that this religious order was established for the defense of the Holy Land and the protection of the fatherland, as its proper final cause. But as this cause is deficient in so far as the Holy Land has not been conquered by these Brethren, and the fatherland which they inhabit has been everywhere made secure upon the conversion of the infidels, therefore, this order is superfluous, nor is it to be tolerated in said fatherland, according to the words of Our Savior where, in His parable of the infertile fig tree, He says (Luke XIII)[73] 'cut it down therefore: why cumbereth it the ground?' the opposite of which is deduced by the writer of this little work. At the very least they ought to be transplanted to another place where they might fulfil the mission that, as they say, was entrusted to them, according to the Savior's words: 'the kingdom of God shall be taken from you, and shall be given to a nation yielding the fruits thereof (Matthew XXI).[74] This suffices for prologue.

At last, I here adduce the first conclusion in this form: 'Although pagans and other infidels should be numbered amongst Christ's flocks by virtue of their creation and redemption by Christ, yet in truth they are wild beasts, perfidious, rebellious, savage and cruel, and thus beasts of the field. Therefore, the Lord's words "Feed my sheep" do not apply to them at all.'[75]

This conclusion expressly denies the plenitude of the keys of the Church promised to the Pope (Matthew XVIII): 'Whomever you shall bind upon earth,' etc., and (John, final chapter): 'Feed my sheep.'[76] For such a grant of authority that does not include a universal pasturage as the end of the conclusion says, does not correspond to the universality of the promise and thus declares Christ to be a liar, Who grants or performs less than He promises. Hence it might be argued: Christ promised the Pope and all his successors care and shepherding of all His sheep, without exception, saying 'Whomever you shall bind,' etc.; indeed this includes all of the human race, fallen in Adam, as he says 'Take care of him' (Luke X).[77] But in no manner did he commit the pagans and infidels to the Pope's care and shepherding although they are numbered amongst His flocks by their creation and redemption, when He said 'Feed my sheep,' as said conclusion has it at the end. Therefore, He has not fulfilled what He has promised. In this way, the writer of such a conclusion is a heretic in the face of this (John XIV): 'I am the way, and the truth, and the life.'[78] The reasoning is clear from the terms employed, and so one of these premises is heretical. This cannot be the major premise, which is Evangelical, and so it must be the minor premise, the conclusion. Therefore, as far as the pamphlet is concerned, it must be revoked and burnt up without dissimulation, just like the evil tree bringing forth such evil fruit as these conclusions must be ordered to be cut down and cast into the fire (Matthew VII).[79]

Secondly thus: All sheep are fundamentally Christ's by reason of their redemption, as they have been purchased by Him in this age, predestined by Him from all time, and property of His by appropriation such as no man may snatch from His hand (John X)[80] as it is impossible for the predestined to be damned, as the Apostle states: 'And whom He predestinated, them He also glorified.'[81] Now, He committed these sheep, principally, to be pastured, by the words of the Lord 'feed my sheep,' because principally they are His. Therefore, pagans and infidels, redeemed by Christ, are principally comprehended in those words, to which the conclusion stands in opposition, and because that idea is Catholic, the proposition contained in the conclusion is clearly heretical. Otherwise, if we take the conclusion: that they are redeemed but not comprehended in the Lord's words because they are perfidious and rebellious beasts, as the second part of the conclusion holds, from this it would follow, contrary to the Apostle, that on account of their temporal malice they may have fallen away from eternal predestination, upon which redemption necessarily follows, as the Apostle states (Romans I)[82] that, according to the flesh,

Christ was predestined by the resurrection from the dead of Jesus Christ, i.e. for the redemption of all lapsed in Adam. Hence, along with the Apostle I do not speak of redemption in terms of sufficiency, but rather in terms of efficiency. Of which the Savior says: 'this is my blood, which shall be shed for many unto remission of sins' (Matthew XXVI)[83] where 'for many' instead of 'for the predestined only,' which locution is used by the Apostle speaking of the predestination by which Christ is the firstborn amongst many Brethren (Romans VIII).[84] And in this manner of efficiency the pamphleteer distinguishes creation from redemption in his conclusion by medial conjugation, grammatically speaking: 'the conjugation links different things.' Now it is clear to the faithful that Christ, the universal Creator and Redeemer, has redeemed all men who could possibly be created, as far as sufficiency is concerned, that is, His sacrifice is sufficient to redeem all, but not all according to efficiency, that is, only those predestined thereunto are saved as is clear from the above. It is their shepherding He commands in the aforementioned words 'feed my sheep,' yet the conclusion states the opposite, which is erroneous. This is confirmed as Christ calls the pagans and infidels sheep who are not of the fold of the Church, saying that He has others as His own, and not as aliens, such as the Father has given Him. And therefore no one can snatch them out of the Father's hands (John X).[85] Thus, by the pronoun 'my' He fundamentally includes them, while the pamphlet's conclusion states the opposite, which is frivolous, erroneous, and contrary to the Evangelical truth.

Thirdly thus: The latitude of the Pope's authority in matters spiritual is just as extensive as that of the Emperor in temporalities. To this the pamphleteer confesses in his fourth conclusion: But the Emperor enjoys sovereignty and has universal care over all the faithful and the infidels, without exception, as he admits throughout his entire argument. Therefore, the Pope has similar authority over all, but only in so far as the Lord's words 'feed my sheep' are concerned. Thus, all infidels and pagans are comprehended under the words 'feed my sheep,' though the conclusion states the opposite.

In confirmation of this, as a sign of his universal authority, the Pope appoints titular bishops to the pagans and infidels, and such deputations would be but frivolously made if the abovesaid words of the Lord were not accepted as being in reference to his care and solicitude for them. Thus, the pagans and infidels are to be comprehended under these same words, but the conclusion says the opposite, in derogation of papal authority. But it is no marvel that he contradicts the Pope and the Church since he contradicts himself by stating that the pagans are sheep such as fall not to the pasturage of Peter.

Fourthly: Speaking conditionally of Himself as the Good Shepherd, Christ concludes with the words: 'And other sheep I have, that are not of this fold,' denoting thus pagans and infidels, 'them also I must bring, and there shall be one fold and one shepherd,'[86] showing that without this bringing-in, the unity of the Church spoken of in the Creed cannot come about in act or *in potentia* — and this bringing-in of the infidels into the Church is effected by the solicitude of the shepherd. Therefore, the care of pagans and infidels is entrusted to the Pope, with that conditional reduction modified even by the verb used in the words of the Lord: 'I must,' which is enunciated here with the imminent penalty of eternal damnation looming in the background. And thus it is confirmed that if Peter was not obliged by the above-cited words to bring in the infidels, which, according to the conclusion, does not belong to him, it follows that he would be committing a mortal sin by meddling in the conversion of the infidels, since it did not pertain to him. This is heretical, repugnant to the revelation made to Peter in the figure of the linen sheet let down by the four corners wherein all manner of fourfooted beasts, and creeping things of the earth, and fowls of the air were depicted, which he was commanded to kill and eat. And which presently were taken up into Heaven, by which vision all the infidels dispersed throughout the four corners of the world are understood as being committed to him (Acts X).[87] But only in these words of the Lord: 'feed my sheep,' which words, I stress, he understood by that vision shown unto him, and extensively interpreted to himself in that way. And thus it follows that the pagans and the infidels, who are reputed to be beasts in the pamphlet before us, and animals by perfidy, rebellion, and savagery, are to be comprehended under these aforesaid words of the vision just mentioned — of necessity, which this conclusion, so heretical, contradicts.

And this is confirmed because it was to Peter that the care of all the Apostles was committed, as Christ's words to him were formulated in the singular: 'feed my sheep' (John, final chapter).[88] But, along with Peter, the Apostles too were commanded to the task of converting all the pagans and infidels, as Christ said unto them: 'Go ye into the whole world, and preach the gospel to every creature,' etc. (Mark, final chapter).[89] Therefore, the care of the universal conversion of all the gentiles by the Apostles was specially commended to Peter, but only in the aforesaid words concluding with 'feed my sheep.'

Thus, pagans and infidels are included in the aforementioned words, although the conclusion holds the opposite. Anyway, as all those to be saved are spoken of as sheep (Matthew XXV),[90] among whom there will be many sinners, publicans, and infidels gathered on the Day of Judgement to the right hand of the Son of God, of whom Our Savior speaks to the Scribes and Pharisees saying: 'Amen I say to you, that the publicans and the harlots shall go into the kingdom of God before you' (Matthew XXI).[91] Yes, sheep erring in this manner must be gathered in by the Shepherd. Indeed, by the words 'Feed my sheep,' He established the Pope as universal shepherd, according to all the doctors of the Church. For this reason it is concluded that pagans and infidels are comprised under that saying of the Lord's.

Otherwise, it must be denied that Christ ever endowed Peter with the universal pastorate, and yet nowhere else in the entire text of the Bible is the actual imposition of pastorate found, save in these aforesaid words. Or that Christ somehow neglected, by mistake, the salvation of those among the infidels predestined, for whom, as for His flock, He has prepared the kingdom of God from the foundation of the world (Matthew XXV)[92] — if He had not provided their gathering-in in the aforementioned words concerning the Shepherd. For man is sufficient unto himself to sin, but not to return, as the Lord says through His prophet: 'Destruction is thy own, thy help is only in me' (Hosea XIII).[93] But unless the shepherd preach unto them, they will not be able to return from their infidelity, as the Apostle says: 'How shall they believe Him, of Whom they have not heard? And how shall they hear, without a preacher?' (Romans X).[94] Thus, in the abovesaid words, Peter is sent out to convert all unbelievers. Because, however, it is sufficient to presume that the Prussians would prefer it if the infidels of neighboring lands not receive the Faith, because, according to their privileges, in that way, and in no other way, would they be empowered to invade the possessions of said infidels, so do they entirely exclude them from conversion and admittance to the pastures of the Church, falsely asserting that they are not to be included in the words of the Lord 'Feed my sheep.' For if that were true, Pope and Church would have no right to mix themselves up with their conversion. Any of the faithful will know just how heretical that is. This from Master Mauricius.

Now,[95] the fact that in the proofs they attempt to set forth for the abovesaid conclusion they also assert that the Pope is bound to wage war against such infidels as do not recognize his authority or that of the Emperor, as they assert them to be pertinacious in their resistance and rebellious, which statement is in concord with conclusion XVI of Brother Johannes Falkenberg, not only is this erroneous in good morals in virtue of how it teaches and encourages the unjust oppression of men, and also contrary to natural law, but further, as it violates the precept of keeping peace contrary to the words of the Apostle (Romans XII):[96] 'If it be possible, as much as is in you, have peace with all men,' etc., it is heretical. Hence St Gregory, in treating of these very words of the Apostle, says: 'The Apostle, wishing to say that we should have peace with all men, yet foreseeing how difficult this is, prefaces the words with "if it be possible," adding thereto in further qualification "as much as is in you"' (which was taken over into the canon *Inter verba*: XI question III). And he who says 'all' makes no exception of any (*De maioritate et obediencia*: *Solite*). Further, the saying in question excludes the Beatitude, coming out against the words (Matthew V):[97] 'Blessed are the peacemakers,' i.e. those who love peace. For they include violence in their assertion, against the Decalogue, and their take on the office of the Supreme Pontiff is repugnant to this (John X):[98] 'Other sheep I have that are not of this fold: them also I must bring,' etc., where the verb 'must,' although it seems to imply necessity, still, this should not be understood as enjoining war or fighting as they pretend by their assertions. Hence we read (in the canon *Qui sincera*: XLV distinction) that one is rather to act so that, provoked by reason and gentleness, they should wish to follow us, not flee us. For Moses goes not to war nor does he fight against his enemies, rather, he prays, and as long as he endured in prayer his people were victorious (the words are to be found in the canon *Si quis sacerdotum*: XXXVI distinction), whose example others, especially Supreme Pontiffs, ought to follow. Finally, as in another proof it is asserted, as it is in this conclusion, that the infidels are in truth beasts and as if lacking in reason, have abandoned the true God to worship idols, believe in a multitude of gods, blaspheme against Christ and persecute Christians, usurping their rights and occupying their lands and surpassing all beasts in their ferocity, etc., and that this appears to be naturally rooted in them — by this statement the author of the pamphlet seems to contradict himself. For if such things are naturally rooted in the infidels, it follows that they are not to be warred against by Pope or anyone else on such grounds. For according to Aristotle (2nd *Ethics*) those things that are natural to us are neither to be lauded nor vituperated, and indeed, to root these vices in nature is to impugn the very First Principle, *scilicet* God, Who, on the contrary, according to Evangelical truth, created all things good! In consequence, such a statement cannot be seen as anything but blasphemy against the Creator.

From these things it is gathered that said conclusion, with its so-called proofs, is false, cruel, and erroneous in good morals and in faith.

The second conclusion is: 'By no title whatsoever are jurisdictions, dominions, principates, and the honors of kingdom, principalities, and realms possibly to be found *de iure* amongst such infidels as utterly refuse to acknowledge the dominion and supremacy of Church or Empire.'[99] And this concurs with a saying of Johannes Falkenberg's, the tenth conclusion in the fourth proof.[100]

To this second conclusion Master Mauricius responds: As by the first conclusion the pamphleteer strives to strip the infidels of the vestment of faith due them by predestination, following such spoliation of the soul he strives in consequence to despoil them of corporal possessions by the second conclusion, which is even more heretical than the first. And because this conclusion is the foundation of the error as a whole, *viz.*, of the conclusions that follow, for this reason we must even more diligently overthrow it by the following argument:

The result of this conclusion is formal heresy, that means, the conclusion is heretical even in all of its parts. This reasoning holds on the basis of the terms, and the antecedent is evidenced in relation to the whole, for it follows that in jurisdictions, etc.: Thus the faithful subject to infidel superiors may withdraw their obedience to them on the grounds of their infidelity. Thus, according to the binding consequence of this conclusion, because of their sin of infidelity, the infidels cease to be lords. By the same reasoning, a bishop in the state of mortal sin, by virtue of his infidelity to God ceases to be bishop and lord — and these ideas are the articles of Wycliffe, which were condemned at the Council of Constance.

Second, this conclusion recalls the ancient heresy of the Jews who refused to recognize the authority of the Emperor on account of his infidelity, for which reason they posed the question to Christ: 'Tell us therefore what dost Thou think: is it lawful to give tribute to Caesar, or not?' (Matthew XXII).[101] For they along with this pamphleteer, reckoned that Caesar, as an infidel, could not possibly have dominion over them, which, however, Christ determined to the contrary, reducing them to subjection to their lord, saying 'Ye hypocrites, show me the coin of the tribute,' which when they did He asked them whose image and inscription they found on the denar, and to their response, 'Caesar's,' He concluded 'Render therefore to Caesar the things that are Caesar's, and to God, the things that are God's,' expressly teaching thereby that they were to acknowledge as their lord the infidel Caesar, who did not recognize the authority of the Church such as it was among the Jews of that time, to whom He said: 'the kingdom of God shall be taken from you' (Matthew XXI).[102] And this is confirmed, Christ paying to the infidel Caesar the tribute on His own behalf as well as that of Peter (Matthew XVII),[103] by which He taught the ecclesiastics to recognize the dominion of the infidels. Similarly, Joseph and Mary submitted to the census of the infidel Caesar (Luke II).[104] And we read that Saint Mauricius along with his companions declared to Maximian: 'We are your soldiers, Caesar, but also the servants of God, which we freely confess. We owe you our military service, but our guiltlessness we owe to Him.' Hence we also read that Christ said to His Apostles: 'when they set you before kings and governors' who recognize not the authority of the church, 'meditate not before, how you shall answer' (Luke XXI).[105]

Thus Christ recognized kingdoms and princely power amongst the infidels.

Likewise, Christ recognized the dominion and jurisdiction of the infidel Pilate over him, who did not recognize the authority of the Church, saying: 'Thou shouldst not have any power against me,' etc.[106] And consequently, He recognized the dominion of Pilate to derive from the dominion of the infidel Emperor who did not recognize the authority of the Church, as He added to Pilate, 'unless it were given thee from above,' i.e. by the Emperor. Thus, Christ recognized dominion and jurisdiction among the infidels, who acknowledged not the authority of the Church.

Third, the kings of the gentiles lord it over them (Luke XXII).[107] Thus, among the gentiles there exist real kingdoms and dominions. This reasoning holds good on the basis of the opposite of consequence.

And it is confirmed because 'beneath' and 'above' are said to be correlatives. But as the pamphlet's conclusion has it, by not recognising the *imperium* of the Church, the infidel Pilate possessed no true authority, and by consequence, was not 'above.' Therefore, Christ did not suffer under him. This consequence is opposed to the Creed and thus heretical. For one of these premises is heretical: it is not the major premise, which is universally known by natural light, therefore it will be the minor premise, which contradicts the light of faith. Likewise, St Paul makes his appeal to the infidel Caesar (Acts XXV)[108] saying: 'I stand at Caesar's judgement seat, where I ought to be judged,' and later 'I appeal to Caesar.'[109] Now, this appeal is worth nothing unless it is made to an ordinary who has jurisdiction. Therefore, St Paul recognized jurisdiction as belonging to an infidel Caesar who recognized not the dominion of the Church. Likewise, seeing that some of the faithful seemed to smack of the same error as found in the conclusion, St Peter let it be known that they were to recognize infidel kings and princes as their lords and kings, honoring them as well, saying: 'Honor the king, be subject to your masters with all fear, not only to the good and gentle, but also to the froward, be subject to every human creature for God's sake, whether it be to the king as excelling, or to governors as sent by Him' (I Peter 2).[110] On his part, Paul asks that supplications and prayers be offered for kings and all that are in high station, that we may lead a quiet and peaceable life, for this is good and acceptable in the sight of God our Savior, Who will have all men to be saved (I Timothy 2).[111] Now, during the days of the Apostles Peter and Paul there were no kings and governors who were not infidels, none of whom recognizes the dominion and authority of the Church, and in regard to those the Apostles confess that they possess true kingdoms, jurisdictions, rule over lands, the honors of kingdom and dominion — against the aforesaid conclusion. Thus, as the recognition of the Apostles is Catholic, it follows that the pamphleteer's conclusion is heretical.

And this is confirmed, because in the days of Christ, temporal kingships and dominions in the world were real, as He said 'when they set you before kings and governors' not acknowledging the authority of the Church, and, according to the Psalmist: 'the kings of the earth stood up, and the princes met together, against the Lord and against His Christ' (as adduced in Acts IV).[112] For such dominions the Church had not, as Christ says: 'My kingdom is not of this world. If my kingdom were of this world, my servants would certainly strive that I should not be delivered' (John XVIII).[113] Therefore, true kingship is to be found amongst the gentiles, and natural dominion, distinct from the dominion of the Church, as the Savior pronounces:[114] 'The kings of the gentiles lord it over them, etc., but you not so,' in which words He does not take away dominion from the Church, but qualifies and distinguishes it, there being a different mode of rule in the Church, as it is in respect to eternal beatitude, and another in the world, in respect to man's natural end, that is, springing from purely natural concerns. Considering which, if this pamphleteer had been aware of this distinction between the dominions of the world and that of the Church, he would never have posited his conclusion, by way of which he vehemently renders the Prussians suspect of seeking earthly rule under the cloak of ecclesiastical dominion. Indeed, I reckon this ambition to be the cause of the composition of this little pamphlet, of which also the following conclusions reeks, which promote the secular dominion of the Church as founded upon the destruction of the kingship of the gentiles, with that natural aim as its goal. And however the supernatural aim never is quite simply a natural aim, still because of relativity it never ceases to be an aim in the manner in which Christ says of Himself (John VIII)[115] 'I am the light of the world.' For still this is not prejudicial to what He says to the Apostles (Matthew V):[116] 'You are the light of the world,' for this is to speak relatively, and of participation.

Thus Master Mauricius.[117]

And besides the above-adduced Doctor Ockham[118] (citied in the third part of his *Dialogues*, book one, chapter XXV), he refers to many other passages from Sacred Scripture pertinent to this proposition, and the sayings of sainted doctors, by which this error is made convincingly and manifestly clear. For example (Acts XXIIII)[119] what Paul says to Lydias the pagan: 'For many years thou hast been judge over this nation,' etc., where Paul acknowledges a pagan as a true judge, and thus of others. And because in the proofs on behalf of said conclusion it is asserted that on account of the unworthiness of the unbelievers all dominions, etc., have been transferred to the Christians, *scilicet* upon the advent of Christ: in this matter it is to be noted that varied and contrary opinions exist, of which two seem to be extreme and one intermediate.

The first is that although Christ is sometimes called a king in Holy Scripture, it is not in the sense of His having dominion over temporal goods, as a man. And even if He had, still He did not commit the same to Peter, and consequently, His vicar does not have power over them. For they say that Christ took upon Himself our poverty, just as He did our other defects, etc. Hence (John XVIII)[120] 'my kingdom is not of this world,' etc.

A second opinion is that of Ostiensis upon which said conclusion is seen to be based, which seems to purport that with the advent of Christ in the flesh, all jurisdiction, power, honor, and dominion were transferred from the unbelievers to the Christians. And to this the testimony of Scripture is manifestly opposed, as has been adduced above.

The third is intermediate and held, commonly, by canonists, *viz.*, that even if supreme and universal dominion over this world has been transferred by Christ to His vicar, as shall become clear from what follows, still (as is proven by I distinction: *Ius gentium*) by this transferral the natural rights of the gentiles by which lands and subaltern dominions of kingdoms have been made distinct and separate are not seen as being violated in any way. Hence St Thomas (*Secunda Secunde*, question IX, article X) states that although it is legitimate that infidels be not constituted again as lords or prelates over the faithful on account of the danger this would present to the Faith, nevertheless, by the same token the pre-existing dominion which they previously held over the faithful is not taken away. And he himself says 'over the faithful,' therefore all the more is this true in the case of their power 'over the unfaithful,' as he says: 'Dominion and prelacy have been introduced by human law, *scilicet* by the laws of the gentiles, whereas the distinction between faithful and infidel comes of divine law. Now, divine law, which comes of grace, does not do away with human law, which comes of natural reason, and on this account infidelity is not repugnant to dominion.'

And although said pamphleteer[121] appeals to Oldradus and Johannes Andreae in support of his conclusion, both of these determine against him, *viz.*, Oldradus in his *Questiones* (question LXXII, which begins with the words 'An contra Saracenos Yspanie,' etc.), and Johannes Andreae (in the chapter *Si a subdelegato*: *De officio delegati*, book VI, on the gloss *Quid dicas*), *scil.*, that even infidels outside the Church possess jurisdiction. What is more, one reads and notes (XXIII question I, canon I), that Andreas and Johannes state that a sentence of excommunication has no power beyond the Church, whereas judgments in civil and criminal cases are binding beyond the Church (argument XI question III: *Iulianus*, noted as well in XXIII question I at the beginning, and the canon *Quisquis*).

And from these things noted above it is evidently clear that the aforesaid conclusion is simply false, and sins not only in the light of canon law, but is also contrary to natural law and divine law, and thus manifestly heretical.

His third conclusion is of no interest here, and for that reason shall receive no response.

The fourth conclusion.[122] '*De iure*, the Emperor wields the very same power over the infidels as over the faithful, especially as far as his use of the exercise of the material sword is concerned.'

This conclusion seems to be based on the second of these extremes, and in effect is in concord with the sixth conclusion of Johannes Falkenberg.[123] Now, concerning this conclusion and certain of my writings against it, the calumnies of some have been directed at me, as if my intent was the diminution of imperial power, as something erroneous. Yet the opinions I adduce there are not of my own invention, but come of the greatest doctors of both laws and exegetes of canon law, whom I quote in the matter.[124] And so that the truth should be more plainly seen, it seems that three things must be considered closely, for a clearer understanding.

The first is the question of whether or not all Christians ought to be subject, or ever were obliged to be subject, *de iure*, to the Emperor in temporal matters, as said conclusion firmly suggests.

And if so:

2) if the same is true of all infidels. And if so:

3) whether or not the Emperor might dispose of their temporal things or dominions as he pleases, in the same way as an owner may dispose of his own property — because in this the foundation of the Prussian Knights of the Cross seems to consist.

On the first questions, *viz.,* whether or not all Christian kings or princes ought to be subject to the Emperor, opinions are at odds. Oldradus determines for the negative (in his *Questiones*, question LXIX), where he speaks above all of the kings of Spain and France, etc., and there see what he says concerning the origin of the Empire. But as to this question I will say no more in reference to our proposition, but move on, rather, to the second.

Concerning which it is to be noted that some posit a dual power or supremacy in this terrestrial world, of which they say that one does not depend upon the other, nor is one subordinate to the other but both come immediately of God, *viz.,* the authority of the Pope in spiritual matters, and the authority of the Emperor in temporalities. And according to others it is said that the Empire was indeed established of God, but still it was instituted by men, *viz.*, by the Romans (XVII distinction: *Concilia*, in the gloss *Habet ergo*). And as evidence of this opinion we have XCVI distinction: *Cum ad verum*, where 'As to the truth, i.e. Christ' it arrives that neither the Emperor shall arrogate to himself the rights of the Pope, nor shall the Pope usurp the name Emperor. And in *Autentica* (*De consulibus*, final § coll. IV) it is said that God has sent the Emperor as if the law animate upon the earth, whereby it is argued that the Emperor is instituted of God (in *Autentica*: *Quomodo oportet episcopos*, at the beginning, coll. V). Hence it is that the Son of God Himself acknowledged the rights of the Emperor as conceded to him by celestial ordination, and proceeded to pay the tribute money, stating that what belongs to Caesar must be given to Caesar, and what is God's, to God (Matthew XXII[125] and XI question I: *Magnum*). Likewise, this is alleged: 'Put up thy sword into the scabbard' (John XVIII),[126] which is also alleged for the contrary. Likewise, that the Emperor is lord of the world and thus other such statements, which, perhaps, might work to the good of the conclusion before us. But the great community of canonists assert the contrary: *scilicet* that both jurisdictions, the spiritual as well as the temporal, belong to the Pope (as proven in XXII distinction, canon I) where it is said that the laws and rights of the celestial and terrestrial empires have been committed to Peter. And in support of this opinion I shall adduce the sayings of some doctors.

Lord Anthonius de Butrio[127] (in the chapter *Novit*: *De iudicijs*, on the gloss II, which conforms to said gloss determining the same thing in this matter), in reference to *Qui filij sint legitimi*: *Causam* by Ostiensis, and the chapter *Per venerabilem* § *Racionibus*, and fully by Innocent, *De foro competenti*: *Licet*, by Johannes, X distinction: *Quoniam* and XCVI distinction: *Cum adverso* and the canon *Duo*; question VII § *Hijs ita*. and he says that this conclusion is commonly held by canonists.

My Lord Francis, Cardinal of Florence, says that the Church has approved this opinion, which has been determined upon in many chapters (especially *De maioritate et obediencia*; *Solite*; *De iudicijs*; *Novit*; *Qui filij sint legitimi*; *Per venerabilem*; *De eleccione*: *Fundamenta*; *De re iudicata*: *Aposolice*, book VI). And this is of the most ancient custom, and there is no memory to the contrary. And according to this authority the Pope, as the Emperor's superior, transferred the Empire from the Greeks to the Germans (accordingly as is noted in the gloss on the word 'transtulit': *De eleccione*: *Per venerabilem*), which transferral was carried out by Pope Stephen, who was later martyred (as we see in *Speculum Historiali* book 24, chapter LVI *et seq.*). It therefore must be admitted, according to this that the Emperor depends upon the authority of the Pope. For to him, the Pope, belongs the examination, approbation or rejection of him who is elected to the Empire. For even the election of the Emperor belongs to the princes, *scil.*, the electors of Cologne, Trier, Mainz, etc. (who are enumerated in *De re iudicata*, in the penultimate gloss of book VI), and thus by positive law, by papal concession (said chapter *Per venerabilem*), however Ostiensis expounds this *de iure*, i.e. by natural reason, which said Cardinal rejects. Thus this right given to said princes is confirmed by custom. Francis, Cardinal. Moreover, whenever there arise any difficulties in the case of contrary opinions, the doctor states that one should hold to what the Church says (for this see the text *De consuetudine*, the final chapter thereof; *De iuramento calumpnie*: chapter 1; *Qui filij sint legitimi*: *Per venerabilem*, where this case is clearly pronounced upon; see also the text *Ut lite non contestata*: *Quoniam* and what is noted in *De foro competenti*: *Licet*). And he who would assert the contrary, is, by the commandment of God, worthy of perishing an evil death (said chapter *Per venerabilem*); in which chapter Johannes Andreae says, following Ostiensis, that where ambiguity of opinion exists, one is to trust canon law over the sayings of the saints or learned men, because to the Pope and to no other is given the interpretation of doubts of this sort, since it is unto him that even the Emperor has recourse (Codex: *De Summa Trinitate*, at the end, likewise Ostiensis). And here the Abbot castigates those legalists who do not base their opinions on cases expressly terminated by a decretal.

In the chapter *Solite*: *De maioritate et obediencia*, Johannes de Lignano[128] says that in this matter laws and canons are well introduced both pro and contra, but he places not much trust in either as the Pope enacts decretals and the Emperor laws and no one is a proper testifying witness in his own case. And thus he sets forth his reasoning (here, and even better in the chapter *Novit*: *De iudicijs*, on gloss II at the end), *scilicet* that both powers reside in the Pope, arguing thus: 'I suppose one thing: that there ought to be one universal ruler in the world, because among things in the universe having an essential order, differing among themselves by species, it is impossible for two to be equally perfect. This is because if they were repugnant one to the other, destruction would be the result, while if they were peers, one would therefore be superfluous, and if they were disparate, ergo, they would not be equal. But as the Emperor is not the greater, therefore, greater is the Pope. For beings do not wish to be badly disposed, a multitude of princes is evil, hence there must be but one prince (this deduction is made by the Philosopher in XII *Metaphysics*, where he demonstrates that there is but One). But the principate of the Pope is spiritual, that of the Emperor, temporal, and as temporalities are ordered towards spiritualities as toward their proper end (I question III, *Si quis obiecerit*), therefore, the authority of the Pope is both spiritual and temporal. This consequence holds, as it implies both end and what is ordered to that end (*ff De procuratoribus*, read *Ad legatum* and *Ad rem*). This is confirmed: the papal authority is over souls, the imperial over bodies. But the soul animates the flesh as the master the slave (as is clear from II *Politics*), hence the master of the master is also the master of the slave. The consequence holds by the rule: If I conquer your conqueror I conquer you as well (*De concessione prebende*: *auctoritate*, book VI). This confirms that the Pope is the lord of the soul and its operations, the Emperor of the body, therefore, of the instrument of the operations of the soul, therefore, etc. The consequence holds because the principal agent is more perfect than the effective agent, as the woodcutter is superior to the axe (II question VII § *Item Balaam*). Likewise, the principate of the Pope is infused by God (XXII distinction, *De novo*), whereas the principate of the Emperor by man (XCIII distinction: *Legimus*), thus the immediate effect of God exceeds the effect of man, arguing from nobility of cause and on nobility of effect (*De celebracione misssarum*: *Cum Marthe*). Likewise, Christ possessed all power and authority, Peter was Christ's vicar, therefore, he came into possession of all power and authority of all sorts. This consequence holds because the vicar enjoys the same consistory as the ordinary (*De consuetudine*, chapter II book IV). Likewise, it is demonstrated that there should be one sole prince, because the optimal principate is there, where one prince chiefly rules (as is demonstrated in II *Politics*) and as is proven by the example of the steward (as we find in I *Economics*). It is therefore necessary to have one sole prince in the world. But this prince cannot be the Emperor, as nothing that is spiritual pertains to his authority, hence it must be the Pope. Likewise, the terrestrial regimen ought to be uniform with the celestial regimen, as on this latter all nature depends (*De Summa Trinitate* chapters I and II and *Meteorologiarum* and I *Celi*), but to the regimen celestial it belongs to arrive, in corporal species, to the most noble celestial sphere, towards which all inferior spheres tend: thus to the species of spirituals it belongs to arrive at the noblest principle upon which all depend together (as in the chapter just adduced). Now, even the noblest of bodies are the instruments of the noblest spirituals, as from that source proceeds all that is spiritual and corporal, thus, therefore, just as it is incumbent upon all in the terrestrial regimen to arrive at the temporal principle, which is the Emperor, so does everything tend thence further to the spiritual principle, which is the Pope. Thus, the Emperor will be the instrument of the Pope. Likewise, arguing from the lights of heaven, the sun illuminates the day and the night, the day by itself, and the night through its minister, *scilicet* the moon; hence, according to the varied aspect of the moon in relation to the sun, the light of the moon varies. Thus, the Pope illuminates the day, that is, the soul, by himself, and the night, that is, the dark temporalities, by his minister, i.e. the Emperor.' Thus Johannes de Lignano infers that authority is one, and it belongs to the Pope, while that of the Emperor follows as it were in its footsteps. Johannes de Lignano.

From these it follows that the monarchy of this globe belongs to the vicar of Christ, who *de iure* possesses both swords, as in custom and origin jurisdiction in regards to laypersons belonged to the Church, but by divine sanction, jurisdiction as to the exercise or actual power in temporal matters was bestowed upon the Emperor by the Church (XCVI distinction: *Cum ad verum*), in line with which Lord Antonius de Butrio, following Innocent, states (in the chapter *Licet*: *De foro competenti*): "The Supreme Pontiffs did not establish this for themselves, but such has been established from the beginning. For in the beginning God created both Heaven and earth and all that they contain, angelic and human nature, spiritualia and temporalia, and these did He rule by Himself as the creator governs his creation, and the goods he creates. Likewise, He gave commandments and established penalties for their transgression (Genesis II: 'Of every tree,' etc.).[129] And indeed He did punish the transgressors, *scilicet* Adam and Eve (Genesis III, where 'To the woman also He said,' etc., and where 'And to Adam He said,' etc.)[130] and thus did He rule Himself, directly, up until Noah, at which time God began ruling His creatures through His ministers, the first of Whom was Noah, and that he was governor of the people is shown by God entrusting him with the government of the ark, which signifies the Church (Genesis IV and VI).[131] Likewise, Noah endowed his sons too with government and laws (Genesis IX),[132] where also, although he had not been a priest (as we read), still he exercised the sacerdotal office in that immediately upon exiting the ark, before he presented his people with the law (Genesis VIII, where 'And Noah built an altar unto the Lord,' etc.),[133] he constructed an altar, which belongs to the sacerdotal office. Abraham did the same, as did Cain before him. In this vicariate there succeeded judges, patriarchs, kings, priests, and others who for a time ruled the nation of the Jews and this endured until the advent of Christ Who was and is our natural Lord and King, of Whom the Psalm says 'Give to the king Thy judgement, O God,' etc.[134] And (Isaiah XXXIV)[135] 'For the Lord is our judge, the Lord is our lawgiver, the Lord is our king.' And Jesus Christ Himself constituted Peter and his successors His vicar when He gave him the keys of Heaven and said to him 'Feed my sheep.'[136] And thus however many distinct the offices and regimens of this world, still, wherever such be necessary, recourse must be made unto the Pope, for example, when doubts arise, or in questions of alleged injustice, or where the administration of justice is seen to be neglected by Emperor or any other secular judge." Thus Antonius de Butrio, following Ostiensis.

But here we may ask, if it is true that the Church possesses both swords in power and custom, why not in act and execution as well?

The answer: The Church did indeed execute the temporal sword at one time through its priests (XI question I: *Relatum*). However, because a minister of the New Testament is a minister of gentleness and the sacrament of unity, and the Sacrament of the altar represents the union of Christ and His Church which in turn signifies the union of the soul and the body, because the soul vivifies the body just as Christ in His Sacrament vivifies the Church, thus the execution of the temporal sword, which divides the soul from the body, does not at all agree with the minister of the sacrament of unity. This is adduced by Johannes Andreae (in the chapter *Novit*: *De iudicijs*), according to Antonius de Butrio (John XVIII)[137] 'Put up thy sword into the scabbard.' And Johannes Andreae also cites St Bernard's letter to Pope Eugenius, in which he says 'Approach your subjects in word, not in deed. Why do you attempt to reach for the sword which you were once commanded to put up into the scabbard?' and (I Timothy chapter 3):[138] 'It behoveth a bishop to be no striker,' for Bernard (see above) states 'The Pope has the material sword at his disposition, the Emperor has it in his command, and the soldier wields it in his hand.' And this too is indicated by the bull of Boniface that begins with the words 'Unam Sanctam.' Antonius de Butrio; likewise Francis, Cardinal of Florence.

And therefore the Church has transferred the execution of the temporal sword to the Emperor and other kings, and having transferred it, can no longer exercise it herself, for we transfer to others that which it is not for us to retain (XXI question II: the fourth; X question I: *Te quidem*). And according to this the imperial jurisdiction also proceeds from God, because it was the will of God that it be exercised by the Emperor and in this way proceed the laws which state 'he impedes him not in temporal jurisdictions, except in certain cases,' etc. And in this way the canon *Cum ad verum*: XCVI distinction is understood, adduced in contrariwise. And furthermore, something of this was observed before the age of Grace, accordingly, from the time following upon Rome's vindication of its empire, whence proceed the arguments by which something may be inferred concerning the independence of Emperor and Pope, according to my Lord Francis, the Cardinal of Florence, who also notes (in the chapter *Venerabilem*: *De eleccione*), that many sharp minds have vexed themselves with this question, inquiring after the beginnings of the terrestrial monarchy, producing many books and many studies on monarchy, but no dispute can be more useless, according to him, because the truth is that the empire was obtained by the Romans through their oppression of other peoples; thus too was the case with other realms which held monarchical sway, such as the Babylonian kingdom and the realm of the Macedonians, which flourished under Alexander, and that of Carthage, which flourished at the time that Hannibal, the Carthaginian general, was devastating Italy, as is clear from Titus Livius in his book on the Second Punic War. There is another work *On Monarchy* too which strives to prove that the power of both swords has always been with the Supreme Pontiff, in the Old Testament as well as in the New; there has also been another book *On Monarchy* that Dante, the Florentine poet, composed. And because he was a Ghibelline he strove to show that the empire in no way depended upon the Pope — it was on account of this tractate that he was close to being burnt at the stake as a heretic. Thus Cardinal Francis.

Lord Petrus de Ancarano[139] (in his discussion of Chapter I of *De constitucionibus*) states that this distinction is equally worthy of general consideration: that there are two jurisdictions, and that in ancient times there appeared to be no doubt concerning which was greater and superior to the other, although as time passed and discords and dissensions arose between the Supreme Pontiffs and the Emperors it was declared that to the Pope belongs the power of both swords, and superiority over the Empire. And this is why it is he who crowns and anoints the Emperor, and sometimes deposes him as well. And this is proven by the most recent laws (in the chapter *Ad apostolice*: *De re iudicata* book VI and *Clementina Pastoralis* towards the end in the same title, and *De iure iurando*: *Clementina* I, and more fully in the bull of Boniface VIII beginning with the words 'Unam Sanctam'). Likewise, during a vacancy of the imperial throne, the pope assumes secular jurisdiction (as in the chapter *Licet*: *De foro competenti*, and there what is noted by Innocent). And Petrus de Ancarano adds: But someone might say: these Roman Pontiffs are making statutes in their own favor, and should not be trusted as no one ought to be judge in his own case, nor witness nor arbiter (as in the Codex: *Ne quis in sua causa*, in rubric and text, and *Nullus*: *De testibus*, brought into canon law in II question IV, etc.). To this Innocent responds (in said chapter *Licet*), as does Ostiensis more broadly (in the chapter *Per venerabilem*: *Qui filij sint legitimi*, and in his *Summa* of that same title § *Qualiter*, the first rubric). The former shows that authority is duplex: spiritual, which belongs to the Supreme Pontiff and secular, at the head of which is the king (to this see *De etate et qualitate*: the penultimate chapter and VI distinction: *Duo*). Now, the spiritual authority precedes the temporal in triple wise: by dignity or majority, in so far as the spirit is greater than the flesh (*De translacione*, chapter II), whence the patriarch Abraham, as the minor party, offered tithes to Melchisadech as his senior (Genesis XIV),[140] and Melchisadech, as his senior, blessed him (with which Hebrews VII concurs).[141] It is of prior institution, as the priesthood of Melchisadech precedes the written law (of which see the chapter *Translato*: *De constitucionibus*, supported by Exodus, Chapter XXVIII towards the end).[142] Likewise, royal power was ordained of God through the priesthood (1 Kings VIII towards the end),[143] where the Lord says to Samuel: 'Make them a king.' Thirdly, it has precedence by authority or power, because the spiritual establishes and judges the terrestrial (as in said chapter *Per venerabilem* where 'Know you not that we shall judge angels? How much more the things of this world?' originally from I Corinthians 6,[144] and XXVI distinction § *Ecce*). Beyond this it is proven by reason of order in said *Autentica*: *Quomodo oportet episcopos*, at the outset. For it is customary to give pride of place to the more worthy (*De maioritate et obediencia* chapter I and the chapter *Statuimus*). According to this it is proven by order of subject, for it is certain that as better fares the governed, so better is the governor considered (in *Autentica*: *De defensoribus civitatum* § *Nos igitur*). Now the soul, which the Pope governs, is to be set before all human things governed by the Emperor (as in codex *De Sacrosanctis Ecclesijs*, *Precipimus*). And finally, this superiority is proven by virtue of the Faith, for just as to accept two principates is heretical, so to accept that there are two equal vicars on the earth seems heretical as far as the law is concerned. Therefore, so that you should not be considered a heretic, let your faith be that just as there is one unchanging God (*De Summa Trinitatis* chapter I) so there should be one universal Vicar of his in the world. It makes no difference that these authorities proceed from the same principle and that the Empire, just like the priesthood, is of God. For the Empire comes not immediately of God, but as a due and subaltern emanation of the Vicar of Jesus Christ. Accordingly, the Apostle states (Romans XIII):[145] 'there is no power but from God,' or, to put it otherwise, the Empire, as he says, is a certain separation of temporal execution from the spiritual, and it is by God's disposition and will that these swords be exercised by divers hands, but these swords are in a certain relation one to the other in that the minor comes of the major.

And whatever is found concerning this distinction of two dignities, it should be understood as a division in fact, but not in law (as the text in the law *Inter tutores, ff De administracione tutorum* reads). Likewise, not only these two powers, but all authority comes from God, even evil authority — with His permission. Hence Christ to the governor Pilate during His Passion: 'Thou shouldst not have any power against me, unless it were given thee from above.'[146] By this, however in no way is done away with that order used in anointing, coronation, and other things of that sort (on which see in *Clementina* I : *De iureiurando*). For this order is kept in regards to kings (*De sacra unccione*, chapter I), and Saul was anointed of Samuel (as we see in I Kings VIII[147] and I question II Judges). Hence if such sacerdotal unction is necessary to the essence of any king whatsoever, all the more so is this true of the essence of him who is above all kings (VII question I: *In apibus*). The Empire is therefore of God as its prime cause and of the vicar of God as of its secondary cause and something of an instrumental agent.

Accordingly, it is of little matter from this perspective that Christ paid the temple tax and commanded that Caesar be given what is his. For He paid the tax Himself so as to avoid scandal (Matthew XVIII[148] and XXVIII question I: *Iam vide*). For in qualifying His command with 'render unto Caesar the things that are Caesar's,' etc., what He commands is a relative command (as I Codex: *De Summa Trinitate*) by which He orders not that all things be given Caesar, but only that which is his — not everything. It is to be noted that, when questioned, He asked His interrogators to show him a coin, upon which He asked whose image and inscription were found thereon. And when the response came 'Caesar's,' it was then He said 'Render unto Caesar the things that are Caesar's,' commanding them thus to return his image to him and responding thus, perhaps, so as to avoid scandal. Nor is it of any moment here that He prohibited Peter the use of the sword, as He did not command him to cast it away, but rather to put it up into its scabbard, as if ordering him to set aside its exercise, but not prohibiting the possession of said authority, whereas of course we gather from another source that the power of both swords belongs to the Church alone by virtue of the words 'behold, here are two swords,'[149] *scilicet* in the Church, and Christ did not say that either of them was superfluous, but rather that they were sufficient.

Furthermore, the same Petrus de Ancarano poses the question, 'in what does this majority of the Pope consist in reference to the Emperor?' And he responds that, first, it consists in what I have said concerning approbation, anointing and consecration, whereby he consequently receives his administrative authority, even though others hold that he is capable of administration even before his approbation (as is noted in *Clementina* I: *De iure iurando* and fully by Oldradus in his question 21). Second, it consists in the maximum difficulty by which the Christian religion might suffer the most grave detriment, either entirely, or in part (as can be clearly seen, for example, from the chapter *Pastoralis*: *De re iudicata*, in the *Clementinae* and in said chapter *Per venerabilem* § *Racionibus* : *Qui filij sint legitimi*). For in such arduous situations it was necessary for one to provide for the common weal (II § *Novissime ff de iureiurando* and the chapter *Pro humani*: *De homicidio* book VI; supported by what Johannes Andreae notes in said chapter *Per venerabilem* on the word 'Casualiter' in *Novella* and the chapter *Quod super hijs*: *De voto* in the major gloss, verset 'Credimus tamen ymmo scimus' and the verset 'De Christianis autem' in *Novella*). But where such difficulty and the gravity of the business is not found, then the contrary has place: according to which the Pope has care over persons, things, and cases ecclesiastical, while their secular cases and things are in the purview of the Emperor, and it is his laws that are to be observed (as in *Leges sacratissime*, Codex: *De legibus*), in which manner the authority and jurisdiction between them are distinct. And he concludes that as far as exercise is concerned, said powers are distinct, but as to propriety both have been conceded to St Peter — although the exercise of the temporal sword has been committed by the Pope to the Emperor. Petrus de Ancarano.

For these things so presented, it is now easier to see that the Emperor possesses no jurisdiction or authority to exercise the temporal sword in regard to those infidels who do not acknowledge his rule, which is the root of the matter before us, because they are not temporally subject to him, but rather to the Pope (as is noted by Johannes Andreae and others, following Innocent, in Chapter I *De constitucionibus*). And even though by divine law they be subject to the Vicar of Christ potentially or passively, they are nevertheless not so actually or actively, *viz.,* by consent or any other natural act. And because the law obliges no person who is not in actuality a subject (as is noted in said chapter I *De constitucionibus*), the divine law, which said infidels never received, does not bind them to actual subjection of that sort, and consequently, the same is true of canon law and civil law. And as it is seen that no law obliges them to obedience to the Pope, it follows that the same is true in regard to the Emperor, whose power is subaltern and dependent on that of the Pope. For the Pope may transfer to the Emperor no more power than he himself possesses, and because he neither had nor has he himself any actual power, that is, reducible to a natural act, even those infidels, therefore, etc. Now the authority of the material sword, which is his by divine right as Vicar of Christ, which as St Bernard (in *Ad Eugenum papam*) says, is 'at his nod,' as noted above, is something he can neither abdicate nor transfer to anyone else, because by that very power he has been made superior to all others, and this he cannot transfer to any others, for in that regard he is quite passive. And so he transferred what he could transfer, what belonged to him, *scilicet* his power to act, to use, his right of exercise, and it is this right of exercise *scilicet* actual or executive power, i.e., that which is in respect to natural action, which is seen to be in the Emperor's possession in temporalities, and in respect to his subjects, as long as they are naturally disposed to the same. Therefore, as said infidels do not recognize this power or right of the Emperor's at all, *viz.,* by actual obedience or consent, and naturally, as no act of any agent is acceptable unless the passive receptor thereof is well-disposed in its regard, it follows that, *de iure*, such a power is of no effect over said infidels. This is also noted by learned men (said chapter I *De constitucionibus*) especially by Johannes Andreae writing in gloss IV, where it reads 'And thus the laws are to be respected by all' (Codex: *De legibus, Leges*), where he notes that, generally speaking, the Pope, the Emperor, the Saracens, and other pagans are exceptions to this rule. Johannes Andreae.

Hence, speaking of the same, my Lord Francis, Cardinal of Florence (in said chapter *Per venerabilem*), notes that said superiority or rule in the world arises in three ways: First, by the will of God revealed in some way to men; Second, by the consent of the governed; Third, by violence. The first and second of these are just; the third is not. According to the first, the authority of the Pope is justified, arising as it does from the authority given to the patriarchs in the Old Testament, and later taken up again by Christ and transferred to Peter and his successors. Moreover, this authority is justified in the second way in respect to Christians and those acknowledging the dominion of the Church, to which the entire Catholic Church, which is the congregation of all the faithful, assents, which is approved by the most ancient custom, nor does anything to the contrary exist in human memory. Now, as it generally cannot be said that the Empire is justified in the rule it claims over the aforesaid infidels in either the first or second manner, the Emperor cannot be said to possess, *de iure*, any sort of authority over said infidels, except in the third manner, by violence and tyranny, in which way the Romans subjected the entire world (or thereabouts) to their rule.

Thus, according to the Archdeacon, the Empire first commenced to be natural and legitimate at the time at which it began to belong to Christ and His vicar, before which it had been founded upon violence. And when it had been confirmed by the Church and also approved in the person of Constantine, who was the first Christian Emperor, it was then purged of its guilt of the violence and oppression it had originally committed, when Constantine, as stated in the *Chronicles* and as noted by the Archdeacon (X distinction: *Quoniam*) gave over into the hands of St Silvester the sword and regal insignia, as a sign that before him there had been no legitimate emperor, nor should there be in the future, unless approved by the Pope and the Church.

And by these statements, the response is made to the second question.

As for the third question, I shall deal with it in my response to the sixth conclusion.

Finally, as a proof of said conclusion, it is further asserted by way of conclusive deduction: 'Therefore, the entire world is governed thus: the Pope presides over spiritual things, and the Emperor over temporalities. Now, indeed, this conclusion tacitly negates the determination of the Church that the Pope possesses authority over both. And moreover, here it is again asserted that said infidels, of necessity, must observe the laws of the Empire, otherwise, they are to be forced to this by the sword, etc., which assertion is also erroneous, as it encourages tyranny, which is prohibited by divine law, and asserts many other unsuitable and untenable things.

From these it is gathered that the aforesaid conclusion, along with its proofs and assertions thus aforesaid, is collectively false. And as it does away with the rights of the Roman Church and those of others, it is intolerably bold. And in so far as it derogates the authority of the Supreme Pontiff, contrary to the determination of the Church, and, what is more, teaches tyranny, which is contrary to divine, natural, and human law, it is tyrannous and savours of heresy and cruelty.

The fifth conclusion:[150] 'Just as the unjust, contumacious, rebellious, and resistant among the faithful may be forcefully compelled by the Roman Emperor when no other way of coercing them exists, so the same sword may be legitimately employed against the infidels, by his declaring war upon them.'

This conclusion concurs with the IX and X conclusions of Brother Johannes Falkenberg. My response to it is sufficiently clear from the foregoing.

The sixth conclusion:[151] 'War may be licitly declared upon unbelievers who do not acknowledge the dominion and supremacy of the Roman Church or Empire *de facto*, especially so as to reduce them to due subjection and obedience.'

This conclusion, similarly to the other, is as easily spurned as proven. It also concurs with conclusions VII and VIII of Johannes Falkenberg. For the Emperor's authority, which he has over those actually subject to him, in that they should accept the same patiently as well-disposed thereunto, he does not exercise over the infidels. And thus, if he should act otherwise, as this conclusion teaches, this would be violence plain and simple, tyrannous and entirely irregular, contrary to divine, natural, and human law. And because infidels are not bound by divine law, canon or civil laws, as laws oblige no one save those actually subject to them, as has been said above, thus by no positive law are they held to acknowledge the superiority of Pope or Emperor. And thus, he who is not obliged to something cannot *de iure* be compelled to it (which is proven in *De baptismo*, chapter *Maiores* § *Verum,* the verset 'Sunt autem,' along with others similar thereto). Therefore, this conclusion, which gives licence to and encourages such a reduction to obedience, is tyrannical and contrary to natural and divine law. Such unbelievers cannot be termed enemies *eo ipso* simply because they do not acknowledge the dominion of Emperor or Pope, nor may they be considered to be in rebellion to the Church or the Empire. Not for this reason can they be attacked as this dreamer raves in his conclusions, because not to acknowledge something is a purely negative state that claims nothing; whereas to be a rebel or occupier or persecutor or enemy, etc., implies something positive, *viz.,* an act of persecution, etc., which, since it does not lie in a person naturally, and as there is no evidence of it, cannot be said to exist *de iure* (according to Innocent in the chapter *Dudum*: *De presumpcionibus*). And by consequence, infidels remaining within the bounds of the law of nature, which is not repugnant to the law of grace, cannot *de iure* be said to be persecutors or rebels to Emperor or Church, and thus numbered amongst our adversities. It is otherwise in cases where, *de facto*, they are in opposition to and perturb the Christians, etc. Nor can this conclusion be sustained even should one hold the opinion that maintains that the Empire is not dependent upon the Pope, but comes immediately of God, or was established through the mediation of the Romans and later transferred to the Emperor according to the statement that the Roman Church has its authority from God (XXI distinction: *Omnes*), but the Emperor from the people (IV distinction § *Leges*, in gloss I and XVII distinction: *Concilia*, in the gloss that begins *Habet ergo*), and that even the Romans transferred to the Pope the authority of installing the Emperor, so that, *scilicet* he should elect the Emperor himself or entrust said election to others. For according to this, although the whole world was at the time subject to the Roman Empire and the Empire itself has never been deprived of rule over any realm whatsoever, for that reason it should be *de iure* above all nations, and, by consequence, above all infidels, even though, according to this, the Emperor is said to possess the plenitude of authority in temporalities and that said infidels *de iure* should be subject to him: still and all he has no right to deprive them of their rights and dominions against natural law, *viz.*, without any regard to the order of law, the cause not being proclaimed and no concession being made to legitimate self-defense. Therefore, nor could he concede these things to the Knights of the Cross. Hence Innocent notes (in the chapter *Que in ecclesiarium*: *De constitucionibus*) that even though a prince may deprive someone of a suit *de facto*, *ex officio* a judge must nonetheless do justice to him who brings the suit, maugre the action of said prince. For such privation of the infidels as is pretended to here, by virtue of a sentence, obtains the quality of a verdict, and such a verdict, even if pronounced by the Emperor, is worth nothing if the party concerned is not summoned, as is noted in the final law of Codex: *De legibus*, and in the text of *Clementina Pastoralis* § *Ceterum*, the verset 'Non predicta supplecio: De re iudicata,' where the verdict was null and void because the party was not legitimately summoned, which is something contrary to nature and law. For judicial order is founded on just this. Because a summons is nothing else than a certain faculty of self-defense (*De maioritate et obediencia*: *Inter quatuor*; II question I: *Nos in quemquam* and the canon *Non sine* and the law *De unoquoque ff De re iudicata*). So to preclude the path of summons is to preclude the path of defense, and defense is a natural right and immutable, such that even a prince may not tamper with it (as in the final § of *Institucionibus*: *De iure naturale, gencium et civili*). And this is upheld by Laudensis in said *Clementina*, by Paulus de Leazaris and Genzelinus, and the gloss may be adduced here and lord Baldus as well (in the law *Princeps ff*: *Que sentencie sine appellacione rescindantur*).[152] Nor would the supplying of defects be to any account here (as we find in said *Clementina*). The rationale: because such a thing refers only to the formal, and not to the material order (as in the chapter *Illa*: *De eleccione*, and as is noted in *Speculum*, the title *De legato* § *Nunc ostendendum*, verset XVIII). It is therefore clear that such deprivations of the infidels is invalid, and in consequence, the donation pretended here is null.

Nor is the emperor the lord of all temporalities to the extent that it is licit or valid for him to dispose of the goods of another accordingly as he pleases. He may do so only in a cause in which the public good is served thereby, as has been expressed above in the first tractate. Hence Naboth the Israelite did not wish to give nor commute nor sell his vineyard to King Achab, for he saw that the king desired it not from any necessity nor in regard to the common good, but solely out of avarice and cupidity (III Kings XXI,[153] and taken over thence into the canon *Convenior*: XXIII question VIII). Nor is the mere fact of refusal to recognize the Empire sufficient cause to deprive the infidels of their dominions, etc. For in the beginning it was not because they failed to recognize their authority that the Romans subjugated others or deprived them of their dominions by waging war against them. Otherwise, they would be sinning grievously thereby, because such wars are illicit, the cause of which is the mere desire of domination (XXIII question I *Quid culpatur*): but rather according to the opinion that they wished not to consent that the Romans should govern the republic of the entire world (as such was expedient), and thus warring, *scilicet*, on behalf of the republic, the Romans were warring justly, justly subjecting those who resisted them, and acquiring just dominion, while those who resisted them were acting unjustly. Thus, the Emperor who claims to have the Empire given to him by the Romans ought not to do otherwise, because the cause that moves the delegating ought to move the delegate as well (as in the chapter *Super litteris*: *De rescriptis*). For, according to Aristotle (X *Metaphysics*), that which is first in every genus ought to be standard and measure for all other things pertaining to the same genus. For sometimes natural reason dictates that one Emperor should not govern all mortals, because in such a case he might be iniquitous and contrary to natural law when this manner of rule might be pernicious and detrimental to the republic and the common weal — which Ockham develops (Third part of his *Dialogues*, book I near the beginning). Hence although it is natural that the optimal principate be that, where one sole ruler chiefly rules (II *Politics*), nevertheless, in some cases it is better to relinquish such optimal regime as something that cannot be had, so that divers provinces be subject to divers princes. For such an optimal mode of government can be impeded by the ire or singular malice of the subject peoples, or on account of the iniquity or insufficiency of the manner in which said rule was assumed. For although all the world's people can form a community with each other in so far as temporal affairs are concerned, and therefore will not be optimally governed unless they are all subject to one prince, still it does not seem to be excluded thereby, that all those who do not wish such a community in common will be optimally governed only beneath one sole ruler. And according to Ockham, it is by the just judgement of God that mortal men have been ordained to be ruled by multiple princes, on account of man's sinfulness. And as it is for just such a reason that a universal government cannot be had today *de facto*, so it is expedient that, for now, it cease *de iure*. Now, as it is not expedient for one sole prince to govern the entire world republic, such being the case, the Emperor may not, *de iure* or licitly, wage war against the infidels in order to reduce them to obedience. Now, when is such expedient and when not? According to Ockham, although this is often hidden from men — especially from the inexperienced and the evil — all things are open and plain to God. And this is the reason why, although it was hidden from those more expert that it was not expedient for them to have kings (I Kings VIII):[154] 'make us a king, to judge us, as all nations have,' etc., their petition was displeasing unto God. For they should not have petitioned for a change in the manner of government ordained by God.

The seventh conclusion.[155] 'Warmaking as a remedy has its place against such infidels as impede the Christian faith, whether by evil blasphemies or by open persecution.' And it is stated that, in this form, the conclusion is that of St Thomas (*Secunda Secunde*, question X, article VIII), which he drags in here in support of his proposition. This conclusion is absolutely true in the sense in which St Thomas asserts it, but it contradicts the conclusion which precedes it as well as those which follow. For, in the sense in which it is distorted here, and for the aims for which it was forcefully introduced, it is false and cruel to the very foundations. This is clear from its conclusions, because those infidels who do not recognize the dominion of Church or Empire are said to impede the Faith, to blaspheme, to persecute, as well as other things here and in other conclusions set forth — but this is false and sins against logic, which states that no affirmative can proceed from a negative. And it is for this reason that such as do not acknowledge Church or Emperor cannot, on this basis, be inferred to impede the Faith or persecute it, etc. For persecution, rebellion, and impediments of such sort are rather something positive. And since after legitimate examination this does not seem capable of being understood here, it is not true that they impede or persecute, for it is one and the same here to appear and to be (*ff De contrahenda empcione et vendicione*: see *In lege*, and in the canon *Solempnitates*: *De consecracione*, distinction I, with others similar thereto). For such enunciative or narrative statements do not introduce, in law, any disposition, nor do they prove anything, according to Innocent (in the chapter *Recepimus*: *De privilegijs*, and what is proven in the same title *Si papa*: book VI in the *Clementina Si summus pontifex*: *De sententia excommunicacionis*; the codex *De probacionibus*: *Raciones*). As, therefore, there is no evidence of persecution by these infidels, or rebellion, or any impediment to the Faith, etc., there is no place for the remedy of warmaking against such infidels, as suggested in the proposal, which is false and counter to the mind of St Thomas as adduced here, and counter to the Apostle as well (Romans VII,[156] carried over into XXIII question I: *Nisi bella*), where the Apostle says that our warring is not against the flesh,[157] *scilicet* against pagans, as long as they are no longer wounding the Christian religion as they did in the past (according to the Archdeacon). Now, because my adversary says that this saying of the Apostle is to be understood as referring to those who recognize the dominion of the Church or the Empire, and thus do not usurp the rights of Christians, nor impede the Faith, nor are they presumed likely to do so in the future, and thus they live without any injury to the Catholics, of which pagans he says 'They are to be treated humanely,' whereas of others he speaks differently, response is made to this that, as can be gathered from the Scriptures, there is no special reason to make a distinction between these here and those there. For the aforesaid words of the Apostle, as well as any other laws or citations from Scripture, which either prohibit war or urge and advise peace (as that found towards the end of II Corinthians:[158] 'have peace, and the God of peace and love shall be with you,' etc.), speak without distinction, generally. And thus, generally and without making distinctions, should these be understood, which is proven by the laws (XIX distinction *Si Romanorum*) in the gloss that begins 'Argumentum quod verbo generali;' and where the law makes no distinction, then neither should we (LX distinction in the final canon; II question V *Consuluisti*, distinction XXXI, final canon). And thus the word 'wars' in said statement of the Apostle has a general application, and every word ought to be generally comprehended (I question I: *Sunt nonnulli*; XIV question III: *Putant*; XX question I *Dilectissimis* and XIII question II: *Non extimemus*). Therefore, etc.

Here it is to be noted that all laws, or at least the great majority of them, adduced here in support of these conclusions, ought to be understood in a contrary sense than that in which they are alleged; indeed, they should be understood as evidence against the conclusion.

The eighth conclusion.[159] 'The secular arm may be used to coerce infidels on account of their sin of idolatry, or their transgressions against the laws of nature, when there is no other way of correcting them, and such wars declared against them are just.' He goes on to state that this conclusion is that of Innocent and the doctors (in the chapter *Quod super hijs*: *De voto et voti redempcione*). Consequently, he says that although Innocent states that such a war is to be declared by the Pope alone, and by no other, unless the case is that of one acting in defense of his rights: nevertheless, he insists that it can be done by the Emperor or on his authority, as is apparent on account of his possessing the exercise of the material sword.

The ninth conclusion.[160] 'That which is said of pacific or gentle infidels, that such are not to be expelled or warred against by orthodox princes or other Christians, is to be understood only of those who without blasphemy, impediment to the Faith, idolatrous worship, or transgression of natural law, and persecution of Christians, *de facto* live under the dominion of Church or Empire, recognising their due authority.' And in support of this he states that such infidels as do not acknowledge the dominion, authority, and law of Church or Empire are trouble-makers and persecutors of the Faith, blasphemous enemies of Christians, hostile and pertinacious rebels, whose resistance is unjust. For this reason they are not, nor can they be said to be, pacific and gentle.

What the response to these aforesaid two conclussions ought to be is sufficiently clear from the foregoing.

It is by these nine conclusions aforesaid that he attempts to establish the authority of the Emperor in respect to the infidels, to the effect of providing the Prussian Knights of the Cross with justification for their warring, just as he proceeds to do in the conclusions that follow, where he would establish the donations supposedly made to their benefit. On which, see what has been said in the Topic section of the first tractate. But he fails in his hopeful scribbling of these insane falsities, as can be seen, nor can they be saved or established in any way. And thus also this pamphleteer is not seen as being excusable from the guilt of error. Hence St Thomas says (in the Quodlibet to one of his conclusions) that in things that pertain to the Faith or to good morals no one is excused for following an erroneous opinion, for facile assent in dubious matters is not to be given. Now, he who assents to the opinion of any master who manifestly speaks contrary to the testimony of Scripture, or likewise, contrary to what is publicly held to, according to ecclesiastical authority, cannot be absolved of the guilt of error, etc.

The tenth conclusion.[161] 'The battling of the Knights of the Cross of the Teutonic House of the Hospital of the Blessed Virgin in Jerusalem, which is undertaken with the authority of Pope or Emperor, truly on their behalf and in the name of all Christendom, against said in fidels at this time, cannot be justly blamed, nor reproved by anyone as illicit.' Said Johannes Falkenberg concurs with this in his XV, XVII, and XVIII conclusions. His proof: because such are blasphemers and troublers of the Faith, etc., as said above. Likewise, he assets that this warmaking of theirs enjoys the common approval of the Holy Fathers and Catholic princes and God's Church; is legitimized by the establishment of these Knights of the Cross for this very purpose, and by the concessions provided them for this purpose by divers privileges, and the aid given them by Kings, princes, and other of the faithful gathered unto them, as he said is noted in fact. Likewise, he would prove that because this sort of warmaking is in line with all that is required for the justification of a war as just:[162] the authority of princes, *viz.*, Pope and Emperor; likewise: just cause, as they are fighting against idolaters, transgressors of natural law, troublers of the Faith, bold usurpers of the rights and lands of Christians, rebels and unjust resisters, as has been earlier brought forth; likewise, on account of their righteous intent, *scilicet,* chiefly the honor of God, the peace and safety of Christians, the preservation and spread of the Faith, the recuperation of the rights and goods of Church, Empire, and the Catholic faithful, as well as the restraint and emendation of error; moreover, he stresses the fitness of these persons to the task of fighting, as thy have been chiefly established with this aim in mind, and marked with the sign of the Cross to do battle against the enemies of the Cross of Christ, etc. beyond this, he adduces a multitude of other horrible proofs, erroneous in both law and Faith, adding towards the end that if many fall at their hands in such a war, this is the result of their own stubbornness. He also introduces many things that speak against the aforesaid conclusion, resolving the same by the aforesaid distinction made, i.e. that all of this is to be understood according to whether or not the dominion of the Church or the Empire is acknowledged.

This tenth conclusion is quite simply false, as are its proofs, and, in rationalising the unjust war of the Knights of the Cross, which is directly contrary to divine law, he thus defends error, is erroneous in both good morals and in faith, and thus also clearly heretical. The falsity of the very supposition is obvious. For he supposes that all such infidels are blasphemous, idolatrous, persecutors of Christians and occupiers of their lands, etc., which, as this does not seem to be understood, *de iure*, as being true, as is said by the laws alleged above, it consequently follows that the conclusion is to be absolutely rejected. For said infidels are not to be understood *de iure* as impeding the Faith, blaspheming against God, etc., unless the evidence thereof is obvious, and because such proposals as must be resolved to facts and verified by factual evidence cannot be said to be true unless evidence of that truth is apparent, and this in one of two ways: either to the senses or the intellect, and because such evidence cannot be apparent to our senses unless that would be to our corporal senses, i.e. that we should see them with our own eyes worshipping idols and hear them with our own ears blaspheming, etc., and as it cannot be said to be apparent to our intellect unless it be demonstrated by legal process and declared so in legitimate law, then, as from the foregoing we have no evidence of such facts in this case, *scilicet* facts apparent to our exterior senses, or legal evidence apparent to our intellect, such things cannot be affirmed as true or notorious merely according to the dreams of this pamphleteer as presented in his proofs. Therefore, etc.

From these it is evidently clear that his statement is erroneous and contrary to what it alleges, in that it would provide excuse for sin, *viz.,* stating that all qualifications to consider this war a just one are present, whereas the opposite is true. For all that is required to declare this war just are lacking here: indeed, all point to the war being unjust: *viz.,* authority, object, cause, animus, and persons (XXIII question II in the summation).

Because it cannot be said that any authority intervened here, given the falsity of the texts, which prove nothing; and even if such were proven, still, according to Ostiensis, the error of a superior excuses nothing (in his *Summa*: *De treuga et pace*, § I, the versicle 'Item error').

For anyway, this warmaking of theirs is not carried out for the recuperation of things or the defense of the fatherland, but rather for the acquisition of the lands of the infidels, their subjection and extermination, as is clear from their own articles and the aforesaid letters, and that this manner of waging war is a sin is proven by XXIII question I: *Militare*, where, following Augustine, it is stated that warfare is not sinful in and of itself, but to make war so as to loot is indeed a sin. And while it is no crime to defend the common weal, it seems damnable to wage war so as to augment wealth.

It is also unjust by cause: for the fighting here is not being waged out of necessity, and necessity is the cause of a just war; no, this is freely-willed aggression, entirely so, and thus contrary to Augustine who says that one should have a will to peace, and go to war only from necessity. For peace is not fostered so that war might be waged, but war is waged so that peace might be enjoyed (XXIII question I: *Noli existimare*).

Furthermore, it is clearly unjust from its spirit, for here we have not only the lust to dominate and to subject the territories of infidels to oneself, but the hunger to loot the goods of others and to occupy another's lands — which is criminal warfare (on the same, also the question *Quid culpatur*, where it is stated that three things are reprehensible in war: *scilicet* the lust to kill, the cruelty of vengeance, and the itch to dominate, etc.).

Fifthly, it is unjust as far as persons are concerned. For these men claim to be religious, and if it is damnable for men who are not religious and profess no vows to engage in this sort of warfare, the same is all the more true for religious on account of their vows. And even granting — without prejudice to the truth — that to do battle with infidels who do not recognize the Empire, etc., with the aim of recuperating lands or rights belonging to the Empire (as is here claimed) were licit or just, still, this would not belong nor could it belong to the religious life, but rather is proper to secular warriors, because such business is not that of religion, which is rather to be immediately concerned with directing oneself to the honor of God and divine worship.

But this warfare is directed at the warriors' own private comfort, *scilicet* to subject said infidels directly to themselves, as clearly appears from their letters and articles. Thus St Bernard, writing to the Templar militia, says that such warmaking is worldly and not religious, stating (in chapter I): 'How truly sacred and safe is that warmaking that is free of the double danger to which men of this sort are frequently subjected, where the sole cause of warring is not Christ Himself! For however many times you engage in worldly warfare, it is wholly to be feared lest in slaying your enemy in the flesh, you slay yourself in your soul. Or perhaps you might be slain, in body and in soul. Indeed it is according to the disposition of the heart, and not the outcome of the war, that the danger or victory of the Christian is assessed,' etc. And because such battling or warmaking aimed at obtaining any worldly goods is contrary to the substance of religion and indeed contrary to all religion, according to St Thomas (*Secunda Secunde*, question CLXXXVIII, article III, and Johannes Andreae and the doctors in the chapter *Sane*: *De regularibus*) thus, this cannot, according to St Thomas, be deemed religion, but rather superstition.

For the religious state is such as, through it, one aims, by supererogatory acts, for example, at the perfection of charity, to which all such warmaking is repugnant, even should it be conceded that it is being carried out as an act of justice, *viz.*, justly despoiling infidels as occupiers, etc. For this does not seem to be based on love of one's neighbor, as the good of one's neighbor is not the principal object here, but it is one's own good advantage that one has here in mind, and this cannot be seen to belong to the active religious life.

By these statements all other things in the contrary argument are resolved. For it is extremely bold to ascribe such error to the Church of God, to the Holy Father or to orthodox princes, and to state that the Church has established this order for such activity, for such warfare, for example. What the truth is here is clear from the foregoing.

And because such warmaking, according to its quality, consists in a fact, and as it is understood that the Roman Pontifex is unaware of facts taking place in particular locales (*De constitucionibus*, chapter I book VI), nor is he understood to approve any order tacitly, but only when such approval has been clearly established (as is proven in *De religiosis domibus*, the final chapter, and the only chapter of the same title in volume II book IV), it follows, in fact, that no concession of any of the privileges granted to them argues for the establishment of their order. Hence the text (in the *Clementina Si summus*: *De sententia excommunicacionis*, II rubric) states, *viz.*, that should the Pope, in word, constitution, or writing, refer to anyone by name or honor anyone by such and such an address, it is not to be understood that by merely using the honorific, he is establishing them in any way, or providing them with any new rights. And therefore, however much the Pope may refer to said Brethren in his letters as the 'Brethren of the Order of the Blessed Virgin Mary of the Germans,' he is not thereby understood as having approved said order, unless such a wish to do so is clearly expressed (which is proven in said *Clementina* in text and gloss on the word 'tractet' and the word 'intelligitur' and the word 'iuris' according the laws there adduced). And because narrative statements induce no disposition (*De privilegijs*: *Si papa*, book VI), therefore, they are also unable to prove approbation in this way (as in the laws adduced). Now, as far as the allegation of the princes and other faithful gathering to their aid, the response is: that as such approbation belongs neither to them nor to any other, but only to the

Apostolic See (as is stated in the final chapter of *De religiosis domibus*, and in the same title, book VI), such a gathering does not indicate any approbation, nor does the frequency of such gatherings nor the multitude of those there congregated in any way diminish or excuse the error of said Brethren, as is plainly seen.

The Eleventh Conclusion.[163] 'In the war of the aforesaid Knights of the Cross, which they are currently waging against said infidels, it is just that they make over the infidels themselves, and their allies in the conflict, when captured, into slaves, and that the goods of the aforesaid, acquired by the Knights of the Cross, have been acquired justly.' This he would prove by the fact that these Knights of the Cross, mighty fighters and champions, have been specially instituted to this task, by edict of their ruler, and indeed are acting on behalf of the ruler himself. And that captives taken in such a war are *de iure* reduced to the condition of slaves of their captors (as in the law *Non dubito* and the law *Hostes ff De captivis*).

This eleventh conclusion is false, injurious, dangerous, and erroneously set forth in support of the aforesaid error, and for this reason suspect. In as much as it justifies such tyrannous and violent captivity against the commandment of the Decalogue, *scilicet* 'Thou shall not kill,'[164] by which all violence is prohibited, as is the acquisition of another's goods contrary to divine law, *scilicet* 'Thou shalt not steal,'[165] it is clearly seen how truly heretical is this dogma, false in the light of divine law, and contrary to Catholic truth. I stress that it is false, and this for two reasons: First, by reason of it being an unjust war, and captives taken in such a war are not *de iure* reduced to the condition of slaves of those who capture them. Second, by reason of the aforesaid Brethren themselves, who, by virtue of their vows, are incapable of dominion (see the chapter *Cum ad monasterium*: *De statu monachorum*, toward the end). Thus, such an acquisition of goods by them is not only illicit and unjust, but by virtue of the law itself null and void. By consequence, it is manifestly clear that this conclusion is dangerous to said Brethren and injurious to many others.

The twelfth conclusion.[166] 'It is meritorious and honorable for princes, nobles, soldiers, and other Christians to gather with the aforesaid Knights of the Cross so as to aid them in making war against the aforesaid wild rebels and impious infidels.' This concurs with the fourteenth conclusion of said Johannes Falkenberg, and with his second proof. And here among the proofs is stated: 'that those who fall in such a war on the side of those waging war on behalf of God merit the reward of Heaven,' etc.

This twelfth conclusion is just as false, overbold, and captious, set forth in order to seduce princes and other Christians in favor of said heresy so boldly posited. Moreover, it is contrary to Catholic truth, *viz.*, in that it would persuade the Christian faithful to gather for participation in such a war as is repugnant to the Faith and Sacred Scripture, etc. And for this reason, as it asserts that such is meritorious, commendable, and redounds to honor, whereas according to the truth it is seen to be illicit, damnable, and dishonest, it is impious, insane, and offensive to pious ears.

The thirteenth conclusion.[167] 'In the case of general indigence or necessity, it is incumbent upon the Church and Catholics in general to ensure that the aforesaid Knights of the Cross be not lacking in victuals, stipends, and all other necessities.' He would prove this by the statement that 'the cause of the Church of the Catholics is furthered by their warmaking against the infidels, as it is the former's security, peace, and common good, as well as the honor of God and the spread and preservation of the Faith that constitute their aim.' And he asserts that to this very thing they have chiefly been instituted, etc.

This thirteenth conclusion is likewise false, brash, and erroneous, aimed at the seduction of Christians, and nutritive of the same heresy. The proofs offered in support of it are in evident contradiction to the letters and articles of these Brethren introduced above.

The fourteenth conclusion.[168] 'The Church, and Catholics in general, ought not to ignore any injury offered to the aforesaid Knights of the Cross by biters, lacerators, or reprovers thereof, on the grounds of their warmaking and fighting, but rather to stifle the same.'

This conclusion is false and bold, an insult to masters and doctors, as well as to just judges to whom belongs the reprobation of errors. And indeed, as such reproofs are offered in this proposal of ours, whether magisterial or authoritative or judicial, as they are to be a canonical remedy for the removal of heresies and errors from the Church of God, which is here attacked in such fashion, in consequence it must be conceded that the entire Church is being tacitly attacked in this assault made upon her remedies. It logically follows that he who forbids such reproofs as mentioned above would necessarily prohibit the extirpating of the above-mentioned error. From which it can be clearly deduced that in this way this sacred Council of Constance, which was chiefly convoked, among other things, for the extirpation of heresies, is being opposed. By consequence, the aforesaid conclusion is disruptive of this sacred Council. And in so far as it urges the Catholics themselves to stifle the above-mentioned reprovers of this error, it is dangerous, and cruel, and impious, and insane, and offensive to pious ears.

HERE FOLLOWS THE SECOND PRINCIPAL PART OF SAID CONCLUSIONS, IN WHICH IT APPEARS THAT THE WAR OF THE POLES IS IMPUGNED BY THE FOUR CONCLUSIONS THAT FOLLOW.[169]

NOW WE MUST MOVE ON to the second principal part of this second tractate, in which we see the struggle of the Poles against the

Knights of the Cross reproved by the conclusions that follow. Now, because following the aforesaid war, it was public knowledge that a report was being spread by these Knights of the Cross amongst kings, princes, and other Christians containing false declarations, *scilicet*, that the King of Poland and the Poles had defeated them[170] with the aid of infidels, etc., therefore, so as to preempt the scandal such as might arise in the minds of the simple, on account of their ignorance of the law, I included in my fiftieth conclusion[171] a statement of Johannes Andreae, as well as the conclusion posed by him in the *Speculum de Iudeis et Saracenis*, *viz.*, that such defensive measures as make use of the aid of infidels are *de iure* permissible, etc. Oldradus writes the same in question LXXI of his *Questiones*. And although in his reply the pamphleteer seems somewhat to defer to these statements of the doctors, nevertheless he strives to co-opt them by way of his glosses for his proposition, although it is more due to his desire than to reason that he infers from them what he intends.

And thus as to the first conclusion he states the following:

The first conclusion:[172] 'If it is possible to sustain the opinion that in case of self-defense a Christian might utilize the aid of peaceful infidels who are not at war, actively or passively, with Catholics, this is to be restricted only to a certain period of time and only to cases of defense and the imminent need of security, and in cases where the party so aided is innocent of wrongdoing, and only thus is this to be understood as possible.'

And first he introduces certain arguments of Oldradus pro and contra said opinion, which I omit here for brevity's sake. And finally he states that such an opinion of Johannes Andreae may be accepted upon the fulfilment of the conditions aforesaid, otherwise no.

In the end, he would prove this understanding of his with seven reasons. He says, *scilicet*, that the defense must be just and the necessity urgent, and that this aid must not exceed its bounds. Otherwise to the extent that it does exceed its bounds, defense becomes attack or revenge, etc. Likewise, he asserts that it is to be presumed against the infidel, who is of an alien type and hostile to the Faith, that his vehement desire is to harm Christians and rage against them, exceeding the bounds of defense. Moreover, he asserts that such mutual aid between faithful and infidel cannot occur without common conjunction and special friendship between them, which as a rule is prohibited. For he says that sharing amongst faithful and infidel regularly meets with the resistance and prohibition of common law. He therefore concludes that said opinion should not be extended or broadened to other impermissible cases, such as attack, revenge, or offensive military action. He tacitly insinuates that the King of Poland, in making use of the aid of infidels, exceeded the bounds of the aforesaid opinion, *viz.*, by going beyond the case of urgent necessity or mere defense. And thus engaging in such traffic with infidels, he proceeded against the law and is presumed to be lacking in good faith, etc. Thus he wishes to state, in effect, and in sum, by these proofs of his.

This aforesaid opinion is evilly twisted, even more badly supported by proofs, and most poorly thought out. Therefore, this screed of his is erroneous in law, injurious to the King and Kingdom of Poland, and even self-contradictory. It is clear that in the aforesaid modifications, attack, revenge, and offensive military action are excluded — which is manifestly clear from the proofs that support said conclusion in reason VI — yet these things are in and of themselves prohibited *de iure* (XXIII question I: *Quid culpatur*, and question II in the summary). For one may not make use of the aid of faithful or infidel for such ends, hence his modification is superfluous, to no effect, and thus the proof is null and void. From which it can be inferred that by excluding such illicit attacks, he would wish to include attacks otherwise permitted by law — of which see what is noted following Innocent (*De restitucione spoliatorum*: *Olim*) which cannot occur absent just war (XXIII question II, canon *Iustum bellum*), because when one of two contraries is negated, the other is affirmed (XXV distinction: *Qualis*). From which there follows a self-contradiction as by said modification nothing is seen to be excluded at all. If indeed he understands that this opinion does not even extend to such warring otherwise permitted by law, this limitation of his is not to the point at all, for we are not speaking of that here, but rather of defense in case of necessity, etc., and that the King of Poland and the Poles exceeded the bounds of self-defense, as is implied here, is understood, *de iure*, to be false, as it is unproven (see the argument in the chapter *Ordinarij*: *De officio ordinarij* book VI, and the laws *Lege* and *Rutilia Polla ff De contrahenda empcione et vendicione*). And thus it is injurious to the King and Kingdom of Poland. And it is also most poorly thought out where he says 'sharing amongst the faithful and infidel regularly meets with the resistance and prohibition of common law,' and that all common conjunction and amity between them is regularly prohibited. Neither of these is true unless he is speaking of conjugal unions sealed by matrimony (see XXVIII question I: *Cave Christiane*). For such things are certainly permitted by natural law (XI question III: *Ad mensam*; XVIII question I: *Omnes*, and *De Iudeis*: *Quam sit laudabile*, following Johannes Andreae). Hence although it is permissible to speak with them and to sit to table with them, following the example of the Lord (XXIII question III: *Infideles*, and said canon *Ad mensam*), the law only prohibits sitting to table with the Jews, as they make a distinction between their food and ours (as is clear from Deuteronomy XIV,[173] which is noted in the first gloss of said chapter *Quam sit*, by the laws there adduced). And where this cause ceases, there too the effect of the prohibition ought to cease (*De appellacionibus*: *Cum cessante*). And the reason for the foregoing is because such things as are not evil by their very nature are not evil save by circumstance or cause, which can make them so. Thus, such things are always understood as allowed unless they are found to be prohibited and vice versa (which is proven by the gloss that begins

'Argumentum' in the chapter *Inter corporalia*: *De translacione*). Since, therefore, commerce with infidels is not prohibited *per se*, it cannot be stated that such sharing or commerce with them is in itself *de iure* prohibited, unless it is expressly prohibited in a given case, for no one should negate what the law of human society allows (XXIII question II *Notandum*, supported by distinction V: *At eius vero*). It is nevertheless prohibited in certain cases, for example if an infidel will not live with his or her faithful spouse without blaspheming the Creator. In such cases cohabitation is prohibited so that sin may be avoided; marriage can even be dissolved on such grounds, whereas otherwise matrimony is not dissolved on the mere account of infidelity (as in the chapter *Quanto*: *De divorcijs*). And thus too in other cases clearly expressed in law.

As to friendship there is no obstacle presented by what we read here (II Paralipomenon XIX):[174] 'Thou helpest the ungodly, and thou art joined in friendship with them that hate the Lord, and therefore thou didst deserve indeed the wrath of the Lord,' etc., as this error is based on a bad understanding of this statement. For this verset prohibits us from offering aid to any power, given that said power is unjust — and this is the opinion of men learned in the Scriptures — nor should we bind ourselves to such as would imply obedience to devils, nor should we be friends to the impious in their impiety. That is what is prohibited here. Otherwise, indeed, friendship with unbelievers is not prohibited in the least. For 'every beast loveth its like,' (Ecclesiasticus XIII).[175] For similarity is the cause of friendship and love, according to Aristotle (VIII *Ethics*) as St Thomas also declares (*Prima Secunde* question 2a, article III), where he states that similarity causes the love of friendship or benevolence, for from this, that two are similar one to another, as if having the same form, they are in some way one in that form, in the manner of two men being one in their humanity, two whites in their whiteness, and for this reason, the affection of one tends to the other as to one and the same, the one wishing the other's good as he wishes his own. Hence Aristotle

(VIII *Ethics*) states that amity and that which is just are found together, for justice is in some way a moral virtue directed at another (as is plain from *Ethics* V), making no distinction between faithful and infidel, thus also to the moral virtue of amity, which likewise is directed at another (VIII *Ethics*), unbelief or the gentile state is not repugnant (which is proven in the canon *Omnes*: XXVIII question I, in text and the gloss which begins with the words 'Non videtur.' However in such infidels virtue does not exist as a theologian understands the term, nevertheless there do exist political virtues, such as are found in many even where charity is lacking). And I say that infidelity is not repugnant to amity, even in the proper sense of the word, between faithful and infidel — amity such as can exist only among the virtuous, *scilicet* on account of the good that is virtue and moral honesty. Because concerning amity on behalf of the good of utility, such may be found even among men who are morally evil, for as the moral virtues, according to Aristotle's deduction (II *Ethics*) are acquired by habit and use, infidelity is not repugnant to such habit and virtue either. So it is impossible to see why infidels should not be virtuous, speaking of infidelity here as that which is in contrast to Faith, which is a theological virtue. It is otherwise where one opposes infidelity to fidelity as a moral virtue. Nor does that which Augustine says create any obstacle here: 'The entire life of the infidel is sinful, and goods which come not of God are worthless. For there, where eternal and immutable Truth is lacking, virtue is false even in the presence of the highest morals,' for that is resolved thus: (said canon *Omnes*: XXVIII question I): 'For just as the validity of the sacraments among the heretics is denied, not indeed on account of their form, but because they lack effective power, so is the existence of the virtues among the infidels negated, not indeed in the sense that they do not exist there at all, as according to the words of Jerome: *the Romans deserved their Empire on account of their virtues*, but because they do not result in eternal salvation — this they lack.'

By this all other things are resolved.

The second conclusion.[176] 'It does not pertain to the aforementioned case of self-defense, nor has the above opinion any place where a Christian makes use of the aid of infidels who do not recognize at all the Church universal's rights of authority and dominion, or those of the Empire, or such infidels who occupy the lands of Christians, or exist in some other way, by virtue of which it is licit for Catholics to declare war upon them.' He would prove this by the opinion that holds that only the aid of such infidels ought to be implored who are peacefully oriented towards us, nor have any active or passive war with us. And such, he states, are not the above-mentioned, in that they are enemies and hostile to the Church and the Empire as touched upon above; therefore, etc.

This conclusion is one false dogma founded in heresy and for that reason erroneous in morals and in Faith and as something contrary to divine, natural, and human law, it is wholly dangerous and iniquitous. Its falsity is evident, both in respect to Christians, to whom it denies the right to invoke the aid of infidels in such times of necessity, which is contrary to natural law, and also in respect to the infidels, in so far as it falsely accuses them of occupying the lands of Christians, which is contrary to good morals, as they hold their possessions justly, by natural right, in agreement with natural law, as is made clear above. And when it is proposed that war may be declared upon such people by Christians even absent just cause, this is contrary to our faith and to divine law, as has been sufficiently dealt with in what is written above. Self-defense is allowed men by both canon law and civil law (Distinction I: *Ius naturale*; *De homicidio*: *Significasti*; *ff De vi et vi*, the argument of Law I § *Vim vi*). And for this reason, all that, without which no defense can be mounted, is *de iure* understood as permitted (XXIII question III § *Item ab aliquo*, near the end; *De officio delegati*: *Preterea*; *ff Ad legem Aquiliam* § *Cum aliter* and in the sole *Clementina*: *De homicidio*, second rubric). Therefore, to take away from

Christian people such a remedy of self-defense, where there is no other remedy, and when the case presents itself in such a way that there is no other manner of effective defense, is to take away from them the faculty of enjoying a natural right. And to teach that this must be done is nothing less than to teach man to tempt God — against divine law and Catholic truth — and thereby to lead men into grave danger, both temporal and eternal, which is just where this wholly pestiferous, erroneous, and iniquitous conclusion tends.

The third conclusion.[177] 'It merits not to be called defense or innocent security measures when a Christian prince, especially absent flagrant violence or at least some other urgent necessity, gathers about himself an innumerable multitude of infidels and invades and wretchedly lays waste a Catholic land, whereby many thousands of Christians are put to death by said pagans with incredible cruelty.' This, in effect, concurs with the conclusion of Johannes Falkenberg. He proves, by eight means, as far as such things may be termed 'proofs,' among which, although the King of Poland is not expressly named, nevertheless it is sufficiently understood about whom he is referring when he speaks of the war waged against the Prussian Knights of the Cross, as he draws all, if tacitly, nonetheless clearly and intelligently, to this fact. I omit this recitation of empty and useless fables for sake of brevity.

This third conclusion is in favor of the aforesaid error, boldly conceived and invented, and thus suspect of heresy, injurious to the King and Kingdom of Poland, false, bold, and iniquitous. The presumptive boldness is made clear, whereby the author pretends to sit in judgement over the King and Kingdom of Poland, declaring that said King, making use of this legitimate aid, exceeded the bounds of self-defense without urgent necessity, and absent flagrant violence, as he claims. And yet such verdicts are not his to make. And although he indeed would see himself as a judge here, declaring that this is a most notorious fact, as he sets forth in his proofs, he is seen to be quite suspect a judge, and a hostile one, who in doubtful matters, at least as far as others are concerned, by ignoring all legal procedure, delivers a sentence contrary to the canons (XI question III: *Grave satis*, with others similar thereto). As in such matters the cause of the deed, the manner and spirit thereof, ought to have greater attention paid to them than the deed itself (*ff De furto*, the law *Verum*; LXXXVI distinction I: *Quisquis*; *De consecracione* distinction III: *Per alium*). As to facts, even the cause of warring is suppressed by my adversary, and thus the truth of the matter is beclouded. As nevertheless said Brethren, contrary to their pacts of perpetual peace, immediately following their letters patent atrociously devastated the King and Kingdom and so devastating finally having destroyed many fortresses and burnt cities and towns to the ground, at last took and kept a notable dukedom known as Dobrzyń. And nonetheless in the following year, scheming the overthrow of the Kingdom, they assembled an immense number of armed men, which obliged said King to oppose so great a danger, and, not wishing to await a greater blow, but rather to avert the same, to enter their territories with his armies. And while he was negotiating a peace with them, he received two swords sent by these Brethren, one of which was addressed to him, and the other to his brother, with such a challenge intimated: 'Behold two swords sent for your defense. Seek not to turn back now, but choose rather a field where we may meet and do battle, for today you may not avoid fighting with us.' After this, suddenly, they fell upon said armies, etc.[178] And these words are witnessed by the obvious truth of notorious fact. Hence the grave and painful hatred and envy, with which in his blindness this pamphleteer wishes to whitewash a notorious truth and with haughty presumption, by way of doctrine to prove here what cannot be upheld in law, which just proves to be injurious, speaking of those immeasurable multitudes with which the King surrounded himself. Having no proof of this whatsoever, he lays the charge of injustice at his own feet. For as to that great devastation of the land of Catholics imputed in the conclusion, the facts themselves demonstrate that, on the part of said King we have legitimate self-defense, not without cause, while on the part of the aforesaid Brethren, their actions were not guiltless. And this is why by such brazen writing equity is dragged into inequity and falsehood is displayed as truth, which, without any doubt, proves that what we have here is slander, pure and simple.

The fourth conclusion.[179] 'The Christian who led the abovesaid unbelievers, in great power and numbers, as has previously been stated, against Christ's faithful, especially those champions fighting on behalf of the Church and the Catholic people, invading their lands, devastating the same and waging war against them, is, as leader, responsible for all evils that occurred during the conflict, and all damages and harms resulting therefrom, for which he is liable to be charged before both courts and should be obliged to a restitution of all damages.' This concurs with the XXI conclusion of Johannes Falkenberg. He would prove that he who caused an unjust war to be waged should be held accountable for all that occurred in said conflict, and should be obliged to make restitution for all harms and damages (*De iure iurando*: *Sicut*). For such a one must be termed a bandit (*ff De verborum significacione*, see *Hostes* and said chapter *Sicud* by Ostiensis, following Johannes Andreae). For war thus waged is unjust, as the conclusion announces, as is clear from the foregoing. Therefore, etc.

This fourth conclusion, just like the preceding ones, is bold in its favoring of brazen heresy, injurious to the King and Kingdom of Poland, false, shamefully brash, and iniquitous. The response to it is simple. For given that the justice of the aforesaid war is not evident and notorious on the part of the Poles, nor do such words of the narrator constitute any evidence to the contrary (as proven by the laws: *De privilegijs*: *Si papa* book VI, with others similar thereto). From which the iniquity of this judge is plain to be seen in handing down so precipitous a verdict against an innocent party, contrary to the laws, which are more prompt to absolve than condemn (*De probacionibus*: *Ex litteris*; *De fide instrumentorum*: *Inter dilectos*, towards the end). For in doubtful matters, the absence of guilt is assumed (*ff De legibus*: *In ambigua*).

And so, briefly and in scholarly fashion, let these things be said so that in bringing this to a conclusion the falsity of the foregoing should not prejudice the truth, nor should iniquity triumph over equity.

In presenting this, I humbly submit it to the correction of this sacred General Council of Constance, and any who should know better.

Endnotes

1. The complicated manuscript issues surrounding this treatise are well analyzed by Belch, *Paulus Vladimiri*, I, 175-180, and his version is to be preferred over the briefer treatment by Ehrlich, *Pisma wybrane*, I, xxxii.

2. This is one of two variant Introductions derived from different manuscript sources. The two-version patterns continues, however, in the treatise. These suggest a difference in the audiences to whom they were directed; see the comment of Ehrlich, *Pisma wybrane*, I, 317, nn. 5-7. Belch, *Paulus Vladimiri*, I, 176-178, has a more complicated explanation. I prefer in this instance to err on the side of simplicity.

3. Johannes von Urbach de Bamberg is known in German scholarship as Johann[es] Urbach or Auerbach and in Polish scholarship often as Johannes (or Jan) de Frebach. A canonist who studied at Erfurt and Heidelberg, his identity was largely unknown until late in the twentieth century. See Hartmut Boockmann, "Aus dem Handakten des Kanonisten Johannes Urbach. Die Satire des Johannes Falkenberg und andere Funde zur Geschichte des Konstanzer Konzils," *Deutsches Archiv* 28 (1972): 497-532. At Constance, he was one of the scholars the Order chose to produce treatises defending against the accusations and arguments mounted by Paweł Włodkowic. Urbach's treatise, entitled *Tractatus*: *De statu Fratrum Ordinis B. Mariae Virginis Teutonicorum et pugna eorum adversus infideles necnon de imploratione adiutorii infidelium per christianos ad defensionem suam,* proved to be a real challenge to Paweł and the Polish position.

4. The implication here is that this was written after Martin V had already been elected by the Council to end the schism (this took place on 11 November 1417).

5. The implicit structure of this treatise is here presented: two parts, in the first of which the legal bases of the Order's establishment are analyzed. What follows in Part One are three main points, each subdivided into three or more questions or considerations. These, in turn,

are subdivided into rubrics or explanatory comments that are analyzed. Part Two directly addresses the treatises of Urbach and Johannes Falkenberg (about whom, see above in the section on *Iste tractatus*, n. 5).

6. Note the absence of Urbach's name in this version.

7. Roughly modern day Latvia.

8. This is apparently a reference to the document known as the "Golden Bull of Rimini" of 1226; see Tomasz Jasiński, "The Golden Bull Allegedly Issued in 1226 by Friedrich II for the Teutonic Order," *Quaestiones Medii Aevi Novae* 3 (1998): 221-244.

9. He has done this in a number of places, but nowhere more fully than in his treatise *Ad aperiendam* of 1416. For it, see the description provided by Belch, *Paulus Vladimiri*, I, 173, and the characterization of it by Paul W. Knoll, *"A Pearl of Powerful Learning." The University of Cracow in the Fifteenth Century* (Leiden and Boston: Brill, 2016), pp. 436-440. The text is printed in Ehrlich, *Pisma wybrane*, I, 144-259 and II, 2-167, with Paweł's treatment of papal letters in II, 2-106, and of imperial letters in II, 106-158 (most of his attention to the latter category—II, 107-152—is devoted to the letters of Frederick II).

10. Johannes Andreae (*ca.* 1270-1348) studied at Bologna, then taught at both Bologna and Padua, serving also from time to time as an ambassador from Bologna. A married layman (only the second to become a professor of canon law), he produced a number of important and influential works. He died of the plague in 1348. See Brundage, *Canon Law*, pp. 216-217.

11. See above in Paweł's *Opinio Hostiensis*, n. 2. In other respects Paweł profoundly disagreed with his views.

12. Here Paweł reprises his argument made in the answer to the seventh question he posed in the first part of his treatise *Saevientibus*.

13. Ex. 20:13.

14. Ex. 20:15.

15. John 10:16

16. Bartolo da Sassoferrato (*ca.* 1313-1357) was a civil jurist rather than a canonist, who studied at Bologna, then taught at Pisa and Perugia. He produced a very large body of work that proved influential regarding theories about the authority of a city-state. He coined the phrase the *civitas sibi princeps*—the city state was its own emperor and did not recognize any superior. See Julius Kirshner, "Bartolo da Sassoferrato," in Joseph R. Strayer, editor-in-chief, *Dictionary of the Middle Ages*, 13 vols. (New York: Charles Scribner's Sons, 1982-1989), here II (1983), 114-116.

17. Peter of Ancharano (*ca.* 1330-1416), may have been one of Paweł's teachers at Padua: see Brundage, *Canon Law*, p. 180 and p. 207.

18. Oldradus da Ponte (d. post 1337), a canonist eventually teaching at Bologna and part of the Colonna household. The family, based in Avignon, was a bitter enemy of Pope Boniface VIII. After his death they were once again in favor when the papacy settled in Avignon. See Brundage, *Canon Law*, pp. 221-222.

19. William Ockham (*ca.* 1285-1347/1349), a Franciscan who studied theology at Oxford. Some of his writings were deemed potentially heretical and he was summoned to Avignon in 1324, but fell out of favor there in a controversy over Franciscan poverty. He fled Avignon and became associated with the court of Emperor Levis of Bavaria, who was enga-

ged in a bitter struggle with the papacy and for whom Ockham wrote many polemical and political works. As a philosopher, Ockham was one of the most important figures in the late middle ages. Paweł found some of his writings congenial and, as will be seen below, referred to him in significant ways later in this treatise. For Ockham' biography, see briefly William J. Courtenay, "Ockham, William of," in Strayer, ed., *Dictionary of the Middle Ages*, IX (1987), 209-214. The still standard English-language biography of Ockham is Marilyn McCord Adams, *William Ockham*, 2 vols. (Notre Dame, IN: University of Notre Dame Press, 1987).

20. The fourth council of this name, held in 635.

21. See above, n. 20.

22. Egidius Colonna (*ca.* 1247-1316, also known as Aegidius Romanus or Giles of Rome). A member of the Augustinian order, he studied theology at Paris, perhaps attending lectures of Thomas Aquinas, and eventually received the first Augustinian chair in theology. Tutor to king Philip IV of France, he wrote the *De regimine principum* and later supported Pope Boniface VIII in his controversy with Philip IV. See Thomas Renna, "Egidius Colonna," in Strayer, ed., *Dictionary of the Middle Ages*, IV (1984), 400.

23. Several biblical allusions may be implicit here: Matt. 26:65; Mark 14:63; Luke 22:71.

24. In the translation at this point, there is a skillful play on words in the Latin: *militia* (military service, warfare, one who engages in war) versus *malitia* (malice). Ehrlich, *Pisma wybrane*, II, 318, n. 29, observes that Paweł is following St. Bernard, whom Falkenberg had also quoted, commenting "Paul may have wished to show that St. Bernard's views supported his own statements."

25. See the material below in this treatise following n. 122.

26. The Archdeacon was Guido de Baysio (*ca.* 1250-1313), who, after studying and teaching at Regio, was named Archdeacon of Bologna by Pope Boniface VIII. Later he became archchancellor of the university and joined the papal curia. He was responsible for an important commentary on Gratian's *Decretum*, which is alluded to by Paweł in his text. For Guido, see Brundage, *Canon Law*, pp. 212-213.

27. Paweł is here referring to his treatise *Ad aperiendam*.

28. Matt. 26:52.

29. Paweł here returns to a thesis often expressed in his writings, i.e., that the documents the Order relies upon are somehow or other fabrications. On this general topic see the effective brief overview of the issues by Roman Czaja and Zenon Hubert Nowak, "An Attempt to Characterise the State of the Teutonic Knights in Prussia," in Czaja and Andrzej Radzimiński, eds., *The Teutonic Order in Prussia and Livonia. The Political and Ecclesiastical Structures 13th-16th Century* (Toruń: Towarzystwo Naukowe w Toruniu, and Vienna: Böhlau Verlag, 2015), pp. 13-30, here pp. 13-14. There is much more detail in Tomasz Jasiński, *Kruschwitz, Rimini und die Grundlagen des preussischen Ordenlandes: Urkundenstudien zur Frühzeit des Deutschen Orden sim Ostseeraum* (Marburg: N. G. Elwert, 2008).

30. Ecclus. 21:2.

31. See above, n. 20.

32. Matt. 21:43.

33. This is Henricus Boic[h] (*ca*, 1310-after 1370, but before 1390), who studied civil and canon law, earning the doctorate in both laws at Paris, where he apparently taught. His

most important works were *repertoria* on the *Liber sextus* and the *Decretum*, but his reputation and influence was limited. See Belch, *Paulus Vladimiri*, I, 298 n. 9; 557; and 581, n. 5; and Ehrlich, *Pisma wybrane,* I, xxxiii.

34. Above, n. 10. Paweł relies upon him in a number of ways in these sections.

35. Johannes Monachus (Jean LeMoine, *ca* 1250-1313), who studied philosophy and theology at Paris prior to his legal studies there. Eventually active in Italy, he became vice-chancellor of the Roman church under Boniface VIII. He was also the author of a number of important legal treatises and commentaries. See Brundage, *Canon Law*, p. 219.

36. Eccl. 5:3.

37. This is a reference indicating that in one or another manuscript or in one or another version a portion of the text has been marked for deletion by being lined out (*cass* or *vacat*), possibly indicating that a number of copies might have been intended with selected content for individual readers. The original text is, obviously, still available.

38. Paweł here implies that whatever kind of order the "Brethren" claim to be—though he denies they are an order of any kind—they never considered themselves nor were considered by others to be mendicants.

39. Ramón de Penyafort (Raymundus, 1180/1185-1275) was a Catalan who studied and taught at Bologna prior to being summoned to Rome by Pope Gregory IX (Hugolinus) to assist in editing existing and composing new decretals, some of which were eventually included in the *Liber extra*, published in 1232. See Brundage, *Canon Law*, pp. 222-223. Geoffrey of Trani (d. 1245) studied at Bologna while Sinibaldo dei Feischi, later Pope Innocent IV, was studying there. Eventually a member of the papal curia and a cardinal, Geoffrey's works include a number of influential treatises. See Brundage, *Canon Law*, pp. 211-212. Ostiensis, with whom in this instance Paweł agrees, quotes the decretal cited.

40. Part of the New Mark (German: Neumark; Polish: Nowa Marchia) came to the Order in 1378 as part of their efforts to unite their Prussian possessions with German territories to the west. They obtained the remainder from Sigismund of Luxembourg, then only King of Hungary, in 1402. See Janusz Tandecki, "Administrative Divisions of the State of the Teutonic Order in Prussia," in Czaja and Radzimiński, eds., *The Teutonic Order in Prussia and Livonia*, pp. 31-56, here pp. 43-44.

41. This is not merely a legal argument; Paweł here is calling upon pope and council to take action against the Order. This is completely in line with the thrust of his arguments about the Order being a heretical sect that must be exterminated, like the heresy of Wycliffe and Hus, that he developed in other treatises, especially *Ad aperiendam.*

42. James 1:27.

43. Paweł is referring here to his mentor at Padua, Franciscus Zabarella (1360-1417, bishop-elect of Florence in 1409, cardinal 1409-1417, and one of the three most important intellectuals at the Constance of Constance 1414-1418); he was arguably the leading canonist at Padua in the late fourteenth century. See Thomas E. Morrissey, "Cardinal Franciscus Zabarella (1360-1417) as a Canonist and the Crisis of His Age: Schism and the Council of Constance," *Zeitschrift für Kirchengeschichte* 96 (1985): 196-208, and reprinted as item VIII, with original pagination, in Morrissey, *Conciliarism and Church Law in the Fifteenth*

Century. Studies on Franciscus Zabarella and the Council of Constance (Farnham, Surrey England and Burlington, VT: Ashgate: 2014).

44. Dinus de Mugello (1253-post 1298), a doctor of both civil and canon law from Bologna who taught at Pistoia and then Rome at the time of Boniface VIII. See, briefly, *Repertorium Fontium Historiae Medii Aevi,* IV: Fontes (Rome: Istituto Storico Italiano per il Medio Evo, 1976), 201-202. He is an unusual citation for Paweł.

45. Matt. 25:40.

46. Heb. 13:16.

47. i.e., the Knights Templar, a military-religious crusading order founded during the crusades but which, after the expulsion of the crusaders from the Holy Land, took up residence in France, from where many of them had come originally. They eventually became wealthy, powerful, and influential and were suppressed by the papacy (at the urging of King Philip IV of France) in the early fourteenth century.

48. This is a reference to documents submitted by the Order to Sigismund in the court of arbitration convened in Buda in 1412 and developments shortly thereafter. Paweł was almost surely present then and involved on the Polish side. For the Buda tribunal see Krzysztof Ożóg, *Uczeni w Monarchii Jadwigi Andegaweńskiej i Władysława Jagiełły (1384-1434)* (Kraków: Polska Akademia Umiejętności, 2004), pp. 189-191. The record of these articles and related materials are printed in *Lites*, 2nd ed., II, 1-88 (subsequent materials in *Lites*, II, 88-360 are related to the activities of Benedictus de Macra); see above in the translation of *Articuli*, n. 10.

49. 1 Cor. 13:2-3.

50. Luke 10:27 and 37. The textual reference to Mark is surely wrong. Ehrlich, *Pisma wybrane*, I, 321, n. 110 cites it as Matt. 22:39, which is possible.

51. Petrus de Tarantasia (1225-1276). He studied canon law at Paris and taught in the Dominican school there. Eventually archbishop of Lyon and cardinal of Ostia from 1273; briefly thereafter (1276), Pope Innocent V.

52. Gal. 5:6.

53. Heb. 10:24.

54. James 2:19.

55. James 2:17.

56. Heb. 11:33.

57. Ex. 20:13 and 15.

58. Gal. 5:6.

59. Gal. 5:19-21.

60. Ps. 35:4 (Vulgate numeration).

61. Ps. 57:9 (Vulgate numeration).

62. Matt. 7:15.

63. This is a characteristic distinction Paweł makes in a number of his treatises. i.e., that between the theoretical (or doctrinal) and a practical (or juridical) process. In his mind, the latter is more effective in achieving his goal of the condemnation and, by extension, the destruction of the Order. See, for example the beginning of his treatise *Iste tractatus*, n. 3 and n. 4. This distinction is further analyzed by Frederick H. Russell, "Paulus Vladimiri's Attack on the Just War: A Case Study in Legal Polemics," in Brian Tierney and Peter Linehan, eds.,

Authority and Power. Studies on Medieval Law and Government Presented to Walter Ullmann on his Seventieth Birthday (Cambridge: Cambridge University Press, 1980), pp. 237-254, especially p. 237, where the distinction is made particularly explicit.

64. This very brief fragment suggests that yet a third version of at least the first part of the treatise had been contemplated. It would probably have been addressed to a different audience than that for whom Versions I and II were intended.

65. This marks the beginning of the end of the first half of the treatise as a whole. The second half is devoted to an explicit response to the treatise written by Johannes Urbach; see above, n. 5.

66. John 20:21.

67. Version II of the conclusion to the first part of *Quoniam error* is briefer and more of a summary than Version I. The substance is, however, much the same.

68. For Falkenberg, see the information above in the translation of the text of *Iste tractatus*, n. 5. The treatise Paweł is referring to here is Falkenberg's *Veteres relegentes historias*, also known as *Liber de doctrina potestatis papae et imperatoris editus contra Paulum Vladimiri Polonum*.

69. Paweł writes here of Falkenberg's polemical treatise *Satira*, which had somewhat earlier been condemned at the Council of Constance. See the section on *Iste tractaus*, n. 14, and—for the condemnation—the treatments by Hartmut Boockmann, *Johannes Falkenberg, der Deutsche Orden und die polnische Politik. Untersuchungen zur politischen Theorie des späteren Mittelalters* (Göttingen: Vandenhoeck und Ruprecht, 1975), pp. 263-296; and, more briefly, Ożóg, *Uczeni w Monarchii Jadwigi Andegaweńskiej i Władysława Jagiełły*, pp. 217-222.

70. The Latin here—*et aperiendo materiam*—consciously reflects the opening of Paweł's treatise *Ad aperiendam,* in which he developed his theory of the *haeresis* or *secta Prussiana*. For that text, see Ehrlich, *Pisma wybrane*, I, 144.

71. What follows are materials drawn from the writings of Maurice (Mařik) Rvačka (d. after 1424). He was an Augustinian canon regular who studied Arts at Prague (BA 1385, MA 1387) and taught Paweł Włodkowic there (note Paweł's phrase about Maurice: "my master"). Maurice later studied theology in Rome, where he earned his doctorate in 1400. After teaching theology at Prague, he came to Kraków, where by 1407 he was teaching theology. He was present and involved at Constance, and was generally a supporter of conciliarism. He was also an aggressive critic of Jan Hus. He cooperated with the Poles at Constance and, as is clear from Paweł's text, he was a supporter of the Polish position vis-à-vis the Order. Following the conclusion of the council, he returned to Poland and remained there. For his biography, see Marian Zwiercan, "Rwaczka Maurycy z Pragi," *Polski Słownik Biograficzny*, 33 (1991) 279; Thomas Wünsch, *Konziliarismus und Polen. Personen, Politik und Programme aus Polen zur Verfassungsfrage der Kirche in der Zeit der mittelalterlichen Reformkonzilien* (Paderborn, Munich, Vienna, and Zürich: Schöningh, 1998), p. 59; and Mieczysław Markowski, *Dzieje Wydziału Teologii Uniwersytetu Krakowskiego w latach 1397-1525* (Kraków: Wydawnictwo Naukowe Papieskiej Akademii Teologicznej, 1996), pp. 107-109.

72. Paweł here seems to imply that Urbach's text has a heretical character and therefore falls into the same larger category of heresy condemned by the fathers at Constance.

73. Luke 13:7.

74. Matt. 21:43.

75. The first fourteen conclusions of Urbach, after a general defense of the Order, focus upon his understanding of pagans and unbelievers and upon the status of the Order and its struggles against the unbelievers. The text of Urbach's treatise has been edited by Belch, *Paulus Vladimiri*, II, 1116-1180. There is an English translation of it in Timothy M. Brennan, "Just War, Sovereignty, and Canon Law: Legal Arguments Over the Lithuanian Crusade and the Rights of Unbelievers at the Council of Constance (1414-1418)," Unpublished Ph.D. Dissertation, University of Kansas, 2005, pp. 422-532. For Urbach's statement of his first conclusion and subsequent argument, see the Latin, pp. 1118-1121 and the English, pp. 425-431. Paweł's four point analysis of it follows.

76. John 21:17.

77. Luke 10:35.

78. John 14:16.

79. Matt. 7:17.

80. John 10:3-5.

81. Rom. 8:30.

82. Rom. 1:4.

83. Matt. 26:28.

84. Rom. 8:17.

85. John 10:5.

86. John 10:16.

87. Acts 10:11-13, 16.

88. John 21:17.

89. Mark 16:15.

90. Matt. 25:33.

91. Matt. 21:31.

92. Matt. 25:34.

93. Hos. 13:9.

94. Rom. 10:14.

95. This begins Paweł's own presentation.

96. Rom. 12:18.

97. Matt. 5:9.

98. John 10:17.

99. For Urbach's second conclusion and subsequent arguments, see the Latin text in Belch, *Paulus Vladimiri*, II, 1121-1133, and the English in Brennan, "Just War, Sovereignty, and Canon Law, pp. 431-452.

100. Paweł here links Urbach's treatise with that of Falkenberg, which—as noted above—was already deemed to have a heretical character.

101. Matt. 22:17-21.

102. Matt. 21:43.

103. Matt. 17:26.

104. Luke 2:4-5.

105. Luke 21:12 and 14.

106. John 19:11.

107. Luke 22:25.

108. Acts 25:10.

109. Acts 25:11.

110. 1 Pet. 2:13-14.

111. 1 Tim. 2:1-4.

112. Acts 4:26.

113. John 18:36.

114. Matt. 20:25-26.

115. John 8:12.

116. Matt. 5:14.

117. Paweł here ends his insertion of Mauricius's comments and renews his own argument, drawing in significant ways upon Ockham.

118. For Paweł's use of Ockham, see above, n. 19, and Ehrlich, *Pisma wybrane*, II, 403, n. 71. Ożóg, *Uczeni w Monarchii Jadwigi Andegaweńskiej i Władysława Jagiełły*, p. 58, notes that Paweł drew upon two of the three approaches to natural law developed by Ockham; see also Tadeusz Jasudowicz, *Śladami Ludwika Ehrlicha: Do Pawła Włodkowica po naukę o prawach człowieka* (Toruń: Wydawnictwo Comer Jacek Waloch, 1995), pp. 60-64. There is, to my knowledge, no systematic study about the relationship of Paweł's thought to Ockham.

119. Acts 24:10.

120. John 18:36.

121. i.e., Urbach.

122. For Urbach's fourth conclusion, see the Latin text in Belch, *Paulus Vladimiri*, II, 1137-1143 and the English in Brennan, "Just War, Sovereignty, and Canon Law, pp. 458-468.

123. See above, n. 100.

124. Paweł's text that follows consists of a number of extracts and conclusions from distinguished canonists, some of whom have already been identified in the notes to this treatise.

125. Matt. 22:21.

126. John 18:11.

127. Antonius de Butrio (1338-1408). He studied canon law at Bologna, Florence, and Ferrara, and was the author of a number of influential works bearing on the Great Schism. See, briefly, *Repertorium Fontium Historiae Medii Aevi,* II: *Fontes* (1967), 379.

128. Giovanni da Legnano (*ca*.. 1320-1383), doctor of both laws at Bologna who also taught there. In his writings—as well as in his experience as a diplomat—he demonstrated considerable expertise on both the study of war and peace and practical matters. See Brundage, *Canon Law*, p. 118.

129. Gen. 2:17.

130. Gen. 3:16-17.

131. Only Gen. 6:14-21.

132. Gen. 9:9-11.

133. Gen. 8:20.

134. Ps. 71:1-2 (Vulgate numeration).

135. Ehrlich's text (I, 353) reads *Ysaye XIII*; should be Is 33:22.

136. John 21:17.

137. John 18:11.

138. 1 Tim. 3:3.

139. Petrus de Ancharano (*ca.* 1330-1416) may have been one of Paweł's teachers at Padua; if not, he most probably knew him. See Belch, *Paulus Vladimiri*, I, ii, 795, n. 1. Peter, who had studied under Baldus de Ubaldis (*ca.* 1327-1400, among the best known canonists of his time), was particularly influential in the last decades of the fourteenth century and the beginning of the fifteenth century; see the comments of Brundage, *Canon Law*, p. 180 and p. 207.

140. Gen. 14:20.

141. Heb. 7:1-2.

142. A vague reference. Exodus 28 deals with raiment and rituals for Aaron and his sons.

143. 1 Sam. 8:22.

144. 1 Cor. 6:3.

145. Rom. 13:1.

146. John 19:11.

147. Though the text says *ut habetur I Regum VIII capitulo*, the reference is actually to 1 Sam. 10:1.

148. The reference should be to Matt. 22:21.

149. Luke 22:38.

150. For Urbach's fifth conclusion and subsequent arguments, see the Latin text in Belch, *Paulus Vladimiri*, II, 1143-1146 and the English in Brennan, "Just War, Sovereignty, and Canon Law," pp. 468-473.

151. For Urbach's sixth conclusion and subsequent arguments, see the Latin text in Belch, *Paulus Vladimiri*, II, 1146-1148 and the English in Brennan, "Just War, Sovereignty, and Canon Law," pp. 473-476.

152. Of the four names mentioned here, only the last is easily identifiable. For Baldus de Ubaldis, see above, n. 139 and Brundage, *Canon* Law, pp. 207.

153. 1 Kings 21:1-3.

154. 1 Samuel 8:5.

155. For Urbach's seventh conclusion and subsequent arguments, see the Latin text in Belch, *Paulus Vladimiri*, II, 1148-1151 and the English in Brennan, "Just War, Sovereignty, and Canon Law," pp. 476-482.

156. An obscure reference, perhaps to Rom. 7:5-7.

157. See Rom. 12:18-19.

158. 2 Cor. 13:11.

159. While hardly perfunctory, Paweł's responses to Urbach's next seven conclusions (with the important exception of his treatment of just war issues in the tenth conclusion) are briefer and in some instances almost dismissive. For Urbach's eighth conclusion and subsequent arguments, see the Latin text in Belch, *Paulus Vladimiri*, II, 1151-1154 and the English in Brennan, "Just War, Sovereignty, and Canon Law," pp. 482-486.

160. For Urbach's nineth conclusion and subsequent arguments, see the Latin text in Belch, *Paulus Vladimiri*, II, 1154 and the English in Brennan, "Just War, Sovereignty, and Canon Law," pp. 486-488.

161. For Urbach's tenth conclusion and subsequent arguments, see the Latin text in Belch, *Paulus Vladimiri*, II, 1154-1162 and the English in Brennan, "Just War, Sovereignty, and Canon Law," pp. 488-502.

162. The analysis by Ehlich, *Pisma wybrane*, II, 408, n. 165, of Paweł's position on the just war vis-à-vis Urbach's treatment is particularly effective.

163. For Urbach's eleventh conclusion and subsequent arguments, see the Latin text in Belch, *Paulus Vladimiri*, II, 1162-1163 and the English in Brennan, "Just War, Sovereignty, and Canon Law," p. 502.

164. Ex. 20:13.

165. Ex. 20:15.

166. For Urbach's twelfth conclusion and subsequent arguments, see the Latin text in Belch, *Paulus Vladimiri*, II, 1163-1164 and the English in Brennan, "Just War, Sovereignty, and Canon Law," pp. 503-504.

167. For Urbach's thirteenth conclusion and subsequent arguments, see the Latin text in Belch, *Paulus Vladimiri*, II, 1164-1165 and the English in Brennan, "Just War, Sovereignty, and Canon Law," pp. 504-506.

168. For Urbach's fourteenth conclusion and subsequent arguments, see the Latin text in Belch, *Paulus Vladimiri*, II, 1165-1167 and the English in Brennan, "Just War, Sovereignty, and Canon Law," pp. 506-509.

169. Urbach's four conclusions are introduced in his text with the rubric "Four conclusions. . . concerning the invocation, namely of unbelievers for help for defense."

170. i.e., in the Battle of Grunwald in 1410.

171. In *Opinio Ostiensis*.

172. For Urbach's first conclusion and subsequent arguments in this part (the fifteenth in his treatise overall), see the Latin text in Belch, *Paulus Vladimiri*, II, 1167-1173 and the English in Brennan, "Just War, Sovereignty, and Canon Law," pp. 509-520. His presentation here, as Paweł notes, is in classic scholastic form: an assertion *pro*, then a response *contra*, and eventually a *resolutio*.

173. Deut. 14:3-21.

174. 2 Chron. 19:2.

175. Ecclus. 13:19. The Latin text here incorrectly places the reference in Ecclesiastes.

176. For Urbach's second conclusion and subsequent arguments in this part (the sixteenth in his treatise overall), see the Latin text in Belch, *Paulus Vladimiri*, II, 1174 and the English in Brennan, "Just War, Sovereignty, and Canon Law," p. 521.

177. For Urbach's third conclusion and subsequent arguments in this part (the seventeenth in his treatise overall), see the Latin text in Belch, *Paulus Vladimiri*, II, 1174 -1179 and the English in Brennan, "Just War, Sovereignty, and Canon Law," pp. 521-529.

178. Paweł is here referring to the outbreak of hostilities in the Battle of Grunwald and the incident of the "two swords," presented by him in *Articuli*; see n. 45 there for details. It is, as noted there, traditionally seen in Polish historiography as an insulting, shaming

maneuver. But see also the different interpretations, including a presentation of Jagiełło's action as based in his own *humilitas*, described by Klaus Militzer, "Kommunikations- und Verständigungsprobleme vor und nach der Schlacht bei Tannenberg," in Werner Paravicini, Rimvydas Petrauskas, and Grischa Verkamer, eds., *Tannenberg—Grunwald—Žalgiris 1410: Krieg und Frieden im späten Mittelalter* (Wiesbaden: Harrassowitz, 2021), pp. 301-305, here pp. 301-302, especially nn. 3-5.

179. For Urbach's fourth and final conclusion and his subsequent arguments in this part (the sixteenth in his treatise overall), see the Latin text in Belch, *Paulus Vladimiri*, II, 1179 -1180 and the English in Brennan, "Just War, Sovereignty, and Canon Law," pp. 529-532.

THE EYES

(*Oculi*, 1420)[1]

Allegations on behalf of the king of Poland[2]

Let thine eyes behold equity, etc. and foregoing.[3]

In speaking of the equitable, three things may be seen as having been brought before you, for your kind consideration. The first of these, certainly, is the very matter of the discord, which has arisen in the territories of Pomerania, Chełmno and Michałów, which lands my lords the Prussian Knights of the Cross presently occupy. The second matter brought before you concerns the extent of other lands similarly occupied by them, that is to say: Dobrzyń, Kujawy, Mazowsze and Żmudź, etc. The third matter concerns the many and oft-renewed injuries perpetrated by the said Knights of the Cross against the Kingdom of Poland and the persons of her Kings at successive times, which injuries are so many and so great as to be well-nigh infinite, and impossible to enumerate exactly. These three matters and points shall form the content of the present discourse.[4]

In the first of these, as far as justice is concerned, the following may be noted.[5] First, I would submit the facts on account of which the present case has arisen, and I say that these are noted facts, well-attested by genuine documents, that is to say by definitive statements and attestations of witnesses, publicly presented and redacted in public instruments, which everywhere are considered sufficient, *de iure*, to be worthy of absolute trust. Second, I shall clear away any inequitable, hedging questions as to the law here, and any impediments to justice in this matter. And thirdly, the lawful remedies in this matter shall be offered, so that justice might shine forth in its full splendour.

Approaching, therefore, the first of these, that is to say, regarding the facts themselves, I would distinguish three periods during which three kings ruled Poland, in immediate and successive sequence. The first reign was that of our late lord His Majesty King Władysław of glorious memory the father of Kazimierz.[6] The second reign was that of that Kazimierz, who succeeded his father to the throne.[7] The third period was, and is, that of our most serene prince and lord, the present King Władysław.[8] During these three periods there arose between these three Kings of Poland and the Prussian Knights of the Cross many disagreements, and much strife, resulting in great slaughter, on account of these territories occupied by said Brethren. Moreover, between the other Kings of Poland who reigned in the times preceding the three periods I have just mentioned, and those same Brethren, there never occurred such disturbances as during these three kings' reigns, nor had the knights so violently occupied the land of Pomerania, nor had they such power to harm.

I would state here first that the aforementioned late King Władysław for many years of his reign held the province of Pomerania in peace and quiet, having his governors and civil officials in place there, just as in all other localities of the Kingdom of Poland. But then, some Grand Master of the said Order then in existence, having gathered together a strong armed force, invaded said province with hostility, besieging with violence the provincial capital, that is to say Gdańsk, along with the fortress that is found there, effecting the slaughter of all Poles there residing, along with many soldiers and other people subject to said King Władysław.[9] Beginning in the year of Our Lord 1306 and subsequently, with continual violent force and the laying waste to said fortress, they came into possession of it and the entire province of Pomerania, which they seized with violence, and continued so to occupy for the following one hundred and thirteen years or thereabout. All of theses facts are borne out by genuine documents.[10]

At length, indeed, the aforementioned Władysław made this all plain in a complaint addressed to the Pope at the time, John XXII, concerning the manner in which said Order, paying no heed to the reasons why his grandfather, Konrad, Duke of Mazowsze, invited them into his territories for the defense of the faith, took possession of them. Believing them to be true defenders of the Catholic faith, he granted them, with liberal hand, some movable goods and real estate, but they, on the contrary, proving ungrateful to this prince, illicitly extended their rapacious hands for his possessions. For they proceeded to plunder the province of Pomerania, known to belong to the Kingdom of Poland, rashly despoiling it of vassals, camps, villages, cities and the goods found therein — against all justice occupying them over the space of eight years and more, retaining the same, which violent occupation continues, as we state in this grievance, etc.[11]

Having listened to these complaints, the aforesaid Pope sent to the King three judge-delegates, namely: Janisław, the archbishop of Gniezno, Domarad, the bishop of Poznań, and Mikołaj, abbot of the Benedictine monastery of Mogilno in the Diocese of Gniezno, as judges according to the power and form of the apostolical mandate. These after due consideration of the facts brought definitive judgment in favor of the Polish King and against the aforementioned Knights of the Cross. Condemning their violent occupation, they enjoined upon them the restitution of said province of Pomerania, along with all things appertaining thereunto. Furthermore, they were ordered to pay damages in the amount of thirty thousand marks as compensation for the goods of the lands that they had consumed. And finally, they were commanded to pay court costs in the amount of one hundred fifty marks, being instructed to comply with all of these verdicts under pain of excommunication. And as such they would be publicly denounced from the pulpit for many years; and this judgment would retroactively obtain to the dead, as well as the living. The sentence was given in Novo Wladislaw,[12] Włocławek Diocese, in the year of Our Lord 1321, on the eighth day of February, the fifteenth year following the occupation.[13]

This being the case, some eleven years after the aforementioned verdict, they invaded Poland again, in hostile fashion, with a strong armed force. Laying waste to the said duchy of Dobrzyń, perpetrating much homicide, arson, and rapine, they despoiled that territory during the reign of Władysław aforementioned, which is to say, in the year 1329.

And lo, these same Knights of the Cross, not content with this occupation of Dobrzyń, invaded the Kingdom of Poland again in the following year, hostilely and cruelly devastating the region of Nakło in Wielkopolska, Sieradz and Łęczyca. These, along with their defenses, cities and the villages belonging to them, they burnt to ash, nearly destroying them completely. Honest women and virgins they foully abused and oppressed, denuding them even in churches. They decapitated many noble men, killing many others, and taking off still other multitudes into captivity. Wherever in the kingdom they found beasts and cattle, these they drove off; whatever thing of value they could find, whether in churches or elsewhere, these they stole. With many other injuries of the most atrocious kind, and damages of the gravest sort, they oppressed the aforementioned King and his subjects, and the Kingdom of Poland as a whole. This occurred in the year 1331, to which facts sufficient testimony is provided by authentic documents and public instruments.

Still not satisfied with the evils they committed up to this time, in the very next year they fell upon the territory of Kujawy with just such great butchery and violence, slaughtering many. Just as before, they committed such homicide, arson, and acts of rapine in the year 1332, as again may be proven on the basis of authentic documentary evidence. What is more, they then built imposing fortresses in that territory of Kujawy, as if the region belonged to them, making themselves the lords of those who for many years previous had held this land, along with Dobrzyń, in their possession. It was then, it seems, that the castle Nieszawa was built in Kujawy, which even until now they retain, along with other villages there, wherefrom the Kingdom of Poland was crucified by these Knights of the Cross during the reign of the aforementioned King, who departed this life so tormented and despoiled of many lands, and saturated with opprobrium. So much for the first period.[14]

The second period was that of King Kazimierz, who immediately preceded the present dynasty, having succeeded to the Polish throne following his father, King Władysław, of whom we have just spoken. This king toiled as diligently as possible to extract the territories belonging to him from the grip of the Order that occupied them. Already having made his complaint to the kings of Hungary and Bohemia, and requesting their assistance, at last he presented the matter to Pope Benedict XII. He, upon hearing the complaints of the King, and considering the reports of the disgraceful actions of the aforementioned Knights of the Cross, who were gravely stained by their violent and sacrilegious acts, their arson and incendiarism, homicide, invasions, malevolent occupations and acts of rapine as described above, sent two worthy men off to the Polish regions, tasked with gathering information concerning all that had been revealed, and administering justice with the aid of the secular power.

Which judges, proceeding judiciously, according to the power and form of the apostolical mandate, brought a definitive finding against the said Knights of the Cross, condemning them on all counts.[15]

First of all, in their decision, these judges state that they have been convinced by the evidence proffered by the proven documents presented them, according to which the above-mentioned Grand Master, and his brethren, who, at the time, with a powerful and hostile force, banners erect, fearing not God but under diabolical persuasion, laid waste to the Kingdom of Poland and churches therein, *viz.* that of Nakło, Warta, Szadek, Bałdrzychowo, Konin, Słup, Pobiedziska, Kaczyna, the Monastery of the Franciscan friars minor and of the Holy Cross before Pyzdry, which they set afire, after having first carried off from them all that they contained, to wit: books, chalices and other sacred items and lockboxes. These places they burnt, along with the relics of the Saints and images within them. And therefore, on this account, the Church declares the Grand Master expressly, the knights of the Order, and whoever else participated in the arson and incineration, or on whose authority such incineration and combustion took place, to be excommunicated, which excommunication declared by the apostolical authority was to be announced by the bishops, prelates, and parish rectors of the cities and dioceses of Gniezno, Poznań, Włocławek, Płock, Kraków, Lubusz, Wrocław, and Chełmno. The judges also ordered the Brethren to rebuild the aforementioned churches and to restore and emend all other property belonging to the injured parties.

Secondly, in this same verdict we find declarations similar to those mentioned above, concerning the evidences and proofs urged dealing with the territories in question. To wit, that the land of Chełmno in Pomerania, the lands of Włocławek, Brześć, Dobrzyń and Michałów, along with their fortresses, cities, villages and all divers things pertaining thereunto are found within the borders of the Kingdom of Poland, subject to that Kingdom, and that the Kings and princes of the Kingdom of Poland, the progenitors of said Kazimierz, possessed and held them during the time of their reigns.[16]

Thirdly in this same verdict it is stated as well that, in accord with the legitimate judgments before mentioned, the said Grand Master and his brethren the knights, did with hostile force invade and occupy the lands of Pomerania, Brześć, Włocławek and Dobrzyń, along with the cities, farms and villages considered as belonging to the above-mentioned King their lord and his progenitors in consistent succession. Such being the case, that these lands were subject to the Kingdom of Poland, great harm was done, offensive to God, to King Kazimierz and his aforementioned father Władysłąw, when with great slaughter these knights invaded and violently occupied the territories, which they continue to hold, to wit: the lands of Chełmno and Michałów. For they, with the cities, fortresses, farms, villages and all that pertain thereunto and are found within their borders, constituting portions of the Kingdom of Poland, subject and pertaining thereto, these same Brethren unduly and unjustly detain under their occupation. For these reasons, sentence is passed condemning them to the restitution of all the above-cited lands in plenary and integral form to the King aforementioned, returning the fruits received and the crops yielded, back to those from whom they had been seized.

Fourthly, in the same verdict it was stated similarly to the foregoing legitimate judgments that the same Grand Master and his brethren aforementioned did enter and invade with strong armed force, with hostile intent and banners erect, the region of Wielkopolska, burning, devastating, and laying waste to the fortresses, farms, villages, cities and towns therein, *viz.*: Gniezno, the metropolitan see of the Kingdom of Poland, as well as other cities, fortresses and towns, along with their territories, farms and villages, which the verdict goes on to list by name, both such as lie within Wielkopolska itself as well as those in other lands of said Kingdom of Poland, that is to say: Sieradz, Łęczyca, Nakło, Bydgoszcz, etc., underscoring the grave destruction wrought upon Żnin, Nakło, Łęczyca, Uniejowo, with Sieradz and its fortress, Warta, Szadek, Bałdrzychowo, Charłupia; all the farms and villages in the territory and district of Kalisz, Pyzdry, with its fortress and the cloister or monastery of the Franciscan friars minor, Konin, Słupca, Środa, Klecko, Pobiedziska, with its fortress and fortified towns and the farms and villages adjacent thereunto, and those constructed in their districts and territories, first having despoiled them of all their movable goods and livestock; having murdered many people and taken many others into captivity, denuding and insulting women, incinerating, devastating, laying general waste and committing other crimes against those subject to his Majesty the King and his Kingdom.

On that account the aforementioned judges required the restitution of all damages or the real, truly estimated value thereof, which they calculated at 194,500 marks, plus additional court costs, calculated at 1,600 Polish pounds. In such manner were the aforesaid Brethren convicted, sententiously and definitively, as being in illicit occupation of those aforesaid lands, detaining the same from their rightful owners and committing the aforesaid excesses. Thus read the verdict, according to the judges' opinion, proven by public documents in which fuller information may be found. The sentence was published in Warsaw, the Diocese of Poznań, in the 1339th year since the Birth of our Lord. The gravity and seriousness of this judgment is clear from the advancement of this suit, as contained in the opinion, which itself is proven and justified on the basis of the trial, otherwise in accord with other public instruments.

And even if the truth of the foregoing were not to be believed, reference can be made to the depositions of witnesses, which have been made public and redacted on judicial authority in public instruments, in which said witnesses record their testimony. These witnesses are such as who had escaped with their lives, who were summoned and examined under oath, and deposed properly, singularly, and separately, truthfully testifying to the above. There were one hundred twenty-three such witnesses giving testimony, among whom were: one archbishop, two senior bishops, three princes of noble birth, abbots, prelates, and canons of cathedral chapters, palatines of many lands and other dignitaries both ecclesiastical and secular.

First, all of the witnesses gave evidence to the case of the region of Chełmno, which lies within the borders of Poland and belongs to the kingdom of Poland. For they assert that the true border dividing Prussia from the Kingdom of Poland is the river popularly known as the Osa, and for this reason the entire surroundings of the region of Chełmno, from the river Wisła to the river Osa, lies within the Kingdom of Poland. They further state that from the most ancient times the Kings of Poland have been in possession of said region of Chełmno, and that there can be no doubt of this fact.

Now, according to the testimony of these witnesses, the manner in which the region of Chełmno came into the possession of the Knights of the Cross was as follows: There was a certain duke in Kujawy named Konrad, who was lord of the region of Chełmno in question.[17] He was the ancestor of the aforementioned King Kazimierz, the great-grandfather of the aforementioned King Władysław Łokietek. It was he who summoned the Knights into his territory as an aid against the neighboring Prussians, who at the time were pagan. In so doing, he conceded them certain possessions. Later, at their petition, he conceded them the region of Chełmno by such a pact that stipulated that when they should have subjugated the Prussians, they were to restore the region of Chełmno to him, or to his successors. And they agreed to this compact. And there are thirty witnesses to this, giving concordant testimony; some of them have seen or read the letters in question with their own eyes. Others have testified that they know this agreement to be true, having heard the same from their forefathers and other men of ancient times, and that this agreement is public, common knowledge.[18]

Janisław, archbishop of Gniezno at the time, and one of these aforementioned witnesses, testified to having seen the documents of the aforementioned Duke Konrad brought into evidence, in which all that was asserted above was indeed to be found.

Similarly, Jan, bishop of Kraków, one of the witnesses who had been made regional chancellor of the Kujawy region by Władysław the father of Kazimierz, was present in Brześć along with the aforementioned Władysław when the Grand Master of the Knights of the Cross sent a certain brother of that order named Sighard of Schwarzburg to the aforementioned King Władysław to treat of peace concerning the Chełmno region and that of Pomerania, both of which King Władysław wished to obtain from the Knights, arguing, among other things, that his grandfather had transferred the region of Chełmno to the Knights by terms of entreaty, and that when they had subjugated the Prussians, they were to restore it faithfully, according to the terms of the pact.

Concerning which pact, he then presented Sighart with the treaty as agreed upon by the Grand Master of the order at that time, and he himself bore witness to having had the documents in hand and seen them.

Likewise, Leszko, the Duke of Kujawy, a literate man,[19] and one of the witnesses, testified to having seen the grant or the documents many times, held them in his own hands, and read them through, and that they contained just what had been testified to above. And that he had last seen it at the seat of Bolesław, the Duke of Mazowsze, his paternal uncle, who showed it to him, declaring 'what rights we should have in the Chełmno region, and that if we were unable to recoup it now, it shall be regained at least by our successors.'

Likewise, a certain Dominican master, an Inquisitor of heretical depravities, one of the witnesses summoned by the former Grand

Knight, the aforementioned Karolus, to Malbork, where amongst many other such bills he was given to read he beheld the grant of the aforementioned Duke Konrad concerning the concession of the Chełmno region, which he read from beginning to end.

Furthermore, all other witnesses who were deposed in this matter, numbering thirty-three in all, were in agreement that Duke Konrad had made a concession of the Chełmno region to the Knights for the purpose of their expelling the Prussians, and that once this had been effected, they were to restore the land to him. All of these witnesses, or nearly all, spoke on the basis of their firm knowledge which had been transmitted to them by their forefathers and other men of those past times and that all this was common knowledge, well known. Besides this, the above-mentioned four witnesses furthermore said that they had also seen the documents themselves — as stated above.

As for the land of Michałów, that it is to be found in the Kingdom of Poland and pertaining thereunto, and that it had been in the possession of the rulers of Poland since the most ancient times, all the witnesses testified to this as a well-known fact, and that the Knights of the Cross were in possession of it by reason of a pledge, which mortgage they had held now for nearly thirty years. Thirty-three witnesses gave testimony to the effect of this being a well-known fact, and all have sworn this to be true.

And in addition to that, this was all common knowledge. Among those giving testimony was Duke Leszko, the lord of said land following his father Leszek Biały and other of his ancestors in succession. He testified to having obligated the Knights of the Cross to a tribute of 280 Toruń marks, some thirty years beforehand, which he had used to redeem himself from captivity after he had been taken captive in Hungary by the King of Bohemia. Salz, the Grand Master of the Knights who was asked to forward this money, was also bound to restore the land once the debt had been repaid. To this he added that the land brought the Knights some 300 marks, and more, annually.

And this testimony was confirmed by his brother Kazimierz, Duke of Kujawy, who was also one of the witnesses.

This same Kazimierz, Duke of Kujawy, and brother of the aforementioned Leszko — one of the witnesses — stated that the Michałów region was a patrimonium belonging to him and his brother, Duke Leszko, and that it lies within the Kingdom of Poland. Furthermore, some thirty years previously, it had been offered as a pledge by his brother Leszko against his, that is, Kazimierz's will and that of their third, deceased brother Przemysław. The same witness testified that, wishing to redeem the land from the Knights of the Cross, he presented them with the money that Leszko had borrowed. These moneys the Knights refused to accept; they also refused to restore the lands in question. He also said that during the time they held the land, it had profited them a sum of two thousand marks.

Then Jan, knight and palatine of Włocławek, also one of the witnesses, testified that he, along with Duke Leszko, had pledged the land in question to the Knights of the Cross for three hundred and eighty marks in Grudziądz. The Grand Master of the Knights at the time was Salz, but it was Gunther, the provincial of the order, who gave them the money. Later, he heard that Duke Leszko had received a greater amount from them on account of the pledge. He also stated that Leszko's brothers, that is to say Kazimierz and Przemysław, wishing to redeem the lands, took them the moneys in his presence and with his aid — but that the Knights of the Cross reneged and refused to accept the moneys and return the lands.

Then Wojciech, palatine of Brześć, a knight and one of the witnesses, testified that he was present when Duke Leszko, who was the senior of the three brothers, in disagreement with the other two pawned their land. The witness also stated that the amount was five hundred Toruń marks and, further, that Leszko's brothers had frequently brought that same sum of money to the Knights of the Cross so as to redeem the land from them, but that the Knights refused to receive it from them.

And all other witnesses testified in agreement with the above, among whom some were able to confirm their knowledge of the pact at first hand, from the time of Leszko's pawning of the land, while others had heard of it from him, and still others heard of it from his brothers or other persons. And all of this is recorded in public instruments.

As to Pomerania being located within the borders of the Kingdom of Poland and its having been in possession of the Kings and Dukes of Poland, and that it had been hostilely invaded and violently occupied by the Knights of the Cross with great slaughter of human life — some sixty-five or sixty-six witnesses testified to these as being well-known facts. Among these witnesses were some men who were present at the time of the invasion, in the army of the Knights, while others gave testimony as having defended the fortresses there on the part of the King of Poland. These testified to the great cruelties perpetrated at the time by the Knights of the Cross: who decapitated, hanged, and otherwise put Poles to death. Amongst these witnesses, Jan, bishop of Kraków, testified that he had taken part in the negotiations between Władysław, who was King of Poland at the time, and the aforesaid Knights of the Cross, and that these same Knights had proposed that the King give them this land in exchange for ten thousand marks of pure silver, and certain possessions, which they held in Kujawy, and beyond this, that they wished to construct and endow a monastery with eighteen brother priests of whatever order he pleased, for the salvation of his soul and their own. And furthermore, they stated their desire to serve said King in his every time of need by providing a certain number of armed men at his disposal. And that all these things can be proven as a matter of public record.

The aforesaid Duke Kazimierz gave testimony to the fact that he, along with his brother, governed said lands in the King's name.

Among other things, he stated that, after the Knights had laid siege to the fortress of Świecie for a month's time, the Knights had finally succeeded in entering it, at which time he and his brother Przemysław were pursued for a good two miles by the Knights, who wished to capture them or put them to death. He testified to many other things as well.

Then another witness, a knight named Antoni, son of Andrzej, of Kujawy, who was a familiar of Kazimierz and had been with him in Tczew, said that when Kazimierz heard that the Knights of the Cross had invaded Pomerania with their army and, having conquered the city of Gdańsk at night, by way of treachery, where they put many people to death, sparing no Pole, he went in person to the Grand Master and his army in the field and begged him to desist from the destruction and occupation of the region in question, saying, 'You had counselled me to accept the governance of this region from my Lord Władysław, the king my uncle, having promised me that you would raise no impediments, but would always aid us.' Then did said Grand Master respond to him, saying that indeed it was more pleasing to him that he and his brothers should hold this land rather than any other more powerful man, but not so that they themselves would rule it as dukes, but rather that he, the Grand Master, should more easily obtain it. At this, the aforesaid duke begged on bended knee, with folded hands, before the Grand Master, that the latter should hold to what he had promised. To which the Grand Master advised him either to lock himself up in his castle and prepare to defend it, or to leave the territory, saving himself and his household and valuables. And when the Duke returned in sadness to Tczew, from which he had earlier departed for his meeting with the Grand Master, he beheld there the banners of the Knights of the Cross already fluttering above the city, and their army stationed beyond the castle. In this way, he was compelled to make his way to the fortress of Świecie, which was subsequently in short order tightly surrounded by the powerful army of the Knights of the Cross, with the siege towers of wood that they constructed so as to facilitate the taking of the fortress. They also built twelve gallows of wood so as to terrify those remaining in the fortress. From each of these gallows they hanged one or two wretches such as they had succeeded in capturing. These facts have been borne out by the testimony of many witnesses, who stated that several such gallows were indeed built and men hanged upon them.

Then Lord Thomas of Zajączkowo, a knight who hails from the Chełmno region, who was with the Knights of the Cross at the time and with their armies everywhere in Pomerania when they violently entered the region, said that they put to death many noble persons and others in order to obtain their wealth. He furthermore testified that, after the Knights had occupied said territory, they had sent to the said King Władysław with the request that he sell it to them. But this the King did not wish to do. The witness said many other things besides this.

Likewise, the Reverend Father lord John, bishop of Kraków, one of the witnesses, testified to having participated in the negotiations between King Władysław and the Knights of the Cross, during the course of which the Knights first offered the King ten thousand marks of pure silver and some properties of theirs in Kujawy. Beyond this, they wished to endow and build a monastery for eighteen brother priests of whatever rule the King himself should choose, to pray for his salvation and their own. And above and beyond this, they stated their wish to serve the aforementioned King at his need with a certain number of armed men.

And thus other witnesses also offered notable testimony that merits attention.

And all of these things can be proven by public record. And many pious persons declared clearly and distinctly that King Przemysł succeeded Prince Mściwoj, and subsequently King Władysław succeeded King Przemysł,[20] all of which were seen to have been in power, in succession; and there also came many witnesses such as the Reverend Father lord Jan, bishop of Poznań, whose nephew Bogusza, a Pomeranian judge, was governor the fortress of Gdańsk on behalf of King Władysław, from which he was expelled by the Knights of the Cross, and Świętosław, the palatine of Pomerania, another of the witnesses who had been expelled by the Knights. Many other witnesses testified to have broken bread with these three in Pomerania, and their testimony was in principle in agreement with all contained in the aforesaid judgment.

Furthermore, though such was the case and it was just that the aforesaid King Kazimierz should consider the judgment pronounced on his behalf and on behalf of his Kingdom to be definitive, still as the aforesaid Knights of the Cross, giving no heed to the ecclesiastical censures, even, as it is believed, dying under their banns, Kazimierz, either not knowing how, or being otherwise unable to extract his lands from their control, was constrained, as it is said, to enter into a pact with them.[21] According to this pact, the Kujawy region was restored to him — excepting the fortress of Nieszawa, along with some villages adjacent thereto, which fact allowed them to invade again and devastate Kujawy at their pleasure — as many subsequent events have proven. Following this pact the Knights of the Cross rejoiced greatly, alleging that they were now in possession of letters patent from King Kazimierz and all the prelates, barons, and municipalities of the Kingdom of Poland, just as they recently alleged at the Gniewkowo Convention — even though they played false to that pact and others of that type many times and in many ways, as shall be explained below.

But I beg your Serene Grace to consider the strangeness of this pact. These Brethren restore three minor territories in order to retain three greater ones in perpetuity, and thus they sell — at a great price — that which they were obliged to restore gratis. And in selling these, they buy the others with someone else's money! They promise peace unto the regions restored, only to have peace in those they retain, and a free hand to engage in rapine such as is forbidden by divine law. And so they play at concord in oppression, simulating peace with the Kingdom while they act tyrannically in reality. And thus underhanded craftiness seeks to purge their guilt of violence, extorting this pact that is in flagrant opposition to laws both divine and human. And yet, such sin cannot be pardoned without the restitution of the fruit obtained by that sin. So much for the second period.

The third period was, and is, that of the present King Władysław, in which we live, and thus remember well the events thereof. Now, this third period may also be divided in three.

The first of these segments stretches from the beginning of the present King's reign and lasts up until the Peace of Toruń.[22] The second: from the conclusion of said Peace up until the amicable agreement arrived at by Your Grace in Hungary concerning the award.[23] The third period is the present day. That the Knights of the Cross continue, frequently and gravely, to crucify the Kingdom of Poland throughout this time, reneging on whatever pact one care to mention, is a notorious fact well known to all.

To pass over the many acts of violence committed at the fortresses of Drezdenko, Santok, and others, we point out that these Knights twice hostilely invaded the land of Dobrzyń, occupying it with their army to the great prejudice and harm of the present King and the Kingdom of Poland.[24] Is it not a notorious fact that they, having loaned a certain amount of money to the Duke of Opole, receiving as a pledge from him the said region, hostilely drove away the people of this Kingdom from the siege of Bobrowniki Castle, appropriating unto themselves the said castle along with all the lands adjacent to it, retaining the same for many years, which constituted a reneging on the pact made with Kazimierz — however faulty that pact was is a secondary matter. They neither wished to restore to said King that land unless they first received from him the entirety of that loan, plus interest at a usurious rate, taking not the slightest account of the profits they had derived from the use of that land, including crops and rents, which exceeded, or at least sufficiently would have reduced the amount of capital initially loaned. And even though another agreement had been made with them in the village of Sławsko in the diocese of Włocławek, they had no intention of honoring it. Rather, defying said King with their letters patent, with their usual boldness they violently invaded said land, committing there arson, lewdnesses, homicides, rapine, and many other disgraceful crimes. They demolished castles, burning them to the ground and destroying them, occupying with violence said region, and remaining in occupation thereof for some two years until the aforementioned King engaged them in the recent battle they provoked, the result of which was their tumbling into the abyss of death along with their armies and wretched people, on account of their very boldness. This took place in the year of our Lord 1410.

And they themselves, the Knights of the Cross, were the cause efficient of that conflict, that battle, and the entire war that then resulted therefrom and is still ongoing, just as has been stated above: by their defiance, their arson, their pillaging, and all the damages they caused, as before noted. Thus they are the guilty party, who is to be blamed for all the ills that have followed upon their deeds, or are to follow.

It was in this manner that the above-mentioned land of Dobrzyń was liberated from their violent hands.

What later resulted following the aforesaid war?[25] The two sides arrived at the agreement, which is popularly known as the Peace of Toruń, according to the terms of which the Knights of the Cross promised to keep perpetual peace with the King — which promise they made just in order to wheedle the cities of Toruń and Raduń, along with their fortifications, from the aforesaid King on the basis of that pact. Then, having in this manner come to occupy said fortresses, they immediately spurned the promised peace, holding the words of the pact in contempt, and invaded the Kingdom with violence — not once, but several times. Banners erect, with their armies, they atrociously devastated all, just as before, according to their old custom. And thus did they resuscitate the war that all had judged concluded, giving rise to much grave evil. Such terrible destruction did they wreak upon the Kingdom in many of its regions or lands by their arson and looting. The Churches in the region were especially pillaged — in particular the metropolitan see of Gniezno, and the dioceses of Włocławek and Płock, the goods of which were not only carried off by the Knights as booty, but the noble structures of which, along with the lands appertaining thereto, they burnt and devastated.

So much for the second segment.

As for the third segment of time, appeal was made to Your Serenity by both sides to be their arbitrator. On the basis of this compromise, you pronounced in Hungary that a perpetual peace ought now to be observed in regard to these and other matters of contention.[26] You suspended pronouncement in other matters, sending, with the agreement of both parties, a commissioner, namely, the noble Benedict de Macra, to the regions of Poland, Lithuania, and Prussia, there to gather information and to carry out what had been pronounced, if these Cross-bearers truly lived up to their name and crucifying reputation. However favorable the pronouncement was to them, and advantageous, nonetheless, disregarding all this and holding it in contempt, they made a frivolous appeal from the aforesaid Benedict to the Imperial Electors, who were no judges of the issue at all. They would not bend to any rules, but proceeded to inhumanly put to the sword and drown all merchants and other people who, trusting to the pact of perpetual peace, came into these territories. In this, they paid no respect to gender, treating women in the same way as men, and robbing them of all their goods. Further, proving incapable of departing from their old habits, again with banners erect they hostilely invaded the Kingdom of Poland with their army, as is their wont, wreaking most cruel devastation, murdering, setting aflame and looting. Above all, they destroyed the greater part of the possessions of the aforementioned Churches in the Gniezno, Włocławek and Płock dioceses. Not only did they just burn these buildings to the ground anew, but the damages done to the Church in Włocławek alone amounted to over one hundred thousand florins or marks. All of this has been sufficiently proven in Hungary, before the Commissioners appointed to this matter, *viz.*, the Most Reverend Father in Christ János, then bishop of Esztergom, and Lord N. de Bara, Palatine. These evidences may be found in their registries.

Although, truly, the aforementioned King of Poland, and the Kingdom itself, were severely disadvantaged by the above-cited pronouncement that confirmed the Peace of Toruń, a peace not only unjust, but, as I shall say below, etc., null and void, in hopes of the pronouncement being amended within the period designated by the Peace, according to the terms of the arbitration, they have borne all these wrongs patiently. Indeed, although the aforementioned King has shown due and precise diligence all throughout the period stipulated in the agreement, sparing neither expense, however great, nor the lobors of his people, however many, to satisfactorily prove his rights to the aforesaid lands occupied by the Knights of the Cross, and establishing the many and varied harms inflicted on himself and his people at their hands, they, on the contrary, have been able to prove nothing, nor could they ever, as will be apparent from the aforesaid registries to which I refer. Thus, it may manifestly appear that: because no declaration, pronouncement, nor sentence of arbitrator has been given in these matters, the King, the Kingdom, and other persons appertaining or subject thereto, have seen their rights trampled, while the Knights of the Cross are seen to have obtained all possible advantages from their insolence and cruelty.[27] In what manner this can be just or proper, let God be the judge.

What has the aforesaid King ever done to be so wronged and oppressed? Unable to do otherwise, he entered the lands held by them with a great force and inflicted so much damage and harm upon them, being powerful enough in that regard; still, among other reasons, at the appeal of Your Serenity, he dismissed his force. And yet, despite the fact that by mutual accord he and they had obliged themselves to obey the sentence of the holy General Council of Constance, or any other such council, nothing resulted therefrom, because the aforesaid Knights of the Cross repudiated the fact of there ever having been any agreement concerning said lands under their occupation. To pass over many other things that took place at the time concerning the aforesaid lands, the aforementioned King, wishing to do due diligence so as to recover them, as the time stipulated in the peace was near its date of expiry, as he had, in the preceding summer, he brought together a great number of men.[28] Having prepared an expedition with so many men and at such a great cost — as it rose to the value of the two lands in question, if not indeed exceeding it — still and all, even though his might was great enough to meet that of his enemies, at the appeal of Your Serenity, restrained by the promise of a good accord, he recalled his entire force from the field and dispersed it, accordingly bearing much grave damage to his land, submitting all disputed matters to the arbitration of Your Serenity, especially in reference to all things unclear concerning the aforesaid lands, such as occurred after the judgment of the arbiters appointed by the Apostolic See. For no compromise dealing with these lands is possible following a binding legal sentence pronounced in their regard, about which there can be no doubt. Concerning which my side protests that there is no doubt but that the lands in question lie within the Kingdom of Poland, nor is there any doubt as to the propriety of the process executed by the aforementioned judges; nor is there any doubt as to the efficacy of the proofs given in this legitimate trial, nor of the probation of the final sentence given in the trial resulting in a proper and legitimate verdict, and of all these things proofs have been provided by public and authentic documents set before Your Sereneness at another time, and which are presented here yet again, as has been said above.

In all of these things, O King of all glory, may Thy eyes see the propriety!

So much for the first, main part of this first matter, *viz.*, the facts of the case.

Let us now approach the second principle,[29] that is to say the removal of all that savours of iniquity in this matter, and stands as an obstacle to equity. These are all the bases upon which the claims of the Knights of the Cross rest, above all, the agreements to which they refer. It is a general statement of fact that there are so many, and so great, pieces of manifest evidence, testified before the law and found in authentic documents, bearing witness to the fact that these brethren have always acted in bad faith in the matter of these lands, from the very beginning. In consequence, they have not the slightest right to ascribe these lands to themselves (*De regulis iuris* c 2° book VI). For as to the third land of Pomerania, which they hold by force, it cannot be 'good faith;' the Chełmno territory was held by so-called precarious tenure, to be in their possession only until such time as conditions of the aforementioned accord had been met. When these had been met this occupation ceased to be precarious tenure and became instead something held in bad faith; the land of Michałów had been held as a pledge for a certain amount of money, the restitution of which or the equal value thereof was to free it *eo ipso* from the aforesaid obligation. And so these Brethren, in continuing to hold it in usurious fashion, cannot be seen to do so in good faith, for he who conducts his business unlawfully is presumed to be of bad faith (the rule *Qui contra, De regulis iuris* book VI). I say of the land of Pomerania that it is held by force, for the same law applies here as does to anyone engaged in a violent crime (*De iudiciis*: *Quia V*), for there is very little difference, as far as danger to one's soul is concerned, between a common thug and someone who unjustly invades the lands and detains the goods of another (This is proven verbatim in the chapter *Sepe*: *De restitucione spoliatorum,* along with its final gloss). It is evidently proven, therefore, by these aforesaid sentences, that these Knights are, and have been, violent, illicit, and unjust detainers of what belongs to others, and thus in possession of these things in bad faith.

Now, as it has been made sufficiently manifest concerning the aforesaid Brethren, that in three periods of time they have inflicted grave harm on the Kingdom of Poland: what is more, both according to facts and according to law it is seen that all pact or concord made with them was — as can be seen from the above — extorted by terror (see chapter *Qui verissimile*: *De presumpcionibus*). For it is not to be presumed that the King should wish to abandon so many and so opulent lands as these, or wish to have them sliced away from the Kingdom of Poland by such accords; or that he should wish to relinquish such rights as he has obtained in their regard by legal verdict at so much lobor and expense. For it is not likely that any person should willingly cast away what belongs to him (which is proven by the first gloss of the attached chapter, appended in support). To such an extent does the law presume that such goods as are in question here have been extorted by force that it does not even admit contrary proofs, as it is simply not likely that a person should, of his own free will, renounce his rights to things of which he had been previously despoiled (as in the chapter *De restitucione spoliatorum* and that which is there noted).

Now, such renunciations made out of fear can be legally binding, because the will coerced is still the will. But this holds only in cases where no other impediment exists (XV question I: *Merito*, where proof is given in chapter *Super hoc*: *De renunciacione* in which clear note of this is made in the gloss). Nonetheless, such cases are rare indeed, and thus legal remedies have been so established by which such renunciations can be rescinded on account of compulsion of the will by fear (see *Quod metus causa lege Metum* § *Violentis manus*, and what is noted in the aforementioned gloss).

Having said that fear or deception do not necessarily render accords null and void if there be no other impediments thereto, I now pass on to proofs of just how other impediments do exist in regard to the agreements at issue here.

From these it necessarily follows that all of these agreements made in such a way are, in general, unjust and iniquitous. They are unjust as they are contrary to law, and iniquitous thrice over, in that they are triply repugnant to equity. First, because they are contrary to the equity of natural law: 'Do not unto others what you would not have done unto yourself.' They are contrary to equity in divine law as well, as they go against the commandments: 'Thou shalt not steal;' 'Thou shalt not covet thy neighbor's goods' (Exodus XX).[30] In treating of these words, St Augustine says that all who illicitly usurp the goods of another are to be known as thieves. This judgment is also moved in Canon XIV question IV: *Dixit Dominus*, in which the taking of things not belonging to one against the will of their rightful owner is known as theft. That it is alleged that the King and Kingdom of Poland agreed to these accords is neither here nor there, for even if that were the case, the law presumes that they did so unwillingly, as according to the previously adduced chapter *Quia verissimile*. For even if one make such a renunciation without being despoiled, it is still presumed that one does so unwillingly, as is noted in the chapter *Super hoc*: *De renunciacione* in the aforementioned glosses thereof. Even stronger is this presumption in a case such as ours, where force is proven to have been employed, which is true both as far as the agreement of King Kazimierz is concerned, and the Peace of Toruń, in which although the King of Poland recuperated in great part the aforesaid lands belonging to him, he was once more presently despoiled thereof by the aforesaid Knights of the Cross, saving a few fortresses, which he still could not easily retain. And even though he dismissed the same on the power of the Peace of Toruń, still he did so unwillingly, as is proven by the texts adduced so many times above. And thus, on account of the violence that preceded the accord of such a type as the Peace of Toruń, the above is true to such an extent as to forbid the admission of any attempts at proving the contrary. See, for example, the chapter *Solicite* and that *Super hoc*, the chief gloss above invoked, in which Johannes Andreae[31] asserts — on this very chapter *Super hoc*, concerning the first gloss — that, following the Abbot,[32] the factual question was settled in the matter of a certain girl who had been snatched while on her way to church, then held in a certain home, where the man who had grabbed her called for witnesses and wed her. When she regained her liberty and he wanted to reclaim her, she proved to have been acting under the duress of fear and violence. He, on his part, wished to prove the contrary, claiming that she voluntarily agreed to the marital contract, even smiling. But this argument of his was forbidden to be entered according to what has been said, according to Innocent. Johannes Andreae. Thus all of the above-mentioned accords go against equity in canon law as well as civil law, for according to the former it is iniquitous to enrich oneself to the detriment of another (as in the rule *Locupletari*: *De regulis iuris* book VI). And as to the latter, no one should impose iniquitous conditions upon another (as *De regulis iuris*: the law *Non debet*, *ff*). Therefore, all accords whereby the Knights of the Cross ought to obtain said territory belonging to the Kingdom, indicate not only an unjust enrichment of the Knights to the detriment of the Kings of Poland, but appear themselves to be the gravest of detriments to the entire Kingdom. For such accords tacitly consent to the division of the Kingdom, etc., and consequently the destruction of the same, as every Kingdom divided against itself shall be brought to desolation.[33]

And from this we arrive at the conclusion that despite any such accords, the aforementioned Brethren are obliged, for the sake of their eternal salvation, to restore and to depart from the aforementioned lands, as much as this lies in their power, for sin cannot be absolved without the restitution of that which has been unlawfully taken (as in the rule *Peccatum*: *De regulis iuris* book VI). Indeed, this seems to follow from the premises.

What is more, in confirmation of the aforesaid, speaking without prejudice to the truth, even if accords of this sort hold up as tacit or express renunciations on the part of the King of Poland, they do not hold up, nor could they have any legal effect as to the aforesaid Knights of the Cross. For such renunciation does not itself transfer the rights of property to any person, because, as the Philosopher[34] says: the legal extent of an act of deprivation ends with the deprivation itself; deprivations cannot, *eo ipso*, be the cause of anyone's acquisition. Thus, whatever rights I myself renounce, they do not, in consequence, redound to the profit of one who has engaged in force (as Johannes Andreae notes in the chapter *Solicite*: *De restitucione spoliatorum* concerning the words 'who renounces' and Johannes de Legnano[35] in the chapter *Accepta eodem titulo*). Nor is that violence purged by such a renunciation, as the turpitude of a pledge is by a voluntary payment (Codex *De hijs que vi metusve causa*, law II, and *ff De condiccione ob turpem causam*: the law *Si ob turpem*). For others state that however odious is the exception of fear, a petition for restitution by one who has been despoiled is to be looked upon favorably (*De ordine cognicionum*, final chapter). And for this reason, the restitution of that which has been paid, except in this exceptional case of fear, is not to be demanded (*ff De condiccione indebiti,* the law *Indebiti* and the law *Qui excepcionem*). It is also said that the one who pays after promising, even after a promise given in a moment of fear, is to be understood as giving freely (*ff De regulis iuris,* the law *Cuius per errorem*). Thus, on account of the payment, the creditor becomes rightful owner, because by that act of payment the promise is fulfilled, its debt resolved, for this reason, that before the payment, which is the fulfilment of the promise, the giver was in possession of means, which he renounced in the act of payment, whereby he freely transferred ownership of the same to another, i.e. to the person he paid. But a renunciation is not an execution of an act of deprivation, nor is it reasonable that the one thus despoiled of something has given it up of his own free will. And therefore, violence is not purged by such a renunciation and, according to the above-cited persons learned in the laws here introduced, nothing may be gained through violence by the one who employs such violent means. And thus it follows that, if on account of fear, I promise you one hundred, nothing is transferred to you by that promise, neither legal ownership nor possession, which can only occur by the act of payment. Now, he who is despoiled is unable to renounce his possession of something that he does not possess. And so, he cannot transfer ownership even if by making such a renunciation he does so to his own disadvantage as far as his property is concerned (see the chapter *Quod in dubijs; De rununcciacione secundum Goffredem,* cited by the learned in the laws introduced above), still the other acquires no rights thereby, unless some positive act of transferring ownership expressly intervenes in said contract or its acquisition by someone occurs, for example, by way of sale or donation or something of that sort. Now, there is nothing at all of this to be found in the aforementioned pacts, and so, according to the law, it is to be understood that such a thing never existed, nor is to follow hereafter, for 'it does not appear' is consonant with 'it is not, such a thing does not exist' (*De eleccione*: *Ut circa* § the final book VI; *De consecracione*: distinction I: *Solempnitates*, and other similar points).

Such a matter is termed faulty, and if this fault not be purged, no acquisition is possible (*Institucionibus*: *De usucapionibus § Quod autem*). Such a thing cannot be acquired by usucapation or prescription, and neither thief nor looter nor anyone else may legally acquire it, though it pass through ever so many hands, and regardless even if it was purchased or taken into possession in good faith (as there, and in Ostiensis[36] in the *Summa*: *De penitencijs et remissionibus § Quibus et qualiter,* the verset *De predam ementibus*).

No such objection can be made, as my adversary seems to have asserted, that the business concerning the lands in question was brought to an end by the agreement, for this is not true, because no such agreement or transaction can take place after a binding verdict has been delivered, according to Ostiensis (in the *Summa*: *De transaccionibus § Et in in quibus esset*, near the conclusion), for such a transaction as suggested concerns questionable and uncertain disputes, not freely made agreements (as is deduced *ff* the same law 1 and noted in the chapter *Super eo*: *De transaccionibus*) according to Ostiensis (in the same place of the *Summa § 1 Et quod dicitur lite incerta*). For if an agreement is made that contradicts a valid judgment that has been pronounced, and which has not been suspended on appeal, or would not be challenged on other grounds such as would cast its provisions into doubt, said agreement would be invalid (*ff De condiccione indebiti; Eleganter* § *Si post rem*).[37] In the same way, should it be denied that a valid judgment has been pronounced, whereas it is known that indeed the judgment is in force, according to Ostiensis (see above, and likewise B. in the chapter *Exposita*: *de arbitris,* in gloss II concerning the laws there cited; likewise H. Boyk[38] in the chapter *Ex parte*: *De transaccionibus*) there can be no negotiations where a firm decision has already been established. And if we use the term 'transaction' (or 'negotiation'), understanding the same in the general sense of an amicable agreement (as in the chapter *Ex litteris*, the chapter *Super eo* and the chapter *Veniens* of the same title): this does not apply here, as there is nothing amicable about it; there is a presumption of violence, as above, and thus any transaction extorted through fear or fraud presents no obstacle to our claim, according to Ostiensis (see above § brought to a conclusion by the laws there cited).

Furthermore, such transactions, stipulations, or pacts concerning the retention of lands belonging to others ought to be understood according to the manner in which they are held by him who retains them: thus, violently, tyrannically, merely *de facto*, for there is nothing else expressly stated here. For acts are not understood in any other way than how those who are acted upon are affected by them. Not for any other cause, such as the purging of a fault, for no other cause is expressly stated, and so the judgment goes against him who might have expressed himself more clearly (as in the law *Contra eum*: *De regulis iuris* book VI, and many other similar thereto), which has a place in pacts and suchlike contracts, according to the same gloss. With good cause this interpretation is to be made against such as commit fraud by way of obscurity, as we claim is the case of these Knights of the Cross. For it is by nature of such fraudulent pacts that they seek to retain lands not belonging to them, which they were, and are, obliged to restore — for which reason they are committing fraud (see the chapter of the book entitled *Dolo eodem*). And so the clause in the Pact of Toruń, in which the Knights of the Cross so rejoiced, namely, that the order ought to hold onto, etc., this region of Pomerania, Michałów, Chełmno, and so on, that these ought to remain in the possession of the order, along with all those lands which they held prior to the war — this clause is merely a statement and confers no new rights upon them. For if this word 'ought' was to signify a right, this pact would contradict the definitive judgment previously handed down, which states that these lands belong by law to the Kingdom of Poland. By this very fact then, their claim would be null and void (as per the chapter *Exposita*: *De arbitris*), and thus the word 'ought' denotes a mere fact and so it ought to be understood: that the order ought to retain them in the manner it has or had them, that is to say *de facto* and by violence, since they did not possess them lawfully, as was declared by the above-mentioned, definitive verdict. Now, this manner of things is contrary to natural law and divine law, for indeed natural law and divine law prohibit the retention of anything belonging to another contrary to the will of that rightful owner. Thus, all such pacts and all such means by which things of another are wrongfully retained are prohibited. The same law ascertains all things accessory to the principal issue in the same way (the rule *Accessorium*: *De regulis iuris* libro VI). And so when something is prohibited someone by law, all things following from that thing are also understood as prohibited (as we see in that same book and rule, the rule *Cum quid*, supported too by the gloss and proven by the chapter *Preterea*: *De officio delegati*, and what is noted in the gloss *Argumentum*). Therefore, just as all rapine and unjust occupation of the aforementioned lands are prohibited to the Knights of the Cross by natural law and divine law, as stated above, so are all things that arise therefrom prohibited them as well.

In consequence, it necessarily follows that all such pacts entered into with them concerning the above-mentioned lands are contrary to natural law and divine law, and because they tend to the detriment of the soul, by this very reason they are to be considered depraved and dishonest and impossible, imposing no legal obligation, which is clearly proven, verbatim, in the concluding chapter *De pactis*, including gloss II, for according to the law a depraved pact is not valid (*ff De verborum obligationibus*: *Generaliter*) and according to canon law as well depraved promises oblige no one. Whence it is said in the canon: 'Break faith in bad promises, etc.' (XXII question IV). And in general all pacts which go against the law, regulations, or good morals are of no moment: all of which is proven in the above-mentioned glosses by the laws put forth in them, and also by the learned men who have written expressly and unanimously on this matter.

And just as this pact is depraved relative to the Knights of the Cross, who retain these lands, so is it depraved relative to the King, should he not demand them back. For he is bound to this by a twofold bond, firstly, by his oath given at his coronation to preserve the rights of the Kingdom in their entirety (as in the chapter *Intellecto*: *De iure iurando*)[39] and also by the nature of his office, whereby it is incumbent upon hm by law to recall and reintegrate all things wrongly disposed of by himself or his predecessor (XXXV *question* IX *Quod quis commisit*) which is proven by gloss I of said chapter *Intellecto*, with which Johannes Andreae is in agreement concerning the term 'bound,' that is to say, even if at his coronation he did not expressly swear such a thing, nevertheless he is bound in this regard. H. Boik is of this opinion in *Nosti*: *De eleccione*, in its first distinction, where he speaks of whether and in what circumstances one might go against one's own act, making reference to B.[40] and to Ostiensis in this very chapter *Intellecto*. And because such a pact, repugnant to the royal office, being contrary to good morals, also sets no obstacle to his requiring a return, it is to such a degree contrary to common law (on which see the canon *Quod quid commisit* cited above, and others similar to it) it is not operative, because 'an agreement of private persons' [cannot alter public law[41]], citing in support of gloss 1 of the aforementioned chapter *Intellecto*.

Nor even is a vow made not to ask for a return of such things binding (which is proven in the rule: *Non est obligatorium*: *De regulis iuris* book VI). For that would be to renounce in perpetuity three important dukedoms which make up one fourth of the entire realm, or more, and such would be tantamount to a resignation, however tacitly, of legal rights, and onerous damage to the kingdom, and such a thing cannot be done as it is prohibited by law, according to Innocent and all learned men in common after him, according to said chapter *Intellecto*, in which the pope reprehends the King of Hungary for having made a certain renunciation detrimental to his kingdom. And the learned men affirm the detriment to have been grave, because there are certain things that can be renounced without grave detriment

(*De donacionibus* chapters I, II, and III and the chapter *De apostolice, De simonia, Etsi questiones*). And because that King had sworn an oath not to contravene said pact, the Pope stated that such an oath was illicit, both as this latter oath contradicted that given at his coronation, which was legitimate, and because according to the law he was bound to preserve the rights and laws of his Kingdom intact.[42] And so the interpretation is that such an oath is not to be honored.[43]

The assent of the prelates, barons, etc. of the Kingdom of Poland to the accords or pacts here mentioned, with which the Knights of the Cross are so delighted, are of no account whatever, because if the principal issue is invalid or prohibited by law, as has been stated, even such assent does not hold any weight, but rather is understood as prohibited as well — for it all refers back to the law (*De constituciones*: *Translato*) concerning the principal matter, which applies to all accessory matters just the same (*regula Accessorium*: *de regulis iuris* book *VI*).

By these same laws it is likewise proven that the King of Poland is not understood has having renounced his rights by the means of such accords or pacts. Because even if such a renunciation had been expressly stated, it would not be recognized as legal, as given the invalidity of the pact, so is the renunciation invalid. Furthermore, since an alienation of such a sort is prohibited by law (as above) so is the renunciation prohibited, by reason of the connections carried back to the same verdict — and a verdict passed on a principal matter holds for all matters accessory thereto as well. From this I infer the conclusion that even if the King of Poland had expressly renounced the definitive judicial sentence or the right he obtained thereby, such a pact would not be valid, by law, maugre the agreement, for reason of the invalidity of the pact itself, as above, *de iure*, and *de facto*. For even if, regardless of the pact, the verdict was renounced, although the lands were not, one might demand their return by initiating a new suit, for a civil obligation is taken away by a judgment while the natural obligation remains (as per the law *Stichum ff De solucionibus § Naturalis*, as Johannes Andreae notes in the chapter *Super spoliacione*: *De ordine cognitionum,* and *Speculo*: *De excepcionibus § Dicto de dilatoriis* in the verse *Sed pone*); however, such a renunciation, which once more sets the affairs if the Kingdom in doubt, since the outcome of the suit is doubtful, and leads to other inconveniences such as expenses, etc., would prejudice the proper dignity and honor of him who renounces. And once again, as something contrary to the law, it should not be legitimate (as above, in the laws cited). And so it is clear that all such accords are unjust and contrary to written law.

But now it remains to be seen, granting that, as stated, according to divine law the answer is no, whether such acts as the renunciation, alienation and transfer of property hold according to canon or civil law, since many things that are forbidden still hold when executed (as in the chapter *Ad apostolicam*: *De regularibus,* where this matter is taken into consideration), similarly, although the first oath, given in convocation, renders the second, contrary oath, invalid (as in the chapter *Tua I*: *De iure iurando*), this, however, does not invalidate a contrary deed to which the oath pertains. For example, if I vow not to sell a book, and later sell it all the same, the sale holds even though I've gone against my oath, as Francis, Cardinal of Florence, notes in the chapter *Intellecto*: *De iure iurando*, and in the chapter *Dilecto*: *De prebendis*, concerning which Johannes Andreae speaks more fully in the question moved by him and the rule of law *Quod semel placuit* in book VI of *Novella,* where it reads: Titius made a will and swore not to contravene it, until he made a second will and then died. He says that it is the second will that is valid, not the first. Concerning which it is to be noted that even if such acts are not null and void by reason of the oath, it is seen that they do not hold, neither on the part of the King, nor on that of the Knights.

On the part of the King this is so, because even though a monarch might renounce his throne, while he is the King he cannot renounce something that is in the interest of his realm. So, should he do something by which the kingdom is notoriously harmed, because this is repugnant to his own dignity and office, and by consequence, to common law, which forbids such things, as noted above, it has no binding power, it is not valid or legitimate, as in the rule *Ea qui fiunt a iudice*: *De regulis iuris* book *VI* where Dinus[44] states: Because he does such things as a private person, not a public person, and so there is no force to what he does, which opinion is in accord with the rule *Ea que contra ius fiunt*, of the same title and book.

For a fuller explication of these things, see H. Boyk in the concluding chapter of *De pactis*, where he makes the distinction: Sometimes it is said that their pact or deed is contrary to natural or divine law and consequently is invalid (XXII question V: *Iuravit*, and the canon *In malis promissis*, and the canon *Non semper*, with the notes there). At other times something is declared to be contrary to canon law or civil law, and thus contrary to public law constituted for the good of all, and for this reason it is invalid (*ff De pactis*, the law *Publicum* and the law *Iure gentium* § *Si paciscar*). Or, it contravenes a law in respect only to individual persons and in respect of laws implemented in individual cases, and therefore is either contrary to a law that forbids intervention or invalidation of a particular act in which case the subsequent act is rendered null and void by law, or such an act is not prohibited by the express letter of the law, even if it be contrary to the spirit of the law, and it holds up until it is annulled. But such rules have no place as far as rescripts are concerned, and the reason for this differentiation is because, in the matter of rescripts, the law contains a clause of derogation, as it states: 'neither damaging to the treasury nor contrary to the law, etc.' as in the law *Rescripta*. In other things the matter stands otherwise, for generally a reservation is provided by the law according to which a person might renounce everything which has been introduced in his favor (as in the codex *De pactis*: *Si quis in conscribendo*). From all that has been said above it clearly follows that by both canon and civil law all the above-said agreements or accords are null and void, were contracted invalidly, and by all the aforesaid laws, that is, both human and divine law, they are of no power or moment whatsoever.

There are also such acts as are null in respect to the passive subject, that is, the Brethren spoken of here, who *de iure* are incapable of any dominion or possession on account of their religious vows, by which they renounce all property (see the chapter *Cum ad monasterium* and that which is there noted: *De statu monachorum* near the end, and XII question 1: *Non dicatis*). For it is said that the vows of the regular orders are three: that is, the renunciation of private property, the preservation of chastity, and obedience, as noted there. Since these Brethren are said to be regulars, it is repugnant to their calling to have possessions, both in general, of the order as a whole, and individually. For the law is the same in its application to the whole as to the parts (XIV distinction, canon 5, speaking to which see gloss I in the chapter *Maioriubus*: *De prebendis,* which is in accord with the foregoing). For those that have professed such vows are comparable in law to slaves (LIV distinction: *Multus*, and the aforesaid *Non dicatis*). And just as the clothes worn by a slave are the property of his lord (*ff De Peculio*: *Illud vestimentum*), not the slave, so even the robes the monk wears cannot be said to belong to him, as if he were a slave (as in the LIV distinction there: *Subire servitutem*). For he possesses nothing that is possessed by another (*ff De adulterijs*: *Sic eveniet*), for the Church owns both habit and monk (*ff De acquirenda possessione,* the law *Cum heredes* in the gloss *De iure*). And since the slave acquires nothing for himself, but the master does (*ff De acquirenda possesione* law I), so here whatever is acquired by the monks is acquired for their cloister or hospital in which they made their profession of vows, or to which they are subject (which is proven in *De officio ordinarij,* chapter 5, and the final chapter of *De regularibus*).

By entering a monastery, or a hospital, or any other institution dedicated to the Order, all a person's rights and entries *eo ipso* are translated thereto, and in this manner their execution pertains entirely to said monastery or hospital — such is what ought to be said in the matter, according to Innocent (*De probacionibus*: *In presencia*). And so such individuals are unable to sue or enter into any contracts in their own name, but only if they are acting in an administrative capacity, and sue and contract in the name of another, as a procurator, in the name of a given hospital, for example. This matter is plainly dealt with in the *Speculum* (in the first part entitled *De accione*: 'An exception is made in the case of the plaintiff, as he is a monk,' and in the following parts). All administrators are known as procurators (I question III: *Salvator*) and thus all who renounce their own in this way ought not to live by rapine, but rather by the fruits of the endowment of their hospital or monastery (as it is noted in the chapter *Johannes*: *De regularibus*, by Johannes Andreae and others). Nor should any hospital or monastery be founded without sufficient endowment (I question II: *Placuit*; *De institucionibus* chapter I, in *Authentica*: *Ut determinatus sit numerus clericorum* at the outset at the outset). In the case of the mendicant orders, alms take the place of an endowment. Johannes Andreae.

So let the aforementioned Knights of the Cross tell us in what hospital is it that they work, or in whose name it is that they possess so many and such territories, cities, fortresses, and so many other worldly goods.[45] Indeed, they call themselves the Brethren of the Hospital of Jerusalem, which hospital may once have existed, but is no more now, nor was it ever really in existence or interpreted to be to at the time; nor has it been since the time at which they acquired such possessions. And if they were Brethren of that Hospital of Jerusalem, they could not acquire things on behalf of a hospital or hospitals not yet in existence. For no endowment can be acquired in the name of a monastery that is not. (For a text expressly dealing with this see the chapter *Abbate Sane*: *De re iudicata, Allegabatur*, book VI). Such a thing would be invalid, nor could anything that does not exist be capable of receiving any donation or easement (*De ecclesijs edificandis*, the chapter *Ad audienciam* II, where this is spoken of). From this it clearly follows that the donation of the dukes of Mazowsze — of the lands of Chełmno, if it were proven what the Knights of the Cross allege in this regard as having been done on their behalf, would still be utterly null *de iure*. Both because they themselves would be incapable of receiving such a donation, and because there neither is nor was there any hospital to which such a donation might be principally made. For whatever is given to these Brethren is understood as being made over to a hospital (*De testamentis*: *Cum in officijs*, and the chapter *Requisisti*). And whatever is bequeathed or donated to a hospital is understood as being given to the poor (as Johannes Andreae notes in his chapter *Dudum*, where the term 'pauper' is spoken of): Because hospitals of this sort are not founded, chiefly, for the sake of the Brethren, but rather for the sake of the poor and infirm (which is proven in the canon *Sanccimus*: XVIII, question VIII).

For as the Philosopher says, the master is not there for the slave, but rather the slave for his master. And so, because a hospital is lacking, which would be, so to speak, the main and final cause, no donation here can have any validity *de iure*, and by law too such would be seen as tending to the prejudice of the King and Kingdom of Poland.

From all this it certainly follows that all contracts in general, by which dominion or possession is transferred from one to another, as in the case of these Brethren, are *de iure* invalid. Similarly, it follows that all verdicts, judgments, or declarations confirming their possession or dominion are null and void. The rationale for both of these statements is clear. For they can neither sue nor contract unless in the name of a hospital, etc., of which they ought to be the procurators, or agents, and not the owners. For all administrators are known under the title 'procurators' (I question III: *Salvator*): for the first, see Johannes Andreae in the chapter *Quanto*: *De officio ordinarij*; concerning the gloss *Hic patet*, where he says that whenever a suit concerns money, or if there be any other civil complaint against a religious, there can be no trial, because the professed religious possesses nothing of his own (XII question I: *Nolo* and the canon *Non dicatis*); as to the second, see Johannes Andreae in the chapter *Cum olim* II: *De privelegijs*, concerning the word 'promotus,' where he states that whether a religious arranges the procurement of something for himself or for his monastery, or enters into any sort of contract, what he acquires belongs to the monastery; should he wish to procure something for a third party, he cannot, because he has no such faculty (on this: *De procuratoribus*: *Constitutus* in gloss 1 along with its reference), nor does he acquire it for his master or his monastery, as such is not his intent (*ff De stipulacione servorum*: the law *Servus*) Johannes Andreae.

And so, from all this it is clear that such use and practices of these Brethren are *de iure* invalid. However much they may call themselves Brethren of the Hospital of Jerusalem, they are, perhaps, unfamiliar with any and all hospitals, and so they sue and contract in the name of their Order, which is illegal; it is not done according to the law; indeed it appears lawless, as things that are too general are repugnant to the law (*De rescriptis*: *Ad hec sumus*, and what is noted there by gloss I with its concordances). For the Order to bring a suit is far too general, as the order as such is a genus that comprises all persons and all monasteries belonging thereto, wherever in the world they may be located, and although it be the case that each monastery has its proper things belonging to it, still none of these possessions are held in common by all. And so, no suit may be made on behalf of all. Furthermore (as the Philosopher says in I *Metaphysics*, and as is noted in *De eleccione*, and in *Genesi*, no suit ought to be made on behalf of any genus unless by reason of the individuals that make it up, for deeds are performed by individuals. And because these individuals have no possessions of their own, consequently, a suit on their behalf is repugnant, as has been said above, in reference to the genus, or Order — to which it is repugnant as well. And I say it is invalid — that practice invented through the error of these brethren (for which see the laws to the contrary, in chapter *Olim* I: *De restituccione spoliatorum*, where in 'nomine domus milicie templi' the case of the Knights Templars is moved, and the chapter *Cum ad sedem* of the same title, 'Ad hospitale Ierusolimitanum spectare,' likewise in the chapter *Inter dilectos*: *De donacione*, where we also find reference to the case of the Hospitallers, *De fide instrumentorum*: *Inter dilectos*, where 'Abbas nomine monasterii sui,' and in many other places similar to these), because whereas it is permitted to secular colleges or chapters, to whose professions the possession of goods and such dominion is not repugnant, to sue and contract in the name of their college or chapter, this is not true of regular religious. For this reason, even if an abbot should from time to time sue on his own behalf or that of his monastery, it is nonetheless improper, as Johannes Andreae notes (in the chapter Abbate: *De re iuridica* book VI, concerning the second gloss toward the end, after Johannes Monachus and the Archdeacon).[46]

From the foregoing, we deduce in consequence that these Brethren, holding in their possession the goods and extensive lands of their Order, and that not in the name of any hospital, etc., are worthy of condemnation by virtue of the very vow they professed, and because of such unlawful possession it is obvious that they ought to be punished by law, because of these offensive deeds of theirs (as according to *Cum ad monasteriis*: *De statu monachorum*). The rationale: Whereas the Hospital of Jerusalem is not in existence, to which the brethren assert that they belong, no possessions may be acquired in its name, for it is said that 'he possesses, in whose name the thing is possessed' (*De resitucione spoliatorum*: *Cum venisset*). Consequently, possessing things in the name of the Order, they also possess them in their own name, for the whole includes its part (according to the rule *In toto*: *De regulis iuris*, Book VI). Whereby the same judgment pertains to the whole and to the part (XIV question V: *Penale*). From this there results their usurpation of another's property: for that which is held in common belongs to me (*ff De verborum significacione* final book: *Pupillus,* further §, in support of the chapter *Cum in Illis*: *De prebendis*, book VI, and what is noted in the final gloss). Therefore, what is said of the three vows that belong to any sort of monastic profession, that is: poverty, obedience, and chastity (as in the above-cited *Cum ad monasterium*), the possession of goods and all such dominion is repugnant to the propriety of the vow of poverty, the will to govern or dominate others is repugnant to the vow of obedience made to God at the hands of others, and as for this Order, apart from the peace, it is held that they are acting against their faith both on account of their dominion and the benefits they derive. This Order appears degenerate, *viz.*, by reason of its occupying extensive territories and holding possessions and dominating others by virtue of a public law, which is contrary to the rationale of monastic vows, and by consequence, contrary to their individual oaths. By so doing, they become unfaithful themselves as it is said in Ecclesiastes (chapter V):[47] 'If thou hast vowed any thing to God, defer not to pay it: for an unfaithful and foolish servant displeaseth Him.'

From the above, it follows that the aforementioned Knights of the Cross have no right whatsoever to the goods they obtain or occupy, nor can they have, especially in regard to the lands here in question — and this lack of rights is very clear indeed. So much for the second principal issue.

And because it is clear from what is said above that all bases upon which the case of the Knights of the Cross rests are invalid, thus they do not affect in any way the verdicts of the judges.[48] For that which by law has no issue presents no impediment (as in the rule *Non prestat*: *De regulis iuris* book VI).

But let us assume, without prejudice to the truth, that the pacts in question are upheld in law, and, consequently, so is the renunciation or alienation made by the King. Now, would such a pact, if valid, create an impediment to the execution of said verdict?

I respond that, if such a pact were *de iure* valid, it certainly would constitute an impediment. However, if it were said that although valid and upheld by law, it could be stricken by virtue of some exception, it would not impede, and in this matter there are many legal remedies by which these bases might be dashed.

And thus, it is impossible to impede execution of the sentence.

For if the donation of the dukes of Mazowsze,[49] or any other thing preceding said verdict be invoked, even assuming that it would in other respects be valid *de iure*, still it would be irrelevant in the face of the sentence legally handed down against it, which upholds the rights of the other party and is recognized as true (as in the chapter *Cum inter vos*: *De sentencia et re iudicata*). Nor should any privileges or confirmations be relied upon in any way, such as the said Knights of the Cross have received and seem to base themselves upon, as arising from the same cause, springing from the same source — for when the principle is invalid, so are all accessories thereto (which is proven in the aforesaid chapter *Cum inter*, in both the text and the gloss beginning with 'Quia donacio,' and *De fides instrumentorum*: *Inter dilectos*, and similar texts). And by these very same laws it is proven that, since the Peace of Toruń is null and void *de iure*,[50] in the same way the arbitrament that followed it,[51] ratifying and confirming it, is also null and void, as it derived its cause or origin from it. Furthermore, it is null and void because it is contrary to the verdict already handed down, and such arbitraments made concerning such things as have already been definitively decided by a binding judgment are null and void by the law itself (which is proven in the chapter *Exposito*: *De arbitris*, where this is spoken of).

And so I have stated that one must not base one's case on such privileges. For according to received convention, privileges are done away with by judgments (as in the chapter *Suborta* of the same title, and what is noted there in the final gloss, of which see chapter 1: *De pactis*, book VI). For a judgment ought not to be withdrawn under the pretext of new documents or items newly discovered, nor should suits be reprised (as in the same chapter *Suborta* at the end, and in the chapter *Inter monasterium*, of the same title, *De re iudicata*).

Now, should an allegation be made concerning an agreement having been compacted: this would be impeded by the presumption of its being extorted by fear or deception, as has been stated,[52] and thus, even if it were somehow valid *de iure*, still it should be annulled because the law takes the part of the deceived, not the deceivers (*De rerum permutacione*: *Cum universorum*).

There impedes also the fact of the faith having been broken by the Knights of the Cross who did not uphold their end of the agreement,[53] and so faith will be broken with him, who breaks his faith (*De iure iurando*: *Pervenit* II); because when one party does not uphold his end of a bargain, the other party may return to his former rights (which is proven in the gloss *Sed nonne* in the chapter *Cum inter*: *De eleccione,* by the laws cited therein). It is not the case that by virtue of agreements of this sort original rights expire, because such agreements have their tacit conditions: 'If the faith be kept,' etc. (*De pactis*: *Cum pridem*). This differs in spiritual matters, where by virtue of a renunciation a right expires, because in such things no conditions are admitted and one simply renounces unconditionally (the aforesaid chapter *Pridem*, which is also proven by the cited gloss to the chapter *Cum inter*, the rubric *Allegato*, while the chapter *Pervenit* by H. Boyk expounds on this fully).

Similarly, should the arbitrament of the King of the Romans, etc., be invoked here, granting for the sake of argument, and without any prejudice to the truth, that such a thing were valid in itself,[54] still it would not impede, since it was not observed or honored by the Knights of the Cross. What is more, the same is impugned by their deeds to the contrary (*De usuris*: *Quia frustra*, and the rule 'Ex eo quis debet comodum sequi': *De regulis iuris* book VI). And so, when one of the contracting parties to an obligation mutually ratified by law contravenes the same, the other party to the agreement is understood as being absolved of his obligation (as is noted in the text of the same chapter *Pervenit* of Francis, the Cardinal of Florence). And thus it necessarily follows that the rights demanded by the King of Poland, arising from the sentence, remain valid and the execution of the verdict *de iure* is to be demanded.

There is yet another remedy to which the King of Poland is entitled by his own right. That is, the right to revoke an alienation of this sort, and by consequence, any pact that is harmful, as stated above, entered into by himself or another. For one ought to revoke any pact made that works ill (which is proven in *De accusacionibus*, the chapter *Quailter et quando* I, with others similar thereto). For successors too may revoke the ill deeds of their predecessors (XII question II *Etsi illi*, XVI question IV: *Si sacerdotes*, *De precario* chapter II). Hence a privilege that is enormously prejudicial to another is to be revoked (*De decimis*: *Suggestam*, and others of the like). A privilege is also lost through an infraction by citizens (XXV question II *Ita nos*). And I say that the King is empowered to revoke by his own right or authority, according to B., the chapter *Intellecto*: *De iure iurando* invoked above.

Nor is any impediment made here by the Codex: let no man take the law into his own hands when involved in a legal dispute. For according to the law, if the thing in question was his, by taking the law into his own hands, by acting as a judge in his own matter, he loses his right (the Codex *Unde vi*: *Si quis in tantam*), and if it was not his, but was rather due him, the same applies (*ff Quod metus causa*: *Extat*), but these rules pertain only when the person in question has no judicial authority to pronounce in his own case. For just as a bishop, though he may be called a procurator or administrator of the Church (XII question I: *Cui privatum*; *De donacionibus* chapter II), may still act as judge in a case involving his Church (argument II question VII: *Si quis ab episcopus*, and the canon *Si quis erga*, where this is treated), as the Emperor is a judge in a case of his treasury, although that be said to be the Emperor's Treasury, as it has become common to note by learned men following Innocent in the chapter *Nosti*: *De eleccione*, where this is spoken of by Francis Cardinal of Florence in the sixth chapter — so, for the very same reason, a king can be a judge in a case involving his own kingdom. For this reason, the King may make a revocation without the usual due process, since the issue in question is notorious — as we find according to the same Cardinal who so understands the matter in his summa. This is repeated by others as well, and I believe it to be true even if the object of the revocation were valid. And on this subject, whether one might be a judge in one's own case, Innocent refers to the note *De foro competenti*: *Cum sit*, and better: *De censibus*: *Venerabili*, and *De verborum significacione*: *Ex parte*, and *De poenis*: *Romana*, book VI. Francis, Cardinal.

But in the matter of whether a person might come out against an act of his own, H. Boyk treats of this in the aforesaid chapter *Nosti*, according to which I state that in extrajudicial matters, where an action is not valid *de iure*, if what a person did was done not in his own name but in that of another, and not as a judge, he may contravene it. As for example if some prelate were to sell a thing belonging to the Church, he may contravene it, not in his own name, but in the name of the Church (as it is put there, and in *De rebus ecclesie non alienandis*: *Si quis presibterorum* and *De iure iurando*: *Sicut nostris*.

And B. and Ostiensis also note this in the same title, chapter *Intellecto*). H. Boyk.

Or make this other distinction, according to Innocent: Either the fact is disapproved by law and thus could not be changed, and then it is permissible to come out against it (*De filijs presbyterorum*: *Veniens*; *De prebendis*: *Cum non ignores;* XII question II: *Non licet*), or it is not disapproved by law, and therefore a contravention is not permitted. Or otherwise again, according to Petrus de Samsona and the Abbot[55] following him, where he also makes reference to Iohannes Andreae and John de Lignano: Either it is not valid on the part of the giver, and thus he may revoke it, since the receiver is not affected, since the gift was invalid in the first place (*De iure patronatis*: *Quod autem*, and the chapter *Cum laici*, where this is proven, and Ostiensis in gloss I), or it is invalid on the part of the receiver who, perhaps, is incapable of receiving it, and in that case the giver, who gave validly, cannot revoke. The second is understood in *Diversis fallacijs*: *De clericis coniugatis*.

And accordingly this should be understood in cases where it is not valid on either part, as here in our proposition.

And even though execution would be difficult in the premises, and because of this many contrarities have arisen *de facto,* still this is true according to the law, *de iure.*

Therefore, Most Serene Prince, as it has been notoriously proven from the foregoing that these aforementioned Brethren are, and have been, the violent and unjust occupiers of these lands, as is stated in the definitive verdict referred to above, it is also established that they have no bases whatsoever to claim these lands *de iure*, nor can they attest anything valid in support of their claims, and by consequence, it is most evidently established that they have no right thereto. And from all this it is necessarily inferred and shall be established also, that You simply cannot pronounce, declare, commend, or in any other way approve their retention and possession of said lands of which up until now they have held in occupation. The manifest reason for this is that such would mean — and far be it from Your Grace! — that You would thus be authorising them to sin, tacitly consenting to their damnation, according to the words of the prophet: 'If thou didst see a thief thou didst run with him, and with adulterers thou hast been a partaker. These things hast thou done, and I was silent.'[56] Thus shall it be, which God forbid, should You favor their cruelty more than justice, and raise inequity above equity, which cannot be done, as the Canon states: 'He who is able to oppose and confound the perverse and does not do so, does nothing less than support them in their impiety' (XXIII question II: *Qui potest*). This would surely be to approve their positions above-stated, which are contrary to divine law, utterly null and iniquitous; such would be to pile iniquity upon iniquity. Furthermore — which God again forbid! — this would be to tacitly consent to the grave oppression of the Kingdom of Poland; yes, to its future destruction. For 'he who declines to oppose a manifest crime is not free of suspicion of being a secret abettor' (LXXXIII, distinction: *Error*).[57] Nor could this be excused or justified on the basis of the King of Poland's extorted consent — as stated above — or any supposed agreement to the aforementioned Brethren being allowed to retain in perpetuity the aforesaid lands, since it has been notoriously established that they are the enemies of the same King and his kingdom, incapable moreover as they are of dominion, as proven above. Indeed, this would rather condemn such consent extorted by violence, as something that adds insult to injury, affliction upon affliction. Especially as the violence of their actions has been manifestly established, such consent, even if made without the duress of a well-founded fear, would not purge such a vice, such a crime, as stated above. Beyond this it would also be to detract from the above-mentioned, definitive sentence of the legates of the Apostolic See, or to define the same in a manner other than what has been definitively decided, and by consequence, to proceed in a manner that is null and void *de facto*, in such a way that does not correspond to the grace and honor of the royal dignity. Such compromises or arbitraments concerning business already decided, contrary to definitive judgments, are null and void in law (see the chapter *Exposita*: *De arbitris*, where this is spoken of). Nor should You be moved to the contrary by the fact that recently, in Hungary, in Buda to be precise, eight years ago, in making a pronouncement by virtue of a similar compromise between the same two parties, Your Serene Majesty approved or confirmed the above-mentioned Peace of Toruń, despite the fact that it contains multiple errors and is null *de iure.* For not to wish to repair something wrongly done is seen as contrary to honesty. So the emperor states in *Authentica* (*De nupciis*, near the beginning of the recapitulation, IV): 'For we should not blush to find that it is proper for us to correct what we earlier stated, not waiting for such correction to be carried out by others. Thus does the Pope at times correct his sentences or acts, as does the Church, as indeed all wise men ought to stand to the task, as noted in *Speculum* in Part II, title *Exceptiones*, chapter IV, verse 'Ut autem').

And so nothing remains for You to do but to set aside all human favor, and, keeping God before your eyes, to conform yourself to the said verdict, from which you may not withdraw any more than may the King of Poland, as stated above. By your arbitrament, You should do away with all difficulties that stand in the way of the execution of said verdict, and provide the manner in which the aforesaid brethren will be made to restore said lands effectively. Because thereby You shall be providing for their salvation, removing from them the dangerous opportunity of destroying the Kingdom in the future, and the Kingdom and King of Poland will be granted their due: justice, truth, and equity, according to both divine and human law. And such is right and just — the contrary is improper and iniquitous. Let therefore thine eyes behold equity.

So much for the third principle, the first matter.[58]

Endnotes

1. This date represents the time Paweł presented it to the imperial *Reichstag* held at Wrocław (Breslau) on 6 January 1420, which was attended by, among others, Sigismund, King of Hungary and Bohemia and emperor elect (as of 1410, crowned 1433). The meeting included arbitration of on-going conflicts between Poland and the Knights of the Teutonic Order. But Paweł, as procurator for the Polish claims, had been mandated to prepare these claims by 17 December 1419 and *Oculi* had probably been completed by then. See Belch, *Paulus Vladimiri*, I, 137-138.

2. The text that follows is Version I of this treatise, but there is a briefer treatment (not presented here) that represents a summary of the fuller arguments and presentation here. Ehrlich, *Pisma wybrane*, III, 79, n. 1 suggests that the shorter version was prepared in vain at the last minute (in Wrocław), where—according to Jan Dlugosz, *Annales*, VIII, 110-125 (*Liber undecimus, sub anno 1420*), here pp. 112-113), Sigismund had already made up his mind on the matter.

3. Ps 16:1-2 (Vulgate numeration): 'O Lord, my justice: attend to my supplication. Give ear unto my prayer, which proceedeth not from deceitful lips. Let my judgment come forth from thy countenance: let thy eyes behold the things that are equitable' [Exaudi, Domine, justitiam meam; intende deprecationem meam. Auribus percipe orationem meam, non in labiis dolosis. De vultu tuo judicium meum prodeat; oculi tui videant aequitates]. The text of this opening quotation ends *ut supra* ("and [the] foregoing"), which is a reference to Paweł's prologue to *Oculi* that is not printed in the edition being translated here. It is briefly discussed by Belch, *Paulus Vladimiri*, I, 185-186 and edited I, 604-605.

4. In fact, it is only the first of these geographical groupings that are treated in this text, though the presentation ranges chronologically over events from the early fourteenth century to Paweł's present. the reign of King Władysław Jagiełło,

5. Thus three approaches: first the evidence or facts as Paweł understands them; second an analysis as to the legal validity of the Order's claims; and third, a proposal of remedies.

6. Władysław Łokietek (*ca.* 1260/1261-1333), King of Poland from 1320.

7. Kazimierz III, later given the sobriquet the Great (1310-1370), King of Poland from 1333.

8. The pagan Grand Duke of Lithuania named Jogaila, who converted to Latin Christianity in 1385, taking the Christian name Władysław (known also in Polish historiography by the Polonized version of his Lithuanian name as Jagiełło). Upon his conversion, he married Jadwiga of Anjou, the ruler of Poland and was recognized thereby as the Polish king. He died in 1434.

9. The circumstances by which the Order obtained rule in Gdańsk (Danzig) have been controversial. It was said at the time that, in that conquest, some 10,000 individuals perished. The matter was the subject of the papal inquiries in 1320-1321 and 1339, and there is an important body of scholarship that has been devoted to it.

For a good overview of the events in 1308, see the treatments by Marian Biskup and Gerard Labuda, *Dzieje Zakonu Krzyżackiego w Prusach. Gospodarka—Społeczeństwo—Państwo—Ideologia* (Gdańsk: Wydawnictwo Morskie Gdańsk, 1986), pp. 256-258; and Paul Milliman, *"The Slippery Memory of Men." The Place of Pomerania in the Medieval Kingdom of Poland* (Leiden and Boston: Brill, 2013), pp. 139-151. More fully, see the materials in Błażej Śliwiński, ed., *"Rzeź Gdańska" z 1308 roku w świetle najnowszych badań* (Gdańsk: Muzeum Historyczne Miasta Gdańska, 2009). The article by Śliwiński and Beata Możejko, "Gdańsk in the Aftermath of the Teutonic Order's Actions in Pomerelia in the First Half of the Fourteenth Century," *East Central Europe* 47, 1 (2020): 29-38 also provides helpful insights.

10. In particular the documents connected with the papal tribunals of 1320-1321 and 1339. See below in this treatise.

11. See above in the translation of the treatise *Saevientibus*, n. 2.

12. Inowrocław.

13. The documents connected with this papal inquiry and court were printed in *Lites*, 2nd ed. I, 7-51 in an edition that had numerous shortcomings, pointed out by Helena Chłopocka, "Dotychczasowe edycje *Lites ac res gestae* w świetle krytyki," *Studia Źródłoznawcze* 10 (1965): 109-115. Subsequently Chłopocka published a revised, and much improved, edition of the 1320-1321 proceedings: *Lites ac Res Gestae inter Polonos Ordinemque Cruciferorum*, vol. 1. *Causa Junivladislaviae et Brestiae-Cuiaviae anno 1320-1321 Acta / Spory i sprawy pomiędzy Polakami a Zakonem Krzyżackim*, vol. 1. *Sprawa wytoczona w Inowrocławiu i Brześciu Kujawskim w latach 1320-1321* (Wrocław: Ossolineum, 1970).

14. Paweł conveniently omits in this listing of campaigns by the Order, the victory won by Łokietek and the Polish army over the Order at Płowce in 1331; see Tomasz Jurek, "Uwagi o bitwie pod Płowcami," *Ziemia Kujawska*, 9 (1993): 77-97. For an overview of Polish-Order political and military relations in the period to which Paweł refers in his text see Biskup and Labuda, *Dzieje Zakonu Krzyżackiego w Prusach*, pp. 342-348; in English see Paul W. Knoll, *The Rise of the Polish Monarchy. Piast Poland in East Central Europe, 1320-1370* (Chicago: University of Chicago Press, 1972), pp. 50, 54-58.

15. The papal representatives were Peter Gervais and Galhard de Carceribus, the latter a long-serving nuncio in Poland who was also involved with collecting the tax, "Peter's Pence," that Poland—almost uniquely in medieval Europe—paid to the papacy. See Stanisław Szczur, "Współpracownicy Galharda z Carcès, kolektora papieskiego w Polski," in Janusz Bieniak, et al., eds., *Homines et Societas: Czasy Piastów i Jagiellonów* (Poznań: Wydawnictwo Poznańskiego Towarzystwa Przyjaciół Nauk, 1997), 337-344. The tribunal over which they presided was held in Warsaw in 1339, and the testimony of witnesses and other official documents have been printed in *Lites*, 2nd ed. I, 65-408. The court's judgment was overwhelmingly favorable to Poland. For a good analysis of the proceedings, the treatment of Bieniak, "Przebieg procesu polsko-krzyżackiego z 1339 roku," *Pamiętnik Bibliioteki Kórnickiej* 23 (1993): 5-22 is very useful. One hundred seventy-six witnesses were

sworn in and 126 actually testified from a broad range of social strata; some were clerics, others were civilians; nearly all had either first-hand evidence or knew documents supporting their depositions directly. Collectively their testimony has proved to be gold-mine for historians in seeking to understand issues of literacy, social status, political and ecclesiastical networks, and the like. See, for example, Anna Adamska, "The Kingdom of Poland versus the Teutonic Knights: Oral Traditions and Literate Behaviour in the Later Middle Ages," in Gerhard Jaritz and Michael Richter, eds., *Oral History of the Middle Ages: The Spoken Word in Context* (Krems and Budapest: Central European University Press, 2001), pp. 67-78.

16. There is a subtle, but important, assumption at play in Paweł's text here, namely that the Kingdom of Poland is an entity within which there are numerous territories that belong to it. This is not simply the idea that an individual exercises authority over specific lands and locations. It is rather that there is an abstract concept of the *Regnum Poloniae* and that it is not complete and whole without all its territories. Thus, for example, although Polish rulers like Łokietek and Kazimierz did not, in practice, exercise rule in the territories Paweł is mentioning, they areas nevertheless, as a kind of *Polonia irredenta*, constitute parts of the Polish kingdom. Thus, for example, Bishop Jan Grot of Kraków could circulate with effect the following epigram through the kingdom in the 1330s: "O, King Kazimierz, you shall never have peace with Prussia/Until you recover Gdańsk, that is, the land of Pomorze [Pomerania];" cited from the contemporary source by Zygmunt Wojciechowski, *Studia Historyczne* (Warsaw: PAX, 1955), p. 221 This concept of what constitutes Polish unity has recently been powerfully developed by Wojciech Drelicharz, *Unifying the Kingdom of Poland in Mediaeval Historiographic Thought* (Kraków: Societas Vistulana, 2019, Polish original 2012); see especially pp. 11-25, especially p. 11: "The unification of the Polish lands did not end with the rebirth of the Kingdom of Poland at the turn of the 14th century. The process lasted till the latter half of the 15th century, and its idea remained topical many years after the coronations of Przemysł II [1295] and Władysław [Łokietek]."

17. This is Duke Conrad of Mazovia (1187/88-1247). See the translated text of the treatise *Saevientibus* above, n. 2.

18. Beyond the thirty referred to here were other witnesses whose testimony bore on a broad range of matters. Paweł then proceeds to summarize the content and relevance of this testimony, attributing it to specific individuals.

19. i.e., able to read the Latin documents.

20. i.e., that legitimate rule of Pomerania passed sequentially from one to the next and then to Łokietek—and by extension to his successors, in particular Kazimierz the Great.

21. Although the judgment of 1339 favored Kazimierz and Poland, the Order refused to recognize it, Four years of political uncertainty followed, until in 1343—urged by a new pope and others—a political and territorial settlement, restoring Kujawy and Dobrzyń to Poland, was concluded between the Polish king at the Order at Kalisz. For the most part this stabilized Polish-Order relations for

half a century. On the Peace of Kalisz, see Szczur, "Traktat pokojowy Kazimierza Wielkiego z Zakonem Krzyżackim z 1343 roku," *Zapiski Historyczne* 56 (1991): 439-464. More briefly, Knoll, *Rise of the Polish Monarchy*, pp. 117-119; and Milliman, "*Slippery Memory of Men*," pp. 137-138.

22. i.e., 1385-1411.

23. i.e., 1411-to the 1412 court of arbitration in Buda.

24. Paweł here is referring to and summarizing many of the points made in *Saevientibus* and *Articuli*.

25. The [First] Peace of Toruń (1411) was remarkably lenient for the Order given their military losses at Grunwald in 1410. In his presentation. Jan Długosz, *Annales*, VII, 119-120 (*Liber undecimus, sub anno 1410*) and VII, 177-178 (*sub anno* 1411), was especially critical of Jagiełło's actions after the battle that severely limited Poland's options and in the negotiations that led to the eventual Treaty of Toruń. For the treaty itself, see the analysis in Sławomir Jóźwiak, Krzysztof Kwiatkowski, Adam Szewde, and Sobiesław Szybkowski, *Wojna Polski i Litwy z Zakonem Krzyżackim w latach 1409-1411* (Malbork: Muzeum Zamkowe w Malborku, 2010), pp. 703-712. Paweł argues here and later in his legal exposition that the treaty's terms should not be observed.

26. In the aftermath of the Treaty of Toruń, there was renewed military conflict between Poland and the Order—in Paweł's eyes the Order breaking the treaty—over territorial claims, As a result the dispute was submitted to Sigismund at Buda in 1412, who urged both sides to abide by the Toruń territorial agreements. He did, however, commission Benedict of Macra to investigate matters in the region. For the Buda decision, see *Lites*, II, 2nd ed, 53-69; and II, 70-71 for the deputation of Benedict. The testimony and evidence Benedict gathered in Prussia, Poland, and Lithuania and his subsequent report are printed in *Lites*, II, 88-356. For Benedict mission, see above in *Articuli*, n. 10.

27. Some of the details lying behind this assertion by Paweł are treated effectively by Szweda, "Zakon Krzyżacki wobec Polski i Litwy w latach 1411-1414," *Prace Historyczne* 141, 2 (2014): 531-553.

28. Paweł is here referring obliquely to developments after the Council of Constance, when twice Poland and the Order entered into military hostilities. It was in the aftermath of these that an armistice was concluded and both sides agreed once again to have Sigismund act as arbiter between the conflicting claims. On 10 September 1419 Paweł, who was then serving as Vice-Rector of the University of Kraków, was appointed Polish procurator for the court of arbitration in Buda; see Belch, *Paulus Vladimiri*, I, 137 for these developments.

29. Paweł begins here the legal analysis of the claims made by the Order.

30. Ex, 20:15, 17.

31. Johannes Andreas (*ca.* 1270-1348) studied at Bologna, then taught at both Bologna and Padua, serving also from time to time as an ambassador from Bologna. A married layman (only the second to become a professor of canon law), he produced

a number of important and influential works. He died in the plague in 1348. See Brundage, *Canon Law*, pp. 216-217.

32. Probably a reference to Bernard of Montemirat (Abbas antiquus); see above in the treatise *Saevientibus*, n. 43.

33. Luke 11:17.

34. i.e, Aristotle.

35. Giovanni da Legnano (*ca*.. 1320-1383), doctor of both laws at Bologna who also taught there. In his writings—as well as in his experience as a diplomat—he demonstrated considerable expertise on both the study of war and peace and practical matters. See Brundage, *Canon Law*, p. 118.

36. Hostiensis (Henricus de Segusio, 1190/1200-1271) studied canon law at Bologna at the same time as Sinibaldo dei Fieschi (the future Pope Innocent IV). He subsequently taught at Paris and was named cardinal-bishop of Ostia in 1261. His important body of canonical writings and his influence ensured he was highly regarded. Dante includes him in *Paradiso* in his *Commedia*: 12:82-97. See Brundage, *Canon Law*, p. 214, and the treatise *Opinio Ostiensis* above.

37. The crucial implication of Paweł's argument here is that once a legal judgement has been made and not appealed (such as, for example, the papal courts in 1320-1321 and in 1339, when the Order simply ignored the decision), no later agreement—whether a compromise or even a treaty—can be valid. The original judgment must stand. See the paragraph below in his treatment of the Peace of Toruń, where the word "ought" (*debet* from *debeo*) is crucial.

38. This is Henricus Boic[h] (*ca*, 1310-after 1370, but before 1390), who studied civil and canon law, earning the doctorate in both laws at Paris, where he apparently taught. His most important works were *repertoria* on the *Liber sextus* and the *Decretum*, but his reputation and influence was limited. See Belch, *Paulus Vladimiri*, I, 298 n. 9; 557; and 581, n. 5; and Ehrlich, *Pisma wybrane,* I, xxxiii.

39. Ehrlich, *Pisma wybrane*, III, 85, n. 70, suggests this is a reference to developments in thirteenth century Hungary that are relevant to issues in Poland.

40. Baldus de Ubaldis (*ca*. 1327-1400), who studied civil and canon law at Perugia and Pisa, then taught at several other *studia*. Among his students were the future Pope Gregory XI (who returned the papacy to Rome, ending the western schism), Peter of Ancharano, and Francisco Zarabella. His extensive writings were very influential; see Brundage, *Canon Law*, p. 207.

41. Translator's clarifying insertion.

42. This is a continuation of the argument referred to above, n. 39. Paweł does, however, move quickly to apply it to Poland.

43. The argument with respect to Poland being developed here by Paweł, i.e., concerning limitations upon royal authority, is striking, though it fits well within the medieval tradition that the ruler (whether king or duke) is not absolute. Further to this principal, see Jean Dunbabin, "Government," in J. H. Burns, ed., *The Cambridge History of Medieval Political Thought c. 350-c. 1450* (Cambridge: Cambridge University Press, 1998), pp. 477-519, esp. pp. 482-519; and Antony

Black, *Political Thought in Europe 1250-1450* (Cambridge: Cambridge University Press, 1992), pp. 136-161, esp. pp. 152-161. For developments on the Polish scene, which was moving toward a *Ständestaat*, see the collection of stimulating articles in Andrzej Marzec and Maciej Wilamowski, eds., *Król w Polsce XIV i XV wieku* (Kraków: Societas Vistulana, 2006); Andrzej Wyczański, *Polen als Adelrepublik* (Osnabrück: Fibre, 2001[Klio in Polen 5], Polish original, 2nd ed. 1991); and Bożena Czwojdrak, "Governance System in Poland during the 15th Century," in Grische Vercamer and Dušan Zupka, eds., *East Central Europe. Power, Ritual and Legitimacy in Bohemia, Hungary and Poland* (Leiden and Boston: Brill, 2022), pp. 291-305, esp. pp. 293-294.

44. Dinius de Mugello (1253-post 1298) studied at Bologna, taught civil law at Pistoia, and eventually became part of the papal curia during the pontificate of Boniface VIII (d. 1303). Dinius participated in the preparation of the *Liber Sextus*. See *Repertorium Fontium Historiae Medii Aevi* IV (Rome: Istituto Storico Italiano per il Medio Evo, 1976), pp. 201-202.

45. This is a recurring theme in many of Paweł's works: the Order was instituted to protect and serve a hospital in Jerusalem during the crusades. They no longer do this. Thus the rationale for their existence no longer obtains and the Order should therefore be dissolved—and, as he argued at Constance—condemned.

46. Johannes Monachus (Jean LeMoine, *ca.* 1250-1313) studied civil and canon law at Paris. He eventually was named a cardinal and served in the curia under Boniface VIII; see Brundage, *Canon Law*, p. 219. The Archdeacon reference is to Guido de Baysio (*ca.* 1250-1313), who studied and taught canon law at Reggio, was named Archdeacon of Bologna by Boniface VIII and eventually became archchancellor of the university there. He joined the papal curia in 1304 and produced a number of influential works. His most famous student was Johannes Andreas, whom Paweł often quotes. See Brundage, *Canon Law*, pp. 212-213.

47. Eccl. 5:3.

48. In the 1339 proceeding initiated by Kazimierz III.

49. In the early 13th century; see the text of *Saevientibus*, n. 2.

50. Paweł's rational here is that, first, the Treaty of Toruń was invalid because the matter had been settled in 1339.

51. See above, n. 23.

52. Paweł's second rational for the Treaty of Toruń being invalid is because it was extorted.

53. And his rationale in the third place is that the Order did not adhere to what they had agreed in the Toruń treaty of 1411. Neither did they, Paweł argues below, honor Sigismund's arbitration in 1412.

54. i. e., implying that it wasn't actually valid.

55. Petrus de Samsone, from France, a master of canon law at Bologna in the middle of the 13th century and author of a *summa* on the *Decretales* of Pope Gregory IX; see *Repertorium Fontium Historiae Medii Aevi*, IX, 1/2 (Rome: Istituto Storico Italiano per il Medio Evo, 2002), pp. 175-176.

56. Despite the attribution of this statement to "the prophet" in Paweł's text, this quotation is from Ps 49:18 and 21 (Vulgate numeration).

57. This is the same canon Paweł quoted at the beginning of his *Quoniam error*: an error unopposed is thereby approved. There is a not-so-subtle implication in this, as Ehrlich, *Pisma wybrane*, III, 90, n. 122, points out, that should Sigismund favor the Order in his decision it will appear he was cooperating with them.

58. The other two matters: (a) Dobrzyń, Kujawy, Mazovia, and Samogitia [Żmudź] and (b) the Kingdom of Poland and its kings, are not, in fact, taken up in this treatise; see above, n. 4.

TO SEE CLEARLY

(*Ad videndum*, 1421)[1]

Composed by Master Paweł so as to impugn the privileges of the Knights of the Cross[2]

In order to see clearly[3] that the Brethren of the Knights of the Cross of Prussia have no right, on the basis of their own claims in the process that is being argued before our Most Holy lord, Pope Martin V, concerning certain lands and dominions, etc., in dispute between His Most Serene Majesty, my lord Władysław, the illustrious King of Poland, on the one hand, and the aforementioned Brethren on the other: It must first be stated that however many and divers privileges have been produced in support of their case by whatever sort of document — even if such documents were authentic — it is clearly to be concluded from these that, not only have these Brethren no rights thereby, but what is more, their very legal status is erroneous, contrary to divine law, and vehemently suspect in the light of the Christian faith.

Circa these privileges, certain articles[4] have been produced in two manners, or in dual form, with subsequent petitions.

The first of these manners or groups of documents, which contain thirty-four articles, pretend to prove the capability of persons, or the institution of the Order, or the propriety of the titles they claim to have, especially concerning the lands belonging to the faithful — that is to say, the Poles.

In the second manner or group, which contains twenty-two articles, the propriety of other titles is deduced, which they claim to have over lands which have belonged to infidels, especially the inhabitants of Żmudź[5] and the tribe of the Sudes[6].

And because the Faith is touched upon and spoken of in both these articles and the privileges:

Three things are to be considered:

First, the facticity of those aforesaid articles and privileges.

Second, the law concerning the same, and

Third — that we shall elicit certain noteworthy things pertaining to the Faith, which must be carefully and clearly considered in regard to this matter.

As to the first, omitting in this place a statement of these articles and privileges, the tedious and diffuse nature of which would distract the reader from what follows — they may be found in an appendix to this text where he may read them[7] — let us presuppose them here as a fact that gives rise to a right being claimed.

Considering the second, it would be well[8] to look into three things. The first: the aforesaid articles, the second: the Privilege of Alexander,[9] which is adduced as an institution and approbation of the Order, and the third: other privileges consequent for the justification of the titles presented.

For the better explication of all these evidences a premise must here be made that, in these very articles and privileges, the aforesaid Brethren confess that they are incapable of possessing any thing or dominion, above all in their own name.

For in their asserting in the aforesaid articles that they constitute a regular order of religious Brethren, which Order has been officially approved, tacitly, by consequence, they assert themselves to be incapable of possessing things of any sort in their own name, because the abdication of the right to hold property is the very substance of a religious order (which is proved in *De statu monachorum*: *Cum ad monasterium*, towards the end, and in XII question I of the canon *Non dicatis*, and similar such texts). Now, the aforesaid Privilege of Pope Alexander IV also seems to bind them to an express profession of a religious vow whereby they solemnly renounce all possessions (as in the laws adduced) and likewise, in other privileges of theirs, especially in the Privilege of Emperor Lewis IV,[10] they confess the same thing expressly. And so I say that they are incapable of possessing things in their own name both individually and in common, for the same judgment binds the whole as it does its parts (XIV question five: *Penale*; *De prebendis*, the chapter *Maioribus*, according to what is noted there in gloss I) and he who swears that something is not his own swears likewise that he does not hold it in common with others (*ff De verborum significacione*, the law *Si pupillus*, the final §, and what is noted in the chapter *Cum in illis*: *De prebendis*, book VI, the first gloss). It is another case when acting in the name of another, *viz.*, in the name of a regular order, for which order nothing can be presumed unless proven. For there is this general rule: All congregations are deemed invalid, which have not been expressly approved (*ff De collegijs illicitis*, the third law). This is especially true concerning regular orders (of which see what Innocent says in the chapter *Dilecta*: *De excessibus prelatorum* and what Francis, the Cardinal of Florence,[11] clearly notes there, following Innocent). Ostiensis[12] takes up this rule (in his *Summa*: *De sindico* § I, and proves in *De religiosis domibus*, in the final chapter thereof, and in chapter I, rubric II, book VI of the same title). For this reason, given that such congregations or colleges are prohibited from possessions, it is understood that the prohibition is held in common, by virtue of the rule *Cum quod prohibetur* (*De regulis iuris*, book VI). Hence, although one presumes of a possessor, *de iure*, that he justly possesses what he has (as we read in and as is noted in the chapter *Olim* II: *De privilegijs*), according to Innocent, Osetiensis, and others writing on the same subject, this is true only where the law allows. For the matter is different where the law commonly resists, as in the case of regular religious, according to the law here adduced, because such are not presumed to possess anything, but are simple detainers and occupiers (for which see H. Boyk,[13] where he clearly pronounces on this in the aforesaid chapter *Olim*). And thus in consequence to all these, unless hard evidence suggests otherwise, judgment must be pronounced according to what follows below.

Besides this, it is to be noted[14] — especially in the first articles, in which the approval of the Order is given or stated, and most especially, that one which appears to be the basis of all the rest, in which it is stated: 'Likewise, amongst other military orders, there was approved a certain order under the name of the Hospital of the Blessed Virgin Mary of the German Nation, etc. which has, except for times of vacancy, a Master pro tem as its head and as many knights commanders and regular Brethren as possible, in service to the Lord and doing battle on behalf of the Catholic faith, etc.' Concerning this, please note that by these general words, *scilicet* 'a certain order was approved,' one cannot understand the specific and determinate substance of said Order, nor whether such a substance might be capable of approbation or possession, for nothing can be approved unless its specific and real substance be stated, or unless its essence be named in such a way that indicates that it is truly capable of possessing something (arg. *ff Si certum petatur*: the law *Certum*). Now, these general terms are not sufficient proof that the order in question may be known as such, above, unless what is affirmed in words really exists, and by consequence, this article does not prove that this order has indeed been approved. Now, the fact that it is stated in this article that except for times of vacancy it has a Master pro tem as its head, would prove that at times this order is vacant, and in consequence, that it is a place, for one cannot properly speak of something being vacant unless the thing in question be a place (as in the chapter *Novit*: *Ne sede vacante*, and there: the entire text plus the rubric). That which is said to have a head must be understood to be a body (II question VII: *Sicut inquid*, with which LXI: *Miramur* is in accord). But where can we find such a body or such a place in existence? That is unapparent, for either this order is taken for the specific body of the Hospital of Jerusalem, which has ceased to exist there, and thus the order itself has vanished, or one grasps, in general, that some sort of college of that hospital is what is noted here, and accordingly, assuming without any prejudice to the truth, that any such genus be in existence, still it is never said of such a thing that it is vacant or lacking a head. For genera are not measured by time or place as are species (as is noted in the chapter *Abbate* § Prefatus: *De sententia et re iudicata*, book VI, there following Johannes Monachus[15] and others). As therefore this article is seen to be the basis of all the following, it will not be capable of being proven since it does not express the essence of any thing nor does it confirm any sort of approval of the order in question. For such a vague and uncertain thing is not to be admitted. And therefore none of the following articles are admissible because nothing can be raised upon such a foundation (I question I: *Cum Paulus*). Hence it is that a claim made in the name of this order must be declared inept, for acts are not carried out by genera, but by subjects (following Aristotle in his preface to the Metaphysics, and as is noted by some others (*De eleccione*: *In Genesi*). Therefore, the Order of the Blessed Virgin Mary of the Germans, etc., is said to be a genus having its colleges as species, and so, etc. Now, lthough it be sufficient for an initial claim to conclude presumptively (as is noted in *De libelli oblacione*, Chapter II, and there by Francis Cardinal of Florence), still in its proofs, in articles and in the positions it sets forth, it is necessary to so prosecute the thing that the intent be necessarily deduced (which is noted in the chapter *In presencia*: *De probacionibus*). It is a different matter if the claim is inept, as is seen in this case, where it ought to be torn to shreds. This is especially true where something of the sort shows itself to be inept from its very inception (following H. Boyk in the chapter *Examinata*: *De iudicijs*), indeed even where it is notorious that the agent is incapable of action even if the claim were apt (which Innocent notes: *De officio vicarij*, c. II, vide: *Collectarum*, *De libelli oblacione*, chapter II just at the end). So it is with these Brethren who are unable of possessing anything individually or collectively, as is alleged above. And therefore.

Next, as to this,[16] let us consider another foundational matter, so that the thing might become even more clear. And so it is to be noted that, in so far as a regular order brings about a state of persons bound to its rule, two things are substantially required for this, *viz.*: propriety of place, which is principally effected by the authority of a superior (*De religiosis domibus*, the chapter *Ad hoc*), for although anyone at all may establish an oratorium in his own house and dedicate his home as an asylum for the poor (the above-cited chapter *Ad hoc*, following Innocent and Ostiensis, and in the same title: *Quia contingit*: *In Clementinis*, antepenultimate gloss by Johannes Andreae[17]), where, however, the licence of the bishop has not been received, the very status of the establishment can also be modified without the bishop's licence (as according to these same laws, and in the chapter *De sinodochijs*: *De religiosis domibus*; also is as noted in *De donacionibus*: the chapter *Inter dilectos*, and as in the Archdeacon's *De consecracione*: distcinction I: *Nemo*).

Secondly, the propriety of the persons, which is effected by their profession to the order (*De statu monachorum*: *Cum ad monasterium*, the whole text). For it is the monastic vow, and not the monastic cowl, that makes the monk (which is proven by the text found in *Porrectum*: *De regularibus*).

By reason of place an order can have its own property, because no hospital or institution of such a type ought to be founded or instituted without sufficient endowment (I question II: *Placuit*: *De institucionibus*, chapter I, and in *Autentica*: *Ut determinatus sit numerus clericorum*, at the start thereof). With mendicant orders alms take the place of property, following Iohannes Andreae (on which see his chapter *De regularibus*).

As to the rationale of persons it is said that the order possesses nothing, because possession is repugnant to persons of this sort. For which reasons the renunciation of possessions as a monastic vow is of the very essence of monasticism, as is alleged above.

From what has been said, it is therefore inferred that on account of both reasons stated, the order is said to hold property in common. Yet because the status of the aforementioned Brethren is lacking substance according to the first matter, since none of their locations, above all in Prussia and Poland, etc., have been legitimately instituted by the authority of a superior or founded or endowed by anyone's favor, but rather tyrannically occupied by the Brethren themselves, or otherwise illicitly acquired, as may be evidently concluded from their own privileges, which will be even more clearly apparent from what follows, so also in the second matter are they substantially lacking, because he who is deficient in the first is consequently deficient in the second, for when matters are so connected, the judgment must be the same in the case of both (*De constitucionibus*: *Translato*, and others similar). Thus of necessity it follows that the aforementioned Brethren effectively have neither the status nor order of religious regulars, but rather constitute a secular association.

Moreover, for greater clarification[18] of this matter, this should be of particular note: that even though this Teutonic Order is seen to claim the two above-mentioned substantial characteristics as conveyed upon them, still, because it is necessary that between these two substances one of them must be of a principal sort, the other accessory, or one must be by way of form, and the other by way of matter, and thereby, possession or any other act of this sort, formally and properly ought to be attributed to the principal substance, or the form, and not the matter, *scilicet*, to the place itself, from which also the denomination would arise (this is addressed by these laws which prove it: *De restitucione spoliatorum*: *Cum ad sedem*, in the text where we find the words 'Ad hospitale Ierosolimitanum spectare,' and chapter *Olim* I of the same title, at 'Nomine domus milicie templi,' and the chapter *Inter dilectos*: *De fide instrumentorum*, where 'Abbas nomine monasterii sui,' *De donacionibus*: *Inter dilectos*, and by many other laws). And although it is sometimes said that an Abbot acts on his own behalf and on that of his convent (*De sententia et re iudicata* in the chapter *Abbate Sane*, book VI), this is, however, improperly stated, according to the note of Johannes Andreae (in the same place in *Novela* concerning the II gloss following the Archdeacon and Johannes Monachus). Hence it is that regular religious of this sort are said to possess something in another's name, for he is said to possess a thing, which is possessed in the name of another (*De restitucione spoliatorum*: *Cum venissent*, with others like thereunto). For all administrators are understood under the name 'procurator' (I question II: *Salvator*, towards the end). And therefore whatever is acquired by them is acquired on behalf of their monastery or hospital (which is proven by *De officio ordinarij*: *Quanto*, and *De regularibus*, the final chapter). For even satisfaction made on account of injuries done to a particular monk is to be made to his monastery, indiscriminately, as what is ever given to a monk is acquired by his monastery (as is noted in the chapter *Parochianos*: *De sentencia excommunicacionis*) and just as he cannot forgive an injury in his own name, nor can he sue (according to the glosses and the learned men there cited), for in the law's eyes such persons are comparable to slaves. (On this matter see Part I of the *Speculum*, the title *De actore,* the verset *Item excipitur contra actorem quod est monachus*, and the two following thereupon).

Therefore, because no territory occupied in Poland, Prussia, etc., by these Brethren can be seen to belong to them, since they have been legitimately appointed to none of these, nor have any of these same places been legitimately instituted for them, but rather acquired by them, for themselves, and in their own name, as has been stated and as will become clear below, and, consequently, neither by virtue of their professed vows are they *de iure* under any obligation or bond to said places, for the acts of agents are not received unless in subjects well disposed: It cannot be said that the aforementioned Brethren possess them in another's name in the role of administrators, but in their own name, as principal owners. Hence in whatever manner it might be stated that they possess them, whether in the name of a community, or that of an order, or that of a house of such sort, in effect, these things are possessed in the name of the Brethren themselves — as no such community or order is seen to be real, but merely personal. Of such personal associations see Innocent (in the chapter *Dilecta*: *De excessibus prelatorum*, and also according to others, by the same Innocent in chapter I and in the chapter *A nobis*: *De iure patronatus*). For according to Ostiensis (in his *Summa*: *De sindico* § I at the verse *Quid sit universitas*) a community is a collection of multiple rational beings who are accorded a particular name. And in particular, a collegium is a collection of multiple persons living together to whom a special name has been given, such as the Canons of St Victor of Paris and the Monks of St Proculus of Bologna. But a corporation is a collection of persons, whether they live together or not, such as millers or bakers, etc., Ostiensis. But *de iure* religious communities may not possess anything in their own name, having become incapable of such by virtue of their professed vows, which, although not obliging them to any certain place or order, as has been said, still obligate them to a regular religious life in general (as in the chapter *Non solum*, and those that follow: *De regularibus*, book VI). From the aforesaid, it can be clearly stated that the aforementioned articles are not to be admitted, howsoever, as the petition made in the name of the order is inept. Consequently, it follows that the aforesaid Brethren, *de iure*, are not to be heard.

Mention has been made above[19] of these articles. But although they appear to be useless to the party producing them, on the contrary, they are indeed of use to the other party, in so far as they testify to what the King of Poland asserts.[20] Concerning which it is to be noted that in the first articles, or the prime group, in the first article it is stated that there existed several dukedoms on the territory of Prussia and in the land of Poland, *scilicet* those of Mazowsze, Łęczyca, and Dobrzyń, each of which customarily had a duke *pro tempore*, certain borders and lands distinct and separate from others. In the fifth article it is stated that the land of Chełmno had been overrun and occupied by the infidel Prussians, who wrested it from the control of the dukes of Mazowsze and Chełmno. In the 6° article it is stated that Konrad, the duke of Mazowsze and Kujawy, offered to provide these brothers with resources from these same lands, following said invasion of infidel Prussians, during which a large portion of Mazowsze and Kujawy had been destroyed and wrested away, and that the Emperor Frederick confirmed them in such if and in so far as the aforesaid Duke Konrad should give it to them as promised. In article VIII it is said that the aforementioned Duke Konrad conferred the aforesaid land upon them, occupied by the infidel Prussians, in the year of Our Lord 1230, for their defense of the faithful in Poland. In the X° article it is said that from the year 1226, and on from then, they recovered this land of Chełmno from the aforesaid Prussians, subjecting those infidels, and that from that time they have been in continual possession of that land up till the present day. And so, from the two articles immediately preceding it is gathered that they had the land in their possession previous to it being granted to them, because in that same year they possessed it, in which the aforesaid Frederick confirmed the donation — that is, in the year 1226, as it appears in the privilege of the same Frederick, and here.[21] Indeed, in the fifth year thereafter, according to their claim, there occurred the donation of the aforesaid Duke Konrad, *scilicet* in 1230, following which they proceeded to fortify the land with castles, cities, and the stoutest of fortresses, just as it reads in their XXII article. Yet this donation is suspect for divers reasons, according to what we say below, and as will become more clearly apparent in its place. In the XXII article it is stated that the Brethren in question overcame the Prussians and, in this way, liberated the land of the Poles from their infestation. They say many things, but prove none. For it is a wonder that the Poles, who at the time were, and still are, more powerful and numerically superior to the Prussians, would be totally incapable of defending themselves, but had to summon the aforementioned Brethren to their defense, calling them here from the most distant regions, whereas they had Christian neighbors at hand all around them, saving for those parts inhabited by Prussians and Lithuanians. Surely these assertions are improbable, nor is it probable that the above-mentioned Brethren, living in convents of ten or twenty persons, who at the time of their beginnings were of little power even in Germany, might be better able, as they claim, of wresting the above-mentioned land of Chełmno from the hands of the Prussians than the Poles, or that they were able to subject the Prussians without the favor and aid of the Poles, especially seeing that the aforesaid Brethren had a march of twenty and thirty days or more from Germany.

It is therefore much more probable what is stated in the chronicles and books of the Poles, and also in the authentic documents, *viz.*, that the aforesaid Duke Konrad, who was at the time in possession of the land of Chełmno, wishing to promote the order of these Brethren, established their convent, made up of some few persons, in that land, and, following their initial molestation of the Prussians, the latter paid them back in kind several times, with both sides rustling the cattle and flocks and whatever the other possessed, and vice versa. At last, the knights made petition unto said duke that he transfer the entire land into their power, so that gaining thus the obedience of the inhabitants and obtaining help from Germany, they might subjugate said Prussians, simultaneously obliging themselves to restore to said duke the land without any hesitation or contradiction once the Prussians had been overcome and vanquished. These things said duke consented to entrust to them, this being at a time when the throne of Poland was vacant and great wars were being waged amongst the princes of Poland. The knights, meanwhile, swelled their ranks with many persons from Germany. Having said land of Chełmno in their power, they made strong their castles, cities, and fortifications and at last brought the Prussians into subjection. Later, when the aforementioned duke required that his land be returned to him, they flatly refused. They hold it to this day. Indeed, after this, they despoiled Władysław, King of Poland and nephew of said duke, of the dukedom of Pomerania, with violence and great cruelty, which land they also hold to the present day. Furthermore, having received the land of Michałów from Duke Leszko, Duke of Kujawy and another nephew of Duke Konrad, as collateral for a certain amount of money lent him, even though Leszko's brothers offered them a return of the sum so that the land of Michałów should be restored, they refused to accept the money, refused to give back the land, and thus retain it to this day. These things are solid facts, the truth, as gathered from the aforementioned books and from public documents or depositions of witnesses who were examined by judges at the time when the matter of this business was of recent date.

And thus they speak the truth in their XXII article when they state that the aforementioned Władysław, King of Poland, wishing to expel them from his territories, waged great wars against them, in which there was great loss of life on both sides. And the same is true, following said King Władysław, of King Kazimierz his son, as they state in article XXIII and those that follow. From these their articles, and also from the privileges attached to them, it can be seen that the part of the King of Poland is sufficiently justified and his claim to the lands in question well-founded.

So, let us first treat of the land of Chełmno. Now, from the Privilege of Pope Alexander IV, given in the third year of his pontificate, it is clear that this Konrad, by whose donation the knights obtained the land, was a Polish duke, the duke of Kujawy and Mazowsze, as is stated in their VI article and in the Privilege of Alexander, that is, according to the tenor of the donation contained in the privilege, etc. Now, these dukedoms of Kujawy and Mazowsze are located in Poland, as is stated in the first article and in the fifth, in conjunction with the XXII article, at the beginning. As to said land of Chełmno, it was inhabited by Polish Christians, that is, the progenitors of Konrad, long before the donation, as is made clear by said Privilege of Alexander. The land was then seized from the dukes of Mazowsze and Kujawy by the infidel Prussians, as we find stated in the fifth article; the land is situated near the border of Prussia, as is clear from the Privilege of Frederick, and was given with the intent that the faithful of Poland should be defended from there. It therefore follows that the land in question is located in Poland, because it is inhabited by Poles, was seized from the Poles by the infidels, and given as a defense of the faithful in Poland by a Pole, i.e. a Polish duke. Indeed, to this very day it is inhabited by Poles who speak Polish as their vernacular, which is clear and common knowledge. Therefore, etc.

As to the land of Michałów, they admit to having it from the hands of Leszko, the aforementioned Duke of Kujawy — as is plain from their XVII article — although they assert that they purchased it from him. Now, there is absolutely no evidence of this being true, but, rather, of its being collateral for a loan.

But concerning the land of Pomerania, although they have attempted by various pretexts to colour and justify their aforementioned violent seizure of that territory, as is clear from their articles and privileges, the truth is that it belongs to the kings of Poland. This they admit in article XV and in article XI along with the pertinent privileges.

Not only do they thus admit the claim of the aforementioned King, they also confess to the fact that a definitive judgment in the matter has been handed down against them, expressly, by the judges delegated to a consideration of the case by our lord Pope Benedict XII in response to the suit brought by the aforementioned King Kazimierz, just as it is clear from article XXVI. However, they claim this verdict to be null and void, asserting the reasons for its nullity in the article immediately preceding this, that is, because it was supposedly handed down in an insecure location, without the full understanding of the case, etc. Now, here, please note this well, because this case of nullity that they have alleged or might allege is done away with by the very privileges they bring forth, which prove them to be stubborn, wayward, and contumacious. For in the Privilege of Lewis IV they assert that consideration of this case belongs to no one else but the Emperor himself, stating that they are members of the Empire, etc., as below, where more on this is said concerning the stated privilege. But that the above-mentioned sentence was handed down against them by those judges, this they confess in article XXIX, in which twenty-ninth article they expressly admit that the proceedings were held and the verdicts handed down against them by such judges as were delegated at the suit of the aforementioned King and prelates of Poland concerning what is said above, and further, in that same article, they admit that numerous judgments have been handed down against them. And not only this; they also confess that whatever is contained in these sentences, judgments, and the public documents in support thereof is true, for they admit that they obtained the aforementioned lands through violence and injury, just as it clearly appears below in the Privilege of Emperor Charles IV, where they petition him to confirm them in these lands acquired through violence and injury, which they ceased to possess through prescription by lapse of time, of which more will be said later. Further, they admit in article XXII that in this fashion they had not only these three lands, as has been said, but also, waging open war against the aforementioned King Władysław in defense of those possessions, they also took and conquered three other dukedoms, namely Dobrzyń, Włocławek and Brześć in the region of Kujawy. And they held on to these dukedoms for numerous years, erecting therein fortifications and divers castles. And so do they justify the judgment handed down against them in reference to these VI lands by our lord Pope Benedict XII. They justify it all the more in reference to the great and divers damages and other evils wrought by them as contained in that judgment, confessing to have inflicted these harms on the aforementioned Kingdom, as clearly evidenced in articles XXII, XXIII and XXVI, in conjunction with the privileges pertinent thereto. Finally, they also admit their unwillingness to acquiesce to the exhortations of the Pope who sought to incline them to concord; nor to obey the proceedings and judgments of the aforesaid judges unless the aforementioned King Kazimierz, with the consent of all princes, prelates and barons of the Kingdom, etc., abjured those lands, *viz.*, Chełmno, Michałowo and Pomerania, as well as the aforesaid damages, and also fulfilled other requirements of theirs as contained in their act of concord, of which mention is made in article XXVII. And that otherwise they had no wish to come to terms with the King, and consequently had no desire of restoring any other of his lands to him either, that is to say: Dobrzyń, Włocławek and Brześć mentioned above, to which they were obliged by the aforementioned judgment, condemning them. This they clearly admit in articles XXVI, XXVII, XXVIII and XXIX. Consequently, they admit the forcible imposition of that concord, which they do even more clearly in the above-cited Privilege of Emperor Louis, where said Emperor commands them not to restore said lands to the aforesaid King, with the assertion that 'our arm is mighty enough to defend you,' etc. And because said concord of King Kazimierz was the foundation or cause whereby all subsequent accords were regulated, including that compacted by Władysław, the present King of Poland, as well as the compromises found in article XX and the following, to the very end, it follows that all of these have a faulty, or defective cause, and by consequence, *de iure*, are invalid.

This suffices for the first articles. On the second we will speak below, along with their privileges.

So much for the first part of this second principal part.

The aforementioned Brethren also rejoice[22] in a certain privilege of the aforesaid Pope Alexander made in the Year of Our Lord's Incarnation 1259, the fifth year of said Pope's pontificate, which they introduce in proof of the institution of their order, or their capability of holding dominions in common.[23]

Concerning which please note[24] that many other privileges of divers donations and confirmations have been produced by them, which precede said Privilege of Alexander in time, and that these donations and confirmations of both Roman Pontiffs and Emperors, who precede Alexander in time, such as Pope Gregory IX, Pope Innocent IV, the aforementioned Emperor Frederick, the aforesaid Konrad, Duke of Kujawy and Mazowsze, etc.

From which it may be deduced in general that if the aforementioned Brethren were first instituted and made capable of holding possessions in common by that Privilege of Alexander, prior to the date of said privilege they were incapable of the same, as at the time not yet having been instituted, for no right is ever acquired unless by one institution, just as by one election (*De eleccione*: *Ut quis duas*, book VI), etc. And when one of two incompatible contraries is chosen, the remaining is removed (the argument of the final law, *ff De divorcijs*, and what is there noted in the gloss concerning the word 'direptum,' with others similar). That there had been no institution precedent to this is seen to be clearly proven by this same privilege of Alexander's, at its very beginning, where it is said 'To my beloved sons, a Master of a religious fraternity,' etc. And later, there too he speaks of a 'new plantation of theirs,' etc., on the basis of which narration the Pope's institution rests, and by consequence no contrary proof seems to be admissible (as according to *Clementinam Litteris*: *De probacionis* and what is noted there). Hence it follows that in the days of the aforementioned Gregory, Innocent, Frederick and Duke Konrad, they were incapable, for all of the aforementioned persons preceded the times of Alexander, as is deduced below in the chapter beginning with the letter [ ].[25] Therefore, it follows that all donations or confirmations of whatever sort of those preceding Alexander, and of Alexander himself before the granting of said privileges, having no basis in legal fact, are invalid, and thus, by consequence, the aforementioned Brethren were occupiers in unjust possession of all those lands. Furthermore, it follows that the above-mentioned Privilege of Alexander, as it makes no reference whatsoever concerning this, and all that follows from it, was null and void, and the claims they seek to stake on its basis are fraudulent (*ff De in ius vocando*, the law *Sed et si hac lege* § *Patronum*; *Ad legem Corneliam de falsis*, the law *Si quis obrepserit*, and what is clearly noted in *De rescriptis*: *Ad audienciam*, and in the chapter *Super litteris*, and there, by H. Boyk, distinction 1). Hence it follows that all of their privileges crumble to the dust and by consequence their lack of right is demonstrated. If it should be stated that another institution, by Pope Honorius III, precedes this, we respond that this would contradict the words of Alexander which speak of their institution 'as a new plantation.' Otherwise, there would be no new plantation, but an old one, nor would it be necessary to address them as a religious fraternity, but rather as a religious order long established, that is, the Brethren of the Order of the Hospital, etc.

These things being said,[26] I now turn to the aforementioned privilege itself. Concerning which it must first be stated that what is contained near its inception, where it reads thus: 'For this reason, my beloved sons in the Lord, we deign turn a clement eye upon your just petitions, granting them and confirming your house or hospital in which you are congregated to the praise and glory of God and for the defense of His faithful, and for the liberation of the Church of Christ, along with all your possessions and goods such as you are known to legitimately possess now, or in the future,' etc. Now, however in this privilege it is pretended that said Hospital was at the time in Jerusalem, that does not seem to be true, because at the time of the aforesaid Alexander, the city of Jerusalem was *de facto* occupied by the infidels. Thus, because such hospital had no place there, nor did said Brethren possess any faculty of congregating there, especially for such a reason as is moved in the privilege, *scilicet* for the wresting of the Church from defilement at the hands of the infidels — etc. More is said of this below in the chapter beginning with the letter [ ]. But even if it were accepted that their order had been instituted long before by Honorius III or any other Roman pontiff, in a form similar to that in which it is somehow stated in Alexander's privilege, there are still other things to be mentioned concerning said privilege.

The first is that such a privilege is chiefly concerned with a hospital or a college, a community of sorts.

2nd, that such a hospital, along with its possessions justly acquired and to be acquired, is to receive the protection of St Peter, etc.

3rd, one order is instituted for them, comprised of two orders.

4th, they have obtained a concession to freely convert to their own use all spoils captured from the pagans, and this is expressed rather as a limitation, that is, for the protection of the Catholic Church and for the wresting of the same, intrepidly, from the defiling hands of the pagans.

The fifth, that they live chastely and without possessions, giving witness to their professed vows in word and deed, etc.

These things having been stated, it is clear to see that this privilege contradicts the intent of these Brethren, since it argues them to be of the genus or order of Hospitallers, whereas in the aforesaid articles they assert themselves to be of a military genus, expressly setting themselves forth as a military order approved among other such. Nor do they say that this Order of theirs be of the Hospital of the Virgin Mary, even though they assert that it is so called.

Second, it is to be noted that this privilege also contradicts all of their imperial privileges, and vice versa. For the imperial privileges are seen to concede to them the task of warring against infidels with a view to subjugating them to a reformation of religion towards the divine cultus, that is, converting them to the Christian Faith, which is not licit, as will be more clearly explained below in the chapter beginning with the letter [ ].[27] Now, as said Privilege of Alexander, establishing them or conceding to them the task of warring in a licit manner, such illicit warring as this is not conceded, indeed, it is negated, even if tacitly, because when one is conceded, the other is negated (XXV distinction: *Qualis*, and others similar thereunto). And again, said Privilege of Alexander concedes to them the right of converting the spoils of the pagans to their own use, but only such as are captured during their defense of the Church or of Christian souls. Now the Imperial Privilege, on the contrary, grants unto them all dominions whatsoever they wrest from the hands of the infidels, when invading their lands with force. On the other hand, in the Privilege of Alexander, mention is made of a defensive rationale, while here, the acquisition of territory is rationalized, *scilicet* lands such as Prussia, Lithuania, and Żmudź. This means, in consequence, the tyrannical and unjust oppression of the infidels. Here, the Pope states that they, along with their goods, ought to be under his and St Peter's protection. There, the Emperor states that the knights, along with their lands, are chiefly subject to his defense, declaring that, under penalty of being deprived of all lands, rights, privileges, etc.

they are to ignore the call of whatever judge, ecclesiastical or secular, should summon them; they are not to appear before them, above all, not at the summons of Kazimierz, King of Poland, or that of any of the prelates of said Kingdom, as stated in the Privilege of Louis aforesaid, of which evidence will be more clearly given below in the chapter that begins with the letter [ ].[28] Furthermore, Pope Alexander states that he has established them as an order, the task of which is the defense of the Christian faithful, and by consequence, as regular religious they ought to be subject to ecclesiastical courts. Louis, on his part, speaks of them as members of the Empire, and asserts that their order was founded, instituted, and endowed by his predecessors on the Imperial throne of Rome for the defense of the Empire and the Christian Faith, in consequence of which they are not regular religious, but rather a secular militia. Considering these privileges then, it follows that these Brethren are duplicitous, and in effect are no regular religious order, neither as militia nor as Hospitallers.

Likewise, for an even clearer proof[29] of the things I have just stated: It is to be said here that Johannes Andreae, summing up the matter of regular religious broadly expounded by St Thomas (*Secunda Secunde* question LXXXVIII) significantly poses (in the chapter *Sane*: *De regularibus*) that religious are distinguished in two manners: First, by reason of their diversity of the aim for which they have been established, i.e., one order ordained to care for pilgrims by sheltering them, another order for the redemption of captives or for tending to the sick, etc. Second, by diversity of their exercises, as in one order the flesh is mortified by fasting; another is characterized by manual lobor or by coarseness of vesture. But because the final aim is most important of all, the great diversity of orders is distinguished by the ends to which they have been established, which is more significant than the diversity in exercise and means. For a comparison of ends is absolute, in that we pursue an end in order to attain it as a final goal, while exercise and means are secondary, conditional — we do not engage in particular exercises as an end in themselves, but only in pursuit of an end. Johannes Andreae.

Second, the words of said Pope Alexander are to be admitted, where he says in his privilege: 'We establish you as an order of the Brethren of the Hospital of Jerusalem in regards to the care of the poor and infirm, and as a Military Order of the Temple as clergy and militia, which is to be observed in perpetuity.' Hence, arguing from the way in which the Pope orders his words, we ought to proceed by acknowledging the first order as principal in this genus, common to both clergy and laypersons; the second ought to be seen as following, accessory to said hospital, and that from that hospital, as its substance, it ought to derive its name. Because although the Order may be composed of two distinct orders, and savour of the nature of both, still, in such a composition, it is necessary for one of these to be taken as the principal, or the form of the thing, and the other as accessory, or its matter, as in one body two orders equally principal cannot exist, otherwise, that same body would be subject to two different laws, which cannot be (as in the chapter *Cum in tua*: *De decennis*, with others similar). For from a diversity of causes arises a diversity of effect (I question I: *Fertur*, and the canon *Necesse*, with those in concord thereunto).

With these things admitted, it follows firstly, that should these Brethren belong, as they assert themselves to belong, to an order of a military type, basing their claim upon said imperial privileges, their Order is not the same as that approved by the Privilege of Alexander, as they pretend. The rationale for this: by asserting themselves to be such a military order, they consequently assert, even if tacitly, that they have nothing to do with any other principal order, as it is clear that by asserting the one, the other is negated (as in the canon *Qualis* adduced above, and those similar to it). Thus, either their Order has nothing to do with the above-mentioned order of said hospital, or this is so only as an accessory — which contradicts the nature of the above-cited order of the above-mentioned privilege. Therefore, etc.

Second, it follows that, if they have not the prime order of the hospital as their principal, as stated above, nor is it possible for them to have the second order, *viz.*, that of Brethren of the temple militant, as an accessory, for the same law applies in connection to both (as stated in the chapter *Translato*: *De constitucionibus*, to which is added the final gloss and its concordances). For when the principal is taken away, the accessories are as well (*De fide instrumentorum*: *Inter dilectis*).

Third, it follows that this above-mentioned military Order of theirs for clergy and laypersons cannot be approved *de iure*, and that for a twofold reason. First, because two things with different aims cannot cohere and be conjoined with one another (XVI question VII: *In nova accione*), which, according to Johannes Andreae, is true of religious orders (which he notes in his chapter *Cum deputatis*: *De iudicijs*, concerning the word 'Studijs'). For it is said that men of diverse professions or disparate confessions should not associate in one office (*De eleccione*: *Cum causam*), and it is true that they should not associate in one body or college (as Francis Cardinal of Florence notes in *Clementina* I: *De eleccione*, shortly after the beginning). For arms and warring are not suitable to clerics (XXIII question VI: *Clerici*, and the canon *Hijs a quibus*). Therefore. Second, because their colleges or congregations, especially in the aforementioned regions of Poland, Prussia, etc., derive their status and manner of waging war from the above-mentioned imperial privileges, and chiefly, as will be said below, from unjust causes. And for this reason, as tyrants, they cannot receive approval, nor should the occasion for nourishing sin be thus given them — that is simply not permissible (XXIII question III: *Qui potest*; II question VII: *Negligere* and LXXXIII distinction: *Error*).

Fourth, it follows that all of their privileges have been surreptitiously, or on false pretences, obtained under the name of Brethren of the aforesaid hospital, and consequently, they crumble to pieces on account of this falsity. By negating them to be of said Order, they cannot be said to be Brethren of said hospital, for words are to be understood as to their effect (*De clericis non residentibus*: *Relatum*).

But, on the contrary, they can neither base themselves upon said Privilege of Alexander, for that privilege concerns itself with the aforementioned hospital in its collegial character, and said Brethren are not of that college in species or genus. Therefore, etc. As to species no, unless the place were also the same in species, because then the privilege granted to that place is extended in perpetuity to all those inhabiting said place together (*ff De censibus*, the law *Forma* § *Quamquam*; XVI question I *Hinc eciam;* XXV question II canon I and III; *De institucionibus*: *Cum venissent*; *De privilegijs*: *Per exempcionem*, book VI). The rationale: because the people inhabiting said place today are those who inhabited it in the past and who shall in the future (*ff De iudicijs*, the law *Proponebatur*). And because said Brethren who live in Prussia cannot be properly said to live in Jerusalem, for the same body cannot be in two places at once (*De apellacionibus*: *Cum Parati*; *De dilacionibus*, the final chapter), nor is this place one and the same in species — therefore. But nor are they the same in genus, or of the same genus as said hospital, and that by a twofold reason. First, because they have no hospital whatsoever by manner of college, especially in the aforementioned regions, where they rather have their colleges in castles, fortresses, and other such places of theirs according to the status of their waging war, a fact so notorious as no tergiversation of theirs might conceal, nor is there any place here for denial. Thus, it is also proven in this way that their establishments are of a genus and a nature different from hospitals, for the nature of a hospital requires that they be established above all on behalf of the poor and the infirm (as in the law *Sanccimus*, included in canon law c. XXIII question VIII; *De religiosis domibus*: *Quin contingit*; in *Clementina*, near the beginning). And so, whatever is given to a hospital is acknowledged as being given to the poor: thus notes Johannes Andreae (in the chapter *Dudum*: *De conversione coniugatorum*, concerning the word 'Pauperum'), the nature of which is not that of said castles, which are rather locales as described above.

Therefore, it necessarily follows that the above-cited Privilege of Alexander does not *de iure* extend to this genus of men. The rationale: because a privilege granted with determination of place or of time does not follow persons who abandon said place (which is proven by that which we read, and which is noted in the chapter *Ex tuarum*, and the final chapter *De usu palij*). For the form of a privilege is to be diligently observed (*De privilegiis*: *Porro*, and the chapter *Recepimus*). Therefore, etc. Second, even were we to accept, without prejudice to the truth, that they had hospitals of the sort spoken of above, because said colleges are of an illicit cause, arising as they do from the above-mentioned imperial privileges, being thus illicit, they cannot belong to any religious order and by consequence, neither can they belong to said hospital.

My dearly beloved,[30] do not overlook in reference to this matter those laws which seem properly applicable in this place, and which state that when a monastery or hospital is destroyed, so are its privileges destroyed as well (as we read and as is noted in the chapter *Abbate*: *De verborum significacione*, towards the end, and there in the final gloss at the beginning, according to the laws there cited), where, concerning this same gloss Johannes Andreae states 'destroyed and not rebuilt; otherwise, according to Innocent, having been rebuilt, it shall enjoy the same privilege' (*De eleccione*: *Quia diligencia*). We presume that those same Saracens who occupy the city of Jerusalem and who destroyed that hospital are not likely to permit such a hospital to remain, in opposition to them. No matter what is noted by Innocent, Ostiensis, and others (in chapter II *De novi operis nunciacione*), *scil.* that whatever hospital may be destroyed by the enemy still and all is said to retain its privileges, for the clergy formerly associated with a church destroyed by the enemy remain clergy

(VII q. I: *Pastoralis*; XIX q. III: *Que semel*). It is a different matter when a city or other place, sacred or secular, is destroyed upon the authority of its superior, for then said clergy could not be said to be the clergy of that particular church, or citizens of that particular place. And likewise, if by the authority of a superior they are transferred from one place to another or are united to others (as in the laws adduced) which Johannes Andreae himself notes (in the rule *Privilegium*: *De regulis iuris* book VI), and the Archdeacon (XVI question VII: *Et hoc diximus*, in the gloss *Adde dicas lacius*, etc.). To this we respond that these laws adduced in proof of the contrary speak of such hospitals as, although destroyed in their species and therefore actually in existence no longer, still remain *in potentia* and in their genus, whereas the genus in question can only be preserved in its species. And thus it is said to retain its privileges in this way, and in no other. Because nothing is said to be retained or received by another if not according to the mode and nature of the receptor (as per the rule *Accessorum*: *De regulis iuris* book VI). And as has been said, the above-mentioned hospital does not exist, above all in the previously mentioned regions of Poland, Prussia, etc., among those Brethren, neither in species nor in genus. Therefore, etc. And even should we admit, for the sake of argument, that said hospital actually did exist, whether in species or in genus, and, consequently, that it retained its privileges, still those privileges would not belong to those Brethren or their places, being as they are of another genus and nature, since, as has been stated, said locales are not hospitals. And just as also has been previously stated, a privilege conceded to a hospital does not follow persons to another place. Therefore, etc. And however a privilege conceded to a genus of persons is transmitted to all future generations of said genus (Codex: *De professoribus et medicis*, throughout; *De excusacionibus tutorum*, the law *Sed et milites*; *De privilegijs*: *Per exempcionem*, book VI) that is only true when the genus remains the same. It is a different matter when the genus or order changes (which is proved in the cited chapter *Abbate* at the conclusion thereof, and XXV question II, the ultimate canon of § where 'Sic viventes,' etc.) because such a substance or nature of the order being changed, it ceases to be a college (according to the very laws just cited) nor truly is there any college when persons are lacking (*ff Ad municipales*) just as a town, when it is dissolved (*ff De legatis* III, the law *Pater filium* § *Tusculanus*, etc., noted in the penultimate gloss of the chapter *Statutum*: *De eleccione* book VI). Hence, whether said order, of which mention is made in the previously stated Privilege of Alexander, is said to have ceased either by the destruction of the hospital, or the dissolution of the college itself, or by the very mutation of its status or location — and the mutation of an order cannot be effected without the permission of the Pope (*De regularibus*, chapter I near the end, book VI), it suffices that when the thing itself is extinct, so all of its privileges become extinct as well (as in the rule *Privilegium* cited above, of which see what Dinus says there, and H. Boyk following him in the chapter *Mandata*: *De presumpcionibus*). From this it follows that said Brethren cannot make use of the Privilege of Alexander without committing the vice of falsehood, being as it is either counterfeit or expired. Second, it is inferred from what has been said that such colleges of theirs, above all those found in the regions referred to, are illicit twice over: firstly, because they are prohibited by law as not found to have been approved (for this, see what is alleged above in the chapter beginning with the letter B). Secondly, there are other reasons why they are illicit, *scilicet* by reason of their sectarian or sinful nature, and as to the laws that apply to such doubly illicit colleges, see H. Boyk (in the chapter *Nos quidem*: *De testamentis*, and there, the laws he adduces). Thirdly, it is inferred of all donations and confirmations of any sort made to them, that these have no strength or significance.

This suffices for the aforementioned Privilege of Alexander.

There yet remains for us to speak of the third,[31] since having taken care of the Privilege of Alexander, wherewith the intention of the aforementioned Brethren is to attempt to establish their claim to a personal capability, consequently it is necessary to consider the other privileges upon which they attempt to base their claim to their fitness to their titles or lands. Considering which it is first to be stated that these privileges are generally three, as some are apostolic, others of some Mindowe,[32] king of the Latvians, or Lithuanians, and some are imperial. Now, however the party producing them attempts to gird themselves in all of them at once and establish themselves firmly in the case of said land, asserting in their articles of the second group — articles XX or XIX — that the Master and the Order had wrested the land of the Sudes from the hands of the infidels on behalf of the Catholic Faith, powerfully conquering them and liberating them, and thereafter continually holding and possessing, as they still do, that land, just as the land of Prussia, by the authority of the Supreme Pontiff and our lords the Emperors: it nevertheless seems that one cannot rely on all of them simultaneously, as said privileges are of diverse authorship and arise from diverse causes. Consequently, they differ amongst themselves, indeed, they oppose each other, being contrary to one another, for which reason it does not seem that they are able to provide any fit title to these lands, for diversity of cause necessarily infers diversity of effect. And what is mine from one cause cannot be mine from another cause, unless it first ceases to be mine (*De fide instrumentorum*: *Inter dilectos*, with many concordances noted in the gloss concerning the word [ ]. For in the apostolic privileges the cause of their concession was the defense of the faithful, while in the privileges imperial the cause was the subjugation of the infidels and the acquisition of their dominions. What is more, in the imperial privileges it is expressly asserted that Prussia, along with other infidel regions, are subject to the rule of the Empire. Now, in the apostolic privileges this is negated, albeit tacitly, by the fact that they are stated to be at the disposal of the Roman Pontiff — which otherwise could not be effected, since nothing can be done to the prejudice of another's rightful jurisdiction, and the Emperor must not usurp to himself the authority of the Pope, etc. (XCVI distinction: *Cum ad verum*). Likewise, whilst in the imperial privileges the lands of Prussia, Żmudź, and others are granted to the knights with full and true dominion, in the apostolic privileges true and direct government of the same are reserved to St Peter and the Roman Church, and to the former is granted merely the usufruct thereof. Many other such contradictions may be gathered from the privileges in question.

Now it must be seen[33] whether they might base their claims upon any sort of such privileges, or any particular one among these.

First, we must take the Apostolic privileges into consideration. Now, because mention is made in these of several Roman Pontiffs, *scilicet* Honorius III, Gregory IX, Innocent IV and Alexander IV, it must be stated that said Honorius began his pontificate in the year of Our Lord 1216, occupying the chair of Peter for ten years, eight months, and twenty-three days. The aforementioned Gregory succeeded him, and his pontificate began in the year of Our Lord 1226, on the fourteenth day of March, and lasted for fourteen years. He was succeeded in turn by Celestine IV, who lived only a short while, and following him, the aforementioned Innocent began his pontificate in the year of Our Lord 1242. He reigned for eleven years and six months, his pontificate coming to an end four days later. And following Innocent the aforementioned Alexander's pontificate commenced in the year of Our Lord 1253 and lasted for seven years. All of this is found in the volume entitled *Recent History of the Church*, books XXI and XXII, in successive chapters,[34] with which the *Chronicle of Martinus* concurs. Concerning this, see Vincencius in *Speculum Historiali* LI. We mention these things in connection with what is to follow. Secondly, it is to be noted here that because the privileges of the aforesaid pontiffs are here produced, that is, those of Gregory,

Innocent, and Alexander, of which the one of Gregory is first, still, because it is introduced by the party producing them to the same effect as the Privilege of Alexander, keeping to the order established by them, we shall speak of both of these together. But as far as the Privilege of Innocent is concerned, which is only one, dated in Assisi two days prior to the Calends of September in the eleventh year of his pontificate (29 August 1253), the knights cannot base their claims upon it, because in it is confirmed some donation of Mindowe, King of Latvia,[35] made in the year of Our Lord 1257 — and at that time Innocent was no longer alive and the aforementioned Alexander was Pope, as is clearly evident from the foregoing. And thus, said privilege, along with the donation it confirms, must be suspected of being counterfeit — for at the time when the privilege was granted, said donation had not yet come about. Secondly, because in such a privilege said donation is confirmed in common manner, in so far as it has been made providentially and to the prejudice of no man, such a confirmation does not provide anyone with any renewed right, although it would reconfirm an ancient right if any such indeed existed (*De confirmacione utili vel inutili*, more or less throughout). Now, it can be stated from the subsequent donations of said King Mindowe, that Innocent caused said Mindowe to be baptized and crowned King of Latvia, subjecting to the protection of the Roman Church both the person of the king and all of his possessions. And so it is proven that said donation, which would be to the prejudice of the Roman Church, is invalid, just as, in consequence, is the confirmation.

And now as to the privilege of the aforementioned Alexander,[36] it is to be seen that there are three of these, and we have already spoken of the third, in which the institution of the order, etc., is contained. Therefore, it behoves us to speak of the two remaining. The first of these is dated in Viterbo on the Ides of July, in the third year of Alexander's pontificate (15 July 1255). In it, a certain other donation of the aforesaid King Mindowe is confirmed, which donation was made in the month of October, in the year of Our Lord 1255. And so, should you incline yourself over these facts, you would see that, similarly, the donation was confirmed before it even came into existence. For, according to what has been said above, the third year of Alexander's pontificate commenced in the year 1255, and from whatever part of the year you choose to compute the third year of this Alexander as commencing, there will be no doubt but that the Ides of July precede the month of October by a long shot. Consequently, the confirmation precedes the donation! And since it is claimed that this confirmation contains the tenor of said donation, he who pretends to such a claim must concede that the donation existed before it came into existence![37] Secondly, this confirmation was made similarly to the former, in common form, *viz.*, providentially, proving that said donation was quite invalid absent consultation with the Roman Pontiff. For the properties being donated are subject to the protection of the Roman Church, just as the other donations of the same King Mindowe declare, as will be seen from what follows. And thus the falsity of the claim is clearly proven, as is the nullity of the confirmation, and the donation, in the same way as the other mentioned above.

The second privilege of the same Alexander, to which such weight is attached, is dated Viterbo, VII Calends of August (25 July) in the third year of his reign, and this contains two principal effects. The first speaks of how a certain Konrad, Duke of Poland, granted to these same Brethren the land known as Chełmno, the tenor of which donation is dated the year of Our Lord's Incarnation 1230, in the month of June. This is inscribed here in this same privilege by said Alexander, and to this end the privilege of the same Alexander is put forward in order that the donation of the above-mentioned Konrad be proven on account of the tenor so inserted, although it is not so proven, as will be explained below. Rather, on the contrary, what is proven is the intent of the King of Poland who sets forth a claim to this land, as in this privilege it is stated that of old the land has been inhabited by the Christian predecessors of Konrad, Duke of Poland, who granted it them for the sake of the rescue of the faithful in Poland. Further, that said duke is the same known as the Duke of Kujawy and Mazowsze (which dukedoms are to be found in Poland, which fact is also admitted by them in their articles, as I have said above in the chapter beginning with the letter F). And therefore, as to its first effect, *viz.*, the region of Chełmno, this privilege is rather to the advantage of the King of Poland than to that of the party producing it. For as I have said, the donation at hand is not proven on account of its tenor here inscribed, for such an insertion does not confirm the trustworthiness of the donation, as the Pope does not thereby declare that he was present at said donation, but that he learned of it from the report of these Brethren. And when a Pope in his writings says that he knows of something from the relation of another, this proves nothing — as Johannes Andreae states (in the chapter *Cum oporteat*: *De accusacionibus*). Likewise, even though the Pope cause the tenor to be inscribed at the insistence of the Brethren, he does not confirm the donation itself thereby, nor is it his wish that such an exemplification should endow it with bona fides, nor that it should have the force of a public document. This is obvious, as he appends to it no decree by which faith would be accorded to it, nor was the party summoned for such purpose, and these very two things are necessary for the document to be admissible as evidence (as noted by Innocent and Johannes Andreae in the chapter *Albericus*: *De testibus*, and the *Speculum de instrumentorum editione* § *Ostenso*, the verse 'Sed numquid,'and the verse 'Qualiter'). Indeed, if said donation had been confirmed, it would not be proven by the insertion of the tenor, but would needs be proven in another manner, as both Ostiensis and Johannes Andreae hold (in the penultimate chapter of *De confirmacione utili vel inutili*). The reason they give is that when a contract is concluded beyond the Curia, the Pope cannot be fully informed of it, and might easily be deceived as to its facticity; it is a different matter when the privilege or act is his own. Now, that this Pope was so deceived here is made plain by the privilege itself, because it was so explained to him as if these Brethren, in proceeding to the region of Prussia, were granted this land by said duke, in which they proceeded to erect castles and towns in it themselves — not without much lobor and expense — and after their damming up the hostile influx of the Prussians, they subjugated a portion of Prussia to the Christian cause, etc. And here, from the order of their words, it is clear, according to them, that the Chełmno region was first granted to them, in which they erected their castles, etc., after which they subjugated a portion of Prussia, as is stated here. And this same order of words is also proven to be found in the Privilege of the Emperor Frederick, where it is stated that the duke promised to provide them with the land known as Chełmno, so that they should take upon themselves the task, etc. But meanwhile, in the privilege of donation of said Konrad, the tenor of which is inserted here, as has been said, it is proven that at the time of the donation the Prussians were already Christians, having their own bishop, of the name of Krystian, who was Bishop of Prussia, and whose name is included in the donation as one of the witnesses. Thus, this donation contradicts itself and the very Privilege of Alexander. By consequence, one suspects it of falsity; this suspicion is increased by the length of time stretching between the donation itself and its confirmation. For the donation indeed was made in the fifth year of the aforementioned Gregory's pontificate, who lived for nine more years. Following him came Celestine IV, then Innocent IV, and at last Alexander, who made the confirmation in the third year of his pontificate. And so the time elapsed turns out to be twenty-four years, and it is not quite probable that such a momentous matter should be made to wait so long upon its confirmation. It is more probable that said Konrad was perhaps deceased by that time, or maybe, that the donation was cooked up shortly before his death, after said land had been made firm in castles and towns. But even should we accept that the documents of donation were proven authentic, this would still be of no advantage to said Brethren, as they would still have been drawn up in their absence. Therefore, they would acquire no right, even if they were to have acquired possession of them by the will of the giver (as is clear from the Codex: *De donacionibus*, the law *Nec ambagi*). This is upheld by Bartolus and Baldus. It is more true, however, that the document itself, the tenor of which is here inscribed, contains no donation but only an admission by which said duke states two things: *scil.* that he gave and granted said land to these Brethren for them to wage war against the Prussians, and conversely, that the Brethren promised to aid him in his struggles against the Prussians, etc. Now, that said documents were drawn up in the manner of an admission, and as a narrative merely, not a disposition intending to prove a donation already made, this is clear from the tenor of the words as formed in the past tense, and is also clearly seen from the conclusion of the same document, where we read: 'Therefore, so that donations and admissions of such sort,' which admissions, being as they are extra-judicial, are prejudicial to no man, therefore, etc.

The second effect of said Privilege of Alexander is the concession of the land of Prussia by this Pope to the rights and property of St Peter, which in assuming he subjected to the protection of the Roman Church. And this privilege is also noteworthy, and it is in the interest of the Roman Church that it be registered with her, as it states that these Brethren have no direct and true dominion in the land of Prussia in the least, as does the Roman Church, in the name of which they strove to obtain and did obtain said land. And for this reason they are bound to pay rent to the Roman Church for this land, as is contained in the privilege. Concerning which please note that it is stated in this privilege in what manner these Brethren came into Prussia, preceded by the power of the Saviour, and having restrained the impetus of the Prussians and secured the safety of the neighboring Christian faithful, who had long been afflicted by the raving of the

Prussians, they restored to the Christian cause that portion of Prussia that they subjugated. And that this was the motive cause for Alexander to make said concession: this is what those who have obtained the privilege are bound to prove. Otherwise, the narrative cannot be used as a basis to the prejudice of another, unless, I say, it is proven. For if in a rescript or privilege another cause is brought forth from which a petition arises, or without which the petition cannot succeed, he who would procure the privilege or rescript must prove it (which Innocent notes in his chapter *Ex parte* I: *De privilegijs*). And that which I have said concerning the narrative not being capable of use as a basis is true, especially as the contrary appears (which is determined by the main gloss of *Clementina Litteris*: *De probacionibus*). Now, what is clear from the imperial privileges, especially that of Frederick II, on the contrary, is that it was not in order to restrain the impetus of the Prussians nor to protect the faithful from attack that they subjected the Prussians, but on account of their desire to obtain their possessions. Consequently, they were motivated by their own greed. And so, the imperial privileges form a basis to the prejudice of the Brethren, which shall be made apparent further on. They themselves expressly confess to this in articles VI and VIII of the first group, which deal with the second privilege of said Frederick, where they assert in what manner said Frederick granted them the authority to invade the Prussians with maximum force — whom they defeated, as they say, concerning which I have spoken above in the chapter beginning with the letter F. Hence it is concluded that a false claim is expressed in said Privilege of Alexander, and in consequence thereof, it is null and void. This is true in regard to its utility and advantage to the aforesaid Brethren who would wish to make use of it for the purpose of committing fraud, but not in regard to the Roman Church, to which no prejudice is done by their deception. And for this reason and by this cause it also follows that quite all other donations of theirs and confirmations of whatever sort, especially such as follow from the Privilege of Frederick previously mentioned, fall to pieces. Furthermore, it is to be inferred from this that the donation of the land of Chełmno, which was inserted into that privilege, is to be presumed fictitious or extorted by violence according to the falsity of the claims it sets forth, which falsity is evidenced by the Privilege of said Frederick. Besides this, furthermore, please note that although said land of Prussia, however it may be seen to have been conceded to them as far as right of use, or usufruct, is concerned, such rights are limited by the qualification or mode that enjoins that they are never to subject the same to the government of any power, as is contained in the privilege. And it is proven clearly from these privileges of theirs that, not being content with their subjection to and protection by the Roman Church, they withdrew from said qualification, and by consequence, from the concession as well, in actuality, by subjecting themselves and all of their possessions to the Empire, as is clearly seen from the Privilege of Emperor Louis IV, dated the year of Our Lord 1338, where they assert themselves to be members of the Empire, instituted by the Emperors for the defense of the Empire and the Christian Faith, and that they are not to present themselves in response to a summons before any other judge, ecclesiastical or secular, unless it be before the Emperor — at the risk of being deprived of all of their lands, rights, and privileges — as is stated more broadly in said privilege. The same is proven on the basis of the Privilege of Emperor Charles IV, given in the year of Our Lord 1354. This Emperor, confirming all concessions, confirmations, and privileges, both of Frederick II as well as those of the Apostolic See and any and all others, expressly forbids all persons, both ecclesiastical and secular, from impeding, perturbing, or molesting said Brethren or their order in anything, adding thereunto the penalty, etc., as is also contained in the same privilege.

Passing by a certain other privilege[38] of a certain Kazimierz, the son of the aforementioned Duke Konrad, which is brought forward as confirmation of the above-mentioned donation of the land of Chełmno (because it falls under the same suspicion of nullity and falsity as the donation itself), it is necessary to consider the Privilege of Pope Gregory IX, spoken of previously. This privilege, as is made clear by article IX of the first group, is brought forward to the same effect as the above-mentioned Privilege of Alexander, *viz.,* in proof of the confirmation of the donation of said land of Chełmno. This is dated Anagni, on II Ides of September (13 September) in the fourth year of his pontificate. In which privilege it is stated that this Gregory has learned from the letter of a nobleman, a duke of Mazowsze, that on account of the pagan Prussians cruelly ravaging the Christians living within the borders of their land, and seeing as he himself and said Christians have been unable to resist them by force of arms, he has introduced into his land the order of these Brethren as an aid to the Christians, conceding to said order the castle known as Chełmno with what pertains thereto, establishing that whatever these Brethren are able to obtain in the land of the infidels, this he cedes to them, and thus, he, the Pope, confirms that which said duke has already done. This is the sum of what it expresses. And so it is clear that this confirmation confers upon them no renewed right. Besides this, please note that, having inspected the date of this privilege and that of the aforementioned donation inserted into the Privilege of Alexander, you will find that this same donation was previously confirmed by the same Gregory, that is, before it came into existence. And yet this Gregory states here that it was made in the past, and for this reason he confirms it, as it had been providentially made. For the fourth year of this Gregory came to an end on the 14th day of the month of March in the year 1230, at which time the fifth year of his pontificate commenced — and consequently, the donation inserted into the Privilege of Alexander, which was made in the year of Our Lord's Incarnation 1230, in the month of June, was made in the fifth year of the Gregory's pontificate, yet it was confirmed by him, according to these Brethren, on II Ides of September (13 September). Thus the donation is fictitious. Besides this, in the Privilege of Gregory the duke asserts that the land is his, and it is only the castle of Chełmno and its appurtenances that he has conceded to them. And here, clearly and openly it is stated that he introduced this order of theirs into the land; meanwhile, in the Privilege of Alexander, he states that he has bestowed upon them the entire region of Chełmno, along with its villages, castles, cities, markets, coinage, tolls, and and water customs duties, along with all things contained within its borders, etc. This is an evident contradiction, and for this reason, neither privilege should stand. And thus it is clearly proven that they are incapable of basing their claims on the apostolic privileges. Concerning which it is to be noted that whereas duplicity is reproved by the law (*De clericis conjugatis*: *Diversis fallacijs*), as the prophet says: Cursed the man who goes along two roads. 'For no man can serve two masters'[39] (and thus also of other of other concordances in this chapter to which I allude), nevertheless, said Brethren, in basing their claims upon Papal and Imperial privileges, travel along two roads, or stumble, rather, in two directions at one at the same time, and thus seem to be in possession of these dominions contrary to common law: to which duplicity they themselves clearly confess in their articles of the second group, where in article XX they assert themselves to have possessed and to possess the land of the Sudes on the authority of the Roman Pontiffs and on that of their Imperial lords; they say the same thing of the land of Żmudź, and by consequence admit to the nullity of their possession, as they hold them merely *de facto*.

Following what has been said above,[40] we need consider the second type of privileges, namely, those of Mindowe, King of Latvia, whose four privileges are brought forth under the guise of transcripts of some sort.[41] But even if their originals were produced as evidence, they would still be seen to be empty things, containing no stipulation nor obligation, nor anything dispositive in expression, being narratives merely, which report some donations or other made by said Mindowe in the past. Indeed, these privileges are to the prejudice of no man, nor do they prove in any way any donations. Concerning which it is to be noted that with these privileges twenty-four articles are produced, which are principally concerned with the lands of the infidels — and this is the second group of the articles brought forward. In these articles and in the afore-mentioned privileges, the aforesaid Mindowe is sometimes referred to as the King of 'Letonia' — spelled thus with an 'n' — as in the third article of the second group, and sometimes as the King of Lithuania, as we find in the seventh article; sometimes as the King of 'Latwia' — using a 'w' — as in the very privileges or donations. Yet because Latvia and Lithuania are not just distinct orthographically, but also geographically, for this reason the aforesaid donations must be suspected of falsehood. A second suspicion of falsehood arises when, in the third article, based on the aforementioned, it is asserted that the land of Żmudź never, ever belonged, nor does it belong, to the dukes of Lithuania. Yet in the privilege of Emperor Louis IV, which said Brethren produce as evidence seemingly to their advantage, it is expressly confessed that this land belongs to the infidel Lithuanians, and as such he has bestowed it upon them, as is clearly seen in said privilege dated the year of Our Lord 1337. Now, on the basis of this privilege, it is the claim of the King of Poland to this land that rather seems to be well founded, claiming it as he does on the basis of his rights to the Duchy of Lithuania. Indeed, even the opposing party admits this claim of his in these same articles. For in the third article it is said that the aforementioned King Mindowe has given them certain lands, or districts, of the Samogitians, that is, the inhabitants of Żmudź, as specified in the privilege dated the year of Our Lord 1255, in the month of October. In the fifth article it is said that he gave them certain other lands or districts of this same land of the Samogitians, specified in his second privilege dated the year of Our Lord 1257. In the sixth article it is said that, once again, he gave them the entire land of the Samogitians, as is contained in his third privilege dated the year of Our Lord 1259, in the month of August. In article VII it is said that, at last, in the year 1260, he granted them the entire kingdom of Lithuania as is contained in the fourth privilege. And thus it is confessed that they possessed the land of the Samogitians by way of donation from the King of Lithuania, and thus, consequently, that it belonged or belongs to the Kingdom of Lithuania.

Concerning which please note[42] that, even granting that it be proven that said King Mindowe indeed possessed any sort of legal rights in this regard, nevertheless the stated donations are worthless. The first reason for this is by the turpitude of the manner in which said Brethren obtained them. For they promised to aid said King in his struggles against the infidels, and yet they seem bound to the acquisition for quite other reasons. Now, the laws forbid one to receive anything for reasons other than that to which one is obliged (*ff De condiccione ob turpem causam*, law I and II, with others similar thereto). Hence it is stated (in said law I, towards the end), that if the cause on the part of the receptor is turpid, the thing may be demanded back, if even if though it were carried through. Now, the aforesaid Brethren had obliged themselves to offer military aid in exchange for said donations, sealed by their very own oaths, just as can be clearly seen from the tenor of the second and third donations mentioned above.

Second, none of the donations in question is valid without the consent of the Pope, given that said King and Kingdom, along with all that belongs thereunto, are subject to the Pope. And, as Ostiensis, Johannes Andreae, and Antonius de Butrio[43] note (in the chapter *Pervenit*: *De arbitris*, and the chapter *Cum tempore*), such things cannot be submitted to arbitration. And Innocent says the same: no prelate can effect any transaction without the authority of his superior (in the chapter *De cetero* and the chapter *Veniens*: *De transaccionibus*).

Third, these donations are invalid, especially the third and fourth, on account of the enormous harm they inflict upon the Kingdom (vide the text *Extra*, in the chapter *Intellecto*: *De iure iurando*, and the chapter *Grandi*: *De supplenda negligencia prelatorum* book VI), because the King is not the owner of the goods and laws of the Kingdom, but rather their administrator. For there are goods that belong to the person of the King and goods that belong to the Kingdom (as is proven in the text of said chapter *Grandi*). Hence (in the chapter *Intellecto* previously adduced), the King swears an oath not to alienate the goods of the Kingdom, which are not his own. If they were, he could dispose of them as he pleased, for each person is moderator and arbitrator of what belongs to him (*ff Mandati*, the law *In re mandata*).

Fourth, it does not appear that the consent of the citizens or inhabitants was given to this act, whose consent is necessary for such a great donation to hold. For no ruler of any city is free to alienate said city without the consent of the people,[44] as Baldus[45] notes in the chapter *Si de feudo controversia fuerit*, c. *In generali*, collation X. The same is noted by Ostiensis, Johannes Andreae, and Lord Antonius de Butrio (in the chapter *Dilecti*: *De maioritate et obediencia*).

And for these last two reasons, *scil.* the third and fourth, all transactions or pacts and compromises made by the King of Poland with these Brethren concerning the lands in question between them are taken away — and for the other two reasons as well, *viz.*, the first and second, the above-mentioned are done away with in so far as the part of the Brethren are concerned. I shall not especially dwell upon these transactions or compromises or privileges of theirs.

Furthermore, it is to be noted that although in the above-mentioned donations it is asserted that the Master and Brethren of the Holy Virgin Mary of the Teutons in Livonia induced said King Mindowe to be babtized through their faithful and diligent persuasion, this is not presumed to be true in the absence of positive proof (*ff Ex quibus causis maiores*, the law *Denique*; chapter I of book VI of *De constitucionibus*). Even should we accept that such were true, it is not to be presumed that this was done in a good and legitimate way, since such an office does not belong to them (by the rule *Ea que fiunt a iudice*, and what is noted in book VI). This is especially true there, where a suspicion to the contrary exists. For it is stated that these Brethren have the power to invade the land of any infidels whatsoever, so as to subjugate them and despoil them of their goods. And it is presumed that causes produce like effects. For even in the third article it is asserted that the aforesaid Mindowe, King of Livonia, was converted to the faith and, consequently, being in the power of said Brethren — perhaps imprisoned, in chains — he made the aforementioned donations, suspicions as to which grow all the more considering that the location in which the donations were made is suppressed, save for the last one, for which the place is mentioned, but in much too general a manner.

Furthermore, please note here that although in the aforesaid donations it is stated that the aforesaid Pope Innocent submitted these lands to the protection of the Roman Church, said Brethren, wishing to be free of said subjection, not being content with the donations themselves, demanded, above all, the land of the Samogitians, with other adjacent lands, from Emperor Louis IV as is contained in the above-mentioned privilege of his, and in thus subjecting the lands to the Empire, they despoiled the Roman Church of its jurisdiction as had existed in that land, to the extent of their ability. From this it is concluded that these Brethren are the enemies of the Roman Church. Even more, it follows that in fomenting such schism between the Roman Church and the Empire, they are doing more harm to the latter by offending it, than good by defending it. Consequently, they prove themselves to be the enemies of the Empire as well as of its Church, even though said Emperor asserts in his privilege that they have been instituted for its defense. Finally, please note the twentieth article of the foregoing, in which they assert that they have wrested the land of the Sudes from the hands of the infidels by force, and following this, they continue to hold the same by the authority of the supreme Pontiffs and their lords the Emperors, just as they have held and possessed the land of Prussia, and continue to hold and possess it. By consequence, they assert that they hold it *de facto* and not *de iure*, as is clearly evidenced by the foregoing, in the chapter that begins with the letter N, near the conclusion thereof.

From these it follows that they are unable to base their claims upon privileges of such sort.

As to the third type of aforesaid privileges,[46] which contains three species thereof, accordingly as they arise from three Emperors, *viz.,* Frederick II, Lewis IV, and Charles IV,[47] it is to be known that the privileges of the aforesaid Emperors appear to contradict one another. For Louis states that these Brethren have been instituted for the defense of the Empire and the Christian Faith, while Frederick, who first placed them in parts of Poland, Prussia, etc., indeed does not say that such is their cause, as is immediately apparent from his privileges, but that their purpose was the conquest of infidel dominions, etc. And because this same Frederick was the cause and origin of their coming to be in said regions, they base themselves rather on his privileges and derive their effective state and principal basis from him. For the aforementioned Charles confirms all of these privileges based on certain knowledge. For this reason, it is now important to enlarge upon these things more fully.

Concerning which, it is first to be stated that the aforementioned Frederick is said to have made three donations.

One of these[48] was of the land of Prussia, where he granted them authority to invade the Prussians with all their might in order to conquer their lands; in which privilege he asserts that Konrad, Duke of Kujawy and Mazowsze, had promised to give them the land known as Chełmno, which is to be found near the Prussian frontier, so that they might take upon themselves the lobor of attacking and obtaining the land of Prussia to the honor and glory of the true God — in which land the same Frederick confirms them, as well as in any other that said duke should give them, as is contained in the same privilege dated Rimini in the year of Our Lord's Incarnation 1226. And to this effect this privilege is produced, *scilicet*, in order to prove the confirmation of this same Frederick concerning the land of Chełmno, although it does not prove that at all, as it is based upon a future donation, as has been sufficiently stated above in the chapter beginning with the letter N. Indeed, there is no proof that said duke even promised to give them it, because one cannot base one's claim on the words of a narrative merely, even though they be the words of a ruler, especially if they proceed into another person's narrative, as Johannes Andreae notes (in the chapter *Cum oporteat*: *De accusionibus*).

The second donation produced here was made by this Frederick in reference to three lands, namely: Courland and Lettonia, and that of the Samogitians, as it is contained in another privilege dated Verona, in the year of Our Lord's Incarnation 1245, in the month of June, the twenty-fifth year of said Frederick's reign.

The third donation, although it was not produced before the Pope, was however produced in this matter before the Roman King as it were before an arbiter. It specifically concerns three lands, *scil.* Prussia, Russia, and Lithuania, as well as all other infidel lands in general, which these Brethren might acquire or at which they might arrive with their banners. This donation was made in Verona in the same year as that immediately preceding, but in another month, as this third privilege was drawn up in May, while the preceding one comes from June. And it is said that they hold this third donation in great veneration. It is displayed to all their guests who visit these parts in order to practice warfare.

The second thing that must be stated here concerns that which one reads in book XXI, chapter XXIV of the *Recent History of the*

Church, and is confirmed by Martinus in his *Chronicle* and Vincencius in the *Speculum,* to wit: that the aforesaid Frederick commenced his reign as Emperor in the year of Our Lord 1220. It was then that he was crowned in St Peter's Basilica by Pope Honorius III, in the fifth year of his pontificate. According to Martinus, he reigned for twenty-nine years, eleven months, and thirteen days. Although from infancy he had been educated by the Church, and raised to the highest honor in the Empire following the condemnation of Otto, still did he not favor the Church as his mother, but rather cut her like a stepmother, as far as he was able. It is for this reason that Honorius, finding him to be a rebel towards himself and towards the Church, first excommunicated, and later anathematized him, releasing all his barons from their oaths of fealty to him (as both Vincencius and Martinus write). This took place in the second year of his reign, and, as the histories report, from then on, that is, from 1221 until the end of his life, he tyrannized and persecuted the Church, just as it is recorded in said book and chapter. Likewise, as is recorded in chapter XXVII of the same book, at this time, Lombardy was divided into two parts, *viz,* into a Papal portion and an Imperial portion; later, these were called by the names Ghibelline and Guelf, after the names of two brothers who divided amongst themselves, for the Ghibellines are of the Imperial part and the Guelfs that of the Church. These two brothers came of Tuscany. They were great nobles, and even today their names continue to be used in this manner, etc. After Pope Gregory IX succeeded Honorius, as we read in chapter XXVIII, he waged a great battle with this Frederick, whom at first he admonished with charity to desist from the malignancies he had initiated. However, as the Pope failed to make any progress with him this way, he then renewed the sentence of his predecessor Honorius against the man, in the second year of his pontificate. Now, when said Gregory wished to call a General Council to Rome, that Emperor impeded access to the city by both sea and land. For example, when two Cardinals, along with many prelates, abbots, and clerics were travelling to the Council by sea, they were seized by Henry, the son of the Emperor, and, as captives, transferred to Apulia, etc. At last, Pope Innocent IV, after long peace negotiations with this same Frederick, because Frederick did not wish to leave off his stubborn persecution of the Church, he was condemned as an enemy of the Church at the Council of Lyons, stropped of his Empire and of all honor — of which privation there exists a legal case (see the chapter *Ad apostolice*: *De sententia et re iudicata*, book VI), where four causes of said privation are indicated. The first of these is perjury, as he did not fulfil the oaths he had sworn to the Church. The second is sacrilege, committed when he kidnapped the Cardinals and other prelates on their way to the Council. The third is stigmatisation for heresy. The fourth is on account of his refusal to pay tribute for the Kingdom of Sicily, which he held in fief from the Church, for eleven years. This privation was effected in the year of Our Lord 1245, on XVI Calends of August, as is recorded in the afore-cited *Recent History of the Church,* book XXII, chapter III. Now here, if you consider this well, you will see that the last two aforementioned donations were made by the aforesaid Frederick to these Brethren in that very year, just previous to his privation, and one of these is from the month of [May], while the other is from the month of June, immediately after which the privation followed on the 17th day of July, that is, XVI Calends of August. And the final donation was made when the Council had been called, on the twenty-fourth day of June, on the feast of St John the Baptist, following which said Council was in session until the octave of the birth of the Blessed Virgin Mary, just as noted in the abovementioned book and chapter. Meanwhile the first donation was made in that same year, when the aforementioned Gregory commenced his reign, *viz.*, in the year of Our Lord 1226, as is clear from the above. From all these things it is clear to see that the aforementioned donations were all made during times of persecution of the Church, and, in consequence of these Brethren taking the part of Frederick, who, as has already been stated, had been excommunicated and stigmatized as a heretic, etc., adhering to him against the Church so as to obtain said donations from him, they are found contrary to the Christian religion and to divine law, as will appear obvious from what follows below, being as they are not without prejudice to said Council, and in contempt of the same.

From this it follows that they ought necessarily to be held suspect by the Church and the Christian religion as a whole. They entered the regions of Poland and Prussia at a suspect time, introduced there by a suspect authority, as they admit in their aforesaid articles of the first group; in article X, for example, where they assert that commencing in the year of Our Lord 1226 and thereafter, successively, they subjected the Prussians to that same Frederick. And if you care to note: at these same times Christians were generally setting out for Jerusalem by sea and land to wage war against the Saracens in defense of the Holy Land, which is clear enough to anyone who chooses to peruse the histories and chronicles. For, as Martinus writes in his *Chronicle*, and as is also written in said *Recent History*, book XXI, chapter XXVIII, the aforesaid Frederick, excommunicated and anathematized, voyaged beyond the sea towards the Holy Land, although he wrought more desolation amongst the Christians there than he brought them any consolation. Vincencius also writes (which is also to be found in chapter V of book XXII of that same *History*) that following Frederick's deposition, a legate was sent from Lyons to France to preach crusade at the behest of King Louis — which resulted in Louis setting out on the crusade with a large force. Taking to ship in the year of Our Lord 1249, he sailed for Damietta, which port he captured, along with the city. Going on from there to do further battle against the Saracens, he lost many men, was captured himself, and remained in captivity in Syria for five years, that is, from '49 until '54, as can be read in chapter VII of said book. Meanwhile, these

Brethren, according to what their privileges teach, were busied at the time in Livonia acquiring the lands of the Samogitians, and the Kingdom of Lithuania, and in Prussia subjugating the Prussians, so that they just couldn't find any free time to set off for the Holy Land in defense thereof and in order to aid the other Christians there. For as they explained to the above-mentioned Pope Alexander, in the third year of his pontificate, as is plain from the above chapter N, that in the land of Chełmno they had built castles and towns, having already subjected a part of Prussia — and it is most probable that this subjugation was concurrent with the times in which said King Louis was battling, and was taken in captivity. For the third year of said Alexander's pontificate falls in the year of Our Lord 1255. And yet, in the fifth year of that same Alexander's pontificate, when they petitioned him to approve their order, they explained that they were gathered in Jerusalem for the defense of the faithful and the liberation of the Church of Christ, etc., as is clearly seen from the chapter above. And yet this story of theirs, this assertion, is not only contradicted by their own privileges, but also by the histories and chronicles of the deeds of arms that took place in those times, since it is well known that the city of Jerusalem had been lost well before then, and was *de facto* occupied by the Saracens. Consequently, there was no place for these Brethren there at the time, nor had they any faculty of gathering there, especially for the aforesaid aims to which they pretend. As we read in the *Recent History of the Church,* book XX, chapter XXXVIII: During the pontificate of Pope Urban III, who was elevated to the see of Peter in the year of Our Lord 1186, after Philip the King of the Franks and Richard King of England had won a great victory in the Holy Land, recuperating many places to their rightful ownership, the Holy City was lost again to the Sultan, who had attacked it with a great army. Upon hearing this, Urban fell ill with great sorrow, died, and was buried in Ferrara. And from that time forward it cannot be read anywhere that the city of Jerusalem was thenceforward ever recovered; indeed, on the contrary, the Kingdom there was successively destroyed so that in the year of Our Lord 1290, during the times of Pope Nicholas IV, in the third year of his reign, Acre and Tyre were lost, and thus the residue of that kingdom was occupied by the Saracens, just as we read in the same history, bookXXIV, chapter XXIII. It is thus clear that these Brethren were not in Jerusalem at the time, as they pretend, but in Prussia, etc., were they gathered, and not for any defense of the Holy Land, 'to the best of their abilities;' by which consequence they are not free of suspicion, nor of guilt. For even if they had some few brothers of theirs in Acre, of necessity they needed the full strength of their power in Prussia and Livonia at that time to fight the Prussians and Lithuanians.

To return to the donations of Frederick noted above,[49] in which mention is made of the Faith, this will be dealt with according to the matter before us, which matter concerns wars, the subjugation of infidels, and the occupation of their dominions in order that they might be converted to the faith. From this arises a question both moral and juridical. Namely, can such wars be just wars? The conclusion, however, is theological, namely: can faith result from such activity? Or can some conclusion of faith be inferred therefrom? And so our consideration will be twofold; the theological consideration, which concerns faith, will be found below in the third principal part.[50] But as far as the law is concerned, it proves that said donations are are worth nothing *de iure*, and consequently, the wars are unjust, etc.

Now, so that the issue be made even clearer, I shall reach ever further with my pen, examining the matter from the perspective of all possible causes, for, according to Aristotle in the first book of his *Physics*, we may only say that we know something when we come to know its causes, to their very elements.

Now, first as to the final cause, which is the most powerful of all causes, it is to be noted here that it is twofold, *scilicet* impulsive or mediate, and principle or immediate. The impulsive is the spreading of the Catholic faith and divine cultus, or the propagation of the Faith. For here the Emperor speaks of how a certain H., Master of the Sacred House, etc., unburdened the will of his pious mind to him, to wit: that he and the Brethren of his house, aflame with a desire to spread the Catholic faith and cult of the Divine Name, would gladly assume the lobor thereof, fervently insisting upon their admittance into these lands so as to win them, etc., to the honor and glory of the true God. And in another privilege he says, 'for the propagation of the Faith, with good will they desire to take upon themselves this lobor.' And so the Emperor states: 'Upon perceiving the devotion of this Master, and the fact that said land is in the governmental power of the Empire,' etc. Hence, although the laws seem to permit a prince to take something belonging to one person and bestow it upon another (*ff De eviccionibus*: the law *Lucius*, and the Codex *De quadriennii prescriptione*: *Bene a Zenone*, with others similar), still, according to the learned, he is able to do so only when public utility is at stake, and upon giving recompense to the party so deprived, otherwise: no (see what Bartolus[51] has to say in the first constitution of the *Digests*, and expressly, in the law *Ne lacius*, as well as the law *Omnes*, the Codex: *Si contra ius vel utilitatem publicam*; the same is upheld by the glosses and the doctors in the law *Rescripta* and the law *Quotiens*, the Codex: *De precibus Imperatori offerendis*, and the Archdeacon,[52] IX question III *Per principalem*). But this cause, *scil.*, the spreading of the faith, although concerning public utility, is not a temporal matter, but merely a spiritual one. It does not pertain to the office of the Emperor to deprive anyone of his dominion for this cause, and by consequence, his donation is invalid. This is proven by XCVI distinction: *Bene quidem*, where although it was good to establish that an ecclesiastical holding cannot be alienated, any statute of the Emperor to the contrary is invalid, because such a thing does not pertain to his office. The same is proven in the rule *Ea que fiunt a iudice*: *De regulis iuris* book VI, where Dinus[53] holds that in doing anything that does not pertain to his office, he is acting not as a public person, but a private one, and thus what he does has no validity. A general rule, therefore, is that it is not sufficient to do good if the same is not done rightly. (For this, see the gloss of that rule and the laws here adduced(. For the cause of the Faith belongs not to the Emperor but to the judgment of the Church (XXIII question I *Quociens*; XII distinction *Preceptis*). For even indulging in the faculty of doing battle on behalf of the Faith belongs to the Church (on which see what Innocent writes in the chapter *Quod super hijs*: *De voto*, and the writings of Ostiensis in his *Summa, De penitencijs et remissionibus*, in § *Quibus et qualiter*, the verse 'Quid de rapina'). Furthermore, even should the spread or propagation of the Faith or divine cultus be a good thing, still the mode here expressed, *viz.* by way of oppression, is prohibited as illicit (XLV distinction *Qui sincera*, and the canon *De Iudeis*; XXIII question I *Iudeorum*, in the first gloss). Such people are to be induced to the Faith not by asperities, but rather blandishments (as is alleged in the laws here invoked). For he who acts otherwise proves that he has his own ends in mind more than those of God (as it says in the text of said canon *Qui sincera*). Therefore, it is clear that as an impulsive cause a manifest error is here committed, contrary to law; a cause illicit and notoriously erroneous. For not even the Faith ought to be the cause of oppression, and, by consequence, the cause of evil, nor, vice versa, should anyone be compelled to the Faith through oppression, for evils are not to be committed so that good might result therefrom. But piling error upon error, said Emperor states this in his privileges: 'Since God has established our Empire elevating it over the kings of the world, widening the frontiers of our authority far and wide throughout the world for the glorification of His Name and Faith in this age, for the propagation of the same among the pagans, accordingly he prepared the Holy Roman Empire for the preaching of the gospel, turning our care and solicitude not so much to the repression as to the conversion of the nations, aware as we are of the grace inherent in this provision by which Catholic men take up the daily lobor of subjecting barbarous people and reforming them to the divine cultus, exposing their goods and their very persons to the dangers of the task,' etc. Behold what intellectual blindness of both, than which the cruelty is no less, that is, of him who provides, and him who is provided thereby. And thus, as is the religious discipline, so is the devotion, and so the authority for waging war. For according to St Thomas (in *Secunda Secunde*, question X article VIII) the faithful of Christ are frequently moved to engage in warfare against the infidels, not in order to draw them to belief, because even should they be victorious over them and hold them captive, still do they allow them freedom of belief, but so as to compel them to refrain from impeding the Faith of Christ. Now, the principal and immediate cause of the aforesaid donations was to favor the aforesaid Brethren who were making petition for said land, which they received, and therefore the Emperor states here: 'We therefore, giving heed to the devotion of said Master,' etc., and a little further on, 'confident in the prudence of said Master that, through his ardour and that of his Brethren he shall mightily initiate, and in manly fashion prosecute, the conquest of said land,' to which after a few sentences interposed, he adds: 'to said Master we concede the right to invade the land of Prussia with all the might and force of his house, confirming said Master and his successors in said land in perpetuity, etc., according to the ancient rights due to our Empire.'

And just as it is said of the land of Prussia in the first privilege, so it is said in all of the other aforementioned privileges, and so it is said of the other lands, using the same words.

From these causes here recalled, it is clearly proven that the aforementioned Brethren did not intend, principally, the spreading of the faith, but rather, under the cover of piety, to occupy the aforesaid dominions of the infidels, against natural and divine law. It is simply not true that this is religious devotion, but truly, the detestable cupidity of a deprived intellect, or ambition. This is no pious yearning, but cruel lust, however boldly the contrary be pretended to in these privileges.

From these it is consequently inferred that the aforesaid Emperor was not moved by any right reason, but rather by private affection; nor from any true or just cause but from a cause erroneous and contrary to the law, and by consequence his act was merely *de facto*, null and void. Beyond this, it is asserted in said privileges that in their ardour for those lands they expose their property and selves to danger, which is a wretched sort of martyrdom. Against which St Bernard, in his book to Hugh, Master of the Temple Militia, writes as follows: 'It is not safe to kill or to die for such causes,' which is to say in any cause arising from motives of irrational anger or the desire of possessing any earthly goods, etc. And later he repeats the same: 'Whoever aims at secular goods or goals I call not a militiaman, but a malicious man, who sins mortally by killing, and when killed himself, perishes eternally.' And a few sentences further on he states: 'Pagans must not be put to death, indeed, if there be any other way of impeding their excessive assault upon or oppression of the faithful.'

From these we conclude that the state of the aforesaid Brethren is perilous in the extreme, entirely illicit, and erroneous, and cruel. Now, because these privileges of theirs contain many impious and insane propositions savouring of heresy, even contrary to the Faith, to which said donations are reduced as if to their foundations — some theological comments will be made concerning them in the proper place, below.

I spoke above of the final cause[54] which moves one to action. Let us now consider this Emperor as agent and donor, who pretended to have some ancient rights to these lands, which claim seems to refer to the days of the ancient Romans. Thus it should first be stated that according to Ockham (in the third part of his *Dialogues*, near the beginning of book 1)[55], that those who seek to justify the dominion of the Romans ought to say that the Romans did not battle down and subjugate others, or deprive them of their dominions because they did not recognize Roman authority, otherwise they would be sinning gravely, but, according to his opinion, because the latter did not wish to agree with them that the republic of the entire world ought to be ruled by one government, which, however, was expedient. And thus, fighting on behalf of the republic, the Romans would be waging a just war, whereas the others would be unjust in their resistance. And thus, they would be acting justly in subjugating these others, etc. But here say: The evidence is lacking to prove that the government of the entire world republic under one government was expedient. For it is not always expedient, according to said Ockham, because natural reason sometimes teaches that such an ordering of things may be iniquitous and contrary to natural law as when, for example, it is to the detriment of the republic. Hence although it be natural that the optimal principate is found where there is one prince who principally rules (according to the *Politics*) still, sometimes it is necessary *de iure* that this is not to be found, *scil.*, when it is better to depart from it and subject divers provinces to divers princes. But when it is expedient and when not — although this is often hidden from men, especially from rude and evil men — to God all things are revealed and open, and thus, when it was hidden from the more experienced it was so because it would not have been expedient for them to have a king (I Kings 8: 'Give us a king to judge us, as all nations have'),[56] but their request was displeasing to God, for they ought not to have asked for a change in the mode of governance that God had ordained (Ockham).

Truly, Francis Zabarellius, Cardinal of Florence, notes (in the chapter *Venerabilem*: *De eleccione*) that rule on earth arises in three ways. First, by the will of God revealed to men in some way. Second, by the consent of the governed. And third: by violent usurpation. Governments of the first and second types are just; governments of the third are not. According to the first, the power of the Pope is justified, as arising from the authority bestowed upon the patriarchs in the Old Testament, and later resumed by Christ and transferred to Peter and his successors. Furthermore, his power is justified according to the second mode in respect to all Christians, and their acknowledgement of the dominion of the Church, according to which the entire Catholic Church, which is constituted of the entire congregation of the faithful, gives consent to this, which is approved by the most ancient traditions, to which no contrary opinion exists. But the monarchy of the Romans, otherwise the Empire, cannot be justified in the first or the second way. Rather, it was a tyranny, according to him, in that it subjugated other nations to itself by violence. He says similar things concerning other monarchies that preceded that of the Romans, such as the Babylonian Kingdom, that of Macedonia, Carthage, etc. For in his *Chronicle*, Martinus states that the first King of the Assyrians was Ninus, who first began subjugating people by force. But even if we accept that the empire of the Romans was ruled by law and not violence, it was translated to Christ all the same (Daniel, chapter II), where, according to Jerome, Daniel the prophet foretold in the dream he interpreted for Nebuchadnezzar that, following four kingdoms, that is, the Assyrian, that of the Medes and Persians, that of Macedonia and that of Rome, the fifth would be subject unto Christ. For in the text it is said that in the days of their monarchies, that is, after these four monarchies should pass away, God would establish the kingdom of Heaven which would not be dissolved unto eternity, nor would His kingdom be transferred to any other people, which is also repeated in the prologue to the aforementioned *Recent History*. Upon this basis Bartolus (in the constitution *Ad reprimenda*, the gloss concerning the words 'totius orbis,' col. XI) writes this: 'The first was the Oriental Empire, *scil.* Babylon. The second was the empire of the Persians and the Medes. The third was the empire of the Greeks, the fourth the Roman Empire. At last, with the advent of Christ, this Roman Empire commenced to be the Empire of Christ and thus, both swords are to be found in the possession of the Pope, Christ's Vicar, that is to say, spiritual and temporal power. For Christ is the stone shaped by no hands, Whose kingdom will have no end, of which Daniel expressly prophesied' (chapter II),[57] where all of these empires are described, and he adds: 'I say therefore that before Christ the Roman Empire depended solely upon God, and the Emperor could justly be described as the lord of the world, to whom all things belonged. After Christ, the Empire is Christ's, and his Vicar's, and by the Pope it is entrusted to a secular prince' (*Extra, De eleccione*: *Venerabilem*). So if we too say 'everything belongs to the Roman Empire, which now belongs to Christ' — it is true. If we speak in reference to the person of the secular Emperor, it is not proper to say that all things are his or under his jurisdiction. Bartolus. For Christ, the Son of God, was naturally Lord of the entire world (Psalm: *Deus iudicium tuum regi da*, etc.[58]) He entrusted to the holder of the keys of eternal life the rights to the Empire, both terrene and celestial (XXII distinction, canon I, both text and gloss); the same is here noted by Laudensis and restated by the Archdeacon (X distinction *Quoniam* on the gloss *Cum ergo*), who says that according to this sentence, which holds that the Pope is in possession of both swords, no Roman Emperor who exercised the sword, not having first accepted it from the Roman Church, especially following the bestowal of the rights of both Empires upon St Peter, has exercised such authority rightly. Accordingly, understanding this, Constantine, in resigning royal power, relinquished to St Silvester the secular sword, signifying that he had not made legitimate use of the power of said sword, nor did he hold it legitimately, having not received the same from the Church, even though this was understood otherwise by the Archdeacon (as is noted in XCVI: *Cum ad verum*). Gloss II in the chapter *Novit*: *De iudicijs*, likewise determines that the Pope was in possession of both powers, to which gloss adhering Antonius de Butrio refers to *Qui filij sint legittimi*: *Causam*, by Ostiensis, and the chapter *Per venerabilem* § *Racionibus* and fully by Innocent *De fori competenti*: *Licet*; by Johannes, X distinction: *Quoniam*, and XCVI distinction: *Cum ad verum*, and the canon II *Duo* II, question VII § *Hijs ita*. And he says that all learned in the canons commonly hold this.

Also, my lord Francis the Cardinal (in said chapter *Venerabilem*: *De eleccione*) states that this conclusion has been approved by the Church, according to the decisions found in many chapters (chiefly *De maioritate et obediencia*: *Solite*; *De iudicijs*: *Novit*; *Qui filij sint legittimi*: *Per venerabilem*; *De eleccione*: *Fundamenta*; *De re iudicata*: *Ad apostolice* book VI) and this is held by the most ancient custom, of which memory to the contrary does not exist. And second, by this power the Pope, as the Emperor's superior, transferred the Empire from the Greeks to the Germans as is noted in the gloss concerning the word 'Transtulit' in said chapter *Venerabilem*, which translation was effected by Pope Stephen (as is found in the *Sepculum historiali*, book XXIV chapter LVI *ff*). It is therefore necessary to state that the Empire depends upon the power of the Pope, for to him belongs the examination, approbation, or rejection of the Imperial election. For according to him the election of the Emperor belongs to the Prince Electors of Cologne, Trier, etc. (of which see *De re iudicata*: *Ad apostolice*, book VI in the penultimate gloss) and this on the basis of positive law and Papal concession (said chapter *Venerabilem*). He also states that many intellects have lobored at this enquiry as to the beginnings of the terrestrial monarchy, and that many books have been produced, as well as many works on monarchy itself, but there can be no dispute more useless, since whatever can be inferred concerning the independence of the Empire from the Pope proceeds from observations that come before the era of grace, from the times, accordingly, when the Romans wished to vindicate their Empire. Another tract on monarchy was composed and drawn up by Dante, the Florentine poet, who, because he was a Ghibelline, strove to prove that the Empire was in no way dependent upon the Pope — and because of this work, he was nearly burnt at the stake as a heretic.[59] Francis.

Now, whenever we come across a difficult question, disputed by those upholding contrary opinions, the learned say that it is the Church's determination that is to be followed (to this, the text *De consuetudine*, final chapter; *De iuremento calumpnione*, chapter 1, *Qui filij sint legittimi*: *Per venerabilem*, where the case is made clear; *Ut libro non contestata*: *Quoniam*; as noted in *De foro competenti*: *Licet*, and he speaking to the contrary is worthy of a wretched death by the commandment of God (said chapter of *Per venerabilem*), in which chapter Iohannes Andreae says, following Ostiensis, that in cases of ambiguity of opinions one should rather follow canon law than the sayings of the saints or the magisterium, because to the Pope and to no other is given such interpretation in doubtful matters; hence, accordingly, following him, the Abbot reproves those legalists who do not rest their case expressly upon the *Decretals*. Beyond this, he refers to the above-said *Recent History*, book XXII chapter X, in which the aforementioned little book of our lord Innocent IV is spoken of, concerning the jurisdiction of the Empire and the authority of the Pope, in which he responds to the presumptuous and haughty definitions of Frederick's official, that is, Peter de Vineis, who later ended as he merited to; the little book is known as *Apologeticus* which later Boniface VIII as well approved via the *Decretals*, as is clear from his bull beginning with the words 'Unam sanctum,' where he expressly states 'Whoever negates that the temporal sword is part of Peter's authority has wrongly understood the words of the Lord: 'Put up thy sword into its sheath.' Concluding thence 'Therefore both are in the power of the Church, *scilicet* the spiritual and temporal swords,' and that it is a necessary condition of salvation for all human creatures to be subject to the Roman Pontiff. From these it is inferred that said donations of the aforementioned Frederick are overbold in that he was attempting to usurp to himself the ancient rights of the Empire, or the ancient dominion generally found in the lands of the infidels contrary to the authority of Christ and His Vicar. From this we see that said Brethren, in basing themselves upon these erroneous donations, are not seen to be justified or excused from their error against the determination of the Roman Church, and, in consequence, are not free of heresy.

All the same, some have been of the contrary opinion,[60] for which reason extensive glosses have been written in this matter. I shall therefore recite some here for greater clarity.

Iohannes de Lignano[61] (in the chapter *Solite*: *De maioritate et obediencia*) says that canons in this matter have been rightly put forth both pro and con, but 'I do not trust them much, for the Pope declares his decrees and the Emperor his laws, yet no one is a proper witness in his own case' and therefore he lays out his reasons (*ibidem*, and better in the chapter *Novit*: *De iudicijs*, on the gloss II at the end), *scil.* in the matter of both swords belonging to the Pope, 'I suppose one thing: that there ought to be one governing power in the world. For any such things as have an essential order in the world, but are of different species, it is impossible for both to be equally perfect, if they are mutually repugnant. The result is destruction. For if they are peers, one is thereby superfluous; whereas if they are disparate they are not equal to each other. But the Emperor is not the greater, therefore, the Pope is, because beings do not wish to be evilly disposed, and as a multitude of rulers is an evil, there can be but one ruler. Such is the deduction made by the Philosopher in XII *Metaphysics* where he demonstrates such unicity. Now the Pope's power is of a spiritual sort, the Emperor's temporal, and temporalities are subordinated to things spiritual, as they are ordained to spiritual ends (I question III *Si quis obiecerit*). Therefore, the Papal authority is both spiritual and temporal. This statement is consequently true, as it implies both an end, and that which is ordered unto that end (*ff De procuratoribus*, the law *Ad legatum*, the law *Ad rem*). And this is confirmed: the Papal power is over souls, the Emperor's over bodies, but the soul dominates the body, as a lord his slave (as is clear from II *Politics*). The lord of the lord is therefore the lord of the slave: this holds, consequently, according to the rule: If I vanquish your victor I vanquish you as well (*De concessione prebende*: *Auctoritate*, book VI). This confirms the following: The Pope is the lord of the soul and its operations, therefore, etc. This holds consequentially, because the principal agent is the more perfect of the two, operating instrumentally as the woodcutter wields the axe (II question VII § *Item Balaam*). Likewise, the principate of the Pope is bestowed by God (XXII distinction *In novo*) while the principate of the Emperor by man (XCIII Distinction: *Legimus*). Therefore, as the immediate effect of God exceeds the effect of men, arguing from nobility of cause and concerning nobility of effect (*De celebracione Missarum*: *Cum Marthe*). Likewise, Christ had power of all sorts, Peter was Christ's Vicar, therefore, he too was possessed of power of all sorts. For it holds by consequence that the vicar has the same consistory as the ordinary (*De consuetudine*, chapter II book VI). Likewise, it is demonstrated that where there is but one prince, power is optimal where one and only one prince principally rules (this is demonstrated in II *Politics*, and is exemplified by the steward, as we find in II *Economics*). It is therefore necessary to have one sole monarch in the world, which cannot be the Emperor, to whom nothing spiritual is subject; hence, it is the Pope. Therefore, earthly rule ought to be subject to heavenly rule, as on Heaven all nature depends (*De summa Trinitate*, chapter I and I *Meteorology*, I *Celi*). But it is inherent in the regimen of the heavens that the corporal genus is to arrive at the most noble celestial sphere, according to the movement by which all inferior spheres are moved, thus it is for the genus of spiritual things to arrive at the first and most noble things on which all depend together (as in the chapter just adduced). But the noblest of corporal things are the instruments of the noblest of spiritualities, since from that Noblest proceeds both the spiritual and the corporal; thus, just as the regimen terrestrial is to arrive at the province of temporalities, which is the Emperor, so, the spiritual arrives at the Pope's, therefore, the Emperor is the instrument of the Pope. Likewise, arguing from the lights of heaven, the sun illuminates both day and night, the latter by its minister, *scil.* the moon, which, according to the variety of its aspect in relation to the sun, so varies the moon's light; in the same way the Pope illuminates the day, that is the soul, and the night, id est the darkness of the temporalities, by his minister, that is the Emperor. We infer from this that the authority of the Pope is the entirety of authority, and that of the Emperor as a follower at his heels. Johannes de Lignano.

It is clear from this that the monarchy of the globe terrestrial is to be found with the Vicar of Christ, as he possesses *de iure* both swords, and originally judgment over laypersons has belonged to the Church, but the exercise of said jurisdiction, or actual authority in temporal matters, by the divine nod, has been given to the Emperor by the Church (XCVI distinction *Cum ad verum*).

Continuing on with this matter, following Innocent, lord Antonius de Butrio (in the chapter *Licet*: *De foro competenti*), states 'These things were not decreed by the supreme Pontiffs on their own behalf; rather, they were established at the beginning of things. For in the beginning God created Heaven and Earth and all things that are found therein, angelic and human nature, spiritualities and temporalities, reigning over them Himself as their Maker over the things He created. Likewise, he established commandments and punishments for the transgression thereof (Gen. II: 'Of every tree,' etc.)[62] indeed, He did punish the transgressors, *scil.* Adam and Eve (Genesis III, where 'Ade quoque,' etc.).[63] Just so God Himself reigned up until the days of Noah, and thenceforward He continued to rule over His creatures through His ministers, the first of whom was Noah. That He was such a ruler to the people is clear from the fact of His giving Noah the governance of the ark, by which the Church is signified (Genesis IV and VI).[64] Likewise, because Noah bestowed rule upon his sons and gave them laws (Gen IX)[65] although he is not said to have been a priest, still he exercised the priestly office upon leaving the ark, before establishing the laws of the people (Gen VIII),[66] for he constructed an altar, which is something that pertains to the priestly office. Similarly, Abraham and Cain did, the latter before him. To this vicariate succeeded the patriarchs, the judges, the priests, and others who for a time ruled over the Jewish people. This lasted until the advent of Christ, our natural Lord and King, of Whom the Psalm 'Give to the king thy judgment, O God,' etc., speaks.[67] And Isaiah XIII, 'For the Lord is our judge, the Lord is our lawgiver, the Lord is our king: he will save us.'[68] and Jesus Christ Himself constituted Peter His Vicar and his successors too when He gave him the keys to the kingdom of Heaven, and when He said: 'feed my lambs.'[69] And thus although the offices and regimens of the world be distinct and various, still it is sometimes necessary to have recourse to the Pope, as for example in matters of doubt, or in cases of alleged injustice, or negligence in the administration of justice on the part of the Emperor or whatever other secular judge. Antonius de Butrio, following Ostiensis.

But can it be debated that, whereas the Church has both swords in its possession by custom, why should it not possess them by act and exercise as well?

The answer: at certain times the Church did indeed exercise such power through its priests (XI question I: *Relatum*) but a minister of the New Testament is a minister of gentleness and the sacrament of unity, for the Sacrament of the Altar represents the union of Christ and His Church, which signifies the union of the soul and the body, because just as the soul vivifies the body, thus Christ through His Sacrament vivifies the Church. Thus the execution of the temporal sword which divides soul from body should not belong to a minister of the sacrament of unity. To this Johannes Andreae adduces (in the chapter *Novit*: *De iudicijs*) following the same Antonius de Butrio (John XVIII):[70] 'Put up thy sword into the scabbard'), and Johannes Andreae adduces Bernardus to Pope Eugene: 'Approach your subjects, but in word, not deed. Why do you reach for the sword, which you were once told to return to its scabbard?' And (To Timothy, chapter III,[71] 'it behoveth a bishop to be... no striker') says Bernard (as above); 'To the Pope belongs the material sword, as far as indication is concerned; to the Emperor belongs its command, and to the solder — its use.' And this is what the aforesaid bull *Unam sanctam* holds. Antonius de Butrio. Likewise Francis, Cardinal of Florence.

And thus, according to the same doctors, the execution of the temporal sword was transferred into the hands of the Emperor and other Kings, and having been thus translated, the Pope cannot exercise it himself, for we transfer to others what is not right for us to retain (XII question II: *Quatuor*; XI question III: *Te quidem*). And according to this, Imperial jurisdiction proceeds from God because by the will of God it was established that the Emperor should wield such power, and in this manner arise those laws which state: he is not to be impeded in temporal jurisdiction, unless in certain cases, etc. This is how the canon *Cum ad verum* (XCVI distinction) is understood. On this matter, further information can be found in the gloss of Johannes Monachus in the aforesaid bull, where he explains the matter more subtly and sufficiently. Now, Pietro de Ancarano (in his recapitulation of chapter I of *De constitucionibus*) also broadly deals with this same matter, saying, among other things, that this distinction is proper, generally considered, for that there are two jurisdictions has never, it appears, been called into question, i.e. that one of these was the greater, the superior, although with the passage of time discords and dissension arose between the supreme Pontiffs and the Emperors; still it was declared that the Pope possessed both swords and superiority in regards to the Empire. And thus it is that the Pope crowns and anoints the Emperor, and sometimes deposes him, as is proven by the most recent laws (see the chapter *Ad apostolice*: *De re iudicata* book VI and *Clementina pastoralis,* to the end of said title, and *De iure iurando Clementina* I, and more fully in the aforementioned bull). Likewise, he says that in the absence of an Emperor the Pope steps in to assume secular jurisdiction (as in the chapter *Licit*: *De foro competenti*, and what is noted there by Innocent). Nor was this established by the supreme Pontiffs to their own advantage, he says, adducing many things in support of this; finally, he goes on to state that the spiritual takes precedence over the temporal in three ways: in dignity and seniority, and in so far as the spirit is superior to the flesh (*De translacione*, chapter II). Hence Abraham the patriarch, as a junior, pays tribute to Melchisadech as his senior (Genesis XIV);[72] Melchisadech, as his senior, blesses him (Letter to the Hebrews, VII).[73] It has priority of institution, as the priesthood of Melchisadech precedes the written law (on this, see the chapter *Translato*: *De constitucionibus*, citing Exodus, at the end of Chapter XXVIII).[74] Likewise, by command of God, the authority of kingship was ordained by the priesthood (I Kings, toward the end of chapter VIII),[75] where the Lord says to Samuel 'make them a king.' Third is priority in power or authority, in so far as the spiritual institutes and judges the temporal (as in said chapter

Per venerabilem, where 'know you not that you will be judging angels? So much the more so, secular things' (originally, directly from the Letter to the Corinthians chapter VI;[76] distinction § *Ecce*, etc.). And finally, the superiority is proven by the power of faith, saying, 'Just as it is heretical to accept two princes (XXIV final question, penultimate chapter) so is it heretical to accept two equal vicars on the earth, as far as the law is concerned. So that you should not be taken for a heretic, just as there is one immutable God (*De Summa Trinitate*, chapter I), so is His vicar on earth one, universally; it being of no moment that both of the swords proceed from the same principle, and that the Empire, just as the priesthood, comes of God.

For the Empire is not immediately of God, but a dependent and subaltern emanation of the Vicar of Christ, or it is of God's disposition and will that these two swords be wielded by diverse agents. But by His ordination, the exercise of these swords has a certain order between them, as the minor proceeds from the major. And whatever is understood concerning the certain distinction between these two dignities, it should be understood that this is a distinction in fact, and not in law (as the text of the law *Inter tutores* II puts it: *De administracione tutorum*). Because in difficulties and arduous cases that arise it was necessary that these be provided for by one, and publicly (the law II § *Novissime ff, De iure iurando*, etc; *Pro humani: De homicidio* book VI). Now, where the difficulty or weight of the matter is not in question, the contrary takes place: for the Pope concerns himself with persons, things, and cases ecclesiastical, judging them according to canon law, while secular causes and their matters are the business of the Emperor and his laws pertain therein. In this way, the two jurisdictions are distinct. And he concludes that whereas the jurisdictions are distinct as far as their execution is concerned, both were conceded to St Peter as belonging unto him, although the exercise of the temporal sword has been delegated to the Emperors by the Pope as indeed to other Kings as well, according to Laudensis, as they too are anointed by a priest just as David and Saul were, by Samuel. Upon this follows their confirmation in their executive office by ecclesiastical judge, as the Archdeacon notes (X distinction: *Quoniam*). And because such an exercise of the temporal sword, in other words, the actual power of the Emperors, cannot be executed by them unless in relation to such as are actually subject unto them, because naturally the act of an agent is properly received only by objects well-disposed thereunto, infidels who do not acknowledge the authority of the Roman Empire at all do not seem well-disposed to its actions, and for this reason, they are not bound by imperial laws or canonical constitutions (which is proven by the Codex: *De legibus*, the law *Leges*, and *De constitucionibus*, chapter 1, although canon law ought to prevail everywhere, as Johannes Andreae says, following Innocent, on the IV gloss with a general exception made for Pope, Emperor, pagans and Saracens). Hence it is that, in reference to them, the jurisdiction of the Emperor is said to cease. Still, they are subject, even in temporalities, to the Vicar of Christ, even though they not be of the Church's sheepfold (John X: 'other sheep I have, etc.'),[77] and it is only he, the Pope, to whom belongs a declaration of war against them, or punishment in the case of their trespassing (as Innocent broadly relates in the chapter *Quod super hijs*: *De voto*).

It is therefore obvious that said donations of the aforementioned Frederick, for the general subjugation of barbarous nations, etc., are of no moment or significance, by reason of defective cause efficient.

There yet remains to be seen[78] what the law is in reference to this matter of the donations. Concerning which it is first to be stated what lord Dominic of San Gemignano,[79] a most expert and renowned doctor, while acting as ordinary in the city of Florence and lecturing there on the *Decretals*, wrote of said donations when it was required of him. Among other things, he said that, although it is asserted in the privileges of these donations that the aforesaid lands of the infidels are subject to Imperial rule, still this is not proven, since not all lands of the infidels are under Imperial rule, as Innocent notes (in said chapter *Quod super hijs*: *De voto*), because even though Jerusalem and other parts had once been under the government of the Empire, the same is not true of Prussia, Lithuania, etc.). Therefore, because the case was delimited to a cause that was not in fact true, the concession is invalid (as in the text *De concessionibus prebende*: *Ex parte*, and noted in the same title: *Dilectus*; and clear on the basis of *De prebendis*: *Si pauper clericus*, book VI: *De treuga et pace*, chapter II). And that the Emperor indeed based his claim upon this very cause it is clear in two places, for he says that they are under the rule of the Empire, and later, he also states that his concession of them is based on the ancient rights that duly belong to the Empire. Now, therefore, if there be no such right of the Empire, it cannot be his intent to grant on the basis of such, because a privilege delimited to a certain quality can have no place if said quality be absent, even though the one granting the privileges might concede them by virtue of some other quality (as is clear from *De rescriptis*: *Susceptum*, and what is noted there in book VI and *De prebendis*: *Cum in illis* and the chapter *Mandatis* and the chapter *Quamvis* in the same title). Thus the conclusion stands, according to the same lord Dominic, that as the lands in question do not belong *de iure* to the Empire, these privileges are of no avail to the Prussian Knights, and if they claim that they do belong to the Empire *de iure*, the burden is on them to prove it. For if some case is based upon a rescript or a privilege, from which arises a petition, or, in the absence of which the petition cannot go forward, it is incumbent upon him who makes the petition for privilege or rescript to prove his claim to it (as Innocent notes in chapter *Ex parte* I: *De privilegijs*). The cause expressed in the Emperor's privilege is of just such a type that requires this sort of proof, because it states that the land is *de iure* the Empire's, and according to the law of the Empire he grants them the power of acquiring said lands. It is therefore clear that this is the concessionary clause, and it is this which they must prove. The idea that the words of the narrative, upon which the Emperor's intention is based, adduce full proof (as in *Clementina Litteris*: *De probacionibus*) is, according to him, irrelevant, because, what is said in *Clementina De probacionibus* applies to the Pope, and as it exceeds common law, it ought not to be extended to any other cause than that, which it precisely addresses (as in the rule *Que a iure*: *De regulis iuris*, book VI, with its concordances). For it is contrary to law that a narrative brought forth when two are compacting should be to the prejudice of a third party (as Innocent notes in *De officio delegati*: *Cum in iure*; and as *De priviligijs*: *Si Papa*, book VI makes clear, and *Clementina*: *Si Summus*: *De sentencia excommunicacionis*). Therefore, the *Clementina* granting said privilege to the Pope in this matter ought not to be extended to any other person, since privileges are not so extended, even on the basis of an identical reason (*De privilegijs*: *Porro* and the chapter *Sane*); and that this *Clementina* is excessive in regard to common law, Oldradus upholds in his consultation upon question CLXI. Lord Dominic.

Indeed, even granting as I said above that the Emperor is the lord of the world in power and by usage, as far as universal dominion is concerned and, by consequence, that the aforesaid lands *de iure* are under the rule of the Empire, even so it holds that other particular lands belong to other particular persons, for the right of possession comes from the natural law of the nations (*ff De justicia et iure*, the law *Ex hoc iure*). Hence Innocent, pursuing this matter (in the chapter *Quod super hijs*: *De voto*) and the same lord Dominic, following him, says: 'Because pagans possess their goods by virtue of the natural law of the nations, therefore, they possess them justly.' Because by law divine, before their occupation, it was allowable to all to occupy whatever untenanted lands there were (Deuteronomy, chapter XI:[80] 'Every place, that your foot shall tread upon, shall be yours') as is plain in regard to Abraham and Lot, of whom one accepted the land to the right, the other to the left (Genesis, chapter XIII).[81] And such things are given by God to all rational creatures, by that God Who 'who maketh his sun to rise upon the good, and bad' and nourishes all winged things (Matthew V near the end, and VI),[82] and in the Psalm[83] 'who gives to all flesh nourishment,' from which Innocent concludes: along with the aforesaid, lord Dominic, that neither the faithful, nor even the Pope is permitted to take away the possessions of the infidel, or the jurisdictions that belong to them, as they possess them rightly, as is clear from the precepts of divine law, which prohibit all violence and rapine, without distinction, by the words 'Thou shalt not kill,' 'Thou shalt not steal'[84] (as in XIV question V, canon 1 and the following). Here say likewise, following St Thomas (in *Secunda*

Secunde, question IX and X), who says the following: 'That dominion and government were introduced according to human law, *scilicet* by the law of the nations, while the distinction between faithful and infidel was instituted by divine law, and divine law, which comes of grace, does not do away with human law, which comes of natural reason, and therefore the state of infidelity is not repugnant to dominion or the possession of goods.' Hence he says that although it is not permissible for the infidels to reconstitute themselves as lords or governors over the faithful, on account of the danger that this would present to the Faith, still, the pre-existing rule that they have over the faithful is not to be taken away from them.

Now, because Ostiensis seems to be of the contrary opinion, for this reason said lord Dominic adduces these words of Johannes Andreae in the *Addicio Speculi De Iudeis et Saracenis*, setting forth here seven most efficacious reasons wherewith to confute Ostiensis' claims, which reasons, according to said lord Dominic, were those given by Oldradus in his counsel. I shall touch upon some of them here.

Now, absent legitimate cause, no prince is permitted to expel peaceful Saracens, otherwise pagans, from those of his territories, which do not appear to have belonged to the Roman Empire. This is proven, first by arguing from natural law and divine law, which teach that whoever wishes to be treated justly, must treat others in that way (Matthew VI[85] and 1 distinction: *Humanum genus*), nor should he do unto others that, which he would not wish others to do unto him (*De maioritate et obediencia*: *Dilecti*). As the prince does not wish to be expelled, nor should he expel others from his realm. Likewise, we are to love the Saracens and pagans in as much as they participate in our human nature, not only in soul, but in body as well (*De penitencia* distinction II: *Cautes*, the verses 'Non illi' and 'Sed proinde' where just as we wish to be aided, so should we aid them, and the conclusion: 'Dearly beloved, with all the power of your love strive so that the good that you wish to receive from others, you should wish for your brother as well'). It is therefore perfectly clear that to expel such persons would be contrary to love. For love of one's neighbor does no harm, whether that be expulsion, or other wrongs (Romans 13),[86] for love 'is not provoked to anger' (1 Cor. 13)[87] and an upright will does no iniquity. This natural law, and divine law, is immutable and thus indispensable (*Institucionibus*, *De iure naturali*; § *Sed naturalia*; VI distinction § *Is ita*), even by the Pope, for its mutation would implicate sin (as is noted in *De iure iurando*: *Etsi Christus*, the gloss *Quedam*); and hence even by law we are obliged to aid them and give alms unto them (XLII distinction: *Quiescamus* XVII distinction: *Si cupis*; LXXXVI distinction *Non satis*).

The second reason for this is that he who has been taken captive deserves to be treated with forgiveness, all the more so where no perturbation of the peace is to be feared on his account. In such cases, such a harsh remedy as expulsion should not be resorted to (XXIII question I: *Noli*). So the ruler is commanded to incline to the fearful and obedient in love, to do them no harm out of cupidity, but from charity and good will to do nothing inhumane (XXIII question V: *Prodest*); nothing is to be done out of fury, but rather, all in charity (XII question II: *Fraternitas*).

The third reason why we should not despoil peaceful pagans of their goods, nor deprive them of their native land and expel them (this is proven by note XXIII to question VII: *Si de rebus* in the gloss *Per hoc*) is because they possess their goods and jurisdictions by natural law, and by just judicial and political determination (XIV question IV: *Quid dicam*; *De vero rum significacione*: *Ius dictum*) and this is clearly held by Innocent (in the chapter *Quod super hijs*: *De voto*; in agreement with what is noted in XXIII question V: *Si papa*). And it is a matter of righteousness, especially the righteousness of kings, never to impose undue force on anyone (VI question I: *Sapiens*). For levity and gentleness are rooted in the Christian religion, which is contrary to all cruelty (XXIII question V: *Unum solum*).

Likewise, the fourth reason is because they are sheep belonging to Christ (John X:[88] 'Other sheep I have, that are not of this fold,' i.e. the Church), and He said to Peter 'Feed my sheep' (John, final chapter)[89] without making any distinction among them. Therefore, the successor of Peter is to feed them and defend them, ergo, he is not to permit them to be battled down or harmed (*De natis ex libero ventre*, chapter I).

Likewise, a text is adduced (in the law *Christianus*: *Codice, De paganis et eciam Sarra*[*cenis*]) which commands that those pagans living at peace must not be molested (and likewise *De Iudeis* chapter II and the chapter *Sicud* and LVI distinction: *Satis perversum* and these words of the Psalmist: 'The Heaven of Heaven is the Lord's, but the earth He has given to the children of men'). Thus they aren't to to be refused what the law of human security grants unto them (XXIII question II: *Notandum*, etc.).

Here say that the lands which are under the power of the infidels cannot be donated to others (this is proven by the text in the chapter *Abbate Sane*: *De sentencia et re iudicata*, the verse 'Allegabatur,' book VI, where this case and the reasons therefore are taken up in gloss VI): because the free man and the land of one's enemies and other things of similar nature cannot be made objects of stipulations (per the law *ff De verborum obligacionibus*: *Liber homo*, and per others cited there). This is true of things which have always belonged to the enemy, according to Pietro de Ancarano, who notes the same there; he says the case is different if they once belonged to us, but are now occupied by the enemy. In such a case they may be donated, deeded, or stipulated according to the hope we have according to the law of *postlimini* (as per the law *Id quod apud ff De legatis* I), where, following him. Bartolus infers in the same law: 'That the concession of the Kingdom of Jerusalem made by the Pope to King Charles and his successors is valid, even though he held none of it, because it was at one time a kingdom only of Christians.' Peter de Ancarano.

From which things it can be evidently stated that also by reason of the object of said donations, they are entirely worthless and contrary to natural and divine law, for a donation made in prejudice to the actual owner is invalid (Codex *De donacionibus*, law II).

To Ostiensis' reasons given to the contrary, lord Dominic makes response; these I omit here for reasons of brevity.

Having stated the above with the aid of Christ,[90] the same may be seen by reason of form. For, assuming that the aforesaid infidels belonged to the Empire by deed of subjugation, and that said Emperor possessed over them a power not only habitual, but actual, still he might not deprive them of their dominium without cognisance of cause. For which it is to be noted that, for such a prevention to be valid, there is required not mere jurisdiction on the part of him who deprives, and proper subjection of him who is deprived, but also a legitimate reason for the privation and a proper form, or legitimate manner of privation. And if even one of these is missing, the act is naturally invalid and contrary to the substance of the thing. For it is the same thing to deprive a person of his rights without legitimate cause and without due cognisance of the cause, for each of these is contrary to natural law, which is proven by what Innocent notes in the chapter *Cum in ecclesiarum*: *De constitucionibus*) stating that although a prince may take up some action *de facto* brought to him by a petitioner, it is nevertheless the judge who *ex officio suo* administers justice to said plaintiff. For it is said that the Emperor's judgment is invalid in cases where the party has not been summoned, as such is contrary to natural law (as is noted in the final law *De legitima*, and in the text that may be found in *Clementina Pastoralis* § *Ceterum*, in the verse 'Nec predicta supplecio': *De re iudicata*) Because the summons allows, in a way, the summoned party to speak in his own defense (*De maioritate et obediencia*; *Inter quatuor*; II question I: *Nos in quemquam* and the canon *Non sine* and the law *De unoquoque ff De re iudicata*). Therefore, to block the path of summons is to block the path of defense, which is a natural right (the law *Ut vim ff De justicia et iure*) and natural rights are immutable, even by a prince (as in the final § of *Institucionibus. De iure naturali gencium et civili*, and this is upheld by Laudensis in said *Clementina*, Paulus de Liazaris, and Genzelinus). Nor, according to Franciscus de Zabarellis, Cardinal of Florence (ibid.) is the repair of defects or lack to any purpose in such a case, because such refers merely to formalities, and not the substance of the process (as in the chapter *Illa*: *De eleccione*, and as is noted in chapter I: *De Transaccionibus* with other scripts similar thereunto, and in the *Speculum*, under the title *De legato* § *Nunc ostendendum*, verse XVIII). Now, if they are not actually subject, they certainly cannot be punished unless their prior culpability is proven, and then it is only the Pope who has the authority to punish them, in certain cases noted by Innocent (the chapter *Quod super hijs*: *De voto*), that is to say, in cases where they have sinned against natural law: thus even the Jews may be punished if they sin against the Mosaic laws. Likewise, if they impede or molest the faithful or occupy Christian dominions, etc. And what I have said concerning punishment at the hands of the Pope is true unless some other is acting in defense of his own right (as is noted in the same place). Hence in his questions, Oldradus, in question LXXII, which begins: 'Is the war of the Spanish against the Saracens a just war?' he says that, even presupposing that now, and in the future, they wish to live in peace with us, as a reason for answering in the affirmative he sets forth the fact that the entire province of Spain was once Christian, where churches, monasteries, and other pious establishments had been founded, in which Christ was worshipped, and they were under the aegis of the Church, while these same Saracens proceeded to occupy them by violence, despoiling us of them. And he adds: 'And thus, if we are acting in order recuperate the fatherland of which we have been despoiled by violence, our war is just, and ought to be judged a defensive action, and not an invasion.' Thus according to him.

And so, as in the aforesaid donations no fault is mentioned as justification for the deprivation, nor can one even be so ratiocinated here as one principal cause to the exclusion of all others (XXV distinction, *Qualis,* with others similar thereto), because diversity of causes implies diversity of effects: it is therefore clear that these privations, and the consequent donations, are null and void because of defect of form and absence of culpability.

What is more, Emperor Lewis IV is seen to be no less in error[91] and cruel than the preceding Emperors, as is clearly seen from his privileges, if they be authentic; of which two privileges are produced. One of these is dated Munich, in the year of Our Lord 1336, and the other from the year immediately succeeding. Concerning which it is to be noted that in the first privilege, which bestows upon these Brethren the land of the Samogitians, that is Żmudź, along with others expressly there mentioned, the Master of the aforesaid Brethren is invested with the temporal administration and jurisdiction, and full governmental authority over said principality. The Emperor names said Master his 'fortunate prince, most dear to the Roman Empire.' In this same privilege he even asserts that the aforementioned lands belong to the pagan Lithuanians, and thus by consequence he asserts that they do not belong to him, as least as far as property and individual dominion are concerned. Therefore, he is not capable of bestowing them or investing anyone with them (per the rights alleged above) nor can he bestow general dominion, if such indeed belonged to him, especially absent the consent of the peoples, according to Baldus, who notes this in the chapter *In generali* and according to others above alleged in the chapter beginning with the letter [ ]. Because he is called lord to whom jurisdiction and care are entrusted (as in XXIII question VIII: *Convenior,* in the first gloss), where it is stated that all things in a given realm are the King's in so far as jurisdiction and defense are concerned, but not as his own property and individual dominion (according to the Archdeacon, on the same cause and question in § *Quamvis*).

The second thing to be noted in this same privilege is the twofold cause set forth as the principle upon which the aforesaid Brethren's warring is based: one is temporal, the other spiritual — and both are erroneous.

The temporal cause is the extension of the Empire, which is touched upon there, where it is said 'they advance into adversity on behalf of the Roman Empire,' which ought to be understood according to the cause which was premised at the outset, where it is stated that the Christian people caused the Roman Empire to be elevated above all other princes of this world, and whatever barbarians there may be, and that the Lord so established all this for future times as well, for what succeeds ought to be understood from what comes before, and vice versa (as in XXXII question VII: *Apostolus*, of which see here in the final gloss, along with its concordances).

Now, the spiritual cause is the spreading of the Faith, and this touches upon what is said here: 'surely because the venerable Master and the aforesaid Brethren and the entire aforesaid Order graciously and laboriously engage in their service of spreading the Catholic faith to the glory and praise of the Divine Name, ceaselessly and valiantly, they present themselves to us as exceptionally gracious and peaceful, etc.' From which causes these Brethren claim their status to to be chiefly constituted, and by consequence that this order is secular and regular at one and the same time. And yet because said causes, so diverse, cannot produce the same effect, it needs to be stated that their military status can neither be termed secular nor regular. For the cause and that which is caused must be of one and the same nature, and whatever the law of the effective cause may be, the same must be the law of the result (I question 1: *Quicunque sacros*, and the canon *Cito turpem*, with others similar to it). For diversity of cause is necessarily followed by diversity of effect, therefore, etc. Now, that their status is founded upon the aforesaid causes is quite clear from their very privilege, in which it is said 'Who abjuring their personal property and abdicating their individual will, regardless of the torments of the flesh, advance into adversity on behalf of the Roman Empire and the house of Jerusalem, fear not to expose themselves to stout battlements, dying the cloaks of their souls crimson in their own blood on behalf of the Catholic Faith and the rights of their fathers.'

And because they admit in this very privilege that they are engaging in incessant warring, however erroneous, it thus must be confessed that they deceived Pope Alexander and the other Roman Pontiffs aforesaid, for in begging their privileges of them, they said nothing of this error or cruelty and tyranny of theirs, suggesting instead a falsehood, something contrary to the truth, as is made clearly evident above in chapter [ ]. And this privilege also provides the clearest basis for the King of Poland's claim to the land of Żmudź, etc. by reason of Lithuania, as it is asserted that said land belongs to the Lithuanians.

The second privilege of this same Louis is dated Frankfurt, on the twenty-second day of the month of July, in the year of Our Lord 1338, to which the appended great round seal attests, bluish-grey in colour and suspended from green ribbons. It is addressed to the Master and the Order at large in response to a complaint brought before said Emperor by this Master. This in effect concerns how Kazimierz, King of Poland, along with the Archbishop of Gniezno and other of his suffragan bishops, had reported to the Roman Curia some acts of violence, etc., committed by these Brethren, of which they bitterly complain, and that said King Kazimierz has initiated a suit against them in an ecclesiastical court concerning these lands, etc. To this, said Emperor responds, commanding them not to respond to the summons and to take no note of the episcopal mandate, etc. As to this, it should be noted that this privilege not only confirms the definitive verdict handed down in the question of these lands, in favor of the King of Poland and against said Brethren, but all public instruments as well, contained in said sentence. For here it is stated that Kazimierz, King of Poland, reported said Brethren to the Roman Curia, and the same is stated in the document of the verdict; they confess in the privilege that said King called them to court before ecclesiastical judges concerning these lands, etc., which is related in the same document, and this same King of Poland, and this same Master of the aforesaid Brethren, and the same year is mentioned, here and there. For it is said in this document that in the year of Our Lord 1338, on the fourth day of the month of December, Theodoric de Aldenburg, Master General, appointed procurators to defend their case, which procurators were invested with sufficient plenipotentiaries to appear before the judges, even though they boldly withdrew from the court. Hence it is evident that in this same year, in the month of July, this privilege was obtained by the Brethren so that they might have the justification — such as it is — to duck away from the court, and now, one may believe, they are attempting to have the judge removed.[92] Nonetheless, said verdict was handed down in favor of said King in the face of the contumaciousness of those Brethren in the year immediately succeeding this, *scil.* 1339, on the fifteenth day of September, as is clear from said document.

Likewise, note well that in so far as they produce this privilege in defense of their case, they tacitly confess to all that is contained in it, and so admit to the triplex cause adduced in the privilege, concerning which later they chose not to reveal to said judges.

The first being that they were members of the Empire and that their Order was instituted by the Emperors and received a donation in return for their defense of the Empire and the Christian Faith, from which it follows that they are no religious order, but secular and lay, and by consequence they deny themselves to be spiritual entities.

Second, it is stated in this privilege that suits brought against them by said King Kazimierz belong to the Empire and the aforesaid

Emperor, and by consequence they deny them to belong to the forum of the Church.

The third is that same Emperor expressly forbade them, under penalty of being deprived of all their territory, rights, and privileges, etc., to place their lands in this way at the mandate of any man beyond his authority, and even to respond to the summons of any judge, ecclesial or secular, whatever, by which they tacitly state that the Emperor possesses a greater authority to prohibit such things than Pope or ecclesial judge, on the contrary, to command them, for by their adducing said privilege in their favor, they wish more to obey the Emperor, by which it is shown most clearly that they were truly contumacious, by which all their objections as to the security of the place are taken away, to say nothing of that which other most expert learned men sufficiently wrote against those objections. What is more, it is clear that the aforementioned Brethren wished to make themselves safe with this privilege from judge as well as from said King, under the protection of said Emperor. For in his exhortation to them, the Emperor states: 'So that your minds might be confirmed in the virtue of constancy toward your task, the above-stated lands you acquire despite manifold dangers and the shedding of your own blood, to secure to secure the same beneath the buckler of our majesty, and so that the purity of your constancy not be assailed by dread, thus our omnipotent hand shall be prompt and liberal in your aid against any invader of your territories, or anyone who seeks otherwise to usurp the same, etc.' And so it is proven that the Emperor, in so defending the aforesaid Theodoric, General Master of the Prussian Knights, whom he names his own prince and prince of the Empire, consents to all the evils perpetrated by this Theodoric in the Kingdom of Poland at the time, such as are contained in the aforesaid document of the verdict, and, in consequence, it is to be concluded that the Emperor himself is guilty of fomenting the tyranny and error of these Brethren, committed not only against the infidels, but against Christians, etc.

It is said that Emperor Charles IV was filled with zeal for the increase of said Brethren in his privilege,[93] which will be spoken of now, last. In it, it is asserted that these Brethren incessantly take upon themselves assiduous labor and effort on behalf of the faith and the glory of the Christians. And this privilege is dated the year of Our Lord 1354, Fourth Nones of January (3 January 1354). Now this privilege, which was produced before the King of the Romans as before an arbiter (or before his deputy) has been produced under another date, *scil.* the year of Our Lord 1355, 13 Calends of January (19 December 1354), and both documents are dated Nuremberg. Concerning which, please note that there exist two privileges of this Charles, one concerning the land of Prussia in which the donation of this land is confirmed as executed by John, the King of Bohemia his father, and both privileges of the father as well as of the son were produced to this purpose. The father's privilege is dated Toruń, in the year of Our Lord 1329, on Invocavit Sunday, while that of the son is dated Włocławek, the year of Our Lord 1337 on the Sunday on which the 'Esto mihi' is sung. Now, it is true that before this time, i.e. in the year of Our Lord 1321, a definitive verdict was handed down against these Brethren on the authority of Pope John XXII, who declared in favor of Lord Władysław, King of Poland at the time, which lands these Brethren at the time had occupied by violence, just as they continue to occupy them now. And this verdict is in the possession of the Poles as a public instrument, and because these Brethren later occupied several other regions in the Kingdom of Poland by violence, once more another definitive verdict was handed down against them on the authority of Pope Benedict XII in the year of Our Lord 1339, according to which the lands of Prussia, Chełmno and Michałów were declared to belong to the Kingdom of Poland, and said Brethren were found to hold said lands of Prussia, as well as those of Chełmno and Michałów, by violence, hence unjustly. Furthermore, they were bound to restore said lands to Lord Kazimierz, King of Poland at the time, according to the public document of which we speak in the chapter above immediately preceding, from which document it is sufficiently clear that the donation and confirmation of the aforesaid John and Charles are null and void on account of prejudice and fraud in relation to the sentence passed. It is with prejudice as well to the King and Kingdom of Poland, and to the benefit of said Brethren, as said John admitted that said Lord Kazimierz was King of Poland, and that between him as such, and said Brethren, he acted as arbiter in the matter of said lands and others, along with lord Charles King of Hungary as is even contained in the privilege of said Kings produced. In consequence, he confesses another to be King of Poland, tacitly acknowledging that his donation made under the pretence of him being King of Poland himself, is invalid.

Now, passing by other matters, we must consider here the privilege of this Charles, of which see above at the commencement of this chapter, and by which all the privileges of his predecessors were confirmed, especially that of Frederick II, and all that is contained in them concerning whatever sort of things, goods, possessions, rights, etc., whether conceded by the Apostolic See or anyone else. Concerning which please note that in this privilege are verified those things which, anent these lands, are contained in the above-stated document of the verdict. For in this privilege it is stated that said Brethren came into the possession of these lands through wrongdoing and violence, and therefore they were charged to restore the same, just as said document holds. And so they assert that they ceased to possess these lands on account of their wrongdoing and violence, and by virtue of this fact they possessed them for such a long time, according to them, and yet they still petitioned for them to be conceded to them anew by Emperor Charles in the fullness of his authority. Hence said Emperor not only conceded this by ratifying them, and by certain knowledge confirming them, but also he forbade by the penalties therein contained that any prince, ecclesiastical or secular, or any other elevated person whatsoever, should impede or molest them in so far as these possessions were concerned, etc. Beyond this please note that the aforesaid Brethren, in admitting that they possessed by prescription lands acquired by wrongdoing and violence, tacitly confess as well to the bad faith of said prescription, and in consequence confess in this privilege to their own turpitude and rapine, for having, for an extended time, not diminished their sinful activity, but rather augmented it. For all the more grave are those sins that hold bound the unfortunate soul for a long period (*De consuetudine*, chapter IV). And here this turpitude and wrongdoing is clearly seen to be confirmed by certain knowledge.

Thus, as it is evidently proven that said inhibition or concession is intended to weaken the jurisdiction of the Church, and to oppress the above-mentioned Kingdom of Poland, so that justice should not proceed from the aforementioned verdict: Therefore, it is also proven that this Imperial authority is not lawful, but merely factual, and in consequence cannot be said to be lawful *de iure*, in the fullness of his authority, but rather in the fullness of cruelty.

From all that has been said above, it is clear enough what is to be thought of the legality of these privileges of theirs, and this suffices for the second principal part of our case.

Endnotes

1. This treatise arises from the aftermath of Sigismund of Luxembourg's arbitration decision delivered in Buda in 1420. That decision was one of the most crucial steps he took trying to balance his own interests between that of a group—the Order—that in general he supported and the Polish monarchy—upon which he was dependents in many ways for support against the Hussites in Bohemia, where rebellion (revolt?) had broken out following the execution of Jan Hus at Constance in 1415 and the death of King Václav (Wenceslaus), Sigismund's older brother and whom he now sought to succeed. The best synthetic work on his approach remains Zenon H. Nowak, *Międzynarodowe procesy polubowna jako narzędzie politiki Zygmunta Luksemburskiego w północnej i środkowowschodniej Europie (1412-1424)* (Toruń: Uniwersytet Mikołaja Kopernika, 1981), here pp. 81-96. Sigismund's 1420 judgment went against the Poles, and in the aftermath the Polish king, Władysław

Jagiełło and his council, were inclined either toward war to achieve Polish goals or to the negotiation of a treaty with the Order to resolve the issues in dispute. Paweł instead proposed an appeal to the pope in an eloquent letter, edited by Belch, *Paulus Vladimiri*, II, 1027-1032; his argument carried the day. Paweł's treatise was among the materials to be presented to Cardinal Guillaume Fillastre (1348-1428), who had been appointed by Pope Martin V to oversee the appeal process. See Krzysztof Ożóg, *Uczeni w Monarchii Jadwigi Andegaweńskiej i Władysława Jagiełły (1384-1434)* (Kraków: Polska Akademia Umiejętności, 2004), pp. 234-241. The best recent study of how these materials were transmitted is Adam Szweda and Anna Adamska, "Notariusz przy pracy. Akcja transumowania dokumentów krzyżackich jesienią 1421 roku," in Grażyna Rutkowski and Antoni Gąsiorowski, eds., *Memoria viva. Studia historyczne poświęcone pamięci Izabeli Skierskiej (1967-2014)* (Poznań: Instytut Historii PAN, 2015), pp. 487-501.

2. Paweł organized his treatise into twenty-three chapters (*capitula*), each beginning with a latter of the alphabet in consecutive order, A to Z, except for J, U, and W; to include K and X (not part of the Latin alphabet) he utilized words with unusual spellings: *Karissime* and *Xpi*, the *nomen sacrum* for *Christi*. The beginning of each *capitulum* is noted below.

3. *Ad videndum clare...*

4. Paweł is here referring to articles prepared by the Order that are to be presented to Cardinal Filiastre in order that he might give them to the pope, He is not referring the his own "articles" in the treatise above *Articuli*.

5. i.e., Samogitia, (Lithuanian: Žemaitije), one of the five central ethnocultural regions of Lithuania and located in the lowlands of Northwestern Lithuania.

6. i.e., the Sudovians.

7. In the manuscript on which this edition is based, these materials are not included and so are absent from the translation.

8. *Bene circa hoc...*

9. Pope Alexander IV (1254-1261).

10. Lewis IV of Bavaria, emperor elect in 1314 (a controversial and contested election), crowned emperor in 1328 (but not recognized by the pope), succeeded as emperor elect in 1346, and d. 1347 (Paweł's treatment of the documents Lewis issued relevant to the Order see the text below following n. 91.)

11. Francisco Zabarella, Paweł's mentor at Padua. Zabarella (1360-1417), Bishop-elect of Florence in 1409, cardinal 1409-1417, was one of the three most important intellectuals at the Constance of Constance 1414-1418); he was arguably the leading canonist at Padua in the late fourteenth century. See Thomas E. Morrissey, "Cardinal Franciscus Zabarella (1360-1417) as a Canonist and the Crisis of His Age: Schism and the Council of Constance," *Zeitschrift für Kirchengeschichte* 96 (1985): 196-208, and reprinted as item VIII, with original pagination, in Morrissey, *Conciliarism and Church Law in the Fifteenth Century. Studies on Franciscus Zabarella and the Council of Constance* (Farnham, Surrey England and Burlington, VT: Ashgate: 2014.

12. Hostiensis (Henricus de Segusio, 1190/1200-1271) studied canon law at Bologna at the same time as Sinibaldo dei Fieschi (the future Pope Innocent IV). He subsequently taught at Paris and was named cardinal-bishop of Ostia in 1261. His important body of canonical writings and his influence ensured he was highly regarded. Dante includes him in *Paradiso* in his *Commedia*: 12:82-97. See Brundage, *Canon Law*, p. 214.

13. This is Henricus Boic[h] (*ca*, 1310-after 1370, but before 1390), who studied civil and canon law, earning the doctorate in both laws at Paris, where he apparently taught. His most important works were *repertoria* on the *Liber sextus* and the *Decretum*, but his reputation and influence was limited. See Belch, *Paulus Vladimiri*, I, 298 n. 9; 557; and 581, n. 5; and Ehrlich, *Pisma wybrane,* I, xxxiii.

14. *Ceterum advertantur...*

15. Johannes Monachus (Jean LeMoine, *ca* 1250-1313), who studied philosophy and theology at Paris prior to his legal studies there. Eventually active in Italy, he became vice-chancellor of the Roman church under Boniface VIII. He was also the author of a number of important legal treatises and commentaries. See Brundage, *Canon Law*, p. 219.

16. *Deinde circa hoc...*

17. Johannes Andreae (*ca*. 1270-1348) studied at Bologna, then taught at both Bologna and Padua, serving also from time to time as an ambassador from Bologna. A married layman (only the second to become a professor of canon law), he produced a number of important and influential works. He died in the plague in 1348. See Brundage, *Canon Law*, pp. 216-217.

18. *Et insuper pro maiori claritate*

19. *Fuit iam supra dictum...*

20. Paweł here begins a summary of Polish claims regarding the way the Order had obtain control of the lands in dispute, an issue he addressed in a number of his writings; see, for example, his arguments on these issues above in *Articuli*, nn. 53 and 54.

21. The reliability of Frederick II's grant in 1226 has long been a subject of controversy (as noted in several instances in the annotations to Paweł's works); see particularly Tomasz Jasiński, "The Golden Bull Allegedly Issued in 1226 by Frederick II for the Teutonic Order, *Quaestiones Medii Aevi Novae* 3 (1998): 221-244.

22. *Gaudent eciam dicti fratres. . .*

23. For the developments that Paweł is alluding to, see Jan Powierski, "Książęta polscy i Zakon Krzyżacki a problem bałtyjski w okresie od schyłku 1258 do połowy 1260 roku," *Komunikaty Mazursko-Warmińskie* 23, 4 (1979): 367-390.

24. From this (polite) imperative in the text, Ehrlich, *Pisma wybrane*, III, 195, n. 13, suggests that here (and elsewhere, in locations he sites) Paweł is addressing someone with whom he was close. This may have been either Cardinal Filiastri, who was responsible for gathering materials to be presented to the pope (see n. 1 above)

or, more probably, an individual in the cardinal's circle who was expected to assist in the preparation of these materials.

25. This space, like other similar instances in the MS, is blank, suggesting it was to be filled in later.

26. *Hoc premisso...*

27. See above, n. 25.

28. See above, n. 25.

29. *Item pro evidencia clariori...*

30. *Karissime...* On Paweł's use of this word, compare the treatment of this by Ehrlich, *Pisma wybrane*, III, 195, n. 13 (though his cross reference to n. 9 of that page is incorrect) with that by Belch, *Paulus Vladimiri*, I, 195.

31. *Loquendum nunc restat de tercio...*

32. Mindaugas, first known Grand Duke of, and after 1253 King, of Lithuania (1203-1263). Originally a pagan, he was baptized a Roman Catholic and forged an alliance with the Livonian Order (a military-religious crusading order originally known as the Sword Brothers that in 1237 became part of the Order of the Teutonic Knights and was known as the Livonian Order. He may later have reverted to paganism. See Steven C. Rowell, *Lithuania Ascending. A Pagan Empire within East-Central Europe, 1295-1345* (Cambridge: Cambridge University Press, 1994), p. 51; and, more fully, Ėvardas Gudavičius, *Mindaugas* (Vilnius: Žara, 1998), which I have not personally seen.

33. *Modo est videndum...*

34. Paweł is undoubtedly referring here to Bartholomew of Lucca (*ca* 1236-*ca*. 1337), whose *Historia Ecclesiastica Nova* in 24 *libri* appeared about 1317; see Ottavio Lavuot and Ludwig Schmugge, eds., *Historia Ecclesiastica Nova: Nebst Fortsetzungen Bis 1329* (Hannover: Hahnsche Buchhandlung, 2009 [Monumenta Germaniae Historica Scriptores, vol. 39]).

35. Paweł here confuses Latvia with Lithuania.

36. *Nunc de privilegijs Alexandri prefati...*

37. Ehrlich, *Pisma wybrane*, III, 198, n. 42, indicates that on this point Paweł's reasoning on the basis of chronology is incorrect. He has accepted the incorrect information of the *Historia Ecclesiastica Nova* that Alexander's pontificate began in 1253, when the date normally accepted is 1254.

38. *Omisso quodam alio privilegio...*

39. Matt. 6:24.

40. *Post predicta... est dicendum...*

41. Paweł's point here is that transcripts are not authentic original documents and can therefore not be used as evidence.

42. Again, the polite imperative to a familiar.

43. Antonius de Butrio (1338-1408). He studied canon law at Bologna, Florence, and Ferrara, and was the author of a number of influential works bearing on the Great Schism. See, briefly, *Repertorium Fontium Historiae Medii Aevi,* II (Rome: Istituto Storico Italiano per il Medio Evo, 1967), 379.

44. Paweł here follows his mentor Zabarella, whose sense of governance was a kind of social contact, such that—apart from a divine order—government derives its legitimacy from the consent of the governed. For his views see Morrissey, "Cardinal Zabarella and Nicholas of Cusa: from community authority to consent of the community," *Mitteilungen und Forschungsbeiträge der Cusanus-Gesellschaft* 17 (1986): 157-176, esp. pp. 158-164 and p. 176: "ultimately authority resides in the community as a whole." This article is reprinted in Morrissey, *Conciliarism and Church Law in the Fifteenth Century,* as entry I, retaining the same pagination as the original.

45. Baldus de Ubaldis (*ca.* 1327-1400, among the best known canonists of his time), was particularly influential in the last decades of the fourteenth century and the beginning of the fifteenth century; see the comments of Brundage, *Canon Law*, p. 180 and p. 207.

46. *Quantum vero ad tercium genus privilegiorum predictorum. . .*

47. Charles of Luxembourg, king of Bohemia 1346-1378, elected King of the Romans (i.e., Holy Roman Emperor elect) in 1346, confirmed by re-election in 1347, and crowned emperor as Charles IV in 1355 (d. 1378).

48. i.e., the Golden Bull of 1226; see above, n. 21, for some of the issues connected with it.

49. *Redeundo ad donaciones Fredrici supradictas...*

50. This part is not included in the MS edition upon which this translation is based, although it may have been added to the document that was eventually submitted to Cardinal Filiastre and given to the pope.

51. Bartolo da Sassoferrato (*ca.* 1313-1357) was a civil jurist rather than a canonist, who studied at Bologna, then taught at Pisa and Perugia. He produced a very large body of work that proved influential regarding theories about the authority of a city-state. He coined the phrase the *civitas sibi princeps*—the city state was its own emperor and did not recognize any superior. See Julius Kirshner, "Bartolo da Sassoferrato," in Joseph R. Strayer, editor-in-chief, *Dictionary of the Middle Ages*, 13 vols. (New York: Charles Scribner's Sons, 1982-1989), here II (1983), 114-116.

52. The reference to the Archdeacon is to Guido de Baysio (*ca.* 1250-1313), Archdeacon of Bologna and Archchancellor of the University of Bologna, author of *Rosarium*, a rich commentary on Gratian's *Decretum*. He was a master teacher, and one of his students was Johannes Andreae (about whom, see above, n. 17). See Brundage, *Canon Law*, pp. 212-213.

53. Dinus de Mugello (1253-post 1298), a doctor of both civil and canon law from Bologna who taught at Pistoia and then Rome at the time of Boniface VIII. See, briefly, *Repertorium Fontium Historiae Medii Aevi,* IV (1976), 201-202.

54. *Supra dixi de finali causa. . .*

55. Paweł is here following the traditional scholastic approach used in disputations—the process of reasoning and arguing—of stating an opinion with which he does not agree, then showing a correct alternative, followed by a conclusion

and—if necessary—a resolution (though in most instances Paweł regards his conclusion as correct and not needing a resolution). See the discussion on his specific methodology by Ehrlich, *Pisma wybrane*, III, 199, n. 66. More generally, the character of the disputation in a scholastic (and juridical) environment is carefully traced, analysed, and illustrated by Olga Weijers, *In Search of the Truth. A History of Disputation Techniques from Antiquity to Early Modern Times* (Turnhout: Brepols, 2013), especially pp. 88-94 ("the juridical disputation"), pp. 119-176 (disputation in medieval universities in general and with examples), especially pp. 164-168 (disputation in law).

56. 1 Kings 8:5.

57. This reference is a bit obscure; chapter 2 in Daniel deals only tangentially with what Paweł is referring two; chapter 7 is more directly devoted to listing the various kingdoms.

58. Ps 71:2 (Vulgate numeration).

59. A reference to Dante Alighieri's treatise *De Monarchia* (1312/1313), in which the poet treats the relationship between secular and religious authority, arguing the former is not subject or inferior to the latter.

60. *Tenebant nichilominus nonnulli contrarium predictis...*

61. Giovanni da Legnano (*ca*.. 1320-1383), doctor of both laws at Bologna who also taught there. In his writings—as well as in his experience as a diplomat—he demonstrated considerable expertise on both the study of war and peace and practical matters. See Brundage, *Canon Law*, p. 118.

62. Gen. 2:16.

63. Gen. 3:16.

64. No clear reference to Gen 4; the second reference is probably to Gen 6:14 and 17.

65. Perhaps Gen 9:15.

66. Gen. 8:20.

67. Ps. 71:2 (Vulgate numeration).

68. Isa. 33:22.

69. John 21:16.

70. John 18:11.

71. 1 Tim. 3:3.

72. Gen. 14:18.

73. Heb. 7:1-2.

74. Ex. 28:41-43.

75. 1 Kings 8:22.

76. 1 Cor. 6:3.

77. John 10:16.

78. *Videndum restat...*

79. Domenicus de Sancto Geminiano, *ca*. 1375-1424, born in Florence, studied at Bologna, where he was a student of Antonius de Butrio and perhaps of Petrus de Ancarano, and where he later taught. Eventually he was an official in papal law

courts and was best known for his commentary on the *Liber Sextus*, among other works. See Johann Friedrich von Schulte, *Geschichte der Quellen und Literature des canonischen Rechts*, 3 vols. (Stuttgart: Enke, 1875-1889, repr. Graz: Akademische Druck- und Verlagsanstalt, 1956), II, 294-296. See also Ożóg, *Uczeni w Monarchii Jadwigi Andegaweńskiej i Władysława Jagiełły*, pp. 228-229 for a brief analysis of Domenicus' opinions being used by Paweł.

80. Deut. 11:24.

81. Gen. 13:9-11.

82. Matt. 5:45 and 6:26.

83. Ps. 135:25 (Vulgate numeration).

84. Ex. 20:13 and 15.

85. Actually Matt. 7:12. The textual reference is incorrect (or incorrectly copied into the MS).

86. Rom. 13:10.

87. 1 Cor. 13:4.

88. John 10:16.

89. John 21:15.

90. *Xρι [Christi] auxilio visis supradictis. . .*

91. *Ymmo Lodvicius Imperator quartus. . .*

92. The "judge" the Order opposed was Antoni Zeno of Milan whom Martin was planning to send as a legate with a fact-finding mission to Poland and Lithuania. See Ożóg, *Uczeni w Monarchii Jadwigi Andegaweńskiej i Władysława Jagiełły*, p. 241. A fuller picture of Zeno's mission is provided by Krzysztof Baczowski, "La misione del nunzio Antonio Zeno in Polonia negli anni 1422-1423," *Prace Historyczne* 96 (1987): 15-27.

93. *Zelum ad incrementum predictorum fratrum dicit se habere Karolus Imperator quartus. . .*

LETTER TO THE BISHOP OF KRAKÓW

(*Ad Episcopum Cracoviensem*, 1432)[1]

To my most Reverend Father in Christ, Zbigniew, by grace of God Bishop of Kraków, Paweł Włodkowic, canon of the same church, the least among all doctors of the decretals, moved by his own free will, recommends himself to your fatherly care, declaring himself to be ever ready to serve you in all things.[2]

Alas, my heart sighs in deep sorrow, wounded at the desolation of my fatherland — namely the two principalities of Dobrzyń and Kujawy, especially the destruction wrought in the diocese of and to the Church in Włocławek.[3] And that the peaceful Kingdom of Poland, lulled into a false sense of security, should be submitted by divine allowance to so horrible a plague! And so much greater is the sorrow that agitates and torments my mind — and I firmly believe that the woe is not confined to me alone, but that many others, indeed the entire generality of the Kingdom, will share in it — to behold so large a number of my lords, so desirous of peace, to be made to proceed on paths so hard and difficult. And that there hardly remains any man to point out to them the right path, and to recall them from error.

For, alas, I watch as they enter upon paths oblique and extreme, now going off to war, now to affirm truces, hurrying now this way and now that, now with a war concluded, flocking together to concord, and now on the contrary, with concord dashed, entering upon war once more, and again turning back and so walking with impious men in a circle, it seems, a circle without end. For they desert the middle road, which is as if a highway leading straight and securely to peace. The roads they travel, alas, as described above, are full of danger; furthermore, they are not the roads of salvation, but those of error.[4]

But alas, what can I say, or what can I do? If those who are placed at high lookouts to watch over and care for the flocks of the Lord cannot see rightly, nor call back those who are erring in this fashion; if they will not exercise the office proper to them, what can I do, as insignificant as I am, who stand far below, occupying the very lowest place on the ground? Who will believe me should I assert that I see more perspicaciously than those who are set in the heights? No one will hear me were I to call out until my throat went raw, my voice hoarse. Should I obtrude onto someone else's office uninvited, I would be reproved for my presumption.

But so that it should not seem that I approve of such errors by remaining silent, erring also along with those who err; lest something worse should befall both flocks and shepherds on account of my holding my tongue, that which my stammering lips are unable to declare, I shall at least indicate here with my pen, with my Lord's permission.

Let therefore the darkness of man's wisdom cede place before the divine, and let the night of human industry and skill not intrude where the sun of the highest knowledge shines. Let all human ingenuity be silent when supercelestial words are spoken. For as the eternal Word of God the Father, Who mercifully became incarnate on our behalf, said: 'Without me you can do nothing,'[5] and elsewhere: 'I am the way, and the truth, and the life,'[6] indeed, the way by which it behooves us to proceed toward true peace, beside which there is no other, is He. For He truly is the truth of light eternal and of supreme peace, without which every other thing is darkness. Nor is any other peace true peace without Him, since without Him nothing at all came to be.[7] And further, He is life, without which there is no salvation, etc. Can you therefore, Reverend Father, imagine it possible to arrive at true peace along with those who go on their way without any path, knowing not where they are headed? Or that anyone might safely walk in the absence of light? Will such a one not knock his foot against a stone, as the Scripture says: 'How might he be trusted to have true peace with others, who is impatient with his own self?'[8] On account of impatience, is not the true peace, Christ, excluded and negated? And how can one in discord with oneself enter into concord with others? He who is evil toward himself, can he be good toward others? It is not to be believed that he should obtain peace, who walks neither in the peace of Christ nor in the truth of God.

Now, if the objection is raised that all the evils that war is wont to produce are taken away, indeed totally doused by concord, why then do you condemn the path of concord?[9] — I would respond that this sort of concord is not the end of evils, but rather their augmentation. Truly, it is the beginning, the means as well as the effect of all evil: past, present, and future. I say the beginning, in respect to evils to come as a result of the existence of such feigned concord, being a lying simulacra of true concord, — and such, alas, has been made clear many times by what has resulted therefrom. For all the while that equity and concord of this sort reigns, it serves but to cloak an unjust occupation and an alien domination, tyrannical inequity and depravity, which is contrary to justice for the Poles, and this, although seemingly as clear as day given the verdicts of the Apostolic See, legitimate and of old standing, still it is so obfuscated by agreements of such sort that truth itself suffers on this account.[10] And so it happens that such 'equity' is but a double portion of iniquity served by those who use it to deceive. Now, such concord[11] is also the means to the accumulation of evils. Because by such agreements, which are mere empty words and nothing real, they continue to practice their iniquity, which they preserve and confirm all the more strongly.

Furthermore, in order to show His faithful what they were to follow and what to flee, Our Lord Jesus Christ, in indicating to us the paths of salvation and peace that we are to follow, also showed us the path we are to avoid, saying: 'Beware of false prophets, who come to you in the clothing of sheep, but inwardly they are ravening wolves. By their fruits you shall know them. [...] A good tree cannot bring forth evil fruit, neither can an evil tree bring forth good fruit,' etc.,[12] manifestly giving us to understand that commerce with heretics and hypocrites is to be avoided, for the former are devoted to pestilent doctrine, and the latter infect true religion with the venom of false piety. These battle against the faith of Christ, while those foam at the mouth against the Church of Christ. The heretics strive to destroy the foundations while the hypocrites demolish the edifice of God, which was raised on a firm rock. The first deny the truth, while the second overturn love, which binds the members of the body to their Head. And for this reason, according to the holy doctors Chrysostom, Gregory, Augustine, and others, it is to these two sorts of perverse men that the Lord refers as false prophets, and it is of these that we must beware. And however much love is known to be the greatest of all virtues, the cruelty of the hypocrites, opposed to the same, is the worst of all crimes or sins. Now, since the order of the Knights of the Cross of Prussia appear in sheep's clothing, the while they display their true nature as rapacious wolves, consequently, by the very testimony of Holy Scripture, it is they whom Christ commands us to avoid as deceitful men and false prophets. By this we conclude, on the authority of the very words of the Lord, that this group of men is that pestiferous, purely hypocritical tribe, and that evil tree that is not capable of producing good fruit. That they are a cruel sect, hostile to the Church of Christ and the Christian religion, is clearly proven by their actions. And consequently, they ought to be sentenced, by the Church of God, to destruction.[13]

However, because this error of hypocrisy seems to be the part of many great men, so that no one should accuse me of insulting them, it is quite proper for me to state that I am the enemy of no person, but only of iniquity and perversity, and so I wish to remain my whole life long, so help me God; and so that the truth of what I have already written should be all the more clear, I shall introduce three proofs, each of which would be sufficient in and of itself to induce faith in what I say. For as the evangelical truth puts it, in the mouth of two or three witnesses every word shall stand.[14]

Now all things doubtful in the way of justice ought to be resolved in one of three probative manners: either the facts are self-evident and need no further proof, because the evidence of the crime committed is such that it needs no cry of prosecutor, or on the basis of the guilty party's own confession before a judge, and so no need is seen for any further proof, or the truth is discerned from evidence, for instance: legitimate witnesses or public documents. Any any of these proofs is sufficient for the charges to be acknowledged as irrefutable.

To speak of the first manner of proof, let Poland, Prussia, Livonia and the other regions in the area and those neighboring it declare how the deeds of the above-mentioned Knights of the Cross are plainly contrary to law divine. But first we should speak of what has recently taken place in the Kingdom of Poland, that is to say in the year of Our Lord 1431:[15] how while his most illustrious majesty, Władysław, King of Poland, was operating far beyond the borders of said Kingdom along with his army, with sacrilegious hand these wicked men did suddenly, and without any warning being given to said King, rupturing all peace accords and violating solemn treaties such as even among barbarian nations are entered into and honored according to the natural law common to all nations, were seen to cast behind them concords recently made, replacing them with the habitual discord which is their use, invading with hostile force the most Christian Kingdom of Poland, devastating the same with the most atrocious cruelty and excessive atrocities in a manner worse than might be expected of pagans, sparing no one, having regard neither to sex nor age. Many notable churches in this Kingdom, such as the metropolitan see of Gniezno, as well as those of Włocławek and Płock, abounding in large possessions, the clergy there in possession of diocesan sees of great extent and breadth, suffered great damage and loss — not only in material possessions, but also as far as the Service of God is concerned. For not only were ecclesiastical benefices destroyed, but the diocesan churches themselves, along with Sacraments, the relics of the saints, books, chalices, and other things pertaining to the divine cultus were combusted and went up in smoke. To state the matter briefly, two renowned principalities belonging to said Kingdom, that is, Dobrzyń and Kujawy, along with their churches and ecclesiastical goods, were almost entirely consumed by the voracious flames and destroyed. See then the profane religion of the iniquitous, the sacrilegious sanctity of arsonists, of wolves covered in the sheep's clothing of devotion — the religious hypocrisy of the Knights of the Cross in the guise of Christianity! Such are the fruits brought forth habitually by that order of wretched men. Such is the diabolical piety concealed beneath the white cloak they wear, that sham, which covers a blackness devilish and cruel — such are those who call themselves the brothers of the Blessed Virgin Mary, yet persecute the glory and honor of the Mother of God, whose magnificent and mighty church in Włocławek they not only gravely damaged, that sumptuous and noble edifice, but the city of Włocławek itself, as well as the diocese thereof, which they nearly completely destroyed and pulverized. And what shall I say concerning the church in Płock, the cathedral of which diocese is likewise dedicated in honor of that same glorious Virgin Mother, and which, along with the churches and ecclesiastical holdings in the diocese, was half reduced to ash? I shall pass over the fate of the metropolitan cathedral of the Virgin Mary in Riga, Livonia, which the same iniquitous author of darkness and father of lies, lurking beneath the black cross they wear, having occupied the things belonging to the churches there, and having expelled the truly pious order of the Canons Regular of St Augustine, occupied that church and installed with hypocrisy the brothers of their own order therein, sacrilegiously desecrating the same. The abundance of material evidence, which could hardly be contained in a voluminous tome, bids me remain silent also concerning their depredations committed against the Lithuanian neophytes. For that same hypocritical demon crucified Christ anew in these neophytes at the hands of his above-mentioned brothers, invading the Lithuanian duchy over the space of many years, and putting to flame their newly-constructed churches, oppressing them severely with the most grievous cruelties. In such a way he wished to extinguish their Christian faith, as the effect of their deeds bears out. At this time, I shall refrain from listing any more of the notorious deeds of this brotherhood.

I now arrive at the second type of proofs, concerning which it behoves me first to mention a notorious truth of which even your Grace is not ignorant, O my Father: how just following the general council held at Constance, his Most Serene Majesty Władysław, King of Poland, being in discord with these same Brethren, the Knights of the Cross, concerning the regions which belong to him, both parties presented their case to the Pope of the Roman Catholic Church through their envoy advocates and legitimately constituted procurators, as before a judge not to be questioned. A time was set them both, before which they were to produce whatever they wished on behalf of their suit, and this indeed they did, producing that which follows:[16]

First, on the part of the aforementioned King, solemn and public documents were produced containing the verdict of the delegates of the Apostolic See, pronounced not long before in favor of the King and Kingdom of Poland and against the aforesaid brothers concerning the lands and possessions of Pomerania, Chełmno and Michałów, as well as the great sums of money owed them in reparations for the damages the Brethren inflicted there.[17]

However, because this same verdict, along with its public document, was many times contested before the Roman Pontiff or his deputy, though it was never invalidated, but indeed confirmed on three separate occasions, as by public documents has been thrice clearly declared: as, therefore, the above-mentioned brother knights agreed to take the matter to trial, and then took the position of objecting to the verdict, by this very fact they can be seen to have agreed to all that arises from said judgment. If not for the impediments arising from the ill-considered and unfortunate agreement,[18] there would have remained nothing more to do with this judgment, than to declare in writing that the verdict handed down by the delegates of the Apostolic See was to be executed. I put it to you now, Father: do you not see what great evil the agreement at hand has done to the King and this Kingdom?

But God, to Whom all times are subject, Who reigns and orders all things, however much He permitted the final victory in this matter to be delayed by allowing this faulty concord to be compacted, with the turning of the times He finally demonstrates that the victory of justice is to follow, at a time more convenable to the suit, by bringing this morbid concord to an end. For just as the cruelties of said Brethren were the impulse for that concord that impeded justice to be done, and by His permission, so now, vice versa, by the will of God the same has become the cause of discord such as shall lead to justice. For He alone knows how to utilize the depraved wills of evil men to work the good.

Second, on the part of the aforementioned Brethren, articles and privileges, many and divers, were produced, among which some were seen at first glance to contain heresies, such as it being permissible to Christians to invade pagan regions with the intent of occupying said dominions, although such is directly contrary to the commandments of the Lord: 'Thou shalt not steal,' 'Thou shalt not kill,'[19] etc., and moreover no one of sound mind doubts but that pagan peoples also possess proper dominions of their own, which are recognized as properly belonging to them by natural law. Among these privileges, produced in order to justify their occupation of lands and dominions formerly belonging to the north-westerly located Lithuanians near Žematija, also known as Żmudź or Samogitia, and which constitute a bone of contention between the parties, are also found such as were granted by Emperor Frederick II — the same who, on account of his heresy and other crimes, was stripped of his empire and all honors due him by Pope Innocent IV during the General Council of Lyons. This sentence of deprivation is to be found in the decretal *Ad Apostolicam*: on Judgements and Legal Pronouncements, Book II. Accordingly, this Frederick, who by these privileges granted said pagan territories, that is, Prussia, Lithuanian Samogitia, as well as Livonia, Latvia, and Russia, and in general, all other lands and dominions of pagans such as the banners of these Brethren might reach, or which might be brought into subjection with the aid of Christian armies, was granting things that were not in his gift, as they did not belong to him, nor ever did they.[20]

Now, since they adduced these privileges, so manifestly erroneous, on their part in the arbitration, as being to their advantage, it logically follows from this that all they contain is likewise acknowledged: First, that they are at fault, and that on account of their error and hypocrisies, committed in the territories belonging to the aforementioned pagans, their criminal sect is deserving of condemnation as the most cruel heresy — as worthy sons of so infamous a father. Second, that all wars waged by them from the time of the granting of said privileges were in consequence illicit, erroneous and unjust. Alas! How many good Christians, from divers parts of the world, were deceived by their call to enlist in the war against these pagans! How many good Christian souls have been deceived, and for so long, by this pestiferous sect, sent to the slaughter on account of this delusion! Oh, the sorrow of it all! What man is capable of narrating it fully? Third, since they never had any right to do what they did on the might of these invalid privileges, in the lands of Russia, Lithuanian Samogitia, Livonia and all other territories however pagan, it follows that they could neither hold on to these same lands nor occupy them, without grave danger to their souls, and that these sins of theirs can never be forgiven unless they first restore all that they have stolen. And all of the above they acknowledge by their acknowledgement of these privileges, even if they do not expressly admit the same.

Having now taken account of two manners of proof, which no objection from the opposing party can overthrow, there remains still a third sort to be briefly adduced — since a string triply bound is more difficult to burst — so that, this error destroyed in the name of the Holy Trinity, human souls might be saved. For even if all the above-stated were suddenly to fall away (which nevertheless is impossible), I shall introduce three sets of witnesses and three authentic and public documents beyond those, by which witnesses and documents it can be clearly proven that this sect is no Christian religious order whatsoever, but rather the contradiction of all law and Christian religion — in short, a hypocritical and erroneous band.

Firstly, I shall introduce twenty-three witnesses,[21] all above any sort of reproach, who although they are no longer alive in this world, live on in their testimony, which is still clear in the memory of men, as well as in one unassailable public document drawn up by the authority of a legitimate judge. By this testimony, sufficient evidence is given of the immense and inhuman cruelties committed by these Brethren against the Poles when, in one way or another, they occupied Polish lands and dominions, that is to say, Chełmno and Michałów, after which they occupied the dominions of the Pomeranian lands, cruelly, by brute force, having driven thence the relatives of the King who was ruling Poland at the time, princes of royal blood, along with other governors and officials of the aforementioned King. And these principalities and dominions they continue to hold and occupy from that time until this present day, with grave harm and prejudice to the King and Kingdom of Poland, as well as to the grave peril of their own souls. Thus it is clear to see that this sect is worthy of condemnation as persons continually persevering in sin.

Secondly, I shall introduce other witnesses from another time, who will testify to the fact that in the year of our Lord 1408[22] these same Brethren did hostilely invade the Kingdom of Poland, perpetrating great evils everywhere, until by the just verdict of God, alas! the swords of the Poles so devoured them that, as it is said, not a single one of them remained following the battle save for a small number of their mercenaries. At last, His most Serene Majesty Sigismund, King of the Romans, desiring to lead both parties onto the path of justice, placed himself between them. With the consent of both parties he appointed a commissioner to visit both sides and examine first-hand the damages incurred by both, receiving and examining witnesses such as were put forward for the purpose, as well as any other rights and claims such as these parties wished to maintain.[23] And indeed this commissioner examined what was to be examined and received many testimonies both on behalf of the King of Poland as well as that of the ecclesial establishment, and many other persons belonging to the Kingdom of Poland as were covered by his commission. Then, on the part of the adversarial party, the aforementioned Brethren, no witness seems to have come forward, nothing being adduced in support of their side save those few aforementioned erroneous privileges. And so these witnesses and their testimonies did not only prove the great and divers harms inflicted upon the King, the churches, and other persons subject to that Realm, but also the most horrible and criminal deeds of the aforementioned Brethren, which are many indeed. No one of sane mind doubts that those acts were deeds of darkness contrary to all religion. Who, therefore, would dare assert that these men constitute a Christian religious order, unless he be a brash contradictor of truth supreme? For Christ Himself, that Truth supreme, declares them to be false prophets when He tells us that by their fruits we shall know them![24] All of these things are also clearly witnessed by authentic documents, namely, by that one special book in which all this is even more clearly contained, brought together by that above-mentioned commissioner, sealed with seals and notarized signatures, as a public document consigned to our trust and belief as testimony to future ages.[25]

Thirdly, I shall introduce other testimonies of those bearing witness at another time to the above-mentioned truth, received and examined legitimately concerning other damages and crimes committed later by the aforementioned Brethren, which a commissioner sent especially for this purpose by the Apostolic See, recently, following the conclusion of the Council of Constance, likewise compiled into a similar book collected of all these things, authentic, that is to say, sealed according to all proper and authentic procedure.[26] And these things done by him, it is said, were confirmed by the Roman Pontiff himself in his apostolic letters. I shall hold my tongue concerning other damages and criminal, detestable deeds that this Order perpetrated later, which, it seems, have not been recorded with such authority. Yet these damages are so great and so many, it is believed, that the Brethren in question would not be able to do complete satisfaction to the Polish Kingdom and Polish nation for them even were they to sell all of the goods they possess in Germany, Italy, and all other places.

Would it be possible for any partisan of this heresy or hypocrisy to excuse these Brethren, under any colour or pretext, without being made to concede that their perverse state is no religious order at all, but rather hypocrisy and error, or without be compelled to assert that Christ is not God at all, no truth-speaker He, when He states truly that a good tree cannot bear bad fruit, nor vice versa?'[27] But that second, so horrible heresy simply cannot be supported in the least. Therefore, there is no doubt as to the truth of the first statement, since, as logicians teach us, such an argument from opposite alternatives necessarily arrives at this: that the denial of one inexorably demands the acceptance of the other.

From all that has been said, we necessarily conclude that there can be no concord between Poles, Lithuanians, and other Christians and the aforementioned Knights of the Cross, who act with such prejudice toward the entire Church militant as well as the Christian religion and faith. For as the Apostle says: 'What concord hath Christ with Belial? Or what part hath the faithful with the unbeliever?'[28]

The second conclusion arrived at is that so notoriously pestiferous as sect as this is not to be tolerated by the Church, but rather thoroughly to be destroyed, according to the words of the Lord: 'Every plant which my heavenly Father hath not planted shall be rooted up,'[29] and elsewhere: 'Every tree that bringeth not forth good fruit, shall be cut down,' etc.[30] And since it is said that the aforementioned Frederick was a great persecutor of the Church, and these Brethren are seen to be his followers in this art, as he is the one who constituted this profane order in these regions, thus, as the original perpetrator is damned, so it follows that his inheritor collaborators shall also be damned.

So far we have spoken of the path of agreement.[31] There remains to be shown, briefly, how the path of war is evil as well as insecure. And so it behoves us to introduce the five conditions wherewith war can be justified, in the absence of just one of which a war is declared unjust.[32] First, persons who are either clergy or hold any other sort of ecclesial office may not spill blood. Second, the reason for engaging in a conflict must be to regain things stolen, or the defense of one's land, meeting force by force. The third is that the cause of war must be necessary, and not arising from one's spontaneous will. The fourth is that the war must not be associated with a thirst for revenge. Fifth, the war must be made only on the authority of legitimate superiors. Thus, it is seen as not being sufficient merely to complain to the Pope of injuries suffered, unless one appeals to him for justice. And should the Pope fail to provide said justice, he tacitly assents to the war and makes of himself the perpetrator of the murders and other evils that are brought about by it. For then the prince or the person waging war is excused on the grounds of necessity, but the Pope who permits such things *eo ipso* must stand before God under the grave accusation of being said to have permitted said war and committed such evils. Since such are the requirements for declaring a war just, it is plain to see that the path of war is a difficult and insecure one. For by no law is war ever permitted to be declared on one's own authority unless it be in armed defense of one's own land, and within the limits of innocent restraint. Therefore, etc.

And from this it is concluded that the aforementioned Knights of the Cross have never waged a just war, but, rather, their warring has always been unjust, taking all of the foregoing into consideration.

First, because they are twice over incapable of dominion, since on account of their professed vows they seem to have renounced all such dominion, both personal and that held in common, because that same reason applies to the whole as it does to its constituent parts, and he who swears that something is not his own, personally, swears as well to it not being his as property held in common with others.[33] Nor can they be said to possess dominion anywhere on the basis of their monasteries or colleges being erected therein, as all of their colleges or congregations are illicit twice over: being erroneous themselves, and, as it has been stated, said holdings having been conquered or occupied tyrannically and unjustly. For this reason, they have not been canonically constituted and by consequence these colleges of theirs, of this sort, or any of their other locales, are unable of possessing any sort of dominium — as they aver, that is, the Brethren possessing, as it were, dominium held in common, purportedly on the basis of these colleges and other locales. Now, in order for colleges or other such places to be considered canonically instituted, first of all, the authority of him who institutes them must be valid. The mere boldness of those who occupy them is no substitute for that! It is furthermore required that the territory of said institution be held properly, by law, and not acquired tyrannically; that it be canonically endowed or acquired lawfully, not occupied tyrannically; it is also required that he who institutes be not the same has he who is instituted; that the possessor and the possessed be not one and the same; that the endower and the endowed be separate entities. Such is not the case of the college of these Brethren.

Secondly, the wars they wage are unjust by reason of their object. For they are not initiated for the recuperation of stolen property nor for the defense of the faithful or their homeland, but rather for the acquisition of territory and the subjugation of infidels, as the above-mentioned privileges confess. From this it is manifestly clear that all of their 'dominiums' which they have usurped from the pagans, viz. in Prussia, Livonia, Lithuanian Samogitia, etc., are tyrannical and unjust. By the same token it is clear that all of their colleges in these dominiums have not been lawfully endowed nor canonically instituted, but are fictive, established merely by the boldness of the Brethren themselves.

Third, they are unjust by reason of their cause. It cannot be said that such wars have been forced upon them by necessity, but rather, they are undertaken merely from their own desire of obtaining the dominions of others and their lust for domination.

I shall pass over the fourth aspect of war, that is, wars conducted in the spirit of revenge. Fifth, all of their wars have been unjust by reason of authority. For they do not wage nor have they ever waged war — against Christians as well as pagans — by any legitimate authority, but rather as animated by their own audacity. For that Emperor was the greatest of heretics, for which reason he was stripped of both his empire and all honors, and thus could not give to others that, which he himself had not in the first place. Now, whether all infidels are by law subject to the Roman Empire, or whether this holds true for all Christians — this I shall not pronounce upon, but rather leave to the vain disputes of those who wish to engage in them. To me, these questions appear as the obscure waters in the clouds of the air. What I hold to, with certainty, is that the Roman Pontiff, as the Vicar of Christ, is the indubitable judge of all the foregoing, and it belongs to him to declare war on the infidels who do not recognize the Roman Church, whenever a reasonable cause for such action arises.

And now, something must be said of the middle road[34] — the short and secure one — which is to say the road of justice. In so far as the present matter is concerned, there appear to be two manners of effectively pursuing justice. That is, by evangelical denunciation,[35] such as is the duty of the bishop, in accord with the Lord's command and as all the writings of the theologians and canonists attest; which denunciation is made so as to turn sinners to penitence. If the case is such that this penitence cannot be effected absent the restitution of goods wrongfully acquired, the other party indirectly receives what is due him, nor is any other monition required, the sin being a public one — especially when it is a question of a large number — and this is the way of charity.

The second manner is that of justice, i.e. judicial denunciation, which is twofold — public and private. It is fittingly public *ex officio*, and arrives in the wake of an official denunciation with no monition required, in notorious cases such as that before us now. It is fittingly private in that he who was harmed receives justice on account of injury done to his private interests. The effects of this are: the correction of sin, the restoration of the thing in contest, and the indemnification of the wronged person. Now, because these manners of pursuing justice and correcting sin seem so easily effected, alas! how great has been the negligence of the prelates, due to which wolves have been tolerated for so long amidst the sheepfolds of Christ, and the aforementioned Brethren have been allowed to persevere for so long in their errors! The danger arising from this state of things cuts two ways, as charity itself commands that those erring souls be aided to their correction, and justice demands of the evangelical pastors to watch over the flocks of the Lord and defend them, as the Lord Himself says:[36] 'The good shepherd giveth his life for his sheep. But the hireling, and he that is not the true shepherd, seeth the wolf coming and leaveth the sheep, because he is a hireling.' Indeed, the Lord castigates such negligent pastors through the mouth of the prophet Isaiah, saying: 'Dumb dogs are not able to bark,' etc.[37] And through Ezekiel he says: 'You have not gone up to face the enemy, nor have you set up a wall for the house of Israel, to stand in battle in the day of the Lord.'[38] Now, according to St Gregory, to go up to face the enemy means to speak out freely in defense of the flocks of the Lord against the powers of this world. And when they stand in defense of the flocks of the Lord they are said to expose themselves to the enemies as a wall to the house of Israel, etc.

And thus, to whatever extent this error infecting parts of Poland and other neighboring lands can be said to have arisen from the neglect of the prelates or bishops, thus, conversely, is it necessary for them to eradicate it by their solicitude and diligence — for whatever things arise from a certain cause, the same are dissolved by the contrary actions of the same agents. And when any sickness is seen to be deeply rooted, so must the care to eradicate it be redoubled, and all the more remedies applied to this purpose. Now, because the fires of such great concupiscence have descended upon these above-mentioned Brethren, blinding them so that they have not, nor can they yet behold the sun of justice,[39] we ourselves must beg mercy of God that they may come to recognize the errors of their ways. For such a demon as possesses them cannot be exorcized but through fasting and prayer. And so we should also be pained more on behalf of those who do such evil than of those who suffer the evil done to them. For the former act on behalf of evil, being proficient therein, while the latter are corrected thereby, according to Isidore (*On the Supreme Good*, Book III, Chapter 41).

Finally, let it be declared unto the Church, the head of which is the vicar of Christ, that it neither can nor should bear such oppressions and errors as we have described above, as the Lord says through Jeremiah: 'Lo, I have set thee this day over the nations, and over the kingdoms, to root up, and pull down, and to waste, and to destroy, and to build, and to plant.'[40] And a strict accounting must be rendered to the Lord concerning such things.

May you turn a lenient eye, Father, upon the prolixity of this letter, which the mind dictating intended to be brief. Yet the matter itself demanded a more prolix pen.

Given at Padua in the year of our Lord 1432, in the month of March, written by the aforementioned Paweł, by his own hand.

[*On the reverse*]: To be presented to the Reverend in Christ Lord Zbigniew, Bishop of Kraków.

(Endnotes)

1. The date is more precisely March 1432 and is determined from the explicit given by Paweł at the end of his text, noting that the letter is written in his own hand. For a facsimile of his signature, see the illustration (fig. 12) by Belch, *Paulus Vladimiri*, II, between 1102 and 1103.

2. Zbigniew Cardinal Oleśnicki (1389-1455) was one of the most important individuals of fifteenth century Poland. He fought at Grunwald in 1410 (apparently saving the life of King Władysław Jagiełło), rose through the royal chancery until his appointment as Bishop of Kraków in 1423, was the leader of the nobility from Lesser Poland (*Polonia minora*), and after Jagiełło's death in 1434 was effectively the dominant political figure in the kingdom. For an overview of his biography, see the

entry (by Maria Koczerska) in *Polski Słownik Biograficzny*, 23 (1978) 776-784; for his role as bishop, see Koczerska, *Zbigniew Oleśnicki i kościół krakowski w czasach jego pontyfikatu (1423-1455)* (Warsaw: DiG, 2004); and for an appreciation of the range of his accomplishments and influence, see the contributions in Feliks Kiryk and Zdisław Noga, eds., *Zbigniew Oleśnicki Książę Kościoła i Mąż Stanu* (Kraków: Secesja, 2006).

3. The tone expressed here by Paweł marks this letter as intensely personal. The region to which he refers was where he grew up, and the destruction to which he refers struck home in a very direct way. (For more on the destruction, see the details he presents in his text following n. 15 below.) Thomas Wünsch, *Konziliarismus und Polen. Personen, Politik und Programme aus Polen zur Verfassungsfrage der Kirche in der Zeit der mittelalterlichen Reformkonzilien* (Paderborn, Munich, Vienna and Zürich: Schöningh, 1998), p. 57, correctly assessed this letter as Paweł's "spiritual testament" ("sein geistiges Testament").

4. The "roads" (the *viae*) of which Paweł speaks form the framework of his advice to Bishop Oleśnicki: they are the road of agreement, that of war, and that of adjudication.

5. John 15:5.

6. John 14:6.

7. John 1:3.

8. Ps. 90:12 (Vulgate numeration).

9. The Latin Paweł uses here is *concordia*, which has the meaning given it in the translation but also can be understood in the sense of an agreement, often in the context of a political agreement or treaty. See the comments of Ehrlich, *Pisma wybrane*, III, 227, n. 4.

10. Papal judgments in 1321 and 1339 had ruled the Order to be in the wrong and Poland to be in the right. See Paul Milliman, *"The Slippery Memory of Men." The Place of Pomerania in the Medieval Kingdom of Poland* (Leiden and Boston: Brill, 2013), pp. 119-124, 135-137.

11. Despite continuing Polish insistence after the Council of Constance on the validity of the fourteenth century papal judgments, the treaty that Paweł is referring to here, the Treaty of Melno of 27 September 1422, changed this somewhat. This treaty ended a two month conflict between Poland-Lithuania and the Order. See the analysis by Sven Ekdahl, "Der Krieg zwischen dem Deutschen Orden und Polen-Litauen im Jahre 1422," *Zeitschrift für Ostforschung* 13 (1964): 614-651. One important part of the treaty included a clause in which the Order ceded the territory of Samogitia to Lithuania, creating a Prussian-Lithuanian border that remained stable for five centuries. Another aspect of the treaty included a clause in which, as apologists put it, for the sake of peace, Jagiełło had consented to annul the papal adjudication of 1339.

12. Matt. 7:15-20.

13. Paweł is here consistent in his long-standing demand that the Order must be destroyed. The question is how?

14. Matt. 18:16.

15. While engaged in Lithuania with matters relating to the succession to Vytautas following his death in 1430, Jagiełło found himself in conflict with his own younger brother, Švitrigaila, whom he aimed to name as the new Grand Duke, though with diminished territorial control. Švitrigaila, however, had different ambitions and allied with the Teutonic Order. Their invasion of northern Poland in 1431 aimed to support Švitrigaila, but broke the 1422 Treaty of Melno. Jan Długosz gives a somewhat one-sided picture of the resulting conflict; see *Annales*, IX, 39-40 (*Liber undecimus* [*continuatio*], *sub anno 1431*). A more balanced account is provided by Marian Biskup, "Najazd krzyżacki na Polskę i bitwa pod Dąbkami 1431 r.," *Zeszyty Naukowe WAP* 48 (1967): pp. 15-28 [*Studia historyczne Stanisławowi Herbstowi na sześćdziesięciolecie urodzin*].

16. Paweł is referring here to a series of hearings and testimonies given to Pope Martin V or his representatives between 1420 and 1423. At issue were the territories gained by the Order in the early fourteenth century that were the subject of the papal tribunals of 1321 and 1339 (see above, n. 10). These Polish claims were presented in a number of venues, in every instance contested by the Order. For an overview of these processes, including Paweł's involvement as Polish procurator in the 1420 court of arbitration in Wrocław (Breslau) and afterward in Rome, see the treatment by Belch, *Paulus Vladimiri*, I, 137-143 and II, 1064-1089. The documents and testimony presented were edited by Tytus Działyński in the first edition (1855-1856) of *Lites*, I, part ii, and II. Their inadequacies from a technical aspect were immediately recognized, but the second edition of *Lites* focused upon the papal tribunals of 1320-1321 and 1339 (1890) and 1412 (1892), edited by Ignacy Kraszewski, and the hearings of 1414 (1935), edited by Jadwiga Karwasińska, with a revised version of the earlier fourteenth century tribunal by Helena Chłopocka (1970). The hearings of 1422-1423 remained unrevised until recently. Now an exemplary edition of them has been published: Sławomir Jóźwiak, Adam Szweda, and Sobiesław Szybkowski, eds., *Lites ac Res Gestae inter Polonos Ordinemque Cruciferorum. Spory i Sprawy pomiędzy Polakami a Zakonem Krzyżackim*: *Akta postępowania przed wysłannikiem papieskim Antonim Zeno z Mediolanu w latach 1422-1423* (Toruń: Wydawnictwo Naukowe Uniwersytetu Mikołaja Kopernika, 2015); see especially the editors' introduction, pp. 13-43. As scholars have the opportunity to analyze more carefully these materials and incorporate them into their own publications, our overall picture and understanding of these sources will surely be influence and modified in certain ways from what has been previously published.

17. This is probably a reference to the 1339 papal tribunal.

18. The Treaty of Melno.

19. Ex. 20:13 and 15.

20. See Paweł's *Articuli*, number 2.

21. This refers to the twenty-three witnesses called to testify on behalf of Polish charges at the 1339 tribunal.

22. Whether Paweł's date is incorrect or this is a scribal error, the date should be 1409, i.e., the beginning of the war that included the Battle of Grunwald in 1410.

23. See above, Paweł's *Articuli*, n. 10.

24. Matt. 7:16.

25. The testimony taken by Benedict of Macra, *Lites*. II, 82, 88-337.

26. Jóźwiak, Szweda, and Szybkowski, eds., *Lites ac Res Gestae. Akta... Antonim Zeno z Mediolanu*, pp. 236-584, for the individual testimonies of witnesses taken by Zeno. Zeno's mission to Prussia and Poland is treated by Krzysztof Ożóg, *Uczeni w Monarchii Jadwigi Andegaweńskiej i Władysława Jagiełły (1384-1434)* (Kraków: Polska Akademia Umiejętności, 2004), pp. 241-249.

27. Matt. 7:18.

28. 2 Cor. 6:15-16.

29. Matt. 15:13.

30. Matt. 7:19.

31. The first *via*, that of concord or agreement, has thus in Paweł's argument to Oleśnicki been shown to be the wrong way to proceed as a response to the Order's invasion of 1431.

32. Paweł here quickly summarizes the five-fold rationale of a just war developed by Ramón de Penyafort, the early thirteenth century canonist (see Brundage, *Canon Law*, pp. 222-223). The classic treatment in English of medieval just war theory remains Frederick H. Russell, *The Just War in the Middle Ages* (Cambridge: Cambridge University Press, 1975).

33. This argument was also made in greater detail by Paweł in his treatise *Ad Aperiendam* (not included in this collection); for the text, see Ehrlich, *Pisma wybrane*, I, 144-259 and II, 2-167; here I, 250. His further points in this letter are also brief summaries of the longer argument made in *Ad Aperiendam*. This treatise, called by Belch, *Paulus Vladimiri*, I, 173, the "definition and detailed description of Prussianism," i.e., that which Paweł called the *haeresis* or *secta Prussiana*. The work has been summarized in detail by Eberhard Schulz, "Paulus Vladimiri und das jagiellonischen Polen. Eine Untersuchung zu den Wirkungen der italienischen Rechtswissenschaft auf den jagiellonischen Staat," (Unpublished Ph.D. dissertation, Göttingen University, 1951), pp. 13-23; and Timothy M. Brennan, "Just War, Sovereignty, and Canon Law: Legal Arguments Over the Lithuanian Crusade and the Rights of Unbelievers at the Council of Constance (1414-1418)," (Unpublished Ph.D dissertation, University of Kansas, 2006), pp. 218-228.

34. i.e., the third *via*: that of adjudication. Given Paweł's view of the pope as the Vicar of Christ as expressed in the previous paragraph, it is implicit that this office is the one able to provide adjudication.

35. See Matt. 18:15-17. Note, however, that Paweł does not fully rely upon this aspect of the third way.

36. John 10:11-13.

37. Is. 56:10.

38. Ezek. 13:5; the reference in Belch, *Paulus Vladimiri*, II, 1102, n. 42, is a misprint.

39. Ps. 57:9 (Vulgate numeration).

40. Jer. 1:10.

BIBLIOGRAPHY —PRIMARY AND SECONDARY SOURCES

Adams, Marilyn McCord. *William Ockham*, 2 vols. Notre Dame, IN: University of Notre Dame Press, 1987.

Adamska, Anna. "The Kingdom of Poland versus the Teutonic Knights: Oral Traditions and Literate Behaviour in the Later Middle Ages." In Gerhard Jaritz and Michael Richter, eds., *Oral History of the Middle Ages: The Spoken Word in Context,* 67-78. Krems and Budapest: Central European University Press, 2001.

The Annals of Jan Długosz. A History of Eastern Europe from A.D. 965 to A.D. 1480. Trans. Maurice Michael. Charlton, Chichester, West Sussex: IMP Publications, 1997.

Baczkowski, Krzysztof. "La missione del nunzio Antonio Zeno in Polonia negli anni 1422-1423," *Prace Historyczne* 86 (1987): 15-27.

Baczkowski, Krzysztof and Janusz Smołucha, eds. *Europa Środkowo-wschodnia od X do XVIII wieku—jedność czy różnorodność?* Kraków: Societas Vistulana, 2005.

Barański, Marek. "Książęta i społeczeństwo wobec zjednoczenia Polski na przełomie XIII i XIV wieku." In Wojciech Fałkowski, ed., *Polska około roku 1300. Państwo, społeczeństwo, kultura*, 9-56. Warsaw: DiG: 2003.

Belch, Stanislaus F. *Paulus Vladimiri and His Doctrine Concerning International Law and Politics.* 2 vols. The Hauge: Mouton, 1965.

Berend, Nora, Przemysław Urbańczyk, and Przemysław Wiszewski. *Central Europe in the High Middle Ages. Bohemia, Hungary and Poland. C. 900—c. 1300.* Cambridge: Cambridge University Press, 2013.

Bieniak, Janusz. "Geneza procesu polsko-krzyżackiego z lat 1320-1321 (inwrocławsko-brzeskiego)." In Zenon Hubert Nowak, ed., *Balticum: Studia z dziejów politiki, gospodarki i kultury XII-XVII wieku ofiarowane Marianowi Biskupowi w siedemdziesiątą rocznicę urodzin.* 49-59, Toruń: Wydawnictwo Towarzystwa Naukowego w Toruniu, 1992.

_____. "Przebieg procesu polsko-krzyżackiego z 1339 roku," *Pamiętnik Biblioteki Kórnickiej* 23 (1993): 5-22.

Birkenmajer, Aleksander. "L'Université de Cracovie. Centre international d'enseignement astronomique à la fin du moyen age." In Birkenmajer, *Études d'historie des sciences en Pologne.* 483-495, Wrocław: Ossolineum, 1972.

Biskup, Marian. "Najazd krzyżacki na Polskę i bitwa pod Dąbkami 1431 r.," *Zeszyty Naukowe WAP* 48 (1967): 15-28.

Biskup, Marian and Gerard Labuda. *Dzieje Zakonu Krzyżackiego w Prusach. Gospodarka— Społeczeństwo—Państwo—Ideologia.* Gdańsk: Wydawnictwo Morskie, 1988. (German translation: *Die Geschichte des Deutschen Ordens in Preußen. Wirtschaft— Gesellschaft—Staat—Ideologie.* Osnabrück: Fibre, 2000.)

Bjork, Robert E., ed. *The Oxford Dictionary of the Middle Ages*, 4 vols. Oxford: Oxford University Press, 2010.

Black, Antony. *Council and Commune. The Conciliar Movement and the Council of Basle.* London: Burns and Oates, 1979.

_____. *Political Thought in Europe 1250-1450.* Cambridge: Cambridge University Press, 1992.

Błaszczyk, Grzegorz. *Burza koronacyjna: Polska-Litwa 1429-1430: Dramatycznych fragment stosunków polsko-litewskich w XV wieku.* Poznań: Instytut Historii Uniwersytetu im. Adama Mickiewicza, 1998.

_____. *Dzieje stosunków polsko-litewskich,* vol, II, part 1: *Od Krewa do Lublina*. Poznań: Wydawnictwo Poznańskie, 2007.

Boockmann, Hartmut. "Aus den Handakten des Kanonisten Johannes Urbach. Die Satire des Johannes Falkenberg und andere Funde zur Geschichte des Konstanzer Konzils," *Deutsches Archiv* 28 (1972): 497-532.

_____. *Der Deutsche Orden. Zwölf Kapitel aus seiner Geschichte*. Munich: C.H. Beck, 1982.

_____. *Johannes Falkenberg, der Deutsche Orden und die polnische Politik. Untersuchungen zur politischen Theorie des spöteren Mittelalters*. Göttingen: Vandenhoeck & Ruprecht, 1975.

Brandmüller, Walter. *Das Konzil von Konstanz*, 2 vols. Paderborn: Schöningh, 1991-1997.

Brennan, Timothy M. "Just War, Sovereignty, and Canon Law: Legal Arguments Over the Lithuanian Crusade and the Rights of Unbelievers at the Council of Constance (1414- 1418)." (Unpublished Ph.D. dissertation), University of Kansas, 2006.

Brundage, James A. *Medieval Canon Law*. London and New York: Longman, 1995.

Brzostowski, Tadeusz. *Paweł Włodkowic*. Warsaw: PAX, 1954.

Bucichowski, Wacław, ed. *Polskie Traktaty Koncyliarystyczne z połowy XV wieku*. Warsaw: Akademia Teologii Katolickiej, 1987.

Burleigh, Michael. *Prussian Society and the German Order. An Aristocratic Corporation in Crisis c. 1410-1466*. Cambridge: Cambridge University Press, 1984.

Chłopocka, Helena. "Dotychczasowe edycje *Lites ac res gestae* w świetle krytyki," *Studia Źródłoznawcze* 10 (1965): 109-115.

Chmielowska, Bożena. "Notatka *Revocatur* w rękopisie Biblioteki Uniwersyteckiej w Gandawie," *Studia Medievistyczne* 30 (1993): 33-39.

Chmielowska, Bożena, ed. *Stanisław ze Skarbimeirza. Sermones Sapientales*, 3 vol. Warsaw: Akademia Teologii Katolickiej, 1979.

Christiansen, Eric. *The Northern Crusades. The Baltic and the Catholic Frontier, 1100-1525*. Minneapolis, MN: University of Minnesota Press, 1980).

Cichocki, Marek A. and Adam Talarowski, eds. *Paweł Włodkowic i polska szkoła prawa międzynarodowego*. Warsaw: Narodowe Centrum Kultury/Teologia Polityczna, 2018.

Colish, Marcia. *Medieval Foundations of the Western Intellectual Tradition 400-1400*. New Haven, CT: Yale University Press, 1997.

Conrad, Karl. "Der Deutsche Order und Karl IV. 1352-1360," *Zeitschrift für Ostforschung* 21 (1972): 20-41.

Courtenay, William J. "Ockham, William of." In Joseph R. Strayer, editor-in-chief, *Dictionary of the Middle Ages*, 13 vols. IX (1987): 209-214-116. New York: Charles Scribner's Sons, 1982-1989.

Coville, Alfred. *Jean Petit. La question du tyrannicide au commencement du XVe siècle*. Paris: A Picard, 1932, reprinted Geneva: Slatkin, 1974.

Curta, Florin. "The Construct of a Tyrant: Feudalism in Eastern Europe." In Curta, *Eastern Europe in the Middle Ages (500-1300)*, 2 vols., I, 463-469. Leiden and Boston: Brill, 2019.

Czaja, Roman and Zenon Hubert Nowak. "An Attempt to Characterise the State of the Teutonic Knights in Prussia." In Czaja and Andrzej Radzimiński, eds., *The Teutonic Order in Prussia and Livonia. The Political and Ecclesiastical Structures 13th-16th Century*. 13-30. Toruń: Towarzystwo Naukowe w Toruniu, and Cologne, Weimar, and Vienna: Böhlau, 2015.

Czaja, Roman and Andrzej Radzimiński, eds., *The Teutonic Order in Prussia and Livonia. The Political and Ecclesiastical Structures 13th-16th Century*. Toruń: Towarzystwo Naukowe w Toruniu, and Cologne, Weimar, and Vienna: Böhlau, 2015.

Czwojdrak, Bożena. "Governance System in Poland during the 15th Century." In Grischa Vercamer and Dušan Zupka, eds. *Rulership in Medieval East Central Europe. Power, Ritual and Legitimacy in Bohemia, Hungary and Poland*, 291-305. Leiden and Boston: Brill, 2022.

Dabrowski, Patrice M. *Poland. The First Thousand Years*, 2nd ed. Dekalb, IL: Northern Illinois Press, 2021.

Davies, Norman. *God's Playground. A History of Poland*, 2 vols. New York: Columbia University Press, 1982.

de Ridder-Symoens, ed. *Universities in the Middle Ages*. Cambridge: Cambridge University Press, 1992. [vol. I of Walter Rüegg, general ed. *A History of the University in Europe*. Cambridge: Cambridge University Press, 1992.]

Długokęcki, Wiesław, Jan Kuczyński, and Barbara Pospieszna. *Młyny w Malborku i okolicy od XIII do XIX wieku*. Malbork: Muzeum Zamkowe w Malborku, 2004.

Donecker, Stefan. "Locals and Immigrants in Medieval Central Europe." In Nada Zečević and Daniel Ziemann, eds. *Oxford Handbook of Medieval Central Europe*, 191-212. Oxford: Oxford University Press, 2022.

Drelicharz, Wojciech. *Unifying the Kingdom of Poland in Mediaeval Historiographic Thought*. Cracow: Societas Vistulana, 2019. (Polish original 2012.)

Dunbabin, Jean, "Government." In J. H. Burns, ed., *The Cambridge History of Medieval Political Thought c. 350-c. 1450*. 477-519. Cambridge: Cambridge University Press, 1992.

Dutton, Paul E., ed. *Carolingian Civilization: A Reader*. Peterborough, Ontario: Broadview, 2004.

Dygo, Marian. "Czy istniał feudalizm w Europie środkowo-wschodniej w średniowieczu". *Kwartalnik historyczny* 120, 4 (2013): 667-717.

Ekdahl, Sven. *Die* "Banderia Prutenorum" *des Jan Długosz. Eine Quelle zur Schlacht bei Tannenberg 1410*. Göttingen: Vandenhoeck & Ruprecht, 1976.

_____. "Battlefield Archaeology at Grunwald (Tannenberg, Žalgiris). A Polish-Scandinavian Research Project during the period 2014-2017," *Przegląd Historyczny* 109, 2 (2018): 239-266.

_____. "Der Krieg zwischen dem Deutschen Orden und Polen-Litauen im Jahre 1422," *Zeitschrift für Ostforschung* 13 (1964): 614-651.

_____. *Die Schlacht bei Tannenberg 1410*, vol. I:*Einführung und Quellenlage*. Berlin: Duncker & Humblot, 1982.

Ehler, Sidney Z. and John B. Morrall, eds. and trans. *Church and State Through the Centuries*. Westminster, MD: The Newman Press, 1954.

Ehrlich, Ludwik. *Paweł Włodkowic i Stanisław ze Skarbimierza*. Warsaw: Państwowe Wydawnictwo Naukowe, 1954.

Ehrlich, Ludwik, ed. *Pisma wybrane Pawła Włodkowica*: *Works of Paul Wladimiri (A Selection)*. 3 vols. Warsaw: Instytut Wydawniczy PAX, 1966-1969.

______. *Polski wykład prawa wojny XV wieku. Kazanie Stanisława ze Skarbimierza* De bellis iustis. Warsaw: Wydawnictwo Prawnicze, 1955.

Fijałek, Jan. *Mistrz Jakób z Paradyża i Uniwersytet Krakowski w okresie soboru Bazylejskiego*, 2 vols. Kraków: Nakładem Akademii Umiejętności, 1900.

_____. "Ostatnie słowo Pawła Włodkowica o zakonie krzyżackim, *Przegląd Kościelny* 1 (1902): 1-13, 92-104, 180-189, 258-273, 342-352.

_____. *Polonia apud Italos scholastica saeculum XV*. Kraków: Typis Universitatis Jagellonicae, 1900.

Filozofia w Polsce. Słownik Pisarzy. Wrocław: Ossolineum, 1971.

Finke, Heinrich, et al., eds. *Acta concilii Constanciensis*, 4 vols. Münster: Regensburgsche Buchhandlung, 1896-1928.

Flanagin, David Zachariah. "Extra Ecclesiam salus non est—sed quae ecclesia? Ecclesiology and Authority in the Later Middle Ages." In Joëlle Rollo-Koster and Thomas M. Izbicki, eds. *A Companion to the Great Western Schism (1378-1417)*, 333-374. Leiden and Boston: Brill, 2009.

Frenken, Ansgar. *Die Erforschung des Constanzer Konzils (1414-1418) in den letzten 100 Jahren*. Paderborn: Schöningh, 1995.

Frost, Robert. *The Oxford History of Poland-Lithuania*, vol. I: *The Making of the Polish- Lithuanian Union, 1385-1569*. Oxford: Oxford University Press, 2015.

Gabriele, Matthew and David Perry. *The Bright Ages. A New History of Medieval Europe*. New York: Harper Collins, 2021.

Garbacik, Józef. "Ognisko Nauki i Kultury Renesansowej (1470-1520)." In Kazimierz Lepszy, ed. *Dzieje Uniwersytetu Jagiellońskiego w latach 1364-1764*, 189-220. Kraków: Uniwersytet Jagielloński Wydawnictwo Jubileuszowe, 1964.

Gąsiorowski, Antoni, Tomasz Jurek, and Izabela Skierska, eds., with the assistance of Ryszard Grzesik. *Metryka Uniwersytetu Krakowskiego z lat 1400-1508*, 2 vols. Kraków: Societas Vistulana, 2004.

Gawlas, Sławomir. "Dlaczego nie było w Polsce feudalizmu lennego?" *Roczniki Dziejów Społecznych i Gospardarczych*, 58 (1998): 101-123.

Gesta principum Polonorum/The Deeds of the Princes of the Poles. Trans. and annotated Paul W. Knoll and Frank Schaer. Preface by Thomas N. Bisson. Budapest: Central European University Press, 2003.

Giedroyć, Michał. "Lithuanian Options Prior to Kreva (1385)." In *La Cristianizzazione della Lituania*. 87-105. Vatican City: Libreria Editrice Vaticana, 1989.

Given-Wilson, Chris. *Henry IV*. New Haven, CR: Yale University Press, 2016.

Gładysz, Mikołaj. *The Forgotten Crusaders. Poland and the Crusader Movement in the Twelfth and Thirteenth Centuries*. Leiden and Boston: 2012. (Polish original 2002.)

Goody, Jack. *The Theft of History*. Cambridge: Cambridge University Press, 2006.

Górecki, Piotr. *A Local Society in Transition. The Henryków Book and Related documents*. Toronto: Pontifical Institute of Mediaeval Studies, 2007.

_____. *The Text and the World. The Henryków Book, Its Authors, and Their Region, 1160-1310*. Oxford: Oxford University Press, 2013.

Górski, Karol, ed. *Jana Długosza Banderia Prutenorum*. Warsaw: Państwowe Wydawnictwo Naukowe, 1958.

_____. "Paweł Włodkowic," *Polski Słownik Biograficzny* 25 (1980) 377-381.

Graff, Tomasz. *Episkopat monarchii jagiellońskiej w dobie soborów powszechnych XV wieku*. Kraków: Societas Vistulana, 2008.

_____. *Kościół w Polsce wobec konfliktu z Zakonem Krzyżackim w XV wieku. Studium z dziejów kultury politycznej polskiego episkopatu.* Kraków: Księgarnia Akademicka, 2010.

_____. "Servants of the Devil or Protectors of Christianity and Apostles among Pagans? Shaping the image of Poland and Poles in the Context of Steps taken by Władysław Jagiełło's Diplomacy against 'Satira' by John Falkenberg," *Folia Historica Cracoviensis* 23 (2017): 143-176.

Gudavičius, Ėvardas. *Mindaugas*. Vilnius: Žara, 1998. (Not personally seen.)

Güttner-Sporzyński, Darius von. *Poland, Holy War, and the Piast Monarchy, 1100-1230*. Turnhout: Brepols, 2014.

Hanke, Lewis. *Bartolomé de las Casas. An Interpretation of his Life and Writings*. The Hague: Martinus Nijhof, 1951.

_____. *Bartolomé de las Casas: Bookman, Scholar, and Propogandist*. Philadelphia: University of Pennsylvania Press, 1952.

Housley, Norman. "A Crusade Against the Poles? Johannes Falkenberg's 'Satira' (1412)." In Helen J. Nicholson and Jochen Burgtorf, eds., *The Templars, the Hospitallers and the Crusades*. 183-198. London and New York: Routledge, 2020.

Ioannis Dlugossii Annales seu Cronicae incliti Regni Poloniae [Libri 12]. Jan Dąbrówski, et al., eds. 11vols. Warsaw and Cracow: Państwowe Wydawnictwo Naukowe and Polska Akademia Umiejętności, 1964-2005.

Izbicki, Thomas M. "The Authority of Peter and Paul: The Use of Biblical Authority During the Great Schism." In Joëlle Rollo-Koster and Thomas M. Izbicki, eds. *A Companion to the Great Western Schism (1378-1417)*, 375-393. Leiden and Boston: Brill, 2009.

Jasiński, Tomasz. "The Golden Bull Allegedly Issued in 1226 by Frederick II for the Teutonic Order." *Quaestiones Medii Aevi Novae* 3 (1998): 221-223.

_____. *Kruschwitz, Rimini und die Grundlagen des preussischen Ordenlandes: Urkundenstudien zur Frühzeit des Deutschen Ordens im Ostseeraum*. Marburg: N.G. Elwert, 2008.

_____. "Okoliczności nadania ziemi chełmińskiej Krzyżakom w 1228 roku w świetle dokumentu łowickiego." In Zenon Hubert Nowak, ed.,

Balticum: Studia z dziejów politiki, gospodarki i kultury XII-XVII wieku ofiarowane Marianowi Biskupowi w siedemdziesiątą rocznicę urodzin, 151-163. Toruń: Wydawnictwo Towarzystwa Naukowego w Toruniu, 1992.

_____. "Złote Bulla Fryderyka II dla zakonu krzyżackiego z roku rzekomo 1236." *Roczniki Historyczne* 60 (1994): 107-154.

Jones, Dan. *Powers and Thrones. A New History of the Middle Ages*. New York: Viking, 2021.

Jóźwiak, Sławomir and Janusz Trupinda. *Organizacja życia na Zamku Krzyżackim w Malborku w czasach Wielkich Mistrzów, 1309-1457*, 3rd ed. Malbork: Muzeum Zamkowe w Malborku, 2019.

Jóźwiak, Sławomir, et al. *Wojna Polski i Litwy z Zakonem Krzyżackim w latach 1409-1411*. Malbork: Muzeum Zamkowe w Malborku, 2010.

Jurek, Tomasz. "Die Entstehung des polnischen Adels." In Eduard Mühle, ed. *Studien zum Adel im mittelalterlichen Polen*, 13-117. Wiesbaden: Harrassowitz Verlag, 2012.

_____. "Polska droga do korony królewskiej 1295-1300-1320." In Martin Wihoda and Lukaš Reitinger, eds., Proměna středovýchodni Evropy raného a vrcholnéo středověku. Mocenské souvislosti a paralely, 139-191. Brno: Matica moravská, 2010.

_____. "Uwagi o bitwie pod Płowcami," *Ziemia Kujawska* 9 (1993): 77-97.

Jurek, Tomasz and Edmund Kizik. *Historia Polski do 1572 roku*. Warsaw: Wydawnictwo Naukowe PWN, 2013.

Jasudowicz, Tadeusz. *Śladami Ludwika Ehrlicha. Do Pawła Włodkowica po naukę o prawach człowieka*. Toruń: Wydawnictwo Comer Jacek Waloch, 1995.

Kadlec, Jaroslav. "The Theological Faculty." In František Kavka and Josef Petráň, eds. *A History of Charles University*, I, 123-148.

Kałuża, Zenon, "Paweł Włodkowic i problem jego doktryny," *Zeszyty Naukowe KUL* 21 (1978): 85-92.

_____. "Podręcznik teologii używany na Uniwersytecie Cracowskim: Komentarz do *Sentencji*, zwany *Utrum Deus Gloriosus*," *Przegląd Tomistyczny* 17 (2011): 235-254.

Kaminsky, Howard. Review of Stanislaus F. Belch, *Paulus Vladimiri and His Doctrine Concerning International Law and Politics*. 2 vols. The Hague: Mouton, 1965, in *Speculum* 42 (1967): 918-920.

Kavka, František and Josef Petráň, eds. *A History of Charles University*, vol. I. Prague: Karolinum, 2001. (Czech original 1995.)

Kejř, Jiři. "The Prague Law Faculty and the Law University." In František Kavka and Josef Petráň, eds. *A History of Charles University*, I, 149-170. Prague: Karolinum, 2001.

Kirschner, Julius. "Bartolo da Sassoferrato." In Joseph R. Strayer, editor-in-chief, *Dictionary of the Middle Ages*, 13 vols. II (1983): 114-116. New York: Charles Scribner's Sons, 1982- 1989.

Kiryk, Feliks and Zdzisław Noga, eds. *Zbigniew Oleśnicki Książę Kościoła i Mąż Stanu*. Kraków: Secesja, 2006.

Kłoczowski, Jerzy. *Młodsza Europa. Europa Środkowo-Wschodnia w kręgu cywilizacji chrześcijańskiej średniowiecza*. Warsaw: Państwowy Instytut Wydaniczy, 1998.

_____. "La Pologne et la Christianisation de la Lituanie." In *La Cristianizzazione della Lituania*, 139-159. Vatican City: Libreria Editrice Vaticana, 1989.

Knoll, Paul W. "Jan Długosz and His *Banderia Prutenorum*," *The Polish Review* 25, 1 (1980):93-97.

_____. "Jan Długosz, 1480-1980," *The Polish Review* 27, 1/2 (1982): 3-28. (Reprinted in Charles Kraszewski, ed., *Fifty Years of Polish Scholarship: The Polish Review 1956-2006*, 259- 295. New York: PIASA Books, 2006.

_____. "The Most Unique Crusader State. The Teutonic Order in the Development of the Political Culture of Northeastern Europe during the Middle Ages." In Charles W. Ingrao and Franz A.J. Szabo, eds., *The Germans in the East*, 37-48. West Lafayette, IN: Purdue University Press, 2008.

_____. *"A Pearl of Powerful Learning." The University of Cracow in the Fifteenth Century*. Leiden and Boston: Brill, 2016.

_____. *The Rise of the Polish Monarchy. Piast Poland in East Central Europe, 1320- 1370*. Chicago: University of Chicago Press, 1972.

_____. "Working for the King (and the Queen): Krakovian Scholars in the Royal Service in Late Medieval Poland," *The Polish Review* 59, 2 (2014): 3-18.

Koczerska, Maria. "Oleśnicki, Zbigniew," *Polski Słownik Biograficzny* 23 (1978): 776-784.

_____. *Zbigniew Oleśnicki i kościół krakowski w czasach jego pontyfikatu (1423-1455)*. Warsaw: DiG, 2004.

Körmendy, Adrienne. *Melioratio terrae: Vergleichende Untersuchungen über die Siedlungsbewegung im östlichen Mitteleuropa im 13-14. Jahrhundert*. Poznań: Wydawnictwo Poznańskiego Towarzystwa Przyjaciół Nauk, 1995.

Kowalczyk, Maria. "Odnowienie Uniwersytetu Krakowskiego w świetle mów Bartłomieja z Jasła," *Małopolskie Studia Historyczne* 6, no 3/4 (1964): 23-42. (reprinted in Kowalczyk, *Colligite fragmenta ne permeant... Studia z dziejów Uniwersytetu Krakowskiego w średniowieczu*. 111-131. Kraków: Societas Vistulana, 2010.)

Kozłowska-Budkowa, Zofia. "Odnowienie Jagiellońskie Uniwersytetu Krakowskiego (1390-1414)." In Kazimierz Lepszy, ed. *Dzieje Uniwersytetu Jagiellońskiego w latach 1364- 1764*. 37-89. Kraków: Uniwersytet Jagielloński Wydawnictwo Jubileuszowe, 1964.

Kozłowski, Wojciech. "Wstęp." In Marek A. Cichocki and Adam Talarowski, eds. *Paweł Włodkowic i Polska Szkoła prawa międzynarodowego,* 6-43. Warsaw: Narodowe Centrum Kultury/Teologia Polityczna, 2018.

Kubon, Sebastian. *Die Außenpolitik des Deutschen Ordens unter Hochmeister Konrad von Jungingen (1393-1407)*. Göttingen: V & R Unipress, 2016.

Kuczyński, Stefan M. *Wielki Wojna z Zakonem Krzyżackim w latach 1409-1411,* 5th ed. Warsaw: Wydawnictwo Ministerstwa Obrony Narodowej, 1987.

Kurtka, Janusz. *Odrozone Królestwo. Monarchia Władysława Łokietka i Kazimierza Wielkiego w świetle nowszych badań*. Kraków: Societas Vistulana, 2001.

Labuda, Gerard. "Staniwisko prawno-polityczne książąt Pomorze Nadwiślańskiego na przełomie XII i XIII wieku," *Zapiski Historyczne* 66 (2001): 195-226.

_____. "Die Urkunden über die Anfänge des Deutschen Ordens im Kulmerland und in Preußen in den Jahren 1226-1235." In Joseph Fleckenstein and Manfred Hellmann, eds., *Die Geistliche Ritterorden Europas*, 299-316. Sigmaringen: Jan Thorbecke Verlag, 1980.

Lavuot, Ottavio and Ludwig Schmugge, eds *Historia Ecclesiastica Nova: Nebst Fortsetzungen Bis 1329*. Hannover: Hahnsche Buchhandlung, 2009.

Lepszy, Kazimierz, ed. *Dzieje Uniwersytetu Jagiellońskiego w latach 1364-1764*. Kraków: Państwowe Wydawnictwo Naukowe, 1964.

Lewis, Anna Lisa Merklin. "Tyrannicide: Heresy or Duty? The Debates at the Council of Constance." (Unpublished Ph.D. dissertations, Cornell University, Ithaca, NY, 1990.)

Liedtke, Antoni. "Jan zwany 'Kropidlo'," *Polski Słownik Biograficzny*, X (1963), 436-438.

Lites ac Res Gestae inter Polonos Ordinemque Cruciferorum, vol. I: *Sprawa wytoczona w Inowrocławiu i Brześciu Kujawskim w latach 1320-1321*, ed. Helena Chłopocka,, 2nd ed. Wrocław: Ossolineum, 1970.

Lites ac Res Gestae inter Polonos Ordinemque Cruciferorum, ed. Ignacy Zakrzewski and Jadwiga Karwasińsksa, 2nd ed. [*editio altera*], 3 vols. Poznań and Warsaw: Nakładem Biblioteki Kórnickiej, 1892-1935.

Łowmiański, Henryk, ed. *Polska w okresie rozdrobnienia feudalnego*. Wrocław: Ossolineum, 1973.

Lukowski, Jerzy and Hubert Zawadzki. *A Concise History of Poland*, 3rd ed. Cambridge: Cambridge University Press, 2019.

Manikowska, Halina. "*Melioratio terrae* and System Transformations on Lands to the East of the Odra during the thirteenth Century and the

Late Middle Ages." In Simonnetta Cavaciocchi, ed., *Poteri economici e poteri politici, secc. XIII-XVIII*, 303-323. Florence: Le Monnier, 1999.

Markowski, Mieczysław. *Burydanizm w Polsce w okresie przedkopernikańskim. Studium z historii filozofii i nauk ścisłych na Uniwersytecie Krakowskim w XV wieku*. Wrocław: Ossolineum, 1971.

_____. *Dzieje Wydziału Teologii Uniwersytetu Krakowskiego w latach 1397-1525*. Kraków: Wydawnictwo Naukowe Papieskiej Akademii Teologicznej w Krakowie, 1996.

Marzec, Andrzej. "New King and New Elites. The Reign of Louis the Great in Poland 1370- 1382." In Dániel Bagi, Gábor Barabás, and Zsolt Máté, eds., *Hungaro-Polonica. Young Scholars on Medieval Polish-Hungarian Relations*, 189-224. Pécs: Történészcéh Egyesület, 2016.

Marzec, Andrzej and Maciej Wilamowski, eds. *Król w Polsce XIV i XV wieku*. Kraków: Societas Vistulana, 2006.

Michałowski, Roman. *The Gniezno Summit: The Religious Premises of the Founding of the Archbishopric of Gniezno*. Leiden and Boston: Brill, 2016. (Polish original 2005.)

Miethke, Jürgen. "Heiliger Heidenkrieg? Theoretische Kontroversen zwischen Deutschem Orden und dem Königreich Polen vor und auf dem Konstanzer Konzil." In Kalus Schreiner, ed., *Heilige Kriege. Religiöse Begründungen militärischer Gewaltanwendung. Judentum, Christentum und Islam im Vergleich*. 109-125. Munich: OLdenbourg, 2008.

Mikuła, Maciej. *Municipal Magdeburg Law (Ius municipal Magdeburgense) in Late Medieval Poland. A Study on the Evolution and Adaptation of Law*. Leiden and Boston: Brill, 2021. (Polish original 2017.)

Militzer, Klaus. "Kommunikations- und Verständigungsprobleme vor und nach der Schlacht bei Tannenberg," in Werner Paravicini, Rimvydas Petrauskas, and Grisha Vercamer, eds. *Tannenberg—Grunwald—Žalgiris 1410: Krieg und Frieden im späten Mittelalter*. 301- 305. Wiesbaden: Harrassowitz, 2012.

Milliman, Paul. *"The Slippery Memory of Men." The Place of Pomerania in the Medieval Kingdom of Poland*. Leiden and Boston: 2013.

Moeglin, Jean-Marie. "Krieg und Vermittlungsverfahren in Europa in den letzten Jahrhunderten des Mittelalteers." In Werner Paravicini, Rimvydas Petrauskas, and Grisha Vercamer, eds. *Tannenberg—Grunwald—Žalgiris 1410: Krieg und Frieden im späten Mittelalter*, 211- 222. Wiesbaden: Harrassowitz, 2012.

Moreau-Reibel, Jean. "Le droit de société interhumaine de la 'Jus Gentium.' Essau sur les origins et le developpement des notions jusqu'a Grotius," *Recueil des Cours de l'Academie de Droit International* 77 (1950): 481-598.

Morrissey, Thomas E. "Cardinal Franciscus Zabarella (1360-1417) as a Canonist and the Crisis of his Age: Schism and the Council of Constance," *Zeitschrift für Kirchengeschichte* 96 (1985):196-208. (Reprinted in Morrissey. *Conciliarism and Church Law in the Fifteenth Century. Studies on Franciscus Zabarella and the Council of Constance*. Farnham, Surry, England and Burlington, VT: Ashgate, 2014, as item VIII, with original pagination.)

_____. "Cardinal Zabarella and Nicholas of Cusa: from community authority to consent of the community," *Mitteilungen und Forschungsbeiträge der Cusanus-Gesellschaft* 17 (1986): 157-176. (Reprinted in Morrissey. *Conciliarism and Church Law in the Fifteenth Century. Studies on Franciscus Zabarella and the Council of Constance*. Farnham, Surry, England and Burlington, VT: Ashgate, 2014, as item I, with original pagination.)

Mühle, Eduard. "Genese und frühe Entwicklung des Adels in polnischer Sicht." In Mühle, ed. *Studien zum Adel im mittelalterlichen Polen*, 1-12. Wiesbaden: Harrassowitz Verlag, 2012.

Mühle, Eduard, ed. *Studien zum Adel im mittelalterlichen Polen*. Wiesbaden: Harrassowitz Verlag, 2012.

Nadolski, Andrzej. *Grunwald 1410*, 3rd ed. Warsaw: Bellona, 2010.

Neitmann, Klaus. "Vom 'ewigen Frieden'. Die Kunst des Friedensschlusses zwischen dem Deutschen Orden und Polen-Litauen 1398-1435." In Werner Paravicini, Rimvydas Petrauskas, and Grisha Vercamer, eds.

Tannenberg—Grunwald—Žalgiris 1410: Krieg und Frieden im späten Mittelalter, 201-209. Wiesbaden: Harrassowitz, 2012.

Nieborowski, Paul. *Der Deutsche Orden und Polen in der Zeit des grössten Konflikts*, 2nd ed. Wrocław [Breslau]: Wahlstaat-Verlag, 1924.

Nikžentaitis, Alvydas. "Die friedliche Periode in den Beziehungen zwischen dem Deutschen Order und dem Großfürstentum Litauen (1345-1360 und das Problem der Christianisierung Litauens," *Jahrbücher für Geschichte Osteuropas* 41, 1 (1993): 1-22.

Noble, Thomas F.X. *The Republic of St. Peter: The Birth of the Papal State, 680-825*. Philadelphia: University of Pennsylvania Press, 1984.

Nowak, Zenon H. *Międzynarodowe procesy polubowne jako narzędzie polityki Zygmunta Luksemburskiego w północnej i środkowowschodniej Europie (1412-1424)*. Toruń: Uniwersytet Mikołaja Kopernika, 1981.

Oakley, Francis. *The Western Church in the Later Middle Ages*. Ithaca, NY and London: Cornell University Press, 1979.

Ożóg, Krzysztof. *The Role of Poland in the Intellectual Development of Europe in the Middle Ages*. Kraków: Societas Vistulana, 2009.

_____. "Stanisław ze Skarbimierza." In Piotr Dymmel, Krzysztof Skupieński and Barbara Treliński, eds. *Droga historii. Studia ofiarowane Profesorowi Józefowi Szymańskiemu w siedemdziesiątą rocznicę urodzin*, 47-61. Lublin: Wydawnictwo Uniwersytetu Marii Curie-Skłodowskiej, 2001.

_____. *Uczeni w Monarchii Jadwigi Andegaweńskiej i Władysława Jagiełły (1384-1434)*. Kraków: Polska Akademia Umiejętności, 2004.

_____. "Udział Andrzeja Łaskarzyca w sprawach i sporach polsko-krzyżackich do soboru w Konstancji." In Ożóg and Stanisław Szczur, eds. *Polska i jej sąsiedzi w późnym średniowieczu*. 159-186, Kraków: Societas Vistula, 2000.

_____. "University masters at the royal court of Hedwig of Anjou and Władysław Jagiełło." In Piotr Górecki and Nancy van Deusen, eds. *Central and Eastern Europe in the Middle Ages. A Cultural History.*

Essays in Honor of Paul W. Knoll, 147-160. London and New York: I.B. Tauris, 2009.

Paravicini, Werner. *Die Preussenreisen des europäischen Adels*, 2 vols. Sigmaringen: Jan Thorbecke Verlag.

Paravicini, Werner, Rimvydas Petrauskas, and Grisha Vercamer, eds. *Tannenberg—Grunwald—Žalgiris 1410: Krieg und Frieden im späten Mittelalter.* Wiesbaden: Harrassowitz, 2012.

Pauk, Marcin R. "Language of Power and Communication in the Piast Dynasty: Toward a Reappraisal of Polish Political Culture of the 12th-13th Century." In Grischa Vercamer and Dušan Zupka, eds. *Rulership in Medieval East Central Europe. Power, Ritual and Legitimacy in Bohemia, Hungary and Poland*, 178-197. Leiden and Boston: Brill, 2022.

Pieradzka, Krystyna. "Uniwersytet Krakowski w służbie państwa i wobec soborów w Konstancji i Bazylei." In Kazimierz Lepszy, ed. *Dzieje Uniwersytetu Jagiellońskiego w latach 1364-1764*, 91-137. Kraków: Państwowe Wydawnictwo Naukowe, 1964.

Piskorski, Jan M., ed. *Historiographical Approaches to Medieval Colonization of East Central Europe.* Boulder, CO: East European Monographs, 2002.

Pluskowski, Aleksander. *The Archaeology of the Prussian Crusade. Holy War and Colonisation*. London and New York: Routledge, 2013.

Podraza, Antoni. "Central Europe as a Historical Region." In Jerzy Kłoczowski, ed., *Europe Centrale entre l'Est et l'Ouest/Central Europe Between East and West*, 30-45. Lublin: Instytut Europy Środkowo-Wschodniej, 2005.

Powierski, J., "Książęta polscy i Zakon Krzyżacki a problem bałtyjski w okresie od schyłku 1258 do połowy 1260 roku," *Komunikaty Mazursko-Warmińskie* 23, 4 (1979): 367-390.

Rácz, György. "The Congress of Visegrád in 1335: Diplomacy and Representation," *Hungarian Historical Review* 2 (2013): 261-287.

Renna, Thomas. "Egidus Colonna." In Joseph R. Strayer, editor-in-chief, *Dictionary of the Middle Ages*, IV (1984): 400. New York: Charles Scribner's Sons, 1982- 1989.

Repertorium Fontium Historiae Medii Aevi, 12 vols. Rome: Istituto Storico Italiano per il Medio Evo, 1942-2007.

Rocznik Traski, ed. August Bielowski. *Monumenta Poloniae Historica*, II, 826-861. Lwów [L'viv]: Nakładem Własnym, 1872.

Rollo-Koster, Joëlle and Thomas M. Izbicki, eds. *A Companion to the Great Western Schism (1378-1417)*. Leiden and Boston: Brill, 2009.

Rowell, Steven C. "Baltic Europe." In Michael Jones, ed., *The New Cambridge Medieval History*, vol. 6: *ca. 1300-1415*, 699-734. Cambridge: Cambridge University Press, 2000.

_____. *Lithuania Ascending. A Pagan Empire within East-Central Europe, 1295-1343*. Cambridge: Cambridge University Press, 1994.

_____. "1386: The Marriage of Jogaila and Jadwiga Emdogies the Union of Poland and Lithuania," *Lithuanian Historical Studies* 11 (2006): 137-144.

Rüegg, Walter. "Themes." In de Ridder-Symoens, ed., *Universities in the Middle Ages*, 3-34. Cambridge: Cambridge University Press, 1992.

Russell, Frederick H. *The Just War in the Middle Ages*. Cambridge: Cambridge University Press, 1975.

_____. "Paulus Vladimiri's Attack on the Just War: A Case Study in Legal Polemics." In Brian Tierney and Peter Linehan, eds., *Authority and Power. Studies on Medieval Law and Government Presented to Walter Ullmann on his Seventieth Birthday,* 237-254. Cambridge: Cambridge University Press, 1980.

Schlesinger, Walter, ed. *Die deutsche Ostsiedlung des Mittelalters als Problem der europäischen Geschichte*. Sigmaringen: Jan Thorbecke Verlag, 1975.

Schulte, Johann Friedrich von. *Geschichte der Quellen und Literature des canonischen Rechts*, 3 vols. Stuttgart: Enke, 1875-1889. (Repr. Graz: Akademische Druck- und Verlagsanstalt, 1956.)

Schulz, Eberhard. "Paulus Vladimiri und das jagiellonischen Polen. Untersuchung zu den Wirkungen der italienischen Rechtswissenschaft auf den jagiellonischen Staat." (Unpublished Ph.D. dissertation, Göttingen, 1951).

Seńko, Władysław. *Piotr Wysz z Radolina i jego dzieło 'Speculum aureum.'* Warsaw: Instytut Tomistyczny, 1995.

_____. "Trzy Traktaty Jana Falkenberga na temat tyranobójstwa przedstawione na Soborze w Konstancji w 1416 r." *Przegląd Tomistyczny* 10 (2002): 87-127.

_____. "Z Badań nad historią myśli społeczno-politycznej w Polsce w XV wieku." In Ryszard Palacz, ed., *Filozofia polska XV wieku*, 20-57. Warsaw: Państwowe Wydawnictwo Naukowe, 1972.

Seńko, Władysław, ed. "Johannes Falkenberg *De Monarchia Mundi*," *Materiały do Historii Filozofii średniowiecznej w Polsce* 9 (20) (1975): v-lvi and 1-289.

_____. ed. *Krakowska redakcja Jana Falkenberga De monarchia mundi.* Warsaw: Akademia Teologii Katolickiej, 1986.

Sieradzan, Wiesław. "Benedek (Benedict) Makrai as a Subarbiter in the Conflict Between the Teutonic Order and Neighbor Countries in 1412-1413." In Sierdzan, ed. *Arguments and Counterarguments. The Political thought of the 14th and 15th Centuries during the Polish- Teutonic Order Trials and Disputes*, 157-168. Toruń: Wydawnictwo Naukowe Uniwersytetu Mikołaja Kopernika, 2012.

_____. *Misja Benedykta Makraia w latach 1412-1413. Z dziejów pokojowych metod rozwiązywania konfliktów międzypańsstwowych w Europie Środkowo-Wschodniej w późnym średniowieczu*. Malbork: Muzeum Zamkowe, 2009.

Sieradzan, Wiesław, ed. *Arguments and Counterarguments. The Political thought of the 14th and 15th Centuries during the Polish-Teutonic Order Trials and Disputes*. Toruń: Wydawnictwo Naukowe Uniwersytetu Mikołaja Kopernika, 2012.

Śliwiński, Błażej. *Pomorze Wschodnie w okresie rządów księcia polskiego Władysława Łokietka w latach 1306-1309*. Gdańsk: Muzeum Archeologiczne w Gdańsku, 2003.

_____. "Wydarzenie w Gdańsku i w okolicach w okresie od września do 12/13 listopada 1308 roku." In Śliwiński, ed., *Rzeź gdańska z 1308 roku w świetle najnowszych badan. Materiały z sesji naukowej 12-13 listopada 2008 roku*, 79-114. Gdańsk: Muzeum Historyczne Miasta Gdańska, 2009.

Śliwiński, Błażej and Beata Możejko. "Gdańsk in the Aftermath of the Teutonic Order's Actions in Pomerelia in the First Half of the Fourteenth Century," *East Central Europe* 47, 1 (2020): 29-38.

Śliwiński, Błażej ed. *Rzeź gdańska z 1308 roku w świetle najnowszych badań. Materiały z sesji naukowej 12-13 listopada 2008 roku*. Gdańsk: Muzeum Historyczne Miasta Gdańska, 2009.

Šmahel, František. "The Faculty of Liberal Arts." In František Kavka and Josef Petráň, eds. *A History of Charles University*, I, 93-122. Prague: Karolinum, 2001.

Šmahel, František, ed., in cooperation with Ota Pavlič. *A Companion to Jan Hus*. Leiden and Boston, 2015.

Smalley, Beryl. *The Study of the Bible in the Middle Ages*. Oxford: Oxford University Press, 1952 and later editions.

Sperka, Jerzy. *Władysław książę opolski, wieluński, kujawski, dobrzyński, Pan Rusi, Palatyn Węgier i namiestnik Polski*. Kraków: Avalon, 2012.

Stopka, Krzysztof. "From Foundation to the Late 18th Century." In Stopka, Andrzej Kazimierz Banach, and Julian Dybiec. *The History of the Jagiellonian University*, 9-76. Kraków: Jagiellonian University Press, 2000.

Stump, Phillip H. "The Council of Constance (1414-1418) and the End of the Schism." In Joëlle Rollo-Koster and Thomas M. Izbicki, eds. *A Companion to the Great Western Schism (1378-1417)*, 396-442. Leiden and Boston: Brill, 2009.

_____. *The Reforms of the Council of Constance (1414-1418)*. Leiden, New York, and Cologne: Brill, 1994.

Supruniuk, Anna."O wyprawach do Prus rycerzy polskich i wojnie domowej w Koronie w latach 1382-1385," *Zapiski Historyczne* 65, 2 (2000): 31-56.

Svatoš, Michal. "The Studium Generale 1347/8-1419." In František Kavka and Josef Petráň, eds. *A History of Charles University*, I, 22-93. Prague: Karolinum, 2001.

Świeboda, Wojciech. *Innowiercy w opiniach prawnych uczonych polskich w XV wieku. Poganie, żydzi, muzułmanie.* Kraków: Societas Vistulana, 2013.

Szczur, Stanisław. *Papież Urban V i powstanie uniwersytetu w Krakowie w 1364 roku*. Kraków: Societas Vistulana, 1999.

_____. "Traktat pokojowy Kazimerza Wielkiego z Zakonem Krzyżackim z 1343," *Zapiski Historyczne* 56 (1991): 439-464.

_____. "Współpracownicy Galharda z Carcès, kolektora papieskiego w Polski." In Janusz Bieniak, et al., eds., *Homines et Societas: Czasy Piastów i Jagiellonów*, 337-344. Poznań: Wydawnictwo Poznańskiego Towarzystwa Przyjaciół Nauk, 1997.

_____. "Zjazd wyszheradzki z 1335 roku," *Studia Historyczne* 35 (1992): 3-17.

Szwede, Adam. "Zakon Krzyżacki wobec Polski i Litwy w latach 1411-1414," *Prace Historyczne* 141, 2 (2014): 531-553.

Szwede, Adam and Anna Adamska. "Notariusz przy pracy. Akcja transumowania dokumentów krzyżackich jesienią 1421 roku." In Grażyna Rutkowska and Antoni Gąsiorowski, eds., *Memoria viva. Studia historycne poświęcone pamięci Izabeli Skierskiej (1967-2014)*, 487-501. Poznań: Instytut Historii PAN, 2015.

Szwede, Adam, et al., eds. *Lites ac Res Gestae intern Polonos Ordinemque Cruciferorum/Akta Postępowania przed wysłannikiem papieskim Antonym Zeno z Mediolanu w latach 1422-1423*. Toruń: Wydawnictwo Naukowe Uniwersytetu Mikołaja Kopernika, 2015.

Tandecki, Janusz. "Administrative Divisions of the State of the Teutonic Order in Prussia." In Andrzej Radzimiński, eds., *The Teutonic Order in Prussia and Livonia. The Political and Ecclesiastical Structures 13th-16th*

Century, 31-56. Toruń: Towarzystwo Naukowe w Toruniu, and Cologne, Weimar, and Vienna: Böhlau, 2015.

Teeuwen, Mariken. *The Vocabulary of Intellectual Life in the Middle Ages*. Turnhout: Brepols, 2003.

Tierney, Brian. *The Idea of Natural Rights. Studies on Natural Rights, Natural Law, and Church Law, 1150-1625*. Atlanta: GA Scholars Press, 1977.

Tulejski, Tomasz. "Paulus Vladimiri and His Forgotten Concept of the Just War," *Archiwum Filozofii Prawa i Filozofii Społecznej* 2019, 2: 39-52.

Tumler, Marian. *Der Deutsche Orden im Werden, Wachsen und Wirken bis 1400*. Vienna: Panorama, 1955.

Urban, William. *The Samogitian Crusade*. Chicago: Lithuanian Research and Studies Center, 1989.

_____. *The Teutonic Knights. A Military History*. London: Greenhill Books and Mechanicsburg, PA: Stackpole Books, 2003.

_____. "The Teutonic Order and the Christianization of Lithuania." In *La Cristianizzazione della Lituania*, 107-138. Vatican City: Libreria Editrice Vaticana, 1989.

Vallery-Radot, Sophie. *Les Français au concile de Constance (1414-1418). Entre resolution du schism et construction d'une identité nationale*, 2 vols. Turnhout: Brepols, 2016.

Valois, Noël. *La France et le grand schism d'Occident*, 4 vols. Paris: A, Picard et fils, 1896- 1902.

van Dussen, Michael and Pavel Soukup, eds. *A Companion to the Hussites*. Leiden and Boston, 2020.

Verger, Jacques. "Patterns." In Hilde de Ridder Symoens, ed. *Universities in the Middle Ages*, 35-74. Cambridge: Cambridge University Press, 1992.

Weijers, Olga. *In Search of the Truth. A History of Disputation Techniques from Antiquity to Early Modern Times*. Turnhout: Brepols, 2013.

Wielgus, Stanisław. *The Medieval Polish Doctrine of the Law of Nations*. Lublin: Wydawnictwo Katolickiego Uniwersytetu Lubelskiego, 1996.

_____. *Polska średniowieczna doktryna* Ius Gentiium. Lublin: Wydawnictwo Katolickiego Uniwersytetu Lubelskiego, 1996.

_____. *Średniowieczna łacińskojęzyczna biblistyka polska*. Lublin: Wydawnictwo Katolickiego Lubelskiego, 1992.

Wiesiołowski, Jacek. "Prace i projekty Pawła Włodkowica—Konstancja, zima 1415 i 1416 roku," *Roczniki Historyczne* 35 (1969): 93-123.

Wiszewski, Przemysław. *Domus Bolezlai: Values and Social Identity in Dynastic Traditions of Medieval Poland, 966-1138*. Leiden and Boston: Brill 2010. (Polish original 2008.)

_____. "Politics and Change: The Silesian Dukes and the Transformation of the Land in the Thirteenth and Fourteenth Centuries." In Sunhild Kleingärtner, et al., eds. *Landscapes and Societies in Medieval Europe East of the Elbe*, 183-203. Toronto: Pontifical Institute of Mediaeval Studies, 2013.

Włodek, Zofia. "Cracowski Komentarz z XV wieku do Sentencji Piotra Lombarda. Część pierwsza: Wstęp historyczny i edycja tekstu Księgi I i II," *Studia Mediewistyczne* 7 (1966): 125-355.

_____. "Cracowski Komentarz z XV wieku do *Sentencji* Piotra Lombarda. W poszukiwaniu tendencji doktrynalnych na wydziale teologicznym Uniwersytetu Cracowskiego w XV wieku. Cz. 2: Tendencje doktrynalne komentarza," *Studia Mediewistyczne* 9 (1968): 245- 291.

_____. "Odnaleziona Satyra Falkenberga," *Studia Historyczne* 14 (1971): 477-491.

_____. "La Satire de Jean Falkenberg. Texte inédit avec introduction," *Mediaevalia Philosophica Polonorum* 18 (1973): 51-120.

Włodek, Zofia, ed., with the cooperation of Ryszard Tatarzyński. *Scripta Manent. Textus ad Theologiam Spectantes in Universitate Cracoviensi saeculo XV conscripti*. Kraków: Wydawnictwo Naukowe Papieskiej Akademii Teologicznej w Krakowie, 2000.

Wojciechowski, Rafał. *Arbitraż w doktrynie prawnej średniowiecza*. Wrocław: Wydawnictwo Uniwersytetu Wrocławskiego, 2010.

Wojciechowski, Zygmunt. *Studia Historyczne*. Warsaw: PAX, 1955.

The Works of Geoffrey Chaucer, F.N. Robinson, ed. 2nd ed. Boston: Houghton Mifflin, 1957.

Woś, Jan W. "Un débat ouvert: Paulus Wladimiri et Francisco de Vitoria," *Mediaevalia Philosophica Polonorum* 20 (1975): 85-88.

_____. "Paulus Wladimiri aus Brudzen—Vorläufer oder Fortsetzer," *Zeitschrift für Ostforschung* 25 (1976): 438-461.

Wróbel, Dariusz, "Zbigniew Oleśnicki a kwestia pruska i krzyżacka." In Feliks Kiryk and Zdzisław Noga, eds. *Zbigniew Oleśnicki Książę Kościoła i Mąż Stanu*, 85-101. Kraków: Secesja, 2006.

Wünsch, Thomas. *Konziliarismus und Polen. Personen, Politik und Programme aus Polen zur Verfassungsfrage der Kirche in der Zeit der mittelalterlichen Reformkonzilien*. Paderborn, Munich, Vienna, and Zürich: Schöningh, 1998.

_____. "Paulus Wladimiri und die Genese des 'realistischen Denkens' in der Lehre von den internationalen Beziehungen: Der Krieg zwischen Polen und dem Deutschen Orden als Stimulus für ein neues politiktheoretisches Paradigma." In Werner Paravicini, Rimvydas Petrauskas, and Grisha Vercamer, eds. *Tannenberg—Grunwald—Žalgiris 1410: Krieg und Frieden im späten Mittelalter*, 27-42. Wiesbaden: Harrassowitz, 2012.

Wyczański, Andrzej. *Polen als Adelrepublik*. Osnabrück: Fibre, 2001. (Polish original, 2nd ed. 1991.)

Zahajkiewicz, Marek T. "Théorie et pratique de l'Évangelisation dans le processus de Christianisation de la Lituanie." In *La Cristianizzazione della Lituania*, 179-192. Vatican City: Libreria Editrice Vaticana, 1989.

Zajączkowski, Stanisław. "Studia nad procesami Polski i Litwy z Zakonem Krzyżackim w l. 1420-1423," *Ateneum Wileńskie* 12 (1937): 282-403.

Zarębski, Ignacy. "Okres Wczesnego Humanizmu." In Kazimierz Lepszy, ed. *Dzieje Uniwersytetu Jagiellońskiego w latach 1364-1764*, 151-187. Kraków: Państwowe Wydawnictwo Naukowe, 1964.

Zawadzki, Roman Maria. "Początki kultu Królowej Jadwigi." In *Jubileusz Sześćsetlecie Wydziału Teologicznego w Krakowie 20 X 1996—20 X 1997*, 283-298. Kraków: Wydawnictwo Naukowe Papieskiej Akademii Teologicznej, 1998.

Zečević, Nada. "Introduction: 'Central Europe': Perceptions, Definitions, and Comparisons in a Historiographical Context." In Zečević and Daniel Ziemann, eds. *Oxford Handbook of Medieval Central Europe,* 1-20. Oxford: Oxford University Press, 2022.

Zientara, Benedykt. "*Melioratio terrae*: The thirteenth Century Breakthrough in Polish History." In J.K. Federowicz, ed. *A Republic of Nobles. Studies in Polish History to 1864*, 31-48. Cambridge: Cambridge University Press, 1982.

Zwiercan, Marian. *Komentarz Jana z Dąbrówki do Kroniki Mistrza Wincentego zwanego Kadłubkiem.* Wrocław: Ossolineum, 1969.

_____. "Rwaczka Maurycy z Pragi," *Polski Słownik Biograficzny* 33 (1991): 279.

Zwiercan, Marian, ed. *Ioannes de Dąbrówka Commentum in Chronicam Polonorum Magistri Vincentii dicti Kadłubek*. Kraków: Polska Akademia Umiejętności, 2008.